# The Cyclopedic Education Dictionary

# The Cyclopedic Education Dictionary

CAROL SULLIVAN SPAFFORD ED.D.

AUGUSTUS J. ITZO PESCE D.ED.

GEORGE S. GROSSER PH.D.

Delmar Publishers

an *International Thomson Publishing company* I(T)P[®]

Albany • Bonn • Boston • Cincinnati • Detroit • London • Madrid
Melbourne • Mexico City • New York • Pacific Grove • Paris • San Francisco
Singapore • Tokyo • Toronto • Washington

## NOTICE TO THE READER

Cover Design: Brucie Rosch

Delmar Staff
Publisher: William Brottmiller
Acquisitions Editor: Jay Whitney
Associate Editor: Erin O'Connor Traylor
Project Editor: Karen Leet/Marah Bellegarde
Production Coordinator: Sandra Woods
Art and Design Coordinator: Timothy Conners
Editorial Assistant: Ellen Smith

COPYRIGHT © 1998
By Delmar Publishers
a division of International Thomson Publishing

The ITP logo is a trademark under license.

Printed in the United States of America

For more information, contact:

Delmar Publishers
3 Columbia Circle, Box 15015
Albany, New York 12212-5015

International Thomson Publishing Europe
Berkshire House 168-173
High Holborn
London, WCI1V 7AA
England

Thomas Nelson Australia
102 Dodds Street
South Melbourne, 3205
Victoria, Australia

Nelson Canada
1120 Birchmont Road
Scarborough, Ontario
Canada, M1K 5G4

International Thomson Editores
Campos Eliseos 385, Piso 7
Col Polanco
11560 Mexico D F Mexico

International Thomson Publishing GmbH
Konigswinterer Strasse 418
53227 Bonn
Germany

International Thomson Publishing Asia
221 Henderson Road
#05-10 Henderson Building
Singapore 0315

International Thomson Publishing—Japan
Hirakawacho Kyowa Building, 3F
2-2-1 Hirakawacho
Chiyoda-ku, Tokyo 102
Japan

1 2 3 4 5 6 7 8 9 10 XXX 03 02 01 00 99 98 97

**Library of Congress Cataloging-in-Publication Data**
Spafford, Carol Sullivan.
    The cyclopedic education dictionary/Carol Spafford, Augustus I. Pesce, George Grosser.
      p.   cm.
    ISBN 0–8273–8475–0
    1. Education—Dictionaries. I. Pesce, Augustus I. II. Grosser,
George S. III. Title.
    LB15.S73 1997
    370′.25—dc21       97–9025
               CIP

# Contents

# Preface

Welcome to a challenging profession in which you must consider many facets and conditions associated with your field. When entering the education realm you must become familiarized with the vocabulary of the profession and be knowledgeable of the subject-matter of your career if you are to optimally serve students in your charge. We believe that this dictionary will give you an excellent introduction into the field of education as well as a resource upon which you can rely throughout your studies from the baccalaureate to the doctoral levels. The information provided here can answer most questions you may have about the meaning of a word, phrase, legal ruling, medical term, name, testing terminology, and abbreviation important to an educator's background. Educators increasingly need to build their knowledge base in a society that is experiencing a rapidly changing information base and is still rooted in many philosophical and psychological schools of thought from previous generations.

This dictionary is a one-of-a-kind resource in that there are several terms that integrate numerous disciplines important to the field of education in one reference guide. There is no other resource of its kind in the education realm. The prospective teacher/learner/ practitioner may consult this guide whether studying physiology; psychology; education; current issues; law; special education; early childhood, elementary, secondary, or middle school education; philosophy; math; reading; literature; language arts; or other courses related to the pedagogy of the profession. Key terms and concepts are explained in easily-understood language which can in turn be used to assist parents, students, other professionals, and nonprofessionals when needed.

Schools today differ from those as few as 10 years ago. There are more and more emphases placed on "inclusionary practices" and "mainstreaming efforts." The advent of important federal legislation (Section 504 of the Rehabilitation Act of 1973, the 1975 P.L. 94-142, and IDEA of 1990) as well as individual state initiatives (e.g., Chapter 766 in Massachusetts) redefined how children with special needs are educated. Instead of substantially separating those with special learning needs from nondisabled learners, educators are now trying to provide inclusive learning experiences within the regular education setting whenever possible. You might wonder what quality integration is, how mainstreaming and inclusion efforts are similar and how they are different, what practices can be used to enhance integrated classroom environments, what legal precedent has been set for such practices, and just what some of that confusing language means (i.e., "decentralized school model," "individualization," "cultural compatibility," "empowered school communities," etc.). Appendix 1, Abbreviations in Education, will help you decipher this educational Morse code and will be useful throughout your entire career as such acronyms always have a way of cropping up during a report, conversation, and in reading materials.

Appendix 2, Legal Terms and Issues Related to Education, provides valuable information for all educators who must address such issues as "What are the schools' legal responsibilities in regard to assessments?" "What does the law say regarding the copying of materials, television shows, and videos?" "Who sets standards for curriculum according to the law?" "What do school systems need to do before students are expelled or suspended?" "Just how far can students go in regard to the freedom of speech?" "What about locker searches—are these legal?" and "Can teachers strike?" Please always keep in mind "the presumption of innocence," "probable cause," and "beyond a reasonable doubt" before someone is charged with an infraction or offense.

Effective teachers rely on systematic and reflective thinking about appropriate instructional strategies and practices. Appendix 3 entitled MARCS and MAPP allows educators to extend their knowledge base by identifying important components to an action-based research classroom (e.g., mathematics). Ideas for portfolio inclusions focus on special sensitivity to ethnic minority students and those factors that help personalize the learning experience for all students.

Computer logos such as "Internet," "RAM," "CPUs," "CRTs" "Software," "Megabytes" and "Gigabytes," "e-Mail," "Muppet Learning Keys," "Mouses," "CD-ROM," "Fortran," "Laser Printers," and "Digitized Speech" can be found in Appendix 4, Computer Terms. You'll be pleased to know that "Worm Disks" are far different than the literal translation. When you hear "wizzeewig!!" don't call an ambulance! You'll also find that "Handshaking" via the computer is actually a part of computer "Protocol." Before you begin to hyperventilate or get "ANSI" after reading this computer jargon, jump to Appendix 4 to find these technical terms described in easy-to-understand and remembered language. You will find that the "virtual reality" of our appendix is that it is very "user friendly."

It is estimated that there will be at least 1 billion users of the Internet worldwide by the year 2000. There are several web sites we have listed that would be of interest to professionals using this dictionary. For example, under the "College" entry, students and parents are provided information regarding how to access web sites for college alternatives, locations, financial aid, SAT preparations, etc. Also, the Orton Dyslexia Society (ODS) links to other national learning disability organizations on the Internet and provides listings of resources and a bulletin board where questions can be posted and answered. As of 1994, WebTV became available to television users who can now dial-up access to the World Wide Web via their television sets. On February 8, 1996, President Clinton signed into effect the Telecommunications Act of 1996 so as to provide the opportunities for every classroom and every child to be connected to the Internet. Read about the nation's technology goals and exactly what "technology literacy" is within Appendix 4 as we move into the twenty-first century.

Descriptions of new technological devices are presented that can assist and improve the life situations of friends, colleagues, students, etc. For example, did you know that closed-circuit television (CCTV), versabraille systems, viewscans, braille embossers, optacons, seeing-eye-dogs, sonic guides, sonic pathfinders, talking books, talking programs, echo speech synthesizers, Hoover canes, large-print books, MIT braille embossers, and laser canes are all technological tools that can assist blind and visually impaired individuals to adapt to academic and social situations? This dictionary might give those who are interested and in a position to assist some ideas as to what is available technologically for individuals with varying special needs to include those with visual disabilities.

You might be wondering what federal guidelines allow expenditures for educational tools for individuals with disabilities. There are a bewildering number of federal laws (e.g., P.L. 90-170, P.L. 91-230, P.L. 101-476, P.L. 101-336, etc.) and related amendments that impact all school-age individuals. We have listed the major educational legislation by public law in the "P" section of this dictionary.

Appendix 5 lists important Federal Legislation, Milestones, and Reports which relate to Education Affairs in the United States, past and present.

A number of studies, reports from foundations and governmental agencies, and legal rulings have greatly impacted our educational system. Perhaps you have heard of the national reports, *A Nation at Risk,* the *Carnegie Foundation Report on Secondary Education,* the *Holmes Group,* or the *College Board Report* but were not sure of the point of each. Many such references have been provided and are cross-referenced with other important information. Additionally, several social issues and reforms have been identified and defined in a nonjudgmental manner so that the reader receives just the facts.

Appendix 6 lists Supreme Court Decisions Related to Education.

Read on and try to decipher the following message (believe it or not, this conversation could very well happen tomorrow in one of our school corridors!):

"An ADHD student has been referred to a SPED program for a CORE or TEAM evaluation. The TEAM must convene in order to prepare for a test work-up that will result in a DSM-IV diagnosis, an IEP, and placement in some PP status. We'll need GE, GP, %ile's, and stanines from an IQ test, the WRAT-R, the KeyMath-R and the GMRT's tests in order to determine appropriate curriculum materials . . ."

Appendix 7 is a sample of an IEP (Individualized Education Plan).

Teachers are also asked to analyze curriculum materials and might not always be sure of the differences among some novel teaching techniques and ideas. Clarification is within reach of this dictionary! You must not forget some of the philosophical positions that have impacted current teaching practices like perennialism, essentialism, realism, behaviorism, existentialism, progressivism, and reconstructionism. We have provided a tie-in between an easily understood definition of terms and the expectations of a teacher who practices the basic tenets seen in these positions. Research has shown that effective schools depend upon teachers collaborating with students, parents, administrators, community members, and other professionals for optimal learning outcomes to occur. The entry "effective schools" details those important characteristics required for "best teaching practices/learning" to occur. Such entries as "grants" allow teachers to explore resources/avenues available for professionals in the field.

After studying this dictionary such questions can be raised as, "What is the meaning of teacher and student empowerment?" "How have Supreme Court rulings impacted our educational system?" "What are teachers' legal rights and responsibilities?" "How can time-honored philosophical positions be updated to current teaching practices?" "What is the difference between affective and effective teaching?" "What are some of the organizational arrangements in the schools?" "What are some different teaching strategies used to teach reading?" "What are some current education trends that must be assessed for effectiveness in years to come?" "What are the brain-behavior pattern relationships in such disorders as depression and schizophrenia?" "What is the difference between whole language techniques and phonics?" "What is the difference between inclusionary practices and mainstreaming?" "What are the different types of hearing problems and can they be corrected?" "How can the current DSM-IV classification system be useful for teacher/educators when categorizing personality disorders?" "What is portfolio assessment?"

Appendix 8 includes sample Literacy Activities for early education and technology literacy for all levels.

Although ethics, values, and values clarification have been defined, it is incumbent upon the reader to become involved in ethical discussions (and concerned with ethical dilemmas) after forming opinions, attitudes, and beliefs with an informed eye. We hope that we have provided a solid foundation for the educator who wishes to become immersed in such issues of the times. Most importantly, it would be incumbent upon the reader to form a philosophy of education that will guide one to practices that optimally meet the needs of the students we serve. Our philosophy of education is to address the needs of the whole person in a comfortable and intellectually stimulating learning environment so that the emotional, social, academic, and psychological well-being of the individual are considered and addressed. You will see such definitions as "personal wellness" and "teacher effectiveness" keying in on strategies/qualities required to accomplish this end. This dictionary provides one avenue for the practitioner in the field to identify and think about a philosophy of education to build on as well as questions, issues, information, and values of the education profession so as to better promote the concept of the "whole person."

# Acknowledgments

We would like to acknowledge the special efforts, support, and guidance of Jay Whitney, editor and friend, from Delmar Publishers. He was always pleasantly accessible and taught us the fine points of an educational publishing "reading road map." To him we are especially grateful. Additionally, the wonderful team of Erin O'Connor Traylor, developmental editor; Karen Leet, Production Manager; Glenna Stanfield, Senior Editorial Assistant; and Bill Brottmiller, Team Leader, provided us with invaluable advise, timely deadlines, and always a helping hand when needed. They're the best!

We are deeply indebted to the fine professionals at Shepherd Incorporated and in particular, Chris Trakselis, Project Editor, for expert technical efforts throughout manuscript preparations. Kelly Bechen provided outstanding copy editing support.

We need to give special acknowledgement to Andre Houle and David Pino, our research assistants, editorial/computer consultants, and friends. Their input, expertise, patience, and high level of competence resulted in a timely completion of the final manuscript. We would like to credit Andre with the introduction of a new word, synthisophy, that we believe may be quite relevant to the field of education.

We would also like to thank the Miguel Roman Family, Henry Benjamin, Dr. Paul Desmarais, Jim Sansalone, Dr. Mel Williams, Dr. Margaret Cassidy, Georgia Parafestas, Ben Swan, Dr. Bryant Robinson, Dr. Ann Courtney, Dr. Barbara Dautrich, Opal Dillard, Stacy Sevigny, Linda Anzalotti, Theresa Fiorentino, Carol Malinosky, Catherine Sargent, Anneta McCabe, Bob McCullum, Nancy Cabana, Dr. Cheryl Stanley, Naomi White, Ann Koenig, Dr. Bernie Berenson, Dr. Chris Ying, Kathy Sullivan, Dr. Candy Budd-Jackson, Mary Frances Peters, John and Cloratha Coleman, Sarah Shapiro, Edwina Grimaldi, Judy Dumont, Mary Lantz, Diane Arnold, Rosalie Tobia, Michelle Hervieux, Taniesha Burton, Kim Scofield, Jennifer Black, Mike Taylor, Danielle Burch, Cory Hulsebus, Richard Hanson, Megan Mantenuto, Neta and Clifford Maddox, Donna Cohen, Kathy Meadows, Jackie Mitchell, Lucretia Polemeni, Eileen Donahue, Tim Dominick, Lorraine Collins, Michelle LaVallee, the Lavins, Ed Hall, Rev. Hugh Bair, Dina and Barbara Rossi, Mary Stacy, Lisa Nettis, Elda Sarah Morgan, Faye Morris, Diane Chira, Barbara Stewart, Melanie

Jennings, Manisha Lalwani, Liz Pappalardo, Renaldo Vega, Alvin Paige, Marsha and Tulius Frizzi, Alan LeBlanc, Elise Blanken, Mauricio Hernandez, Beth Jones, Diane Cohen, Lena Lefebvre, Janet Scott, Eva Soalt, Jodi Nomi, Lisa Sotirion, Elliot Best, Eric Butler, Ben Mathis, Simone Matlock, Dr. Joy Fopiano, Mildred McKenna, Howard Cherry, Marie Stevens, Marcie Gruskin, the Netkoviks, Stephanie Wilson, Susan Blackington, Arlene McKenzie, Khan Tai, Meredith Boone, Stephen Freed, Harold Collins, The Bartolomeis, Phil DiPietro, Carol Doty, Eve Green, Aleyda Torres, Jeanne Kinney, Mary Broderick, Miriam Santiago, Jo-Jo Wooden, James Hector, Joanne Guiel, Marie Smythe, Kim Stone, Bill Daley, Harry Orr Gonzalez, Huelette King, Ester Figueredo, Kim and Julie Leonard, Debby Lavendar, Mary Anderson, Eileen Pisarski, Daquall Brown, Charlie and Judy Collins, Flo and Bill Checile, Nellie Duong, the Furlanis, Sharonda Sanders, Robert Chagnon, Linda Lee, Valerie Church, Sonya Martinez, Rene Sandoval, Brian Welch, Ester Figueroa, Mary Louise Rutherford, Cathy Torres, Tyron McAllister, Tony Mason, Justin Dalessio, Forrest Traylor, Marie Baez, Kathy Lynch, Dr. Jeannette Goggins, Diane and Richard Cole, Celia Cauley, Marjorie Zackheim, Anouk Ewald, Scott Anderson, Ingrid Cuevas, Carrie Sarkozi, Doris Simmonds, and Doris LeBlanc (students who "never gave up"), Jennifer Stevens, Tina Toohey, Megan Thomas, Betty Bonfitto, Jeanne Hebert, Henry Renelus, Edna Proulx, Leticia Matos, G. Oliver Layne, and Debby McCarthy for their inspiration throughout this project.

Special recognition should be given to Betty Gandy-Tobin who was our primary computer specialist. Betty was instrumental in organizing and editing new entries. We could always count on her to meet deadlines with outstanding results. We're proud of her. On a personal note, the first author would like to give a special note of thanks to Aida King (a great teacher!), the VNA, Sister Mary Caritas, The Sisters from St. Thomas, the Trembles, and the D'Amours.

Finally, we would like to thank those special individuals in our lives who provided inspiration, guidance, and a helping hand: close family members Ken, Kenny, Irene, Rose and Jim, Gerry, and Richard Spafford; Edward, Yvonne, and Joseph Pesce, and Denise Boratgis; Edward and Eleanor Hickey; Louis and Edith Pesce, and especially Grace Pesce; Richard, Carol, Janice, Pat, and George Sullivan; and Eleanor Grosser—all of whom were especially supportive and helpful. They're the best! We hope that this dictionary will provide you with a vehicle for reflective thinking in your chosen field of study. The authors may be contacted on the Internet at: @Spafford@Spafford.Com.

Our best to you and your families! Happy Reading!

# About the Authors

**Carol Sullivan Spafford** is Education Chair and Associate Professor of Psychology and Education at American International College in Springfield, Massachusetts. She has been involved with college accreditation programs at several colleges and is active in a number of professional organizations including the Massachusetts Reading Association, serving as Co-President of the local Pioneer Valley Reading Council. Dr. Spafford was recently named to Who's Who in the East and has published several articles and books in the areas of learning disabilities and education. She has presented workshops at the National Orton Dyslexia and NCTM conferences.

**Augustus J. Itzo Pesce** is Director of Special Education and Associate Professor of Psychology and Education at American International College in Springfield, Massachusetts. He was a former Superintendent, Assistant Superintendent, Director of Special Education, and Principal. Dr. Pesce serves as an educational consultant and member of a site-based management team for a local public school. He has been a featured speaker at several local and state conferences and is a member of Phi Delta Kappa, and the Divisions of Teacher Education and Learning Disabilities (DLD) of the Council for Exceptional Children.

**George S. Grosser** is Associate Professor of Psychology at American International College in Springfield, Massachusetts. Named to Who's Who in the East, he is the author or co-author of seven books and over 25 journal articles. Dr. Grosser has been actively researching and writing about the nature and causes of learning disabilities for several years. He serves as the chair and a committee member for several doctoral committees. He is a member of the New York Academy of Sciences, the American Psychological Society, and the Division of Learning Disabilities, Council for Exceptional Children. Previous to his education career, Dr. Grosser was a distinguished scientist.

# Dedication

This book is dedicated to Ken Spafford, Grace Pesce, Eleanor Grosser, Miguel Roman, Tim Sunstrom, Carrie Sarkozi, Doris Simmonds, Doris LeBlanc; and our children, family, students, mentors, and colleagues.

**A posteriori ideas**   The things one knows as the result of experience. Philosophers who subscribed to materialism in metaphysics and empiricism in epistemology would say that only these things can be true; they would deny any credibility to the truth of a priori ideas. SEE: *a priori ideas, empiricism, epistemology*

**A priori ideas**   Those things we know because we are born having a human brain; the self-evident truths. The possession of a priori knowledge is a necessary assumption of an idealistic metaphysics, the idea that reality is by nature mental or spiritual. Kant attempted to describe a priori knowledge in detail. Empirical philosophers such as Hume, however, had no use for this concept. In epistemology, a priori ideas are compatible with the method of rationalism. SEE: *a posteriori ideas, empiricism, epistemology, idealism, metaphysics, rationalism*

**AAC**   SEE: *Augmentative Communication*

**Abasement**   The condition of feeling humiliated or lower in rank, prestige, or self-esteem.

**Abasia**   Motor incoordination as it concerns walking. An inability to walk as a result of impaired coordination.

**ABC model**   A system of behavioral analysis that examines three components; namely, antecedents to the behavior, the actual behavior, and the behavioral consequences.

**Abduction**   A term used in physical therapy to indicate movement of a leg or arm away from the middle of the body.

**Aberration**   A severe straying from what is considered normal.

**Ability**   A student's or person's capacity to effectively perform tasks or skills already learned. SEE: *aptitude*

**Ability grouping**   The placement of students into homogeneous groups in accordance with their intellectual or academic abilities. Such placement can result in tracking.

**Ability tracking**   SEE: *Appendix 2: Legal Terms and Issues*

**Ablation**   The removal of a part of the nervous system. This may be done to a lower animal for research on brain-behavior relationships. This may also include the removal of any other part of the body through surgical means.

**Abnormal behavior**   Behavior that is not in line with what is considered appropriate or average within a group or society at large.

**ABR**   SEE: *Auditory Brainstem Response*

**Absence seizures**   Temporary mental inattention in the form of epileptic seizures that occurs for brief periods of time (usually less than 30 seconds) and that may occur dozens of times per day. Sometimes called petit mal.

**Absences, excessive school**   SEE: *Appendix 2: Legal Terms and Issues*

**Absolute standard**   A measurement standard whereby arbitrary points are set for obtaining different letter grades. For example, if a 2.0 (generally a "C" average) cumulative average is set as passing for college graduation, cumulative averages falling below that point "fail" and averages falling above "pass."

**Absolute threshold**   The least amount of sensory stimulation that can be detected. For example, the sound of a ticking watch at a distance of twenty feet from the listener. Another example would be the sight of a candle flame at 1.5 miles.

**Abstract**   A short summation of a research article, including the problem under investigation, the research method employed, the data, and the conclusions. An abstract of an article often appears in a brief paragraph as a research summary. Many education/psychology associations/publications print such abstracts for the benefit of the reader who is then able to determine whether or not obtaining the full manuscript would fulfill an education/psychology need (e.g., when preparing a master's thesis or doctoral dissertation).

**Abstract concept** A product of the abstract reasoning process, which involves the selection of one particular aspect of a perceived stimulus, thinking about this one feature, and remembering both the perception of the feature and the results of the thoughts about this feature at future times. Such a feature may be stated in general terms so that it may be applied to a great many objects or stimuli.

**Abstract reasoning** The ability of a student or other person to think about known facts, concepts, ideas, and information in order to infer additional ideas that are reasonable and probable in nature.

**Abstraction** A straightforward three-step process as follows: 1. the student focuses her/his attention on some feature or experience; 2. the student holds onto this experience or feature as the immediate object of thought, and 3. the student is able to recall this feature or object of thought at a later time.

**Abulia** An absence or an inability to control one's will. A loss of ability to make decisions or initiate action.

**Academic aptitude** A student's or person's ability or capacity to effectively master a school or academic program that is yet to be presented or taken. SEE: *aptitude, ability*

**Academic disciplines** The different branches in academia that deal with the acquisition of knowledge. For example, in some Western societies, such disciplines include the study of English, math, science, art, music, and history.

**Academic freedom** The freedom of a teacher to present and discuss subject matter in such a way that is deemed appropriate by the teacher without the interference of administrators. Academic freedom is a privilege and those who have been given this privilege should consider the law, community standards, morality issues, developmental appropriateness, and curriculum standards within the school district.

**Academic learning disability** A condition that causes great difficulty for a student or person when learning to read, spell, write, or compute arithmetically.

**Academic learning time** The time consumed by students when learning material successfully. Academic learning times differ depending on the age, developmental levels, achievement level, intelligence, and so on of the learner. Individuals with learning disabilities, for example, may require accommodations that would permit extended learning times during the school day because cognitive processing speeds/abilities may be impaired to some degree.

**Academic plateau** The tendency for students with some learning problems to reach a plateau in academic achievement before high school graduation (e.g., the mentally retarded frequently do not go beyond a concrete level of functioning).

**Academic socialization** The procedures used to teach children how to be students and the ways in which children are taught to value learning.

**Academic support** Support that is considered part of the regular classroom curriculum, including supportive services for the major goals of the school or system.

**Academic tasks** Work that a student is required to complete, including coverage of content materials. Academic tasks include the necessary mental steps (problem-solving procedures, making inferences, using deductive logic, etc.) to complete assigned work. Examples of academic tasks would include a measurement problem in math, completing a spelling exercise, performing a science experiment, giving an oral speech, conversing in a foreign language, and so on.

**Academic year**   Generally speaking, the regular school year, normally from September through June in elementary, middle, and secondary schools and September through May at the college level. Current trends indicate that the school year will be expanded to 190 or more days in the not-too-distant future.

**Academy**   1. A term used to describe a school usually above the elementary level, that is, at the high school or college level; frequently, a private high school or preparatory (prep) school. 2. A term used to describe an early American secondary private school.

**Acalculia**   SEE: *dyscalculia*

**ACALD**   Association for Children and Adults with Learning Disabilities.

**Acataphasia**   A lack of ability or an inability to coherently express oneself verbally. The condition is a result of a brain lesion. The student or person has great difficulty using words to form meaningful sentences.

**Accelerated program**   The rapid advancement of students with high academic abilities and performances through school. Students can accelerate their programs by "skipping" grades or by taking courses not ordinarily taken by classmates at that grade level. Teachers can also provide individual enrichment for those students who need to be challenged. SEE: *acceleration*

**Acceleration**   An educational process in which the student progresses through the grades at a faster-than-normal rate. It can involve early admission to school, skipping grades, combining grades, early graduation from high school, and advanced placement at the college level.

**Accommodation**   1. This term refers to the changing of the lens shape in the eye, the lens bulging into a rounder shape to focus upon objects that are less than 20 feet in distance. 2. In Piaget's theory, the modification of existing cognitive patterns. One's cognitive schemes are changed to accommodate new experiences or information.

**Accountability**   1. A monetary term referring to expenditure of funds per pupil for optimal learning to transpire and 2. a professional understanding that an educator should be able to at least verbally explain his/her actions with regard to any aspects of job performance.

**Accreditation**   An approval given to a school by an outside agency which certifies that the school or agency is able to deliver the type of education or program it was designed to provide. For example the New England Association of Schools and Colleges would accredit a local high school or college in the State of Massachusetts.

**Acculturation**   The process of acquiring the predominant characteristics of the dominant culture (including attitudes, values, beliefs, language, and behaviors).

**Acetic acid**   Vinegar; it is also one of the breakdown products of the neurotransmitter acetylcholine.

**Achieved role**   A social role one has acquired voluntarily such as that of being a spouse, church leader, and so on.

**Achievement**   A level of accomplishment that is usually measured via a test of knowledge or skill.

**Achievement motivation**   The individual's intention of performing well, which involves placing a high value on excellence and success.

**Achievement test**   A test intended to measure a person's rate of learning acquisition in a particular subject area. For example, a math achievement test might measure an individual's acquired problem-solving strategies and/or abilities to perform math computations. SEE: *norms*

**Achondroplasia**   A condition characterized by a defect in the formation of the long bones of the body resulting in a form of "dwarfism."

**Achromatic vision**   A state of visual colorlessness or being totally color blind.

**Achromatism**   SEE: *color blindness, achromatic vision*

**Acoustics** The science of sound to include its perception; that is, its origin, transmission, and effects.

**Acquiescence** A philosophy or attitude amongst test takers wherein the student or person tends to agree with test statements made regardless of how the statements would apply to the individual concerned.

**Acquired** A term used to indicate the onset of any situation, disease, problem, disability, and the like that occurs some time after the birth of a child. SEE: *acquired aphasia, acquired dyslexia*

**Acquired aphasia** A condition characterized by an inability to speak or comprehend a language, occurring after language skills have been learned and used. SEE: *aphasia*

**Acquired dyslexia** A condition of reading disability (acquired after birth) resulting from brain damage. This is in contrast with developmental dyslexia. SEE: *developmental dyslexia*

**Acquired Immune Deficiency Syndrome (AIDS)** A virus-caused disease that involves a weakening of the body's immune system, making it vulnerable to any number of infections it could normally ward off. It is most often a fatal disease that is caused by one of the HIV group of viruses. AIDS is typically the final stage of infection by the human immunodeficiency virus (HIV), often occurring about seven years after the initial infection. The two modes of transmission that account for a majority of AIDS cases are 1. sexual contact among homosexual and bisexual men, and 2. the sharing of needles during intravenous (IV) drug use. However, the number of male-to-female and female-to-male transmissions of the AIDS virus continues to increase. Although the HIV virus has in some instances been found in the saliva and tears of infected individuals, there is no evidence to demonstrate that AIDS can be spread through casual contact. No cure has been discovered as of this writing. It should be noted that some individuals may be infected by the HIV virus without succumbing to full-blown AIDS. Some

behaviors that can minimize the risk of developing AIDS are 1. reducing the number of sexual partners, 2. use of condoms to prevent the exchange of semen, 3. abandoning illegal intravenous drug use, 4. avoiding the sharing of syringes, 5. sterilizing needles, and 6. sexual abstinence. Unfortunately, the increase in the number of individuals with the AIDS virus continues to be a major concern. SEE: *HIV*

**Acquisition** 1. In classical conditioning, the increase in strength of a conditioned response (CR) after several pairings of the conditioned stimulus (CS) with the unconditioned stimulus (US). 2. In operant conditioning, the increase in the rate of emitting an operant response after that response has been reinforced. 3. In rote learning of math material, the acquisition stage would involve the memorization of math facts.

**Acrocephaly** A condition in which the top of the cranium (head) is pointed. The eyes are slanted and widely set and the toes and fingers may be webbed. Mental retardation can be present.

**Acromegaly** A chronic disease of middle-aged persons in which enlargement and elongation of the bones of the head, especially the jaw and frontal bones, as well as the extremities, occurs. The soft tissues of the nose, lips, and face are also enlarged. It is caused by overactivity of the pituitary gland's growth hormone.

**Acronym** A term artificially formed from the use of the first letters of a series of words. Acronyms are often used as memory aids and may be considered a mnemonic device. An example of an acronym serving as a mnemonic device is HOMES, the word formed from each of the first letters of the five Great Lakes (i.e., Huron, Ontario, Michigan, Erie, Superior).

**Acroparesthesia** A condition characterized by a tingling or numbing of hands and fingers usually following a period of sleep.

**Acting-out** A response to a stimulus or condition wherein a student or person openly releases tensions or frustration in an adverse behavioral manner. It can be a student's response to pent-up feelings of insecurity, frustration, anger, immaturity, etc.

**Action component**   The part of one's attitude(s) that governs actions toward the person(s) or object(s) of the attitude(s).

**Action research**   Diagnostic teaching or experimentation with new teaching tools or techniques.

**Action zone**   That part of a classroom in which the greatest number of interactions actually occur. The action zone in most traditional classrooms occurs in the vicinity where children are seated at their desks (i.e., front and center of the classroom).

**Activation**   The amount or degree of arousal experienced when stimuli are presented.

**Activation-synthesis theory**   Hobson's theory which specifies that our dreams result from subcortical nerve impulses that are randomly stimulating portions of the visual area of the cerebral cortex. The stimulated visual cortex, in turn, produces the sequence of events known as "dreaming."

**Active teaching**   Teaching activity that includes a great deal of explaining and demonstrating. The active teacher also does a good deal of interacting with the students. Examples of active teaching would be writing journal entries with students, solving math problems as a group on the board, reading and making predictions in small or large groups, debating current issues, etc.

**Activities of daily living**   SEE: *daily living skills*

**Activity curriculum**   Designing curricula in which the interests, learning styles, and learning purposes for children determine the educational program. Teachers and pupils cooperatively select and plan activities.

**Activity group therapy**   In education, a system of group therapy involving counseling sessions, work/activity

projects with common goals, and so on for students/adults who share common personal/behavioral/academic problems.

**Activity theory**   The theory of aging which presumes that the best psychological adjustments to aging occur with individuals who remain mentally and physically active.

**Actor**   The person whose behaviors are under study.

**Acuity**   The sharpness or keenness of the senses, especially used for describing the senses of hearing or vision.

**Acupuncture**   The ancient Chinese practice of inserting and rotating needles into the skin at various places on the body in order to alleviate pain. The place stimulated by the acupuncture needles may be far removed from the painful area being influenced. Although some believe the pain relief to be a placebo effect, physiological psychologists attribute the analgesic effects to the release in the brain of endorphins and enkephalins, the body's own opiates.

**Acute**   A term used to refer to a condition that has a rapid and severe onset. It is usually of short-term duration. SEE: *chronic*

**ADA**   SEE: *Americans with Disabilities Act or P.L. 101-336 (1990)* SEE: *Average Daily Attendance*

**Adaptation**   1. An individual's ability to adjust to prolonged stimulation of a sense organ by lowering the response level to that stimulation. For example, working in a restaurant for a day lowers an individual's sensitivity to food odor. 2. An individual's ability to cognitively and psychologically adapt to the stressors and required actions for everyday living.

**Adaptation level**   The average level of stimulation at which an individual or organism adapts to the environment. For example, in the middle of summer, the level of cold that forces a Texan to shiver would not stimulate this reflex in an Alaskan.

**Adaptive behavior** 1. The degree to which an individual meets societal goals for personal independence and social responsibility for a particular age, sex, cultural group, and even disabilities group (e.g., mental retardation). 2. Responses of organisms to various environmental stimuli that allow for survival and successful adaptation to the environment.

**Adaptive devices** Learning/social tools that allow individuals with special needs to adapt and function within their work/school/home environments.

**Adaptive fit** The match that exists between a student's or person's needs, talents, and/or abilities and the requirements of a particular job/task/academic assignment/social situation.

**Adaptive fitness** A set of behavioral and anatomical characteristics of a species that affect its ability to survive and reproduce.

**Adaptive instruction** Instruction that is amended or changed to meet the unique learning/social needs of a learner(s). The instructional changes can involve slight or major changes to the teaching/learning situation at home, work, or in the school environment. SEE: *adaptive skills*

**Adaptive physical education** A modified physical education program that is intended to meet the individual needs of a student with special learning challenges.

**Adaptive reflexes** Inborn automatic reflexes that are not under our conscious control. Newborns have a number of adaptive reflexes that include grasping, sucking, and the Moro reflexes.

**Adaptive skills** Skills acquired to adapt to one's work/home/school environment that promote optimal functioning in such areas as written/oral communication, leisure, academics, health, safety, community living, citizenship, self-care, vocational skills, home living, etc.

**ADD** SEE: *Attention Deficit Disorder*

**Addiction** A strong obsessive/compulsive need, usually for ingestion of a given drug. In the case of drug addiction, there is usually a buildup of tolerance (the individual must ingest more and more of the drug in order to obtain the same effect), strong behavioral dependence (the directing of great efforts toward obtaining a supply of the drug), and withdrawal symptoms (the real or seemingly apparent development of illness and suffering when the individual abruptly stops taking the drug).

**Addison's disease** (Thomas Addison, English Physician, 1793–1860.) A disease or deficiency of the adrenal cortex due to chronic underactivity. Symptoms include pigmentation of the mucous membrane and skin, vitiligo (milky-white skin patterns), weakness, nausea, vomiting, weight loss, and black freckles on the neck and head. Proper treatment yields an excellent prognosis.

**Addition** In the areas of special education and specifically articulation disorders, it is a condition characterized by the adding on of sounds that are not part of the word or words spoken by a student or individual (e.g., says "dictionaryrio" for "dictionary").

**Adduction** A term used in physical therapy to indicate movement of a leg(s) or arm(s) inwardly toward the middle of the body.

**ADHD:** SEE: *Attention Deficit/Hyperactivity Disorder*

**Adhesions** A holding together by fibrous bands of two structures in the body that are normally separated. It can be as a result of surgery, inflammation, scarring, or trauma.

**Adiadochokinesis** A condition wherein an individual is unable or has impaired ability to perform alternating movements in a rapid fashion. It is sometimes indicative of brain dysfunction.

**ADM** SEE: *Average Daily Membership*

**Admissions test scores** The standardized admissions tests or special admissions tests students are required to take in high school or college. These are used to make decisions about admitting students to a particular school or program.

**Adolescence**   A transitional period between childhood and adulthood. Adolescence starts with puberty (ages 11–13) and continues to the age of majority (from 18–21).

**Adolescent egocentrism**   The assumption on the part of the adolescent (ages 11–13 to 18–21) that all people share in one's emotions, concerns, and opinions. The egocentric adolescent, for example, might think that everyone around him/her has a bad attitude because he/she has a bad attitude.

**Adrenal glands**   Glandular organs attached to each of the two kidneys. The adrenal medulla glands secrete hormones that help the individual cope with an emergency by either fighting or fleeing. The adrenal cortex glands release hormones that organize the body's defenses against environmental stress, such as injury, infection, or extremes of temperature.

**Adult education**   Courses of instruction provided by public or private institutions, educational and otherwise, to persons who are normally beyond high school age. The courses normally do not lead to a high school diploma or college degree. These courses are usually taken by part-time students and can be in a variety of areas such as education, recreation, vocational, and avocational.

**Advanced organizers**   This is a form of expository teaching whereby the teacher describes in outline or abstract form what is to be expected in a unit or lesson. Advanced organizers summarize major features of material to come.

**Advanced placement**   Courses or programs coordinated between high schools, colleges, and/or universities that allow the student to take courses at the college level. Frequently the courses count for both high school and college credit as well.

**Adventitiously blind**   Any student or person, after being born with normal vision, who develops severe visual impairments or blindness as a result of illness, disease, or accident. SEE: *blind, legally*

**Adventitiously deaf**   Individuals who are born with normal hearing but through disease or illness lose their sense of hearing. These individuals have benefited in the past from hearing so that speech and language have been acquired through normal means. The impact of this hearing loss is less than for the individual born with a complete hearing loss. SEE: *congenitally deaf*

**Advocacy**   A concept in which professionals, parents, or other interested adults work in an assertive and informed manner to obtain better academic, social, or psychological services for individuals with disabilities.

**Advocate**   A person usually involved in the special education process who represents the special needs child and/or parent in order to ensure due process and to obtain an appropriate Individualized Educational Plan (IEP) while protecting the rights of the individual. SEE: *IEP*

**Aerobic exercise**   Exercise that uses the oxygen inhaled at a continuous level over an extended period of time. For example, a healthy person maintains a minimum pulse rate of 120 beats per minute over at least an 18-minute period of exercise. Such exercise at least three times a week would provide an individual with appropriate aerobic conditioning. Note: Recommended pulse rates vary with a person's age and health.

**Aesthetic reading**   A style of reading wherein the reader experiences feelings in a vicarious fashion as a result of what has been read. Aesthetic reading elicits feelings of past and present experiences and allows the reader to live the experience of the written material as it relates to the individual.

**Aesthetics**   The domain of values that search for the creation and appreciation of beautiful things. A course involving aesthetics could be the teaching of art appreciation.

**AFDC**   SEE: *Aid to Families with Dependent Children*

**Afebrile convulsion**   A convulsion or seizure that is not accompanied by or caused by a fever.

**Affect**   The feelings, positive or negative, that accompany an emotional condition.

**Affective disorder**   A condition of mood disturbances wherein the student or person has alternating feelings that reach extreme highs and lows; that is, elation and sadness. The feelings are unrealistic but very intense on the part of the individual concerned.

**Affective domain**   An area of learning that concerns itself with feelings, beliefs, and values. It involves the student's attitudes and emotions toward learning. This domain or territory deals with feelings rather than intellectual pursuits.

**Affective education**   Any educational procedures intended to foster the emotional growth and maturity of the student. Proponents of affective education believe that the emotional/social wellbeing of the individual is critical to the overall functioning of that person. Affective education/ideas/curricula include socialization skills training, activities to build self-esteem and self-concept, and the provision of positive reinforcement systems to foster acceptable behaviors/functioning.

**Affective learning**   Learning that involves the acquisition of feelings, attitudes, emotions, and other aspects of social and psychological development gained through feeling rather than through cognitive intellectualization.

**Afferent**   Messages that are carried toward a center, as illustrated by a sensory nerve carrying a message to the brain. It is the opposite of efferent. SEE: *efferent neurons, peripheral nervous system*

**Affirmative action**   Legislated plans governing personnel policies and hiring practices that try to ensure that women and members of minority groups are not discriminated against during the hiring process.

**Affix**   A prefix or a suffix. SEE: *prefix, root, suffix*

**Affricate**   Sounds combining stops and fricatives such as the "ch" sound in "child" and the "j" sound in "jump." SEE: *fricative*

**African-American English**   An African dialect or variation of the English language. SEE: *dialect*

**African-American language**   SEE: *Ebonics*

**African-American vernacular English**   SEE: *Ebonics*

**AFT**   SEE: *American Federation of Teachers*

**Afterimage**   The visual image that persists on the retina for a brief time after a visual image is removed. A negative afterimage is seen in colors complementary to the colors of the original stimulus. For example, after staring for two minutes at a green circle, looking away to a white screen will result in the sight of a red circle the same size as the original green stimulus.

**Age discrimination**   SEE: *Appendix 2, Legal Terms and Issues*

**Age-equivalent scores**   An age-equivalent score is computed by finding the mean raw score of a performance measure for a given group of children at a specific age. If the average score for a particular group of 12-year-olds on a particular reading test is 30 out of 50, then any child receiving a score of 30 would have an age-equivalent of 12. These scores do not seem to be used as much as percentiles, stanines, standard scores, and grade equivalents.

**Age norms**   Test scores or standards based on the average performance of individuals for a particular age. SEE: *age-equivalent scores*

**Age of onset**   The age of a student or person at the time of onset of any disability, disorder, syndrome, etc.

**Age of Pericles (455–431 B.C.)**   Named after Pericles, an Athenian statesman, it is a special period of Greek history during which great strides and interest in formal education and human advancement were made.

**Age of Reason**   A period of modern educational thought that emphasized the importance of reasoning in education. Voltaire (Francois Marie Arouet, French writer 1699–1778) was a great influence in this movement and the so-called "father" of rationalism. SEE: *rationalism*

**Ageism**   Discrimination against an individual based on that person's age (too young or too old).

**Ageusia**   A condition characterized by an absence or partial loss of the sense of taste; in effect, impaired taste.

**Aggregate membership**   The sum of all students present and absent for a given period of time for each day in that period (usually quarterly, half-year, or more typically a full school year).

**Aggregate present**   The sum of all students present for all of the days in a given period, (usually quarterly, half-year, or more typically a full school year). Note: It does not include absent students.

**Aggression**   The motivation to inflict bodily harm on another organism. The term usually refers to the tendency to attack another member of the same species. Aggression is one of the main symptoms of asocial personality disorder, according to the DSM-IV (Diagnostic and Statistical Manual of Mental Retardation, 4th Ed.).

**Aggressive personality**   A personality disorder wherein the individual has little patience with others as well as a low frustration level. A person or student can be bully-like in nature, throw temper tantrums and exhibit destructive behavior as well as verbal abuse.

**Agitated depression**   A form of depression characterized by a state of excessive restlessness on a continuing basis. Patients are restless, agitated, pick and rub themselves, and cry. They feel depressed, guilty, persecuted, and suffer from fears and obsessions.

**Agitolalia/agitophasia**   A condition of very rapid and cluttered speech with omissions, slurring, and distortions of sound.

**Aglossia**   No tongue; absence of a tongue. The removal of a tongue in part or totally is called a "glossectomy." SEE: *glossectomy*

**Agnosia**   The inability to place meanings to sounds, words, or visual experiences. This condition also includes an inability to recognize objects and experiences through the other senses as well.

**Agnosticism**   The view that it is not possible to decide whether or not there is a god.

**Agonist**   A chemical that activates (or mimics the action of) some drug or chemical neurotransmitter.

**Agraphia**   A condition caused by a central nervous system lesion or lack of muscular coordination wherein the student or person has lost the ability to express oneself in writing. Writing or copying from the board or dictation may still be possible. It is associated with motor aphasia. SEE: *aphasia, dysgraphia*

**Agrypnia**   A condition characterized by sleeplessness or an inability to sleep. It is a synonym for insomnia.

**AI**   SEE: *Artificial Intelligence*

**AIDS**   SEE: *Acquired Immune Deficiency Syndrome*

**AIDS-Related Complex (ARC)**   A condition caused by the AIDS virus in which the patient tests positive for AIDS but the symptoms are often less severe than the classic AIDS.

**Aid to Families with Dependent Children (AFDC)**   A special program that provides funds to qualifying low-income families with dependent children. Such factors as death of a parent, no or inadequate parental support, parental disability, an unemployed parent, a missing parent, and other such reasons that deny or deprive children of proper and adequate support can qualify children and families for AFDC payments.

**Air conduction (AC) test**   A hearing test that uses pure tones ranging from 125 Hz to 8000 Hz through headphones. This test assesses the amount of hearing loss a child has if a hearing loss is present. The results from AC testing and bone conduction (BC) testing reveal whether or not a hearing loss is conductive, sensorineural, or mixed. SEE: *bone* conduction (BC) testing, conductive hearing loss, sensorineural hearing loss, mixed hearing loss

**Akinesia**   A condition characterized by a loss of voluntary muscle movement.

**Akinetic seizure**   A seizure or an attack wherein the individual has an absence or loss of muscular movement. SEE: *seizure, akinesia*

**Alalia**   A type of aphasia wherein the student or person has lost her/his ability to speak due to damage or paralysis of the vocal organs. It is the loss of functional speech.

**ALAN**   An acronym for the Assembly on Literature for Adolescents.

**Albinism**   An inheritable condition that is characterized by a severe deficiency or total lack of pigmentation in the eyes, hair, or skin. This condition can be and many times is accompanied by photophobia (extreme sensitivity to light), astigmatism (blurred vision), and nystagmus (involuntary movement of the eyeball). SEE: *photophobia, astigmatism, nystagmus*

**Alchemy**   1. A speculative science occurring during medieval times involved with the transmutation of base metals into gold. 2. In education, the term is used to describe the transformation of something or someone ordinary into something or someone of great worth. The changing of an ordinary student into a talented or gifted individual, an academic blossoming.

**Alcohol embryopathy**   SEE: *fetal alcohol syndrome*

**ALD**   SEE: *Automated Learning Device*

**Alerting device**   A device used by individuals with disabilities that signals to them that something of note is happening. For example, a blinking light signals a telephone call for the deaf. The device can use sight, sound, or vibration to signal the individual.

**Alexia**   A condition characterized by an inability to comprehend written language symbols (words) as they relate to real-life experiences and objects. It is a serious reading disability related usually to brain dysfunction. SEE: *visual aphasia*

**Algorithm**   1. A strategy for thinking. Math algorithms or procedures, for example, involve well-defined and sequential steps. For instance, the main algorithm involved in subtraction is solving from right to left. 2. SEE: *Appendix 4: Computer Terms*

**All-group share**   A type of classroom activity wherein a student shares her/his writing(s) with a group and elicits responses and reactions to the shared writing(s).

**Alliteration**   A term (poetic terminology) that describes the occurrence of two or more words having the same beginning sound(s) such as: "Johnny Johnson joyously jumping."

**Allocated time**   The amount of time set aside for learning activities. Times allocated for different learning activities differ depending on the needs of the learners, the importance of the curriculum, imposed curriculum mandates, etc. Generally, teachers allocate more time for language arts activities (reading, writing, spelling) than any other subject as fundamental literacy is dependent on this important area of study.

**Alpha level**   The level of statistical significance established.

**Alpha waves**   A type of Electroencephalogram (EEG) record, in which the rises and drops in voltage occur from 8 to 12 times every second (i.e., the frequency of these waves equals 8 to 12 hertz [Hz]). Alpha waves occur when the individual is resting quietly with the eyes closed. Meditation is often practiced by individuals in order to produce alpha waves, which indicate comfortable relaxation.

**Alphabetic principle**   In language arts, the concept that children exposed to printed material and read to begin to understand that sounds and letters are related. It is an early phonemic or phonetic stage of development and mainly written with the use of consonants; one or more letters may represent a complete word. Example: "R CT JMP DN" = "Our cat jumped down."

**ALS**   SEE: *Amyotrophic Lateral Sclerosis*

**ALT (Academic Learning Time)**   This is the actual time spent on a learning task as opposed to the total time spent in class or school.

**Alternative education**   Educational experiences outside of the conventional educational experiences for students who cannot or do not want to be taught in traditional public school classes. Alternatives include home schooling, schools without walls, street academies, and free schools.

**Alternative futures**   A system or method used by persons who predict the future (also called futurists) based upon current knowledge. The idea is to take current trends and project them into the future in order to arrive at possible future alternatives.

**Alternative living unit**   Any type of residential setting other than a student's or individual's family home or residence. Alternative living units include but are not limited to foster homes, group homes, supervised dwellings (apartments, flats), and residential care placements and facilities.

**Alternative school**   A school designed to meet the needs of a special education student who is unable to progress effectively in a regular school program. It can be private or public. Such schools can also accommodate regular education students who are in need of new, different, and/or innovative programs.

**Altruism**   The disposition to act unselfishly for the benefit of other persons or for the sake of a larger group, such as one's country or all humanity. SEE: *egoism, ethics*

**Alveolar ridge**   The ridge of the mouth just above the upper front teeth.

**Alzheimer's disease**   (Alois Alzheimer, German neurologist, 1864–1915). A chronic and organic mental disorder classified as a dementia and sometimes referred to as "premature senility." It is accompanied by pathological changes in the cerebral cortex such as the appearance of "tangles" (the remains of dead nerve cells) and "plaques" (the accumu-

lation of abnormal protein material called amyloid). Most of the degenerated neurons are those that synthesize and release the neurotransmitter acetylcholine (ACh). The symptoms include forgetting (with loss of personal, biographical memory a prominent feature) and the loss of the ability to think clearly. Patients frequently will walk away from home and become lost. Other dementias are less frequent; these are Pick's disease and Creutzfeldt-Jakob disease.

**Ambidextrous**   The ability to use and work effectively with either the left or right hand.

**Ambivalent affect**   A condition wherein a student or person has mixed feelings toward another individual or some situation or event; that is, strong positive as well as negative feelings.

**Amblyopia or lazy eye**   Poor vision in a structurally sound eye. This condition involves an inability to focus both eyes on a fixed point. Thus, one eye is out of focus. If not corrected, this condition will continue to cause impaired visual functioning.

**Amblyopia ex anopsia**   A condition characterized by a dimness of vision as a result of nonuse of the eyes. It is usually in one eye and thus the brain suppresses the vision of the unused eye and uses the other. Squinting and poor visual acuity are associated with this condition. SEE: *amblyopia*

**Ambulation**   A term used to describe acts of walking or moving about at large.

**Amentia**   Seriously impaired intelligence (IQ usually 70 or below) or feeblemindedness; in effect, subnormal mental capacity or development.

**America 2000**   SEE: *Goals 2000*

**American Association on Mental Retardation (AAMR)**   An organization of persons and professionals from various backgrounds who monitor and interact in the treatment of individuals with mental retardation or retardation in general. The AAMR is an offshoot of an early advocacy group organized by

Edward Seguin in 1866. In 1876, with Seguin as its president, the group was named the "Association of Medical Officers of American Institutions for Idiotic and Feebleminded Persons." It was then renamed the American Association on Mental Deficiency and is now known as the American Association on Mental Retardation.

**American Federation of Teachers (AFT)**  A teachers organization, long affiliated with the AFL/CIO (American Federation of Labor and the Congress of Industrial Organizations). It is a professional organization committed to improved education for students and improved working conditions for teachers. John Dewey (U.S. philosopher and educator, 1859–1952), became the first card-carrying member in 1916. It is one of two of the largest professional organizations in the nation, the other being the National Education Association (NEA). SEE: *The National Education Association (NEA)*

**American Sign Language (ASL)**  One of the manual language systems for the deaf and hearing impaired. It is understood to be a method of communication that has its own language and grammar rules but is generally aligned with the linguistics standards of spoken English. ASL is a language unto itself. It is also known by the name of Ameslan. SEE: *Signing Exact English (SEE II), Seeing Essential English (SEE I)*

**Americans with Disabilities Act (1990) (ADA)**  A civil rights bill also known as P.L. 101-336. Its major premise is to eliminate discrimination against persons with disabilities. It guarantees equal opportunity in the areas of public accommodations, telecommunication, public services to include transportation, and employment. SEE: *Appendix 2: Legal Terms and Issues*

**Ameslan**  The nickname for American Sign Language. SEE: *American Sign Language (ASL)*

**Amimia**  Inability to use signs and/or gestures to express oneself. This may be complete or partial but in any case it may contribute to a severe inability to communicate.

**Amnesia**  A loss of memory in part or totally. It is frequently associated with hysterical, epileptic, traumatic, senile, and alcoholic episodes as well as other organic brain syndromes.

**Amniocentesis**  A medical procedure that analyzes amniotic fluid taken from the uterus in which the embryo is suspended. The fluid is drawn through a needle and inserted through the abdomen and into the uterus. Analysis of the watery fluid helps to determine some types of genetic defects (e.g., Down Syndrome).

**Amplification device**  Any mechanical device used to increase the volume of sound (typically for hearing-impaired individuals).

**Amplitude**  The intensity or strength of an energy wave, such as a light wave, sound wave, or EEG wave.

**Amputation**  1. The absence of a limb that might occur congenitally in the fetus in utero or 2. surgical removal of a limb or part of an organ.

**Amputee**  A person who has had one or more limbs surgically removed.

**Amygdala**  A structure in the limbic system that is part of the cerebral cortex located in the base of the temporal lobe. The amygdala is involved in our emotions. Damage to the amygdala can cause fighting or the eating of inappropriate substances. SEE: *limbic system, cerebral cortex, temporal lobes*

**Amyotonia congenita**  A deficiency or lack of muscle tone. One's ability to walk or even sit or stand is adversely affected. It normally appears at or shortly after birth and the lower extremities are usually involved first. It is also known as Oppenheim's disease (Herman Oppenheim, German neurologist, 1858–1919).

**Amyotrophic Lateral Sclerosis (ALS)**  A disease characterized by muscular weakness and atrophy of the muscles. It is a motor neuron disease that is sometimes called Lou Gehrig's disease for the great New York Yankee baseball player whose career and life were cut short by ALS.

**Anacusis/anacusia**   A condition of complete deafness; total loss of hearing.

**Anal stage**   The second stage of personality development as proposed in the psychoanalytic theory of Sigmund Freud. It begins at the age of one and lasts until age four. It is during this stage that the superego, the third of the three parts of the mind, takes form. Supposedly, the way in which this is achieved is by means of toilet training; the child learns to anticipate the demands of adults rather than continuing to act in an unrestrained way.

**Analgesia**   Pain relief.

**Analogical thinking**   A heuristic technique. Analogical thinking involves attempting to solve a problem by looking at solutions from other problems whose solutions resemble the current problem situation. Example: (vocabulary analogy) River is to boat as road is to_____. A correct response could be "car." By analogical thinking one arrives at a possible solution—a boat is used to travel on a river; therefore, a car could be used to travel on a road.

**Analysis of Covariance (ANCOVA)**   A type of statistical method that attempts to estimate if two or more groups would have differed on a particular criterion variable if the effects of variables associated with the criterion variable are eliminated.

**Analysis of dreams**   A technique of psychotherapy developed by Sigmund Freud. The assumptions behind it are that unacceptable wishes and shameful memories are repressed into the unconscious part of the mind and that these repressed thoughts will produce neurotic symptoms and the contents of dreams, among other things. When the patient reports the content of his/her dreams, the Freudian therapist treats these details as "manifest content;" this apparent dream material is considered to be a mask for the true thoughts, the "latent content." By explaining the "true

meaning" of these dream images to the patient, the psychoanalyst is supposedly providing the patient with the insight necessary for a cure to be achieved.

**Analysis of free associations**   One of the psychoanalytic techniques developed by Sigmund Freud. The patient keeps on saying whatever comes to his/her mind as a response to each stated word. When an expressed thought is followed by a delay, the psychoanalytic therapist regards this as a "block," and the just stated word is regarded as a very important key to the material repressed in the patient's unconscious. As more and more important keys are brought out, the analyst gains the ability to understand the patient's deeper problems. The analyst then provides the patient with insight, which is the first step in exposing repressed material to the patient's consciousness and the patient regaining his/her mental health.

**Analysis of resistance**   A therapeutic technique used by psychoanalysts somewhat after the analysis has begun to interpret the patient's repressions. The patient seldom accepts the interpretation immediately, usually expressing disbelief. This so-called resistance is worked through, with the analyst pointing out to the patient that the vehemence of the patient's denials supposedly amounts to an admission that the information has some validity after all.

**Analysis of teaching**   A self-evaluation technique for teachers. The concept is to recommend and encourage teachers to critique themselves and their teaching techniques. The ultimate goal is an improved teacher and thus improved education for students.

**Analysis of transference**   During a lengthy psychotherapy, the patient usually develops extreme attachment and/or dependence on the therapist. The therapist uses this inappropriate emotion to show the patient that he/she is supposedly treating the therapist as one of the patient's parents or lovers. The transference is then thought to be an opportunity for further interpretation, bringing on insight on the part of the patient.

**Analysis of Variance (ANOVA)**   A type of statistical procedure or method that allows one to examine the probability that differences among two or more groups are a result of chance. The use of ANOVA is important when comparing: 1. mean values between experimental and control groups in a study (e.g., an experimental group is given instruction in the writing process and a control group of students is given no instruction; 2. pre- and post-test comparisons of mean scores for two groups of individuals or subjects (e.g., math achievement scores of first and third graders are compared at the beginning of the school year and then at the end of the school year); and 3. the comparison of mean values/scores between several groups of subjects individuals (e.g., comparing males to females at various age levels; individuals with learning disabilities to those without disabilities at different grade levels; third, fourth, and fifth graders' performance in field day activities; etc.).

**Analytic instruction**   A type of instruction that involves the analyses of students' cognitive learning styles and metacognitive strategies. The students' conceptual knowledge base is continually assessed and strengthened. SEE: *cognitive styles, metacognitive strategy instruction*

**Analytic listening**   The act of hearing what is said or communicated and critically evaluating or interpreting what one hears.

**Analytic philosophy**   The investigation of the meaning of certain terms such as "causation," "mind," "equal opportunity," "affirmative action," "justice," etc. This investigation is done in a skeptical manner by philosophers who are not interested in founding entire systems of thought. For example, Nietzsche or Russell would be a better example of an analytic philosopher than Socrates or Plato. SEE: *prescriptive philosophy, speculative philosophy*

**Analytic phonics approaches**   These are phonics approaches that focus stu-

dents first on mastering a number of easily learned words. Letter sounds, phonics rules, and generalizations are discovered through inductive reasoning. Analytic approaches are best used with beginning readers who appear not to have reading/learning problems. SEE: *synthetic phonics approaches*

**Analytic scoring**   A system for scoring essays in which separate grades are recorded for organization, spelling, and accuracy of content. The opposite approach is known as "holistic scoring."

**Analytic touch**   A system of mental reconstruction. The student mentally reconstructs various parts of an object(s) that he/she is handling.

**Anaphia**   A term that refers to an individual's loss of the sense of touch.

**Anathria**   A central nervous system disorder that results in one's lack of ability to speak (loss of speech).

**Anchoring ideas**   The notion that new material can be "anchored" or related to material that is familiar. The familiar material helps the learner conceptually to assimilate and accommodate this new information.

**ANCOVA**   SEE: *Analysis of Covariance*

**Androgen**   A male sex hormone. Androgens are examples of steroids. Testosterone is one of the androgens.

**Anecdotal record**   A brief written description of a subject's performance on one occasion. This may be obtained during the course of a study of behavior using the method of naturalistic observation.

**Anemia**   A disorder of the red blood cells characterized by an inability of the cells to carry a sufficient amount of hemoglobin, resulting in a lack of oxygen carried within the cell. Symptoms of anemia include weariness, paleness, weakness, and jaundice. SEE: *hemoglobin, sickle cell anemia*

**Anencephaly**   A condition characterized by failure of the development of the brain.

**Aneneia**   A condition characterized by mutism as a result of deafness.

**Aniseikonia**   A medical visual condition in which the ocular image of one eye differs in size and shape from the other.

**Ankyloglossia**   A condition in which the flap that holds the tongue to the floor of the mouth is attached too far forward or too short limiting the ability to produce tongue-tip sounds; a condition of being tongue-tied.

**Ankylosis**   A medical condition characterized by an unusual and abnormal stiffening or fixation of a joint of the body as a result of pathological changes within the joint or surrounding tissue.

**Annual goals**   The general goals listed in a student's Individualized Educational Plan (IEP). It is required by IDEA (P.L. 101-476) (formerly EHA, P.L. 94-142) for special needs children. SEE: *IDEA, P.L. 94-142, IEP*

**Annual increments**   The standard steps based upon years of service and experience; found in teacher salary scales/contracts. The step compares to the number of years taught and thus determines salary levels.

**Anodontia**   No teeth; the absence of teeth.

**Anomaly**   A term used to describe an organ or structure that is abnormal. It is frequently a congenital malformation. SEE: *congenital*

**Anomia**   Difficulty with or an inability to recognize names or to remember objects; recall and recognition of names and objects may be partially or completely lacking. SEE: *nominal aphasia*

**Anomie**   A social condition wherein a person has feelings of not belonging and alienation to social norms, standards, and especially accepted codes of conduct. It was coined by a social theorist named Emile Durkheim during the 1890s.

**Anophthalmos**   Also called anophthalmia, it is the absence of one or both eyes as a result of a congenital anomaly.

**Anorexia nervosa**   An eating disorder in which the patient avoids eating in the attempt to become slim. There is a distorted body image to the extent that even a very thin person may see himself/herself as being obese. This self-starvation process may be carried to the point of fatality.

**Anosmia**   The loss of the sense of smell.

**ANOVA**   SEE: *Analysis of Variance*

**Anoxia**   A serious lack of oxygenated blood severe enough to cause brain damage. Anoxia of brain tissue could cause mental retardation.

**ANS**   SEE: *Autonomic Nervous System*

**Antecedent**   Events/stimuli that precede measurable behavior changes.

**Anterior**   Toward the front of the body.

**Anterograde amnesia**   The inability to form relatively permanent memories (i.e., Long-Term Memories (LTM) or the constituents of LTM) resulting from an injury to the hippocampus, even though preinjury LTM is intact.

**Antianxiety drugs**   Psychoactive drugs that are used to relieve anxiety (vague fears). These drugs are also known as the minor tranquilizers. Prozac is one example; another is Valium.

**Anticonvulsant**   An agent or medication that relieves or prevents a convulsion or seizure. SEE: *seizure*

**Antidepressant**   A drug given to relieve depression.

**Antidiscrimination**   SEE: *Appendix 2, Legal Terms and Issues*

**Antimania drugs**   Psychoactive drugs that relieve mania, a condition of irrational euphoria and overconfidence carried to a psychotic extreme. Examples of such drugs are lithium carbonate and reserpine.

**Antipsychotic drugs**   Also called neuroleptics, these psychoactive drugs are used to relieve the positive symptoms of schizophrenia. Positive symptoms are manifest and overt; they include paranoid delusions, hallucinations, catatonic motor symptoms (e.g., waxy flexibility), speaking in gibberish, etc.

**Antiretroviral agent**   Any agent that inhibits the function of a retrovirus (the common name for Retroviridae,

RNA-containing tumor viruses). These viruses involve the reversal of the transfer of genetic information (in this case, a molecule of DNA from an RNA model).

**Antisocial personality disorder** A personality disorder marked by impulsiveness and lack of ethical restraint. Criminal acts can be performed readily by such an individual because there is a lack of moral control and an absence of the ability to experience feelings of guilt. SEE: *psychopath*

**Antonym** In language arts, a word directly opposed to another in meaning. For example, *hot* is the antonym of *cold.*

**Anvil (or incus)** One of the bones in the middle ear involved in carrying sound vibrations through the middle ear to the inner ear. SEE: *incus*

**Anxiety** A troubled feeling, a state of emotional unrest, or tension to the degree that it causes apprehension and fear. The distress produced may be from a real or imagined threat to one's physical or emotional well-being. It is particularly tied to fear of the future. SEE: *anxiety neurosis, neurosis*

**Anxiety disorder** Any of several kinds of neurotic conditions involving irrational or vague fears that cannot be attributed to objectively present dangers.

**Anxiety neurosis** A functional disease in which fear is out of proportion to actual circumstances. Symptoms of anxiety such as sweating, palpitations, trembling, and others are not a result of any disease or organic cause. The individual may or may not be conscious as to the reasons for this feeling of anxiety and abnormal fear from an imagined or real but minor threat. SEE: *neurosis, anxiety*

**Anxiety-withdrawal** A type of deviant behavior in which the child shows symptoms that may include timidity, shyness, withdrawal, sensitivity, submissiveness, extreme dependency, and depression.

**Apert's syndrome** A narrowing of the skull to such a degree that the development of the brain is adversely affected. It can result in mental retardation unless surgical intervention takes place. It is a congenital condition marked by a peak-like head with manifestations such as malocclusion and webbed fingers and toes.

**Apgar score** (Virginia Apgar, Contemporary American Physician 1909–1974.) A system for scoring an infant's physical condition one minute and five minutes after birth. Developed in 1952, it measures heart rate (beats per minute), respiratory effort, muscle tone, reflex irritability, and skin color. It is scaled 0 (low), 1 (middle), and 2 (high and best). All are then totaled for the final Apgar (10 is highest possible score).

**Aphagia** A loss of interest in eating as the result of brain damage. The individual may starve to death unless fed intravenously.

**Aphasia** A language impairment presumably resulting from central nervous system damage that involves impaired comprehension or an inability to communicate clearly.

**Aphonia** The impairment or inability to produce sounds of speech from the larynx as in the case of laryngitis or the complete loss of voice.

**Appeal** SEE: *Appendix 2: Legal Terms and Issues*

**Appellant** SEE: *Appendix 2: Legal Terms and Issues*

**Appellee** SEE: *Appendix 2: Legal Terms and Issues*

**Applied behavioral analysis** An approach to teaching behavior management that involves charting and observing behaviors and then analyzing the frequency, duration, and context of those behaviors. Behaviors are task-analyzed and recorded so that applied teaching techniques and reinforcement schedules can be assessed before and after for effectiveness. Student behavior is monitored and recorded during all phases of this approach.

**Applied research** Research conducted so as to apply or test a hypothesis/theory and then evaluate usefulness of data in problem solving.

**Appreciative listening**   The act of enjoying what one is hearing and liking what one hears (e.g., listening to one's favorite singer).

**Approach-approach conflict**   A conflict of motives is a clash of two different tendencies to act, with the two actions being incompatible with one another. An approach motive is a behavior tendency having a positive goal, such that the organism having that motive will approach the goal in an attempt to attain it. When two approach tendencies are both active at one time, the tendency to approach one of the two goals may carry the organism farther away from the second goal. In that case, the organism is involved in one type of conflict, namely, one between two opposed approach tendencies, or approach-approach conflict. For example, if you have limited funds, you may be able to afford a desktop computer or a CD player, but not both. If you want to get both, you are in an approach-approach conflict.

**Approach-avoidance conflict**   A conflict of motives is a clash between two different motives. Sometimes a part of one's environment has ambivalent features, meaning that it is partly desirable and partly feared. The individual therefore has a tendency to approach the ambivalent stimulus as well as a tendency to move away from it. These two tendencies are incompatible with one another. The individual, as a result, is in a condition of approach-avoidance conflict.

**Approximation**   A condition of language development wherein young children have not quite mastered the rules of language. An example of approximation would be nontraditional spelling in writing by young children such as, "I hva new ct," which approximates, "I have a new cat." Such invented spelling is encouraged during beginning writing tasks so that the stress is on the ideation/creative aspects of writing versus the mechanics (i.e., spelling/grammar).

**Apraxia**   The loss of the ability to perform a particular motor task; this usu-ally results from a specific injury to a part of the cerebral cortex.

**Aptitude**   The capacity to perform a specific type of activity. The activity involved is usually more narrowly defined than an activity related to "an ability." One may show an aptitude for mathematics or for music, as examples.

**Aptitude-achievement discrepancy**   A comparison or the difference between scores on a standardized test of achievement versus a student's actual potential. An example of such a discrepancy would be a bright student who scores very low on a standardized achievement test in reading. Thus, a discrepancy would exist between real ability and actual achievement.

**Aptitude tests**   These are tests that measure a student's general or specific abilities within a narrowly focused field of study such as art or music.

**Aptitude Treatment Interaction (ATI)**   The interaction of individual differences among students with methods of instruction. (e.g., Method A works best with students of Type T.) For example, some students with learning disabilities perform best when material and exams are given via an oral/aural presentation.

**Aquaphobia**   A fear of water.

**Aqueous humor**   A watery substance between the cornea and lens of the eye.

**Arbitration**   Part of the collective-bargaining process that involves having two parties (e.g., teachers vs. school committee) who are deadlocked on an issue and appointing a third party to hear both sides of an issue (e.g., pay increase). The arbiter studies the facts presented and makes a decision that is generally binding for both parties involved.

**ARC**   1. A National Organization on Mental Retardation, "The Association for Retarded Citizens." This is a support group that works and lobbies on behalf of persons (e.g., improved and expanded services). ARC also provides support services/ common meeting facilities for family members and friends. 2. SEE: *Aids Related Complex*

**Archetypes**   In Carl Jung's theory, each of us has an unconscious part of the mind that we share among ourselves simply because we are all human; that is, the racial unconscious or the collective unconscious. The elements of that part of the mind are neither linguistic nor logical; they are mental images that are found to be present in all human societies. Such images are termed archetypes in the terminology of Jung's analytical psychology system.

**Architectural barrier**   A barrier or condition in the physical environment that prevents individuals with disabilities or other conditions from using the facilities or moving about as optimally as possible. For example, staircases in relation to persons using wheelchairs.

**Area vocational center**   A facility that provides instruction in vocational education (e.g., auto mechanics, medical assistants) to students from a school system or region. Students attending an area vocational center receive academic programs in regular secondary schools or other institutions.

**Arnold-Chiari deformity**   (Julius Arnold, German Pathologist, 1835–1915; Hans Chiari, German Pathologist, 1851–1916) A malformation of the cerebellar hemisphere. It is one of the factors in hydrocephalus and is usually associated with spina bifida, and meningomyelocele. SEE: *hydrocephalus, spina bifida, meningomyelocele*

**Arousal**   Any physiological or mental reactions that could be classified as increased alertness or greater attentiveness.

**Arraignment**   SEE: *Appendix 2: Legal Terms and Issues*

**Array of services**   Refers to the availability of a group or battery of educational personnel, services, and/or placements that are available to a student or person.

**Arson**   SEE: *Appendix 2: Legal Terms and Issues*

**Arteriosclerosis**   A hardening and thickening of the walls of the arteries, resulting in high blood pressure.

**Arthritis**   Inflammation of a joint of the body, which frequently includes changes in structure, swelling, stiffness, and pain.

**Arthrodesis/arthrodosis**   The fixation of a joint through surgery. Cartilage is removed and thus the bones are allowed to grow together.

**Arthrogryposis**   A congenital condition in which poorly developed muscles result in contraction or crooking of the joints.

**Articulation**   The altering of the flow of air from the lungs by the movement of the mouth and tongue to shape sounds into speech.

**Articulation disorder**   Disorders that involve the omission, substitution, or distortion of speech sounds or segments.

**Articulators**   The body structures used to alter the passage of air through the vocal tract such as the larynx, pharynx, velum, tongue, lips, teeth, etc.

**Artifact**   In regard to assessment, the concrete learning outcomes generated from learners (e.g., written work, art work, a taped speech, a videotaped lesson, etc).

**Artificial Intelligence (AI)**   A special area of computer science in which the computer is programmed to work out procedures by the use of logic. The study of the psychology of thinking can benefit from developments in AI, and some of the work in AI may be derived from some principles of cognitive psychology. SEE: *Appendix 4, Computer Terms*

**Artificial larynx**   An alternative method of speech used by persons who have had a laryngectomy (removal of the larynx). This alternative speaker uses a device that is hand-held and battery-powered. This device is pressed against the neck and produces a vibrating sound that passes through the neck and into the throat. The speaker pantomimes the words to be spoken by shaping the articulators and thus produces mechanically sounding speech. SEE: *articulators, esophageal speech, larynx*

**Asian-Americans**   1. Americans who are from the Far East or related to peoples from the Far East. 2. Asians from the Far East living in the United States.

**ASL** SEE: *American Sign Language*

**Asphyxia** A condition characterized by a lack of oxygen. A lack of sufficient oxygen can cause or contribute to many and varied handicapping conditions such as anoxia resulting in brain damage. SEE: *anoxia*

**Assault** The act of intentional physical contact without an individual's permission, causing fear or apprehension of battery. SEE: *battery, Appendix 2: Legal Terms and Issues*

**Assertive discipline** An attitude toward child-rearing or early education involving firmness and clarity but not including threatening or harshly punitive procedures.

**Assertiveness training** Training in the social art of expressing oneself openly and forcefully, without resorting to rudeness or aggressiveness.

**Assessment** The general process of gathering data and analyzing those data to assist in making decisions about class procedures. Information is collected about teacher and/or student performance, student behaviors, and classroom atmosphere. SEE: *Appendix 2: Legal Terms and Issues*

**Assessment error** Any systematic inaccuracy in data gathered in the assessment process. There may have been a poorly administered test, a fault test, unreliability of test responses as a result of guesswork by respondents, etc. At least a small amount of error should be expected in any set of assessment data. SEE: *Appendix 2: Legal Terms and Issues*

**Assessment portfolios** SEE: *portfolio*

**Assimilation** A process of cognitive development, described by child psychologist Jean Piaget, in which new data are fitted into already present knowledge systems or schemes.

**Assistive communication** Any type or form of communication that replaces, supports, or supplants speaking. SEE: *augmentative communication*

**Assistive listening devices** Devices that aid hearing-impaired students or persons such as hearing aids, cochlear implants, FM transmission devices, audio loops, etc. SEE: *audio loop, FM transmission device*

**Assistive technology** Refers to the positives of technological advances as they help individuals with disabilities and other conditions function and cope with the environment. Such technology can range from low-tech adding machines to high-tech word processors.

**Associate degree** Degree based on less than four years of work beyond high school. Typically, associate degrees involve a two-year program in the liberal arts areas and two to three years in nursing (e.g., students with associate degrees frequently transfer their two to three years of credits into four-year institutions of higher learning in order to obtain baccalaureate degrees or bachelor's degrees). SEE: *bachelor's degree*

**Association** A term used to describe one's cognitive/thinking ability to connect and to see the relationship between knowledge, data, concepts, and/or information from differing sources.

**Association areas** Areas of the cerebral cortex that are neither the terminals of direct neural pathways from sense organs nor the starting points of direct nerve pathways to the muscles and glands. Many of these areas are used for various higher mental processes.

**Astereognosis** The inability to recognize familiar objects. SEE: *agnosia*

**Asthenia** Without strength. While it can be any weakness, it particularly pertains to muscular or cerebellar disease.

**Asthenopia** Painful vision resulting from a weakness of the eye muscles.

**Asthma** A respiratory problem involving episodic difficulties in breathing (dyspnea). Individuals who are asthmatic have more intensified or induced asthmatic attacks (wheezing/breathing problems) when under stress, poor weather conditions, or when in contact with allergy-causing items (e.g., pollen).

**Astigmatism** Blurred vision due to differences in the refraction of light at different parts of the cornea; the result of this uneven bending of light rays is that when some parts of the visual stimulus are brought into focus, others have to remain out of focus.

**Asymbolia** An inability to use any type of symbol, especially in music and math. It may also include signs, words, or gestures. It is a form of aphasia. Also called asemia or asemasia. SEE: *aphasia*

**Asymmetrical Tonic Neck Reflex (ATNR)** A natural reflex in very young infants (up to four months of age) that involves turning the head to the side, causing the arm and leg on that particular side, to automatically extend toward the head. The opposite arm and leg fall into a flexed position. Physicians will look at the ATNR reflex carefully as an abnormal reflex action; after the age of four months this sometimes indicates brain injury.

**At-home reading** As the term implies, time outside of the classroom involving a student with his/her parent, guardian, or tutor in the home in reading situations. The adult supervises the reading whether it be aloud or silent.

**At risk** Usually refers to children who are "at risk" for school failure because of learning/environment/medical problems.

**Ataxia** A condition involving discoordination problems of balance, posture, directionality, and general orientation in space. Both fine and gross motor skills and movements are affected. The individual with ataxia has noticeable difficulty in performing simple tasks such as reaching for an object or taking a step. This condition can be considered a type of cerebral palsy. SEE: *cerebral palsy*

**Atheism** The view that it is possible to reach a conclusion about the existence of God and that answer is negative (i.e., the atheist states positively that there is no God).

**Atherosclerosis** A type of arteriosclerosis involving a roughening of the normally smooth arterial linings.

**Athetoid** Involuntary, meaningless, and uncontrollable movement. SEE: *athetosis*

**Athetoid cerebral palsy** A type of cerebral palsy. SEE: *athetosis*

**Athetosis** A severe muscular condition that involves sudden and involuntary jerky movements with writhing movements of the fingers and wrists most evident. This condition can be considered a type of cerebral palsy. SEE: *cerebral palsy*

**Athletics, access to** SEE: *Appendix 2: Legal Terms and Issues.*

**ATI** SEE: *Aptitude Treatment Interaction*

**ATNR** SEE: *Assymetrical Tonic Neck Reflex*

**Atonia** The absence of or a deficiency in muscle tone.

**Atonic cerebral palsy** A type of cerebral palsy whereby the individual lacks muscle tone (e.g., floppiness).

**Atresia** A physical condition of the external auditory canal in which the external canal is not completely formed.

**Atrophy** The degeneration or destruction of tissue(s).

**Atropinization** Administration of atropine, which dilates the pupils of the eyes as a means to treat cataracts (the clouding-over of the lens of the eye).

**Attainment value** Placing a value on good performance or the relationship of success on a task to one's own needs. Attaining good grades in school would be a higher priority or have higher attainment value for a student who is trying to seek a scholarship.

**Attendance center** A legal and/or administrative area that sets boundaries to determine which children will attend which school.

**Attention** The selection of particular sensations, memory images, and/or thought processes for cognitive elaboration from the complex totality of all present sensations, images, and thoughts.

**Attention Deficit Disorder (ADD)** A childhood disorder similar to attention-deficit/hyperactivity disorder except that hyperactivity is not present. SEE:

*Attention-Deficit/Hyperactivity Disorder (ADHD)*

**Attention-Deficit/Hyperactivity Disorder (ADHD)**   According to DSM-IV, this is a childhood disorder (diagnosed in approximately 5–10 percent of school-age children) that involves both an attention deficit and hyperactivity, which persist for at least six months. The ADHD child is not always able to function satisfactorily both at school and at home because of 1. difficulty following directions and executing tasks to their completion, 2. difficulty in maintaining adequate attention during schoolwork and at play, 3. excessive fidgeting, squirming, moving, and running around, 4. difficulty listening to others, and 5. an inability to wait one's turn while speaking. Other signs of ADHD are: absent-mindedness, frequent mood swings, clumsiness, a poor sense of direction, being easily irritated and hot-tempered, disorganization in play and at work, an inability to follow through with tasks (especially tasks requiring sustained attention), low frustration tolerance, haphazardness in strategies used to problem solve, and being easily overwhelmed even by small tasks. This disorder is diagnosed in two to eight times more boys than girls and can be found in many cultures. The treatment for adults and children is generally the same with medication, counseling (e.g., channeling energies into productive avenues), and appropriate education interventions combined for those with severe cases of ADHD. The primary medications used are Ritalin, Dexedrine, and Cylert (stimulant medications). ADHD tends to run in families with approximately one-third of all diagnosed cases also involving another immediate family member. There are also positive aspects to ADHD as many individuals (both children and adults) successfully adapt and become very productive/contributing members of society. Specifically, this population has many individuals who are "resilient," with good self-esteem and a sense of optimism. The resiliency, in particular, allows the individual to be persistent and achieve goals even after repeated failures. Some believe that Albert Einstein, Winston Churchill, and others were ADHD as adults, which demonstrates that this disorder need not be disruptive/negative to one's life. Regardless, trained professionals need to be consulted when an individual experiences ADHD or any other learning disability. SEE: *Learning Disability (LD)*

**Attention deficits**   A condition frequently associated with students or persons with learning disabilities. Individuals with this condition have difficulty staying on task and paying attention to instruction for any length of time. SEE: *Attention Deficit Disorder (ADD), Attention-Deficit/Hyperactivity Disorder (ADHD)*

**Attention span**   The length of time a student can attend to tasks or concentrate on an activity before losing her/his concentration and interest.

**Attentive listening**   The ability of a student or person to focus out other stimuli and listen and concentrate on one source or stimulus being heard.

**Attitude**   A disposition to behave favorably or unfavorably toward some object, person, event, or idea. An attitude has emotional and cognitive components. Examples of emotional components of an attitude would be love and hate; examples of cognitive components might be favorable biases and prejudiced opinions.

**Attitude inventory**   An assessment instrument used that typically involves a series of questions that stimulate and initiate thought/discussion regarding a particular topic (e.g., attitude toward mathematics). Many times statements are presented and the individual is asked to agree or strongly agree, disagree, or form no opinion.

**Attribute chart**   One method of categorizing information (attribute = a characteristic) gathered as the result of reading, experimentation, observation, and the like. Typically a subject area (attribute) is designated, such as "height," and subcategories might include "short," "average," and "tall" and this information is charted for visualization/understanding. In language arts, this is an effective post-reading strategy in that students are condensing important information and are making connections. Students can classify by more than one attribute (e.g., classifying by shape, color, and size in mathematics).

**Attributes**   In education, a term that describes general characteristics of a group. A more general meaning would include a quality or characteristic of any student, person, or thing.

**Attribution**   Attempts to account for our own behaviors and thoughts. The explanation of these attempts constitutes a sub-field of social psychology called "attribution theory."

**Attribution theories**   Theories that explain how an individual tends to account for his/her own motives and/or actions.

**Audience inhibition**   The unwillingness of a bystander to offer assistance to someone in need of help when other bystanders are also present.

**Audio loop**   An Assistive Listening Device (ALD) that aids a hearing-impaired person through the use of a special hearing aid. The instructions are heard directly in the ear of the learner. Sound may be looped by wire or radio waves and the listener must sit within the loop.

**Audio-visual material**   Any educational material or device that uses either sight or sound or both to facilitate learning (e.g., a tape recorder, video cassette recorder, video player, cassette player, maps, charts, etc.).

**Audiodescription**   A technique that involves the use of FM transmission or the available (extra) sound track on stereo televisions. A trained specialist narrates what is happening on stage, in a film, or in a television program through the use of FM transmission directly to the hearing-impaired listener. SEE: *FM transmission device*

**Audiogram**   The charting of pure tone conduction and bone conduction results on a grid or chart. Frequencies tested run across the top of the grid with the amount of hearing loss in decibels running down the side of the grid. The type or kind of hearing test used along with the ear tested are noted in symbolic form. SEE: *decibel, frequency, hertz*

**Audiologist**   A person trained to identify types of hearing losses, to interpret audiometric tests, and to recommend equipment and procedures to assist the hearing impaired.

**Audiology**   The science that deals with the diagnosis of hearing problems and, if possible, their remediation.

**Audiometer**   A special instrument or machine used to measure hearing acuity.

**Audiometric zero (zero decibel level)** This is the lowest level at which individuals with normal hearing can detect sound.

**Audiometry**   A method of testing using an audiometer to measure the hearing of a person. SEE: *audiometer*

**Audition**   SEE: *hearing*

**Auditory acuity**   The sensitivity of the ear to sound stimuli with the ability to detect sound falling in the range of 25–60 decibels (dB) with frequencies of 500–2000 Hertz (Hz). SEE: *hertz (Hz), decibel (dB)*

**Auditory analysis**   An ability of a student or person to separate and comprehend various components of an auditory communication.

**Auditory association**   The ability of a student or person to connect the meanings of words or information that are verbally presented.

**Auditory blending**   The ability of a student or person to synthesize phonemes (smallest units of sound) of words when the words are pronounced with pauses between the phonemes.

**Auditory Brainstem Response (ABR)** Measurement of changes of electrical brain-wave activity. This medical procedure involves electrodes that are attached to the scalp. It is used with infants, young children, and those adults who are unable to participate in audiometric testing on a voluntary basis.

**Auditory canal**   A passageway from the inside of the head to the middle ear. SEE: *external auditory canal*

**Auditory cortex**   That area of the cerebral cortex that receives the neural inputs from the hearing organs (the cochleae of the two inner ears). The auditory cortex is located on the uppermost convolution of the temporal lobe.

**Auditory decoding**   One's ability to gather (glean) meaning from verbally expressed information.

**Auditory discrimination**   The ability to detect differences between sound stimuli that may vary (e.g., loudness or pitch). The ability to distinguish between similarly sounding words, such as *ice cream* and *I scream*, is important for beginning readers.

**Auditory figure-ground**   The ability of a student or person to separate out a certain sound or word from other sounds or words being heard at the same time.

**Auditory group trainers**   Sound amplification apparatus, usually an FM system, used to communicate with a group of hearing-impaired students or persons. The system is wireless and thus removes restrictions upon the movements of the teacher or presenter and the hearing-impaired members of the group.

**Auditory integration**   The ability of a student or individual to connect a sound or sound combinations, as in the case of spoken words or sentences, with past and present experiences.

**Auditory localization**   The ability to differentiate among sounds with various pitch and loudness so as to be able to locate the sound's source or point of origin.

**Auditory memory**   The ability to retain information originally acquired by hearing.

**Auditory nerve**   The nerve running from the cochlea the hearing organ to the medulla of the brain. It is part of the eighth cranial nerve. SEE: *cochlea, auditory processing*

**Auditory perception**   The ability of a student or person to not only understand what he/she hears but to meaningfully interpret what he/she has heard in an organized fashion.

**Auditory processing**   The act of hearing or listening wherein sounds are channeled through the external auditory canal, to the tympanic membrane (ear drum) and middle ear (ossicles), and then past the oval window via the auditory nerve to the brain for interpretation of what has been heard by the brain. SEE: *auditory nerve, cochlea, ossicles*

**Auditory receptive language**   A general term used to describe one's ability to understand what has been heard. SEE: *auditory perception, auditory sequential memory*

**Auditory sequential memory**   The ability of a student or person to correctly repeat what she/he has heard in proper sequence. SEE: *auditory receptive language*

**Auditory training**   Procedures for training individuals who are hard of hearing to make the best possible use of their residual hearing.

**Auditory-visual integration**   The ability of a student or individual to connect sounds with symbols in the form of understanding of the relationship; for example, phonetic symbols used to indicate certain sounds.

**Auditory vocal association**   The ability of a student or person to meaningfully relate to what he/she hears; relating appropriately to the spoken word.

**Augmentative communication**   Systems, programs, methods, teaching strategies, etc. used to expand or enhance the communication skills of students whose speech is unintelligible or who in fact do not speak at all. A child who has great difficulty communicating verbally can use gestural and/or electronic assistance to explain ideas and to understand and communicate more effectively. Such would be the case if a child with cerebral palsy used a pointer, keyboard, computer, etc. SEE: *Appendix 4: Computer Terms*

**Aura**  A perceptual sensation, sometimes experienced before an epileptic seizure, involving the perception of such things as sounds, odors, and visual images.

**Auricle (pinna)**  That visible portion of the ear that is composed of cartilage. The auricle is responsible for collecting sounds from the environment and then funneling those sounds through the auditory canal to the eardrum.

**Authentic assessment**  An assessment of student learning based on a comparison to practical and real-world situations. Outcomes and achievement are measured in as close a fashion as possible to the style or way the student learned. Portfolios are a type of authentic assessment. SEE: *portfolio*

**Authentic tests**  Assessment methods testing how the individual performs in real-life situations, meanwhile revealing his/her levels of ability in various skills.

**Author study**  An in-depth exploration of literature wherein all the works of an author are studied. This also applies to in-depth studies of illustrators. Students are expected to become somewhat expert at identifying the writing style of an author or illustrator. SEE: *illustrator study*

**Authoritarian parenting**  Parent disciplining that includes the setting of rules/consequences/expected behaviors/responsibilities for a child.

**Authoritarian personality**  A personality type characterized by an eagerness to control one's subordinates and to obey the orders of one's superiors to the letter. It is often accompanied by an overzealous identification with one's group and a bigoted attitude toward members of other groups.

**Authoritarianism**  A philosophy that encourages respect for and confidence in persons or institutions of authority. Individual rights must defer to the rights and power of the authority or the person(s) in charge.

**Authoritative/contractual**  The use of language that refers to contracts, laws, regulations, etc.

**Authoritative parenting**  A style of parenting wherein the parent sets limits for the child and enforces the limits in an appropriate way, usually in a spirit of warmth and love. This type of parenting style lets the child have some say in what the rules and consequences of behavior are to be.

**Authoritative truth**  The notion that authority provides us with the knowledge of what is true. The authority may be ancestral, religious, or political. SEE: *epistemology*

**Autism**  A severe childhood psychosis that involves complete withdrawal from the world, cognitive impairments, a lack of ability to interact in social situations, a lack of appropriate affect, and self-stimulating behaviors.

**Automated Learning Device (ALD)**  Any adaptations to a device (e.g., an appliance, steering control, etc.) that allows it to be used by persons with disabilities.

**Automatic processing**  The elaboration of incoming perceptual data without having to use deliberate mental effort. Such processing will not affect the performance of any unrelated active behaviors that may be going on at the time.

**Automaticity**  The performance of an activity smoothly and automatically as the result of having previously learned the task very thoroughly. As an example, *automaticity* in word recognition is an important prerequisite to comprehension proficiency. If too much time is spent on sounding out or identifying words, fewer cognitive energies can be spent on trying to derive word meaning.

**Autonomic nervous system (ANS)**  That part of the peripheral nervous system which communicates to the smooth muscles and glands. The ANS has two divisions: the parasympathetic nervous system (PNS) and the sympathetic nervous system (SNS).

**Autonomy**  The ability to carry out a task or set of tasks independently. Independent learners are autonomous in the sense that they can follow a set of directions and complete a task with little direct supervision.

**Autonomy versus shame and doubt**
The second of Erik Erikson's eight stages of personality development, occurring in the second year of age. Successful development of this stage involves obtaining a minimum amount of independence from one's parents. This stage of development is roughly equivalent to the anal stage in Freud's psychoanalytic theory of personality development.

**Autosomes**    A term used to describe any of the 22 pairs of chromosomes other than the sex (gender) chromosomes, which are the 23rd pair (XX female, XY male).

**Auxiliary materials**    Refers to such items as workbooks, reproducibles, maps, bulletin-board products/ideas, overheads, computer programs, Internet programs, lesson ideas, etc. that accompany a text or curriculum materials in a complementary fashion.

**Average children**    Refers to children who fall in the IQ range of 90–110, which is where approximately two-thirds of all children are functioning.

**Average Daily Attendance (ADA)**
The aggregate attendance of a school during a reporting period (usually quarterly, half-year, or more typically a full school year) divided by the total number of days the school is in session during this time frame, or, the number of students in attendance every day of the school year divided by the number of days in the school year. Frequently, funding from the state and federal governments requires paperwork with attendance figures. SEE: *aggregate present*

**Average Daily Membership (ADM)**
The aggregate membership divided by the days in session (usually quarterly, half-year, or more typically a full school

year) equals the average daily membership. SEE: *aggregate membership*

**Aversion therapy**    The correction of an undesirable behavior by pairing the usual cue for that activity with an unpleasant (i.e., aversive) stimulus. For example, alcoholism might be treated by dosing the patient with Antabuse, so that consumption of an alcoholic beverage makes him/her feel nauseated.

**Avitaminosis**    A disease resulting from a lack of vitamins in one's diet. It is a nutritional deficiency that may cause neurological and psychological problems that can interfere with the learning process.

**Avoidance-avoidance conflict**    A choice between two incompatible behaviors, each of which involves removing oneself from an undesirable (aversive) situation. Expressions that refer to this state of affairs include "between Scylla and Charybdis," "out of the frying pan into the fire," and "between a rock and a hard place."

**Avoidance learning**    Learning to avoid the onset of an aversive stimulus by responding promptly to a warning signal. In most cases, the warning signal is terminated after the response. As a result, the aversive stimulus is not delivered (i.e., it has been successfully avoided).

**Avoidant personality disorder**    This is a type of personality problem that involves the avoidance of personal interactions and communications because of the fear of rejection or criticism from others. The individual is overly sensitive and preoccupied with social rejection.

**Axiology**    A study of values, morals, and ideals. It is a philosophy that deals with values and value systems; that is, what is right, wrong, good, bad, moral, immoral, ethical, unethical etc.

**Babbling**  Repeated consonant-vowel sounds normally produced by infants from about 6–9 months old (e.g., "mamama"); it is not meaningful speech as such. Sometimes called canonical or reduplicated babbling.

**Baby talk**  Immature speech at a level substantially below the child's age-mates.

**Bachelor's degree**  A four-year degree conferred by a college after high school. Students usually have a wide selection of majors ranging from liberal studies to sociology, pre-med, science, math, English, history, psychology, etc.

**Back to basics**  A general grassroots movement by the public as a result of declining test scores, especially in math and reading, to return to a basic curriculum presentation with great emphasis on the three R's (reading, 'riting, and 'rithmetic) and also science as a means of curriculum improvement and expanded student competencies. The "back to basics" movement has been a concern of parents, teachers, and the public at large for over 30 years and may have been a reaction to the launching of Sputnik (a space satellite launched October 4, 1957, by the Soviet Union). Many Americans felt they were falling behind other countries, especially the former Soviet Union, in the space race as well as in basic curriculum content areas, as is the case presently. SEE: *back to teaching basics*

**Back to teaching basics**  A movement during the latter half of the twentieth century to return school curriculum back to a basic set of core requirements deemed essential for literacy, technological competence, and a competitive academic force in the world. Many educators would agree that courses like English, science, math, U.S. history, and reading comprise to a large extent this essential listing.

**Backward conditioning**  The presentation of an unconditioned stimulus before the presentation of a neutral stimulus when attempting to make the latter a conditioned stimulus, in classical (Pavlovian) conditioning. Pavlov's research established that backward conditioning is not an effective procedure.

**Bacterial meningitis**  The result of inflammation of the membranes of the central nervous system (CNS); namely, the spinal cord and/or the brain. While meningitis can be aseptic, usually resulting from viral infection, this type is caused by bacterial infection.

**Balance**  1. Generally, the use of gross motor movement in connection with the ability to maintain one's equilibrium. 2. The ability of an individual to maintain one's mental or emotional stability.

**Balance theory**  The explanation of attitude consistency or attitude change that involves 1. one's own position and 2. the position of other people. One retains the same attitude if other people whom one respects share the attitude, or disagrees with other people for whom one has little or no respect. One is likely to change positions if other people whom one respects disagree with one's position, or if others whom one dislikes agree with one's original attitude. In this way, one's beliefs, opinions, and feelings are kept in balance with one's attitude toward others.

**Bandwagon**  1. Terms of persuasion used in writing to effectively appeal to the need of a person to "belong" to a group. 2. Frequently used in commercials, "the bandwagon effect" (join the group because everyone is doing it) can be aimed at any age group. For example, a product that appeals to youngsters (e.g., some brand of clothing) because someone famous wears that particular style.

**Barbiturates**  A group of depressant drugs that are often prescribed as treatments for insomnia.

**Barlow's disease**  Named after Sir Thomas Barlow, English obstetrician, 1845–1945. Commonly known as "scurvy." SEE: *scurvy*

**Barrier-free facility**  A school, house, building, or other facility that is accessible to persons with disabilities. Comfortable access/entry throughout the building interior occurs as well with specific accommodations for persons in wheelchairs also available.

**Barrier games**  A teaching method that encourages student development of language. The idea is to have students describe an object while others attempt to identify what is being described.

**Barylabia/barylalia**  Terms used to refer to speech that is so thick, indistinct, and husky that it cannot be understood.

**Basal ganglia**  A group of brain areas that has motor functions. They are involved in the planning and execution of muscular movements. Disruption of the functions of some of the basal ganglia may lead to schizophrenia, a form of psychosis (severe mental illness). Basal ganglia of the cerebrum include the septum, the caudate nucleus, the globus pallidus, and the putamen. Basal ganglia of the midbrain include the substantia nigra, the red nucleus, and the ventral tegmental area.

**Basal metabolic rate**  The minimum use of oxygen measured in an individual while he/she is completely rested.

**Basal reader**  A reading series that has been designed so that the books therein are systematically sequenced to continue to expand and improve the reading development of the student in a logical and orderly fashion. Basal readers are designed with controlled vocabularies and repetition of key words. Typically,

basal readers consist of literary collections of stories, poetry, essays, folktales, and so forth that are carefully sequenced across grade levels. This approach to reading is based upon the average ability level of a particular grade or group. Teacher manuals, assessments, and other auxiliary materials are usually available to support the basic reading material. Some basals may emphasize meaning-based instruction, and there are skill-based basals whose primary focus is on decoding skills.

**Basal reader approach**  A teaching method for reading development, sequential in nature, that gives basic skills instruction to students through the use of a basal reader. The basal series determines the reading content, skills, vocabulary development, and successive stages of reading development. The basic philosophy to this approach is that children will learn to read best by a predetermined scope-and-sequence of skills using reading/literature (usually excerpts—not complete literature works) selections in a student reader with reinforcement of skills work provided in student workbooks. A teacher's guide provides step-by-step instructions/ideas/format/extensions for the teacher. Specifically, instructional strands include but are not limited to word analysis skills, vocabulary development, guided silent reading, comprehension checks/discussion, and study-skills work. Student texts and workbooks are frequently organized by themes (e.g., becoming friends) and teacher input most often follows that of Directed Reading Activities (DRA). Although there is an emphasis on meaning-based instruction, this is considered a "bottom-up" approach because of the emphasis on skills work. SEE: *bottom-up philosophy of reading, Directed Reading Activities (DRA), reading instruction, basal reader*

**Baseline**  The initial recording of behavioral data in behavior-intervention approaches. The data recorded measures the frequency of behaviors (typically unwanted behaviors) before interventions are implemented.

**B**

**Baseline design**   A research design (or plan) in which the same subjects who are observed in the baseline situation with no treatment are then given the experimental treatment. The behavior of these subjects is examined to see if the treatment produces any difference in behavior.

**Baseline measure**   A level of behavior measured before the implementation of a management program or instructional program/procedure that will also be measured or evaluated later.

**BASIC**   SEE: *Beginner's All-purpose Symbolic Instruction Code*

**Basic anxiety**   One of neo-Freudian analyst Karen Horney's theoretical concepts. This is the feeling of insecurity established in a child when the parents show harshness of discipline, indifference, inconsistency, and disparagement in their treatment of the child.

**Basic hostility**   One of neo-Freudian analyst Karen Horney's theoretical concepts. When a child experiences basic anxiety, a deep resentment or hostility takes form. This results in one of three possible "neurotic trends": Moving against people, moving away from people, or moving toward people.

**Basic Interpersonal Communicative Skills (BICS)**   A standard basic conversation between two or more persons face-to-face. It is not a complex linguistic ability but merely a face-to-face conversational skill.

**Basic research**   Research done in order to add to the world's fund of knowledge. The purpose of such research is to satisfy the scientist's curiosity about nature, and not necessarily to increase the immediate happiness of any human being. Historically, benefits of humankind have accrued from the knowledge generated by basic research.

**Basic sight words**   Typically, lists of high-frequency words developed first during the early 1900s by people such as E. W. Dolch (220 basic sight-word list). Nouns are included on sight-word lists; the criteria for selection typically involves the frequency of appearance of the word in basal reading materials or other readings.

**Basic skills**   1. The individual skills that can be combined for a well-integrated complex performance. These basic skills are learned first, in a step-by-step manner. Later, the basic skills are put together into a structured complex action. For example, students learn the basic skills of counting to 12, counting by fives, understanding fractions of an hour, understanding clockwise and counterclockwise directions, etc. before they learn the complex skill of how to tell time. 2. The term "basic skills" often refers to the subject matter of reading, writing, and mathematics as the basics to our total functional literacy. SEE: *back to basics*

**Basilar membrane**   One of the membranes of the inner ear. The basilar membrane is narrowest at its origin (which is at the oval window separating the middle ear from the inner ear) and widest at its ending in the center of the snail-shaped cochlea. On the basilar membrane rests the organ of Corti, which contains the hearing receptors known as the hair cells.

**Battered child syndrome**   The abuse of children, whether it be physical (beatings), sexual (rape), or psychological (deprivation of love). This abuse can be life-threatening or permanently damaging to the child. Anyone who witnesses battered children is required by law to report this abuse to the police or other appropriate authorities. Anonymity can be given if an individual reports the abuse to a social-service agency in most states.

**Battery**   The intentional physical touching of an individual without consent, which causes fear or anxiety in the victim. SEE: *assault, Appendix 2: Legal Terms and Issues*

**Before-during-after reading guide**   A system or strategy wherein a reading student is assisted in intervals (before, during, and after reading a selection) with the understanding of what is about to be read and the comprehension of what is being read and finally what has been read.

**Beginner's All-purpose Symbolic Instruction Code (BASIC)**   A language used to program computers.

**Behavior checklist**   Checklist that contains a listing of the typical behaviors and characteristics of a normal child or group of children. In special education such lists are used to help determine whether or not a child is exhibiting abnormal behavior and may be in need of special support services. Such lists may be used to compare any student to the norm represented by the listing.

**Behavior content matrix**   An educational planning technique. Expected educational outcomes are examined along with particular course topics. These outcomes and topics are put together so that clear behavioral objectives can be specifically stated.

**Behavior contract**   A written contract typically signed by a nonconforming student and teacher/school caretaker. Parents are also typically involved in behavior contracts. Behavior contracts usually specify acceptable or expected behaviors, consequences for good/bad behaviors, and criteria for evaluation and follow-up.

**Behavior disorder**   A type of disorder where observed behaviors deviate from the average or typical. Behavior disorders extend past what would be considered "temporary" (e.g., depression as a result of a death in the family) and are extreme in intensity and frequency (e.g., individuals with conduct disorders).

**Behavior excesses**   Behaviors exhibited by a student or individual that are extremely socially unacceptable. This requires that the unacceptable behavior is not of a transient nature but occurs with great frequency over a long period of time and occurs with intensity at inappropriate times.

**Behavior genetics**   The study of the hereditary causes of some aspects of behavior, emotionality, personality, and/or intelligence.

**Behavior guidance**   An approach for guiding young children's development of self-control and intrinsic moral standards.

**Behavior management**   Any system used for behavior control of students or persons such as the principles of B. F. Skinner's operant conditioning or behavior modification. SEE: *behavior modification*

**Behavior model**   The model of behavior that assumes that one's behaviors and actions result from inappropriate learning and that conditioning techniques can be used to reinforce or extinguish wanted or unwanted behaviors. SEE: *reinforcement, conditioning*

**Behavior modification**   The application of the principles of Skinnerian (operant) and/or Pavlovian (classical) conditioning to the modification of antisocial and/or neurotic behaviors. The behaviorists adhere to the position that behaviors are learned and can be conditioned and reinforced. Behavior modification techniques are specific techniques involved in changing or reinforcing wanted and unwanted behaviors. Behavior modification procedures that can be used to increase wanted behaviors include: modeling, shaping, token economies, praise, contingency management, and self-reinforcement. Behavior modification procedures that can be used to decrease unwanted behaviors include: extinction, punishment, timeout, contingency contracting, response cost, and the reinforcement of incompatible responses. SEE: *conditioned response (CR), reinforcement, each procedure as listed above*

**Behavior therapists**   Those clinical psychologists who use the behavior-therapy approach when dealing with emotional or mental disorders. SEE: *behavior therapy*

**Behavior therapy**   1. A type of clinical psychology in which the therapist selects a type of behavior to be changed and sets up a program to cause the desired change. The concern is with removing the unwanted behavior rather

**B**

than with "curing" some mental disease. 2. The position that maladaptive behaviors can be treated effectively by following the conditioned-response principles as established by Pavlov, Skinner, and their followers. Accordingly, adherents of this view are skeptical about the value of psychotherapy, the "talking cure."

**Behavioral assessment** The detailed observation and recording of a subject's behavior for a specified time. This assessment may be a preliminary step in planning a behavior-therapy program.

**Behavioral contingencies** Arrangements for the delivery or removal of punishing or reinforcing stimuli following specific behaviors. Examples of a reinforcement contingency would be: 1. in the classic sense, the delivery of corn to a pigeon after it pecks a plastic disk set in the wall of a Skinner box. A particular pattern for providing the reinforcement of some responses of a specified type is known as a *schedule of reinforcement,* and 2. providing a treat or special time together to a child after a good report card.

**Behavioral factor** Behaviors and activities that could contribute or cause disabilities and/or mental retardation. Some examples are: driving to endanger, ingesting drugs and/or alcohol, smoking, etc.

**Behavioral learning theories** Those theories of learning that emphasize environmental stimuli as the chief cause of the learner's observed responses. For example, B. F. Skinner proposed that people learn by responding to environmental stimuli and reinforcers via schedules of reinforcement. SEE: *reinforcer, schedules of reinforcement*

**Behavioral model** This model is based upon the premise that students misbehave and are behaviorally disordered as a result of improper or inappropriate learning. The model postulates that the best way to prevent or to treat behavior disorders is to control the student's environment in order to teach the student just what comprises appropriate behavior and to ensure that proper learning takes place.

**Behavioral object** A specific objective or goal that a student needs to learn and demonstrate in order to show competence or mastery at the conclusion of the instruction/learning period.

**Behavioral objective** This is a precision statement of what a learner should demonstrate after being exposed to a specific lesson that should contain stated goals, methods, materials, and follow-up. The behavioral objective usually states the criteria used to assess lesson effectiveness as well as a measurable behavioral response to indicate the level of mastery. For example, the following could be considered a behavioral objective: When given the education dictionary, Juana will choose 15 unknown terms to master in a cooperative flash-card exercise (after choosing a partner) with follow-up testing indicating 95 percent mastery.

**Behavioral Observation Audiometry (BOA)** The observation of a child's responses to audiometric test stimuli.

**Behavioral perspective** The point of view that behavior can be explained by reference to environmental influences such as punishment, reinforcement, and/or extinction.

**Behavioral preparedness** The doctrine established by Garcia, Seligman, and others that some neutral stimuli are much more readily conditioned to particular unconditioned stimuli than most other neutral stimuli. These preferential links are a result of the life cycle of the animal species involved. The evidence for behavioral preparedness constitutes an important correction to the views of Skinner and Pavlov.

**Behavioral theory** The theoretical position that emphasizes the measuring of overt responses to specific environmental stimuli or reinforcers. Behavior change is implemented after initiating programs of reinforcement in a variety of timed conditions. SEE: *stimulus, response, reinforcer, programs of reinforcement*

**Behaviorism** 1. The doctrine that the appropriate subject matter of scientific psychology is observable behavior and that subjective mental processes cannot be scientifically studied. 2. It is also a philosophy of education concerning the idea that, psychologically speaking, the causes of behavior or misbehavior are rooted in learned responses.

**Behaviorist approach** The theoretical stance that an individual's behavioral makeup is determined by environmental influences. Therefore, behavior management and behavior modification techniques are recommended for educators and criminal justice authorities. SEE: *behavior management, behavior model, behavior modification, behavior therapy, behavioral learning theories, behavioral model, behavioral perspective, behavioral theory, and behaviorism*

**Being needs** The three higher-level needs in Maslow's motivational theory. They are also known as "growth needs."

**Bell's palsy** An acute inflammation of the facial nerve. It causes pain and paralysis of the facial muscles, which control expression. The face is distorted and appears to droop. The condition is usually of short duration.

**Beriberi** A disease of malnutrition that is endemic in the Orient and the Pacific Islands. Mostly found in areas where large amounts of highly milled rice are eaten, it is caused by a lack of thiamine (vitamin B) in the diet. Its symptoms include impairment of peripheral nerves, loss of appetite, cardiovascular changes, insomnia, lassitude, and edema.

**Between-class ability grouping** A way of assigning students to different classes. The class to which a student is assigned depends on her/his measured ability and/or achievement. For example, a teacher might assign math groupings based on students' abilities to compute and problem solve. Students who can compute addition and subtraction problems proficiently might be in one group; students with multiplication/division proficiency assigned to another group; and students with fractions/decimals proficiency assigned to a third group.

**Beyond a reasonable doubt** SEE: *Appendix 2: Legal Terms and Issues*

**Bias** Any systematic distortion of the outcome of a research study. The bias could result from 1. uncontrolled subject factors such as expectations and attitudes, 2. the expectations and/or attitudes of the researchers, or 3. the action of an uncontrolled variable or set of variables that would affect the outcome variable. In a well-controlled experiment, for example, the outcome variable should be affected by the independent variable only.

**Biased responding** An inclination or a predisposition by a test taker or respondent to answer questions in a particular fashion regardless of what the question might be.

**Bibliotherapeutic** A term used in reading to indicate the assistance a teacher gives to a reader in using texts and other books so the reader will better understand the reading(s). Thus, the student is expected to develop his/her self-awareness and be able to use the new knowledge to solve personal problems.

**BICS** SEE: *Basic Interpersonal Communicative Skills*

**Big books** Enlarged versions of regularly published picture books. Increasingly being used at the kindergarten and early-primary level for young children, these books allow students to interact in group settings. A variety of story and language arts activities can be built around the use of "big books." For example, the teacher can demonstrate by reading a "big book." The children then can collaborate with the teacher and share in the reading and, finally, the children can practice and perform together by exploration and sharing.

**Bilateral** A term used to indicate two-sidedness or both sides.

**Bilingual** A term used in education to describe the use of two languages as part of the learning process (bi = two; lingual = language).

**Bilingual education** A type of education program developed for non-English speaking students or students who speak two or more languages. Started in the late 1960s as a result of new waves of immigration, bilingual education was intended at first to give new immigrants a good start in U.S. schools. However, many students did not benefit from these early bilingual education efforts, which led to Title VII of the Elementary and Secondary Education Act of 1968 (Bilingual Education Act). This act required supplementary services for all non-English speaking children. Specific criteria for bilingual education programs have not been prescribed but generally the students' language skills are more fully developed and refined in both their native language and in English.

**Bilingual Education Act**   Title VII of the Elementary and Secondary Education Act of 1968. This act propelled bilingual education to a priority position with funding provided from the early childhood level through adult literacy. Additionally, vocational programs and meeting the needs of low-income students were important parts of this act.

**Bilingual immersion approach**   Programs designed for language-minority students that use both the student's primary language and the majority language of the school (English in the United States). The Canadian schools developed this model for their language-majority students. Program components involve early total immersion efforts in the child's primary language to partial immersion through grade 12. The 90/10 model is used by many schools in the United States with the child's primary language used almost exclusively (90 percent of the day) in grades K–1 so as to develop proficiency in the child's primary language. In grades 2 and 3, English instruction is added (one to two hours) with academic instruction provided half of the day for both languages by grade 6. High-school instructional efforts involve the majority language 60 percent of the day and the student's primary language 40 percent of the day.

**Bilingual learners**   Students who vary in both English-language and native-language proficiency. There have been

three types of bilingual learners cited in the literature: 1. LEP or Limited English Proficient students—these essentially non-English speaking learners speak/communicate in a language other than English. English-language skills are quite limited. 2. ELP or English Language Proficient—these learners cannot quite function independently in English-speaking classrooms (i.e., require bilingual education specialists/programs/assists) and most often communicate socially in their native language. The learner is English proficient but not fluent. 3. FEP or Fluent English Proficient—bilingual learners who have satisfactory English-language written/oral communication skills and can function independently in English-speaking classrooms. SEE: *bilingual immersion approach, language minority student, language minority programs, sheltered English, transitional language programs*

**Bilingual maintenance approach**   A method of teaching bilingual students using the English as a Second Language (ESL) approach. The main theme is teaching students partly in English and partly in their primary language in order to maintain proficiency in both. SEE: *bilingual education, bilingual learners, bilingualism, bilingual transitional approach, English as a Second Language (ESL)*

**Bilingual transitional approach**   An approach to bilingual education wherein most of the academic instruction is presented in English; however, some instruction is given in the native or primary language of the student. The idea is to use this approach until the student is able to master English sufficiently enough to operate effectively in his/her regular academic program. SEE: *bilingual education, bilingual learners, bilingualism, bilingual maintenance approach, English as a Second Language (ESL)*

**Bilingualism**   An ability to speak two languages. Individuals who are bilingual generally speak the language of their country and the language of an adopted country.

**Bimodal distribution**   A particular shape of a frequency distribution of

B

scores. The frequency distribution presents scores or measures on the X-axis of a graph and the frequency of each score (i.e., the number of people who get that score) is given on the Y-axis. When two very different scores (one rather low and the other somewhat high) both show the highest frequency (e.g., as many as 10 people receive the lower score and another 10 people receive the higher one, while no other score had a frequency over nine), these two scores are tied for the mode. Centrally located scores will fall into a "saddle" between the two higher parts of the curve. As a result, in a bimodal distribution, the mode cannot be used as a measure of the central tendency of the distribution. SEE: *central tendency, frequency distribution, mode, shape*

**Binet-Simon scales** An intelligence (IQ) test/scale developed in France by Alfred Binet and Theodore Simon in 1905. This assessment tool was revised at Stanford University (California) by Lewis Terman in 1916 and then called the Stanford-Binet Intelligence Scale. SEE: *Stanford-Binet Intelligence Scale, Wechsler Intelligence Scale for Children (WISC)*

**Binocular cues** Those cues to visual depth (i.e., the judgment of front-to-back distances) that require the use of both eyes. Such cues include convergence and visual disparity.

**Binocular disparity** The difference between the visual images on the two retinas (because of the fact that the eyes occupy different positions in space) constitutes a cue to visual depth or distance. This cue to depth is also called retinal disparity or binocular parallax.

**Binocular vision** This is the ability of a person to merge the image from each eye into a single image, thus enabling one to see clearly and not doubly.

**Biochemical imbalances** A condition based upon an imbalance in the metabolic process, which causes a variety of biochemical disorders.

**Biofeedback** A type of training in which a person is helped to control his/her own responses, responses that most laypersons would think cannot be altered by learning. Biofeedback has been used to change such autonomically controlled processes as blood pressure or finger temperature, as well as the electrical activity of the striated muscles and the brain waves measured by the EEG. The procedure involves giving the person a light or tone signal to indicate whether or not the targeted response is changing in the right direction.

**Biographical inventory** An individual's personal history. This is background information that provides a sketch of one's activities, achievements, life highlights, awards, etc.

**Biological psychology** SEE: *biopsychology*

**Biomedical factors** Factors relating to biological causes that often are used to explain some causes of mental retardation/physical and/or mental disabilities. These can include, but are not limited to, poor nutrition and genetic anomalies.

**Biophysical model** SEE: *biophysical theory*

**Biophysical theory** A theory that emotional and behavioral disorders are founded in biological causes; that is, the biological imbalance (dysfunction) in effect causes the emotional disorder.

**Biopsychological perspective** The point of view that behaviors and emotions are best understood by examining their causes in nerve physiology and biochemistry.

**Biopsychology** A subfield of psychology dealing with the relationships between behavioral variables and biological processes such as embryology, genetics, neurophysiology, endocrinology, and biochemistry. The field of biopsychology has also been called physiological psychology, psychobiology, biological psychology, and behavioral neuroscience.

**Biopsychosocial** An adjective used to describe human behaviors and attitudes as the result of interactions between biology (genetics, neurophysiology, biochemistry, etc.), psychology (the mind

**B**

and personal behavior), and society at large (home, family, school, work environment, etc.).

**Bipolar disorder**   The type of mood disorder (often called manic-depressive disorder) that involves drastic swings between mania (feeling very high, elated, euphoric, overconfident) and depression (feeling very low, "down in the dumps").

**Bits**   A computer processes information by a series of on/off signals. One (1) on/off signal, the basic unit of information in a computer, is called a bit (for binary digit). SEE: *bytes, kilobytes*

**Black English**   SEE: *Ebonics*

**Blacks**   In the United States, individuals of African-American descent.

**Blend**   Two consonants in a sequence that form a sound recognized as two phonemes rather than one sound (e.g., as in a digraph). Examples of blends are: "bl," "gr," and "sk."

**Blended families**   Sets of parents, children, and stepchildren resulting from the second (or later) marriage of at least one of the parents.

**Blind, legally**   The condition where vision acuity measures 20/200 or less in either eye with the best corrective lenses/contact lenses. This means that an individual can see, from at least 20 feet, an object that a person with 20/20 vision can see from 200 feet. Also legal blindness includes corrected vision in the better eye with a field of view of 20 degrees or less.

**Blindism**   A condition characterized by repetitive (stereotypical) movements such as head nodding, eye rubbing, rocking, leg vibrating, hand wringing, etc. Sometimes this is indicative of disturbed and/or retarded children or persons.

**Block grants**   Federal grant monies that are consolidated into a multipurpose fund. States have freedom to disperse these monies for educational purposes, thus allowing state and local agencies more discretion in educational matters.

**Blocking**   The phenomenon by which a neutral stimulus presented just prior to an unconditional stimulus (US) fails to become conditioned to that US because an already established conditioned stimulus is presented along with that neutral stimulus.

**BOA**   SEE: *Behavioral Observation Audiometry*

**Board of Education of Central School District No. 1, Town of Greenbush v. Allen (1968)**   The Court ruled that the loaning of books to nonpublic schools alone did not show an unconstitutional degree of support for a religious institution.

**Board of Education v. Rowley (1982)**   The so called "Rowley" decision was the first time the Supreme Court considered an Education of All Handicapped Act case (EHA P.L. 94-142, now renamed IDEA P.L. 101-476). This case determined that states must provide an appropriate but not necessarily optimum education as per the requirements of P.L. 94-142.

**Boards of education**   Agencies instituted at the state and local levels that are responsible for formulating and implementing educational policies. Members are sometimes appointed by the governor's office but are more frequently elected at the local level. School committees for individual communities are considered boards of education. Consolidated schools frequently have boards of education or school committees comprised of members from several different communities.

**Body image**   A term used to indicate one's awareness and opinion of one's own body in relation to its parts and the environment. Also, how one sees oneself in relation to the physical characteristics of others.

**Body localization**   One's ability to locate one's body parts. SEE: *body image, body spatial organization*

**Body senses**   Sensations from the body referring to the positioning of parts of the body and the pattern of high and low muscle tone in the various muscles of the body. The body senses include the senses of balance and kinesthesis.

**Body spatial organization**   The ability of a student or person to appropriately move her/his body in an organized and controlled fashion within the spatial environment. SEE: *gross motor skills*

**Bond**   SEE: *Appendix 2: Legal Terms and Issues*

**Bone conduction (BC) test**   A hearing test that assesses the responsiveness of the sensorineural mechanisms of the inner ear as opposed to outer- or middle-ear functions. A comparison of the BC thresholds from this test and the air conduction (AC) thresholds from AC testing will reveal whether or not hearing losses are conductive, sensorineural, or mixed. SEE: *air conduction (AC) test, conductive hearing loss, sensorineural hearing loss, mixed hearing loss*

**Book binding**   The process of writing, illustrating, and binding a book. In the classroom, students need paper/computer-generated materials for individual pages, endpapers, adhesives or threaded needles, cover material (e.g., wallpaper samples, original illustrations, shelfliner, pictures, fabric, etc.), and sometimes drymount tissue and an iron. There are many different types of books students can make, including pop-up books, picture books, big books, etc.

**Borderline children**   Also known as slow learners. "Borderline" functioning is a somewhat outdated term that refers to IQ functioning in the range of 70 to 85.

**Bottom-up approach to curriculum development**   A model of curriculum development that begins with the identification of the very basic educational skills and behaviors, the so-called "entry level" of a curriculum. Once this level is established, the curriculum is arranged sequentially and builds on the base or preceding step with subsequent steps upward toward mastery of the skill or behavior.

**Bottom-up philosophy of reading**   The view of reading that instruction should begin with skills work (i.e.,

phonics skills/word recognition skills). Typically a scope-and-sequence of skills taught involves word analysis and word comprehension work before the comprehension of text. This approach differs from the top-down philosophy of reading, which focuses on reading-literacy instruction beginning in the natural context of language and text presentations (e.g., story books) with skills instruction given only as the need occurs. SEE: *bottom-up processing, top-down philosophy of reading*

**Bottom-up processing**   The perception of stimulus patterns (e.g., printed sentences) as the result of separately identifying individual features of stimuli (e.g., print) and combining those features into what seems to be a sensible pattern. For example, bottom-up processing in reading refers to mastering sound/symbol correspondences before reading word parts, words, phrases, sentences, and paragraphs. Comprehension is seen as beginning at the level of sound/symbol correspondences before the reading of connected text is meaningful.

**Braille**   A system that allows blind persons to read with their fingertips invented by Louis Braille (France, 1809–1852). It consists of communication based on a code of raised dots arranged in two columns of three embossed/raised dots. This six-position rectangular system, depending on the dots raised, would indicate letters, numbers, sound, and grammar meanings to the braille reader.

**Braille bills**   Refers to legislation passed in several states that makes braille available to students with vision problems and learning disabilities. SEE: *braille*

**Braille code**   SEE: *braille*

**Braille embosser**   A printer similar to a typewriter that produces braille. SEE: *braille*

**Brain**   That part of the central nervous system that is encased by the skull. The human brain is about the size of a grapefruit and weighs approximately three pounds. The brain has approximately 100 billion nerve cells (also called

**B**

neurons), which are responsible for processes that control learning and other behaviors. The field of biopsychology is concerned with how the brain regulates processes related to behavior and neurology. SEE: *biopsychology, cerebral cortex, forebrain, hindbrain, midbrain, neuron*

**Brain damage**   A term used to describe any injury or damage to the brain tissue that can be identified; brain damage of an organic nature.

**Brain dysfunction**   A term used to define brain problems involving learning, motor, perceptual, and other functioning when no apparent damage is evident. A brain malfunction without an apparent organic cause.

**Brain injured**   A person who has received brain injury during or following the birth process. The damage to the brain can be as a result of accidental trauma or infection. This can affect mental development, learning, and behavior.

**Brain stimulation**   The application of mild alternating current electrical or chemical stimuli to particular areas of the brain in order to observe the behavioral correlates of the stimulation.

**Brainstem**   The brain structure that is the top end of the spinal column that widens to form the midbrain. Also, the narrower portion of the brain that is connected with the spinal cord. From the spinal cord forward, the three parts of the brain stem are the medulla, the pons, and the midbrain. Life-sustaining functions of the body are controlled by the brainstem.

**Brainstorming**   A method used by a group of persons wherein solutions to a problem are proposed by any member. It is a collective effort and any member can throw out an idea for consideration. Those multiple answers can be built upon or expanded by any member of the group. No criticism is allowed of any solution. Eventually, evaluation of the many possible solutions is made by the group and the best answer or answers are accepted by the group as the brainstorming session is concluded. It is also a prereading or written-language

activity in which students generate a collective fund of existing ideas that will assist in the task at hand. All ideas offered by students related to the topic are accepted and recorded.

**Branching hierarchy**   A teaching or learning method that employs the use of a graphic organizer, flow chart, topical listing, etc. in the form of a structured overview of the main topics or themes of concern. Each topic or theme is then further separated into divisions and subdivisions until all major and minor points are covered.

**Breach of contract**   The termination of a contract by one of the contractual parties without the consent of the other party(ies). For example, a teacher who signed a contract for a year would be considered "in breach of contract" if he/she left the school system in the middle of the contract year without permission or proper notification.

**Breadth model**   A method model of identifying gifted children based upon the concept that a battery of assessments and tests are needed and not any single test. The model requires that the student exhibit superior levels on more than just one measure such as a superior level of performance on an IQ test, achievement test, aptitude test, etc.

**Breathiness**   A whisperlike speech sound created by air rushing through the vocal folds (cords) without causing them to vibrate such as in the case of heavy breathing.

**Brightness constancy**   The ability to judge the illumination level of an object correctly, despite variations in both the lighting of the object and the lighting of its surroundings.

**Bright's disease**   (Richard Bright, English physician, 1789–1858) A general term used to describe acute and/or chronic kidney diseases. SEE: *nephritis*

**Brittle bone disease**   SEE: *osteogenesis imperfecta*

**Broad discretion**   A legal term used to denote the range or leeway found within the framework of the law, or an agreement that allows for wide interpretations of the issues presented. For example, schools are given broad discretionary powers in life-threatening situations whereby student rights might be curtailed (e.g., pushing a student [i.e., could be considered battery in other circumstances] into a classroom if a danger is perceived in the hallway).

**Broca's aphasia** (also called motor aphasia) The inability to utter most of the sounds of speech as a result of damage to a specific, small part of the frontal lobe of the cerebral cortex. In most persons, this area of the cortex (Broca's area, area 44) is in the left hemisphere of the cortex.

**Broca's area** An area of the cerebral cortex (usually in the inferior frontal lobe of the left hemisphere) that when damaged results in an inability to form the sounds of speech. This disability is known as Broca's aphasia.

*Brown v. Board of Education of Topeka (Kansas)* The May 17, 1954, Supreme Court ruling that outlawed de jure (by law or practice) segregation in the schools. The Supreme Court asked—and answered—the question, "Does segregation of children in public schools solely on the basis of race, even though the physical facilities and other tangible factors may be equal, deprive children of the minority group of equal educational opportunities? We believe that it does." SEE: *de jure segregation, de facto segregation*

**Buckley Amendment** P.L. 93-380 (1974), also known as the Equal Education Opportunity Act of 1974, included an amendment known as the Buckley Amendment or the Family Educational Rights and Privacy Act. This act guaranteed parents the right to access and examine their children's school records. It also guaranteed specific control of parts of the school records to the parents.

**Building drug-free schools** A term used to indicate a commitment of communities to present drug education programs at all levels (K–12) so that students consciously decide not to take drugs (resulting in drug-free schools).

**Bulimia** SEE: *bulimia nervosa*

**Bulimia nervosa** An eating disorder that involves binges in eating, which alternate with purging or fasting. The individual many times uses life-threatening or harmful weight controls such as excessive use of laxatives, diuretics, self-induced vomiting, or excessive exercise.

**Buphthalmos** A condition characterized by abnormal protrusion and enlargement of the eyeball.

**Burglary** SEE: *Appendix 2: Legal Terms and Issues*

**Burkitt's lymphoma** (D. P. Burkitt, Ugandan physician) A disease associated with the Epstein-Barr virus originally noted in African children. It is a malignant lymphoma that is a growth of tissue in the lymphatic system.

**Burnout** A term in education used to describe teachers, guidance counselors, principals, and other school professionals who become stressed and/or tired of the teaching profession because of associated stressors.

**Bursitis** A condition characterized by inflammation of the bursa (a padlike sac or cavity), especially between bony prominences and muscles or tendons located in such places as the shoulder, knee, and elbow.

**Busing** A method of transporting students to various schools or sections of a city or town as a means to solve the problem of de facto or de jure segregated schools that are segregated racially or ethnically in order to obtain a more balanced student placement representative of the community, state, country, etc. Busing may be voluntary or involuntary. SEE: *de facto segregation, de jure segregation*

**Bystander intervention** The helping behavior of a witness to another person's need for aid.

**Bytes** A unit of information in the operations of a computer. A byte is comprised of eight bits. A byte represents a number, letter, or symbol. SEE: *bits, kilobytes, Appendix 4: Computer Terms*

**C-print**   A computerized speech-to-text translator used for the benefit of a hearing-impaired learner. C-print requires a trained operator who listens to what is being said and types special codes that are immediately shown as words on a special screen that sits atop an overhead projector. This projector in turn displays what has just been said. Once the statement or lecture is completed, the hearing-impaired person can obtain a printout of the presentation.

**CA**   SEE: *Chronological Age*

**Caffeine**   A stimulant drug, found in such beverages as tea, coffee and cola drinks, that produces increased alertness.

**CAI**   SEE: *Computer-Assisted Instruction*

**Caldecott Medal**   A special award given to the most outstanding book illustrator of the year. The Caldecott Medal is named after Randolf Caldecott, children's illustrator, and has been awarded since 1938. It is one of two major annual awards in the United States given to outstanding books. The other is the Newbery Medal for the most distinguished children's book. SEE: *Newbery Medal*

**CALP**   SEE: *Cognitive/Academic Linguistic Proficiency*

**Cancer**   An abnormal growth of cells that can affect the skin or any other organ of the body. Many cancers are treatable, but early detection is critical before massive spreading of the disease causes destruction of vital organs.

**Cannabis sativa**   The generic name for the hemp plant that produces the drug marijuana.

**Cannon-Bard theory**   The theory of emotion that states that the nerve impulses from the perception of the emotional stimulus are routed to the brain's thalamus. From there, some nerve impulses are sent to the cerebral cortex for recognition and some to the sympathetic nervous system for the fight-or-flight emergency response. As a result, this theory says that we know the meaning of the emotion at the same time that we are performing the emotional behavior.

**Canterbury aid**   A special electronic device for visually impaired students or persons used to assist and improve mobility. Objects are located for the user by means of echoes.

**Capital outlays**   These are expenditures for buildings and land serving the public domain such as the construction of and additions to buildings and the maintenance and purchase of large equipment items (e.g., heating system for a school).

**Captions**   Subtitles shown usually at the bottom of a screen that represent what is being said on a television program, film, or video. Captions may be "open" (able to be seen by all viewers) or "closed" (seen only by those with a decoder or those who subscribe to a service).

**Carcinoma**   A growth or malignant tumor.

**Cardiac disorder**   A malfunction or disease of the heart or cardiac orifices that affects the heart's operation and/or normal functions.

**Cardinal trait**   In the personality theory of Gordon Allport, a behavioral disposition of an individual that reveals itself repeatedly in different situations. Not every person has such an overriding trait. In the relatively few that have one, the cardinal trait serves as a general organizing principle in their lives.

**Career** One's chosen field of work, which spans a period of time or even a lifetime. For example, a teaching career is considered by many to open many opportunities for professional and personal growth. The rewards are considered intrinsic to a large degree.

**Career awareness** Knowledge obtained through programs, readings, interactions with others, etc. concerning opportunities, requirements, and background needed for one's career.

**Career education** Educational opportunities that provide preparatory experience(s) for a chosen field of work or job. Many high schools have work-study programs that allow non-college-bound students to work part of the day (career preparation) and take regular academic subjects the rest of the day in school. Career education can also involve college-bound students. Students looking toward college must take certain prerequisite courses (e.g., algebra) and exams (SATs). Many high schools prepare students by providing guidance counselors (for appropriate course selections) and administering pre-SAT practice exams.

**Career ladder** The career history of a person or professional (e.g., a teacher), which shows the steps or rungs of progress as one gains experience in one's chosen career area. The idea is that performance, responsibilities, and professional requirements are in an ascending scale or ladder of complexity and accountability.

**Caries** Decay and disintegration of a tooth or bone. Also called a "cavity" as concerns the progressive decalcification or rotting of the enamel and dentine of a tooth. SEE: *enamel, dentine*

***Carnegie Foundation Report on Secondary Education*** This 1986 report was prepared by the Carnegie Task Force on Teaching for the 21st Century and focused on reforms in teacher education. Recommendations were made and included some of the following: improving teacher salaries to become more competitive, requiring bachelor's degrees in the arts and science areas as a prerequisite for teaching, developing new material at the graduate level leading to master's degrees, creating a National Board of Professional Teaching Standards, and encouraging new ways to recruit minorities into the field.

***Carnegie Report*** A special educational report written and published by the "Task Force on Teaching as a Profession." The report relates to teacher education reform and incentives for teachers (both monetary and professional) as a means to improve teacher preparation and status as well as to provide improved education for students. It also called for the establishment of a board for national teaching standards.

**Carnegie unit** Usually the hourly time unit (or clock time) established for the earning of credits toward graduation. The Carnegie unit of credits is normally used at the secondary level (one Carnegie unit for each course that meets five times weekly).

**Carrels** Sometimes referred to as study carrels. They are small reserved spaces that are normally enclosed to reduce distraction for the studying student. They usually include a desk, chair, and bookshelf.

**Cascade of services** A series of levels that ranges from the most restrictive to the least restrictive placements for students with special learning challenges; services for students with disabilities must be provided in the educational environment (least restrictive setting) that best suits the students' needs. A substantially separate and isolated program would be an example of a most restrictive program (and might be the only viable alternative for a student with severe difficulties or learning challenges) while placement in the inclusionary model or regular classroom would be typical of a least restrictive model. SEE: *inclusion, Least Restrictive Environment (LRE), continuum of service*

**Case finding** Any procedure used by a school department designed to seek out and make initial contact with targeted populations, such as in the case of an outreach identification program to locate and identify children aged three and four years who may be in need of special education services, etc.

**Case history**   The main part of a case study. SEE: *case study*

**Case management**   The process of following diagnosis wherein a planned program of intervention is monitored to ensure success of the treatment, plan, or program.

**Case study**   A thorough study of the past history and present circumstances of an individual. In most cases, the purpose of such research is to understand the person with an eye toward the modification of his/her behavior.

**CAT**   SEE: *Cognitive Abilities Test*

**CAT scan**   SEE: *Computerized Axial Tomography*

**Cataract**   A condition of the eye involving clouding of the lens which, in turn, obstructs the passage of light through the eye to the retina. Vision is impaired but can be corrected through medical interventions to include surgery.

**Catatonia**   A phase of schizophrenia in which the patient is unresponsive. It is characterized by the patient's refusal to talk and a tendency to remain in a fixed position.

**Catatonic schizophrenia**   A variety of schizophrenia involving unusual motor symptoms, such as a waxy flexibility of the limbs, immobility of the limbs, strange actions, extreme excitability, and/or unresponsiveness to environmental stimulation.

**Catatonic stupor**   This is a condition wherein a student or person withdraws to such an extent within oneself that the individual becomes practically immobile and disconnected to surrounding stimuli. It is a form of withdrawal of an extreme nature with little or no responsiveness on the part of the patient. SEE: *catatonia.*

**Categorical aid**   Financial aid to local school districts from state or federal agencies for specific, limited purposes only. This type of funding (pre-1981) many times restricted states in decision making regarding educational matters because funds had to be used for very specific purposes. Block grants are now available for states to use, giving them more discretion and decision-making authority in the educational realm. SEE: *block grants*

**Categorical imperative**   Philosopher Immanuel Kant's basic rule of conduct. One should act as one would have other people act and not do anything that one would not want anyone else to do. Therefore, one's own actions should be usable as a general guideline for right conduct in all persons. One is constantly being made responsible for laying down a universal moral law. SEE: *ethics*

**Categorical system**   A system of labeling or classifying students by their category of ability (e.g., mentally retarded, learning disabled, gifted and talented, hearing impaired, blind, deaf, etc.).

**Categorizing**   A term used to describe a particular thinking skill or ability to group, classify, or place correctly in a specific category students, handicaps, concepts, ideas, items/objects, programs, and/or other things with common characteristics.

**Catharsis**   The outpouring of emotional energy (previously bottled up by the process of repression) when a psychoanalytic patient first achieves insight into the nature of the motives and memories he/she has long been unable to acknowledge.

**Catheter**   A tube inserted into some part of the body to drain fluid, to insert stents, and inject medication, or open a pathway. SEE: *catheterization*

**Catheterization**   A surgical procedure involving the insertion of a tube into the urethra in order to drain urine from the bladder.

**Caudal**   Toward the tail or hind end of the body.

**Causation**   The effective influence of an independent variable (e.g., as a particular kind of stimulus) upon a dependent variable (e.g., a given type of behavior).

**CBA**   SEE: *Curriculum-Based Assessment*

**CBI**   SEE: *Community-Based Instruction*

**CCC (Certificate of Clinical Competence)**   A certificate granted by ASHA (speech-language-hearing association) to professionals at the master's degree level who have clinical experience and have passed national exams in the areas of speech-language pathology (CC-S), audiology (CC-A), or both (CC- S/A).

**CCTV**   SEE: *Closed-Circuit Television*

**CD-ROM Compact Disc-Read Only Memory**   These compact discs look like the typical music CDs. The computer can read these programs but cannot change them. They are able to store a great deal of information—up to 550 MB (megabytes). CD-ROMs store text, graphics, and sound information. SEE: *megabyte, Appendix 4: Computer Terms*

**CEC**   SEE: *Council for Exceptional Children*

**Ceiling effects**   A level built into test problems or questions that restricts a student's ability to perform at his/her actual level of ability and achievement. In effect, this is an artificial cap that prevents the measuring of a student's full capacity in the area being tested.

**Cell body**   That part of a nerve cell (neuron) that most resembles an unspecialized animal cell. The cell body contains the cell's nucleus as well as most of the cell's cytoplasm. The fibrous parts of the neuron (i.e., the dendrites and the axon) are attached to the cell body.

**Celsius scale**   (Anders Celsius, Swedish astronomer, 1701–1744) A scale of temperature at which water boils at 100 degrees and freezes at zero degrees. It is also known as centigrade.

**Center for the Study of Reading**   A resource for all teachers and a research center established by the National Institute of Education at the University of Illinois in 1976. Through the years, the Center has focused on the connection between the reading comprehension process and the relationship between writing and reading.

**Centers**   A term used in education and in general to denote an area of learning devoted to a certain subject or activity.

Examples include but are not limited to language arts centers, media centers, health centers, life-skills centers, science centers, math centers, computer centers, foreign-language centers, etc. A math center might contain math manipulatives, flashcards, games, teacher-made activities, calculators, computer activities, banking materials, etc.

**Centile**   Any of 99 scores on a test or response measure such that, between any two adjacent centiles, one percent of the sample subjects are to be found. The first centile is that score below which the lowest-scoring one percent of the subjects in the test group are found. The 99th centile is that score below which the lowest scoring 99 percent of the group are found. SEE: *percentile rank*

**Central auditory disorder**   A term used to describe a condition wherein a disorder of auditory discrimination, perception, and/or comprehension exists even though there is no apparent damage or disorder to peripheral mechanisms of hearing.

**Central canal**   A part of the central hollow or lumen of the brain and spinal cord. The entire lumen is filled with Cerebrospinal Fluid (CSF). The central canal runs through the spinal cord and the lower (caudal) half of the brain's medulla.

**Central lisp**   The sibilant sounds produced with the tongue between the teeth such as "thun" for "sun."

**Central nervous system**   SEE: *CNS*

**Central nervous system disorder**   Disorders or diseases that affect those parts of the nervous system encased in bony covering such as the spinal cord and the brain. SEE: *CNS, central nervous system*

**Central Processing Unit (CPU)**   In actuality, the brain of the computer that controls all operations. It is usually the largest or one of the largest chips on the internal circuit board. A chip is usually made of a semiconductive material such as silicon. SEE: *Appendix 4, Computer Terms*

**Central sulcus** (also called the Fissure of Rolando)   A major groove in the

C

gray matter of the cerebral cortex. It runs down the outside of the cortex, forming a natural boundary between the frontal lobe (anterior to the central sulcus) and the parietal lobe (posterior to the central sulcus). The central sulcus does not quite reach the temporal lobe; just below and in front of it lies Broca's area for motor speech, which is in the third frontal convolution. The frontal lobe gyrus just anterior to the central sulcus is area 4, the primary motor cortex. The parietal lobe gyrus just posterior to the central sulcus contains areas 1, 2, and 3, the projection area for the general body senses of touch, pressure, pain, temperature, and kinesthesis.

**Central tendency**   The middle of a frequency distribution of scores. In a frequency distribution, the set of scores is presented with the scores listed in order of size, usually from the lowest to the highest. There are various ways to identify the central tendency (sometimes called the location) of a frequency distribution. The three best known measures of central tendency are the mean, the median, and the mode. SEE: *frequency distribution, mean, median, mode*

**Central trait**   In Allport's personality theory, a behavioral disposition that is often shown by an individual, although it is not exhibited quite as often as the cardinal trait. It is a long-lasting attribute to a person's behavior so that it is more characteristic of him/her than a short-term secondary trait.

**Central vision**   A term used to describe a person's main field of vision as not being able to see a wide area but only what is directly in front, usually no greater than an angle of 20 degrees.

**Centration**   A limitation of one's ability to attend, so that the individual can attend to only one aspect of a stimulus at a time. This is typical of the preoperational stage in Piaget's theory of mental development.

**Cephalad**   Toward the head or anterior part of the body.

**Cephalocaudal**   The principle of embryological growth that states that the anatomical and functional growth of the head end of the organism will be the fastest, and the growth of the tail end will be the slowest. The process of maturation begins at the head (cephalo) and moves to the lower part of the body (caudal).

**Cerebellum**   The part of the brain that uses sensory inputs to guide motor activity.

**Cerebral cortex**   The outermost portion of the cerebrum (i.e., the highest part of the brain). The cortex, which contains most of the gray matter of the brain, is responsible for our higher cognitive processes.

**Cerebral hemispheres**   The left and right sides of the cerebral cortex including the neocortex, the old cortex, most of the basal ganglia, and many of the limbic structures.

**Cerebral Palsy (CP)**   A nonprogressive disorder of the central nervous system that affects motor functioning and performance. It has also been known as Little's disease. This neuromuscular disorder is based on damage to the motor areas of the cerebral cortex of the brain.

**Cerebrospinal Fluid (CSF)**   A colorless fluid found in the hollow center (lumen) of the central nervous system (CNS) and in the subarachnoid space around the brain and spinal cord. The lumen's fluid seems to be an extension of the arterial blood, supplying nutrition (but not oxygen) to interior brain and spinal cord cells. The subarachnoid CSF helps to provide a protective cushion around the CNS. It communicates with the venous blood, disposing of chemical waste products.

**Cerebrovascular accident**   An unexpected and sudden disruption, blockage, or leaking of cranial blood vessels that causes damage to the brain tissue.

**Cerebrum or telencephalon**   The largest part of the brain consisting of two separated but connected hemispheres (the left and the right) and other structures anterior to the diencephalon. This division of the brain controls higher-level thought and language processes. SEE: *forebrain, cerebral cortex*

**Certification** Educationally speaking, the area of competence in which a state department of education certifies the teacher to be qualified to teach. Thus, the credential or teaching certificate authorizes an agency to hire a teacher in accordance with state standards at the professional level.

**Cerumen** Commonly known as earwax.

**Chain mnemonics** A type of memory aid in which the first item of a series is linked to the second, the second is associated with the third, and so on.

**Chaining** The control of a complex sequence of behaviors by operant conditioning. Each of a series of responses is reinforced for occurring at the correct time and place. At the completion of the training, the organism is given the reinforcing stimulus only after the entire series of actions has been performed correctly.

**Chancroid** A venereal disease characterized by a highly infectious venereal ulcer nonsyphilitic in nature. It is caused by the hemophilius dicreyi bacillus. Approximately three to four days after exposure a purulent (pus-like) ulcer forms on the penis, anus, urethra, or vulva. SEE: *Venereal Disease (VD)*

**Change agent** The professional role an educator or person plays as an active member of the school system or society. It is the responsibility a person assumes as part of one's duties to improve (change) and develop the education system.

**Chapter books** Books arranged in a chapter format popularly used in language arts programs and as part of reading programs. For example, in the case of novels, arranged by chapters, teachers can intersperse other activities in language arts such as the writing process, vocabulary skills, punctuation, and grammar in between the chapter readings. Students may be grouped or paired for chapter readings.

**Chapter 1 and Chapter 2 funds** (formerly called Title 1 and 2; then Chapter 1 and 2; now, back to Title 1 and 2) Chapter 1 makes federal funds available to all states that offer educational support for minority, low-income, and underachieving students and Chapter 2/Title 2 provides financial support for curricular materials. These programs must give pre- and post-testing to students enrolled in these programs in order to assess program effectiveness and subsequent funding. Typically, math, reading, language arts, and counseling services are provided under these funds. Although communities qualify for Chapter/Title 1 and Chapter/Title 2 funding because of poverty or low income, any student in a particular qualifying school is eligible for services. Parent support is strongly encouraged in these programs with funds available for parent training and support. Parochial schools may apply for these funds but must secure classroom space off premises (separation of church and state); thus, students attend Chapter Title 1 classes outside the school setting. Chapter/Title 1 instructional models include the "pull-out model" and "in-class model." SEE: *pull-out model, in-class model*

**Charcot-Marie-Tooth disease** (Charcot; Pierre Marie, French neurologist, 1853–1940 and Tooth, Howard, English physician, 1856–1926) A heredity disease characterized by progressive weakness of the distal muscles of the arms and the feet. It is a form of neural muscular atrophy. SEE: *distal*

**Charter schools** Independent outcome-based public schools that are designed to promote innovative teaching and education practices/strategies. Minnesota was the first state to pass charter legislation in 1991, followed by California in 1992. Several states now have charter schools that call for original "charters," or agreements specifying learning outcomes the students will accomplish and that are signed by the school's founders and a sponsor. There are several commonalities in the various charter schools but specific practices vary widely. Some common model components include: 1. accountability of the charter school for student performance to the sponsoring public institution and parents; 2. because of strict accountability, state and federal laws do not apply except in the cases of those related to health, discrimination, and safety of those agreed on by the charter school; 3. various private and public organizations can sponsor a charter school that is nonsectarian and tuition-free and a school of choice for students, teachers, and parents alike; 4. charter schools have fiscal autonomy to expend allocated resources; 5. states typically allow a certain number of charter schools and allow any individual to initiate a charter school petition to include teachers (usually more than two), parents (usually more than 10), a local school district, a country board of education, etc.; 6. outcome-based expectations include desired learning outcomes/gains; 7. site-based decision making involves expanding decision making to cooperative partnerships of professionals, students, parents, and community members; 8. innovative practices and technology applications, as well as new approaches, are encouraged; 9. many charter schools have extended school days for both students and teachers. Concerns have been expressed regarding the following aspects of charter schools: (a) funding is sometimes a problem as state/federal vouchers are often not enough—grants, foundation monies, contributions, etc. are often needed; (b) some charter schools have not hired certified teachers, which raises qualifications concerns; (c) longer-than-normal workdays are required for extra paperwork/charter requirements; and (d) teachers desire collective-bargaining activities to ensure fair remuneration and benefits.

**Checklist** A written list of behavior descriptions. The observer marks an item (e.g., with a checkmark) when he/she observes the subject perform the behavior described. A checklist yields only yes-or-no data; there is no qualitative assessment involved. Checklists should be tested for their interjudge reliability before they can be put to use throughout a school or district.

**Chemical dependency** A physical and psychological need for tobacco, alcohol, or other drugs that interferes with social, job, and psychological functioning and overall adaptation to the environment.

**Chemotherapy** The use of drug treatments to control or cure diseases, disorders, or other problems. Some forms of chemotherapy are now available to control or cure certain forms of cancer (e.g., leukemia).

**Chest physiotherapy** The treatment of the chest through physical agents such as exercise, heat treatments, massage, radiation, etc. in a therapeutic fashion.

**CHI** SEE: *Closed Head Injuries*

**Chi square** A statistical procedure that relies on frequency counts (nominal data) in assessing the degree of relationship of one distribution to another. Chi square tests allow one to estimate the probability that a trend or pattern of performance/scores is a result of chance from an unexpected distribution of those same scores. For example, if one was to throw a quarter 20 times on a table and one recorded 15 times that heads appeared and 5 times that tails appeared, one could determine the likelihood that these results were due to chance from the expected outcome of 50 percent probability of either heads or tails appearing (i.e., expected outcome = 10 times heads and 10 times tails).

**Chief state school officer** An executive head or chair of a state department of education.

**Child abuse** Intentional sexual, psychological, and/or physical injury or trauma of a child such as rape, incest, child beating, and threats of violence at a child. SEE: *child neglect*

**Child advocacy movement** A movement in the direction of ensuring the rights of children. Advocates spell out requirements and protect children in their best interests, while making sure that children's/students' rights are protected within the process.

**Child benefit theory** A criterion used by the U.S. Supreme Court to determine whether or not services provided to students in the public and nonpublic sectors benefit children only and not any school or religion. If the children benefit only, the courts have ruled that services may be funded by public funds (e.g., public monies may be used to bus children to parochial schools as this has been deemed a safety issue for the children alone).

**Child-care center** SEE: *day-care center*

**Child-centered** SEE: *child-centered instruction*

**Child-centered instruction** Instruction designed for the interests, abilities, and needs of individual students that is rooted in existentialist philosophy. SEE: *existentialism*

**Child find** A method or system usually required by federal, state, or local law (or regulation) that actively seeks out students that may be in need of special education or other services such as "children at risk." Such a system also includes a referral process. SEE: *students at risk*

**Child neglect** A serious lack of or no concern about the upbringing of a child by the parent, adult in charge, or other family members to a point where the child's physical and emotional well-being are ignored to a great degree or even completely. Thus, the child's physical and emotional growth is restricted. For example, a child left at home alone on a repeated basis; no recognizable signs of real love, caring, and nurturing; poor nutrition; and lack of medical attention. SEE: *child abuse*

**Childhood psychosis** A disorder occurring during childhood with symptoms that include impaired speech development, bizarre social behavior, and abnormal motor behavior. SEE: *psychosis*

**Children at risk** Children who potentially are at risk for academic/social failure because of a variety of learning impediments which could include but are not limited to the following: disease, health conditions (i.e., asthma), poverty, lack of nourishment, abuse, parental drug addiction, etc. SEE: *at risk*

**Chiropodist** A synonym for a podiatrist (one who treats foot problems and diseases).

**Chiropractor** A trained professional and expert in the manipulation of the spine in the form of spinal adjustments. Chiropractics is a medical system that regards diseases as being caused by impingements upon the spinal nerves and thus spinal adjustment and correction is necessitated.

**Chisanbop** A method of math calculation especially recommended for the visually impaired. It is a system developed in Korea that uses the fingers to calculate.

**Chondrodystrophy** A condition characterized by defects in the cartilage formation at the extremities of the long bones, especially that of the hip bones and shoulders.

**Choral and choral repeated reading** This is a whole-class reading activity that involves students reading aloud and in unison. Students should be active participants in constructing meaning. The teacher should demonstrate good oral reading behaviors by phrasing properly, changing tempos, voice intonation, and expression.

**Chorea** Also known as Saint Vitus's dance, it is any number of nervous diseases organically caused or caused by infection. It is characterized by involuntary and spasmodic bodily movement, particularly of the limbs or facial muscles.

**Choreiform** It is a condition characterized by spasmodic twitching or jerking of the arms and legs and/or the facial muscles. It is a common symptom of Huntington's disease or chorea. SEE: *chorea*

**Choreoathetoid cerebral palsy** A type of cerebral palsy where the individual has abrupt involuntary motor movements and great difficulty maintaining posture or stance.

**Chorionic Villi Sampling (CVS)** A type of prenatal examination of the fetus to screen for signs of abnormality in development. The villi are threadlike projections extending from the chorion (the membrane around the fetus); the villi can be examined for their chromosomes and the genes on the chromosomes.

**Choroid** The layer of blood vessels located between the sclera and retina in the eye that provides nourishment to the retina. SEE: *retina*

**Choroidoretinal degeneration** Degeneration or deterioration of both the choroid and the retina in the eye. SEE: *choroidoretinitis, choroid, retina*

**Choroidoretinitis** Inflammation of both the choroid and retina of the eye. SEE: *choroid, retina*

**Chromosomal abnormalities** A defect, damage, or abnormality of one or more of the normally 23 pairs of chromosomes in an individual. SEE: *chromosome*

**Chromosome** A threadlike or rodlike microscopic body developed from nuclear material, namely Deoxyribonucleic Acid (DNA). The human chromosome contains hundreds of genes, which determine our characteristics of heredity. A person normally has 46 chromosomes, 23 from the mother (ovum) and 23 from the father (sperm); that is, one from each parent, making 23 pairs. The first 22 pairs are autosomes; they do not contain any sex (male/female) determinants. The 23rd pair, the sex chromosome, is designated either XX for female or XY for male. Thus, if the embryo has an XX pair, a female would be born, and if XY, a male. SEE: *autosomes, genes*

**Chronic** A term used to refer to problems, diseases, and disorders of various natures that repeatedly reoccur or are present over long periods of time.

**Chronic enuresis** A chronic or continual case of bedwetting over a long period of time.

**Chronological Age (CA)** The exact age of a student or person. It is normally expressed in years but is more accurately expressed in years and months. Ex: A CA of 15–4 means the student is 15 years, 4 months old. SEE: *Intelligence Quotient (IQ), Mental Age (MA)*

**Chunk** A meaningful unit of information in Short-Term Memory (STM). The grouping of bits of information into chunks enlarges the amount of information one can store in STM.

**Chunking** The grouping of individual items of knowledge into larger units, preferably meaningful ones. This approach to learning helps the consolidation of Short-Term Memory (STM) into Long-Term Memory (LTM).

**CIC** SEE: *Clean Intermittent Catheterization*

**CIDI** SEE: *Composite International Diagnostic Interview*

**CIJE** SEE: *Current Index to Journals in Education*

**Ciliary body** That part of the eye that is directly behind the iris. It secretes aqueous humor (fluid) and also contains the ciliary muscle, which controls the focus of the eye as concerns changing the shape (refraction) of the lens. SEE: *iris*

**Cilium** (singular) or **cilia** (plural) 1. Cilia are hairlike projections in the bronchi, inner ear, etc. They are constantly moving (i.e., beating, recovering, and beating). These projections serve to propel and/or repel dust and mucus. 2. An eyelash is also classified as a cilium.

**Cinefluoroscopy** Refers to the taking of x-ray motion pictures.

**CIRC** SEE: *Cooperative Integrated Reading and Composition*

**Circadian rhythms** Behavioral cycles that occur once a day, such as going to sleep and waking up.

**Cirrhosis** A deterioration of the connective tissue of an organ. The term is often used to imply cirrhosis of the liver, a degenerative and chronic disease caused by many factors, including nutritional deficiency, poisons, viral or bacterial inflammation, and chronic alcoholism.

**Civil Rights Act of 1964** This act deals with discrimination against individuals. It is considered landmark federal legislation and it permits the federal government to intervene in state cases involving discrimination on the basis of race, religion, sex, or national origin.

**Civilian labor force**   The total of all civilians who fall in one of two categories: employed or unemployed. Members of the armed forces, merchant marines, national guard, etc. who are stationed either in the United States or abroad are included in the labor force.

**Clairvoyance**   One of the talents claimed as a type of Extrasensory Perception (ESP) by ESP advocates. Clairvoyance is the ability to know about far-off events without having to depend on the use of one's sense organs.

**Class journal**   A technique in the teaching of language arts wherein the students keep representative writings of classwork, homework, multicultural participation/activities, stories of mystery and adventure, cooperative learning ventures, travel, vacation trips, etc. The students share their experiences with the class at an appropriate time and these experiences are recorded in the format of a class journal, perhaps to be shared with parents/other classes or displayed.

**Classical conditioning**   The type of conditioning originally studied by Ivan Pavlov. In classical conditioning, a neutral stimulus, such as the sound of a bell, is presented to a hungry dog just before meat is presented to the dog's mouth. After several such bell-meat pairings (called conditioning trials), the dog will salivate to the sound only (i.e., the sound can now elicit the salivation response).

**Classification**   The grouping of individual items into classes or categories.

**Classification sort**   A term used in language arts to describe a system of using word cards to interest students in reading and to build vocabulary connected to the reading(s) being experienced. Two multiple sets of word cards are prepared, which address the passages/stories about to be read. The teacher gives the cards to small groups of students to arrange in logical categories. Then one student from each group shares the group decision with the class.

Thus, classification sort builds new knowledge upon previous knowledge/experiences. This approach is a variation of Connect Two. SEE: *Connect Two*

**Classifying**   A term used to describe one's ability to categorize or place correctly in a specific group items, objects, persons, things, etc. that share a common characteristic.

**Classroom analysis systems**   These are clearly articulated sets of procedures and written materials that can be used to analyze and objectify the behavioral interactions between teachers and students and interactions among students.

**Classroom environment or classroom climate**   The characteristics of a classroom; that is, the physical set-up, the psychological or emotional atmosphere, and the general learning climate or environment that exists within the educational setting.

**Classroom library**   In general, a collection of printed material kept in a classroom on a permanent basis such as Big Books, literature books, paperback books, leisure-types of readings, magazines, newspapers, talking books, workbooks, etc. Nonprint materials such as videos, films, cassettes, computer disks, CD-ROMs, listening centers, etc. may be integrated as well.

**Classroom management**   A multifaceted term used to describe the total classroom teaching and learning situation in terms of content, curriculum, methods, and teaching approaches; also, the general classroom environment and behavioral and disabling practices and systems. SEE: *classroom environment, behavior modification*

**Classroom paraprofessionals**   Professionals who typically do not hold 4 year degrees but have some experience in working with children. These classroom assistants usually work one-on-one with students in need of assistance or with small groups under the direction of an assigned teacher. Lesson planning/curriculum matters are determined by the cooperating practitioner and not the paraprofessional.

**C**

**Classroom performance**   An educational term used to describe a student's progress in class, one's so called "academic" achievement or behavior. Such performance is usually judged by grades earned, such as "A", "B", "C", etc. or by some similar or other marking system.

**Classroom teacher**   The professionally qualified/certified person assigned to the classroom to teach students in self-contained, inclusive, or departmentalized (separate subjects) situations. Students are assigned to the classroom and teacher as well.

**Claustrophobia**   A condition wherein a person has an abnormal fear of closed places or spaces, or being confined, enclosed, or locked in.

**Clean Intermittent Catheterization (CIC)**   A medical procedure that requires the inserting of a sterile tube (catheter) through the urethra into the bladder. The schedule for an intermittent (CIC) is usually every three to four hours.

**Cleft lip/palate**   A congenital malformation of the upper lip or palate in the roof of the mouth. This takes place during the embryonic process of development and can lead to communication disorders of voice and articulation.

**Clinical experience**   An on-the-job training experience that is part of the teacher-training preparation. It may be in a classroom or a related clinical setting, such as an internship, in preparation for certification as a school psychologist or school counselor. Most of this takes place outside of the classroom.

**Clinical psychologist**   A psychologist who is trained to work with individuals who experience relatively severe psychological (e.g., suicidal depression) and/or behavior (e.g., aggression) problems. SEE: *psychologist*

**Clinical psychology**   The field of psychology concerned with the diagnosis and treatment of emotional/behavior disorders.

**Clonic**   In effect, a condition characterized by alternate muscular relaxation and contraction. SEE: *clonic phase*

**Clonic phase**   The phase of an epileptic seizure when the muscles alternately contract and relax in rapid succession.

**Closed caption**   A system for the seriously hearing impaired or deaf wherein subtitles are flashed upon the movie or television screen, thus providing the dialogue for the program being viewed. Sometimes called line-21 because the caption is viewed on the blank 21st line of the picture. SEE: *closed captions*

**Closed caption decoder**   A device used for television sets or VCRs that allows closed-caption display.

**Closed-Circuit Television (CCTV)**   A system of magnified images displayed on a monitor or television screen— which are televised programs closed to the general public but available to subscribers of a service on a part-time or full-time basis.

**Closed Head Injuries (CHI)**   An injury characterized by damage to the brain without penetration of the skull. For example, injuries caused by falls, sports, auto accidents, etc.

**Closed institution**   A closed organization that purposely is set apart from the rest of a group or society at large. Closed institutions form a total social environment and address only the needs of their members (e.g., certain religious sects).

**Cloze procedure**   A special technique used in reading comprehension for testing and teaching. Words are deleted in a prescribed manner from the text or story and are replaced with blank spaces. The idea is that the student is able to fill in the blank spaces with appropriate words she/he has learned and mastered.

**Clubfoot**   A congenital defect that involves one or both feet turning at an incorrect angle at the ankle. This condition can be corrected with surgery, braces, or casts. Children with clubfeet may be taught to walk in a normal fashion. Also known as "Talipes."

**Cluster programs**   A breaking down of a regular class into subgroups based on ability or some common need, as in the case of an advanced reading group and regular reading group or gifted students being grouped for part of the day for an enrichment activity or for advanced work (e.g., math).

**Cluttering**   A speech problem characterized by an excessive rate of speech accompanied by articulation problems and repetitive speech patterns or words. Cluttering symptoms include but are not limited to part and whole-part repetitions, rapid speech or tachylalia, interjections, grammatical problems, articulatory and motor problems, writing disorders, restlessness and hyperactivity, and garbled articulation. In effect, it is basically an imbalance of the central language process that affects communication and behavior in general.

**CMI**   SEE: *Computer-Managed Instruction*

**CMV**   An acronym for Cytomegalovirus, a virus in the herpes-virus family, which affects newborns. SEE: *Cytomegalic Inclusion*

**CNS (central nervous system)**   The central nervous system includes those parts of the nervous system encased in bony coverings such as the spinal cord and brain.

**Coaching**   Teaching specific skills and then providing guided feedback.

**Cocaine**   A highly addictive stimulant that produces both alertness and euphoria. Cocaine abuse can result in severe damage to several body organs including the heart and lungs.

**Cochlea**   A coiled cone-shaped tube forming a portion of the inner ear. Snail-like in appearance, it contains the organ of Corti, the receptor for hearing. SEE: *organ of Corti*

**Cochlear implant**   A special medical technological process involving an electrode implantation in the inner ear that is connected to a sound processor, transmitter/receiver, and an external microphone. Thus, the cochlear is stimulated and the student or person is able to perceive sound.

**Code of ethics**   A formal declaration of correct and appropriate behavior to be followed by the professional person as a guide to proper professional conduct. SEE: *ethics*

**Coding**   1. The arrangement of sensory nerve impulses to represent an aspect of a physical stimulus. For example, the loudness of a sound may be coded by the number of axons in the auditory nerve simultaneously firing nerve impulses. 2. SEE: *Appendix 4: Computer Terms*

**Coefficient of correlation**   An index of the relationship between the numerical value of one variable and the size of a second variable, obtainable when the same subjects are measured for both variables. For example, the individual's Scholastic Aptitude Test score is correlated to that person's grade point average in college. When higher scores on one variable accompany higher scores on the other, the two variables are positively correlated. When higher scores on the first variable are associated with lower scores on the second, the two variables are negatively correlated.

**Cognition**   The higher mental processes in general, including reasoning, strategy use, understanding, problem solving, etc.

**Cognitive Abilities Test (CAT)**   A group of intelligence tests used in many classrooms throughout the United States.

**Cognitive/Academic Linguistic Proficiency (CALP)**   Abilities beyond basic language to abstract language capabilities that are requisites to academic performance and work.

**Cognitive appraisal**   The subjective evaluation of the severity of a stressful stimulus.

**Cognitive approach**   An approach or method that focuses on cognitive processes such as self-monitoring and reflective behaviors, self-pacing oneself through learning exercises, self-talk or talking oneself through a particularly difficult problem, self-questioning, and self-evaluation. An example of such an approach is the "Detective Q Squirt Approach," developed by Spafford.

**C**

**Cognitive behavior modification**
Teaching wanted behaviors by providing the individual with self-monitoring techniques and learning strategies. SEE: *behavior modification*

**Cognitive behavioral training** An approach that teaches students to control their own thought processes so as to internalize strategies of speech when responding to questionable situations and problems.

**Cognitive development** The intellectual acquisition of information, facts, and/or data to include their concepts and principles. This mental development includes reasoning, understanding, problem solving, etc. SEE: *cognition, cognitive functioning*

**Cognitive-developmental theory** A theory of the development of gender roles emphasizing the child's understanding of the meaning of gender as a concept before that child can be expected to learn the activities appropriate to his/her gender role.

**Cognitive dissonance** Festinger's theory that an unpleasant, tense condition arises whenever one's attitudes are not consistent with one's behavior or knowledge of the facts. This condition may sometimes be relieved by changing one's attitude (e.g., the reduction of a physiological drive such as hunger by ingesting food). SEE: *theory of cognitive dissonance*

**Cognitive domain** That part or area of learning that is involved with gathering information and putting the acquired knowledge to use.

**Cognitive evaluation theory** A theory concerning intrinsic motivation in relation to a reward offered for going along with the motivated activity. If the reward is perceived to have an informative function, the motivation will increase, whereas if the reward is perceived to be a tool for controlling one's motivation, the motivation will decrease.

**Cognitive functioning** That which has to do with thinking. In effect, how one processes knowledge and information

and the level of proficiency at which it is processed. SEE: *cognition*

**Cognitive learning styles** Individual differences in ways of perceiving information and organizing it into higher-level cognitive structures.

**Cognitive map** A mental representation of the spatial relationships of different locations in an individual's environment. The representation may consist of visual and/or kinesthetic memory traces.

**Cognitive mediation** A thinking technique in which students develop an "internal dialogue" that directs skilled reading. The teacher first models appropriate dialogue, which frequently takes the form of questioning strategies. By thinking aloud, in response to a specific text, the teacher makes explicit some internal cognitive reasoning. Gradually, the student is able to verbalize his/her own dialogue.

**Cognitive monitoring** One's self-examination of one's own thinking processes and learning procedures.

**Cognitive objectives** Those educational objectives that pertain to higher mental processes.

**Cognitive perspective** The point of view that the way that one understands one's experiences, the nature of the mental organization of one's perceptions, and the processing of information are the major factors in deciding how one thinks, feels, and acts.

**Cognitive psychology** The school of psychology that stresses the study of higher cognitive processes, including thinking, perception, discrimination, judgment, problem solving, etc.

**Cognitive restructuring therapy** A type of cognitive therapy in which the patient is influenced to change negative self-imagery and pessimistic expectations.

**Cognitive theory** The view that thoughts and information processing involve personal choices that are goal-directed and cognitively monitored. This theory is different from behavioral theory, which emphasized the role of environmental stimuli eliciting responses from organisms, rendering thought processes as insignificant. SEE: *behavioral theory*

**Cognitive therapy**   A type of psychotherapy intended to eliminate irrationally negative views of oneself, other people, and the world.

**Cognitive training**   A system of training in which the major goal is to change thought or patterns of thought. SEE: *cognitive approach*

**Cognitive view of learning**   The attitude toward learning that treats it as an active way of acquiring, retaining, and utilizing knowledge.

**Cognitivist theory**   A theory based on the work of Jean Piaget, Noam Chomsky, Richard Cromer, and others that advances the notion that language is a result of intelligence and not a product of behavior. Cognitivists believe that regardless of environmental factors, logical thinking proceeds through a series of sequentially identifiable stages. The idea is that cognition preceeds language and thus cognitive development determines language development. The ability to think is the foundation for acquisition of language. SEE: *constructivism*

**Cohabitation**   Living with another person and having close and personal relations with that person, without being married to the cohabitating partner.

**Coherent instruction**   A type of instruction that focuses students on the learning connections within the lesson and across the curriculum. The role of the teacher is to assist students in integrating new knowledge with prior experiences and to build a sound knowledge base.

**Coherent reading**   In language arts, continuous reading by the student from a book or text in a meaningful way. That is, the reading makes sense to the student and is normally done for an extended period of time.

**Cohort**   Those people who comprise a given category such as age. Cohorts may

also be set around other factors besides age, such as a companion.

**Coleman Report (1966)**   A report that helped initiate programs for bilingual students, as this report demonstrated that non-English-speaking students tested below all national norms in reading and math. The study concluded that the most influential factor regarding student achievement was family background.

**Coleman Report (James Coleman, 1981)**   An educational study that concentrated on a comparison of the effectiveness of private v. public schools. SEE: *Coleman Report (1966)*

**Collaborate**   Working with others in a cooperative manner toward a common objective or goal.

**Collaborative consultation**   The collaboration of professionals to generate strategies/ideas to more effectively deal with the unique learning needs/styles of individuals with special needs (e.g., learning disabilities).

**Collaborative instruction** or **collaborative teaching**   1. A type of instruction that involves interactive negotiations and reciprocity between the student and teacher/learner. The teacher assumes the role of student/learner at times when material or concepts are unfamiliar and the students can provide information or guidance. 2. Teaching teams that work together in planning and instruction efforts. Teams sometimes divide subject matter according to the background/strengths/interests of each participating teacher. 3. Teaching teams within one classroom setting (e.g., regular classroom teacher, resource teacher, and home-school adjustment counselor).

**Collaborative research**   (within education settings) The process of initiating teacher-research partnerships between teachers and teachers; college faculty and college faculty; teachers and researchers; teachers and college faculty; teachers and community members/families, etc. The major goal of collaborative research activities within the classroom is to better meet the learning styles and needs of all children. Typically preliminary activities involve brainstorming appropriate topics/issues to research (e.g., how to better meet the needs of bilingual learners) along with goal setting, model implementation, problem identification, assessing one's knowledge base, identifying all likely participants/resources, researching classroom research models, etc. The following 8 steps provide a foundation for collaborative research endeavors: 1. establish goals, objectives, and problems identification(s); 2. coordinate data collection (e.g., journal writing, maintaining anecdotal records, observation recordings, videotaping of classes, surveying students, conducting ethnographic observations, conducting home visits, etc. 3. schedule times where the collaborative research team engages in continuous and ongoing discussions regarding data collection, redefining mission ideals and goals, restructuring methods/techniques, discussing how to implement findings, etc.; 4. analyze data; 5. implement findings/theory into new practices by revising previous methods, reviewing/selecting alternative placements, etc., 6. provide ongoing self-assessment and evaluations of research applications; and 7. disseminate information to school personnel, parents, colleagues, and students when appropriate.

**Colleague consultation**   Refers to the process of soliciting input from peers (teacher-to-teacher; special needs resource teacher-to-speech therapist) regarding the education planning of students.

**Collective bargaining**   A bargaining procedure wherein a group, such as an association or union, represents the employees and representatives from this employee unit bargain contractually with representatives of the employer. Procedures are usually specified in writing and a written contract ensues as a result of the negotiations between the parties concerned. The contracts or agreements cover salaries and working conditions as well as conditions of employment and the like. SEE: *collective bargaining agent*

**Collective bargaining agent**   An organization such as the National Education Association, American Federation of Teachers, etc. recognized by an educational institution, either voluntarily or through elections, as representing the interests of faculty in collective bargaining.

**Collective monologue**   A type of speech used by children in a group. They may be speaking, but they are not really interacting or communicating with one another.

**Collective unconscious**   The portion of the unconscious mind that, according to Jung's theory, is shared by all human beings. It contains the archetypes (i.e., the universal mental images) originating from the animal ancestors of present-day humans.

**College**   A post-secondary (after high school) school that offers a two-year (associates') or four-year (baccalaureate) degree and other advanced or graduate degrees such as a Master's Degree. There is a World Wide Web site for high school students who would like to look at college and career alternatives at http:// www.tpoint.net/~jewels/college.html. Students can visit different college sites at http://www.collegeview.com. Financial aid information can be obtained via the U.S. Department of Education at http://www.ed.gov/prog_info/SFA/StudentGuide. To prepare for college SAT tests, access http://www.testprep.com for the Testprep.Com home page. SEE: *associates' degree, bachelor's degree*

**College board report**   A set of norms or standards of achievement that cover areas of mastery that a high school student should attain before considering and attending college.

**College work-study program**   A program designed to employ college students on a part-time basis. It is normally used to assist students with financial needs.

**Colomba**   A degenerative visual disease characterized by incomplete formation of the peripheral and central areas of the retina resulting in impaired vision. SEE: *retina*

**Color blindness**   The inability to detect different hues, which is usually an inherited trait. Persons who are totally color blind see the world in grayish blues. Partial color blindness is the more common type and frequently involves a person's inability to see red and green and to distinguish between them. Color blindness is also referred to as achromatism.

**Color constancy**   One aspect of perceptual constancy. Color constancy is the ability to recognize the true color of an object despite viewing it in colored illumination or through colored filters or lenses. For example, objects are perceived to have the same color at sunset as they have at noon, even though the daylight at noon is white and the daylight at sunset is reddish.

**Commit**   The act of placing a student or person into the charge of another person or an agency in the person's best interest. For example, a court sends a student to juvenile hall or a family commits a person who is mentally ill to a hospital or clinic for the mentally ill, etc.

**Committee of Fifteen (1895)**   Another historic National Education Association Study that reversed some findings of the Committee of Ten in 1892 as concerns secondary education. SEE: *Committee of Ten (1892)*

**Committee of Ten (1892)**   In 1892 a committee was established by the National Education Association to study U.S. high schools and it established several recommendations that influenced secondary education, such as: 1. high schools should include grades 7–12, 2. courses should be sequential, 3. very few electives should be offered, 4. a Carnegie unit of one should be awarded for each course so long as it meets four or five times weekly.

**Common elementary schools**   An early plan designed to provide basic education for all elementary students. Such schools were in operation from about 1820–1852. Horace Mann

(1796–1859), secretary of the State Board of Education in Massachusetts, helped establish these common elementary schools. In 1852, Massachusetts passed the first compulsory elementary school attendance law in the country.

**Common fate**   One of the principles of perceptual organization in Gestalt psychology. If some parts of the visual stimuli are moving in the same direction and at the same velocity, they are perceived as belonging together to the same group.

**Common school**   A school that is open to the general public and the curriculum of which is offered to all children regardless of background or social class.

**Communication**   The process of making one's ideas and thoughts known to others, as well as receiving thoughts and ideas from others. In effect, an exchange of transmitted/received messages and information and their meanings.

**Communication board**   A board used to display an alphabet, yes/no answers, and other choices to be selected/pointed to by the student, such as in the case of keyboards for facilitative learning. SEE: *facilitative learning*

**Communication disorder**   A generic term used to indicate any significant disability or serious impairment that interferes with normal communication, such as a cleft palate, stuttering, etc.

**Communication signals**   Any type of message that provides information about a person, one's emotions, activities, or some immediate event about to take place. For example, the ringing of a school bell could indicate that the class has ended or the period is about to begin, etc.

**Community-Based Instruction (CBI)**   A practical teaching approach which posits that students learn best in an environment that relates to the skills being learned. For example, shopping skills can best be taught in a shopping mall or retail store rather than in a school store.

**Community catalog**   An assessment strategy that involves four curriculum areas; namely, vocational, recreational, domestic, and community. It is an assessment used to designate the settings where students with disabilities will work, learn, play, and/or live. The plan is usually developed by a team of teachers on behalf of the student; working together they identify the skills and activities needed by the student and the appropriate areas/settings in which they will be learned and/or performed.

**Community living arrangement** A living situation and arrangement that allows and encourages placement of mentally retarded persons in homes within a regular neighborhood. This provides a more normal living setting than institutionalization.

**Community mental health clinics or centers** Local community and sometimes regional health centers that are specifically operated to serve the local and/or regional mental health needs of its citizens.

**Community-referenced instruction** In education, this is the teaching or training of students with the skills needed in a number of community settings (a broad range) in order to prepare students for current and future work settings or environments.

**Community Residential Facility (RF)** Usually a group home for a small number of retarded adults within a residential or urban setting. These retarded adults live in the neighborhood in groups of usually less than 10 and under supervised conditions.

**Community school** A school primarily for children but designed to provide for the educational and sometimes recreational/social needs of the general public within the local area.

**Comparative psychology** That area of psychology dealing with the similarities and differences of various species of animals.

**Compensation** The idea that gains (or losses) in one area of behavior are offset by changes in another type of activity. An individual with a learning disability might compensate for a reading problem by becoming a prolific speech maker.

**Compensatory education** Normally, an enriched course of study or curriculum presented to underprivileged children. Frequently, these children represent low-income families such as in the case of the Head Start program. SEE: *Head Start program*

**Competency** A student's ability to perform specific tasks at a certain skill level and to perform such tasks with accuracy. SEE: *ability*

**Competency-based certification** The process by which the state (or an agency designated by the state) provides a teaching credential to an individual. Several steps are usually required and may include demonstrated mastery of minimum essential generic (e.g., reading and writing) and specialization (e.g., special education) competencies. Usually comprehensive written examinations and other procedures (e.g., demonstration lessons) may be prescribed by the board responsible for the educational examinations.

**Competency-based education** A system of learning based on the acquisition of certain selected skills that have been determined to be desirable curriculum goals in the education of the student. The skills/concepts are geared toward achieving these goals.

**Competency-based teacher education** or **performance-based teacher education** SEE: *competency-based certification*

**Competitive employment** A type of work environment where most of the employees are nondisabled and receiving at least the minimum wage.

**Complementary discipline units** A model more commonly found in secondary-level learning wherein courses or units that bear some relation to each other are studied together; for instance, the case of a humanities course that would study the arts, music, culture, history, and literature of ancient Athens.

**Complex partial seizure** A nonconvulsive seizure sometimes referred to as a psychomotor or focal seizure. The electrical dysfunction localized in the brain causes automatic behavior which the student is unaware of during the seizure. Sometimes this behavior and confusion is erroneously interpreted as a student clowning around and just misbehaving. SEE: *seizure*

**Complex psychosocial motives**  Also known as psychogenic needs and/or wants, these motives are not derived from biological needs but result from learning and experience.

**Compliance**  An agreement to conform to a request presented, whether or not there may be some degree of coercion involved.

**Components**  The basic problem-solving processes that comprise general intelligence, according to the information-processing view of intelligence.

**Composite International Diagnostic Interview (CIDI)** (Core Version 1.1) A fully structured interview that can be scored by computer. Intended for clinical use in a variety of cultures. American Psychiatric Press, Inc. 1400 K Street, MN. Washington, DC 20005.

**Composition**  A term used to describe creative writing of a brief nature in language arts but, in the film industry, it is a term used to describe how people, objects, and places are arranged within a scene.

**Compound words**  Individual words connected or joined together to form a new word and generally a new meaning. For example, air and port = airport; class and mate = classmate; school and board = schoolboard.

**Comprehend**  To understand what is presented; a concept through cognitive strategies/observations that promotes reasoning/thought processes.

**Comprehension monitoring**  A self-monitoring system wherein an individual keeps track of his/her own comprehension of reading material. Adjustments are made during the reading process to improve comprehension by the individual involved. It is a system that frequently does not work well with

individuals who experience learning disabilities.

**Comprehensive secondary school**  Usually the typical high school found in the United States today. There are a variety of program offerings such as business, general, college, industrial, technology, vocational, etc. The vast majority of students, however, are enrolled in the general nontechnical, vocational, or occupational programs.

**Compulsion**  A condition wherein a person engages in an activity that the person considers irrational but just cannot prevent him/herself from doing it. The person feels compelled to perform the act.

**Compulsory education**  The requirement by every state that children must attend school when school is in session. The normal requirement includes ages 6–16.

**Computer**  SEE: *Appendix 4: Computer Terms*

**Computer-Assisted Instruction (CAI)**  Usually a two-way (also small group) teaching/learning communication between a student and instructional computer software via a computer set-up. Computer-assisted instruction can provide supplementary enrichment or practice in a self-paced and self-directed format. Computer graphics can provide highly motivating and rewarding learning experiences. SEE: *Appendix 4: Computer Terms*

**Computer-enhanced instruction**  Any software program that is used to expand, enhance, or enrich regular instruction. These programs, while frequently used to replace drill and practice, can also involve enrichment/advancement materials.

**Computer-Managed Instruction (CMI)**  The tracking of student performance by using computer recordkeeping procedures. SEE: *Appendix 4: Computer Terms*

**Computer-managed learning**  Refers to learning systems that use computer programs to prompt responses from the learner/user. The responses are then analyzed statistically and performance ratings provided.

**Computer simulations** Computer programs that require students to use their knowledge and abilities to solve problems in lifelike settings.

**Computer skills** The ability of a student or individual to properly and appropriately use computers with hardware accessories such as a modem, a scanner, a mouse, a laser printer, etc. Also, computer skills involve the informed use of various types of software such as word processing programs, data analysis, and file storage. Other skills include the proficient use of computer-language programs such as Apple Soft, Basic, CAM, Cobol Logo, Pascal, etc. SEE: *Appendix 4: Computer Terms*

**Computer software** Programs and procedures that provide the instructional component for computers via disks.

**Computer terminology** SEE: *Appendix 4: Computer Terms*

**Computer tutorials** Computer programs that teach by presenting questions to the students and reacting to the students' answers.

**Computerized Axial Tomography (CT scan or CAT scan)** A method of visually examining the intact brain, which is done by taking a linear series of x-ray pictures from the anterior end of the brain all the way to the caudal end. CAT scans may also be used to examine any other part(s) of the body.

**Concentric method** A system or approach to learning to speak for deaf students. Groups of sounds are progressively arranged. The student masters the small group of sounds orally and learns to accompany them with finger spelling. The student then proceeds to the next group of sounds, learns them orally along with finger spelling for clarity and correctness, and so on until an appropriate age-related vocabulary is developed.

**Concept** A way to classify or categorize thoughts or ideas so that there are distinguishing features that are commonly held. For example, the concept of

goodness can be described in a number of ways but there are commonalities in what we all believe to be good.

**Concept attainment** Teaching that involves the development of thinking skills via concept generalizations.

**Concept mapping** A method of diagram used to explain the meaning of a concept.

**Conceptual intelligence** The type of intelligence measured by IQ tests that assess verbal reasoning abilities. Conceptual intelligence refers to cognitive or thinking processes that are involved in problem solving, schema development, social awareness, and metacognition.

**Conceptualize** A mental thought, opinion, or idea formed by making generalizations from particulars. One generates questions in one's mind in order to form abstract ideas.

**Concrete operational stage** The stage of Piaget's model of cognitive development that fits the child ages 7–12. The child can reason logically, but the objects of reasoning have to be physically present.

**Concussion** Usually the result of a severe head injury or blow to the head. The brain is violently jarred and partial or prolonged loss of consciousness may be present. Other symptoms include headache, transient dizziness, vomiting, rapid pulse, flushed face, and restlessness. Symptoms may last from 12 to 24 hours.

**Conditional knowledge** The knowledge of when and where it is appropriate to apply one's procedural and/or declarative knowledge.

**Conditioned play audiometry** An auditory activity tied to instruction or demonstration to condition a child to a specific play activity such as dropping a ball into a pail of water (when hearing a certain sound or command).

**Conditioned response (CR)** Sometimes referred to as conditioned reflex or conditioning, it is a learned reaction or response to a specific condition or stimulus. An example of a conditioned response would be students preparing to

C

leave a classroom (response) just prior to the ringing of the bell signaling the end of class (stimulus). SEE: *operant conditioning*

**Conditioned stimulus (CS)**   In Pavlov's classical conditioning model, an originally unrelated or neutral stimulus is made to elicit a reflexive response such as salivating by presenting it just before the conditioned stimulus (e.g., food in the mouth), which already does elicit that response.

**Conditioned taste aversion**   A dislike for a particular food developed after the individual has experienced gastrointestinal upset or illness following the ingestion of that food.

**Conditioning**   A process characterized by response to a certain stimulus, wherein new circumstances will elicit the same responses that previously were reactions to the original stimulus.

**Conduct disorder**   A type of behavior disorder involving patterns of aggressive acting-out behaviors that frequently are delinquent in nature (e.g., fire setting, assaults, etc.). Both verbal and nonverbal behaviors reflect an antisocial and anti-authority attitude that is evident in both the school and community settings.

**Conduction aphasia**   A specific loss of language ability as a result of damage to the arcuate fasciculus, which is the band of nerve fibers linking Wernicke's area for speech recognition to Broca's area for motor speech. With conduction aphasia, one has great difficulty repeating anything as well as in carrying on a sensible conversation.

**Conduction deafness**   SEE: *conductive hearing loss*

**Conductive education**   A special education method developed in Hungary following the World War II. It is commonly used throughout Europe today. The idea is that education and rehabilitation go together; they are not taught separately. They are presented in an inclusionary manner as concerns instruction in the school.

**Conductive hearing loss**   This is a type of hearing loss involving damage to the

outer or middle ear that is caused primarily by middle ear infections, also known as otitis media. Otitis media causes a malfunctioning of the eustachian tube. Other problems that can cause this disorder are a buildup of earwax, excess fluid in the eustachian tube, and the lodging of a foreign object in the ear. Conductive hearing loss many times is correctable by using a hearing aid, by surgery, or by medical treatment. The two other types of hearing loss are sensorineural and mixed. SEE: *sensorineural hearing loss, mixed hearing loss*

**Confabulation**   It is the tendency of a person or student to fill in gaps in memory with imaginary tales or experiences.

**Confederate**   An experimenter's assistant who pretends to be one of the research subjects. A laboratory slang term for such a confederate is a "stooge."

**Conference** (student)   1. In general education, a meeting and discussion between a teacher, counselor, administrator, and student about some special topic or concern. 2. In language arts, a conference is an opportunity to meet with a student (student-to-student or student-to-teacher) to discuss a writing project, an assignment, a book, student grades, etc. Conferencing is part of the writing process in language arts. SEE: *writing process*

**Confidence interval**   A range of scores within which an individual's true score lies, at a specified probability, such as 95 percent or 99 percent.

**Confidential school records**   The private file, folder, or records of a student. SEE: *confidentiality requirements*

**Confidentiality requirements**   A system of regulation required by law and/or regulation for processing of student records and information. These requirements regulate the release and custodial care of permanent and temporary information such as the student transcripts and medical records (permanent) and report cards and behavior reports (temporary).

## C

**Confirmation bias** In problem solving and inferential reasoning, confirmation bias is the tendency to notice evidence tending to confirm one's expectations and to overlook evidence tending to disprove one's own hypotheses.

**Conflict** A clash of motives resulting from the fact that the behavior required to satisfy one motive is not compatible with the behavior that would satisfy another motive. Being subject to conflicting motives is stressful for an individual.

**Confluence model** The view that the nature of a child's familial environment decides his/her intelligence. The familial factors include the intelligence level of the parents, the intelligence level of the child's siblings, the birth order of the child (first-born, middle, youngest, etc.), and the times between the birth of the child and siblings.

**Conformity** The apparently unforced altering of one's own actions so that they match more closely the actions of other people.

**Congenital or congenital anomaly** A condition that is present in a child at birth. A congenital anomaly would be a birth defect or deviation from the normal.

**Congenital anophthalmos** A condition usually characterized by a lack of development of the eye and certain parts of the brain. It is usually accompanied by mental retardation.

**Congenital aphasia** A condition present at birth characterized by an inability to speak or understand a language. SEE: *aphasia*

**Congenital aural atresia** A birth condition in which the external auditory canal is malformed or missing entirely.

**Congenital condition** SEE: *congenital or congenital anomaly*

**Congenital heart disease** A condition that exists at birth involving defects or anomalies of the structure of the heart or of its functioning.

**Congenital rubella** Also known as maternal rubella and German measles, it is a disease that is contracted by the mother during pregnancy. It can cause serious defects in the newborn such as visual and hearing impairments, deafness, blindness, mental retardation, and other problems neurological in nature. SEE: *maternal rubella*

**Congenital syphilis** Syphilis transferred by the mother during pregnancy to the unborn child. It is known to cause spontaneous abortion or miscarriage, stillbirth, and a variety of problems in the newborn. SEE: *syphilis*

**Congenital visual impairment** A visual impairment usually of a severe nature that was present at the time of birth.

**Congenitally deaf** The condition of those individuals who are born deaf and never have the benefit of hearing. Their loss of hearing makes the acquisition of speech and language more difficult than for individuals who have residual hearing or lose hearing after a disease or illness. SEE: *adventitiously deaf*

**Congestive heart failure** Improper functioning or failure of the heart caused by excessive fluid buildup around the heart. It is characterized by breathlessness, weakness, abdominal discomfort, and edema in the lower body as a result of venous stagnation and flow of blood. SEE: *edema, heart failure*

**Conjugate eye movements** The movement of both eyes together in a coordinated manner.

**Conjunctiva** A thin protective transparent layer of tissue that lines the eyelids and covers the front of the eye. This tissue protects the eyes from dust and other particles.

**Conjunctivitis** Commonly called "pink-eye," this is a highly contagious inflammation of the conjunctiva, the mucous membrane that lines the eyelids and covers the eyeball. This type of infection must be treated with antibiotics prescribed by a physician.

**Connect Two** Refers to a prereading technique wherein the teacher puts two lists of words on the board or provides a handout, both of which relate to a certain topic or reading. Students then decide which words go together by arrangement in sets of two. The sets of words are connected on the board or the handout by lines drawn by the teacher or student. This system can be used to associate three words as well and is then referred to as "Connect Three." The matching of words in this system supports building on known words and integrating new ones. SEE: *classification sort*

**Connect Three**   SEE: *Connect Two*

**Consciousness**   The awareness of our environment and of our own cognitive and emotional processes.

**Consensus**   The degree of consistency of behavior, on a given occasion, of the members of a group of people. Also, it is the willingness of all group members to support the prominent group decision whether or not it is one's first or personal choice.

**Consent**   Educationally speaking, it is the act of obtaining written approval. In the sense of special education, in order to evaluate and/or place a student in a special needs program, written consent must be supplied by the parent, guardian, or by the student if 18 years of age or older. SEE: *due process*

**Consequences**   The after-effects of an action. These may be reinforcing, raising the chances that the action will be repeated, or punishing, lowering the probability of the action.

**Conservation**   The realization that altering the shape of a container does not change the amount of liquid inside a container. A child develops this ability when his/her cognitive development has arrived at the stage of concrete operations, in Piaget's model of cognitive growth.

**Consigliere**   SEE: *second stage facilitator*

**Consistency**   The extent to which an individual behaves the same way in a given type of situation whenever that situation occurs.

**Consolidation**   Usually meant as the combining of smaller schools into a larger school or the inclusion of a school into another. Programs and courses of study can also be combined or consolidated.

**Constant dollars**   Dollar amounts that have been adjusted by means of price and cost indices to eliminate inflationary factors and allow direct comparison across years. Constant dollars are expressed in two ways: 1. according to the calendar year and 2. according to the school year.

**Constants**   The learning experience or steps that are taught and comprise the offerings of the academic or vocational track in a secondary school.

**Constricted-response format**   Assessment procedures requiring the student to organize and express one answer. These correction procedures are sometimes called "objective tests."

**Construct validity**   Refers to the ability of a test to measure a theoretically valid hypothetical construct such as character or intelligence. No one statistical test (e.g., a correlation coefficient) can measure this type of validity. Rather, the test scores should constitute a variable that is strongly related to several other sets of data, including the outcomes of experiments, surveys, case studies, etc.

**Constructive alternativism**   The process by which a person makes use of personal constructs in order to select an appropriate course of behavior in a given situation.

**Constructive recall**   The alteration of the memory of an event by addition, omission, or change in the details so that memory is better suited to some mental organization (schema) the individual has developed.

**Constructivism**   According to Spafford and Grosser, a method or approach to teaching that keys in on having learners "construct" their own meaning/knowledge base/learning experiences. Constructivism allows teachers to become student/learners and students to become facilitators of knowledge acquisition because there are interactive communications/activities and discovery/rediscovery learning experiences. The teacher serves as a facilitator of learning versus an imparter or director of knowledge. Scaffolding is important to this learning approach because the adult scaffolds or structures the learning experience at first until the child reaches independence in performance/achievement. Constructivism is popular in the math and science areas where discovery learning can facilitate a broader conceptual knowledge base. This learning theory is similar to cognitivism in that there is an interaction between the cognitive (thinking) function of a child and the environment (both linguistic and nonlinguistic), resulting in the development of complex language structures. Such an interactive approach considers the environment as important in providing learning in context and giving context to learning. SEE: *cognitivist theory*

**Constructivist view of learning**   Based on the work of Lev Vygotsky (1896–1934), this approach to learning provides strategies/activities that allow the learner to constantly build and rebuild or "construct" ideas based on previous information. The learning process is characterized by making mistakes and refining knowledge as a result of realizing that earlier ideas may not be correct. Teachers can adapt learning activities to foster students' construction of knowledge. This view stresses the active role of the learner in building together his/her understanding of the presented information.

**Constructivist view of reading**   A view of reading based on the tenet that the reader interacts with the printed page or text. It is posited that the reader can create meaning by using prior knowledge/experience and knowledge about language in general to derive meaning. This view of reading is based upon the constructivism theory of learning. SEE: *constructivism, "constructivist view of learning"*

**Consultative services**   Assistance provided to teachers in general educational settings in order to assist/help them in dealing with special education students. For example, a special education teacher could advise a regular classroom teacher on techniques and wherewithall to better serve a child with special learning challenges (e.g., a child with mild disabilities within the regular classroom setting). Also, consultative services involve any other specialist(s) who provides assistance to a regular class teacher such as a counselor or psychologist. The intent of the consultant is to improve the educational and/or the planned program of intervention for the child with special learning challenges.

**Consulting teacher**   A specially trained teacher in the area of special needs or other areas who assists the regular classroom teacher in adapting the regular education curriculum to the needs of the child with special needs.

**Consumer unit**   1. All members of a particular household who are related by blood or legal arrangements; 2. persons living alone or sharing a household with others; or 3. two or more persons together who are making joint expenditure decisions. All units are considered financially independent.

**Contact hour**   An hour of classroom instruction time for students. SEE: *credit hour*

**Content**   A term used to indicate subject matter or course content.

**Content area text**   SEE: *expository text*

**Content validity**   Refers to whether a test or diagnostic instrument measures what it purports to measure. For example, a geography test should ask a question such as "Where is Rio de Janeiro?" but should not ask for the value of the gravitational constant or the chemical formula for water.

**Context**   The physical, social, perceptual, and/or emotional environment in which an event takes place.

**Context clues**   Information in a text or book that would assist a reader to identify word(s) or written material (e.g., a description of a scene would help identify the location; nursing rhymes have predictable word patterns that give the reader clues as to identity/meaning).

**Context dependent memory**   The tendency for memory to be more accurate when recall is done in the same environment where the material was originally learned.

**Contiguity** The mental association of two events as the result of their being presented together.

**Contingency contracting** A contract between educational personnel and a student usually in writing but sometimes orally wherein an agreement is reached concerning the student's behavior. That is, the punishment/awards appropriate for improper/proper behavior.

**Contingency management or contingency contracting** A type of behavior modification technique that can be used to increase or decrease wanted or unwanted behaviors. For example, if a child does not like to do math homework but loves to watch television, a contingency contract could be set up. That is, every time the child completes a math homework assignment, a 30-minute TV program could be allowed (watching television) = contingent on completing homework). Also, if a child has a bad habit (e.g., throwing a temper tantrum), one could again make watching television contingent on no tantrums for the day.

**Continuing education** A renewed or extended opportunity for students to continue their education after the completion of full-time schooling. Sometimes used by dropouts to finish a program, it can be used at any level of education but frequently refers to college-level programs or education and training beyond high school.

**Continuous Reinforcement Schedule (CRF)** The presentation of a reinforcer to the learner every time the correct response is made.

**Continuum of educational services** The full range of special-needs services available to students with disabilities. The range extends from regular class placement (the least restrictive) through inclusion and mainstreaming to residential placement, full-time, full-year, and substantially separate (the most restric-

tive). SEE: *mainstreaming, least restrictive environment, inclusion*

**Continuum of placements** The range of educational placements as per the Individuals with Disabilities Education Act (P.L. 101-476). This can range, for a child with special needs, from placement in a regular classroom to a separate resource room, or even to a home or hospital program. It may also include placement in a day school or even a residential setting out of district.

**Continuum of services** SEE: *continuum of placements*

**Contract system** A behavior-modification approach to education. For example, a student agrees prior to the taking of a college course to achieve a set of standards in order to earn a particular grade.

**Contracture** A permanent shortening or contraction of a muscle as a result of spasm or paralysis to a point where limbs, bones, and/or posture are distorted.

**Control group** Those subjects who do not receive a particular treatment; their behavior is compared with that of the subjects who do receive the treatment.

**Control subjects** Those subjects in an experiment who are not given the treatment under investigation. The behavior of the control subjects is used as a standard to which the behavior of the experimental subjects (those who do receive the treatment) can be compared.

**Control theory** A theory that contends that we fashion our behavior in order to keep control of ourselves but also to gain control of others.

**Controlled drinking** A technique for curing alcoholism in which the individual is taught how to drink in moderation.

**Controlled processing** The use of deliberate mental effort to affect the processing of information. This often interferes with other cognitive activities. A spectacular example of controlled processing is lucid dreaming. SEE: *lucid dreaming*

C

**Controlled vocabulary** A system in reading wherein the use of words are carefully sequenced for the reader/learner in order to allow the individual to systematically develop vocabulary competence.

**Contusion** 1. In effect, a bruise that is an injury in which the skin remains intact and is not broken. 2. A head injury wherein the brain is pressed against a side of the skull, out of position to a point causing bruising of the neural tissue.

**Conventional level** In Kohlberg's model of the moral development of children, this is the level of development in which the child is concerned with conforming to the values and laws of his/her society and with acceptance of authority.

**Conventional spelling** A stage of spelling development wherein the student has reached a level of mastery of phonemic and rule-governed spelling patterns as well as recognition of word derivations so as to be able to spell most words without consciously thinking about correct spelling.

**Convergence** The turning inward of the two eyeballs when a stimulus object approaches the individual. This allows that object to be viewed directly and in focus by both eyes. The word refers to the convergence or coming together of the two lines of sight.

**Convergent learning** Learning in which there is one answer to a proposed question or problem. For example, 1 + 1 always equals 2.

**Convergent questions** Questions that have a single particular correct answer.

**Convergent thinking** Sometimes referred to as nondivergent thinking, it is the ability to think deductively (reasoning from the general to particulars), rather than inductively (reasoning from the particular to the general). SEE: *divergent thinking*

**Conversion disorder** The appearance of a loss of sensory or motor functioning (i.e., somatoform disorder), which apparently has no physical cause and which is accompanied by inappropriate behavior on the part of the patient. Such symptoms were formerly labeled "hysterical."

**Conversion reaction** An hysterical neurosis wherein the student or person displays sensory or motor dysfunction for which no known organic reason exists.

**Convulsion** An abnormal spasm or contraction and relaxation of the muscles. It is involuntary and can violently interfere with normal functioning. SEE: *seizure*

**Cooley's anemia** SEE: *thalassemia*

**Cooperative Integrated Reading and Composition (CIRC)** A cooperative learning arrangement. Pairs of students work together on various reading/writing tasks. The teams are later rewarded, according to the level of their joint performance.

**Cooperative learning** A type of learning based on the notion that students can learn from each other by coordinating/networking efforts in a format that promotes the exchange of dialogue and ideas. Brainstorming together is one type of cooperative learning example.

**Cooperative learning groups** Learning groups consisting of 2–6 students whereby cooperative input/networking are implemented when confronted with learning challenges. Typically group role assignments exist to include some or all of the following: a chair(s), observers, recorders, coordinators of special activities, checkers, researchers, coaches, and so on.

**Cooperative teaching** SEE: *collaborative instruction*

**Core curriculum** Curriculum design in which one or more subjects become the focal point around which all other subjects are correlated. Teacher education programs usually have a core curriculum of liberal arts courses (e.g., English, science, art, music, psychology, sociology, philosophy, etc.) that are related and integrated into education courses (e.g., introduction to education, methods courses, and student teaching).

**Core evaluation** SEE: *evaluation team*

**Core home** A group of residential homes clustered in a community and designed to meet the needs of students or individuals with mental retardation or other serious disabilities. Homes are arranged within the cluster so as to meet the individual needs of the disabled population. Persons may move from one home to another based upon their individual abilities and needs.

**Cornea** It is the transparent frontal and external covering that covers the eyeball and, in particular, the pupil and iris. It allows light to refract and enter the eye.

**Corporal punishment** A disciplinary procedure wherein physical (bodily) punishment is administered to a student by a school teacher, administrator, or other employee; for example, beating a student's fingers with a switch, spanking, and paddling. Twenty-one states still allow some form of corporal punishment. The U.S. Supreme Court ruled in 1977 that states may allow corporal punishment. SEE: *Ingraham v. Wright (1977)*

**Corporate-education partnerships** Businesses or companies that donate time, resources, or monies to schools on an ongoing basis and consider such involvement as collaborative/participatory in the education of youth. Involvement could include advocacy; access to technology; the donation of recycled paper and other materials; mentoring or buddy programs; reading to children on a regular basis; the provision of incentives for learning/good behavior; educational use of corporate facilities; scholarship programs; adopt-a-school programs; intern programs; inservice programs for parents and teachers; participation on site-based management teams; consultation/advice; grants for innovative programs/practices; business basic training for disadvantaged students; etc.

**Corpus callosum** The brain structure that consists of bands of fibers connecting the right and left hemispheres and is the largest commissure of the brain. A commissure is a band of axons linking a part of the brain on the right side to its counterpart on the left. The corpus callosum links the left hemisphere of the cerebral cortex with the right hemisphere. It is severed in the operation called "split-brain surgery."

**Correlation** The strength of a relationship between two variables (e.g., height and weight) expressed as a numerical value called a correlation coefficient. Correlation coefficients range from $-1.00$ to $+1.00$. The closer the correlation value to plus or minus 1.00, the stronger the relationship. Negative correlations indicate inverse relationships (e.g., better pitching averages result in lower ERAs) and positive correlations point to direct relationships (e.g., taller individuals tend to weigh more). See: *correlation coefficient*

**Correlation coefficient** (known as $r$-meaning relationship) A numerical value that signifies the strength of relationship between numbers and typically most correlation coefficients are adaptations of the Pearson coefficient. Correlation coefficient values range from $+1.00$ to $-1.00$ with zero showing no relationship between values on two measures. Typically values above + or − .75 show strong relationships between scores or values. There are relatively few perfect correlation coefficients of + or − 1.00 in the social sciences. An example of a strong correlation coefficient value (generally between .80 and .90) would be one that results from the study of the relationship between one's IQ and reading performance on standardized achievement tests. Remember that the strength of the correlation coefficient is not affected by the sign. Negative correlation coefficients indicate inverse relationships (e.g., increased school attendance generally results in lower drop-out rates).

**Correlational analyses** A type of statistical analysis that looks at data in terms of whether or not a relationship exists between two or more variables that can be quantified. The two most popular correlational statistical analyses are the product moment correlation coefficient (Pearson $r$) and the rank difference correlation coefficient (Spearman rho). See: *Pearson r, Spearman rho*

**Correlational research** Research done in order to determine whether or not two factors are correlated with one another (or whether more than two factors are correlated among themselves).

**Correlational statistics** Statistical procedures that provide an index of the extent of the correlation between two variables; one well-known example is *r*, the Pearson product-moment correlation coefficient.

**Correspondent inference theory** A theory of how people develop causal explanations (attributions) of the behavior of others. It holds that we are swayed by such factors as the voluntary nature of that behavior and the social desirability of it.

**Cortis' organ** SEE: *organ of Corti*

**Cosmology** That area of philosophy that is concerned with the origin of the universe as well as the subsequent development of the universe. Relevant concepts include time, space, and causality. SEE: *creationism, evolution*

**Cost-effectiveness analysis** A mathematical analysis of an undertaking (e.g., building a school) that looks at the extent to which the project accomplished its objectives in relation to its cost.

**Council for Exceptional Children (CEC)** A special education organization of major importance in the field of special-needs education. It has many divisions to include TED (division of teacher education) and DLD (division of learning disabilities). It regularly publishes the magazine *Teaching Exceptional Children* and the periodical entitled *Exceptional Children* in addition to many other publications. The home page for the CEC is "Foundation for Exceptional Children" at http://cec.sped.org.

**Counseling psychologist** A psychologist who is trained to work with individuals who experience mild psychological (e.g., mild depression) and/or behavior (e.g., truancy) problems.

**Counseling psychology** That specialty within psychology that deals with the analysis and correction of personal problems. The counseling psychologist usually does not diagnose or treat severe mental/emotional illnesses. Examples of workers in this field are vocational counselors and marriage counselors.

**Counseling service** These are services designed for students in order to assist them in making educational, career, and vocational choices. It helps them plan, develop, and make choices concerning their personal development and future endeavors.

**Counter theory model** A model that focuses on advocacy for a disordered or deviant child and delivery of services to the behaviorally disordered child that are effective and appropriate to the child's needs. The idea is also to change social values and expectations that lead to a narrow view of what behaviors are considered "normal" and the view that if behaviors are not classified as "normal" they must be deviant.

**Counterconditioning** A behavior-therapy technique in which an undesirable response is eliminated by presenting the usual conditioned stimuli for that response while (simultaneously) eliciting, by unconditioned stimulation, a competing, incompatible response. The result is that the conditioned stimuli become attached to the new activity and lose their tendency to elicit the older, unwanted response.

**CP** SEE: *Cerebral Palsy*

**CPU** SEE: *Central Processing Unit*

**Cranial nerve** One of 12 nerves connected to one side of the brain (in other words, there are 12 pairs of cranial nerves). The first cranial nerve is connected to the olfactory bulb at the front tip of the brain and nerves II–VI are respectively the optic, oculomotor, trigeminal, abducens, and facial. Cranial nerves VII–XII are connected to the medulla at the caudal end of the brain and are respectively the vestibulo-cochlear, glossopharyngeal, vagus, spinal accessory, and hypoglossal.

**Craniosynostosis**   A fusing of the bones of the cranium at an abnormally early stage of development; in effect, premature fusion of the bones of the skull especially the part enclosing the brain.

**Cranium bifidum**   A condition wherein the brain protrudes through the back of the skull. Sometimes the protrusion is inward into the throat and the nasal cavity. Also called "encephalocele."

**Cranmer abacus**   A type of Japanese abacus for individuals with vision problems. This device consists of beads that can be manipulated to solve math problems.

**Creationism**   The speculation that the universe originated from the action of a "first cause" or divine creator. SEE: *cosmology, evolution*

**Creative reading**   The ability to use novel ideas and problem-solving abilities during the reading task.

**Creativity**   The cognitive ability to problem-solve in novel and original ways.

**Credit**   The accumulation of points (e.g., 120 credits can be earned in order to achieve a bachelor's degree) by recognition of course completions and/or performance in an instructional activity (course or program). The recipient can apply these credits to requirements for any educational degree, diploma, or certificate.

**Credit course**   When successfully completed, credit toward the number of courses required for achieving a degree, diploma, or certificate.

**Credit hour**   A single unit of measure (e.g., at the college level, one credit hour usually equals 15 hours of instruction) that represents an hour of instruction that can be applied to the total number of hours required for a degree, diploma, or certificate.

**Cretinism**   A medical condition that results from a disorder of the thyroid gland. Persons with cretinism have delayed bone development, large muscles, short heavy-thick hands, and mental retardation as well as poor bone and brain development. SEE: *hypothyroidism*

**CRF**   SEE: *Continuous Reinforcement Schedule*

**Crisis intervention room**   Frequently referred to as a "time-out" room, it is a separate area in a school where a student may go or be sent in order to calm down, compose oneself, or even to obtain counseling for a personal and immediate crisis. Once things are returned to normal the student is usually reintegrated into the regular school mainstream.

**Criterion-referenced**   Rating the caliber of a student's test performance or work performance by comparing it with predetermined standards (e.g., curriculum texts). For example, a criterion-referenced assessment comment could read, "Jose could draw conclusions, sequence material, make inferences, define vocabulary, and make predictions for 80 percent of the material in his grade-level reading basal." Based on this informal criterion-referenced assessment, it is logical to assume that Jose should do well in his content-area reading subjects. Predetermined standards for criterion-referenced measures are often derived from the scores of a large standardization group; in that case, the term "criterion-referenced" is synonymous with "norm-referenced."

**Criterion-referenced assessment**   Assessment based on locally established levels of mastery. A student's performance is in reference to the local criterion or level established and not to the performance of others. SEE: *criterion-referenced, norm-referenced*

**Criterion-referenced grading**   The assessment of each student's success, according to how well she/he mastered the objectives of the curriculum.

**Criterion-referenced test**   A test designed to measure a student's achievement/knowledge in an academic area based on locally established standards. It determines what level of achievement the student should master and thus what the student has learned and still needs to learn based on the locally established needs and standards. SEE: *norm-referenced test*

**C**

**Critical instruction** A type of instruction that promotes the development of a questioning attitude on the part of teachers and students alike, with a focus on the "why" of learning.

**Critical pedagogy** A current philosophy that suggests reconstructing a new society through the use of critical thinking skills. It is another and more current term for "reconstructionism." SEE: *reconstructionism*

**Critical period** A period of development in the young in which learning of a particular type is maximally sensitized. For example, about 12 hours after hatching, a young precocial bird (e.g., chick or duckling) will learn the visual form and the typical sound of its mother and begin to follow the parent bird around. SEE: *sensitive period*

**Critical reading** Reasoning, interpreting, and predicting what is read in order to evaluate presented reading material.

**Critical thinking** One's ability to analyze situations by using logic and reasoning skills.

**Cross-categorical definitions** A system wherein students are grouped according to the severity (severe, moderate, mild) of the exceptional need in the areas of behavior or learning disorders. Thus, students are not categorically grouped according to the major exceptionality in the traditional way, such as visually impaired, mentally retarded, learning disabled, etc.

**Cross-curricular** A term used in education to indicate the study of material by using a unit, topic, or theme approach wherein multiple academic areas or disciplines are included, (e.g., math, science, writing/composition, social studies, and multicultural studies include content all related to a unit on "How to Become Good Citizens").

**Cross-sectional research** An approach to designing research in developmental psychology in which separate samples are taken of people of different ages. The responses of all of these subjects are observed and recorded at the same time. This approach contrasts with the longitudinal research approach, which involves repeated observations of the same subjects over a period of time.

**Crowding** The belief that one's space or territory is violated or too restricted when persons are placed too close together (less than 18–24 inches on average).

**Crystallized intelligence** That portion of the individual's intelligence that is acquired from education, training, and experience.

**CS** SEE: *conditioned stimulus*

**CSF** SEE: *Cerebrospinal Fluid*

**Cue words** Key words or word phrases that cue the learner into the meaning of something. For example, cue words in a math problem (e.g., "the difference" or "altogether") assist the learner in choosing the appropriate algorithm to solve the problem.

**Cued speech** A method of communication for the hearing impaired in which gestures are used in combination with speech reading. These hand signals clarify sounds/words that are identifiable by not reading alone, thus providing the speech/necessary additional information.

**Cueing** The provision of a stimulus that sets the stage for a particular response to be successful.

**Cultural approach to labeling** In effect, categorizing students in accordance with the standards of normality of their given culture. SEE: *developmental approach to labeling*

**Cultural bias** The notion that one's own cultural values are the most valid for society.

**Cultural-deficit model** The view that ethnic/minority students fail to learn academic subjects as well as other students because their cultures are educationally inadequate and fail to prepare them for good academic performance.

**Cultural-familial retardation** An outdated term that applies to the exceptional child, indicating that the condition might be a result of both genetic factors and sociocultural conditions.

**Cultural label** or **labeling**    A system wherein the standards of normality are defined relative to the social structure or culture of a particular group.

**Cultural literacy**    Core knowledge of the people, traditions, places, events, language, and concepts of a particular culture.

**Cultural pluralism**    A way of describing societies that are made up of many different cultural groups (e.g., African-American, Hispanic, Asian, European, Indian, etc.). The individual ethnic groups maintain their cultural identity while at the same time they contribute to a unified whole (e.g., United States).

**Cultural transmission**    A theory promulgating that behaviors of various types are taught and passed on to succeeding generations in the same manner as are one's culture and traditions.

**Culturally compatible classrooms**    Classrooms in which the teaching methods and subject matter do not clash with the students' culturally acquired learning styles and social customs.

**Culture**    The beliefs, traditions, habits, and values controlling the behavior of the majority of the people in a social/ethnic group. These include the people's way of dealing with their problems of survival and existence as a continuing group.

**Culture-fair or culture-free tests**    Tests that supposedly eliminate or greatly reduce cultural bias in their content (e.g., SOMPA). SEE: *System of Multicultural Pluralistic Assessment*

**Curie, Marie**    (Polish-born chemist, 1867–1934, married to Pierre Curie) 1. Discovered polonium and radium. She was awarded the Nobel Prize in physics with her husband in 1903 and she alone in chemistry in 1911. 2. Curie: the standard unit of quantity of a radioactive element such as radon (named after Marie Curie).

**Current dollars**    These are basic dollar amounts that do not include any cost-of-living or inflation adjustments.

**Current expenditures**    The required expenses for operating local public schools that do not include capital outlay (i.e., building schools) and interest on school debt. These expenditures include such items as salaries, busing transportation, school maintenance, school texts and supplies, and energy costs.

**Current expenses**    The cost expenditures that are necessary for daily school operations and maintenance.

***Current Index to Journals in Education (CIJE)***    A periodical published through the ERIC network that keeps educators current on various topics/issues covered in the various education-related journals. CIJE is published on a monthly basis and a cumulative index is published at the end of each year. SEE: *ERIC*

**Curriculum**    Educational objectives that are applicable to a specific academic area or area of study. SEE: *core curriculum*

**Curriculum adaptations**    Changes or modifications to regular curricular activities/materials which suit the individual learning styles and needs of the learner. For example, a curriculum adaptation for a blind student might be a "talking book."

**Curriculum-Based Assessment (CBA)**    An evaluative testing method whereby student performance is evaluated by giving students sample items from the curriculum of their school from which they have been taught. Thus, this type of assessment determines if the students are learning what has been taught in their school rather than comparing their performance with national norms that do not necessarily reflect the curriculum content of the school.

**Curriculum compacting**    A system that allows gifted and talented students to move ahead. The normal time for regular academic instruction is reduced to make additional time available for enrichment and advancement of the curriculum. The process involves three basic steps: 1. determine what the student knows prior to instruction,

2. arrange to briefly teach any remaining concepts or skills not understood, and 3. provide the student with academic experiences that enrich or advance one's curriculum. This three-step approach is an example of "curriculum compacting."

**Curriculum development**   The process of planned development/evolvement of curriculum pedagogy/instruction/ presentation modes that is ongoing and reflective. Continual self-assessment and ongoing change allow teachers and schools to achieve major goals and specific objectives.

**Curriculum frameworks**   Guides for creating/implementing curriculum, classroom assessment procedures, professional development, etc.

**Curriculum specialist**   A professionally trained person who provides supportive and consultative services to regular classroom teachers and special needs teachers in the area of curriculum development and implementation. SEE: *curriculum*

**Cushing's syndrome**   (Harvey Cushing, American surgeon, 1869–1939) A disease that results from hypersecretion of the adrenal cortex. It may be caused by a tumor of the adrenal gland. Symptoms include fatigue, weakness, impotence, edema, diabetes mellitus, obesity, skin discoloration, excess hair growth, and other physical as well as psychological problems.

**Custodial**   A common term used to describe the category as well as the needs of a seriously retarded person or student. That is, one whose IQ is below 35–40 points and is seriously lacking life and self-care skills and adaptive behavior. Even basic needs require special care and supervision.

**Custodial student**   A student who requires institutional care or constant supervision because of severely dehabilitating psychological, social, physical, or emotional conditions.

**CVS**   SEE: *Chorionic Villi Sampling*

**Cyanosis**   A blue skin discoloration caused by a lack of oxygen in the blood.

**Cylert**   Also known as pemoline, a psychostimulant drug used to treat Attention Deficit Disorder (ADD) and Attention-Deficit/Hyperactivity Disorder (ADHD). SEE: *ritalin*

**Cystic fibrosis**   A type of inherited disease that results in a reduced life span and an intensification of symptoms. Respiratory problems necessitate daily treatments and digestive problems also have to be addressed.

**Cytomegalic Inclusion (CMV)**   A cytomegalovirus infection in newborns. It is a condition that is transmitted to the fetus from a mother. This herpes virus rarely causes problems in the newborn, but when it does produce illness usually death results.

**Daily living skills**   Those basic skills needed by a person for self-help or societal living. These include but are not limited to grooming and personal hygiene, independent living skills, vocational or job skills, social skills, and skills needed to travel and live independently.

**Daily response to reading**   A technique used in reading instruction wherein on a daily basis students react in writing to the daily reading(s). Responses may involve journals, logs, and group responses in writing to the daily readings.

**Dame school**   A type of early elementary school in which the children were taught by a housewife or other untrained woman in one's own home. This occurred during colonial and post-colonial times.

**DAP**   SEE: *Developmentally Appropriate Education*

**Dark adaptation**   The optical process by which the eye adjusts to a dimly lit environment. After the dark-adaptation process, the individual is sensitive to very faint lights (so faint that they would not be noticed in broad daylight).

**DAT**   SEE: *Differential Aptitude Test*

**Data-based instruction**   A method of academic assessment that employs daily or weekly measures of the mastery of particular skill areas. For example, in mathematics, a teacher might give daily math problems to assess fact or concept mastery.

**Day-care center** (or Child-Care Center)   A place, school, or institution that cares for young children who are either not yet in school (pre-schoolers) or school-age children during non-school times such as after school, school vacations, summertime, etc.

**De facto segregation**   Actual or real segregation that exists with or without governmental sanction of any kind. SEE: *de jure segregation*

**De jure segregation**   The segregation of students because of school policies, laws, or other governmental practices intended to segregate based on race, sex, or other attributes (e.g., until recently apartheid in South Africa).

**Deaf**   Having a severe hearing loss to the extent that understanding speech or hearing sounds via the ear alone is impossible, with or without sound amplification (e.g., hearing aid).

**Deaf-blindness**   A term used to describe a disorder wherein the person has hearing and vision impairment at the same time or together.

**Deaf-mute**   A term used to describe a student or person who cannot speak or hear.

**DEAR**   An acronym used in language arts that stands for the "Drop Everything And Read" program.

**Debriefing**   An ethically required procedure for experimental psychologists doing research in which deception of the research subjects is part of the experimental plan. The subjects are informed, after the study has been completed, about the true nature and purpose of the research. The debriefing process allows the psychologist to deal with any doubts, fears, and/or misunderstandings that the subjects may have developed during their participation in the experimental procedure.

**Debt service**   The repayment of principal and interest on loans incurred by school districts.

**DEC talk** (DEC-Digital Equipment Corporation)   A speech synthesizer to be added to a computer; manufactured by Digital Equipment Corporation.

**Decay**   The gradual weakening of memories as time passes.

**Decay theory**   A view of the forgetting process as the gradual fading away of physical memory traces (engrams) stored in the brain.

**Decentering**   Placing the focus of instructional efforts on more than one aspect of a subject at a time.

**Decentralization**   A situation in which authority and responsibility are delegated to subordinates. The central authority or supraordinate allows those lower in the chain of command to be in charge of certain things as determined by the central authority (sometimes it is a collective decision).

**Decibel (dB)**   One tenth of a Bel, it is a relative measure of the loudness or intensity of a sound.

**D**

**Decile** This is a marker for every successive 10 percent of a set or population of scores. A decile represents any of nine scores on a test or other behavioral measure such that, between any two adjacent deciles, 10 percent of the subjects may be found. Below the first decile may be found the lowest-scoring 10 percent of the subjects. Between the first and second deciles one may find the second-lowest-scoring 10 percent of the subjects, etc.

**Decision making** The act of examining several possible behaviors and selecting from them the one most likely to accomplish the individual's intention. Cognitive processes such as reasoning, planning, and judgment are involved.

**Declarative knowledge** Knowledge of the facts; "knowing" that something is true. The type of knowledge tested by the Information Subtest on the Wechsler Intelligence Scale for Children (revised) taps into declarative knowledge.

**Declarative memory** A part of long-term memory. Declarative memory consists of memories of facts. It has two subdivisions; namely, episodic memory and semantic memory.

**Decode** A term used in language arts and reading to mean a student has received a phonetic or language message and extracted the appropriate idea or ideas from the message received phonetically or in print. SEE: *decoding*

**Decoder** Any electronic device that permits closed captions to be seen on a television screen. SEE: *closed captions*

**Decoding** This is the extracting of ideas out of the phonetic code or language we receive. We are, in effect, receiving a message. In regard to reading, decoding is that print-to-speech match that relies on one's recognition of phoneme/grapheme correspondence and ability to combine such correspondences into whole words.

**Deductive reasoning** A logical procedure wherein one reasons from generalities to arrive at specifics. It is the opposite of inductive reasoning. SEE: *inductive reasoning*

**Deep structure** The underlying, essential meaning of the printed page as opposed to the grammatical arrangement of the words or surface structure.

**Defective syntax** A condition in which a student or person has difficulty putting words together to express meaning and ideas. Sentence structure and grammar are adversely affected. SEE: *syntax*

**Defense mechanisms** Freud discovered that people often have characteristic but unconscious ways to protect their ego or self against anxiety-provoking situations or strong feelings of anxiety. The particular defense mechanism one adopts becomes characteristic of her/his personality. These defense mechanisms include denial, repression, projection, fantasy, regression, reaction formation, identification, rationalization, intellectualization, displacement, and sublimation. The use of defense mechanisms is considered normal as they help everyone cope with daily stressors. However, when used to an extreme, defense mechanisms are considered maladaptive.

**Deficiency needs** The four lower types of needs in Maslow's motivational theory. These needs must be satisfied before one can attempt to satisfy the higher-level needs.

**Defining attributes** Those distinguishing features that are common to all items belonging to a given category (e.g., all women can be defined by certain attributes that distinguish them from men and vice versa).

**Degree** An award (e.g., bachelor's degree, associate's degree, high school diploma, doctoral degree, etc.) conferred by a high school, college, university, or other educational institution as recognition for successful completion of an outlined program of studies.

**Degree-seeking students** Students enrolled in courses for credit who have been formally accepted by the institution as seeking a particular degree (e.g., master's program) or formal award.

**Degrees of freedom** This term is the index that is used to look up table values when interpreting inferential statistical tests. When using parametric tests like the *t* test, degrees of freedom relate directly to the number of subjects/observations studied. Nonparametric tests (e.g., chi square) use degrees of freedom to represent the number of categories used in the analyses. Degrees of freedom usually appear in parentheses after a statistic. For example, *t* (2, 23) allows the practitioner to read the *t* table at 2 and 23 degrees of freedom.

**Deindividualization**   The process by which individuals within a group become less aware of their separate personal identities and become less personally concerned with how they and their actions will appear to other persons or society in general.

**Deinstitutionalization**   Refers to the placement of individuals with disabilities outside of hospital and other residential types of institutions into more homelike settings (e.g., apartments for persons with disabilities).

**Deism**   The view that God exists and is the source of natural and moral law. A deist holds, however, that organized religious services are not necessary and a person need not adhere to any formal religion. George Washington and Thomas Jefferson were deists.

**Deja vu**   This is a French phrase meaning "already seen." It refers to a subjective feeling that one has already encountered some objects, persons, or scenery despite the fact that the objects, persons, and scenery were never experienced before.

**Delayed language**   The inability of a student or person to develop his/her speech and understanding of a language in a timely and normal fashion.

**Delayed response task**   A task which the subject is required to perform based on a signal given some time before arrival of the opportunity to act. This tests the subject's ability to hold a signal in memory and act on it later.

**Delayed speech**   A condition wherein the student or individual speaks at a level of proficiency indicative of a person much younger.

**Delinquency**   A term normally used to describe a youth and/or teenager who violates the norms of behavior of a society. The behavior may also violate laws as well as traditions.

**Delirium tremens**   Also known as tromomania, it is a psychic disorder characterized by trembling and visual as well as auditory hallucinations. It is frequently accompanied by raving and/or incoherent speech and found commonly amongst habitual and chronic users of alcohol. It is often improperly referred to as delirium tremors.

**Delusion**   An irrational belief that a person will defend with great determination even though there is little or no evidence to support such a belief. Thus, a delusion has no real basis in reality.

**Dementia**   (senility) A state of deteriorative mental capacity. It is normally part of the aging process as in the case of senile dementia and is progressive. There is a loss of memory, especially for short-term or recent events, coupled with occasional attacks of excitement and disorientation.

**Demographics**   The statistical data used to describe or profile a society at the international, national, regional, state, city, town, or local levels. The data includes information about race and/or ethnicity, family, gender, education levels, occupations, culture, etc. Thus, a general societal picture of the population studied is formed.

**Denasality**   A condition characterized by a deficiency of air passing through the nasal cavity, thus creating a voice resonance problem.

**Dendrite**   A fibrous extension of a neuron or nerve cell. A dendrite is thickest at the cell body and tapers down as it continues away from the cell body. It in turn gives off branches that are also tapering in shape. Since this is much like the arrangement of a tree and its branches, the dendrite gets its name from the Greek word *dendron,* meaning "tree."The dendrites are the message-receiving fibers of the neuron.

**Denial**   A defense mechanism whereby an individual does not acknowledge threatening feelings.

**Deno's cascade**   A hierarchy of seven service placement options that range from regular classroom participation with no additional support services to homebound and hospital programs. Level 1—exceptional children in regular classrooms with or without support services; Level 2—regular classroom plus additional instructional assistance; Level 3—part-time special class; Level 4—full-time special class; Level 5—special schools within the public system; Level 6—homebound; and Level 7—hospital, residential or total care placements.

**Dentine or dentin**   The main tissue of the tooth that surrounds the inner pulp and is covered by the hard exterior enamels. SEE: *enamel, pulp*

**Department of Education (ED)**   Refers to the U.S. Department of Education, a cabinet-level agency that establishes federal education policies, finance policies, program providers, etc.

**Dependent variable**   The variable measured during a scientific experiment. In psychological research, the dependent variable is almost always some kind of response. The dependent variable may (or may not) increase or decrease in accordance with changes of the independent variable. SEE: *independent variable*

**Depolarization**   The activation of a neural impulse by the conversion of the normal (resting) potential on the membrane of a neuron's axon from a positive to a negative charge. The normal resting voltage is a considered a state of polarization. Therefore, changing it would be a depolarization. SEE: *excitatory synapse.*

**Depressant**   A drug that lowers mood and slows behavior.

**Depression**   A lowered mood-state, feeling "blue" or "down in the dumps." It may be situational (appropriate to a grief-causing real-life event), neurotic (relatively mild), or psychotic. The latter is referred to as "major depression" or "clinical depression;" the patient must be put under medical care, as he/she may be a threat to the welfare and survival of oneself or of others.

**Depth model**   A model that identifies gifted individuals through measures of achievement. This model requires only one criterion for giftedness (e.g., a high IQ).

**Depth perception**   The perception of the front-to-back distance of an object from the observer. The observer judges how far in front the object is.

**DES**   SEE: *Diethylstilbestrol*

**Descriptive-correlational-experimental loop**   A research schema that involves 1. observation to identify variables worth exploring, 2. the study of relationships among the variables, 3. finding statistically significant correlations, and 4. using teaching procedures that are based on such established data.

**Descriptive data**   Data used to objectively describe a student, school day, school climate, etc. Typically, information is gathered and categorized or classified in some way (e.g., types of schedules available for students, the number of students present on a given day, professional development offerings available for teachers, etc.).

**Descriptive positivism**   The position in analytic philosophy that only descriptions of observations are acceptable statements in natural science. Even the abstract results of inductive reasoning, such as the hypothetical concepts of the atom or the electron, are rejected as nonsensical. The early twentieth century advocate of this view was Mach. Induction of general laws (statements of relationships among sets of observations) was the only logical procedure acceptable to descriptive positivism. The originator of the viewpoint was Sir Francis Bacon. A modern psychologist who attempted to work within the framework of this approach to scientific practice was B. F. Skinner, the behaviorist. SEE: *behaviorism, logical positivism*

**Descriptive research**   The systematic recording of observed behaviors. The observer may have a prearranged data sheet as a checklist, or may write long-hand descriptions of what he/she observes; alternatively, the observer might use some combination of the two.

**Descriptive statistics** Statistical measures of various facts about the numerical data yielded by a research study such as a survey or experiment. Examples of descriptive statistics include the mean, mode, median, range, and standard deviation. SEE: *mean, mode, median, range, standard deviation*

**Descriptive video service** A type of service offered by public television stations to individuals with vision impairments. The service provides an audio narrative to important visual information.

**Desegregation** A position that opposes racial segregation with efforts made to eliminate any segregation. Some white suburban school systems, for example, have programs that allow for the busing of African-Americans and other minorities into their school system so as to promote integrated schools. This is one method for desegregating schools.

**Desktop publishing** Producing written and/or graphic material of a high quality and in publication format with a microcomputer (desktop size). Special software is required for desktop publishing.

**Detective Q Squirt** A cognitive approach developed by Spafford in 1993. SEE: *cognitive approach*

**Detention** The retention of students during school at times usually devoted to recreation (e.g., recess) or after school because of school or classroom infraction(s).

**Determinism** The assumption that human events have observable and measurable causes. Most psychologists hold a deterministic view of human behavior.

**Development** Systematic and adaptive changes of body and mind that the human being undergoes in the period from birth to death.

**Developmental aphasia** A disorder of language in young children characterized by impairment of the formulation, use, and comprehension of written or verbal language. This partial or complete loss is caused by damage to the brain. SEE: *aphasia*

**Developmental approach to labeling** In effect, categorizing students or children in accordance with what is considered normal growth and/or development. SEE: *cultural approach to labeling*

**Developmental bilingual education** SEE: *maintenance bilingual education*

**Developmental crisis** An emotional conflict arising during development that prepares one for the emergence of a new adjustment to the environment.

**Developmental delay** A term used in special education and in general to indicate a delay in a student's progress when comparing the student with her/his peers. Developmentally, the student is doing less than expected and is not up to par with others in such areas as cognition, self-core skills, language and communication, physical ability, social growth, etc.

**Developmental disorders** Severe delays or disorders involving the acquisition of developmental skills in the areas of cognition, motor, language, and social or any combination thereof.

**Developmental dyslexia** A form of reading disability that is acquired at birth and follows a developmental progression of the disorder. Generally, individuals with developmental dyslexia evidence more language manifestations (e.g., spelling errors, word recognition errors) of the disability with increased age. As the individual gets older, the reading problems increase. This is also known as the "Matthew Effect." SEE: *dyslexia, Matthew Effect*

**Developmental label or labeling** A system wherein labeling takes place based upon the difference in development of the child under study or diagnosis as compared to abnormal development of the average child.

**D**

**D**

**Developmental model**   1. In education, this is an approach based on certain standards of so-called normal development. It is also referred to as the developmental milestone assessment model. This approach posits that children develop abilities and skills in a sequential manner (not necessarily age related). Thus, children can be compared to these developmental milestones to see if they are indeed developing in accordance with what is expected for a normally functioning child. If not, the curriculum is modified so that the students can progress in a sequential order (regardless of chronological age) from the mastery of lower-level skills before going on to the next higher-level skill. 2. In psychology, stages of developmental growth that are tied to a particular perspective or field. For example, Freud described five stages of psychosexual development: (1) oral stage (birth to 1 year), (2) anal stage (1–3 years), (3) phallic stage (3–5 years), (4) latency stage (age 6 to puberty), and genital stage (after puberty). Freud believed that one's personality evolved during these overlapping stages of development. Kohlberg developed a theory of moral development (i.e., the evolution of one's moral reasoning abilities) that also involved stages of development. Level 1: obedience, punishment orientation, and naive egotism emerges; Level 2: authority control results in "good boy" or "good girl" orientation where children seek to maintain the approval of adult figures (moral standards are blindly accepted); and Level 3: one's morality is a reflection of internal standards that are embraced for the good of one's self and society in general.

**Developmental period**   As defined by the American Association on Mental Retardation (AAMR), it is the period that covers birth to age 18.

**Developmental placement**   A system of placing students into a grade level that is not based on their chronological age but instead considers a student's academic achievement, physical and mental development, social competencies, etc.

**Developmental psychology**   A special field of psychology that studies the changes in behavior, emotion, language, and intelligence of people as they pass through the various stages of life from birth to old age.

**Developmental retardation**   A term used to describe a delay in a student's progress that is not a result of a learning disability, mental retardation, or some such factor but is instead a result of psychosocial causes such as poverty, abuse and neglect, malnutrition, and other environmental factors.

**Developmental task**   A task that arises at or about a certain time frame in one's life (e.g., walking at age 1).

**Developmentally Appropriate Education (DAP)**   Those educational programs and methods that are intended to match the needs of the students in the areas of cognition, physical activity, emotional growth, and social adjustment.

**Deviance**   Behavior that is different and not in conformity with the accepted norms of the day. When behavior or psychological deviance or abnormalities are noted, social and cultural factors dictate what is considered abnormal. What is considered deviant in one culture might be commonplace in another. Even within one's own culture, what is considered normal in one situation (e.g., laughter and the telling of jokes, eating and drinking, and dancing at a party) might be considered deviant or unacceptable in another situation (e.g., a church service). SEE: *deviant*

**Deviant**   A term used to indicate a student or person who is different from the norm. The individual's behavior is usually inappropriate as concerns socialization and interpersonal relations.

**Deviation IQ**   A score on an intelligence test based on a comparison of the individual's performance with the average performance of other persons in the individual's age group.

**Dexedrine**   A stimulant drug; trade name for dextroamphetamine sulfate. It is used to combat mild depression and has also been used as an appetite suppressant. Its value as an appetite-control tool is not medically accepted. SEE: *ritalin*

**df** SEE: *degrees of freedom*

**Diabetes** SEE: *diabetes mellitus*

**Diabetes mellitus** A chronic health problem wherein the pancreas produces an inadequate supply of insulin. As a result, the body is unable to properly metabolize fats, proteins, and carbohydrates. This incurable genetic disorder is characterized by sugar in the urine (glycosuria), elevated blood sugar (hyperglycemia), excessive urine production (polyuria), excessive thirst (polydipsia), and increased food consumption (polyphagia). It can lead to low resistance to infection, poor circulation to extremities, cardiovascular problems, and disturbances of vision. Treatment includes insulin therapy and control of sugar through a proper diet.

**Diabetic coma** A medical condition caused by a severe lack of insulin available to the body, resulting in an excessive production of acetone. An abnormal deep stupor occurs and the individual is unconscious. SEE: *diabetes mellitus*

**Diabetic retinopathy** A condition resulting as a spin-off from unchecked diabetes. A poor blood supply to the retina can lead to blindness.

**Diagnose** To identify a student's strengths and weaknesses in learning, perhaps with a hypothesis added to account for the particular pattern of strengths and weaknesses exhibited. Formal and informal assessment measures should be gathered before making any diagnostic decision. SEE: *diagnostic label*

**Diagnosis** The process of identifying student strengths and weaknesses in a number of areas following the identification of a problem (e.g., learning disability, school failure, or psychological distress). Informal and formal measures of assessment are used to obtain a well-rounded view of the child's academic/ social/psychological functioning. Additional sources of information include cumulative records, parent input/interviews, psychological profiles, and medical information. The diagnostic process should be ongoing and subject to change/modification. A presenting question(s) or hypothesis(es) (e.g., "I believe that this child is learning disabled") should be related to assessment instruments chosen with the goal of academic and/or social/psychological improvement. SEE: *formal assessment, informal assessment*

**Diagnostic label** A label given to an individual (e.g., learning disabled, mentally retarded, etc.) after a careful analysis of assessment information and the presenting problem(s). Diagnostic labels should be based on specific criteria abstracted from reputable systems in the field such as the Diagnostic & Statistical Manual of Mental Disorders IV (revised) (DSM-IV). SEE: *diagnose, Diagnostic and Statistical Manual of Mental Disorders, IV (revised) (DSM-IV)*

**Diagnostic prescriptive center** A special facility in which children are placed in order to determine their special needs and individual educational plan. The placement is usually on a short-term basis.

**Diagnostic and Statistical Manual of Mental Disorders IV (revised) (DSM-IV)** A manual currently published in its fourth revised edition. It deals with general as well as specific information concerning mental disorders. This is a multiaxial assessment system that includes five diagnostic axes: clinical syndromes, personality disorders, general medical conditions, psychosocial and environmental problems, and global assessment of functioning. The DSM-IV is used to diagnose psychiatric problems, learning disorders, learning disabilities, psychological conditions, etc.

**Diagnostic teaching** Instructional practices that incorporate knowledge of student strengths and weaknesses, changing developmental characteristics, and social/psychological/emotional needs/ interests/attitudes in order to provide an optimal learning environment. A

**D**

focus is made on early intervention and prevention of learning problems. Diagnostic teaching usually involves both formal and informal measures of assessment. SEE: *formal assessment, informal assessment*

**Diagnostic test**   A test aimed at detecting an individual's weaknesses or identifying any specific learning disability. Some diagnostic tests are group-administered while others are given individually. Diagnostic tests differ from survey tests or achievement tests in that they key in on specific skills like vocabulary knowledge, phonemic awareness, spelling proficiency, etc. These formal measures of assessment are most often norm-referenced. SEE: *formal assessment, norm-referenced*

**Diagnostician**   A trained person qualified to administer, score, evaluate, and interpret the testing of students in order to determine areas of strength and weakness as they relate to a finding of special needs (e.g., school psychologist). This highly qualified specialist is able to assist in setting educational goals and plans for the students tested.

**Dialect**   A language variation. Dialects are usually influenced by history, culture, ethnic, and regional factors (e.g., English spoken with an Hispanic, German, Italian, or Southern accent and such English as Cajun, Black, Elizabethan, Patois, etc.). Dialects usually vary in three ways: 1. the phonology or how people produce certain phonemes (e.g., in South Carolina, fee/sh is often the pronunciation used for *fish*), 2. grammatically or the sentence structure (e.g., in Puerto Rican English dialects, verbs often precede nouns), and 3. lexically or the meaning of what is spoken (e.g., a toilet is known as a "john," "flush," "lav," "restroom," etc. depending on the location/dialect spoken).

**Dialectic**   1. A term used to describe the conflict between one's personal desires and needs and those of the collective society. 2. The conflict that results when opposing views, opinions, and beliefs meet.

**Dialetical materialism**   The philosophy of history developed by Marx. He used Hegel's dialectic but imposed it upon a metaphysical foundation of materialism.

**Dialogue journals**   Journal-writing diaries that require students to write to one another dialoguing what they are reading in a type of book-chat format.

**Diaphragm**   A musculomembranous wall that separates the abdominal cavity from the chest cavity. Breathing requires the activity of the muscular component of the diaphragm.

**Diathesis-stress viewpoint**   A theory of the development of emotional disorders stating that the emotional/behavioral problems are the result of an interaction between biological/constitutional factors and environmental stress factors.

**Dichromats**   Individuals who inherently can detect only two of the three primary hues (colors).

**Diethylstilbestrol (DES)**   A synthetic estrogen taken in the past to reduce the risk of a miscarriage. The use of DES may result in vaginal or cervical cancer in females and female offspring and testicular cancer in male offspring. It should not be taken during pregnancy.

**Difference threshold**   Also known as the just-noticeable difference (jnd), the difference threshold is the smallest amount of change in stimulation that can be detected by the senses.

**Differential Aptitude Test (DAT)**   A particular standardized test of vocational aptitudes, it covers such areas as mechanical reasoning, clerical speed, clerical accuracy, and arithmetic ability.

**Differential pay**   Refers to the awarding of extra pay or incentives awarded to education professionals on the basis of merit.

**Differential psychology**   That field of psychology studying the ways in which individuals differ in emotionality, personality, intelligence, and physical traits.

**Differentiated curriculum**   A curriculum that allows for content mastery and in-depth learning as well as the investigation of concepts and issues. SEE: *differentiated education*

**Differentiated education**   Normally meant to indicate an educational curriculum that is suited to the needs, abilities, and interests of gifted and talented students. However, programs for special needs students are also usually differentiated depending on the requirements of the Individualized Education Plan (IEP). SEE: *IEP*

**Differentiated staffing**   The determination of educational positioning of staff so that optimal use is made of their aptitudes, interests, education preparation, and experience.

**Difficulty index**   A descriptive feature of an individual item on an objective test. The item's difficulty index is the proportion of pupils who have answered the test incorrectly; the more students who get the item wrong, the tougher the item must be.

**Digital grasp**   The act of holding or grasping an object with the fingers (digits) only, rather than the entire hand.

**Digitized speech**   Recorded speech in a digital format used in electronic communications and especially by computers.

**Dignity of risk**   The concept that taking ordinary risks is part of a child's normal development. Taking chances is part of growing up and is to be expected in children as normal behavior.

**Digraph**   Two letters that represent one phoneme such as "th," "cl," and "ai."

**Dimensional classification**   A system of classifying behavior disorders that statistical analyses show tend to occur under similar circumstances. This typing or classifying group disorders of behavior sharing similar characteristics can be used when prescribing treatments.

**Diphthong**   A vowel sound followed by a (w) or (y) sound as seen in "oy" "oi," "ow," and "ou." It is a colliding single syllable sound like the "oy" in "toy."

**Diplegia**   A condition that involves paralysis of the same or similar part on each side of the body. SEE: *paraplegia*

**Diploma**   A document attesting to the completion of a formal course of study by a student (e.g., a high school diploma).

**Diplophonia**   Two or more simultaneously present tones or pitches when one speaks. This can occur when one needs to clear one's throat of saliva globules or it may be of a more permanent nature and indicates problems dealing with the vocal folds (cords).

**Diplopia**   A condition of seeing two images when presented with only one, often called double vision. SEE: *polyopia*

**Direct instruction/explicit teaching** Instruction provided by an active teacher in the ways to perform particular types of skilled action. This type of instruction is well suited for math and reading. The teacher structures lessons, develops strategies for solutions to problems, and selects examples for students. SEE: *direct teaching*

**Direct observation**   A research method in which an observer records and times the activities of the subjects, without any manipulation of the subjects' environment.

**Direct teaching**   A type of instructional practice whereby the teacher directs and structures the classroom environment. Typically, subject matter is presented in a developmental manner (i.e., scope-and-sequence) with student practice and teacher evaluation/feedback following lesson presentations.

**Directed Reading Activities (DRA)** (similar to DRTA approach)   The primary instructional approach used in many basal reading programs. Students are prepared for the reading task by building/activating background knowledge; setting a purpose for the selection at hand; guiding student readings in the form of questions; discussing questions following readings with a focus on main ideas, details to support main ideas, character development, etc.; encouraging rereadings (especially oral readings following silent readings); reinforcing vocabulary usage and fluency; and providing extension activities that involve

**D**

word analysis work, vocabulary usage, comprehension development, literature extensions, writing, and other such skills development. SEE: *basal reader approach, Directed Reading-Thinking Activity (DRTA)*

**Directionality**   A term used to classify one's ability to recognize direction. For example, front and back, up and down, left and right, etc.

**Disability**   An inability to perform physical or mental tasks which one can normally be expected to do. Usually more severe than a disorder, it involves loss of physical functioning and great difficulty in learning and/or normal social or growth development. SEE: *disabled, disorder*

**Disability rights movement**   An advocacy movement for individuals with disabilities with a focus on 1. guaranteeing the constitutional rights of individuals with disabilities and 2. affecting legislation that improves the life situations of individuals with disabilities.

**Disabled**   A student or individual that has a disability (usually more severe than a disorder) in contrast to a disorder. SEE: *disability, disorder*

**Disarticulation**   A term used to describe an amputation through a joint of the body.

**Disc**   Record-player-type plastic discs that are used in a computer. They are usually produced in two sizes, 3.5 and 5.25 inches and store information to be used in a computer. Discs can be floppy (bendable) or hard (not bendable). Recently, compact discs composed of metal have been adapted for use with computers. These discs resemble compact discs for audio systems.

**Discipline**   A branch of learning that trains the mind and character (e.g., academic discipline = humanities; behavior discipline = behavior modification). Emphasis is upon self-control or management of one's behavior/learning in the context of what are considered appropriate actions.

**Discourse**   Conversation or the ability to communicate orally.

**Discovery learning**   A type of instruction preferred by Jerome Bruner in which the student is required to work out basic principles of learning for himself/herself.

**Discrepancy analysis**   An educational assessment procedure wherein the tester first identifies activities to be analyzed. The student is then observed performing the skills needed to effectively participate in the activity. The tester then records whether or not the student has performed the skills effectively and independently. Results are then analyzed, discrepancies are noted, and conclusions drawn.

**Discrepancy formulas**   Formulas used by local, regional, or state educational agencies to identify the discrepancy, if any, between a student's actual achievements and the student's expected achievement based on that student's known Intelligence Quotient (IQ).

**Discrepancy scores**   The scores used by some school systems and/or state educational systems in order to determine eligibility for special services designed for students with disabilities or mental retardation. For example, some schools will accept students who score below the 30th percentile in reading for special education services or assistance in reading.

**Discriminate**   1. To respond appropriately to a given stimulus and refrain from responding to a similar (but inappropriate) stimulus. 2. To deny access to equal opportunities under the law (e.g., an education) based upon a person's gender, sex, race, or ethnicity.

**Discrimination**   1. To respond in different ways to different stimuli that resemble one another to some extent. 2. A condition wherein it is concluded that an individual or group has been denied legal rights under the Constitution. Although not in constitutional violation, it can include unfair practices, educational or otherwise, to an individual or group.

**Discrimination index**   A descriptive feature of a test item on an objective test. The discrimination index is given by the similarity between the proportion of students answering the item correctly and the proportion scoring well on the whole test. A biserial correlation coefficient between the two sets of scores (item and total test) would be an example of such an index.

**Discrimination learning** A type of conditioning that may be identified as a variety of either classical (respondent) conditioning or instrumental (operant) conditioning. In classical conditioning, the ability of the conditioned stimulus (CS) to elicit the conditioned response (CR) is transferred to other stimuli that have some resemblance to the CS in the process known as generalization. One of these is selected as a stimulus to be presented in contrast with the CS. For example, if the CS is a strong light and the response is salivation, the contrasting stimulus (e.g., a weaker light) is presented without the unconditioned stimulus (US) while the CS is presented to the subject along with the US. The animal then learns to continue to respond to the CS but to withhold salivation to the other stimulus (the one used for contrasting) when given the other, generalized stimulus. This result is a learned respondent discrimination. In operant conditioning, the pressing of a lever, for example, may bring the subject a food reinforcement. If the set-up is changed so that pressing the bar while a light is on is followed by reinforced bar-pressing but pressing the bar when the light is off is not followed by food reinforcement, the subject learns to work on the lever while the light is on and to stop working on the lever when the light is off. This outcome is a learned (operant) discrimination. Any generalization that occurs will have to follow the discrimination learning, in the case of operant discrimination.

**Discriminative stimulus** A stimulus that, in operant conditioning, sets the stage for a given operant response to be reinforced. In the absence of the discriminative stimulus, such responses are not reinforced. The organism learns to make the response only when the discriminative stimulus has been presented. For example, some students will study only in the presence of a television or radio. The television or radio can be a discriminative stimulus.

**Disequilibrium** According to Piaget, an unstable condition that develops when the individual learns that his/her approach to problem-solving is failing to yield a solution.

**Disfluency** A condition in which words are spoken in a halting or pausing manner. Frequently the speaker backs up and repeats or revises what is being said. The most often encountered fluency disorder is stuttering. SEE: *stuttering*

**Disorder** In education, a term used to indicate a malfunction of a physical or mental activity. Usually less severe than a "disability." Disorders can be physical, mental, or psychological.

**Disorganized schizophrenia** That variety of the psychosis known as schizophrenia in which the patient exhibits very bizarre responding, incoherent speech, and the disintegration of his/her personality.

**Disparagement theory** The view that the effectiveness of humor derives from its allowing the audience to feel superior to others.

**Displacement** 1. A personality defense mechanism that involves directing one's behaviors or motives to another person or object. For example, if one is angry and kicks a chair, the anger is displaced to the chair. 2. A feature of language that allows one to refer to events and objects that are not in his/her immediate environment.

**Dissociation** A separation of components of the mind or personality that are usually integrated. In extreme cases, there may be totally separate streams of consciousness, as in the multiple personality disorder.

**Dissociative disorder** A separation of the emotions and/or memories from the rest of the components of the mind or personality, especially the parts that remain accessible to conscious awareness. Examples of dissociative disorders include hysterical paralysis or amnesia and multiple personality. Each of the defense mechanisms (e.g., repression, reaction formation, or denial) involves some degree of dissociation.

**Disruptive behavior disorders**  Behavior conditions involving difficulty in paying attention and attending to tasks (e.g., direction taking, socializing and/or interacting with others, taking turns, listening, reacting to negative situations with aggression, etc.).

**Distal**  The area farthest from the center, the outside.

**Distance education**  The use of telecommunications to present live instruction to a student not physically present but actually a long distance away. An example would be the use of a telephone link for the audio component of a class or a television broadcast for both audio and visual learning. Such services are necessary for students with terminal medical conditions (e.g., cancer) and other conditions that prevent on-site school participation.

**Distance senses**  Senses such as hearing and vision that alert us to information beyond/outside of our bodies.

**Distinctiveness**  The extent to which the individual behaves in a consistent manner in various settings.

**Distortion**  This occurs in speech when the individual alters speech sounds although attempting to say the phoneme or word correctly, such as "shumtime" instead of "sometime" or "brlu" for "blue."

**Distractability**  A condition of "mental wandering" wherein a student or person is continually distracted and responds to the various extraneous stimuli about oneself and is therefore unable to really attend to the relevant stimuli and thus unable to focus on the matter at hand.

**Distractor**  The technical term for any of the incorrect choices presented with an item on a multiple-choice test.

**Distributed practice**  Having one's rehearsal of a verbal learning task or practicing of a new motor skill spread over a relatively long time period, leaving room for resting between practice trials. This seems to improve the retention of the newly learned information or skill.

**Distribution**  The form or shape a group of scores takes in a group under study. A "normal" distribution takes the shape of the normal curve while "skewed" distributions can be represented by asymmetrical curves. Extreme scores (very high and very low) fall either at the upper end (positively skewed mean or the mean is greater than the median and mode) or at the lower end of the distribution (negatively skewed mean or the mean is less than the median and mode). A negatively skewed distribution looks like the left half of a cursive "m" and a positively skewed distribution looks like the right half of a cursive "m."

**Divergent learning**  Learning that involves more than one answer, perspective, or point-of-view. For example, there is more than one way to study.

**Divergent questions**  The types of questions that do not have a simple right or wrong answer.

**Divergent thinking**  The style of thinking in which the individual considers a variety of possible problem solutions. In divergent thinking, one's thought processes are not confined to linear paths (as in deductive logic).

**Diverse instruction approaches**  Education practices/programs which recognize cultural/gender/special needs issues/problems/needs.

**Diversity**  1. In the most general sense, difference or variety. 2. Individuals whose ethnic heritage is different from the mainstream culture. 3. Students with special learning challenges with no outward physical disabilities (e.g., the learning disabled). 4. Students with physical disabilities or challenges (e.g., the hearing or vision impaired). 5. Students who come from different socioeconomic/home backgrounds. 6. Students with varying religious backgrounds. 7. Students with unique value systems.

8. Gender/age differences in classroom situations. 9. Individuals within a particular culture/race/ethnicity who differ in other ways (e.g., general category = Hispanic-Americans—within the general category = Mexican-Americans differ in a number of social/cultural ways from Puerto Rican Americans). 10. Students considered to be in minority categories established by the census bureau or other such agency (e.g., African-Americans). 11. Students with developmental differences within the same age/grade (e.g., children will learn at various learning rates and will display various learning styles). 12. Individuals with different emotional adjustments or emotional diversity (e.g., differing social skills, differing responses in interpersonal interactions, and unique family interactions).

**Dizygotic**   (twins) A term used to describe twins who are products of two separate eggs.

**Doctoral degree**   The highest academic degree conferred by an institution of higher learning such as a college or university, including Ph.D's in any field, doctor of education, doctor of juridical science, doctor of public health, doctors of medicine—M.D.'s etc.

**Dolch list**   A popular sight word listing used in primary classrooms to assess reading ability.

**Domain-specific knowledge**   Information that is useful in a given situation or is appropriate to just one subject matter.

**Doman-Delacato**   The theoretical school of thought that would treat learning disability by supervised retraining of motor activities, including the ones acquired in early infancy. One assumption is that learning disabilities result from the incorrect acquisition of sensory-motor coordinations during early childhood; a second assumption is that this incorrect learning can be cancelled out and replaced by the correct response patterns. Most authorities in the field of learning disability do not accept this theory.

**Dominant genes/genetic traits**   Genes are the basic units of heredity. Heredi-tary traits are controlled by gene pairs. Each pair may be dominant or recessive or may contain one dominant and one recessive gene. A dominant gene will express its effect without assistance from its partner. Dominant genes override the effect of recessive genes. If one parent has a dominant gene for a specific trait (e.g., hair color), then there is a 50 percent chance that this trait will be passed on to all offspring. SEE: *recessive genes/genetic traits*

**Door-in-the-face technique**   A negotiating strategy in which one begins by presenting a demand that will almost certainly be rejected. After the expected rejection, the negotiator introduces a more modest request, hoping that the other party will now be more ready to comply with this more reasonable-looking suggestion.

**Doppler effect**   It is the raising and lowering of the pitch of a sound as it approaches, passes, and moves away from the listener. For example, an emergency vehicle with a wailing siren passing by.

**Double-aspect theory**   The view that reality is basically very complex and largely unknowable. Humans, however, are able to gain limited knowledge of two aspects of the complex whole; namely, the material and the mental. This outlook is a monism in metaphysics (i.e., it holds that the universe is one complex reality) but a dualism in epistemology. We are able to know material things and mental things. Two supporters of the double-aspect view were Spinoza and Fechner. SEE: *dualism, epistemology, idealism, materialism, metaphysics, monism*

**Double-blind technique**   A control procedure used by psychologists when doing experiments. Neither the subject nor the experimenter who records the subject's responses is aware of whether the subject has been given the experimental treatment or the control condition. This procedure rules out both subject bias and experimenter bias.

**Double dissociation of function**   A demonstration that a given functional

**D**

problem is linked with specific damage to a particular part of the brain. It involves collecting data on people with damage to either one or another of two parts of the brain. These subjects are given two behavioral tests, each of which is supposed to depend on one (but not the other) of the two parts of the brain involved in the study. The result is a double dissociation if each type of brain damage is shown to correlate with just one functional disorder and not the other.

**Double-entry journal**  (Vaughn, 1990) A type of journal, diary, or recording method with two facing pages allocated per entry. The left page is reserved for the initial response to a writing prompt (e.g., illustrate or write about Independence Day). The right page allows students to consolidate and apply this knowledge in a personal way (e.g., What does it mean to be independent?). This allows students to think about what will be read and then to organize what has been learned. SEE: *journal*

**Double hemiplegia**  A condition of paralysis of the body on both sides but one side is more affected than the other. SEE: *hemiplegia*

**Down syndrome**  (J. Langdon Down, British physician, 1828–1896) Caused by a nondisjunction of chromosomal pairs. Formerly referred to as "mongolism," a term now not preferred. Also known as "trisomy-21." It is a congenital condition of moderate to severe mental retardation that usually but not always affects the 21st set of chromosomes. The infant has 47 (the 21st pair has an extra chromosome). It is characterized by a sloping forehead and oriental appearance of the eyes, a nose that is flat, and generally a short and dwarflike appearance. SEE: *translocation, chromosome, mosaicism*

**DRA**  SEE: *Directed Reading Activities*

**Dream**  A fantasy occurring during sleep in which a series of visual images passes through the sleeper's awareness. Usually, these visual images occur during the Rapid-Eye-Movement (REM) stage of sleep.

**Drill-and-practice programs**  Computer or non computer programs that provide a learner with exercises on which to practice his/her skills.

**Drive**  An arousal or motive that is initiated by some biological need such as thirst or hunger. When the need is met, the drive is reduced.

**Drive-reduction theory**  The theory that all behavior is motivated by the reduction of drives aroused by various types of biological needs.

**Drop Everything And Read (DEAR)** In language arts, a philosophy and method of teaching students to read for extensive periods of time. This system employs silent reading for the students and allows the teacher the freedom to work with individuals, groups, and to hold conferences. SEE: *Sustained Silent Reading (SSR), Uninterrupted Sustained Silent Reading (USSR)*

**Dropouts**  Individuals who do not complete a diploma or degree program (e.g., high school dropout/college dropout).

**DRTA or the Directed Reading-Thinking Activity**  A reading technique that focuses on developing independent and active thinking strategies. Students make predictions about the ideas and concepts of small portions of text based on headings or topic sentences. Students read the segment to confirm or amend their predictions. The cycle of predicting and confirming or proving is continued throughout the reading. SEE: *Directed Reading Activities*

**Drug therapy**  The medical/behavioral use of drugs to control a student for a specific problem, disease, disorder, or disability. Drugs may include antipsychotics, anticonvulsants, depressants, stimulants, etc. For example, Ritalin, a stimulant, is sometimes administered to children with Attention-Deficit/Hyperactivity Disorder (ADHD). SEE: *Attention Deficit/Hyperactivity Disorder*

**DSM-IV**  SEE: *Diagnostic and Statistical Manual of Mental Disorders IV (revised) (DSM-IV)*

**Dual marking system**   A system of giving two grades, one for achievement and one for effort.

**Dual sensory impairments**   This term typically applies to students or persons with seriously impaired sensory loss in the areas of vision and hearing. It includes persons that are both blind and deaf. Such sensory impairments create educational and developmental difficulties and can result in serious communication problems. Such persons may require extensive educational support from trained specialists.

**Dual-track system**   Refers to an outdated European tradition of providing separate but equal schools for various groups/classes of students.

**Dualism**   The metaphysical belief that there are two types of reality in the world. Some things belong to the realm of the material and other things belong to the realm of the mental or spiritual. Champions of the dualistic viewpoint were Descartes and Leibnitz, who each had a particular way of accounting for the relationship between each segment of reality. For Descartes, the materal interacted with the spiritual; whereas for Leibnitz, the material and the mental worlds each had to follow separate but parallel courses. SEE: *interactionism, metaphysics, monism, parallelism*

**Duchenne's disease**   Guillaume B. A. Duchenne, French neurologist, 1806–1875) A form of muscular dystrophy, it is hereditary and affects children between one and six years. This disease of progressive muscle deterioration is considered a fatal disease. SEE: *muscular dystrophy*

**Due process**   With respect to special needs and nondisabled students, it is a set of legal procedures established in order to guarantee an individual's constitutional rights and/or appropriate educational opportunities. It gives the student (depending on age) and/or the parent an opportunity to become involved in the consent to an educational evaluation and decision for placement in a special education program. Due process also protects the rights of any student to appeal educational decisions and placements. SEE: *Goss v. Lopez*

**Due process hearing**   A hearing that is a noncourt procedure at which parent and school personnel in disagreement appear. When there is disagreement each party has an opportunity to present its side of the case to an impartial hearing officer for resolution. SEE: *due process*

**During reading strategies**   In language arts, an activity or strategy (e.g., relating picture cues to paragraph sense or relating what is read to previous similar experiences) that relates to what is being read by the student in such a fashion as to enhance the student's understanding of the reading material.

**Dyad reading**   A language arts term that describes readers of unequal or equal ability being paired and assigned a reading task. The first student finished reviews the material silently until his/her partner is done. One student is designated as the "recaller" and the other "the listener." The recaller summarizes the reading aloud while the listener clarifies and comments during the summary. Thus, both students discuss, debate, and internalize the reading as a team and conclude together what strategies, skills, and knowledge have been learned.

**Dyadic relations**   Relationships that occur between two persons. It can also be a relationship of two parts.

**Dynamic assessment**   Sometimes referred to as a variation of the "test-teach-test" model, it is an approach wherein a teacher integrates a student's readiness to learn with direct and immediate instruction. In effect, a test-as-you-go-along approach. The teacher gets immediate feedback using this approach. Dynamic or ongoing assessment has been recommended for use with students who come from diverse backgrounds.

**Dysacusis**   A condition of the inner ear wherein a student or person has difficulty understanding speech.

**Dysarthria**   An impairment in speech processing involving muscular

**83**

functioning of the articulatory, phonatory, and/or respiratory processes.

**Dysbulia**   A condition characterized by an inability to fix one's attention. The student has difficulty thinking and paying attention.

**Dyscalculia**   A type of learning disability wherein a student or person has great difficulty or an inability to calculate/perform mathematics.

**Dysfluencies**   Interruptions of the patterns of speech are frequently seen in young children during their speech development process and are considered part of normal speech acquisition.

**Dysfluency**   The inability of a student or other person to speak effortlessly in a smooth and/or flowing manner, quickly and without hesitation.

**Dysgraphia**   A condition characterized by an inability to write properly. It can be caused by a brain lesion and is commonly a result of poor small or fine muscle control, which results in poor handwriting.

**Dyslexia**   Dyslexia is a specific type of learning disability involving a severe impairment in reading ability that affects and disrupts a person's language development and functioning. It is estimated that at least 2.625 percent to 5 percent (and perhaps even more) of the entire population suffer from dyslexia, which is the most prevalent type of learning disability. Spafford and Grosser cite three distinctive subtypes of dyslexia (noting that there is no consensus in the field as to a definitive classification system): 1. a visual-dysphonetic type, 2. an auditory-linguistic type, and 3. a mixed type with symptoms from both 1. and 2. Current research supports academic interventions related to the reading and language problems associated with dyslexia. It is believed that dyslexia is caused by neurological anomalies that are either enhanced or intensified by environmental and social factors. Correlating behaviors of dyslexia include but are not limited to delayed language development, verbal deficits, deficits in phonemic awareness, a familial history, gross motor problems, sequencing difficulties, oral reading miscues, written expressive language deficits, spelling errors, reduced reading rates as children and as adults, time and directional confusions, less on-task behaviors, attention problems, less independent behaviors, poor study skills, social behavior problems, memory deficits, and less follow-through. Not all individuals with dyslexia will display all of these symptoms. Most individuals with dyslexia, however, evince several of those listed. Individuals can ask questions about the subject matter of dyslexia on the Internet bulletin board of the Orton Dyslexia Society (ODS) at "http://ods.org."

**Dysmenorrhea**   A term used to describe painful and/or irregular menstruation.

**Dysphasia**   The impaired ability of an individual to call out or write out an appropriate word when given a visual or auditory signal to do so. Note that dyslexia can be viewed as a specific example of a dysphasic condition.

**Dyspnea**   Labored breathing, shortness of breath, lack of air, difficulty with breathing, etc. SEE: *stridor*

**Dyspraxia**   The impaired ability to make a specified kind of motor response. Note that dysarthria can be viewed as a specific example of a dyspraxia.

**Dystrophy or dystrophia myotonica**   An hereditary disease involving the wasting away of the muscle tissue. The term is sometimes used as another name for muscular dystrophy. SEE: *muscular dystrophy*

## Early childhood special education

Educational programs for children with special needs; that is, children who differ from the norm and when school age would more than likely not progress effectively in regular school programs. The early childhood classification covers children from nursery or preschool age to kindergarten (usually age 5). In some states like Massachusetts early childhood programs encompass prekindergarten or nursery school through grade three. SEE: *early childhood education, special children or special needs children*

## Early-exit transitional programs

Bilingual programs that use the individual's native language for part of the instructional program for less than two years. SEE: *late-exit transition programs*

## Early infantile autism

An autistic condition expressed at a very early age (from infancy) wherein the child seems unable to come out of his/her shell, so to speak, and has great difficulty or is unable to relate to things outside himself/herself. SEE: *autism*

## Early intervention

Preschool services for disabled children who are infants and toddlers ages 0–3. Preschool ages (3–4) are sometimes included in early intervention programs as well. Such comprehensive services usually include educational assistance, social or psychological assistance, and health care or medical services.

## Early multiword communication

A type of communication where children or persons use very basic word combinations in a primitive manner, such as "daddy cook," "mommy fix roof," "me drink soda," etc. Most of these verbalizations are characterized by the use of two or three words and sometimes four.

## Early phonemic spelling

In language arts, the early use of the correct letters for sounds. It is the developmental stage that follows the earliest stage of spelling called "prephonemic spelling." It is characterized by short strings of letters, one to four, wherein single letters are used to represent sounds in words or whole words. While spellings are very incomplete, consonants are used to express initial sounds and final sounds as well. SEE: *prephonemic spelling*

## Earwax

Also known as "cerumen," it is the waxy substance deposited in the auditory canal of the outer ear.

## Eastern philosophy

A philosophy that in practice was established in the Near East, Middle East, or Far East areas of the world. These philosophies emphasize mysticism, proper attitude, reduction of stress, tranquility, and the inner peace of an individual. These philosophies, the roots of which are steeped in the inner world rather than the outer world, are spread throughout the East in such countries as Arabia, India, China, Japan, etc.

## Eating disorder

Conditions that involve fear of eating, misunderstanding of one's body image, poor nutrition, binge eating, and/or weight loss from abnormally eating too little (anorexia) or deliberate regurgitation (bulimia). SEE: *anorexia nervosa, bulimia nervosa*

## Ebonics

Also known as African-American language, African-American vernacular English, and Black English, Ebonics is a term that blends the words "ebony" and "phonics" into what is known as a second language for people of African-American descent. There are some basic linguistic differences between what is known as "mainstream American English" and "Ebonics," which is derived from African languages. For example, in ebonics, the past term of the verb "to be" would include such plurals as "we was" and "they was"; whereas in mainstream American English the correct usage would be "we were" and "they were." In ebonics, the more negatives in a sentence, the more negative the meaning (e.g., "nobody just don't have no excuses to give" means "everyone lacks an excuse"). In mainstream American English two negatives in one sentence convey a positive statement. There is continued debate regarding whether or not ebonics constitutes a dialect, vernacular, or language.

**Echo**   A brief auditory memory for something heard for up to two seconds. This would be the ringing aftereffect following the ringing of a doorbell. SEE: *echoic memory*

**Echo reading**   (or the "Neurological Impress" method) This method can be used with students with severe reading disabilities. Essentially, the teacher and student read together side-by-side and the teacher does not correct oral miscues or errors. At first, the teacher reads louder and slightly faster than the student so that the student can "echo" the teacher's reading. Eventually they read in unison. This is a multiple rereading exercise that builds reading fluency and accuracy.

**Echo speech synthesizer**   A speech synthesizer that can be used as an add-on to a computer. This device adds speech to a software program and is produced by Echo Speech Corporation. It can be used for the blind or severely visually impaired or for persons who are incapable of speech. It is adaptable to the Apple II and IIGS, MacIntosh, IBM, and Tandy computers.

**Echoic memory**   The immediate memory of a recent auditory stimulus. An auditory memory trace or "echo" may last as long as four seconds or more.

**Echolalia**   The echoing or repetition of meaningless sounds and words after listening to someone speak or after viewing television, as examples.

**Echolocation device**   (invented by Kay and developed by Bower) A device that emits high-frequency sound waves that bounce off environmental objects. When loud sounds are heard, the visually impaired or blind know an object is close by. This device allows individuals with vision problems to detect the size of an object with the pitch emitted from the device clueing the individual to an object's distance.

**Eclecticism**   The practice of using several approaches or methods as part of one's pedagogy. The emphasis is on diversity of presentation, diversity of behavior management techniques, multiple measures of assessment, and different performance outcomes. For example, an eclectic reading teacher might use phonics approaches, sight-word recognition cards, whole language activities, writing-process activities, DRT (Directed-Reading-Thinking) activities, the newspaper, big books, paperback books, the great books, poetry, choral reading activities, plays, a class newspaper, book reports, etc.

**Ecological approach**   An approach that is focused on how the individual interacts in the environment with the different systems to which he/she belongs. That is, one could belong to a family system, school system, peer system, religious system, etc. Behaviors are seen as interactive and when problems arise, blame does not reside with the individual but with the systems to which he/she belongs. Treatments must reflect a community effort with all relevant parties involved.

**Ecological assessments**   Assessments usually conducted by persons trained in the techniques of observation in the field. Such assessments are typically based on observed behavior of the student in a classroom subject or activity (i.e., within the context of a natural environment). Observed information is gathered in this ecological and natural setting and is organized in the light of how the student, subject, or individual interacts in a natural environment.

**Ecological inventory** An individualized approach to education that posits the necessity for a curriculum to address the needs of students from the point of view necessary to prepare them to operate independently within the current environment. Specific skills are identified for teaching, which are required by students to live within their present and probable future environments.

**Ecological model** SEE: *ecological approach*

**Ecopathy** A bizarre pathological condition in which a student or person mimics the actions, speech, or behavior of another in a silly or senseless fashion.

**ECT** SEE: *Electroconclusive Therapy*

**Eczema** A term used to describe a variety of skin diseases and disorders to include chronic dermatitis, rashes, scales, scabs, sores, etc. The skin may be dry or watery, itching and/or burning.

**ED** SEE: *Department of Education*

**Edema** An excess accumulation of serous fluid (watery) in a tissue or cavity.

**Editing** 1. In language arts, the process of having the teacher, another student, or a reviewer read what has been written and proofread by the writer. Suggestions are made by the editor as to content, punctuation, spelling, grammar, and any adjustments to the writing with specific recommendations. 2. In films, it is the process of cutting, moving, revising, and splicing in order to visually create the desired effect.

**Educable Mentally Retarded (EMR)** A term applied to the mildly mentally retarded, emphasizing their ability to profit from instruction in basic academic subjects such as reading, mathematics, and science. Vocational training is usually possible. Independent living in adulthood is also possible. The IQ range for this category of persons is 50 to 70. EMR is a term not in popular use but is still used by some educators. SEE: *mild mental retardation*

**Educate America Act** SEE: *Goals 2000*

**Educated citizenry** The goal of a society to provide its citizenry with educational opportunities so that all members are productive participants. Technology today has provided the means for global resourcing via the Internet. For example, *The Global Schoolhouse* can be accessed on the World Wide Web at: http://www.gsh.org/ and allows teachers to discover/access resources that connect the classroom to the Internet. To visit the Internet, teachers need only a modem, access to a telephone line, and an Internet provider.

**Education expectation/educability** A category that describes the probable level of educational achievement of a student. It is a prediction of the educational boundaries a student is expected to operate within.

**Education for career** Special educational programs that are geared toward preparing a student for post-secondary schooling and/or careers in a vocational sense.

**Education major** A specialty area in which a student's program concentrates on subject matter relating to the field of education as well as fulfilling the basic college requirements for a degree. For example, a student preparing to become an elementary teacher would concentrate on courses needed in order to gain experience and knowledge in elementary education.

**Education of All Handicapped Children Act** A special education act passed by Congress in 1975. SEE: *P.L. 94-142, P.L. 101-476*

**Education web site** Multimedia sites within the Internet that provide text/graphics/sound/video/interactive formats/animation so as to simulate real-life situations and transform the learning environment into a dynamic, motivating, interactive, current, and extended network of knowledge and information sharing. World Wide Web pages have their own addresses or web sites written in hypertext markup language (HTML). For example, http://www.nmia.com:80/~cram is the

**E**

address for "Doc's Education Resources Pages," a K–12 web site that contains lesson plans for teachers in all subject areas and information for students from current events to the arts to the classroom. SEE: *Appendix 4: Computer Terms*

**Educational blindness**   A term used to describe students who need to use braille for reading. SEE: *braille*

**Educational integration**   The combining of students with disabilities and/or those in need of special educational services in the regular classroom setting with non-special-needs students. Educational inclusion is also referred to as "mainstreaming" or "inclusion." SEE: *mainstreaming, inclusion*

**Educational lockstep**   An educational approach to grade-level placement that is based upon the chronological age of children only. For example, all students who are 10 years old are to be placed in grade five. There is no exception or consideration given to other factors that might affect grade-level placement.

**Educational malpractice**   Neglect by a teacher (whether found legally guilty or not) in the performance of his or her duties as an education practitioner (e.g., abuse of a child).

**Educational park**   Refers to a type of architectural style involving a large campus-like school facility with several units housing a variety of facilities. Often these school facilities contain many grade levels and programs with rich cultural resources.

**Educational placement**   The arrangements made for a student's education in regard to her/his classroom setting. For example, placing a student in a regular classroom, in a special needs resource room, in a vocational school, in a day or residential school, etc.

**Educational psychology**   That field of psychology that concerns itself with the search for the most effective teaching methods, the most appropriate tests of academic aptitudes, and the testing of achieved knowledge. Educational psychology draws on the psychology of

learning and memory, developmental psychology, psychometrics, and statistics.

**Educational synthesizer**   A teaching system that includes supportive services within the regular classroom setting. The teacher arranges for a special service delivery to a student as part of the student's regular day as in the case of speech or physical therapy services, etc. No pull-out is required.

**Educational Television (ETV)**   Usually broadcast by stations outside of the school system especially for consumption by the general public and at various times of the day and night. Programs of an educational nature are broadcast. Schools are also able to receive such broadcasts. Typically, public television stations generate such broadcasts.

**Educational vouchers**   A type of payment or grant that represents the cost of educating a child(ren) for a school year. Parents or students are given permission for out-of-district/school placements and payment vouchers are given to the accepting school.

**Educationally blind**   A term used for any student who requires braille reading materials in order to be capable of learning. SEE: *braille*

**Educationally disadvantaged**   SEE: *students at risk*

*Edwards v. Aguilard*   The 1987 Supreme Court ruling that overturned the practice of presenting a balanced view of creation with Biblical and scientific concepts. The Court ruled that the teaching of the Biblical creationist view was unconstitutional in that the Louisiana state statute ruled on was not religiously neutral. The statute clearly had the purpose of advancing a religious doctrine.

**EEG**   SEE: *Electroencephalogram*

**Effective schools**   Effective schools are those schools responsive to the learning styles and needs of students served within a safe, nurturing, interactive, and positive environment with students achieving maximum learning gains as measured by standardized and authentic (e.g., portfolios and observations) assessments. Additionally, effective schools respect the diversity of the population and strive to eliminate prejudice/bias. Research has generally shown that effective schools: 1. develop clear goals and mission statements; 2. employ site-based decision making with parents, teachers, administrators, professionals, the community, and students as cooperative partners in defining the school agenda; 3. use curriculum guides or frameworks and specific and varied teaching principles/methods/materials based on proven research in the field; 4. incorporate multicultural education/activities throughout the school day; 5. view parents as partners in the education process; 6. provide an emphasis on basic skills (academic-English, math, spelling, science, social studies, the arts, foreign languages, etc.); life-communicating a message effectively, interrelating appropriately, working in group/team situations, etc.; 7. reflect friendly, orderly, and disciplined school environments where behavior expectations are clear; 8. connect with community organizations/individuals/programs and maintain positive community relations; 9. have well-maintained buildings/clean facilities/good breakfast/lunch programs; 10. continually self-assess/assess learning/social gains; the school environment; teaching/services, etc.; 11. develop continuity regarding instruction across the various grade levels; 12. develop curricula that reflects interdisciplinary connections; 13. develop instruction based on the needs/learning styles of all students; 14. have adequate supplies and updated learning materials; 15. provide consistent and immediate feedback to students; 16. keep classroom interruptions to a minimum (especially school announcements, students releases, etc.); 17. provide professional development opportunities to discuss new/proven behavioral/multicultural/teaching methods/materials/strategies; 18. provide services/ guidance/programs in areas where students need support

(e.g., music directors, coaches, drug/alcohol prevention programs, and conflict resolution programs); 19. provide incentives or recognition for a job well done, good behavior, etc.; 20. hold high expectations/standards for all learners; 21. use technology in the classroom and plan to give computer and Internet access to all students; 22. provide career preparations/guidance/foundations; 23. key in on interest levels/motivation of students served both academically and in extracurricular offerings; and 24. strive to develop well-rounded and contributing/productive citizens. The U.S. Department of Education provides information and resources that allow schools to implement/initiate school reform efforts. As examples, "The Role of Leadership in Sustaining School Reform: Voices from the Field" can be obtained via the World Wide Web at: http:// www.ed.gov.pubs/Leadership/; "MiddleWeb" delves into the issues and challenges of education reform efforts at the middle school level in urban settings and is available on the World Wide Web at http://www.middleweb.com.

**Effective teachers**   Effective teachers are reflective lifelong learners who are enthusiastic, positive, nurturing, responsive, and dedicated to the overall well-being of the students served. Research has shown that effective teachers carefully develop and structure their lessons and continually assess student progress, providing feedback every step of the way. During lesson presentations, effective teachers solicit/provide probing questions and clarify directions as well as initiate learning prompts, learning cues, and learning examples. Larger tasks are broken down into smaller components and organization formats/study-skills training encourage independent learning to occur. Good modeling/demonstration behaviors provide necessary learning assists. Teaching prerequisite skills and background building provide necessary learning foundations. Effective teachers are able to key in on those students who experience learning challenges and can adapt the learning environment to meet the unique challenges of all children. Effective teachers also are resourceful and keep abreast of technology changes/usages. Internet sites like "Teams Distance Learning Site" at http://teams.lacoe.edu from the Los Angeles, California Office of Education give additional resource Internet sites that contain lesson ideas and project and unit planning that allow teachers to gain up-to-date information and new classroom strategies. Similarly, "ERIC Lesson Plans" at gopher://ericir.syr.edu//11/lesson is designed for K–12 level teachers in all curriculum areas. SEE: *effective schools*

**Effective teaching** Sometimes called "effective schools or schooling," it is a movement based on outcomes of educational research. Its main goal is to use the research information to improve teachers and teaching.

**Efferent neurons** Neurons that carry messages from the brain and/or spinal cord to the muscles and/or glands. Hence, efferent neurons are motor. (The antonym of *efferent* is *afferent*.) Efferent fibers go to the muscles and glands, which are the body's effectors. SEE: *afferent*

**Efferent reading** A term used in reading to describe an approach to reading where the reader focuses on what information needs to be acquired from the reading. For example, "What is the purpose of and information to be learned from the reading?" or "What are some probable actions or problem solutions to be carried out as a result of the reading?"

**Ego** 1. One of the three components of personality in Freudian theory. The ego is attuned to reality and mediates between the other two components; namely, the id and the superego. The ego permits a person to adapt to what might have been an unpleasant experience. 2. A common term for self. SEE: *id, superego*

**Egocentric** A term applied to an individual who assumes that other people look at the world in the very same way that he/she does.

**Egocentrism** An inability to view reality from the standpoint of another person. This is the limitation of the child in the preoperational stage of cognitive growth in Piaget's theory.

**Ego-involved learners** Students who monitor their own progress, judge how well they are doing, and check on how others rate their performance.

**Egoism** The tendency to do what is best for oneself, regardless of the impact of that action upon others. SEE: *altruism*

**Eg-rule method** A teaching technique that begins with specific examples and moves on from them to the development of generalized rules.

**Eidetic imagery** Also known as photographic memory, it occurs when the person has a visual image clear enough to be scanned mentally and retained in memory for longer than 30 seconds. The individual with this ability can reconstruct a complex picture in full detail. For example, a painting of a crowd scene can be shown to a subject for one minute and then turned over. The subject is then asked to describe the painting as fully as possible. Individuals with this ability achieve remarkable accuracy in doing such tasks. This ability is found mostly in children; it is estimated that eight out of 100 children possess eidetic imagery.

**EKG** SEE: *Electrocardiogram*

**Elaboration** Adding to the meaning of a word or a passage by associating other bits of information to the already established meaning of the word or passage.

**Elaborative rehearsal** The reorganization of newly learned material (e.g., adding a mnemonic device to it), making it more meaningful, and actively adjusting it to other memories. Elaborative rehearsal allows the new material to be readily retrieved from storage at a later time.

**Elective mutism** A childhood condition wherein the child refuses to talk in spite of the fact that he/she is able to do so. The child deliberately chooses not to speak.

**Electra complex**   In psychoanalytic theory, the female equivalent of the Oedipus complex. SEE: *Oedipus complex*

**Electroacoustic aids**   A general term to describe any electronic device that enhances a person's ability to hear. For example, a hearing aid, telephone amplification for the hearing impaired, etc.

**Electrocardiogram (EKG)**   A medical diagnostic procedure involving electrodes attached to the patient's torso. The voltage changes picked up by the electrodes reflect the ups and downs of heart muscle activity. This results in a record of heart rate that indicates whether the heart is beating at a normal rhythm or otherwise. SEE: *heart rate response audiometry*

**Electroconclusive Therapy (ECT)**   The treatment of mental disorders by administering an electric current to the patient's head; the shock is applied either bilaterally (to both cerebral hemispheres) or unilaterally (to one hemisphere). A mild electric current is sent across the head from one ear to the other for 1/25th of a second. ECT will at times produce convulsions and temporary comas. Inasmuch as the current can destroy brain cells, this treatment is controversial. It is to be used only when medication and behavioral therapies have been attempted and have proven unsuccessful.

**Electrodermal audiometry**   A special technique used for testing the hearing of very young children or students who are difficult to test. It is accomplished by measuring skin resistance and reaction to controlled sound.

**Electroencephalogram (EEG)**   A medical diagnostic procedure involving electrodes attached to the patient's scalp. The voltage changes that take place in the cerebral cortex of the brain are picked up by these electrodes. The rate at which the voltage alternates between positive and negative values is recorded individually for each of several head locations.

**Electronic mail (e-mail)**   This refers to a system of mail delivery that involves sending messages, instructions, or information via the computer from a person, group, or organization to other individuals, groups, or organizations as well as to governmental agencies, etc.

**Elementary school**   An education setting/institution/private facility for children in grades (sometimes K) 1–6 or (sometimes K) 1–8.

**Eligibility determination**   The decision made by a teacher, a group of teachers, or educational professional in determining whether or not a student qualifies for a specific program or service. An example would be a determination as to whether or not a student has a special education need or if a student meets the criteria for placement in a gifted and talented program, etc.

**Elimination diet**   A diet intended to eliminate toxic chemicals from the dieter's body. The Feingold diet is intended to serve as an example, or perhaps the model, for this concept.

**Elimination disorders**   A condition or behavior involving loss of bladder and bowel control (that is, wetting and soiling oneself) without any apparent physical problem. Elimination problems are considered disorders when they occur in older children beyond the age when control is expected (usually after the second year). SEE: *enuresis, encopresis*

**Elitism**   Typically, this term describes a group that has been given preferential treatment, attention, and/or favor as a result of the fact that they are supposedly superior in some area of academics or performance.

**E-mail**   SEE: *electronic mail*

**Embolism**   A common term used to describe an obstruction of a blood vessel by a clot or a foreign substance.

**Embryonic stage**   That portion of the prenatal life of the human organism from the end of the second week after conception through the eighth week. Before the embryonic stage is the germinal stage; the stage following the embryonic stage is the fetal stage.

**Emergence of Common Man**   The education movement usually associated with Rousseau during the Age of Reason. This was a time when the rights of the common people for a better life (academically, politically, economically, and socially) were emphasized. Previous to this time, education opportunities were thought to be open only to the elite.

**Emergence theory**   The view that certain complex arrangements of material objects can lead to the emergence of a qualitatively new phenomenon, the mind. The author of this theory in its original form was Henri Bergson. He compared this idea to the mixture of two gases, hydrogen and oxygen, that produce the liquid $H_2O$ (water). This view has been incorporated by Gazzaniga into his modern version of mind-body interactionism. SEE: *epistemology, interactionism, materialism, metaphysics*

**Emergency certificate**   A temporary certificate for teachers who have not met all the requirements for certification. These certificates are usually given when qualified teachers are not available for certain positions (e.g, bilingual teachers, special education certified individuals, etc.).

**Emergent literacy**   A reading and writing theory that posits that if children are exposed to meaningful print that is read to them and with them they will emerge into readers and writers gradually on their own.

**Eminence**   In education, a term used to describe superior ability.

**Emmetropic eye**   A synonym for a normal eye. During refraction, parallel rays focus on the retina exactly. SEE: *retina*

**Emotional lability**   Changes in mood, usually on a frequent basis.

**Emotionally disturbed**   1. In education, a term used synonymously with behavior disordered. 2. Disturbances involving one's feelings. SEE: *behavior disorder*

**Empathetic listening**   Extracting the emotional significance and inferring the motivation associated with what someone else says, then paraphrasing these inferred emotions and motives and reflecting them back to the speaker.

**Empathy**   The sharing of the experience of another person's feelings, which makes one more likely to behave with more than just sympathy and with true understanding toward that person.

**Emphysema**   A medical condition characterized by improper functioning of the lungs, which creates a shortness of breath particularly during exertion; frequently, a condition related to persons who smoke.

**Empiricism**   The philosophical position that emphasizes the study of reality through observations and the scientific method. This position holds that knowledge is obtained through the senses.

**Employment**   Work situations involving civilian, noninstitutionalized persons such as: 1. paid work during any part of a week; work in a business, profession, or farm; or unpaid work for 15 hours or more in a family-owned enterprise, and 2. employment in situations of temporary absence because of deaths, births, illnesses, bad weather, vacation, labor-management problems or disputes, or other personal reasons, despite the fact another job might be sought.

**Empowerment**   1. A term in education normally employed to designate teacher/parent control or participation in school decision-making. Areas of empowerment include but are not limited to curriculum development, selection of texts, school-discipline policies, selection of technology materials, etc. The concept of parent empowerment necessarily involves the formation of school-family partnerships where parents are viewed as equal partners in the learning process of a student. 2. Student empowerment refers to the concept of giving students the skills/strategies needed to become better learners/school citizens/family members.

**EMR**   SEE: *Educable Mentally Retarded*

**Enamel**   The hard exterior of the tooth that surrounds the dentine and forms a crown or covering for the tooth. The enamel is the body's hardest substance. SEE: *pulp, dentine*

**Encephalitis**   An inflammation of the brain, either by a viral disease that attacks the brain directly or as the after-effect of other infectious conditions such as rubella, influenza, measles, chicken-pox, cowpox, etc.

**Encephalitis lethargica**   Sometimes called "sleeping sickness" or Economo's disease, it is an infectious disease viral in nature and is characterized by lethargy and prolonged sleep. It is sometimes called epidemic encephalitis.

**Encephalization**   Refers to the developing brain that increases in size, with higher brain areas taking over control of behavioral functions from lower areas.

**Encephalocele**   SEE: *cranium bifidum*

**Encoding**   This is the process involved in expressive language; in effect, the sending of language messages. Framing the words of a spoken phrase or sentence. SEE: *coding, decoding, engram, memory trace, echoic memory, iconic memory, linguistic code, motor code*

**Encoding specificity**   The law of memory specifying that the best retrieval of stored material occurs when the retrieval is done in the same environment as the one in which the original learning (i.e., the encoding) of that material took place.

**Encopresis**   A lack of bowel control resulting from incomplete toilet training rather than from disease or injury.

**Encounter group**   A type of group therapy in which the members frankly express their feelings to one another. Such groups are employed by therapists of the humanistic psychology school.

**Enculturation**   The process of acquiring a particular culture(s), which is done in the home (informally) and at school (formally and informally).

**Endocrine disturbances**   Behavioral problems resulting from the malfunction or absence of one of the endocrine glands. For example, some children with ADHD are thought to have problems with their pituitary, thyroid, or adrenal glands. SEE: *endocrine gland*

**Endocrine gland**   Any of the ductless glands that releases its secretion(s) into the bloodstream rather than into a duct. A glandular product released into the blood is called a hormone. The hormones produced by the endocrine glands help to regulate internal bodily processes. The hormones are chemical messengers that circulate in the bloodstream to reach the parts of the body that they affect.

**Endocrine system**   Those glands that release their secretions (i.e., hormones) directly into the bloodstream.

**Endogenous**   Refers to something that originates from within.

**Endogenous mental retardation**   A term used to describe mental retardation causes that originate internally such as those caused by genetic abnormalities and heredity. SEE: *exogenous mental retardation*

**Endorphins**   Opiate-related neurotransmitters in the brain that are involved in the sensation of pleasure and pain. The term comes from "*endo*genous *morph*ines."

**Endowment**   That part of an institution's income derived from donations. Many private schools and colleges subsist in large part on endowment funds from alumni and other donors. SEE: *endowment funds*

**Endowment funds**   Donations received from a giver who designates that the money principal is not expendable. The use of the interest benefits an organization without depleting the fund.

**Engaged time**   The time spent by the student while actively learning.

**Engineering psychology**   That field of applied psychology involving the use of psychological knowledge in the design of machinery, vehicles, and buildings, etc. It is also known as human engineering or human factors engineering.

***Engle v. Vitale***   The 1962 Supreme Court ruling that overturned the New York State Board of Regent's practice of using prayers to open the school day. The Court held that mandatory prayers

**E**

violated the First Amendment of the U.S. Constitution.

**English as a Second Language (ESL)** Bilingual education programs that are designed to instruct students whose primary language is not English. SEE: *bilingual learners*

**English grammar school** An eighteenth-century private American school that was an alternative to the Latin grammar school. These schools focused on accounting, bookkeeping, navigation, engineering, and commerce skills.

**Engram** The physical basis of a memory in the brain. Sometimes it is referred to as a "memory trace."

**Enrichment** In education, a term that refers to a curriculum that allows any student but particularly the gifted and talented to expand their knowledge base and their creative and thinking skills beyond what is regularly presented in class.

**Enrichment triad/revolving door model** This model arranges for periodic participation in activities for 15–20 percent of the students in a class or school. It is a program designed to encourage and develop creativity, thinking skills, and problem solving. In this model, more students get a chance to participate than in other programs designed only for the gifted. In a typically designed gifted program, only about 3 percent of the students are involved. The rotating approach of the enrichment triad/revolving door model obviously allows a larger percentage of students to benefit.

**Enrollment** The total number of students in a school or a school system. In other words, the membership of the school or system on any given day or other period of time such as a school quarter, semester, full year, etc.

**Entitlement program** A state or federal government program that funds any institution (i.e., school system) or individual who meets the requirements for eligibility for such a program. Funds allocated and granted must be used in accordance with specific criteria for services designated by the program requirements.

**Entity view of ability** The belief that an individual's ability level is fixed and unchangeable.

**Enuresis** A lack of control of the bladder; especially beyond the age that control is expected and usually achieved. Normally children establish bladder control after the second year. A child who feels neglected may deliberately wet himself or his bed for attention. Also known as incontinence, lack of bladder control may be a result of urethral irritation, drinking excessive liquid, or of a pathological or neurological basis such as old age, diabetes, epilepsy, or even laughing, crying, or coughing.

**Environmental adaptations** Changes or modifications to the regular classroom environment which suit the individual learning styles and needs of the learner. For example, an environmental adaptation for a student with cerebral palsy might be a ramp or elevator access.

**Environmental bias** A point of view that is subjective in nature and based upon the social and cultural background or environment of the person(s) involved.

**Environmental education** In effect, studies that deal with our environment. An analysis of causes and conditions of such topics as natural resource management, pollution, population growth, energy, environmental waste, preserving the earth's atmosphere (ozone layer), and hazardous waste are some but not all of the topics included. In general, environmental education is concerned with the keeping of the earth in proper environmental balance.

**Environmental psychology** The field of applied psychology dealing with the improvement of the physical environment (e.g., buildings, noise levels, air spaces, landscaping, etc.) in accordance with known principles of psychology.

**Epicanthic fold** A condition characterized by a fold or flap of skin over the inside corners of the eye. It is a vertical field of skin extending from the root of the nose to the middle end of the eyebrow.

**Epiglottis**   A fold of cartilage that covers the glottis (the opening between the vocal folds in the throat) during swallowing. It is located at the back of the tongue and prevents liquids or food from entering one's airway. SEE: *glottis*

**Epilepsy**   A disordered brain-functioning condition characterized by various types of organic, recurring, and intermittent seizures or convulsions. Sometimes the person is rendered unconscious. The seizures are a result of malfunctions of the brain's physiochemical and electrical activities. SEE: *convulsion, seizure*

**Epileptic**   A person with recurring transient attacks of disordered brain functioning. A person with "epilepsy." SEE: *epilepsy*

**Epileptic aura**   The strange sensation or funny feeling experienced by epileptics just before an attack. SEE: *aura, seizure*

**Epiphenomenalism**   The view that the mind is just a product of the brain's activities. Although the mind seems to be very real subjectively, it has no ability to cause events. In this view, the mind is analogous to the buzzing sound emitted by an electric razor. The whirring blades do the job of shaving, while the sound is only a side effect. SEE: *materialism, metaphysics*

**Epiphora**   A condition of obstruction of the lacrimal (tear) ducts of the eye characterized by an overflow of tears.

**Episodic memory**   One of the two major parts of declarative memory. Episodic memories are for particular events that have occurred in the individual's life. These memories are the most easily lost in retrograde memory.

**Epistemology**   The branch of philosophy that deals with the nature of knowledge and how we obtain knowledge.

**Epperson v. State of Arkansas**   The 1968 Supreme Court ruling that overturned an Arkansas antievolution statute. The Court ruled that forbidding the teaching of evolution in the schools violated the First Amendment.

**Epstein-Barr virus**   (M. A. Epstein and Y. M. Barr) A virus herpeslike in nature and believed to cause mononucleosis and Burkitt's lymphoma. SEE: *mononucleosis, Burkitt's lymphoma*

**Equal educational opportunity**   The legal and/or social premise that every student deserves the opportunity to experience educational opportunities that develop fully special aptitudes, talents, interests, and innate abilities without regard to race, color, national origin, sex, physical or mental condition, or socioeconomic status.

**Equilibration**   The attempt to find a balance between one's cognitive schemes and information obtained from the environment.

**Equity**   The assurance that teachers and students have equal access to programs, materials, and other educational opportunities.

**Erb's palsy/paralysis**   (Wilhelm H. Erb, German neurologist, 1840–1921) Paralysis of muscles of the upper arms and shoulders. Generally the arms hang limply at one's sides with the hands rotated inward. Lost regular movement involves the cervical roots of the fifth and sixth nerves of the spine. SEE: *palsy*

**ERIC**   The Educational Resources Information Center or the U.S. federal information network of 16 clearinghouses. The various clearinghouses provide information that relates to an area of specialization (e.g., special education) with computer access available in most college and area libraries. SEE: *Current Index to Journals in Education (CIJE)*

**ERPs**   SEE: *Event-Related Potentials*

**Erythroblastosis fetalis**   A condition in which there is an Rh factor imcompatibility, which results in the destruction of red blood cells in the fetus. Bilirubin, an orange-red bile pigment, is secreted. Untreated, this condition will cause brain damage.

**Escape learning**   That form of learning in which the correct response is

E

reinforced by the removal of a harmful stimulus such as a very loud noise or an electric shock. Escape learning and avoidance learning are two types of operant conditioning by negative reinforcement.

**ESL** SEE: *English as a Second Language*

**Esophageal speech** An alternative method of speech used by persons who have had a laryngectomy (removal of the larynx). Air is swallowed into the top of the esophagus and shaped into words as it is "burped" out. The speech produced is low-pitched and guttural and the amount of speaking is limited by the volume of air swallowed. SEE: *larynx, esophagus, artificial larynx*

**Esophagus** A muscular tube or canal that passes down the neck from the pharynx (a passageway for food from the mouth) to the stomach. It's about 9 inches long.

**Esophoria** A tendency for the two lines of sight to diverge inwards from the normal, almost parallel, orientation. In the school of optometry known as syntonics, this is a result of overactivity of the parasympathetic nervous system and is likely to lead to a learning disability. In syntonic visual therapy, treatment with red light (a sympathetic nervous system stimulant) is used to produce a balance in the autonomic nervous system between the sympathetic and parasympathetic divisions, restoring the normal phoria and correcting the associated learning disability.

**Esotropia** Also known as esophoria. SEE: *esophoria*

**ESP** SEE: *Extrasensory Perception*

**Essentialism** In education, a premise that an educated person must have a common core of learning/skills. Schools are expected to design their curriculum around this concept so as to provide this "essential" education to all students.

**Establishment clause** That section of the First Amendment that states, "Congress shall make no law respecting an establishment of religion." This clause in our Constitution prohibits public schools from teaching religion. SEE: *Appendix 2: Legal Terms and Issues*

**Estimated pregnancy rate** An estimated pregnancy rate that is mathematically derived from the sum of births plus abortions plus miscarriages as a percentage of a total population (e.g., pregnancy rate of a particular high school, pregnancy rate of a particular community, etc.). Miscarriages are estimated to be 20 percent of all pregnancies and abortions another 10–15 percent.

**Estradiol** An estrogen (female sex hormone).

**Estrogen** Any of a number of female sex hormones to include specifically estradiol and estrone and their metabolic product estriol. These hormones are produced by the ovaries.

**Ethics** The domain of values that involves our principles of good conduct in our daily lives. Certain ethical standards are usually universally accepted in our schools (e.g., no plagiarism, respect for one another, no stealing, etc.).

**Ethnic group** A subcultural group with the larger societal culture, such as Hispanic-Americans, Italian-Americans, etc.

**Ethnic pride** Having a positive self-concept in relation to one's racial or national heritage.

**Ethnicity** The shared cultural heritage of a people. The collectiveness of a particular group is based upon a shared common identity derived in part from a common ancestral past and a common set of values/beliefs/lifestyles. Ethnicity is different from race because members of an ethnic group may or may not be from the same race but they all share common cultural characteristics such as religion, language, political ideologies, etc. The terms *ethnicity* and *race* are frequently used interchangeably. Race is considered to be more biologically-based, and ethnicity more culturally influenced. Also, one can change one's ethnicity based on a changing lifestyle, whereas racial distinctions are more permanent in nature.

**E**

**Ethnocentrism**   Essentially, a form of prejudice and discrimination wherein a person believes his/her group or culture is superior to others, not merely different.

**Ethnography**   Collecting data over an extended timeframe on several variables in a naturalistic setting. Some professionals use the terms "ethnography" and "qualitative research" interchangeably, while others believe that ethnography is one type of qualitative research. SEE: *qualitative research*

**Ethology**   ("ethos" = "behavior" in Greek) The experimental study of the behavior of higher animals (birds and mammals) under natural conditions.

**Ethyl alcohol**   That form of alcohol found in alcoholic beverages. It is a psychoactive drug that depresses behavior and mood, although in smaller doses it may elevate mood and act as a stimulant. The latter effects are release phenomena resulting from the removal of inhibitions. Like other depressants, ethyl alcohol can be addictive in that one develops a physical need for it and exhibits uncomfortable withdrawal symptoms when trying to go without it.

**Etiology**   Refers to the causes, roots, or factors involved in the development of a disorder. For example, the etiology of schizophrenia is thought to result from anomalous levels of certain neurotransmitters.

**ETV**   SEE: *Educational Television*

**Eugenics**   An attempt to breed healthier and more intelligent people by selecting reproductive cells from a chosen group of donors and preventing other (presumably defective) persons from reproducing. Such thinking produced laws at the beginning of the twentieth century that prohibited individuals with mental retardation from having children (also forced sterilization).

**Eustachian tube**   This tube leads from the middle ear to the pharynx allowing air to move in and out of the middle ear space, thus balancing pressure on each side of the tympanic membrane (eardrum).

**Eustress**   A positive response to a stressor, which is considered a challenge rather than a threat.

**Evaluation**   1. An educational, medical, and/or diagnostic process that uses a battery of medical, mental, social, psychological, and/or educational tests to analyze, evaluate, and determine a student's or person's strengths and weaknesses and/or condition. 2. Analysis of test and measurement results in determining just how effective a school program, course of instruction, and/or teaching method is. Quality and progress are also determined.

**Evaluation team**   Sometimes referred to as a CORE evaluation team, a former term still in use. Those persons are charged with writing an Individualized Educational Plan (IEP) for a child with special needs. This team includes persons who are knowledgeable about the child and understand the evaluative data and the implementation of services required in different placement options. This process may include professional and paraprofessional personnel as well as parents, the student, and other appropriate individuals such as social workers, counselors, medical personnel, etc. The evaluation team is listed on the IEP on the front cover sheet. However, the signatures that make it a legal document are on the sign-off page at the end. These signatures usually include those of the parent, guardian, or student (if 18 years old), the principal or the director of the facility, and the special education administrator. SEE: *IEP*

**Event-Related Potentials (ERPs)**   EEG patterns that regularly accompany particular psychological events. An example is the P300 wave, a positive voltage swing occurring 300 milliseconds after the onset of a meaningful stimulus.

**Evoked potential**   A modification of the EEG (Electroencephalogram) in which the EEG record is examined for changes following a specific stimulus presentation. Since the EEG is the cluttered recording of many neurons, it is usually necessary to average the EEGs over a number of stimulus presentations before a change in the EEG can be detected. Accordingly, the technique is often called the AER (for Average Evoked Response).

**Evoked-response, audiometric**   A special procedure that uses an Electroencephalogram (EEG) to measure the brain's electrical impulses in response to sounds, thus measuring brain wave changes in response to sound stimuli.

**Evolution**   The speculation that the universe just happened to evolve by itself and that no sweeping burst of creation was necessary to bring it about. SEE: *cosmology, creationism*

**E**

**Exceptional**   Especially in education, this refers to a student or person who is different from the normal/average. Generally the person's mental, physical, or behavioral characteristics are substantially higher or lower than the average, so that special needs/education services are required for the individual.

**Exceptional children**   Children who vary from average mental, physical, or behavioral characteristics to such an extent that they require special schooling, training, or other special treatment. The category includes those who are mentally retarded, those who are learning disabled, and those with emotional or behavioral disorders as well as those who are highly intelligent and gifted.

**Exceptional learner**   One whose growth and development deviates from the average student so markedly that he or she requires modification of the regular school program. Exceptional learners extend from those with gifted or superior abilities to those individuals who are mentally retarded. Both ends of the continuum require highly intensive, individualized educational programming.

**Exceptional student**   SEE: *exceptional learner*

**Excess cost**   The educational expenses beyond the regular per-pupil cost for a special needs program. The excess cost is the difference between the cost of a program for children with disabilities as compared to children without disabilities.

**Exchange transfusion**   Blood replacement with blood that is normal and fresh.

**Exclusionary definition**   Defining a concept or condition by what the concept or condition is not. For example, the term *dyslexia* is frequently defined by researchers as to what it is not. As such, it cannot include individuals with a below-average IQ, primary emotional disturbances, primary sensory disorders, cultural disadvantages, etc.

**Executive control process**   Certain perceptual or cognitive processes that affect the encoding, memory, storage, and/or retrieval of information. These processes include attention, rehearsal, elaboration, and organization.

**Exemplar**   A given example of a particular concept or category that can be used to help make decisions about the classification of other items.

**Exhibition**   A public demonstration of a learned achievement (e.g., a piano recital). Such achievements require the learner to spend time preparing for the performance.

**Exhibitionism**   Obtaining of sexual gratification by exposing one's genitalia to strangers. This behavior has to be habitual if there is to be a diagnosis of pathology.

**Existential psychology**   A school of psychology that concerns itself with subjective experience, free will, and living a meaningful life, while deemphasizing the scientific research aspects of psychology. SEE: *existentialism*

**Existential psychotherapy**   The attempt to deal with a client's emotional problems by addressing such major philosophical issues as the meaning of life, the inevitability of death, the responsibilities of free choice, and the isolated existence of the individual.

**Existentialism**   A philosophical position considered by many to be the fifth "pure" philosophical position.

Proponents of this school of thought believe that existence (being) comes before essence (meaning). One's destiny is in large part determined by one's choices and attitudes toward the future. Famous existentialists are Kierkegaard (1813–1855), Sartre (1905–1980), and Camus (1913–1960). The role of the teacher is to guide the student into independence so that he/she can make good choices. Curriculum is student-centered with student freedom a priority. The nurturing and development of the student-teacher relationship is critical to the existentialist.

**Excitatory synapse**   A kind of synapse is which an excitatory effect is produced in the receiving (or postsynaptic) neuron as a result of the release of a chemical neurotransmitter from the sending (or presynaptic) neuron that depolarizes (excites) a receptor site on the receiving neuron's cell membrane. SEE: *synapse*

**Exogenous**   Refers to something that originates from external causes.

**Exogenous mental retardation**   A term used to describe mental retardation causes that originated outside of the body; that is, caused by infection, injury, or trauma before, during, or after birth. SEE: *endogenous mental retardation*

**Exophoria**   A tendency for the two lines of sight to diverge outward. According to the school of optometry known as syntonics, this condition is a result of overactivity of the sympathetic nervous system leading to a form of learning disability. In syntonic visual therapy, treatment with blue light (a parasympathetic nervous system stimulant) is given to produce normal "phoria" in the individual and to correct the associated learning disability. SEE: *esophoria, exotropia*

**Exotropia**   An exaggerated outward turn of one or both eyes, also known as divergent strabismus or "wall eye."

**Expansions**   The act of taking what the child says and expanding it into a more grammatically correct statement (i.e., the child might say "daddy sleep" and the adult would say "your daddy is sleeping").

**Expatiations**   Expanding upon what the child says and adding something new to its meaning (i.e., the child states "play toy" and the adult says "play with the red truck"). SEE: *expansions*

**Expectancy**   The perceived probability of success in performing a task. The measurement of expectancy levels is done during research on the level of aspiration or in studies of achievement motivation.

**Expectancy and value theories**   Theories of motivation that emphasize the learner's expectation of success as well as the value placed by the learner on the goal.

**Expenditures per pupil**   Charges incurred for individual students by school districts for a particular period of time. The per-pupil expenditure is the total school budget divided by a student unit of measure (e.g., average daily attendance or average total school-district enrollment).

**Experiential intelligence**   The type of intelligence exhibited by people while performing either 1. tasks with which they have hardly any experience at all or 2. tasks with which they have a great deal of experience. SEE: *triarchic theory of intelligence*

**Experiment**   The research procedure that best enables the investigator to draw inferences about cause and effect relations. The variable that may cause a change in some behavior is set at various values; this is the independent variable. The behavioral measure that may or may not show changes related to the values of the independent variable is called the dependent variable. Factors that could affect the dependent variable (other than the independent variable) must be held constant or otherwise controlled.

**Experimental group**   Those subjects in a psychological experiment to whom some amount of treatment is actually administered. Other subjects, those in the control group, do not receive the treatment.

E

**Experimental method**   A research method in which one variable, the suspected cause, is manipulated by the researcher. Other variables are controlled by averaging them out or holding them constant. The researcher observes still another variable, the dependent variable, to see whether it changes in accordance with the prearranged changes of the independent variable.

**Experimental mortality**   Changes in group performance or outcomes resulting from the fact that some of the subjects dropped out of the experiment or study, subsequently impacting resulting outcomes. The only way to avoid this problem is to prevent the "dropping out" of individuals or subjects before a study is concluded.

**Experimental psychology**   A subset of areas in psychology dealing with experimental research on basic psychological processes such as sensation and perception, learning, memory, motivation, emotion, and cognitive processes.

**Experimental schools**   These are schools in which new curricula, programs, teaching methods, etc. are field tested. The application and administration of the new programs, methods, materials, etc. takes place under controlled conditions.

**Experimentalism**   A system of problem solving based upon the concept that the physical world is in a constant state of flux. Problems are considered within the context of social sciences and this serves as the framework for solutions.

**Experimentation**   The research method allowing some variables to be manipulated (the causal factors) and other variables to be recorded (the result variables). This research method permits generalizations to be made concerning cause-effect relationships.

**Experimenter bias effect**   The effect that experimenters' expectations have on the outcome of their research. If specific steps are not taken to prevent experimenter bias, a psychological experiment may result in an incorrect conclusion.

**Expert computer systems**   Refers to computer systems that are designed by computer experts and "human experts" (i.e., teachers) to meet the needs of the instructional setting/learners/instructor.

**Expert system**   A computer program that contains information about a particular field of knowledge and is capable of working logically with that knowledge. Expert systems belong to the field of computer science known as artificial intelligence.

**Expert teachers**   Teachers who are experienced and effective and who have worked out solutions for the routine problems that often arise in the classroom. They have a well-developed knowledge of the teaching process.

**Explanatory links**   Such words or phrases as "so that" or "because" that indicate how ideas are interrelated. Explanatory links are studied by syntactics; they have no content so that they cannot be studied by semantics.

**Explicit learning**   Knowledge that can be clearly acquired and restated or conveyed to others through oral and/or written communication.

**Exploratory education**   Educational procedures, techniques, or devices that emphasize the individual's need to discover answers by himself/herself.

**Explosive personality disorder**   A disorder whereby the individual will "fly into a rage" that is beyond normal reaction to provocation. Temper tantrums, physical assaults, and emotional outbursts will occur with even the slightest frustration or anxiety.

**Expository teaching**   The teaching method spelled out by Ausubel. The teacher first presents very broadly stated ideas, then works down to more specific points. This approach is the opposite of the Eg-rule method.

**Expository text**   1. Refers to text that is written to convey factual information, ideas, concepts, etc. Sometimes referred to as "content area text," expository materials can be associated with social studies, math, science, and other content area subjects. 2. In language arts, books, text, or other written materials that are organized to show cause-and-effect relationships, problem-solution relationships, and/or comparison/contrast concepts. SEE: *text structure*

**Expressive language** Written or oral language sent or communicated to others. It is also said to be encoding language. SEE: *encoding*

**Expressive language disability** SEE: *expressive language disorder*

**Expressive language disorder** Problems with producing language. The student suffers from an inability to verbally express herself/himself.

**Expulsion** The exclusion of a student from school (i.e., usually over 10 days of time and sometimes a school month, quarter, the remainder of the school year, and even on a permanent basis) because of a school infraction (e.g., repeated fighting, carrying a weapon, and/or being a threat to the health, well-being, and safety of others).

**Extended family** Normally, these would be close relatives of the family such as aunts, uncles, cousins, etc., that are in frequent contact with the immediate family. However, today this may include close friends and even members of a school or group as well as members of human services, religious organizations, etc.

**Extensor muscles** Muscles that provide for movement of a body part such as in the case of extending one's arm in reaching for an object, thus opening the angle of a joint. SEE: *flexor muscles*

**External auditory canal** A part of the outer ear, it is an irregular tube-shaped canal about one to two inches long. It extends from the auricle (outside of the ear) to the eardrum (tympanic membrane). SEE: *auricle, tympanic membrane*

**External locus of control** A condition of control wherein a student or person feels that factors for success and achievement are controlled by forces outside of oneself. In effect, one has little or no control over one's destiny. SEE: *locus of control, internal locus of control*

**External otitis or swimmer's ear** An infection of the external auditory canal of the ear. SEE: *otitis media*

**External validity** The extent to which the results of a research study can be correctly generalized to the entire population. The appropriateness of the sampling method used to obtain subjects for the research is the most important factor in the external validity of the research.

**Externalizing behaviors** Behaviors usually of an external (i.e., observable) nature directed toward another student or person. For example, externalizing behaviors are often found in students who are hyperactive, impulsive, and inattentive. SEE: *internalizing behaviors, Attention-Deficit/Hyperactivity Disorder (ADHD), hyperactivity*

**Extinction** The gradual fading away of a learned behavior as a result of the continued absence of reinforcement for that behavior. Also, extinction is the process of withholding the unconditioned stimulus during respondent (classical) conditioning, which leads to a reduction in the strength of the conditioned response or (in operant conditioning) the withholding of reinforcement after a correct response occurs, resulting in a lower rate of performing the conditioned operant behavior. For example, if a teacher would like to eliminate a temper tantrum, an extinction procedure could be implemented. This could involve ignoring the tantrums until the child (hopefully) becomes aware that such behaviors are not reinforced in any way, thus eliminating the unwanted behavior.

**Extracurricular or extracurriculum** Refers to that part of the school day/life outside of the academic setting—sports, clubs, newspaper, theater, band, chorus, etc. Such experiences are considered by many educators and parents to be helpful in building such desired traits as good sportsmanship, teamwork spirit, leadership, cooperative work, etc.

**Extrapyramidal cerebral palsy** A type of cerebral palsy caused by brain damage outside of the pyramidal cells of the cerebral cortex. These individuals experience muscle stiffness, involuntary

**E**

movements, or a floppiness of the limb muscles.

**Extrasensory Perception (ESP)** The alleged ability to perceive events without having to use the sense organs. Among the ESP skills are mental telepathy, clairvoyance, and psychokinesis (also known as telekinesis).

**Extrinsic motivation** The willingness to perform a response only because of the prospect of obtaining reinforcement (e.g., money, praise, or high grades), rather than for the pleasure of responding.

**Extrovert** An outgoing individual who is alert to things going on around him/her and who tends to be talkative, open, self-confident, and assertive. Extroverts are not inclined to be passive and silent. The term comes from Carl Jung's analytic theory, although Jung used it in a more complex manner.

F

**Faces of intellect** The three basic classes of mental ability according to the theory of J. P. Guilford: operations, products, and contents.

**Facial feedback theory** The theory of emotion that attributes an emotional feeling to the facial expression of the person. Setting the muscles for a given expression provides proprioceptive sensory information to the brain, which is used in deciding on what emotion to feel.

**Facilitative communications** SEE: *facilitative learning*

**Facilitative learning** Also known as facilitative communications, this is a system of physical support provided by a teacher or aide; usually the holding or touching of the hand, wrist, or arm of the student. When using this technique, the student selects/points to letters or answers on a communication board or device. The teacher or aide facilitates but does not guide the student's hand as it works the board. The student actually brings the facilitator's hand along. This type of technique is used extensively with autistic children. It should be noted that some critics have expressed doubt that the performance is totally free of influence from the facilitator. In effect, the student answers questions or communicates through the use of a communication board, keyboard, or other device but not by speaking.

**Fact finding** A process initiated to resolve conflict in which a neutral third party examines the problem(s) and issue(s) surrounding the problem. The fact finder generally makes published recommendations that are not binding. However, many times the parties involved agree to honor the fact finder's recommendations beforehand.

**Factor analysis** A statistical method that reduces a large number of trait names to a manageable few by combining related traits into larger units. Correlation coefficients are obtained among the tests of the numerous traits. A group of traits with high positive correlations among them is formed into a single factor.

**Faculty** Generally refers to the teaching professionals in an educational setting such as an elementary or secondary school and institutions of higher learning (colleges and universities).

**Faculty teams** Teams of teachers created at various grade levels and/or by subject areas according to the expertise/interests of the teachers and the curriculum requirements of the school/district. Members of the team often make decisions regarding student placements, instructional materials, resource allocation, scheduling, etc.

**Fading** The gradual removal of stimuli such as letters or prompts during the instruction process. This gradually increases the difficulty of the task. The goal of this technique is for the learner to acquire the ability to produce the material independently. A teaching method where assistance given to a child is gradually cut back until the child becomes able to perform the task or skill on his/her own.

**FAE** SEE: *Fetal Alcohol Effect*

**Fair local contribution** An amount of money generated by local property taxes (for school use) as mandated by state governments.

**False negative** An incorrect assumption derived from a test or other diagnostic tool that indicates an individual is free of a specified condition, where in fact the individual does indeed have the specified condition. SEE: *false positive*

**False positive** An incorrect assumption derived from a test or other diagnostic tool that indicates an individual has a specified condition, where in fact the individual is free of that specified condition. SEE: *false negative*

**Familial retardation** This refers to instances of mental retardation found in several members of the same family but with no signs of a biological cause for the retardation.

**Family** Defined for research and educational purposes as two or more persons (to include at least one person in whose name the housing unit is owned, leased, or rented; and residing together within),

usually family members who are related by birth, adoption, or marriage. However, nonrelated persons may also be considered part of the so-called extended family when residing together or sometimes even when they are not. SEE: *family household*

**Family consultation** or **family counseling** A type of supportive counseling given to several or all members of a family in order to help them cope with and assist one or more family members who might experience some type of disability, disorder, and/or physical illness. SEE: *disability, disorder*

**Family dynamics** The social forces at work in that microcosm of society, the nuclear family (parents, children, and siblings).

**Family household** A household containing biological/adopted family and any unrelated persons (unrelated subfamily members, other individuals, or both) who may be taking residence there. The number of family households in a society is equal to the number of families. The number of family household members is not the same as the number of family members, however, in that the family household members include all persons living in the household, whereas (adopted/biological) family members include only the head of the household and his/her relatives.

**Family psychotherapy** A type of psychotherapy used to improve the psychological well-being of an individual within the context of that person's family. Lines of communication are opened among the family members in order to facilitate more positive interactions than those that prevailed before the start of the therapy. Each family member is encouraged to identify and help satisfy the needs of other family members. The goal is to have the family function as a cohesive, whole unit.

**FAPE** SEE: *Free Appropriate Public Education*

**Farsightedness** An inability to see at close range. Also known as hyperopia. SEE: *hyperopia*

F

**FAS** SEE: *Fetal Alcohol Syndrome*

**Fear of failure** The reluctance to take on a challenging task because the possibility of failure is too unpleasant to consider.

**Feature analysis** The perception of a complex stimulus such as an object or a scene by consideration of the separate elements of the stimuli. Neurons in the cerebral cortex are selectively sensitive to particular features, such as lines with 30 degree slants. SEE: *feature detectors*

**Feature-detector theory** The concept that visual perception is based on the ability of individual sensory neurons to react selectively to particular features of stimuli. For example, a neuron in the visual cortex may respond to linear stimuli that have a 30 degree slope, but will not respond to any other lines presented to its visual field in the retina. Such a neuron is a specific detector of the 30 degree slope feature.

**Feature detectors** Cortical neurons that are selectively sensitive to lines of a given slant, to a particular width, to motion in a given direction, etc. SEE: *feature analysis*

**Federal aid** Monies generally raised through federal government taxation and appropriated for educational purposes. Such federal money or aid is usually given to and distributed by the states but occasionally it is granted directly to a community or educational entity, private and public.

**Feeblemindedness** A term meaning "weak of mind." Presently, it is an outmoded term that had been used in the past to signify mental retardation. The term is no longer popular and its use is considered insensitive.

**Feingold diet** A special diet that is low in sugar and avoids artificial flavorings and colorings. Care is also taken to reduce salicylate intake. The Feingold diet is also known as the Kaiser-Permanente diet, because Feingold's work was done at the Kaiser-Permanente hospital. The diet is supposed to correct the learning disabilities that, according to Feingold, are attributable to improper diet. SEE: *Feingold diet for hyperactives*

**Feingold diet for hyperactives** A diet prescribed for hyperactive individuals. It includes food free of artificial coloring and artificial flavorings. Although research has shown positive outcomes only for a small percentage (10 percent) of hyperactive children, there does seem to be evidence for physiological ill-effects from certain food additives. For example, red dye #3 has been reported to alter the permeability of neural membranes.

**Fellowships** Grants in aid and trainee stipends to graduate and doctoral students. Students usually perform services for the institution such as research or teaching.

**Feminist** A female who supports equality of the sexes in the areas of politics, salaries, social causes, work opportunities, work loads, etc.

**Fenestration** A medical and surgical term used to indicate an operation wherein an opening is made in the labyrinth of the ear. This operation is used to treat deafness associated with "otosclerosis," an inherited disease involving progressive deafness.

**Fernald-Keller approach** The VAKT approach developed by Fernald in 1921. This method utilizes four sense modalities (i.e., Visual, Auditory, Kinesthetic, and Tactile) in the process of teaching word recognition.

**Fetal Alcohol Effect (FAE)** A condition wherein full Fetal Alcohol Syndrome (FAS) cannot be documented. There is enough evidence, however, involving mental retardation to associate it with the consumption of alcohol by the pregnant mother. No amount of alcohol during pregnancy has been determined to be safe. SEE: *Fetal Alcohol Syndrome (FAS)*

**Fetal Alcohol Syndrome (FAS)** The occurrence of mental retardation and physical problems in a newborn infant as the result of the mother's abuse of alcohol during pregnancy. The danger point is estimated to be the daily consumption of 89 milliliters of ethyl alcohol (about three ounces). The safest way is for the pregnant mother to avoid drinking alcoholic beverages altogether. The possible symptoms of this condition include mental retardation (the level of which can vary from one baby to another), hyperactivity, lowered alertness, motor difficulties, heart defects, and facial abnormalities.

**Fetal stage**   The prenatal period lasting from the beginning of the ninth week after conception to the moment of birth. It follows the embryonic stage.

**Fetish**   1. An object or charm thought to have special or magical powers such as a rabbit's foot or horseshoe. 2. Psychiatrically speaking, the object of fetishism or the love of an object that represents a person such as a lock of hair, a personal item, etc. 3. A type of mental illness wherein a person is sexually stimulated by the sight of some body part, object, or article such as a shoe, glove, toe, etc.

**Fetoscopy**   A medical procedure used to directly examine the fetus in utero with a flexible fiberoptic device known as a fetoscope.

**Fetus**   An unborn infant who is mature enough to look like a human being. This stage of development is reached at the ninth week of pregnancy (i.e., during the third month).

**Fictional finalism**   The setting up of a goal by an individual so that the goal can serve to guide that individual's behavior, even if the goal is never actually attained.

**Field dependence**   An approach to perception of the environment. People who are field dependent respond to the environment as a totality; they find it difficult to differentiate such separate features as shapes, colors, sizes, attributes of individual objects, etc.

**Field independence**   An approach to perception of the environment. People who are field independent readily perceive the separate elements of the environment as clearly distinct from one another. They have difficulty perceiving the total environment as a whole.

**Field of vision**   That area of visible space when looking directly ahead with both eyes that is measured in degrees of visual angle.

**Fifth amendment**   The constitutional amendment which clearly states that no person shall be deprived of life, liberty, and property without due process of law and that private property shall not be taken for public use without just compensation to the owner(s). The "due process clause" has been used frequently by educators and students in court cases involving property rights and discipline.

**Fifth-year teacher education program**   A type of teacher preparation program that requires a provisional bachelor's degree or appropriate baccalaureate program as well as a permanent or fifth year graduate program. The fifth year of study is generally regarded as a time to implement theory into practice (e.g., see clinical experience) and to develop advanced pedagogical skills.

**Fight-or-flight response**   The activity of the sympathetic nervous system. It is an aroused condition, involving the inhibition of routine functions such as digestion and elimination. The organism goes into the optimum mode either for combat with an enemy or for flight from danger.

**Figure-ground perception**   The distinction between a clearly defined and centrally placed object (the figure) from the other aspects of the surrounding environment (the ground).

**Figure-ground perception ability**   The ability of a student or person to separate out one particular part of a visual field and concentrate on that particular aspect. Other aspects of the visual field are relegated into the background.

**Final-offer arbitration**   The process invoked when two parties are in dispute (e.g., over contract negotiations) and agree to have an arbitrator choose one of two (or more) proposals as the final offer for the recipients of a negotiated settlement.

**Fine motor skills**   Skills involving the voluntary, coordinated movements of small muscles, especially hand muscles, that are needed to demonstrate

**F**

dexterity. These skills may be applied to mechanical puzzles, drawing, rotating and stacking cubes, etc. SEE: *gross motor skills*

**Fine motor skills/control**   Use of fine or small muscles in a controlled fashion so as to perform detailed hand-eye tasks such as threading a needle. SEE: *gross motor skills*

**Fingerplay**   In language arts, a system of learning poetry by using poems that require hand or body motions as part of the reading or recitation.

**Fingerspelling**   A form of sign language in which a student or person spells out words in English by using various positioning of the fingers. SEE: *sign language*

**First amendment**   The constitutional amendment that specifies the separation of church and state, freedom of speech, freedom of press, freedom of assembly, and freedom of religion.

**First professional certificate**   An award, diploma, certificate, or degree that is given to an individual who has completed a program of study that leads to one's first professional certificate. For example, an associate degree or bachelor's degree.

**Fiscal**   A term used to refer to the financial affairs of an organization such as a school department.

**Fiscal neutrality**   Refers to the legal precedent of determining education expenses based on the needs of the students in the district as opposed to the wealth of its citizens.

**Fit**   SEE: *convulsion, seizure*

**Five basic subjects**   The core curriculum subjects recommended by the *A Nation at Risk* report: four years of English; three years of mathematics, science, and social studies; and one semester of computer training.

**Fixation**   1. A condition characterized by an abnormal and unrestrained attachment (e.g., a child to a parent or person). 2. A condition wherein a person develops to a certain stage and stops developmentally at that point. This fixated state

of development is usually accompanied by feelings of anxiety. 3. A brief stoppage of eye movement after a saccade.

**Fixed interval schedule of reinforcement**   A schedule arranging for the reinforcement of some correct responses by a student, but not all of them. In a fixed interval schedule, a given time interval must expire after reinforcement has occurred before another response can be reinforced. For example, with a fixed interval of 30" (FI30"), the student must wait 30 seconds before the response is given reinforcement. Responses made earlier than that will not be followed by reinforcement.

**Fixed ratio schedule of reinforcement**   A schedule for the arrangement of partially reinforcing the correct responses made by a student, such that every "nth" response results in reinforcement while all other responses are not reinforced. The name "fixed ratio" refers to the ratio of the number of responses made before the reinforcement is given to the reinforced response. For example, a fixed ratio of 5 (FR5) means that five responses are made before reinforcement is provided.

**Fixed-role therapy**   A therapeutic approach derived from Kelly's theory of personal constructs. Fixed-role therapy involves encouraging the client to select new roles in life, in order to develop and sustain a better-adapted set of personal constructs.

**Flashbulb memory**   Long-term memory (or memories) of emotionally charged events or persons on a particular day and time. For example, remembering where you were when President John F. Kennedy or Martin Luther King were shot; the details about a person's first date, etc. are examples of flashbulb memories.

**Flat affect**   An emotionless display with little indication of either positive or negative feelings. A person with flat affect frequently speaks in a monotone voice and shows little facial expression. Schizophrenics are known to display flat affects.

**Flexibility disorder** An impairment or disorder of articulation, quality, and/or voice pitch. It is characterized by rigid or stiff speech.

**Flexible grouping** A type of grouping that is widely used in reading classes because individual learning styles/characteristics can be addressed. Students are typically separated into learning groups based on some level of achievement or level of academic functioning. Movement from one group to another occurs as well as individualized instruction when the need arises. Temporary instructional groups within this model allow teachers to address deficit areas of need as they arise. Group dynamics can also change as the curriculum changes.

**Flexible scheduling (schedules)** The type of scheduling that allows students to attend classes of different lengths during the school day or week.

**Flexor muscles** Muscles that provide for movement of a body part toward the body's midline as in the case of pulling an extended arm back toward the body and closing or decreasing the angle of a joint. SEE: *extensor muscles*

**Flooding** A behavior-therapy technique in which the client's phobia is treated by intense exposure to the fear-evoking stimulus, causing intense fear in the client. The anxiety response is expected to undergo extinction when the fear stimulus does not produce any painful aftereffects.

**Fluency** The condition of speaking effortlessly in a smooth and flowing manner as well as quickly and without hesitation.

**Fluency disorder** An oral language disorder such as stuttering that involves prolonged or repetitive speech sounds, syllables, words, or phrases.

**Fluent English proficient** SEE: *bilingual learners*

**Fluid intelligence** The kind of intelligence that does not result from training or experience. This type of intelligence involves the ability to handle novel problems and situations. This kind of

ability reaches a peak during the teens and declines gradually thereafter. SEE: *crystallized intelligence*

**Fluoride** A salt of hydrofluoric acid (fluorine compound with a radical) frequently added to water supplies and toothpaste as a method of preventing dental caries (cavities).

**FM transmission device** An electronic device or equipment used to allow hearing-impaired students to hear through a closed FM/frequency modulated radio system. The teacher wears a portable microphone and the instruction is broadcast directly to the students wearing special hearing aids or receivers. SEE: *audio loop*

**Focal seizure** A partial seizure resulting in limited motor or sensory problems. It results from a discharge in a limited part of the brain. SEE: *generalized seizure, partial seizure*

**Focus of attention** The ability to focus one's undivided attention on a particular stimulus or situation.

**Focused instruction** A type of instruction that involves the development of several main ideas or skills as opposed to focusing on several disconnected informational sources. The role of the teacher is to identify key concepts and ideas for students to master.

**Folkways** Societal practices dealing with correct or incorrect behavior, conduct, mores, etiquette, and/or attire (dress).

**Follicle-Stimulating Hormone (FSH)** A hormone from the anterior pituitary gland (the master gland) that leads to the preparation of the follicle in the ovary of the female (which means increased estrogen production and the development of an ovum) and to the production of sperm in the testis of the male.

**Follow-up study** As the name implies, it is a continuation at some later date of the evaluation of the results of a study. This follow-up provides later/ongoing information for continued evaluation and diagnosis.

**F**

**Foot-in-the-door technique**   Raising the odds that someone will comply with a request by first demanding something so outrageous that the person would reject it immediately. The follow-up request should be so much more restrained that the person might be relieved and feel inclined to oblige.

**Forebrain**   One of the three main parts of the brain. The forebrain includes the cerebral hemispheres, the diencephalon, the rhinencephalon, the limbic system, and most of the basal ganglia. The other two main parts are the midbrain and the hindbrain.

**Forensic psychology**   The application of psychological knowledge and methods to legal problems, such as improving police work and analyzing the behavior of witnesses in the courtroom.

**Forgetting**   A condition wherein a student or person has difficulty or cannot remember information previously known or learned. SEE: *memory*

**Forgetting curve**   The graph showing the amount retained in memory as a function of elapsed time. The graph shows that most forgetting occurs soon after learning, while the small portion retained is held for an indefinite time.

**Form**   A term used in education to describe the rules and regulations of language. It includes phonology, syntax, and morphology. SEE: *morphology, phonology, syntax*

**Formal assessment**   There are several standardized test instruments that are norm-referenced. Typically formal assessments are used to measure "how much" students have learned as opposed to informal assessments that stress "why" and "how." Formal assessments should be related to instructional programs with a purpose set for any test administration. Information from formal assessments is typically used in curriculum planning efforts within a classroom, school, or school district. Most diagnosticians/professionals combine formal and informal measures of assessment to optimally understand children's learning strengths and weaknesses.

**Formal operation stage**   The most mature stage in Piaget's stage model of cognitive growth. It begins about age 12 and is shown by an ability to use abstract reasoning and to solve problems logically.

**Formal supports**   Refers to direct support and intervention services for students or persons with disabilities that are government funded at the local, state, or federal levels (such as public schools, Title I programs, etc.).

**Formal tests**   These tests, usually standardized, include specified tasks and procedures that must be adhered to very strictly so that the test results can be comparable to those from other administrations of the test.

**Formative assessment**   An assessment process that is ongoing while teaching and learning are occurring. The purpose of such an assessment is to further the education process rather than to decide on a grade. This is the opposite of a summative assessment. SEE: *assessment, instructional assessment, summative assessment*

**Formative evaluation**   In education and in general, a process of ongoing evaluation during the learning process that provides feedback and direction for continued learning. SEE: *summative assessment*

**For-profit schools**   Schools operated by private companies, organizations, or foundations that agree to provide teaching programs that allow students to achieve optimal learning outcomes/gains/achievement in exchange for operating at a profit. Frequently, school systems or districts will give the private organization the same per-pupil funding for participating students as the students who actually attend the public schools. The for-profit school is accountable for student progress/achievement/attendance. For example, the Edison Project plans to build more than 1000 for-profit schools by the year 2010.

**Foundation programs**   These are state funding programs that determine the dollar value of basic educational opportunities that are required in a state for meeting the educational needs of children and adolescents. This foundation level of funding involves specification of the minimum standard of local education efforts. A determination is made regarding an equitable way to distribute monies to school districts based on local wealth.

**Fourteenth Amendment or equal protection clause**   The constitutional amendment that guarantees certain rights and privileges to all U.S. citizens as concerns due process of law and equality under protection of the law. Passed in 1868, it also assured citizenship, personal liberties and rights for slaves who were freed.

**Fourth Amendment**   The constitutional amendment that protects citizens against search and seizure activities unless a warrant is first obtained.

**Fovea**   A small area directly in the center of the retina. The fovea contains only cones and provides maximum visual acuity and color-perception ability.

**Fragile X syndrome** (also: fra (X) syndrome)   An abnormal development of the X chromosome in the 23rd pair, the sex gender chromosome. Males have an X and Y chromosome and females an X and a second X. Males have a greater chance for a defect and in fact the syndrome is typically found only in males. Fragile X or fra (X) usually results in moderate to severe mental retardation. Males usually have abnormally long faces, large ears, and large testes as adults. Fra (X) has been known only since 1969. The fragile X chromosome of the male has a constriction near or at the end of the long arm of the X. Fragile X individuals show a noticeable decline in IQ during puberty in contrast to males with Down syndrome who show a steady decrease in IQ with age.

**Framing effect**   The bias introduced into a problem-solving task by the manner in which the problem is presented to the would-be solver.

**Framing questions or interactive frames**   Guided question formats for a particular subject that provide stimulation for effective responses on the part of the students.

**Free Appropriate Public Education (FAPE)**   In accordance with P.L. 101-476, the Individuals with Disabilities Education Act (IDEA), students with disabilities/special needs on Individualized Education Plans (IEPs) are entitled to appropriate educational services in reference to their special education needs and at no cost to the student or family. SEE: *IEP, P.L. 101-476*

**Free will**   The view that people can make effective decisions that change the direction of their future lives. This view implies that people are responsible for the consequences of their own actions and that they can be justly rewarded or punished for their own deeds. The leading philosophical ethicists advocated free will. Aristotle, Thomas Aquinas, Descartes, Hobbes, Locke, Rousseau, the Mills, and Russell can all be considered supporters of the idea.

**Frequency**   This refers to a speech frequency measured in hertz (Hz), the number of cycles per second. We perceive frequency of this type as "pitch." Any energy wave can be described by its frequency, or alternatively, its wavelength. The higher the frequency, the shorter the wavelength.

**Frequency distribution**   The set of scores obtained after measuring the behavior of (or administering a test to) a group of subjects. The scores are arranged in order of size, usually from lowest to highest. Occasionally, several people will get the same numerical score. The number of people getting the same score is defined as the frequency of that score. The accurate presentation of scores in order of size will include the frequency data. For example, if the presentation of a frequency distribution is a graph, the score is represented on the x-axis (the abscissa) and the frequency is given by the y-axis (the ordinate). As graphed, a frequency distribution has various descriptive features (e.g., shape, central tendency, and variability). SEE: *central tendency*

**F**

**Frequency histogram**   This is a graph of a frequency distribution (i.e., a display of scores v. the frequency of each score) in which the frequency of a score is indicated by the height of a rectangle. For example, a bar graph.

**Frequency of sound**   The number of vibrations per second of sound measured by a unit called hertz (Hz). Sound vibrations involve molecules of water, wire, air, etc. High sound frequencies are high-pitched while low frequencies are low-pitched. The ear can hear from about 20 Hz (low) to 20,000 Hz (high). Speech usually falls between 250 and 4000 Hz (cycles per second).

**Frequency polygon**   This is a graph of a frequency distribution (i.e., a display of scores v. the frequency of each score) in which each frequency is marked by a point in Cartesian coordinates (distance along x-axis = size of a score and distance up y-axis = frequency of that score). Each point is connected to the following point by a straight line. For example, the bell-shaped curve expressing normal frequency distribution.

**Frequency theory**   A theory explaining the ability to discriminate the pitch of a sound; it is also known as the telephone theory. According to this view, the number of cycles per second in the sound wave is matched with the number of impulses per second in the auditory nerve axons. The theory may be workable for low-pitched sounds, but cannot account for the pitches of sound frequencies over 1000 cycles per second. This is because an axon cannot conduct more than about a thousand nerve impulses in one second, due to the absolute and relative refractory periods.

**Freud, Sigmund**   Austrian neurologist and psychoanalyst (1856–1939). His teachings involved investigation of mental functioning through the use of free-association, analysis of resistance and transference, and dream interpretation. Although known as the "father" of psychoanalysis, Freud considered "psychoanalysis" as not scientific but as a means to elucidate the recesses of the mind and soul in order to assist an individual to live with peace of mind and at a level of maturity that would help the individual lead a better life. SEE: *developmental model, id, ego, superego*

**Fricative**   Consonant sounds made by forcing air through a narrow opening. Fricatives include the sounds in the letters f, v, and th.

**Friedreich's ataxia**   A condition that is inherited and affects the spinal cord. The hardening of the spinal cord results in the paralysis of the lower limbs.

**Fringe benefit**   Benefits given to employees that are above wage earnings such as sick leave and personal leave.

**Frontal lobe**   One of the four lobes of the cerebral cortex that is situated directly back of the skull's frontal bone. Since the cortex is divided into two hemispheres, there are a left and a right frontal lobe. The caudal or posterior edge of the frontal lobe is marked by the central sulcus (or fissure of Rolando). The inferior or ventral boundary of the frontal lobe is the lateral fissure (or fissure of Sylvius). In most people, the left frontal lobe contains Broca's area for the motor production of speech sounds. In each frontal lobe resides the motor areas that send out motor commands to the contralateral muscles. The very front or anterior end of the frontal lobe, the prefrontal area, was the part excised in the frontal lobotomy operation, which was faddish in the 1930s and 1940s. This lobe is involved in how we sequence information, think abstractly, form concepts, problem-solve, and attend to tasks. Damage to this lobe can affect speech, thinking, and gross and fine motor skills. SEE: *prefrontal lobotomy*

**Frustration**   The blocking of goal-directed behavior and/or the emotion associated with the experience of being prevented from reaching the goal.

**Frustration-aggression hypothesis**   The hypothesis that the experience of frustration leads to an outburst of aggression.

**Fry list**   A popular sight-word listing.

**Fry readability graph**   SEE: *readability formulas*

**FSH**   SEE: *Follicle-Stimulating Hormone*

**Fugue**   A serious condition characterized by a student or person who runs away from home, job, or current life impulsively. This condition may last for days, weeks, or years. Usually recovery from this condition involves loss of memory of what occurred while the person was in the fugue state. It is sometimes called personality dissociation or psychogenic fugue. SEE: *psychogenic fugue*

**Full inclusion**   Complete integration of all children in need of special education services into the regular classroom with children who do not experience special learning challenges. SEE: *inclusion, integration, mainstreaming*

**Full-time staff**   Educationally speaking, all faculty, staff, and administration, as well as any other workers who work a full school schedule (school day and school year) or a 40-hour work week.

**Function**   Any action by a student or individual in response to the demands of one's general needs. Human needs or functions include existence, the need for communication with others, adaptations to one's environment, the learning process, leisure or relaxation time, recreation, travel, sports, etc.

**Functional**   A term used to describe disturbances of function of an organ although no known organic change or physical cause is present.

**Functional academics**   An academic program that teaches practical skills and not just academic learning.

**Functional articulation disorders**   Disorders of articulation that are apparently a result of environmental/ecological or psychological reasons. Such problems apparently are not a result of neurological difficulties nor of structural defects.

**Functional assessment approach**   An assessment approach that highlights the connection between an individual's educational functioning and the environment as concerns learning, living, and working.

**Functional communication**   The ability to communicate both orally and in writing in a functionally literate way and in such a way as to positively adapt to the environment.

**Functional curriculum**   An approach to teaching and learning based upon curriculum skills that are age-appropriate for the students. Further, the curriculum emphasizes skills that have immediate and functional application.

**Functional disorder**   A disorder characterized by a disturbance in organic functioning; it may involve disease, emotional responses, psychosis, etc. No known organic cause is evident.

**Functional fixedness**   The inability to find a novel use for a familiar object when that kind of flexibility would help to solve a problem.

**Functional hearing loss**   A hearing loss that is caused by psychological or social factors rather than causes of an organic nature. Sometimes such a loss is considered psychosomatic or hysterical in origin.

**Functional learning handicap**   A condition wherein a student develops learning problems and difficulties as a result of a lack of ability to function effectively and appropriately within one's environment. This may occur for any number of factors, such as social, psychological, environmental, etc.

**Functional life/compensatory approach**   An approach to education that teaches skills of practical value so as to prepare a student for the world of work. Social skills, self-care skills, and occupational skills are emphasized.

**Functional literacy**   The attainment of a high-enough level of reading, writing, and speaking to enable one to function effectively among other literate persons.

**Functional print**   In language arts, a term used to indicate classroom print that has a specific learning purpose.

**Functional psychosis**   A severe mental disorder for which no pathology can be found; no known physical reason is evident nor apparent within the central nervous system (CNS). SEE: *psychosis, autism*

**F**

**Functional retardation**   A condition that may exist in a student or other individual that seems to be related to one's environment. Events and actions within the environment shape and affect the individual's adaptive behavior in a negative way. This results in retarded adaptive behavior (i.e., functional retardation).

**Functional skill**   A task or skill that a student or person would be expected to know and use in one's daily living and within one's normal environment.

**Functional skills model**   A model of instruction for students with special needs that emphasizes presenting curriculum materials tied in to life situations. Hands-on life experiences are stressed.

**Functionalism**   A psychological school of thought (subscribed to by the followers of William James) that placed emphasis on the workings of the conscious mind in helping the individual adapt successfully to the environment.

**Functionally illiterate**   A term used to refer to an individual who is unable to read or write at a level that is considered necessary for adequate functioning in a society.

**Fused curriculum**   A type of curriculum organization that involves "fusing" or "merging" a smaller number of subjects into one subject category. For example, spelling, grammar, speech, reading, and literature are frequently merged into language arts curricula.

**Future problem solving**   A national project and special instructional program developed by Torrance, E. P. and Torrance, J. P. (1978) that emphasized future problem solving in a creative way and in an area of need. For example, problems included what to do about the depletion of the ozone layer, motoring with solar energy, etc.

**Future shock**   A term that refers to the accelerated lifestyle of modern living and the impact it has on our immediate future. Standards, values, mores, etc. have changed at a very rapid pace. People who become confused and disoriented as a result of lack of ability or inability to make adjustments for what is changing and what probably will change are said to be suffering from future shock.

**Futurism**   A philosophy that deals with the prediction of the future. Within this philosophy, development of plans and techniques to deal with coming change/situations are embraced. In effect, prediction is accompanied by planning probable future actions and/or solutions.

**"G" loading**   A common term used when factor-analyzing data on intelligence. The term "g" refers to one's general intelligence. "Loading" refers to a type of factor-loading in the statistical analysis that is represented as a correlation value. Performance on a subtest measure of intelligence would indicate how highly correlated the skills measured are with general intelligence. For example, a g loading of .75 on a vocabulary subtest of an intelligence measure would indicate a moderately high correlation between the vocabulary measure and one's overall general intelligence.

**Gait training**   A system of instruction for persons with physical disabilities wherein their abnormal and normal walking movements are evaluated in order to better assist the person with correct walking techniques.

**Galactose**   A simple sugar, crystalline in form.

**Galactosemia**   A genetic disorder that involves the body's inability to metabolize galactose. This disease can result in mental retardation.

**Gallaudet University**   A special university for the deaf that was first named the National Deaf Mute College. It was founded in 1864 and is located in Washington, D.C. Gallaudet University was named for Thomas Hopkins Gallaudet (1787–1857), who established the American Asylum for Education of the Deaf and Dumb (now the American School for the Deaf in Hartford, Connecticut). He was an early pioneer in the field. Gallaudet University is a federally funded school and has both undergraduate and graduate programs. It is the only university of its kind in the world.

**Ganglion** (plural: ganglia)   A cluster of the cell bodies of neurons in the peripheral nervous system (e.g., the dorsal root ganglia or the sympathetic chain of ganglia). One exception: the basal ganglia are really nuclei within the brain.

**Gastrostomy feeding**   Feeding food directly into the stomach via a feeding tube. A procedure used when a child has some physical difficulty dealing with the sucking and swallowing reflexes or perhaps a malformed esophagus. SEE: *nasogastric feeding*

**Gate theory**   A theory of pain sensation and analgesia. According to this view, there is an area either in the spinal cord or the medulla that receives pain-nerve impulses and that can also receive inputs from other senses. The other sensory inputs may inhibit pain neurons so that the pain messages are prevented from traveling toward the forebrain (i.e., the gate is closed).

**GED**   SEE: *General Educational Development test*

**Gender bias**   Different views of, and also attitudes toward, the abilities of males and females. Often, this may become detrimental to one gender and favorable to the other.

**Gender identity**   The sex that a person identifies with, accepting it as the person's own. Ordinarily, this is decided by whether the sex chromosomes are XX (female) or XY (male). As a result of androgen insensitivity syndrome, or abnormal groupings of sex chromosomes, the picture can become more complicated.

**Gender roles**   The behaviors that a given culture defines as appropriate for males and females.

**Gender schema theory**   A theory of the development of gender roles that appeals to a combination of social learning theory and cognitive-development theory.

**Gene**   The basic ultramicroscopic unit of heredity. This genetic particle is responsible for characteristics of heredity. Genes are arranged within the chromosomes of a cell. The average person has about 100,000 genes, distributed among 46 chromosomes. SEE: *chromosomes, genes*

**General adaptation syndrome**   Dr. Hans Selye's model of the body's response to stress. The first phase consists of an alarm reaction, in which the emergency situation is acknowledged. The second phase, that of resistance, involves specific attempts to correct the problem. The third phase, exhaustion, follows when the first two phases have been unsuccessful. Exhaustion can result in severe fatigue, death, or stress-related disorders.

**General education**   Usually a basic curriculum that is required to be taken by all students. Such programs are also known as "common" or "core" curriculums.

**G**

**General Educational Development test or GED** An equivalency test which is an alternative means for high school dropouts to complete their high school education experience. Passing this test earns a high school equivalency diploma. SEE: *high school equivalency*

**General knowledge** Information about a number of unrelated subjects that can be put to good use in various situations.

**General paresis** An organic mental disease caused by syphilitic infection that leads at first to a partial or complete paralysis and, ultimately, to a progressive and fatal ending. It is chronic and irreversible.

**General Welfare Clause** Article 1, Section 8 of the U.S. Constitution, which enumerates the various powers of Congress to include providing for the general defense and welfare and levying and collecting taxes. The courts have generally ruled that education matters fall under this general welfare clause. Congress, with its implied powers, can pass legislation concerning the general welfare of its citizens regarding education issues. SEE: *implied powers*

**Generalization** The tendency to respond the same way to a group of different stimuli because of some degree of similarity among these stimuli. In education, generalization is the ability of a student to formulate new information and conclusions from past and present knowledge.

**Generalized anxiety disorder** A persistent condition of chronic anxiety that cannot be attributed to any particular stressful situation.

**Generalized reinforcer** A type of reinforcer that is really a kind of secondary reinforcer, as its reinforcing qualities result from associations with several primary reinforcers. Money is a generalized reinforcer because it can result in food, buying this dictionary, and other positive things. SEE: *secondary reinforcer*

**Generalized seizure** Unlike a focal seizure, this type of seizure affects a large part of the brain, not just a limited area. SEE: *focal seizure, seizure*

**Generativity** That feature of human language involving the ability to combine words in ways that have never been experienced earlier by the speaker.

**Generativity vs. stagnation** A stage in Erik Erikson's theory of personality development. Successful development at this stage is reflected by increasing concern for the welfare of others and a lowering of self-absorption.

**Generator potential** The electrical response of a sense receptor that starts nerve impulses going down the afferent neural axons, thus indicating the reception of a stimulus.

**Generic special education teacher** SEE: *resource teacher*

**Generic supports** Public services and benefits to which all nondisabled persons have access, providing they meet eligibility requirements. Sometimes all people have generic support eligibility and access as in the case of public schooling, public transportation, etc.

**Genes** Cell structures (made of DNA) on specific locations in the chromosomes (the ribbon-like objects within the nuclei) of all body cells. Genes are our genetic markers; they are responsible for our hereditary characteristics.

**Genetic blueprinting/engineering** The genes are the blueprints for the body. Genes and chromosomes determine the characteristics of heredity that are transmitted to our children. With our new-found knowledge of genetic engineering, scientists/doctors are able to alter or repair the genes through synthetic approaches and thus prevent or limit the passing on of genetic aberrations to offspring. SEE: *gene, chromosome, genetic counseling*

**Genetic counseling** Meetings or sessions with a genetic specialist and counselor who provides information to prospective parents or parents concerning the possibility of and the probability of children inheriting some abnormal or disabling condition. SEE: *genetics, genetic blueprinting/engineering*

**G**

**Genetics**   The science of the biological basis of heredity.

**Genital stage**   The final stage of Sigmund Freud's theory of personality development. It is associated with the onset of puberty and a mature adjustment to that event. The individual develops sexual interest in persons of the opposite sex. This stage corresponds to Erikson's stage of identity versus role confusion.

**Genius**   A student or person with an IQ of 180 or above or a person of rare and unusual ability not necessarily academic.

**Genotype**   The genetic influence (on a specific trait such as eye color) carried by an individual.

**Genre**   1. A term used in general to describe a type, classification, category, or class of art, literature, painting, etc. 2. In language arts, "genre" is a term used to describe a type of writing style or type of book such as a classic, a mystery, an autobiography, science fiction, etc.

**German measles**   Measles that can cause retardation during the first 90 days of a pregnancy as well as hearing and vision impairments in the fetus. SEE: *congenital rubella*

**Germinal stage**   The first part of the prenatal period, lasting from conception through the second week. It precedes the embryonic stage.

**Gestalt**   A complex entity involving the integration of component parts so that the whole is superior to the sum of the parts (e.g., seeing the forest through the trees).

**Gestalt psychology**   That school of psychology that emphasizes the study of patterns or whole units. "The whole is greater than the sum of its parts" is the gestaltists' theme.

**Gestalt therapy**   A form of psychotherapy introduced by Perls in which the client is encouraged to face her/his own true feelings and to accept full responsibility for them.

**Gifted**   Individuals who display learning styles and characteristics that allow them to acquire literacy skills at levels considered to be developmentally advanced. Sometimes the term "gifted" is used synonymously with "talented." It is usually applied, however, to a person who has superior cognitive abilities and not just raw talent. It is someone who can perform, create, and achieve at exceptional levels, such as a high honors student, a composer, an extraordinary artist, etc. Generally, to be considered gifted, one's IQ falls above 130. Demonstrated abilities and potential are evident in at least one of the following areas for gifted individuals: 1. overall intellectual ability, 2. specific academic aptitude, 3. creativity, 4. leadership, 5. ability in one of the visual and performing arts, and 6. psychomotor ability. Individuals who are truly gifted most often have several areas of "giftedness." Gifted individuals most often are highly intelligent, good abstract and critical thinkers, self-confident, curious, or inquisitive. Such individuals have a good sense of humor and an advanced vocabulary. They have a small circle of friends, are independent, and like solitude in social and academic settings. They are highly empathic or sensitive to those around them and possess a serious disposition. Being gifted also has its problems in the academic and social realms. Many gifted individuals lack organizational skills and do not complete an assigned task/job because there are so many "irons in the fire." Some gifted individuals are socially isolated or have difficulty relating to and interacting with age-appropriate peers. Students who are gifted many times require enriched educational programs so as to challenge, stimulate, and tap into the individual's learning strengths. Because a disproportionate number of gifted students "drop out" of school, it is believed that more can be done to address the educational needs of this population. Some states such as Connecticut require IEPs for gifted students. The National Research Center on the Gifted and Talented (NRCGT) provides research and information opportunities for those who are committed to servicing gifted students.

**G**

The NRCGT website is http://www.ucc.uconn.edu:80/~wwwgt/nrcgt.html.

**Gifted learning-disabled**   A term used to refer to individuals who are gifted and learning-disabled at the same time. SEE: *gifted, learning disability*

**Gillingham-Stillman approach**   A type of synthetic phonics method offered by Gillingham and Stillman in 1935 that teaches the names and sounds of letters, the names for spelling, and the sounds for reading. It is a multisensory approach.

**Gland**   An organ or structure of the body that secretes a substance that is used in another part of the body. Glands are either 1. mucous; that is, they produce a slimy viscous secretion or 2. serous; that is, they produce a clear watery secretion or 3. mixed; that is, they produce both types of secretion.

**Glaucoma**   An eye condition that usually occurs during or after middle age, involving excess pressure on the eyeball leading to severe vision loss or blindness if untreated.

**Glial cells**   Cells in the nervous system that perform various support functions for the nerve cells (i.e., the neurons). They supply nutrients, remove waste material after damage has occurred, help make the myelin sheaths that surround some axons, and in the peripheral nervous system guide the regenerating axon to its proper position during the recovery after an injury.

**Glioma**   A cancerous neuroglial tumor.

**Global retardation**   An outdated term used to describe a student or other individual who has a broad spectrum of learning disabilities, resulting in severe or profound difficulty in learning. Such a delay in learning is across the board rather than a specific or single area (e.g., reading), giving rise to the description "global" delay or retardation in learning.

**Global self-concept**   A term used to refer to one's total self-concept or how one feels about oneself and one's accomplishments. These are feelings in general as opposed to foci on particular situations, persons, or events.

**Glottis**   The opening between the vocal folds (cords) in the throat. This is covered by the epiglottis during swallowing. SEE: *epiglottis*

**Gluten**   A simple protein or albumin from vegetables that is prepared from wheat and other grains as well.

**GNP**   SEE: *Gross National Product*

**Goal-directed actions**   Actions that are purposely directed toward the attainment of a specific goal.

**Goal setting**   Deciding on a particular level of accomplishment to strive for in the future.

**Goal structure**   The manner in which a number of persons working toward a particular goal are interrelated to one another.

**Goals 2000**   Education goals established by President George Bush and 50 state governors in February of 1990 who placed a high priority on the basic subjects of English, science, mathematics, history, and geography. The six national goals were enumerated as follows: By the year 2000, 1. All children will enter school ready to learn. 2. High school graduation rates will increase to at least 90 percent. 3. Students in grades 4, 8, and 12 will demonstrate (through testing) basic literacy/competency in English, mathematics, science, history, and geography. Students will also be critical thinkers and productive/contributing members of society. 4. American students will excel in science and mathematics achievement. 5. American adults will be literate in a global economy and will exercise their rights and responsibilities of U.S. citizenship. 6. American schools will be drug/violence free. Disciplined environments will nurture the learning process. In 1994, two additional goals were added: 7. Teachers will continue to grow as reflective practitioners by participating in a number of professional development activities. 8. Parents will be involved partners in their child's education programs. Note that these goals are also referred to as "America 2000," "National Educational Goals," and "The Educate America Act."

**Gonad**  One of two paired endocrine glands related to sexuality and reproduction. The female gonads are the ovaries and the male gonads are the testes.

**Gonorrhea**  A venereal disease of the genital mucous membrane, it is caused by the gonococcus Neisseria gonorrhoeae and infects both sexes. In the male, a purulent discharge from the penis is noted as a result of inflammation of the urethra. Sometimes in the female it is asymptomatic but it usually includes urethral or vaginal discharge. Painful urination is frequently present in both sexes. Gonorrhea may cause health and learning problems. SEE: *Venereal Disease (VD), urethra*

**Governance**  A formal system of management by governmental agencies of the educational system.

**Gower's sign**  (Sir William Gower, British neurologist, 1845–1915) A symptom of muscular dystrophy associated with the Duchenne type of dystrophy. It is characterized by a student's inability to stand after having been seated on a chair or on the floor. One must place one's hands on one's knees and thighs and "walk up" the legs, pushing oneself into an upright position. The individual might also grab onto a post or pole or push off a desk top in order to straighten the back into a vertical position. This is a result of a weakening of the stomach, thigh, and back muscles in the disease process. SEE: *Muscular Dystrophy (MD)*

**Grade**  A number or letter used to indicate how well (or how poorly) a student has performed (either on a single examination or on all the student's work in a given subject throughout a given time period).

**Grade equivalent**  A grade-equivalent score is computed by finding the mean raw score for children at each grade level. If the mean score for a group of fourth graders on a reading test is 40, then a child with a score of 40 would be performing at the fourth-grade level. These scores are generally reported in whole number and decimal form. So, a child with a 4.2 grade equivalent in reading would be performing at the fourth grade, second month level.

**Grade membership**  A rating of the extent to which a particular item fits into a given category.

**Graded schools**  Schools that place students in year-long programs or levels such as the first grade, second grade, etc. Most school systems are organized with grades from kindergarten through grade 12.

**Grading on the curve**  The norm-referenced type of scoring; an individual's performance rating depends on how that performance compares to the average performance of the whole group.

**Grading system**  The procedure used by a teacher to arrive at a number or letter expressing the quality of a student's performance in an academic subject.

**Graduate student**  A term used to describe a student who already holds a first degree or is studying at a post-baccalaureate level such as a student in a master in education (M.Ed.) or a master in teaching (MAT) program.

**G**

**Grammar school**  1. The ancient secondary school in Greece where young men between the ages of 12 and 16 were taught Greek classics and *grammar.* 2. The American colonial secondary school that focused on the classics and preparing individuals (mostly men) for college. 3. The current American conceptualization of an elementary school where classical literature is still taught. The instruction of grammar is considered most appropriate at an elementary level (i.e., grades 1–6) with refinements continued at the secondary levels. Notice the focus of what a grammar school should be has changed from a secondary level to its current elementary conceptualization.

**Grammatical rules**  The manner in which we are to use properly words, groups of words, phrases, clauses, and sentences in relation to the requirements of a particular language. Such rules are concerned with the placement of nouns, verbs, subjects, predicates, and other parts of speech, as well as with the tenses (present, past, and future), etc.

**Grammaticus**   One of the teachers who taught in ancient Roman grammar schools.

**Grand mal or grand mal seizure**   A typical epileptic seizure characterized by loss of consciousness. The person collapses, becomes rigid, has involuntary muscle contractions, may bite his/her tongue, and pass urine. If you are in the presence of someone experiencing a grand mal seizure, do not try to stop the attack; align the head and turn the patient to one side to aid breathing. Prevent the person from swallowing his/her tongue, and place a pad between the teeth if possible. Contact a medical authority and allow the person to rest following the attack. SEE: *petit mal seizure*

**Grants**   Money stipends awarded typically after a grant proposal (e.g., for curriculum projects, computers, research, etc.) has been submitted to a funder for acceptance. Grant writing usually involves submitting an abstract or brief summary of the proposed project, objectives and goals for the project, a needs assessment, a time table of activities/implementation, planned assessment of outcomes, and budgetary information. Some Internet sites for grant information include: The United States Department of Education Grants and Contracts at http://gcs.ed.gov; The Foundation Center at http:// fdncenter.org, and Yahoo! Education Grants Link at http://www.yahoo.com/Education/Grants.

**Graphic organizers**   Written diagrams or outlines that illustrate the main structure of the material to be read. Key terminology is used to create a "skeleton" that depicts the sequence and organization of the textual material.

**Grasping reflex**   In infants, a response in which the child grasps objects placed in the palm of the hand.

**Grave's disease**   (Robert J. Graves, Irish physician, 1797–1853) SEE: *hyperthyroidism*

**Gray matter**   In the central nervous system (CNS), collections of neuron cell bodies present an off-white, dirty yellow appearance. This is in contrast to the white matter also of the CNS.

**Great books**   Refers to the timeless classics in literature (e.g., Homer and Shakespeare). Leaders of the perennialist school of thought have used the "Great Books" to help establish an education philosophy. SEE: *perennialism*

**Gross motor skills**   Voluntary, coordinated activity of large muscles. Such skills are exemplified in running, throwing, swimming, sliding, vaulting, etc.

**Gross National Product (GNP)**   The sum total value of goods and services generated by the members of a nation during a specific time period.

**Group**   A set of at least two persons who interact with one another and are each influenced by the other. Sometimes this is referred to as a "face-to-face" group.

**Group auditory trainers**   A wireless FM device that amplifies sound for groups of hearing impaired students or individuals. The FM nonwire system allows complete freedom of movement for both the teacher and student(s).

**Group consequences**   The assignment of rewards (and/or punishments) to an entire group for the extent to which the group members obey their orders and are well-behaved.

**Group facilitator**   An individual who leads a group by giving constructive feedback to members who interact with one another in such a way that positive facilitative growth is the major outcome.

**Group focus**   The extent to which most group members continue to be involved in the group's activity.

**Group investigation**   A type of learning that involves working in a cooperative manner and brainstorming. SEE: *cooperative learning, brainstorming*

**Group polarization**   An effect of group membership in which the participants adopt a more extreme form of behavior than they would have done as individuals.

**Group test**   A testing instrument designed to be given to groups such as a class of students, rather than to an individual. For example, Iowa Test of Basic Skills (ITBS) and the Scholastic Aptitude Test (SAT). Group tests can be given to many students at the same time. SEE: *individual test*

**Group therapy**   SEE: *activity group therapy*

**Grouping**   Also called homogeneous grouping, it is the placement of students together based on their abilities and interests. This is sometimes referred to as "ability" grouping. SEE: *flexible grouping, heterogeneous grouping, homogeneous grouping*

**Groupthink**   The tendency of the members of a small and cohesive group to place the cohesiveness of the group ahead of rationality in arriving at a joint decision.

**Growth spurt**   The rapid increase in height and weight that precedes full-blown adolescence; usually during ages 8–10 for girls and 10–12 for boys.

**GRP**   SEE: *Guided Reading Procedure*

**Guide dogs**   These are also known as seeing-eye dogs. They are specially trained dogs to assist the seriously visually impaired or the blind for mobility and travel. An additional factor to consider is the companionship provided by the dog.

**Guide-o-ramas**   Commercial or teacher-made reading guides that assist the reader to note certain information while reading.

**Guided discovery**   A modified form of discovery learning; the teacher is permitted to use a limited amount of direction.

**Guided reading procedure**   A reading method developed to improve an individual's ability to generate questions while reading and to organize reading material for enhanced recall (developed by Manzo, 1975).

**Guilty knowledge test**   A system for using the lie-detector apparatus or polygraph. The individual is asked a set of neutral control questions and a few questions that the individual, if he/she had never been on the scene, should not be able to answer. If the physiological responses (breathing rate, heart rate, blood pressure, and galvanic skin response) to the guilty-knowledge questions are radically different from those to the control questions, the subject is deemed to have failed the test.

**Gustation**   The sense of taste. The taste buds in the papillae of the tongue detect and interpret chemical taste stimuli in the saliva. There are four taste qualities; namely, sweet, salty, sour, and bitter.

**Habilitation**   Unlike rehabilitation, this is the training of a student or other person in skills, knowledge, and/or information that heretofore were not part of one's past experience. In other words, habilitation is the teaching of new skills and knowledge.

**Habitual pitch**   The range of sound (high or low) or a specific level of tone that a person normally uses when speaking.

**Hair cell**   A type of receptor cell associated with the inner-ear senses of hearing and balance. There is a hair or cilium extending from the receptor cell into a surrounding fluid-filled canal. The fluid moves in response to stimulation, leverage on the hair is exerted, and a generator potential results.

**Halfway house**   Usually, a residential home or other small facility used to bridge the gap for students with disabilities from institutional placement to community living. Persons who are unable to live independently in the community (e.g., the mentally retarded) are frequently placed in halfway houses as a first step in the deinstitutionalization of the disabled.

**Hallucinogens**   Also known as psychedelics. These psychoactive drugs alter consciousness to the extent that visual or auditory perception of nonexisting stimuli takes place. There is also a disturbance of time perception.

**Halo effect**   The influence of the general impression of a person upon the rating of one particular type of performance by that person.

**Hammer**   One of the three bones of the three-bone chain in the middle ear. It is shaped like a hammer and is commonly referred to as the hammer and technically referred to as the malleus. SEE: *malleus*

**Handedness**   The preference for using one hand rather than the other (left-handed, right-handed).

**Handicap**   A disadvantage of some sort. It may be the result of a physical disability or a learning disability, for example.

**Handicapism**   A term now in use by activists who are opposed to the unequal treatment frequently received by those with handicaps. The term has connotations similar to the use of the word "racism" (unequal treatment based on race compared to "handicapism," or the unequal treatment based on a handicap).

**Handicapped**   A handicapped person is one who displays several of the exceptionalities regardless of whether or not he/she requires special education. There are several handicapping conditions or problems that require special attention or consideration in our schools and communities. These include: 1. *Educable mentally retarded:* A type of mental retardation that includes students who are educable in the academic, social, and occupational areas, even though some supervision may be necessary. 2. *Trainable mentally retarded:* A form of mental retardation that includes students who are capable of very limited meaningful achievement and adaptive functioning in social and academic areas but are capable of benefitting from training in self-care and rote or simple job skills. 3. *Hard of hearing:* A type of hearing impairment, permanent or temporary, that can adversely affect a student's educational performance. The individual has some residual hearing and may benefit from hearing aids and other adaptations for the hearing impaired. 4. *Deaf:* A severe hearing loss that impairs processing of language (acquisition and usage) with or without amplification. The deaf are at a great educational disadvantage. 5. *Speech-impaired:* A communication/language disorder that may include stuttering, articulation problems, language usage, or other voice impairments that can negatively affect a student's academic and/or social functioning. 6. *Visually handicapped:* A visual impairment that, even with correctional lenses, adversely affects a student's academic and/or social performance. This category includes both partially seeing and blind children and adolescents. 7. *Seriously Emotionally Disturbed (SED):* A cognitive/behavioral disorder whereby the individual exhibits one or more of the following symptoms over a long period of time (usually more than six months) and to a marked degree with adverse effects on academic/ social/psychological functioning: (a) an inability to learn at

H

expected levels, which cannot be explained by intellectual, sensory, or health factors; (b) an inability to create or maintain satisfactory interpersonal relationships with family members, peers, teachers, and other adults; (c) inappropriate behaviors or feelings under normal circumstances (i.e., abnormal behaviors would be expected when there is a death of someone particularly close, for example); (d) a general pervasive mood of sadness, unhappiness, or depression; and (e) a tendency to develop physical symptoms (e.g., stomach ache, headache) or fears related to personal or school problems. The term SED includes individuals who are schizophrenic or autistic. 8. *Orthopedically impaired:* A severe orthopedic (related to bones and bone structures) impairment that can adversely affect an individual's educational and social experiences. The term includes problems caused by congenital anomalies (clubfoot) or diseases as well as those from other causes (e.g., accidents). 9. *Other health-impairments:* There are acute health problems that can limit a child or adolescent's physical strength, alertness, and cognitive functioning and, as a result, negatively impact educational experiences. These would include problems like heart conditions, AIDS, venereal diseases, tuberculosis, rheumatic fever, nephritis, asthma, sickle-cell anemia, hemophilia, epilepsy, lead poisoning, cancer, leukemia, or diabetes. 10. *Specific learning-disabled:* Disorders in one or more of the basic psychological processes involved in understanding or using language, spoken or written, which may be manifested in impairments in listening, thinking, speaking, reading, writing, spelling, or math. The term currently includes children who have learning problems that are primarily the result of visual, hearing, or motor handicaps, of mental retardation, or of environmental, cultural, or economic disadvantage. Learning disabilities are thought to be a result of some type of neurological dysfunctioning, persisting over time, which is familial in nature, cross cultural, and involves social

misperceptiveness. 11. *Deaf-blind:* A combination of hearing and visual impairments that can result in severe language/communication problems and other developmental, social, and educational problems that require very specialized programming. 12. *Multihandicapped:* Concomitant impairments (such as mentally retarded-deaf, mentally retarded-epileptic, etc.) excluding the deaf-blind students who make up another category. Usually the problems associated with multiple handicaps cause severe social and educational problems that cannot be accommodated in regular/special education programs solely for one of the impairments. See the above italicized terms for more information.

**Haptics** The science of tactile and kinesthetic sensation (i.e., the sense of touch).

**Hard-drive program** Some computers use hard disks, usually called hard drives, and these are frequently built right into the base of the computer. A hard drive has a large storage capacity (20 megabytes [MB] to 80 or more MB) and is suitable for special education programs in that they can store frequently used paperwork data and programs. SEE: *CD-ROM, megabytes*

**Hard of hearing** SEE: *hearing impaired*

**Harshness** A term used to describe a quality of speech that is strident, discordant, perhaps coarse, loud, and/or obtrusive, as well as unpleasant to hear.

**Hashimoto's struma** (Hakura Hashimoto, Japanese surgeon, 1881–1934) Sometimes erroneously called Hashimoto's disease, it is a condition characterized by chronic inflammation and enlargement of the thyroid gland. SEE: *thyroid*

**Hawthorne effect** A change in performance by a group of research subjects, workers, or students, primarily resulting from their knowledge that they are being observed rather than from a variable being manipulated by the observers.

**Head Start program** Federally funded programs at the preschool level that are designed to provide learning/social experiences for underprivileged and children with disabilities. SEE: *handicapped*

**Head teacher** 1. The early American educational practice of having a teacher serving as a principal (administrator) and a teacher at the same time. 2. The current practice of having a particular teacher who is well versed in the pedagogy of the level served become a mentor or leader of other teachers at that level or discipline.

**Health disability impairment** A chronic condition resulting from health problems that interferes with the physical and emotional well-being of students or persons. Normal development to include schooling may be interrupted. Such impairments require special-needs equipment, accommodations, or programs. For example, students with asthma, diabetes, epilepsy, allergies, etc. Normally, these conditions are chronic and require continued medical attention.

**Health disorder** A medical condition or disease not as severe as a disability that is disruptive to one's overall living or to a specific activity but does not necessarily interfere with one's ability to move about physically in general. Such conditions include but are not limited to heart problems, asthma, AIDS, anemia, etc. SEE: *health disability impairment*

**Health psychology** A field of applied psychology in which psychological knowledge is employed in the prevention and/or treatment of medical complaints. An example of health psychology in action would be the modification of health-impairing behavior patterns.

**Hearing aid** An electromechanical apparatus used to amplify sound and used to assist persons with hearing impairments in order to compensate for any loss of hearing.

**Hearing impaired** A hearing loss from mild to severe wherein it is difficult but not impossible to comprehend speech or to hear sounds with the ear alone, with or without sound amplification (e.g., a hearing aid).

**Hearing impairment** A term used in special education and in general to indicate a student or other individual having some type of hearing loss. This loss might be mild (–27 to –40 decibels), moderate (–41 to –55 dB), or moderate-severe (–56 to –70 dB). These classifications are considered "hard of hearing." To be classified as "deaf," hearing losses must be as follows: severe (–71 to –90 dB) and profound (–91 dB or greater). Note: dB is the symbol for decibel(s), units of loudness. SEE: *decibel (dB)*

**Hearing loss, types of** There are three major types of hearing loss: conductive, sensorineural, and mixed. A conductive hearing loss results from damage to the outer or middle ears, which impedes sound transmission to the inner ear. A sensorineural hearing loss involves damage to the inner ear and auditory nerve. The third type of loss, or mixed type, involves both conductive and sensorineural impairments. SEE: *conductive, sensorineural, and mixed hearing loss*

**Hearing threshold** The point or level at which a student can hear the softest sound at each frequency tested.

**Heart failure** 1. Stoppage of the heart beat. 2. A condition wherein the heart fails to maintain adequate blood circulation. May be caused by the failure of either the left or right ventricle or both. SEE: *congestive heart failure, ventricle*

**Heart Rate Response Audiometry (HRRA)** Used to determine auditory thresholds through changes in electrocardiogram responses to auditory stimuli. SEE: *electrocardiogram*

**Heat exhaustion** Also known as heat prostration, a condition characterized by nausea, headache, weakness, and collapse. While the body temperature is usually normal the skin is clammy, pale, and cold, and the pupils are normal. Students or persons should be taken to a cool place, clothes should be loosened and the head placed low. Usually caused by exposure to heat and loss of normal body fluids and salt from the body. Heat exhaustion should not be confused with heatstroke (sunstroke). SEE: *heatstroke*

H

**Heatstroke** Also known as hyperpyrexia or sunstroke, a condition characterized by headache, fast pulse, numbness, confusion, delirium, and cessation of perspiring. The body temperature is very high (105 degrees and up), the face is red and dry, and the skin is hot and dry. Students or persons should be taken to a cool place and preferably placed in an ice bath or covered with wet sheets. Keep head elevated. Usually caused by exposure to the sun. Heatstroke should not be confused with heat exhaustion. SEE: *heat exhaustion*

**Hebephrenia/hebephrenic** An older name for the disorganized form of schizophrenia. Its usual age of onset is before 20 years. The person exhibits bizarre and silly childlike behavior. A student with hebephrenia may be bouncing off the wall (so to speak) one minute and then down and depressed another. It is not uncommon for students to show senseless thought processes, hallucinations, and delusions. Sometimes these students will laugh out loud for no apparent reason, babble incoherently, make funny faces, and posture in a strange and absurd fashion. SEE: *schizophrenia*

**Heimlich maneuver** (H. J. Heimlich, contemporary American surgeon, 1920) A special technique used to dislodge food or a foreign object lodged in the pharynx or trachea that is preventing the flow of air to the lungs. It is an effective method that forces air against the obstruction and thus dislodges it. The Heimlich maneuver consists of three steps as follows: 1. wrap both arms from behind around the person's waist, 2. make a fist with either hand and place it against the abdomen between the rib cage and the navel, and 3. clasp your fist with your other hand and press inward and upward in a forceful manner. Repeat several times and continue as necessary. Call 911 if needed.

**Heller's disease** A cerebral degenerative disorder. The degeneration of the brain causes speech and language disabilities as well as impaired mental development and loss of normal motor functioning.

**Hemianopia** A condition characterized by no vision for half of the normal field of view (e.g., left hemianopia allows only vision on the right side of the usual visual field).

**Hemiplegia** A condition that involves paralysis of one half of the body (the right or left half).

**Hemispheres** The two sides of the cerebral cortex. At first glance, the left hemisphere seems to be a mirror image of the right. However, there are differences in detail. The left hemisphere extends farther back and the right hemisphere extends farther forward. Also, certain structures are much larger on one side than the other. SEE: *hemispheric differences*

**Hemispheric differences** The unique functions of one hemisphere of the cortex that are not matched by the other. For example, the control of expressive language and of language reception is normally restricted to one hemisphere (the so-called "dominant hemisphere"), which is (in most persons) the left hemisphere.

**Hemispheric specialization** The concept of the lateralization of certain behavioral and physiological functions in either the left or the right side of the brain. Usually, such specialization is confined to the cerebral cortex, but the thalamus is involved to some extent as well. SEE: *hemispheric differences, laterality*

**Hemolytic disease** A disease characterized by destruction of red blood cells in the fetus as a result of opposite and incompatible Rh factors between the mother and the fetus. SEE: *Rh incompatibility*

**Hemophilia** A genetic sex-linked blood disorder (almost always affecting males) that is transmitted by a recessive gene from the mother. The hemophiliac's blood is not able to clot properly, causing excess bleeding with injuries. Frequent blood transfusions are needed with injuries. These individuals are

**H**

excessively sensitive to any blow to the body and are easily bruised.

**Herbartian teaching method**  An organized method based on the principles of Pestalozzi that stresses learning by association and consists of five steps (preparation, presentation, association, generalization, and application).

**Heritability**  A statistical index of the extent to which variations in a given trait (anatomical or behavioral) can be attributed to hereditary factors.

**Hermaphrodite**  A person exhibiting the characteristics of both a male and a female. A true hermaphrodite has one testis and one ovary; such cases are very rare. Most hermaphrodites are "pseudo-hermaphrodites"; for unknown reasons, they have not matured completely either as males or as females.

**Heroin**  A narcotic drug that is very addictive in nature. It is derived from morphine and usually is in the form of a white crystalline powder. It is not currently used medically. SEE: *morphine, opium*

**Herpes genital**  A type of herpes wherein lesions appear on the genitals. It is considered a form of Sexually Transmitted Disease (STD).

**Herpes simplex**  A recurring infectious disease caused by the herpes simplex virus (Herpesvirus hominis). Usually, it affects the eye and especially the gums and lips. This disease is commonly referred to as "cold sores" or "fever blisters." SEE: *herpes zoster*

**Herpes zoster**  An infectious disease that is caused by the virus "varicella-zoster," the same virus that causes chicken pox. It affects only a limited number of cranial or spinal nerves. Eruptions that are almost always unilateral occur along the nerve pathways. This disease is commonly called "shingles." SEE: *herpes simplex*

**Hertz (Hz)**  Cycles per second. A measure of the frequency of an energy wave such as light, sound, or the Electroencephalogram (EEG) waves.

**Heterochromia iridis**  A condition in which the eyes are of different colors (i.e., both eyes are not the same color).

**Heterogeneity**  In education, the mixing of students regardless of ability level. One finds many variations of ability in a class of students grouped together in this fashion. SEE: *homogeneous grouping*

**Heterogeneous grouping**  The grouping of students for instructional purposes into classes with the make-up of the class consisting of individuals with a wide range of abilities and talents (as opposed to homogeneous grouping where students are grouped because of similar levels of ability or functioning). SEE: *P.L. 94-142*

**Heuristic**  A general approach to solving a problem. It has a guiding function but, unlike an algorithm, it is not an exact procedure that inevitably leads to the solution.

**Hidden observer**  In Ernest Hilgard's theory of hypnotism, this is part of the hypnotized person's consciousness that remains independent of the hypnotist's controlling influence.

**Hierarchy of needs**  In Abraham Maslow's model of motivation, this is a five-level categorization of human motives. The basic level consists of physiological motives. In ascending order, the other levels are: safety/security needs, social/love needs, self-esteem motives, and the need for self-actualization (total fulfillment of one's potential).

**High achievers**  Students or persons who do well because they expect to be successful and in fact are. Such persons view their success as an incentive to even greater achievement.

**High-risk children**  A term used to describe children who because of an assortment of physical, mental, and/or developmental problems, will in all probability be in need of special education services in the future. This includes physical, health, medical, psychological, and/or educational services, etc.

***High School: A Report on Secondary Education in America***  A Carnegie

**H**

Foundation for the Advancement of Teaching Report in 1983 which recommended 12 priority reforms needed to restructure and improve the quality of education services at the secondary level.

**High school diploma** A high school diploma or certificate certifies that a student has successfully completed a course of study at the secondary level (usually grades 9–12).

**High school equivalency** A certificate which verifies that an individual has successfully completed a battery of examinations that are considered equivalent to the general educational level of a high school graduate. These equivalency diplomas are normally awarded by state departments of education. A GED diploma (General Educational Development) is awarded. SEE: *General Educational Development test (GED)*

**High-stakes testing** A situation of heavy reliance on standardized tests on the part of administrators and/or employers in guiding their decisions about students or workers.

**High-tech devices** Any technical device used to enhance learning or to assist the handicapped, the physically disabled, and/or the health impaired. Examples would include but are not limited to computers, infusion pumps (for persons with diabetes), and the Xerox Kurtzweil Reading Machine for the blind.

**Higher-level processes** Cognitive processes more complex than rote memorization. These include problem-solving, analysis, and interpretation.

**Higher-level questions** Test questions that require testees to use their knowledge in order to solve novel problems or to apply it in novel situations. These questions may require students to analyze or synthesize concepts and/or make evaluations.

**Higher-order interaction** A statistical concept. An interaction occurs when one independent variable (causal factor) modifies the effect of another independent variable on some behavioral

(result) variable. When more than two independent variables are involved, the interaction becomes a higher-order interaction.

**Hindbrain** One of the three main divisions of the brain. The hindbrain includes the medulla, the pons, and the cerebellum.

**Hippocampus** A structure in the limbic system that is part of the "old" cerebral cortex, the hippocampus is involved in the storage of memories. Individuals with damage to this area cannot retain new memories (anterograde amnesia). SEE: *limbic system, cerebral cortex*

**Hippocrates** (Greek physician, fifth and fourth century B.C.) Commonly known as the "Father of Medicine" and author of the "Hippocratic oath." SEE: *Hippocratic oath*

**Hippocratic oath** A system of ethical standards written by a fifth and fourth century B.C. Greek physician. Many of these standards are still applicable to the medical community today. SEE: *Hippocrates*

**Hirsutism** A condition characterized by excessive body hair.

**Hispanics** Refers to individuals of Spanish heritage who are descended from the peoples of Latin America, Spain, or Portugal.

**Histogram** A graph of a frequency distribution in which the frequency of each score is represented by the height of a rectangle (bar graph).

**Historicism** An approach to the history of knowledge that requires viewing the past in its own terms, as opposed to criticizing the contributions of ancient and medieval thinkers for not reflecting an understanding of modern science and/or technology.

**HIV (Human Immunodeficiency Virus)** HIV is a virus of the immune system that is transmitted from person-to-person contact (e.g., sexual relations, sharing needles during intravenous drug use) and not casual contact (e.g., hugging, kissing). The person's immune system usually weakens over a period of

**H**

years (i.e., around seven years) until the individual is quite disabled. AIDS is the final stage of the HIV infection. AIDS is mostly fatal but being infected with the HIV virus is not the equivalent to having AIDS. SEE: *Acquired Immune Deficiency Syndrome (AIDS), Human T-Lymphotrophic Virus Type III (HTLV-III), lymphadenopathy associated virus*

**Hoarseness**   A term used to describe a quality of speech that is coarse or rough in sound, such as in the case of someone with a cold or laryngitis.

**Hodgkin's disease**   (Thomas Hodgkin, British physician, 1798–1866) A lymphatic disease of unknown origin. It produces progressive enlargement of the nodes of the lymphatic system as well as the liver and spleen along with other tissue. There is lymphoid infiltration of blood vessels and bone marrow resulting in anemia (a disorder of the red blood cells). Lymphogranulomatosis may be present; that is, the development of multiple granular tumors. SEE: *anemia*

**Holism**   A philosophy that dictates that individuals function as a complete whole unit and cannot be separated in parts as such. Originally presented by Jan C. Smuts.

**Holistic scoring**   The grading of any learning outcome (e.g., essay) with one score representing the quality of the essay or work being assessed as opposed to a number or letter grade. For example, a holistic reading score for a book review could involve evaluating 1. comprehension and meaning, 2. topic familiarity/prior knowledge, 3. presentation style, 4. adherence to writing standards specified by the teacher, and 5. logical/sequential development of the topic. The opposite approach is called "analytic scoring." SEE: *analytic scoring*

**Holmes group**   A group of individuals from large research-based universities who believe that undergraduate training should focus on a strong liberal arts curriculum with teacher-preparation program requirements primarily given at the graduate (i.e., master's degree) level. SEE: *Holmes Group Report*

**Holmes Group Report**   A report published in 1989 by a group of education college deans from major universities which recommended that teacher education requirements be offered only at the master's level after students have obtained liberal arts degrees at the bachelor's level. Standards for faculty in higher teacher education were recommended along with specific commitments and goals on the part of the institution. The *Holmes Report,* which was written by deans from colleges of education around the country, urged teacher-preparation programs to institute entry-level standards for teachers, to be committed to increased diversity in program planning efforts, to develop university-school partnerships, to stress intellectual soundness, etc.

**Holophrases**   Single words that convey complex ideas.

**Holophrastic speech**   Using single words in the place of entire phrases or sentences. This is an early stage in the acquisition of language by an infant.

**Home or hospital teacher**   SEE: *home study, hospital and homebound instruction*

**Home study**   A more and more popular method of instruction designed for students who live at a distance from educational institutions, those who are too ill to attend school, or for students whose parents are not satisfied with the community school programs. Instructional materials can be provided to students and students must be subject to standardized assessments to measure achievement, which in turn are submitted to school boards or teaching institutions for evaluation. SEE: *hospital and homebound instruction*

**Homeostasis**   The ability of the body to maintain steady states for such variables as blood pressure, temperature, blood-oxygen level, blood glucose level, and salt/water balance. This is often referred to as an internal equilibrium.

**Homogeneous grouping**   The grouping or classifying of students according to one or more attributes. Students are usually grouped by ability level (as opposed to heterogeneous grouping where students with differing ability levels are grouped). Frequently, schools will provide homogeneous tracks or groups for math classes and the like whereby students at certain levels of functioning would be in the same group or class. Homogeneous grouping can be done within a class or between classrooms.

**Homographs**   Words that have the same spelling but different meanings. For example, the word *run* has at least 130 different meanings (as in a *run* down the street, a *run* for political office, a *run* in one's stocking, a truck *run* down the highway, etc.).

**Homonym** or **Homophone**   Words that sound alike but have different spellings and meanings (e.g., too, to, and two; see, sea; fare, fair).

**Homophenes**   Sounds that are identical when articulation lip movements are made. For example, lipreaders cannot differentiate between the letter p and b when others are speaking. Context and other letters allow one to fill in the missing gaps.

**Homophile**   A homosexual person. Someone who is attracted to another sexually of the same gender.

**Homophone**   SEE: *homonym*

**Homosexuality**   Typically, being attracted to and preferring to have sexual relations with members of one's own sex.

**Honig v. Doe**   A legal decision regarding the suspension and expulsion of students with disabilities. A Supreme Court decision, 108 S. Ct 592 (1988), stating that suspension of up to 10 days does not constitute a change of placement in an IEP under the EHA/IDEA but suspensions of over 10 days or indefinite suspensions violate the EHA/IDEA's "stay put" provision. The Court further ruled that expelling a student when a student's misbehavior is caused by his/her special need or disability is illegal. SEE: *P.L. 94-142, Education for All Handicapped Act (EHA); and P.L. 101-476, Individuals with Disabilities Education Act (IDEA)*

**Honors section**   Special sections or classes established for high-achieving students in an academic area.

**Hoover cane**   A long white cane usually tipped in red or a fluorescent color (e.g., orange) that is used by the blind or severely visually impaired for mobility and travel.

**Hormone**   A secretion from an endocrine or ductless gland. The secretion from a ductless gland has to travel via the bloodstream to its site of action. Most hormones chemically are polypeptides. The hormones from the gonads and the adrenal cortex, however, are chemically classified as steroids.

**Hornbook**   A common teaching tool in colonial times. Single-page pieces of paper were attached to a sheet of cow's horn which was then tacked to a piece of wood resembling a paddle. This paddle was worn around the neck for easy carrying. Papers on the hornbooks contained math facts, the alphabet, words, prayers, etc. and were frequently the child's first book or preprimer.

**Hospice**   A medical facility that provides terminally ill patients with total psychological and physical care. The three tenets of the hospice concept include pain control, providing care if possible in the familiarity of the patient's home, and allowing control of treatment and care to remain in the hands of the patient, caregiver, and family.

**Hospice movement**   A movement advocating that care for the terminally ill should be provided in the familiarity of the patient's home when possible, or in comfortable settings similar to the home environment. It also advocates alleviation of pain with proper medications and allowing control of treatment and care (decision making) to remain in the hands of the patient, caregiver, and family.

**Hospital and homebound instruction**   While this service may be provided to any regular day or special-needs child, it is normally a service delivered to a child who is on an individual education plan in a hospital or home setting so long as the student is unable to attend regular school. This type of service is usually temporary in nature except in the case of severe illnesses or disabilities.

**Hot line**  A 24-hour telephone service to assist persons; that is, to provide comfort and/or information in a very timely fashion, such as a suicide hot line, 911 emergency line, prayer lines, abuse and neglect lines, etc.

**Household**  Consists of all individuals (related and unrelated) who occupy a household unit. A condominium, house, apartment, multiple-family dwelling, single room, etc. are regarded as housing units when occupied. A household includes related family members (biological and adopted) and all unrelated persons, roomers, foster children, wards, or other individuals who share the housing unit. A person living alone in a housing unit is also counted as a household.

**Householder**  The actually named person or persons in whose name(s) the dwelling is listed as owners, rentees, or leasees. If property is owned, rented, or leased jointly, then each person (husband and wife) is considered a householder. SEE: *household*

**HRRA**  SEE: *Heart Rate Response Audiometry*

**HTLV III (Human T-Lymphotrophic Virus Type III)**  Also known as one of the AIDS viruses. SEE: *Human Immunodeficiency Virus (HIV), Acquired Immune Deficiency Syndrome (AIDS)*

**Human ecology**  The study of a total system of influences/situations that affect the actions/lifestyles of the people of that system. A classroom environment is a study of human ecology as several influences/variables/individuals influence the social/emotional/cultural qualities of the classroom.

**Human Immunodeficiency Virus** SEE: *HIV*

**Human T-lymphotrophic VirusType III**  SEE: *HTLV III*

**Humanism**  The approach in the philosophy of education which holds that humans are essentially good but are corrupted by the social order. Therefore, the task of the schools is to be liberating and to allow human freedom to find expression. This view is related to the philosophy of naturalism that was founded by Rousseau. According to this philosophy, the individual student should be allowed to make the important choices relating to the student's own education. A modern educational humanist was A. S. Neill, author of the influential book *Sunmerhill.* SEE: *existentialism, naturalism, philosophy of education*

**Humanist**  An individual who is focused on the human needs and interests of his/her learners. SEE: *humanistic approach*

**Humanistic approach**  The approach that focuses on psychological or emotional conflicts within the individual that influence behaviors. Proponents of this approach believe that these internal conflicts interfere with the coping mechanisms of the individual. Treatment involves being open to alternative approaches and the individual learning styles, interests, and needs of the individual. The teacher is encouraged to become a friend of the student and a facilitator of his/her learning.

**Humanistic teacher education**  A type of education concerned with training prospective teachers as real and caring persons. Emotional and attitudinal growth and development activities as well as reflective practices are employed. SEE: *humanistic approach*

**Hunter's disease**  (C. H. Hunter, Canadian physician, contemporary) A metabolic disease also known as mucopolysaccharidosis, it is characterized by mental retardation, skeletal abnormalities, heart disease, enlargement of the liver, and clawlike hands. Children usually die in the first 10 years of life but with milder forms they may live into their 60s. SEE: *Hurler's disease*

**Huntington's chorea**  (G. Huntington, American physician, 1850–1916) A genetically transmitted disease of the central nervous system (CNS), its onset is usually between 30 to 50 years. It is a presenile dementia characterized by bizarre and spasmodic movements of the limbs as well as strange behavior and mental retardation.

**Hurler's disease** (Gertrud Hurler, Austrian pediatrician 1889–1965) A hereditary disorder of the metabolism also known as lipochondrodystrophy, it can cause mental retardation in a child if left untreated. There is a congenital abnormality of the bones and cartilage, kyphosis (hunchback), and other physical abnormalities such as a flat, broad nose, thick lips, and cloudy corneas. SEE: *Hunter's disease*

**Hydrocephalus** A condition that involves excess pressure from cerebrospinal fluid buildup inside the head precipitated by tumors, meningitis, encephalitis, etc. The fluid in essence is blocked and cannot circulate resulting in excess pressure and an enlargement of the head. This condition results in mental retardation, the degree of which depends on how early the condition is detected and treated. Treatment involves placing a shunt or tube in the head area to drain the fluid. SEE: *Cerebrospinal Fluid (CSF)*

**Hyperactivity** Higher-than-normal levels of expected physical activity. There is an increased tendency to fidget, move about in one's seat, move from place-to-place, and not attend to tasks for long periods of time. Such individuals may require medical interventions (e.g., drug treatment). SEE: *Attention-Deficit/ Hyperactivity Disorder (ADHD)*

**Hyperglycemia** A condition characterized by abnormally high levels of glucose or sugar dextrose in the blood, it is often related to diabetes (excess sugar in the blood). It can make one more susceptible to infection and can result in coma (diabetic coma). SEE: *diabetes*

**Hyperkinesis** A condition characterized by a high rate of sustained motor activity. Persons or students with this condition just cannot seem to sit still; they are always on the "go," so to speak. SEE: *hypokinesis*

**Hyperkinetic behavior** Behavior that involves excessive physical activity in an inappropriate fashion. Hyperkinetic behavior is a component of Attention-Deficit/Hyperactivity Disorder (ADHD). SEE: *hyperactivity, Attention-Deficit/ Hyperactivity Disorder (ADHD)*

**Hypermnesia** 1. Hypnotically induced recall. The validity of hypnotically induced memories is questionable. Hypnosis leads to an increase in the number of reported memories, some of them true and some false. 2. An outstanding/ extraordinary ability to remember names, dates, and other facts.

**Hypernasality** A disorder of speech involving voice resonance. Too much air passing through the nasal cavity gives the voice of the speaker a higher pitched, irritating, whining sound which most listeners find to be unpleasant. SEE: *hyponasality*

**Hyperopia** Farsightedness. The inability to see close objects clearly. This is attributed to a shortening of the eyeball so that the focal point for rays of incoming light is behind the retina.

**Hypertelorism** A cranial facial anomaly characterized by an excessive distance between the eyes. It could also be an excessive or abnormal width between two paired organs other than the eyes.

**Hypertension** A medical term for high blood pressure. It is usually a result of constriction of the peripheral blood vessels but it can be psychological as well. It is usually reported as a set of numbers such as 150 (systolic) over 90 (diastolic); this is also the generally accepted limit for high blood pressure. Systolic means the amount of blood ejected from the heart during contraction of the ventricle. Diastolic means the least pressure in the arterial system while the heart dilates and fills with blood.

**Hyperthyroidism** Also called Grave's disease, it is a medical condition caused by an overactive thyroid gland that produces too much thyroxin (the thyroid hormone). Students or persons with this condition have a higher rate of metabolism. Such persons are tense, anxious,

H

inattentive in class, have finger tremors when the hand is extended, have weight loss, and are generally nervous in nature. Students with hyperthyroidism find it difficult to sit still. SEE: *hypothyroidism*

**Hypertonicity**   SEE: *hypertonus*

**Hypertonus**   Greater than normal muscle tension in the form of spasms.

**Hyperventilation**   A term used to describe very rapid and deep breathing. Such activity can cause one to become lightheaded or dizzy as a result of carbon dioxide depletion. This condition is usually accompanied by very marked anxiety. Breathing into a paper bag (nose and mouth in bag) or pressing one nostril closed as well as keeping the mouth closed and thus breathing only through one nostril will relieve these symptoms by returning carbon dioxide levels to normal.

**Hypnosis**   An altered state of consciousness actively induced by another person, the hypnotist. The hypnotic subject responds to the commands of the hypnotist by altering her/his sensations, behaviors, and cognitive processes.

**Hypoactivity**   A term similar to hypokinesis that indicates a lack of activity and lethargy. Activity is abnormally low and severely restricted. SEE: *hypokinesis*

**Hypochondriacal delusion**   A condition in which a person believes he/she is suffering from some sort of bizarre and exotic disease or medical disorder.

**Hypochondriacal neurosis**   A condition in which a person always thinks that something is physically, mentally, or medically wrong with himself/herself. Such a person is anxious about bodily functions as well as preoccupied with the idea that he/she is ill or suffers from some medical disorder or disease. SEE: *hypochondriasis*

**Hypochondriasis**   The tendency to interpret any slight internal sensation as a dangerous symptom of some disease process. This is classified as a somatoform disorder in the *Diagnostic and Statistical Manual of Mental Disorders, IV*

**Hypoglycemia**   A condition wherein the blood contains abnormally low amounts of glucose or sugar dextrose, as it is sometimes called. Persons suffer acute fatigue, general weakness, and malaise. In severe cases delirium, coma, and death may result.

**Hypokinesis**   A condition in which movement and motor activity is severely restricted. Persons with this condition tend to be sluggish, listless, and poky. It is the opposite of hyperkinesis.

**Hyponasality**   A disorder of speech involving voice resonance. Too little air passing through the nasal cavity gives the voice of the speaker a quality of sound as if one has a head cold. SEE: *hypernasality*

**Hyporesponsive**   A student or person who is slow to respond such as in the case of some persons with learning disabilities.

**Hypothalamus**   A part of the forebrain involved in emotional and motivational processes. It helps to regulate eating, drinking, sexual activity, sleeping and waking cycles, body temperature, and emergency reactions. The hypothalamus is directly connected to both the anterior and the posterior pituitary glands. Its functions are also linked to those of the autonomic nervous system.

**Hypothesis**   An educated guess or proposed relationship between events that are either observed or imagined. It is also, in research, the primary assumption or prediction of the results of a study or experiment.

**Hypothetic-deductive reasoning**   An approach to problem solving, with the individual identifying all the variables that could be involved in a problem situation, then going on to deduce the logical consequences of the action of each of those variables, and finally testing to see if those consequences do occur. The process continues until all the deduced possible solutions have been tested.

**Hypothyroidism**   A medical condition characterized by slow metabolism as a result of an underactive thyroid gland that does not produce sufficient thyroxin

**H**

(the thyroid hormone). It is in fact a lesser form of cretinism. Symptoms include obesity, lethargy, low blood pressure, sluggishness with low tolerance for sustained activity, and in general a lackluster approach to schooling or life. It is the opposite of hyperthyroidism. SEE: *hyperthyroidism, cretinism, thyroid, thyroid hormones*

**Hypotonia** Loss of muscle tone to a point where it is difficult to move body parts. It is considered a type of cerebral palsy. SEE: *cerebral palsy*

**Hypotonicity** SEE: *hypotonia*

**Hypoxia** A condition that prevents enough oxygen from reaching tissues in the body.

**Hysteria** A condition of emotion and excitement characterized by excessive anxiety, sensory motor disturbances, and sometimes organic disorders for which no organic cause is apparent, such as an inability to walk, deafness, blindness, etc. SEE: *hysterical neurosis, hysterical personality*

**Hysterical neurosis** A physical or psychological state of anxiety in which a person involuntarily loses some normal bodily or mental function. The individual completely denies that the anxiety exists and may be the reason for the loss of normal function. SEE: *hysteria*

**Hysterical personality** A category of personality wherein the individual appears to be emotionally unstable. Further characteristics include an abnormal desire for attention, overdependence on others, self-dramatics, and egocentric behavior. SEE: *hysteria, hysterical neurosis*

**"I" message** The announcement in clear, unambiguous language that one is being affected by something. This type of statement, moreover, is not accusatory or blaming. Example: "I" am feeling very tense about our upcoming final exam.

**ICF** SEE: *Intermediate Core Facility for the Mentally Retarded/Developmentally Disabled*

**Icon** A brief visual mental image that will persist for about one-half-second. This would be the image you see after you stare at an object and then close your eyes.

**Iconic memory** Visual sensory memory. Our iconic memories can hold between nine to ten items as opposed to about five items one can store in echoic (auditory) memory. Typically visual stimuli remain in iconic memory for less than half a second after stimuli(us) have been removed. Most physiologists believe that iconic memory involves more than receptor functions; that is, higher level visual processing. SEE: *engram, memory trace, encoding, echoic memory, motor code, linguistics, linguistic code*

**Id** One of the three components of the personality, in Freud's psychoanalytic theory. The id houses the primitive, instinctual, animal drives (including sex and aggression) and acts in accordance with the pleasure principle.

**IDEA**   The Individuals with Disabilities Education Act, P.L. 101-476, (1990), which was formerly called Education of the Handicapped Act (EHA), P.L. 94-142 (1975), ensures that special-needs students receive an appropriate education in the least restrictive environment. SEE: *P.L. 94-142, Appendix 3: MARCS and MAPP*

**Idea mapping**   A method of representing the structure of expository text by using visual-spatial conceptions for diagramming ideas and the relations between ideas (e.g., cause and effect) (developed by Armbruster and Anderson, 1982).

**Idealism**   The pure philosophical position that adheres to the belief that the senses deceive us. Deductive logic is necessary as reality exists in the human mind. The idea of a physical thing such as a school is what is real, for example, and not the physical structure. Idealists study the great and enduring ideas of great thinkers (e.g., Martin Luther King and Mother Theresa) and search for universal truths (e.g., What is beauty?). The role of the teacher is to be a good role model and to be the transmitter of the cultural heritage of the times. Kant (1724–1804), Hegel (1770–1831), and Plato (427–347 B.C.) were famous idealists from previous centuries.

**Identical (or monozygotic) twins**   Twins having the same genes because their birth has resulted from a single fertilized egg or zygote. The zygote splits into two identical cells, with each cell having exactly the same genome (set of genes) as the other. If these two were each to split in the same manner again, identical quadruplets would result. Identical twins have to be of the same sex. Out of every thousand births, there are about four sets of identical twins. SEE: *twin, identical*

**Identification**   Any system that is designed to seek out disabled students. Prekindergarten screening to identify students with potential special needs would be an example. One of the Freudian defense mechanisms. One protects oneself from anxieties and painful feelings by taking on the characteristics of someone else, a person stronger and better-equipped than the individual is. Children often resort to identification and it may be part of the natural process of gaining maturity and confidence. In pathological extreme cases of this defense, paranoid schizophrenics may believe themselves to be incarnations of great military conquerors or godlike figures.

**Identity**   Erikson's definition of our stable sense of self where we depend on ourselves rather than others (e.g., parents) for direction in such areas as conduct, decision making, etc.

**Identity (in Erikson's theory)**   The answer to a person's struggle to define himself/herself.

**Identity achievement**   The commitment to an approach to life that has been reached after the free consideration of several alternatives.

**Identity diffusion**   A state of doubt and confusion about the future direction of one's own life.

**Identity foreclosure**   The acceptance of a life choice provided by parents (or other authority figures) without freely considering other options.

**Identity versus role confusion**   In Erikson's stage theory of personality development, this is the stage reached by most people at the onset of adolescence. Successful growth is reflected in the establishment of a clear sense of personal identity. This stage corresponds to Freud's genital stage; in Erikson's system, further personal growth is required beyond this stage, whereas in Freud's theory this is the most mature stage.

**Idiopathic**   Symptoms of a problem or a disease that are present without clear causation. Spontaneous symptoms appear to emerge with no known cause.

**Idiopathic epilepsy**   Epilepsy with no clear etiology. One can not determine its cause.

**Idiot savant**   A mentally deficient, retarded, or mentally impaired individual who displays a special ability or talent in a single or limited area (e.g., memorizing dates, playing the violin, etc.). The term "savant" or "savant syndrome" is replacing the less flattering term, "idiot savant." SEE: *savant syndrome*

**IEP (Individualized Education Plan)** A written individualized educational plan that is prepared for students with special needs; an educational plan developed by a team that decides on the general goals and specific objectives for a special-needs student. An IEP presents current levels of functioning, background data, test information, long-term and short-term goals and objectives, services to be provided, time frames for service delivery, and plans for assessing progress and planned programs. The IEP must be signed by the parent or guardian, the principal or director of the facility, and the special education administrator after a team evaluation and appropriate assessments have been completed. While parental signatures are required, students can sign after the age of 18. This is a requirement under P.L. 94-142. SEE: *P.L. 94-142, evaluation team*

**IFSP (Individualized Family Service Plan)** A special needs program or plan that not only identifies and meets the needs of a young child but includes the family as well. An IFSP usually refers to plans implemented with preschool children whereas an IEP usually refers to plans implemented with grade school students. However, the family is involved in both programs and the terms can usually be used interchangeably. SEE: *P.L. 99-457*

**IGE** SEE: *Individually Guided Education*

**IIS** SEE: *Integrated Instructional System*

**ILE** SEE: *Individual Learning Expectation*

**Illusory contours** The perception of edges that do not belong to any actual stimuli. These are demonstrated by Gestalt psychologists who employ incomplete pictures that we, the observers, tend to fill in automatically.

**Illustrator study** An in-depth exploration wherein all the works (illustrations) of an illustrator are studied. Students are expected to become familiar at identifying the works of a certain illustrator with this particular learning structure. SEE: *author study*

**ILS** SEE: *Integrated Learning System*

**Imagery** The formation of mental images based on past sensations. Imagery may result from such processes as memory, dreaming, hypnosis, meditation, drug effects, and imagination.

**Imaginative** In language arts, the use of words to create images or mental pictures in a creative and novel fashion.

**IMC** SEE: *Instructional Materials Center*

**Imitation** A kind of learning that partly involves the formation of stimulus-response associations, as in conditioning, and also requires a higher-order cognitive process such as perceptual judgment. The learner watches another individual, the model, perform the response to be learned. The model may receive reinforcement, punishment or neither. The watcher learns the response in all three cases, but will perform the response (imitation) if the model's action has been reinforced. This type of learning is also called observation learning, modeling, or social learning.

**Immersion** 1. In language arts, the system of totally involving or flooding the student from infancy with language. 2. In the United States, total immersion would mean classes in English-only for immigrant or non-English-speaking children.

**Immune system** Bodily system that protects the body from viruses, bacteria, and other dangers to health. The major active body parts or materials that participate in immunity are 1. antibodies, which are usually produced in reaction to a vaccination and/or 2. the body cells themselves, reacting against the antigens, which include red blood cells, pollen, transplanted tissue, or even the patient's own tissues.

**Immunohistochemistry** A technique of labeling nervous system tissues by using the immune system. This method results in the staining of a particular protein or peptide wherever it occurs in the brain.

**Impairment**   A term used in a general way that implies a person is functioning in a less than normal fashion as a result of some disability or handicap, whether it be academic, social, psychological, etc.

**Impedance audiometry or immitance audiometry**   The measurement of changes in ear pressure in the auditory canal, which provides information about the eardrum, the bones in the middle ear, the functioning of the eustachian tube, and acoustic reflexes. This technique can estimate hearing sensitivity when conventional audiometry is unsatisfactory.

**Implied powers**   Refers to powers that are not specifically enumerated in the U.S. Constitution but are implied from general clauses such as the General Welfare Clause as determined by the U.S. Supreme Court. SEE: *General Welfare Clause*

**Impotence**   The inability to have an erection of the male sex organ.

**Impression formation**   Forming a judgment about another person on the basis of a first acquaintance, an examination of something written by the person, a photograph, or other information.

**Impression management**   The deliberate attempt to control the type of personal impression that other people will form about oneself.

**Imprinting**   A rapid kind of learning that takes place in a single trial. The stimulus that is to be imprinted must be presented to the learner at a particular age (usually measured in hours or days). The required age-range is called the critical period or sensitive period. Once the stimulus has been experienced, its effect is supposedly stamped in for good, which is why this kind of learning is called "imprinting." The acquisition of the species-specific song by male songbirds is one example of imprinting. In species that depend on imprinting, if the sensitive period expires with the young male never having heard the song, the bird, when mature, will never be able to deliver the song.

**Impulsive**   Tending to respond quickly, whether accurately or inaccurately. This tendency may be exhibited by a person often enough to be labeled as that person's cognitive style.

**Impulsivity**   A personality trait wherein the student or person tends to act or react quickly without thinking, so to speak. Time is not taken to consider alternatives or possible consequences.

**In loco parentis**   A term meaning "in place of the parent," which refers to the implied responsibility of teachers and schools to function in a parenting role while students are under their care.

**In utero**   A term used to describe the development of a child (fetus) in the uterus before birth. In utero defects or abnormalities occur during this developmental period.

**In vivo desensitization**   A type of counterconditioning. The subject is kept in a relaxed state while a phobic stimulus is introduced. The object itself, not a picture or recording of it, is used; hence, the phrase "in vivo."

**Inactive learners**   A term used in education to describe students who do not fully participate in the educational process. Their lack of involvement leads to nonparticipation in extreme cases but usually to unacceptably poor interest and participation. Such students are not seriously involved in learning; they normally do not ask questions or seek help from a teacher or instructor. Their motivation is virtually nonexistent.

**Incentive**   An external stimulus that directs motivated behavior. An incentive increases the desirability of the goal.

**Incentive value**   The perceived worth of the reward(s) that accompanies the completion of a goal-directed behavior.

**Incidence**   A term used in education and in general speech to indicate the number of individuals in a given population who exhibit a certain characteristic. That characteristic may be a particular behavior exhibited in the past or one likely to occur in the future. This measure of the extent to which something occurs is taken over a certain period of time or the lifetime of the individuals in question. SEE: *prevalence*

**Incidental learning**  Knowledge and information that a student or other person gains indirectly as a result of studying an entirely different area that is not expected to provide such knowledge. According to psychologists who have studied learning and memory, dependence on incidental learning does not yield reliable results or build strong memories; these experts prefer intentional learning if one desires good retention of learned information.

**Inclusion**  Inclusion can vary in meaning from 1. integrating all students regardless of disability in general education programs for the entire school day, to 2. the placement of students with disabilities with their chronological-age peers in general education classes to the greatest extent possible ("partial inclusion"). Inclusion under (1) would involve having special education staff working with regular classroom teachers within the regular classroom setting. Responsibilities and program planning would involve preplanning efforts and coordination. Under (2), students are provided supportive staff or education programs in the general education classroom whenever possible. Appropriate services may be provided in other settings, however, where the student is pulled out of the regular class for a specified time frame (e.g., physical therapy three times per week for half-hour intervals). The early inclusion efforts were referred to as a type of mainstreaming. Mainstreaming efforts tended to focus on physical program efforts; that is, planning programs based on where the child/student would receive supportive/academic services (e.g., the resource room vs. the regular classroom). Inclusion efforts now focus more on the interactive/social components and benefits of regular classroom participation. Individualized Education Plans (IEPs) and individualized transition plans are necessary to document how students with disabilities will be serviced within the school setting.

It is thought that integrating special-needs students within a regular classroom setting promotes improved opportunities for employment following graduation, academic/social outcomes, and preparation for independent living and community life. Legal precedent for inclusionary practices is grounded on the principle of "equal education opportunity" and can be found in the legal cases of the *Pennsylvania Association for Retarded Children v. Commonwealth of Pennsylvania (PARC); Mills v. D.C. Board of Education;* and P.L. 94-142 (renamed in 1990 as P.L. 101-476). Various teaching methods/approaches have been used (with varying degrees of success) to support students with special needs within the regular classroom setting. These include cooperative learning/peer tutoring, specialist/colleague consultation, team teaching, classroom paraprofessionals, special-needs assistive technology, curriculum and environmental adaptations, planning systems, behavior modification plans, integrative facilitator support, collaborative/team teaching, and providing heterogeneous learning groups. Some of the basic tenets specified in Goals 2000 pertain to inclusionary practices. From Goals 2000: All children will be ready to learn, the high school graduation rate will improve to 90 percent, all adults will be literate and possess the skills necessary to compete in a global economy, teachers will have access to programs that will enhance professional development, and schools will nurture and foster parent partnerships. Inclusionary practices involve providing support services to students (rather than removing students from classrooms to other locales) within the regular classroom setting. Inherent is the assumption that inclusive classrooms provide for the individual learning styles and needs of all students and do not require that all students "keep up" with the standard curriculum. The education commitment of implementing educational curriculum/practices/ technology to special needs and non-special needs students to the maximum extent possible within the regular classroom setting. SEE: *Appendix 3: MARCS and MAPP, Goals 2000, inclusion, mainstreaming, P.L. 94-142.*

**Inclusion goals**  The National Association of State Directors of Special Education (NASDE) has stated that inclusion goals must focus on reducing the drop-out rates and increasing the numbers of students receiving regular high school diplomas, increasing the numbers of students participating in post-secondary programs such as college, and increasing the numbers of students with disabilities participating within instructional settings with students without disabilities.

**Inclusive schooling**  Refers to schools that embrace a nurturing and supportive environment in order to meet the social/emotional/academic/psychological needs of all students/teachers/participants in the learning experience. SEE: *P.L. 94-142*

**Income support**  Any government program in which an individual receives money that is directed toward everyday living needs.

**Income tax**  A tax that generates revenues from an individual or business based on income. .

**Incongruity theory**  A theory of humor that emphasizes the putting together of previously separate objects in an unexpected way that surprises the reader, listener, or viewer.

**Incontinent**  A condition characterized by the lack of ability or the inability to partially or completely control the bladder or bowels. Sometimes referred to as incontinence, which is really the condition of being incontinent.

**Incremental view of ability**  The belief that a person's level of ability is changeable. This is the opposite of the entity view of ability.

**Incubation**  Work performed (apparently in an unconscious part of the mind) toward the solution of a problem while the person is (temporarily) not engaged in purposeful activity directed toward solving the problem.

**Incus**  One of the bones of the three-bone chain in the middle ear. It is shaped similarly to an anvil and is commonly called the anvil. SEE: *stapes, malleus*

**Independent learners**  Refers to individuals who are able to use a variety of strategies to facilitate learning/ knowledge acquisition. Independent learners are reflective and are able to self-monitor, self-regulate, self-evaluate, and self-pace; in other words, independent learners possess good metacognitive abilities or skills.

**Independent school**  A school that is not affiliated with the public sector in any way. This is also a school that is not part of a religious institution nor affiliated with any other agency. In effect, this is a totally independent private school.

**Independent study**  1. An approach to learning that allows a student to study individually, in depth, and at one's own rate, topics not generally covered in the regular curriculum. This approach is popular in enrichment programs for the gifted and talented. 2. Any course or topic studied on an individual basis by a student independent of a regular class.

**Independent variable**  The experimental or causal variable in a cause-and-effect relationship. Also, the activity/ variable/characteristic that directly impacts some behavior (although not necessarily causal).

**Individual approach to labeling**  SEE: *identity (in Erikson's theory), identity versus role confusion*

**Individual comparisons tests**  Refers to post hoc tests. SEE: *post hoc tests*

**Individual differences**  Differences amongst students when considering such areas as intelligence, vision, hearing, interests, social development, maturity, physical size and strength, speech and language development, etc.

**Individual Learning Expectation (ILE)**  A student's average score, which is subject to constant recalculation in order to keep it up-to-date.

**Individual psychology** That branch of psychology that attempts to understand the individual's experience in terms of behavioral/psychological principles.

**Individual test** A test designed to be administered to one student or individual at a time as opposed to group tests. SEE: *group tests*

**Individualization** Education practices/programs which recognize the unique learning styles, special needs, similarities, and differences of all students/teachers/participants in the learning experience. SEE: *P.L. 94-142*

**Individualized Educational Plan (IEP)** SEE: *IEP*

**Individualized Family Service Plan (IFSP)** An educational plan that provides for services for preschool children under the age of three and their families. This plan is similar to the IEP written for school-age children and is required by P.L. 99-457. The IFSP for each infant or toddler must include the following: 1. the young child's present knowledge level, 2. the resources, needs, concerns, and priorities of the family, 3. the major goals and outcomes for the family and child (including the criteria to be applied), and 4. the specific interventions and services needed, the date of program start-up, the expected duration of the services to be provided, any plans for transition to other services, the extent to which the services will be delivered in the child's regular environment, as well as the assignment of a plan manager. SEE: *IFSP*

**Individualized instruction** A type of teaching in which the lessons are especially tailored to fit the needs and abilities of each individual student. SEE: *IEP, Individually Prescribed Instruction (IPI)*

**Individualized Transition Plan (ITP)** Mandated by P.L. 101-476 (Individuals with Disabilities Education Act), a student's IEP (Individualized Education Plan) must include a statement concerning planned student transition services and information dealing with the transition from schooling to a changed program of instruction in another school or for on-the-job training and/or community living. This written plan, which is the ITP, should reflect the special goals, objectives, and skills that the student will require in order to effectively make such changes. The plan should also include the short-term and especially the long-term training components needed in order to meet the goals and objectives of the transitional plan. The ITP specifies not what is needed as the student moves from program to program or school to school so much as the services needed to allow the student to move on to independent adulthood. SEE: *transition teams*

**Individually Guided Education (IGE)** An individualized instructional program in which teachers and students coordinate and implement learning objectives, goals, materials, etc.

**Individually Prescribed Instruction (IPI)** A systematic step-by-step sequential method of instruction that is particularly concerned with behavioral objectives. These carefully arranged behavioral objectives become instructional objectives as well. SEE: *individualized instruction, Individually Guided Education (IGE), Individualized Education Plan (IEP)*

**Individuals with Disabilities Education Act (IDEA)** SEE: *IDEA*

**Induction** The type of reasoning that starts from a set of particular statements and proceeds to a general proposition. SEE: *deduction, logic*

**Induction programs** Supportive programs (e.g., teacher mentor programs) that are designed to help education professionals during their beginning years. These programs often assist teachers during their first year in order to enhance successful implementation of pedagogy and instructional strategies, to provide a support system, to improve retention of promising new teachers, to ensure system/state/national standards are maintained, and to more fully expose the teacher to the school culture. Typically, these beginning teachers have completed an approved college teacher-certification program. SEE: *internship programs*

**Inductive discovery learning**   Learning that is based on experiences that are very specific with generalizations formed thereafter.

**Inductive hypothesis**   Making or creating a generalization/hypothesis based on an observation(s).

**Inductive reasoning**   An act of logical thinking wherein one reasons from specific information to conclude generalities or general statements. The formulation of generalized propositions on the basis of known, detailed items of information. It is the opposite of deductive reasoning. SEE: *deductive reasoning, eg-rule method*

**Industrial/organizational psychology**   An area of applied psychology in which psychological knowledge and theoretical principles are used for the benefit of business organizations, government agencies, and public institutions.

**Industry**   The positive motivation to work constructively.

**Industry versus inferiority**   A stage of personality development in Erik Erikson's theory. Successful growth in this stage produces a sense of competence. This stage of development corresponds to the latency period in Sigmund Freud's theory of personality development.

**Infancy**   The period of life from birth to the age of two years.

**Infant stimulation approach/program**   Programs designed to stimulate learning amongst children aged from birth to three years. This involves the use of stimuli in the areas of vision, hearing, motion, touch, taste, and smell.

**Infantile autism**   A behavioral/mental disorder of children and young adults that begins before the age of two-and-a-half years. It involves a lack of responsiveness to social stimuli, very poor language ability, and bizarre behavior.

**Inference**   A term used in education and in general speech to identify opinions or decisions derived from reasoning about information. Inferences are not fully developed opinions or decisions; they fall into the category of suggested ideas or possibilities rather than the category of specifically stated, absolutely solid conclusions.

**Inferential comprehension**   The ability to apply reasoning and metacognitive skills to the reading task in order to understand what is presented. Inferential comprehension is also called "reading between the lines."

**Inferential statistics**   Statistical procedures that determine whether or not the researcher is justified in generalizing the outcome of an experiment done with small groups of subjects (i.e., samples) to the entire population of all possible relevant observations. A finding (from statistical inference) that the result of an experiment could easily be the result of chance requires that the researcher should not make a general statement on the basis of that study alone. If the result is given an acceptably low probability (the lower the better, but five chances out of 100 is often considered the highest acceptable probability) that it is a result of chance, then the result may be generalized to the entire population. In that case, the result is considered "statistically significant."

**Infoglut**   A term used to refer to the information overload we experience in our society because of the electronic media and the explosion of our knowledge bases within this century.

**Informal assessment**   Supplementing the standardized formal tests that can be given to a group of examinees and such other measures as observations, teacher-made classroom tests, sample behavior situations, anecdotal records, checklists, etc. Most diagnosticians combine formal measures of learning with informal assessments to optimally understand a child's learning strengths and weaknesses. Informal assessments tend to stress the "why" and "how" students are learning as opposed to formal assessments that focus on "how much" students are learning (e.g., informal reading inventory). SEE: *formal assessments*

**Informal reading inventory**   A process of administering sequentially graded and increasingly difficult reading paragraphs in order to determine a student's reading level of competence in certain areas.

**Information age** Society's current information explosion resulting from technological advances (e.g., television, mass production of written materials, and other media), with concomitant problems in dealing with vast amounts of changing information.

**Information processing** 1. The study of how we encode, store, and retrieve information from the world around us. A computer-based model is used by individuals from this school of thought who believe that our thinking processes somewhat model the operations of a computer (which must encode, store, and retrieve data upon request). 2. The intake of information, the storage of such information, the retrieval of the information, and the application of the retrieved information by an individual or computer.

**Information processing model** The view of learning and memory that is based on the similarity between the brain and a computer. Information is considered to be encoded during acquisition, stored during the formation of memories, and retrieved at the time of recall.

**Information processing theory of learning disabilities** A theory that the causation of learning disabilities is based on a student's inability to organize one's thoughts in a systematic way. Further, the theory specifies that the student lacks the ability to approach the learning task in an organized fashion. SEE: *Learning Disability (LD)*

**Infused** A term used in education to describe the expansion of the regular curriculum to include enrichment materials and activities. This is often the case in programs for the gifted and talented.

**Infusion approach** In effect, a philosophy of education positing that "career education" should be included as an integral part of the curriculum and not presented separately as an isolated area of study.

*Ingraham v. Wright, 1977* In this case, the U.S. Supreme Court ruled that states may constitutionally establish corporal punishment and authorize such without prior hearing or notice to a student's parents. Consent of parents is not required. Further, the ruling held that the administration of corporal punishment does not violate a student's rights under the eighth amendment. On the other hand, states may elect to eliminate or limit the use of corporal punishment. The corporal punishment must be reasonable in nature and degree.

**Inhalants** Psychoactive drugs that are consumed by inhaling their vapors. Inhalants may be depressants, stimulants, opiates, or hallucinogens.

**Initiative** The motivation to start new activities and to be creative.

**Initiative versus guilt** In Erikson's stage theory of personality development, this is the stage in which the child is successful when he/she can act spontaneously in a socially responsible manner. It corresponds to the phallic stage in Sigmund Freud's model of personality development.

**Innate** 1. A condition that reflects the basic nature of things, 2. a condition present from birth, 3. originating in the mind, not from external sources and not learned as a result of experiences.

**Innate response system** The motor responses that a child has at birth. They appear to be unlearned and instinctive. For example, crying.

**Inner directedness** A personal condition wherein one relies upon oneself for advice and direction in order to come to solutions with problems one faces. SEE: *internal locus of control*

**Inner ear** The fluid-filled cavity that is often called the labyrinth because of its complex functions and parts. The inner ear is divided into two sections: the cochlea (responsible for converting mechanical sound waves to electrical impulses via the cochlear nerve) and the vestibular mechanism (responsible for our sense of balance). After the cochlear nerve is stimulated and electrical impulses are relayed to the auditory cortex, sound is heard.

**Inner-ear deafness** or **nerve deafness** The loss of hearing as a result of damage to the cochlea or to the auditory nerve.

**Inner language** A form of self-dialogue that forms the basis of self-thinking. Frequently, students with learning disabilities are taught to talk to themselves in the sense that self-questioning, self-monitoring, and self-evaluation can be acquired.

**Innumeracy** The inability of an individual to deal readily with number concepts or to understand how random probability works.

**Inquiry** A questioning process that can be developed in students. Methods of inquiry are particularly necessary when teaching subject matter involving higher cognitive processing and evaluation skills (e.g., hypothesis testing in science) as opposed to rote types of learning (e.g., memorizing math facts).

**Inquiry teaching** An approach to teaching. The teacher presents a problem and the students are required to solve it by acquiring data and testing hypothesized solutions.

**Insanity** A legal term (that does not fit precisely into the language of clinical psychiatry and psychology) that denotes the condition of an individual who is not legally responsible for his/her actions. Such an individual may be committed to a mental hospital rather than to a penitentiary.

**In-service education** In effect, continuing education for teachers on-the-job and teaching. In-service programs are frequently provided within the school-system setting. An example of an in-service workshop would be an activities session on teaching teachers how to use math manipulatives with children.

**Insight** 1. A psychoanalytic term that indicates one's awareness of inner drives or unconscious conflicts that are causing distress or psychological problems. Psychoanalytic sessions involve free association, transference, and dream analysis, which focus on developing insight. 2. A

Gestalt psychology term for the sudden awareness of the solution to a complex problem, based on the mental assembling of the elements of the problem that had earlier seemed to be unrelated or whose interrelationships were previously misunderstood. Some Gestaltists speak of such a sudden understanding as the "Aha!" experience.

**Insight therapy** A type of psychotherapy focused on the patient's obtaining an understanding of his/her own motives and actions in order to improve the patient's well-being. SEE: *psychotherapy*

**Insomnia** An inability to sleep over prolonged periods of time. Generally, individuals who are under stress during the day are more prone to sleep losses. Also called agrypnia. SEE: *agrypnia*

**Instability** Refers to the pattern or tendency of an outcome or result to change from time-to-time or situation-to-situation because of the use of small groups, unreliable assessments, experimenter bias, etc.

**In-state student** A student who is in fact a legal resident of the state in which he/she attends school.

**Instinctive drift** The tendency of an animal to return to actions typical of its species despite its having obtained numerous reinforcements for nontypical actions.

**Instincts** Inherited and unlearned behavior patterns (e.g., blinking when something comes close to your eye).

**Institution** 1. The formalized educational system, the school district. 2. In the light of special education, it is a place, usually a school or campus where students with like disabilities are sent for special educational services. Normally, it would be residential in nature and both schooling and daily living take place on the site.

**Institutional practices** The operational behaviors that give structure and power to an organized group.

**Institutions of higher education** Refers to postsecondary education institutions that are legally authorized to offer programs of college-level study, which lead to the conferring of a degree.

**Instruction**   The art of teaching in the sense that strategies or methods of material presentation are created in order to maximize the learning experience for all. There are various types of instruction that include analytical instruction, coherent instruction, collaborative instruction, critical instruction, focused instruction, and meaningful instruction.

**Instructional assessment**   The collection of data and the analysis of the data to assist in the planning of future instructional activities. SEE: *assessment, formative assessment*

**Instructional events model**   Gagne's theory of learning. The theory coordinates phases of instruction with stages of information processing.

**Instructional expenditures**   Money that is spent in support of curriculum as well as other educational costs relating to the curriculum. Such money is dedicated to the instructional costs of the school organization or institution.

**Instructional faculty**   A full-time teaching professional whose main job is to instruct students. Such full-time staff work through the regular school year as designated by the school system, school, organization, or institution.

**Instructional interactions**   These are interactions between a teacher and student(s) resulting from previous or ongoing instruction.

**Instructional Materials Center (IMC)**   A center where students can use library periodicals and readings as well as media equipment.

**Instructional objectives**   The planned goals that a teacher would hope that a student would achieve. The goals and objectives help determine what the curriculum will be and what methods are best, as well as materials and supplies that will be needed.

**Instructional technology**   The application of the scientific method to instructional lessons. This application of the scientific method can be intuitive (class brainstorming on how to recycle) or with the use of machines and other technological tools (e.g., computer).

**Instructional Television (ITV)**   Lessons that are telecast via a television hook-up from educational institutions to a home or hospital setting, as examples. ITVs are usually provided to students with medical problems or special disabling conditions. May also be televised to a regular classroom.

**Instrumental conditioning**   SEE: *operant conditioning*

**Instrumentalism**   John Dewey's particular version of pragmatism. According to instrumentalism, a proposition's truth or falsity depends on the utility of that proposition. When asked if a statement is true, an instrumentalist should retort, "True in relation to what human purpose?" On the issue of whether there is a purpose underlying world history (teleology), the instrumentalist should say, "Not automatically, but by our own efforts we can provide such a purpose." SEE: *pragmatism, progressivism, teleology*

**Insulin**   A hormone released by the beta cells of the pancreas. Insulin reduces the level of glucose (blood sugar) in the blood; the glucose is chemically changed to glycogen (animal starch) and stored in the liver. People with diabetes mellitus (sugar diabetes) have excessive blood sugar because their beta cells are no longer manufacturing insulin.

**Insulin infusion pump**   A battery-operated device used by persons who are insulin-dependent diabetics. This device injects insulin of varying doses subcutaneously into the wall of the abdomen in accordance with the needs of the patient. SEE: *diabetes mellitus*

**Insulin shock**   A condition characterized by too much insulin in one's system. This condition can be remedied by the ingestion of a drink or food high in sugar. Symptoms of this condition include sweating, weakness, lightheadedness, paleness, and dilated pupils of the eyes. SEE: *diabetes, insulin*

**Integrated function** A learning process that involves more than one modality. An example of integrated functioning would be visual-motor or auditory-motor combinations for learning.

**Integrated Instructional System (IIS)** A set of computer programs that teach various subjects at multiple grade levels while recording the performances of each student.

**Integrated language arts** The concept that reading, writing, speaking, spelling, and listening should be considered as a whole and not as separate subject areas.

**Integrated Learning System (ILS)** A curriculum software system used between networked computers. It is comprehensive in nature in that it includes management tools for teachers and instructional software. SEE: *network*

**Integrated service delivery system** A system of teaching students with and without disabilities together. Students of the same age are kept together and taught in the same classroom during the course of a normal school day. This approach is synonymous with "inclusion." SEE: *integrated settings, inclusion*

**Integrated settings** 1. Educational settings or environments which include students with and without special needs. 2. Integration can also refer to settings that are open to students from different ethnic, racial, or cultural backgrounds.

**Integration** The act of placing students of different races together in the same school and classrooms as a means to overcome segregation.

**Integrative facilitator** An individual who is trained to create and implement integrative programs/support systems. This individual is often a liaison between the home and school and actively seeks to facilitate successful academic/social integration for assigned students. Integrative facilitators provide advice and resource support for regular educators, administrators, parents, and other professionals in order to enhance the integration of students who might otherwise not be "mainstreamed" or "included" within the regular classroom setting. SEE: *P.L. 94-142*

**Integrity** A realization that one's life is acceptable and is a record of fulfillment.

**Integrity versus despair** The eighth and last of Erikson's stages of personality development, one appropriate to a retired, elderly person. Looking back on his/her life, the person judges whether or not it has been meaningful and has been a positive contribution to the history of humanity.

**Intellectual abilities** General cognitive skills in such areas as overall intellectual capacity, reasoning, conceptual understanding, language proficiency/usage, and critical thinking.

**Intellectual functioning** SEE: *intellectual abilities, intelligence*

**Intellectualization** A defense mechanism identified by Sigmund Freud. This involves avoidance, not having to face one's own feelings by developing a superficial type of insight into one's inner problems. There is a rational and well-thought-out analysis of oneself and one's own motives, but feelings are buried and are covered by logical thinking. SEE: *defense mechanisms*

**Intelligence** An overall ability to carry out one's intentions, to solve problems, and to cope with the environment successfully. Psychologists continue to debate whether or not intelligence is a single concept definition or a concept with multiple meanings. 1. An advocate of the view that there are a number of intelligences (plural), Howard Gardner offers this definition: An intelligence is the ability to solve problems or to create products; such solutions or products are valued within a particular cultural setting. 2. Advocates of the view that there is a single overall capacity, however, would use the following: Our capacity to think rationally, act purposively, communicate linguistically, and interact socially so as to adapt to our environment. Even without a basic one-dimensional definition, intelligence can be considered as the capacity to understand and function in the world about us and to strategically/resourcefully adjust/cope with problems/challenges presented. Intelligence is impacted by heredity and by environmental stimuli and situations. Generally, IQ assessments are thought to tap into our innate intellectual abilities or capacities as these are global measures in cognitive/behavioral functioning.

**Intelligence Quotient (IQ)**  The concept of "intelligence quotient" was developed by the German psychologist Wilhelm Stern on the basis of the "mental age"/"chronological age" dichotomy utilized by Alfred Binet, the originator of the intelligence test. The division of the individual's mental age-scaled score by the same person's chronological age was intended to yield a description of the person's intelligence as if it were one's inherent feature, by analogy with eye color. The adoption of Stern's idea by Lewis Termen for his American version of Binet's test, the Stanford-Binet, led to the widespread acceptance of IQ measurement among educators and psychometricians in the United States. The intelligence quotient is based specifically on an individual's performance (usually verbal and perceptual areas are measured) on an intelligence test. The IQ is purported to measure the testtaker's global ability to adapt effectively to the environment. It supposedly reflects such cognitive variables as memory, problem-solving ability, reasoning, judgment, etc. After the age of six, someone's IQ is relatively stable unless there are complications from illness, drug or alcohol abuse, or brain trauma. Generally, an IQ score in the range of 90–110 is considered to fall in the average range of performance. Lower scores generally mean that there are general intellectual lags or mental deficit areas. Higher scores, especially those above 130, indicate giftedness or superior intellectual functioning. Performance on intelligence tests may be impacted by: 1. genetic factors that may place some individuals at a disadvantage, 2. cultural differences, 3. motivation/ health issues, 4. education/economic opportunities, and 5. other environmental factors.

Therefore, any IQ scores obtained must be examined with caution and in the context of other measures of intelligence (e.g., measures of creativity).

**Intelligence tests**  Tests that specifically assess intelligence or IQ. SEE: *Wechsler scales, intelligence*

**Intensity**  This is a measure of the relative loudness of sound, sometimes referred to as volume. In speech, it is controlled by the amount of air pressure that causes the vocal folds (cords) to be blown apart.

**Intensive-care specialists**  In reference to infants, professional persons trained especially to provide care to newborns (e.g., doctors, nurses, etc.). These neonatal specialists provide services to infants who are seriously disabled or ill and are at risk medically speaking.

**Interactional**  A term used in language arts to indicate the use of language in a practical way in order to facilitate getting along with others.

**Interactionism**  The view that the mental and material worlds, although fundamentally of different natures, can influence one another. This view was originally stated by Descartes. It has recently come back in a modern version authored by Gazzaniga. SEE: *dualism, idealism, materialism, mind-brain problem, monism*

**Interactive journals**  The use of journal entries in language arts education wherein the student and the teacher maintain a dialogue in writing. The use of interactive journals becomes an efficient way for the teacher and learner to communicate in writing, answering questions, make brief comments, and allowing open and private sharing of information on any topic.

**Interactive teaming**  An approach to meeting the needs of all students including special-needs students in a regular classroom setting. A team comprised of teachers, students, parents and other professionals work together toward this common goal of "inclusion." SEE: *inclusion, mainstreaming, transdisciplinary team*

**Intercranial neoplasm** Technically, a new growth in the brain (i.e., a brain tumor).

**Interdisciplinary instruction** An educational approach usually taken with gifted and talented students although it can be used with regular or even special-needs students. In this approach, the students study a topic and its related issues in the context of various academic areas or disciplines. For example, the invention of the chimney; How did it affect family life (sociology)? How was the first chimney constructed (mechanics; technology)? How does the chimney relate to food preparation (home economics)? In this example, the topic of the chimney crosses several academic and/or technological areas or disciplines.

**Interdisciplinary team** An evaluation team that maintains separate evaluations and treatments for each discipline. Usually these individuals confer to create an Individualized Educational Plan (IEP) and remain separate for delivery of IEP services. There is, however, more cooperative effort by this team than the multidisciplinary team. This team is more concerned with a united approach to solutions. Its cooperative approach falls between the multidisciplinary team (the least cooperative) and the transdisciplinary team (the most cooperative and communicative). SEE: *multidisciplinary team, transdisciplinary team*

**Interest boosting** A type of behavior-management technique that involves controlling restless or bored students by showing an interest in their work or providing lesson materials that key in on areas of great interest for the student(s) serviced.

**Interest centers** These are centers that provide independent learning activities for students from which to choose. Centers are created keeping in mind the developmental levels of the children involved and specific interest areas of the students involved.

**Interference** The blockage by the memory of certain information in the memory bank/store.

**Interference theory** A view of forgetting in which some of one's memories increase the difficulty of recalling others.

**Interindividual** A term used in education to describe a comparison of a student's achievement/performance with that of another(s); how one compares to a norm. SEE: *intraindividual, norm*

**Intermediate Care Facility for the Mentally Retarded/Developmentally Disabled (ICF)** A residential care facility designed to meet the needs of mentally retarded and/or developmentally delayed students or other persons who are unable to live at-large or attend regular schools or training programs. Residential care and training are provided during the person's life span.

**Intermediate school** A synonym for middle school.

**Intermediate unit** A subdivision of the elementary grades. It normally consists of grades 4 and 5. SEE: *intermediate school, middle school*

**Intermittent reinforcement schedule** The presentation of a reinforcer after some, but not all, correct responses.

**Internal locus of control** A condition wherein the student or person believes that he/she is in charge of his/her destiny. Personal decisions account for success and failure. Others are not in charge of one's life; one is in fact in charge of oneself. SEE: *locus of control, external locus of control*

**Internal validity** The extent to which the changes of a dependent variable in an experiment can be correctly attributed to the variations of the independent variable. To the extent that one or more confounding variables can be identified that would explain variations of the dependent variable, the internal validity of the research is impaired.

**Internalizing behavior** A term to describe the actions of a person such as a student who is in the process of withdrawing into oneself, particularly in the case of a socially withdrawn individual.

**International education** The study of historic, educational, social, political, and economic factors and information about other countries.

**International Reading Association (IRA)** A nonprofit reading organization dedicated to promoting worldwide literacy. Members address a number of literacy issues to include international trends in reading, current research in the field (through various publications and journals), updates in children's literature offerings, teachers as readers, teachers as writers, teachers as researchers, assessment, adult literacy, community outreach, legislative action, technology and reading-writing connections, working with learners experiencing special learning challenges, etc. Professional development opportunities are suggested and local/state reading councils can network with and belong to the IRA.

**Internet** SEE: *Appendix 4: Computer Terms*

**Interneuron** A neuron that is neither a sensory or afferent neuron bringing messages from sense organs into the brain or spinal cord nor a motor or efferent neuron carrying messages from the central nervous system to the muscles and/or glands. An interneuron (by definition) must belong to the central nervous system (i.e., to the brain or spinal cord).

**Interneurosensory learning** When learning takes place between two or more systems as an interrelated function.

**Internship** 1. On-the-job teaching. The intern is fully employed as a teacher and is supervised by the local school system or a cooperating college or university. Internships replace the traditional student-teaching requirement and usually involve twice the amount of time required by student teaching (i.e., 30 weeks instead of 15 weeks for an initial or first certificate or 300–400 hours instead of 150–200 hours). The time requirements depend on the certification requirements set by each state. The intern normally teaches in his/her own classroom without direct supervision of a cooperating certified teacher. 2. The service by a recently graduated physician of a one-year postgraduate training

prior to becoming licensed to practice medicine. The internship is usually done in a hospital/medical facility. SEE: *student teaching, certification*

**Internship programs** Programs designed to assist beginning teachers in acquiring professional skills necessary for successful/optimal teaching delivery. These programs are typically designed for individuals who have not fully experienced a teacher preparation program, especially the student teaching experience. SEE: *induction programs, internship*

**Interpersonal skills** Social skills that allow one to interact and react positively to others in a variety of contexts and situations.

**Interpreter** In education, a term used to describe a student or person who translates oral speech into sign language for individuals who are seriously hearing impaired or deaf.

**Intersex** An individual whose sexual development is between the male and the female; a hermaphrodite.

**Interval data or scales** A type of data or scale that is based on equal numerical intervals between each point on the scale (e.g., IQ points, test scores), where a true zero point rarely exists. Many education variables can be represented via interval data/scales.

**Intervention** A proposed educational, social, or medical strategy or program that is designed to improve the academic, psychological, or social status of a particular student or group of students.

**Intervention assistance** A term used to describe the educational assistance given to a student prior to referral for special-needs services. In many cases, such assistance (which includes but is not limited to extra help, additional time, a modified teaching approach, remedial aid, etc.) preempts the need for referral for a special needs evaluation.

**Intimacy versus isolation** The fifth stage of Erikson's personality development model (i.e., the first one to go past Freud's fourth and final stage). In late

I

adolescence or early adulthood, the individual demonstrates successful growth by being strongly attached and committed to another person.

**Intoxication**   1. The state of being drunk and/or under the influence of alcohol or drugs. 2. Educationally and medically speaking, this refers to deficient mental or intellectual development resulting from some poison or toxin to include lead, mercury, alcohol, and other drugs.

**Intraindividual**   A term used in education to compare a student's performance in various areas to that student himself/herself. Students are not compared to other individuals as is in the case of interindividual comparisons. Intraindividual comparisons show the student's own abilities and weaknesses. SEE: *interindividual*

**Intrasensory integration**   The ability to process sensory information through more than one sensory system at one time. For example, reading entails visualizing words and hearing the sound components and in some instances pointing to words (integrating visual, auditory, kinesthetic, and tactile sensory systems).

**Intrinsic motivation**   The tendency to perform an action that is rewarding in itself without the need for an incentive to be added to the situation.

**Intrinsic** or **interest value**   The positive rewarding effect of doing something without expecting any reinforcements afterward. The task is its own reward.

**Introvert**   A term derived from Carl Jung's theory. An introvert is concerned mostly with her/his internal life and inner consciousness. She/he will be extremely reserved in social situations.

**Intuitionism**   The concept that the basis of knowledge is direct awareness of the universe. This view is championed by the Eastern philosophies. Techniques of controlled meditation are usually prescribed as aids to the fullest use of intuition. SEE: *epistemology*

**Intuitive thinking**   Progressing by leaps, instead of going step by step, to the correct solution of a problem.

**Invented spelling**   Spelling used by young children or a new learner of a language that approximates correct spelling. The spelling is considered functional enough to be understood when read. Invented spelling is also known as "temporary spelling."

**Invertebrate**   An animal without a backbone. Invertebrates include a great variety of living forms. The lowest animals on the evolutionary scale, such as the one-celled animals, the worms, the starfish, etc. are invertebrates. But some invertebrates, notably the ants and the honeybees, represent comparatively high levels of evolutionary progress.

**IOP relief drawing set**   A special set of drawing materials used to draw raised lines for the seriously visually impaired as well as some figures, maps, and graphs.

**IPI**   SEE: *Individually Prescribed Instruction*

**IQ**   SEE: *Intelligence Quotient*

**IQ-achievement discrepancy**   An academic difference in which a student's performance is greatly and significantly different from the student's verbally measured intellectual ability as in the case of individuals with learning disabilities. SEE: *Learning Disability (LD)*

**IRA**   SEE: *International Reading Association.*

**Iris**   A ring of muscular tissue situated behind the cornea of the eye. Depending on which of two sets of muscles contracts, the pupil (an opening for incoming light set in the center of the iris) will either dilate (widen) or constrict (narrow). It is the color of the iris that imparts the eye's color, such as blue or brown.

**ISO standard**   The International Standard Organization. In reference to hearing, it standardizes average hearing levels based upon dB (decibel) losses as follows: 1. up to a 26 dB loss is normal, 2. 27–55 dBs is mild, 3. 56–70 dBs is moderate, 4. 71–90 dBs is severe, and 5. 91 or more dBs is a profound hearing loss. SEE: *decibel (dB)*

**Itinerant service** Those services provided by a traveling or visiting teacher in a classroom, school, home, or hospital program for special-needs students. The services include therapy, instruction, curriculum assistance, counseling, and other services required by Individualized Education Programs (IEPs). SEE: *IEP, itinerant specialist teacher.*

**Itinerant specialist teacher** A specialist or special teacher who travels from class to class, school to school, school to home, school to hospital programs, etc. This person assists teachers in providing special-needs services to children or in fact provides the service himself/herself. SEE: *itinerant service*

**ITV** SEE: *Instructional Television*

**Jacksonian epilepsy** A type of epilepsy that affects limited parts of the body. The site of the seizure is found on one part of the brain specifically. SEE: *epilepsy, petit mal seizure, grand mal seizure*

**Jaeger Chart** (Edward Jaeger von Jaxtthal, Austrian opthamologist, 1818–1894) A chart or card with lines of type of assorted sizes. It is used to check near vision. The smallest type one can read at the closest distance is the information sought. It is felt that this information can aid teachers in selecting reading materials for students with visual impairments. SEE: *Snellen chart*

**James-Lange theory** The theory of emotional experience put forth by William James. The emotional feeling is a result of the response made to the emotion-arousing stimulus rather than to the stimulus itself. The model for this viewpoint has been given in these three short sentences: "I see a bear. I run away. I am afraid."

**Jaundice** A condition in which the skin appears yellow as a result of deposits of bile pigments in the skin as well as the mucous membrane. This condition frequently indicates problems with the liver or the biliary apparatus.

**JigSaw approach** A cooperative learning technique that involves giving members of the group only bits and pieces of a learning problem(s) with students then pooling their resources to brainstorm and solve the presented problem(s).

**JigSaw II approach** A cooperative learning technique that involves giving members of a group only bits and pieces of a learning problem(s) with students then pooling their resources to brainstorm and solve the presented problem(s). This approach is the same as the JigSaw approach but with added pre- and post-assessments to measure learning gains. Assessment scores are averaged and the group score is given to each individual member of the group.

**JND** SEE: *Just Noticeable Difference*

**Job coach** An individual who assists adults with physical/learning disabilities in the areas of vocational guidance, college training/planning, job planning, interactive assistance with current and prospective employers, interactive assistance with social service/government agencies, etc.

**Job corps** A federally funded program for disadvantaged men and women that

**J**

provides comprehensive job/social training skills such as basic education proficiency in reading, math and writing skills; counseling; and health services.

**Job developer**   A specially trained individual who searches out job opportunities within a community or region for persons with disabilities. The idea is to discover or design job-placement opportunities appropriate to the abilities of the persons with disabilities for whom employment is being sought.

**Job-related academic skills**   These are abilities which when taught as skills can be related to vocational or job skills required for employment in the workforce. The use of specialized equipment (e.g., for mechanics), texts (e.g., manuals for mechanics), facilities (e.g., simulated garage), etc. provide hands-on experiences.

**Job Training Partnership Act (JTPA)**   A law passed by Congress in 1982 that provides block grants to states that support job/social training programs for disadvantaged groups of citizens. SEE: *block grants*

**Joint referencing**   SEE: *language modeling*

**Journal**   1. A type of periodical reserved in libraries for research in a particular field (e.g., special education journal, autism journal, reading journal). 2. A personal diary of activities, lessons, thoughts, reflections, etc. Journals are becoming popular learning tools in the language arts area. SEE: *double-entry journal, literature-response journals, vocabulary journals*

**JTPA**   SEE: *Job Training Partnership Act*

**Judicial hearing**   As part of due process for students, there is a set of legal procedures that the students' parents have the right to use. They can insist on a due process hearing and a judicial hearing if they disagree with the school system (teachers, principal, school committee, school superintendent, etc.) concerning their children's education. A judicial hearing is a hearing before a judge in a court of law. SEE: *due process*

**Judicial review**   The process by which the U.S. Supreme Court is empowered to judge the constitutionality of a law. The Court will decide which powers are implied as "necessary and proper" for the federal government and the individual states.

**Just Noticeable Difference (JND)**   A term for the difference threshold (i.e., the slightest difference between two similar stimuli that can be detected as a difference).

**Juvenile delinquency**   An educational and legal term used to describe juveniles; that is, adolescents or teenagers who commit acts of wrongdoing, crime, vandalism, etc.

**Juvenile diabetes**   A disease of childhood that involves inadequate secretion of insulin causing excess sugar in the blood and urine. Diet and/or medication (e.g., insulin) is used to control this condition which, if left untreated, can cause severe vision loss, amputation of limbs, coma, and death. Juvenile-onset diabetes is a term used to describe diabetes mellitus that occurs prior to age 25. This insulin-dependent Type I diabetes is also known as brittle diabetes and is extremely difficult to control. Note Type II diabetes is non-insulin dependent. SEE: *diabetes mellitus*

**Juvenile paresis**   Usually occurs 5–15 years after a child is infected; normally resulting from syphilis contracted by a child from its mother during the prenatal period. It is progressive and tends to be fatal. This chronic condition may cause partial paralysis, organic mental disease, and other degenerative changes.

**Juvenile rheumatoid arthritis**   A chronic form of arthritis in youths or children. The most severe cases can cause paralysis. SEE: *rheumatoid arthritis*

J

**Kernicterus** A form of erythroblastosis fetalis. It is so severe in nature that death usually results during the neonatal period. SEE: *erythroblastosis fetalis*

**Ketoacidosis** A medical condition characterized by an excess of ketone bodies in the blood of a diabetic student or person. The diabetic student may have a fruity breath odor and suffer the symptoms of drowsiness, dehydration, vomiting, breathing difficulties, and frequent voiding.

**Keyword method** A memory-aiding system. New concepts are associated with cue words that sound like the names of the concepts.

**Kilobytes** A computer memory-capacity measurement. Kilobytes are called "Ks," whereby one K is the equivalent of 1024 bytes. A 128K computer would store about 128,000 bytes (actually 131,072). SEE: *bit, bytes, megabytes*

**Kindergarten** Refers to the first year of schooling for children in the age range of 4–6. This movement was started by Froebel with the intent of gradually easing young children into the normal routine and rigors of a regular school day. Some kindergarten programs are half-day and others are full-day programs. The usual admittance to kindergarten is five years of age.

**Kinesthesis** The sensation of muscles, tendons, and joints as they pertain to movement of the body. SEE: *kinesthetic senses*

**Kinesthetic approach** A system of teaching or an instructional technique wherein the student learns through the use of one's movement sensations or the spatial application of movement, such as visualizing shapes of letters as one traces them in space.

**Kinesthetic senses** Our senses that involve movement, posture, and orientation in the environment (e.g., our sense of direction). The receptors for kinesthesis are found in the muscles, tendons, and joints.

**Kinesthetics** To learn by doing; the hands-on visual/spatial application and processing of information.

**Kleptomania** Stealing for just sheer pleasure goods that are not needed to survive. This is considered an impulse-control disorder or an obsessive compulsion to pilfer or steal.

**Klinefelter's syndrome** An abnormality of the sex chromosomes. A person with Klinefelter's has three sex chromosomes, two X and one Y. The result is incomplete male development. There is a high-pitched voice, a tendency to obesity, and limited beard growth.

**Klippel-Feil syndrome** (Maurice Klippel, French neurologist, 1858–1942; Andre Feil, French physician, 1884–?) A congenital condition that causes the neck muscles as well as the vertebrae of the neck to develop abnormally. The neck is short and wide and the central nervous system (CNS) can be affected.

**Kluver-Bucy syndrome** A combination of symptoms produced by destruction of parts of the temporal lobes bilaterally, with some subcortical brain damage as well. The individual will pick up small objects and put them into the mouth, will show an absence of normal fears, will be unusually tame and docile, and

K

will attempt to copulate with inappropriate animals or objects.

**Knowledge base**   A term that refers to basic foundation knowledge in a particular subject area. This is the basis from which to build subsequent knowledge.

**Korsakoff's syndrome**   Apathy, confusion, and the general impairment of memory. It is a consequence of chronic alcoholism. The immediate cause is thiamine deficiency; the vitamin is needed for the proper nourishment of cortical neurons. The rapid death of cortical neurons in turn produces the behavioral symptoms.

**Kurzweil personal reader**   A computerized version of the Kurzweil reading machine (for IBM and Apple computers).

**Kurzweil reading machine**   A machine that converts written materials to spoken English. It requires training to use effectively and appears to be best suited for older students and adults. Now also known as the Xerox-Kurzweil Reader.

**Kwashiorkor**   (Ghanese term) A disease caused by a nutritional deficiency in infants or the very young. It is a condition of malnutrition characterized by retarded growth and changes in internal organs, the skin, and the hair. A potbelly is present in spite of the gauntness of the body. This disease occurs after the child is weaned, that is no longer suckled.

**Kyphosis**   This is a musculoskeletal disorder in which the area surrounding the shoulders is rounded with treatment required in order to forestall severe physical deformity.

**L1**   A term used in education to designate a student's primary language. The language spoken at home is usually the student's dominant language. It is also the language the child has learned first.

**L2**   The second language of a student. The language is learned secondly and is usually not the student's dominant language, although it could become so.

**Labeling**   Classifying students according to a particular syndrome, disorder, disease, disability, or problem. This is done in order to 1. provide appropriate remedial strategies, 2. provide specific directions for research endeavors, and 3. provide categorical information for funding and program purposes.

**Labor force**   Generally, a term used to describe the civilian workforce whether currently employed or unemployed. Sometimes members of the armed forces are considered as part of the country's total labor force. SEE: *labor force participation rate*

**Labor force participation rate**   The proportion of the noninstitutional population that is in the workforce (labor force). This civilian labor force participation rate is a ratio of the civilian labor force and the civilian noninstitutional population. Participation rates are usually examined to determine participation by race, sex, educational attainment, economic status, etc.

**Laboratory**   A controlled environment or setting with stringent control of conditions (e.g., the type of stimulation given) so that the "pure" effects of variables or stimuli can be measured or assessed.

**Laboratory school**   A school that falls under the jurisdiction or guidance of a teacher-preparation institution of higher learning, with school facilities used for lesson demonstrations, research, and practice teaching.

**Land grant college**   Refers to a type of college created to carry out the purposes of the first Morrill Act of 1862 and subsequent supplementary legislation (e.g., Hatch Act of 1887), which provided public lands to states for the establishment of colleges for practical education purposes (e.g., agriculture and mechanical arts).

**Language**   The code or symbols used to represent letters, words, and sentences needed for communication purposes. The four components of the study of language are phonology, semantics, syntax, and pragmatics. SEE: *each language component as listed*

**Language deficit**   A measurable loss or void in some language skills area whether it be in oral language (speech) or written language.

**Language delay**   A term used to describe a condition in education whereby the student develops at a normal rate except in the area of language. SEE: *language disorder*

**Language disorder**   An inability or poor ability to express or understand language; thus, developmental language sequences can be severely impaired and/or interrupted. SEE: *receptive language, expressive language disability*

**Language impairment**   An inability of a student or other person to comprehend and learn effectively the systems and rules of language. Thus, communication is impaired and learning is affected. SEE: *language disorder*

**Language-minority programs**   Programs designed to meet the needs of language-minority students. Three variables have been researched and found to be key influences in academic achievement gains for language-minority students: 1. use both the primary language of the child and English when teaching the academic curriculum with an emphasis on the constructivist approach, discovery learning, and learning that involves real-life connections; 2. provide complex and challenging instruction in both English and in the child's primary language; and 3. provide an inclusive and safe, nurturing environment where the student is willing to take risks, and communicate with others in both English and in the primary language.

**Language-minority student**   Refers to bilingual students who are in English-speaking schools and are therefore considered to be language-minority students.

**Language modeling**   This refers to a situation in which the speaker and the child both look at the same object or scene, thus jointly sharing and talking about what they are observing and doing. It provides language stimulation and is sometimes referred to as joint referencing.

**Language of acceptance**   A nonjudgmental positive affirming language approach where individuals willingly share and express feelings.

**Language stimulation**   SEE: *language modeling*

**Language theorists**   Scholars who study the acquisition and use of language as it applies to everyday functioning and to the problems/disorders of individuals with language deficits.

**Large-print books**   Sometimes referred to as large-type books. These books are enlarged as well as clearly printed and with large spaces between words as assists for the visually handicapped or impaired. SEE: *talking books*

**Laryngectomy**   The surgical removal of the larynx. Many times this procedure is done as a result of cancer of the larynx, wounds to the throat, etc.

**L**

**Laryngitis**   Inflammation of the larynx which can result in an impairment of speech characterized by hoarseness and impaired (reduced) intensity or loudness of voice.

**Laryngologist**   A medical doctor who specializes in diseases and treatments of the throat (larynx and nasopharynx).

**Larynx**   A structure in the throat made up of cartilage and muscle, also known as the voice box and sometimes referred to as the Adam's apple. It houses the vocal folds (usually called the vocal cords).

**Laser cane**   A cane that uses laser beams to identify obstacles for individuals with serious visual problems. This device emits three beams of infrared light: one up, one down, and one straight ahead. When the beams strike an object within a range of about 5–12 feet it sends an audio signal to the user.

**Latchkey children**   This refers to the phenomenon of modern times in which children must leave for school and/or come home from school without adult supervision. This frequently happens because the parent(s) or guardian(s) must work to provide a home for the child(ren).

**Late-exit transition programs**   Bilingual programs that involve the student's native language as part of the program from kindergarten through grade 3 or for a period of time over two years in length. SEE: *early-exit transitional program*

**Latent**   Knowledge, ability, or talent that is hidden but potentially able to become manifested at a later date.

**Latent learning**   Learning that takes place before correct responses have been practiced. A student is given a strong motive but no way to gratify that motive (i.e., no reinforcement). For example, a motivated individual is encouraged and drilled on the "12" math multiplication facts. After several rote sessions of drill exercises, the individual misses all of the answers to the "12" tables on a quiz. After a night's rest, a reinforcing stimulus is made available (e.g., a day without homework). The individual is quizzed on his/her "12" tables and scores an 80 percent. This phenomenon shows that learning must have been happening all along even when it was not overtly demonstrated.

**Latent power**   Power seen in maintaining the status quo.

**Lateral**   Pertaining to one side. Lateral structures in a bilaterally symmetrical organism come in pairs (e.g., a left arm and a right arm). The opposite of lateral is medial; medial structures may be single (e.g., there is only one nose).

**Lateral dominance**   A term used in education to designate a preference for one side of the body or the other in regard to motor behavior and activities. For example, a student may write with her/his left hand, kick a ball with her/his left foot, and thus be considered left-lateral dominant (i.e., left-handed). A student may perform those actions with her/his right hand and leg (i.e., be right-handed). In the case of mixed dominance, or lateral confusion, some professionals claim it to be associated with poor reading and with learning disabilities in general. An example of this would be a student who throws a ball left-handed but kicks a ball right-footed or vice versa.

**Lateral lisp**   This refers to the situation when a person speaks by directing air along the sides of the tongue instead of down the middle creating a slushy "s" or "sh" sound.

**Laterality**   The tendency for a response or physiological function to be performed by a part of the brain on one side of the midline, but not by its mirror image on the opposite side. The process by which one-sided brain parts become specialized is known as lateralization. It is usually held that men's brains evidence a greater degree of laterality than do women's.

**Lateralization**   The tendency for a given behavior to be organized in just one side of the brain (e.g., the relation of the control of language functions to Broca's area, Wernicke's area, and the arcuate fasciculus in the left cerebral hemisphere, in most persons).

**L**

**Latin grammar school**  Schools that were in existence from 50 B.C. to 200 A.D. that emphasized the study of Latin, grammar/literature, history, mathematics, music, and dialectics.

**LAV**  SEE: *Lymphadenopathy-Associated Virus*

**Law of effect**  The principle of learning introduced by E. L. Thorndike that specified that positive behavior outcomes lead to the repetition of a behavior(s). When this law was first stated, it was taken to mean that learning has to be a "trial-and-error" process. Many came to believe that the negative lessons we learn from our failures are far less significant than the positive lessons we learn from our successes. Accordingly, the principles of reinforcement began to emerge, replacing the old "law of effect." SEE: *reinforcement, schedules of reinforcement*

**Lazy eye**  SEE: *amblyopia*

**LC**  SEE: *Library of Congress*

**LD**  SEE: *Learning Disability*

**LEA**  SEE: *Local Education Agency*

**Learned bias**  Behavior that involves prejudging a person or group of individuals after having distorted learning experiences rather than objective personal contacts.

**Learned helplessness**  A condition wherein a person becomes dependent on others as a result of the belief that it is easier to let someone else do it for you. Also, the belief that no matter how hard one tries, one is only going to fail anyway. SEE: *theory of learned helplessness*

**Learning**  A relatively permanent change in behavior or cognition that results from exposure to environmental stimuli and experiences with accompanying physiological changes (e.g., increased firing of neurons in some areas of the brain). SEE: *cognition*

**Learning Disability (LD)**  1. As defined by the Association for Children and Adults with Learning Disabilities (ACALD): Specific learning disabilities are chronic conditions of presumed neurological origin that selectively interfere with the development, integration, and/or demonstration of verbal and/or nonverbal abilities. Specific learning disabilities exist as a distinct handicapping condition in the presence of average to superior intelligence, adequate sensory motor systems, and adequate learning opportunities. The condition varies in its manifestations and in degree of severity. Throughout life, the condition can affect self-esteem, education, vocation, socialization, and/or daily living activities (ACALD). 2. As defined by the National Joint Committee for Learning Disabilities (NJCLD): Learning disabilities is a generic term that refers to a heterogeneous group of disorders manifested by significant difficulties in the acquisition and use of listening, speaking, reading, writing, reasoning, or mathematical abilities. These disorders are intrinsic to the individual and presumed to be a result of central nervous system dysfunction. Even though a learning disability may occur concomitantly with other handicapping conditions (e.g., cultural differences, insufficient/inappropriate instruction, psychogenic factors), it is not the direct result of these conditions or influence (NJCLD). 3. As defined by P.L. 94-142: Specific learning disability means a disorder in one or more of the basic psychological processes involved in the understanding or use of language, spoken or written, which may manifest itself in an imperfect ability to listen, think, speak, read, write, spell, or do mathematical calculations. The term includes such conditions as perceptual handicaps, brain injury, minimal brain dysfunction, dyslexia, and developmental aphasia. The term does not include children who have learning problems that are primarily the result of visual, hearing, motor handicaps, mental retardation, emotional disturbances, or environmental, cultural, or economic disadvantages (U.S. Office of Education [USOE], 1977, p. 65083 of the Federal Register). According to Spafford and Grosser, current practice points to the following: 1. learning disabilities reflect discrepancies between an individual's innate (as measured by IQ) abilities and

L

actual reading/language/math performances; 2. learning disabilities most often appear to stem from neurological dysfunctioning of some type; 3. there appears to be varying subtypes of learning disabilities that appear on a continuum to range from mild problems to severe impairments; 4. learning disabilities can appear with concomitant disorders such as mental retardation, emotional disturbance, motoric handicaps, etc.—individuals with such problems were generally not included in learning disabilities definitions before the late 1980s; 5. learning disabilities persist through to adulthood; 6. social misperceptiveness or social problems appear to go hand-in-hand with learning disabilities, with social misperceptiveness ranging from mild to severe; 7. there are several correlating behaviors of learning disabilities (e.g., directional problems, spelling errors, organizational difficulties, etc.), with individuals who have learning disabilities not exhibiting all symptoms and in varying degrees; 8. learning disabilities appear to run in families or are genetically linked; 9. most individuals with learning disabilities have reading/language deficiencies (estimates range from 5–10 percent of the total population); 10. males and females appear in the learning-disabled population in equal proportions although males tend to be overidentified and females underidentified; 11. individuals with learning disabilities require specialized assistance when not achieving in school (e.g., see VAKT method); and 12. individuals with learning disabilities frequently have lowered self-esteems and self-images and need much positive reinforcement when deserved.

**Learning disabled**   SEE: *Learning Disability (LD)*

**Learning disorders**   A term used to describe persons or students whose performance is well below average when compared to others of the same age or expected developmental level. SEE: *Learning Disability (LD)*

**Learning goal**   The intended amount of improvement in the learner's ability and understanding, which is to be pursued even if one's performance level has to be lowered.

**Learning potential assessment device**   An inventive technique for measuring a student's potential ability to gain from instruction. The method is based on Vygotsky's theory of cognitive development.

**Learning resource center**   A specially designed educational space that has a full line of special equipment and supplies appropriate to the individual needs of a student or a small group of students who are studying on an independent basis. SEE: *Instructional Materials Center (IMC)*

**Learning strategies**   General approaches to various types of learning tasks.

**Learning style preferences**   A student's preferred options in studying. For example, the student might prefer studying with others over studying alone, prefer to learn from pictures rather than from print, etc.

**Learning styles**   Approaches, behaviors, and specific ways of responding by which an individual learns and interacts with the environment. Learning styles are impacted by the environment, genetics, and culture and are embedded in one's personality. Cognitive, social, affective, and physiological characteristics all contribute to one's learning style. There are many dimensions involved in determining one's learning style. Some individuals learn best in formal, structured settings—others respond better when participating in more relaxed, informal settings. Some individuals respond to what has been termed "right-brained" learning endeavors while others appear to be more involved in "left-brained" activities. Authors and journalists tend to favor linguistic learning/applications while scientists and math teachers enjoy logical-mathematical learning activities. In regard to culture, research has shown that effective learning environments for Native Americans include but are not limited to many opportunities for teacher-student interactions and use of visual-kinesthetic curriculum materials as these learners are strong in the area of visual-spatial awareness. A student with learning disabilities may require assignments to be broken down into small steps with tape recordings available for books, notes, and lectures. The concept of learning styles is variable and might be more appropriate for some students than for others. Self-awareness of one's learning style and that of students in the classroom enables educators to impact instruction so that it is more closely aligned to the learner's communication and learning characteristics. Caution needs to be given regarding generalizing specific learning styles to particular groups of individuals. There are intra-group differences always observed within groups that may display certain learning styles commonalities (as in the example of Native Americans, Alaskans and Hualapai Native Americans share commonalities and differences in regard to learning styles).

**Learning tactics**   Techniques for doing specific learning tasks; tactical methods might include annotating or highlighting, for example.

**Least Restrictive Environment (LRE)** An educational setting in which a special-needs student is mainstreamed (placed with regular students) as much as possible and can still achieve the educational goals of the Individualized Education Plan (IEP). SEE: *IEP*

**Least restrictive setting**   SEE: *Least Restrictive Environment (LRE)*

**Lecture recitation**   Traditional lecture-style, teacher-directed lesson presentations followed by student responses centered on the concepts and ideas that were presented by the teacher.

**Lecturing**   The spoken delivery of learning materials organized and delivered by an instructor.

**Left-brained**   Supposedly, a type of person who is serious-minded, analytical, focused, attentive, uses logic, and expresses herself/himself with carefully considered words and phrases. Left-brained individuals like structured

activities and like being organized and can be perfectionists. The left-brained person tends to avoid open-ended formats and enjoys language words. The assumption behind the left-brained vs. right-brained typology is that people will differ according to which cortical hemisphere, the left or the right, is predominantly in charge of their more typical actions. SEE: *right-brained*

**Legally blind**   A student or person whose visual acuity is rated at 20/200 or over (20/200) with correction in the better eye or whose field of vision is an arc of 20 degrees or less.

**Legg-Calves-Perthes' disease**   SEE: *Perthes' disease*

**Legislation**   (State): Any laws passed by a state legislature and signed by the state's governor. (Federal): Any laws passed by the U.S. Congress and signed by the President.

**Lens**   The crystalline, transparent, and colorless structure just behind the pupil of the eye. Its principal function is to focus or refract light rays on the retina in such a manner as to produce a sharp image.

**LEP**   SEE: *Limited-English Proficient*

**Lesch-Nyhan syndrome** (M. Lesch, born 1939, and William L. Nyhan, born 1926, U.S. pediatricians)   A hereditary metabolic disease, this disorder affects males only. It is characterized by mental retardation, self-mutilation, aggressive behavior, and kidney failure as a result of the excessive production of uric acid.

**Lesion**   A given injury to a part of the body. A brain lesion is accidental or pathologically caused damage to an area of the brain. In research, a brain lesion may be specifically inflicted in an effort to learn more about brain-behavior relationships.

**Lessons and/or units**   A subsection of the curriculum that concentrates on certain goals that are part of the general curriculum. A clear set of specific objectives are taught during the lesson or unit presentation, which relate directly to the established goals of the curriculum

L

offered. Typically lessons follow this format in writing: 1. general goals, 2. specific objectives, 3. materials and equipment needed, 4. introduction and procedure, 5. lesson conclusion, 6. lesson follow-up, 7. lesson evaluation by student, and 8. lesson evaluation by a cooperating practitioner or mentor.
The Internet can be visited for lesson-plan ideas and information. Some sites include: TeachNet at http://www.teach-net.com (includes discussion forums); Collaborative Lesson Archive at http://faldo.atmos.uiuc.edu/TUA_Hom e.html; and Busy Teachers' Website at http://www.ceismc.gatech.edu/BusyT/ TOC.html.

**Letter-name spelling**   A term used in language arts to define a condition wherein the student is aware that specific letters stand for certain words with no silent letters. It is still incomplete spelling on the part of the student and some sounds in words are regularly omitted, such as vowels in unstressed syllables and "n's" before other consonants and short vowels; verb tenses and plural sounds are spelled as they sound. This stage of development follows the prephonic and early phonic stages of spelling. For example, "Me dog luvs bonz, i giv him a bon" (My dog loves bones, I give him a bone). This condition is typical of beginning readers such as first and second graders. SEE: *prephone-mic spelling, early phonic spelling*

**Leukemia**   A type of blood cancer, chronic or acute. The symptoms of the various forms are similar. As a result of the failure of the bone marrow to function properly the patient develops infections, anemia, fatigue, and bleeding. There are abnormal functionings of the spleen, liver, lymph nodes, and nerves as well as other organs.

**Level of confidence**   The establishment of an acceptable risk of Type I error (or alpha error) that the outcome of an experiment is a result of chance alone leads to the establishment of a level of confidence that the outcome is a result of the action of the independent variable rather than to chance. For example, if

the level of alpha-error risk is set at 5 percent, then the confidence level is 95 percent. If the level of alpha decided upon is 1 percent, the confidence level is 99 percent. The existence of the inevitable sampling error(s) assures that the confidence level can never reach precisely 100 percent. SEE: *independent variable, level of significance*

**Level of significance**   The probability level established that signifies how the results of a statistical procedure or test could have resulted in relation to chance and chance alone. Three levels of significance are commonly used: .05, .01, and .001. For example, if a group of students was said to differ from another group of students because of an intense training program at the .01 level, that would mean that there is less than one chance in 100 that the two groups are equal and that the observed differences measured via outcomes (i.e., a quantifiable score) were probably not a result of chance and the result perhaps of the training program. The lower the number cited in the level of significance, the more confident one can be that chance differences did not affect the outcomes. Typically researchers do not use levels below .05 (95 percent confidence), as chance occurrences are more likely to occur below this level. As a rule, levels of significance are reported in three ways: 1. the groups differed significantly (p < .01 or p < .001 or p < .05), 2. the groups differed significantly (alpha = .01 or alpha = .001 or alpha = .05), and 3. the groups differ at the .01 or .001 or .05 level of significance. Computerized programs can give exact probability levels. The three major tests of statistical significance are the *t*-test, analysis of variance, and chi-square. SEE: *each test as listed*

**Levels of processing perspective**   The view put forth by Craik and Lockhart that is an alternative to the popular model of memory involving the three stages of sensory store, short-term memory, and long-term memory. Instead of being weak or strong according to their age, memory traces differ in strength in relation to their depth of processing.

Shallow information processing leads to quick forgetting of information; deeper processing means retention for a longer time. An example of shallow processing of a word would be considering the appearance of the word as printed, while an example of deep processing would be thinking of how the word could be correctly used in a sentence.

**LGL approach** The list-group-label approach developed by Taba in 1967 157. Better known as "semantic webbing." SEE: *semantic webbing*

**LH** SEE: *Luteinizing Hormone*

**Liability** A legal term used to describe the condition where one is legally responsible for damages or a loss if one is in a position of supervision or authority and is negligent in these duties. For example, a teacher with assigned recess duties could be held liable for monetary damages if a child gets hurt on the playground if the teacher unreasonably (e.g., left for a coffee) left the child unsupervised. Otherwise, the school system would be held liable for any damages if the teacher exercised proper care in fulfilling duties (i.e., an accidental fall off a swing).

**Libertarianism** The view that the expansion of government into many walks of American life is excessive and must be cut back. The implication of this viewpoint for educational practices is that parents ought to be the primary educators of their own children and that schools as government institutions should be disbanded. Private schools could be retained because people are free to choose whether or not to use them. Some libertarians go so far as to reserve the right to be the principal educator for the students themselves. On reaching high school age, each student should make her/his own educational choices by selecting an apprenticeship, for example.

**Libido** Basic sexual desire. According to Freud, the sexual and other biological urges provide the psychic energy that pushes individuals toward pleasurable experiences such as sexual encounters. Freudian psychologists believe the libido is the source of all mental energy. According to Jung, the libido is the individual's total biological energy.

**Library** An organized collection of printed materials and audiovisual materials that are cataloged systematically and available to take-out for periods of up to two weeks to one month. Libraries consist of material holdings and audiovisual materials, as well as necessary equipment and services of a staff as needed to maintain the facility.

**Library referencing, access** Providing access to sources of information, technology, and instructional aids in various subject areas to enhance student learning and expand one's knowledge base. Providing access means preparing students with a working knowledge of where to go and how to use the information available. Teachers need to provide library strategies regarding the ways libraries work and how to become "library-intelligent." Some useful library Internet sites are: 1. The American Library Association at http://www.ala.org 2. The American Library Association Booklist at: http://www.ala.org/alaorg/alsc/notbooks.html and 3. The Library and Information Technology Association at http://www.lita.org

**Library of Congress (LC)** A federal government library that provides a number of informational services. The mission of the Library of Congress is to make its resources available and useful to the Congress and peoples of the United States and to maintain and preserve a collective knowledge base of documents for future generations. Access to the Library of Congress on the Internet can be made at: http://www.loc.gov

**Life-adjustment education** Experiences through which the unique and total resources of each individual are discovered and developed.

**Life history data** Information abstracted from school, job, and personal records that provides insight into an individual's habits, strengths, weaknesses, and social, emotional, and psychological growth and development.

L

**Life skills**   Those everyday skills one needs for personal living, including home management, food preparation, shopping, etc. SEE: *daily living skills*

**Likert scale**   A type of test or assessment instrument that requires an individual to agree or disagree with a statement. For example, an individual could strongly agree (SA), agree (A), disagree (D), strongly disagree (SD), or have no opinion (HNO).

**Limbic system**   The structures in the cerebral cortex that are important to memory and emotion. It is thought that the limbic system controls what information is processed through the cerebral cortex, which subsequently becomes recorded as lasting neural traces in the cerebral cortex. The two main structures in the limbic system are the amygdala and the hippocampus. SEE: *amygdala, cerebral cortex, hippocampus*

**Limited-English Proficient (LEP)**   Refers to students who have a limited ability to understand, speak, or read English because the language spoken at home is other than English. SEE: *bilingual learners*

**Line**   Sometimes referred to as the "chain of command," it is the arrangement of an organization from the bottom to the top wherein a subordinate is directly responsible to a supervisor. That supervisor in turn is subordinate to his/her supervisor, etc.

**Line 21 system**   Another name for closed-caption programs. SEE: *closed-caption*

**Line graph**   Also known as a frequency polygon. The x-axis (horizontal axis; abscissa) of the graph represents the scores continuously, from the lowest score at the left to the highest at the right. The y-axis (vertical axis; ordinate) represents the number of persons obtaining a score (i.e., the frequency of the score). The frequency of each score is represented by a dot in the appropriate position (over the score's place on the x-axis and at the appropriate height for the score's frequency). All the consecutive dots are connected by straight lines.

If necessary, a lower score than the actual lowest one is added and given a frequency of zero, while a higher score than the highest one obtained is added and recorded as having a zero frequency. This ties the polygon to the x-axis, closing the figure completely. The geometric figure thus produced is an irregular polygon.

**Linguicism**   According to Tove Skutnabb-Kangas, a term for language discrimination. In other words, using structures or ideologies to create unequal divisions of resources and power between groups on the basis of language (e.g., when unequal education opportunities exist for children because the primary language in the classroom cannot be understood).

**Linguistic comprehension**   The student's understanding of the meaning of a prose passage.

**Linguistic diversity**   Diversity between and within languages. For example (within a cultural group), the cultural characteristics of Japanese descendants who settled in Hawaii are different than those characteristics of immigrants who settled in California because of differing lifestyles/experiences.

**Linguistic functioning**   The ability of a student or other person to effectively use language in order to communicate with others.

**Linguistic skills**   Acquisition and use of vocabulary and the syntactic aspects of language in order to communicate in the oral and written realms.

**Linguistics**   The study of language that involves speech units, phonetics, syntax, semantics, and the origins of language. SEE: *syntax, semantics*

**Linguistics of visual English**   A system that is used for young children with hearing impairments, especially for preschool- and primary-level students. It is a manual sign system that follows the pattern of word order in English. SEE: *American Sign Language (ASL)*

**Lip reading**   Part of speech reading, it is the interpretation of visual clues of the

L

movement of the mouth in speaking.
SEE: *speech reading*

**Lipid**   A fat or fat-like substance that does not mix with water.

**Lisp**   A speech error that affects the class of sounds known as sibilants. SEE: *sibilant*

**Literacy**   Refers to the acquisition and use of basic written and oral language skills necessary for adequate communication and life-functioning in a society. Literacy includes the notion of cultural literacy or the importance of possessing necessary cultural information in order to be socially productive and accepted. There are different types of literacy that include but are not limited to the following: 1. *multicultural literacy*—knowledge of the ideas, politics, economic policies, values, social/cultural attributes, and linguistics of various minority groups in an effort to promote diversity in the learning/social environment; 2. *functional literacy*—basic knowledge required to function adequately in one's immediate environment. Students are expected to maintain a minimum level of competency in writing/reading/speaking/listening skills so as to enter the workforce upon high school graduation with at least a fourth to sixth grade reading/writing level; 3. *specialized literacy*—knowledge of specialized skills/ language in highly technical and/or professional areas (outside of functional literacy); for example, military terms, computer terminology, legal terms, etc. 4. *critical literacy*—knowledge of the fine points of written and oral language to the extent that the individual is an active and interactive participant in social change/progress, cultural forums, text interpretations, etc. SEE: *literacy levels*

**Literacy levels**   The levels at which individuals attain varying levels or degrees of reading/writing proficiency. Based upon levels detailed by The United States National Assessment of Educational Progress (NAEP), five levels of literacy can be identified: 1. *rudimentary* or the level at which individuals can

follow through with simple reading tasks such as identifying a word, phrase, or picture; 2. *basic* or the level of literal comprehension at which isolated specific reading skills are mastered and used such as locating facts in a story or newspaper; 3. *intermediate* or the level at which an individual can make connections and inferences about what is read and then generalize to other situations such as finding the main idea or purpose of a selection; 4. *accomplished* or the ability to interact in meaningful ways with the text presented and to organize, summarize, and reiterate knowledge and complex ideas or information about what was read (at this level, the individual possesses metacognitive knowledge and skills that allow one to react to the text and to self-evaluate, self-monitor, and self-pace the reading situation); 5. *Advanced* or the highest level of literacy whereby the individual can analyze, synthesize, and restructure ideas/information about abstract/complex reading material as in the case of mathematics and science articles and literary essays and fully comprehend what is presented. SEE: *literacy*

**Literature-based approach**   The basic philosophy to this approach is that children will learn to read best by using literature several ways in the classroom—by responding to predetermined literature selections or a "core" collection of books, to integrate subject matter across the curriculum, and to foster an interest/love of reading. Frequently, small reading groups are formed where children read and respond to literature selections. An emphasis on constructivism or having children construct their own meaning is facilitated by discussion prompts from the teacher. Children can also respond in journals or reading logs. Core reading selections are chosen by the teacher/librarian/reading specialist and include but are not limited to nonfiction (i.e., biography, autobiography), fiction (fantasy, mysteries, realism, science fiction, folktales), poetry, and plays. SEE: *top-down philosophy of reading, reading instruction, reading response groups*

**L**

**Literature-based reading** SEE: *literature-based approach*

**Literature conferences** Conferences that allow professionals and other interested parties to come in contact with literature through books, authors, panel discussions, visuals, and workshops. The IRA (International Reading Association) and other state reading associations frequently sponsor such conferences. SEE: *IRA, ALAN*

**Literature log** In language arts, a system wherein the student reader keeps a log or journal of what books or materials have been read. Reactions and written responses are recorded in reference to the readings.

**Literature-response journals** Journal writing that encourages children to think and write about ideas abstracted from literature selections. Teachers or other students can respond, react, and interact to each other's responses. Teachers can provide writing prompts (at least initially) to help facilitate the student's active construction of text meaning (e.g., Can you relate to any character in the story? Does anything in the story happen that is similar to something that happened to you?). The exchange of ideas is encouraged as opposed to any focus on spelling or the mechanics of writing. SEE: *literature-based approach*

**Litigation** As part of due process, a legal proceeding or a lawsuit (which is a claim) brought before a court for judgment.

**Little's disease** An outdated term used for the condition of cerebral palsy or cerebral spastic infantile paralysis. This disease is named for William John Little (1810–1894), who first described the symptoms. SEE: *cerebral palsy*

**Lobotomy** SEE: *frontal lobotomy, prefrontal lobotomy*

**Local Education Agency (LEA)** 1. a public board of education or other legally administered public agency within a particular state that is responsible for various administrative duties related to educational functions in the public elementary or secondary school sector. 2. The local school committee or board of a town, city, or regional school district.

**Local norms** Test norms that are quantified such that a student's performance is compared to students in the same locale (i.e., class, school, city, or district).

**Localized** Refers to a behavioral or physiological function confined to a particular area of the brain, usually to a part of the cerebral cortex. An example would be the ability to demonstrate color constancy (perceiving the true color of an object despite viewing it through a colored filter), which is localized in area 19 (visual area IV) of the occipital lobe.

**Loci method** A memory-assisting technique. The concepts to be learned are mentally placed in specific locations.

**Locus of control** The perception of ownership over control of one's destiny or fate. An internal locus of control involves the perception that one's actions, thoughts, beliefs, etc. are under one's own control or action. Possessing an external locus of control means that an individual believes that what happens in terms of one's fate is under the control of others or environmental influences. Individuals with learning disabilities, for example, many times possess an external locus of control. That is, these individuals believe that their learning and social problems result from the negative actions of others.

**Logic** One's ability to reason and draw conclusions based on heuristics or algorithms. SEE: *heuristic, algorithm*

**Logical concept** A category that includes objects having at least one feature in common. Concepts are the objects that we manipulate when we reason. How we manipulate concepts is a matter of establishing what kind of relationships they have with one another. Logical propositions are statements about how concepts are interrelated.

**Logical consequence** This is an event (e.g., praise for a good job) that is a logi-

L

cal follow-up to a particular behavior. Many times a logical consequence involves actions that follow misbehaviors (e.g., withholding a privilege like television for bad behaviors).

**Logical error**   The use of either incorrect or inappropriate assessment information in the judging of a pupil's performance or in making a decision about the pupil's future instruction.

**Long cane**   A type of cane used by individuals with vision impairments. The individual sweeps the cane in a wide arc in front of him/her and thus allows mobility for the blind, especially when traveling. SEE: *Hoover cane*

**Long-term health care**   A term used in reference to the longtime continuing needs of persons with long-standing health care requirements. Such persons may require health care for years or even a lifetime.

**Long-Term Memory (LTM)**   The relatively permanent storage of learned information that results from the consolidation of short-term memory.

**Longitudinal research**   A way of doing research that involves reinvestigating the actions of the same subjects from one time to another. The one independent variable that all longitudinal studies have in common is the amount of time elapsed. Developmental psychologists and geriatric psychologists have found this type of research to be useful. The main drawback is that this type of research takes a great deal of time to complete.

**Looping**   A term used in writing wherein the student focuses or narrows a topic in the following manner: 1. the writer writes about a topic for a few minutes without regard for spelling and grammar; 2. the writer then circles interesting words; 3. the writer then writes quickly and freely about the circled words, again with no real regard for spelling and grammar; 4. the writer again circles interesting words or phrases and writes about them; 5. the writer continues this approach a third time and thus it is assumed that by now

the writer has focused/narrowed the topic.

**Lordosis**   This is a debilitating musculoskeletal condition where the spine is curved inward, which results in swayback and a protruding abdomen.

**Lou Gehrig's disease**   SEE: *Amyotrophic Lateral Sclerosis (ALS)*

**Loudness**   The intensity of the sound of one's speaking voice or the relative intensity of any sound. Relative loudness is measured in units called decibels (dBs). SEE: *decibel (dB), intensity*

**Loudness perception**   The subjective experience of the intensity of a sound stimulus and the judgment of the amount of intensity in the stimulus. The physical correlate of loudness is sound amplitude, which is the amount of energy in the sound wave. Loudness perception can be modulated by other factors such as the frequency of the sound wave, the presence of other sounds, the presence of strong non-sound stimuli, the emotional condition of the subject, etc.

**Low achievers**   Students or other persons who are either not motivated to do well or lack the intellectual capabilities/abilities to perform well. Sometimes low achievers expect and are willing to accept poor performance and even failure. SEE: *high achievers, inactive learners*

**Low birthweight**   A term used to describe an infant at birth (frequently a premature birth) who is 2500 grams or five-and-a-half pounds or less.

**Low-incidence disability**   An exceptionality or disability that occurs in the general and in the school population in low numbers. The disability occurs infrequently and the number of new cases is low. An example of a low-incidence disability would be the case of students who have orthopedic impairments. Students with orthopedic impairments represent about 1.1 percent of the students in special education. SEE: *orthopedic impairment*

**Low-road transfer**   The easy transfer of skills that are very well-practiced.

**L**

**Low-tech devices** Noncomplicated aids or devices designed to be used to assist persons with disabilities. Examples of such devices include but are not restricted to ramps providing access to different levels in a school building, railings in a classroom or bathroom, and homemade cushions or pads.

**Low vision** The ability to see objects only if they are close to the eyes. Generally some type of magnification or enlarged print is required. In the case of low vision, the student or person is still able to see enough to learn and/or to execute tasks albeit with some difficulty.

**Lower-level processes** A term used to refer to cognitive processes in which memorization is the principal component (e.g., writing-out spelling words, recitation of number facts, or declaiming a memorized passage of poetry or prose).

**LRE** SEE: *Least Restrictive Environment*

**Lucid dreaming** The type of dreaming that is guided by one's conscious decision to dream about some topic. The dreamer follows the action of the dream and can change events in it.

**Lupus** A disorder of the connective tissue of the body. The tissue becomes inflamed and in "lupus vulgaris" tuberculosis of the skin the skin breaks down by patches and scars upon healing. In "erythematosus," a systemic lupus, pathological changes take place in the vascular system. It is chronic and usually fatal. The term "lupus" in the past has been connected with various forms of chronic and progressive skin diseases.

**Luteinizing Hormone (LH)** A hormone from the anterior pituitary master gland that affects the gonads. LH directs the female ovary to construct the corpus luteum, which releases the hormone progesterone. It directs the male testis to release the male hormone, testosterone.

**Lymphadenopathy-Associated Virus (LAV)** One of the AIDS viruses. SEE: *Human Immunodeficiency Virus (HIV)*

**Macroculture** A nation or social group with shared cultural/political values.

**Macroglossia** A condition in which the tongue is too large for the mouth or an excessively large tongue. This condition is the opposite of microglossia. SEE: *microglossia*

**Macropolitics** Politics occurring within the society at large (e.g., presidential and gubernatorial elections). SEE: *micropolitics*

**Magnet schools** Schools that have special offerings in curriculum and/or noncurriculum presentations or activities that are not normally found in similar schools as a means to attract students into their programs. These schools are normally open to students on a space-available basis and sometimes by lottery. As examples, magnet schools have been developed in the areas of science and math where the primary emphases are on those subject areas across the curriculum. There have also been magnet schools developed just for the gifted and talented.

**Magnetic Resonance Imaging (MRI) or Nuclear Magnetic Resonance (NMR)** A method for picturing the detailed structures of a living brain. A magnetic field coupled with a radio frequency field is used to make brain atoms with odd-number atomic weights rotate in the same direction. Removal of the radio field leads to the release of electromagnetic energy by the atoms. The measurement of that energy as it is released produces the brain image. MRI procedures can be used for many areas of the body.

**Mainstream assistance team** That group of professionals and paraprofessionals that provide on-going support and assistance to special needs students in the regular classroom and to their teachers. The team visits the classroom, analyzes the student's needs, and assists the teacher in planning intervention strategies. The "team" can also deliver services directly and indirectly to students with special needs.

**Mainstreaming** The process of educating children with special needs with non-special-needs children and placing them together, whenever possible and appropriate, in regular classes (i.e., art, music, science, etc.). This should be done to the greatest extent possible and in the least restrictive setting. SEE: *least restrictive setting*

**Maintenance** or **developmental bilingual education** An attempt to preserve, respect, and develop a student's first language while he/she is acquiring a second language.

**Maintenance rehearsal** The retention of information in working memory by continuous repetition.

**Major depression** Also called clinical depression, this is a mood disorder much more severe than run-of-the-mill "feeling low" or "having the blues." There is great sadness and despair, with a strong possibility of suicidal thought and action. Major depression is considered a psychosis (i.e., an emotional disorder serious enough to require hospitalization and medical treatment).

**Malformation** An abnormal formation or development of a body part or of a system of the body during the developmental stage. It may be caused by genetics, disease, teratogens, or drugs and may occur during prenatal development or during or after birth. It may also be a result of accident or trauma.

**Malingerer** A student or person who feigns illness or disability in order to avoid some undesirable task or activity from the point of view of the malingerer. SEE: *Munchausen syndrome*

**Malleus** The outermost bone of the three-bone chain in the middle ear. It is shaped like a hammer and thus is commonly known as the "hammer." Its function is to transmit sound waves. SEE: *incus, stapes*

**Malocclusion** The misalignment of teeth or an improper relationship between the upper and lower teeth such as an "overbite."

**Mania** A mood disorder in which the patient is extremely elated, cheerful, and hyperactive. There may be delusions of self-importance and a tendency toward aggression if one's plans are blocked.

**Manic depression** A bipolar kind of mood disorder. The individual swings between mood extremes that are abnormally high (the mania) or dismally low (the depression). The condition is attributed to abnormal levels or activity of a brain neurotransmitter, which might be norepinephrine or serotonin.

**Manual communication** SEE: *manual communication systems*

**Manual communication systems** Systems that are used in place of speech by the seriously hearing impaired and the deaf in order to communicate. For example, fingerspelling, sign language, and speech reading. SEE: *American Sign Language (ASL), speech reading*

**Marfan syndrome** (Bernard-Jean Antonin Marfan, French physician 1858–1942) A hereditary condition characterized by a tall lean person with an unsteady gait, stooped over with long lanky arms and legs. It affects the connective tissue, muscles, ligaments, bones, and structure of the skeleton. It can cause displacement of the lens of the eye, thus contributing to poor vision or blindness, curvature of the spine, and a pigeon-chest (pointing out) breastbone, as well as weakness of the heart valves. Sometimes fingers and toes are abnormally long and slender. It has been said that Abraham Lincoln suffered from Marfan syndrome.

**Marginal glosses**   Personalized comments authors or teachers make in the margins of books such as asides, notes of clarification, vocabulary highlights, summary statements, interpretations, trivia notes, etc.

**Marginal listening**   A condition wherein part of the auditory input received by an individual is placed in one's background while the individual concentrates on a primary area of listening. An example of this would be hearing background music while concentrating on a two-way conversation one is having with a friend. No deliberate attempt is made to block out the background music. SEE: *selective listening*

**Marijuana/marihuana**   A drug that is a derivative of the cannabis plant (Indian hemp or cannabis sativa). It is an excitant drug that is psychologically habit forming. It is composed of the leaves and flowers of the cannabis plant and is usually smoked in the form of cigarettes. It is an illegal drug in the United States and has no substantial recognized medical value as such in that other legal drugs can do what it does as well or better (i.e., in the case of relief for nausea or glaucoma). Its main use is recreational in nature. There is continued controversy regarding its use for medical purposes and otherwise and issues surrounding legalization.

**Marital and family therapy**   Therapy for married couples and families in order to identify problems and find solutions. Therapy includes learning how to communicate more effectively individual to individual and collectively

as a family unit. In education today, approximately one out of every three students is a child of divorce. Thus, marital and family therapy plays a more important role than ever before.

**Masking**   The prevention of hearing in one ear of a student or individual by stimulating that ear with controlled noise while the other ear is tested by sending it specific tones or spoken words.

**Massed practice**   A type of training in which the learner is given one trial after another in rapid succession. A college student about to take a comprehensive final examination who has not been keeping up with reading assignments may try to memorize the entire semester's material the night before the test. Most of the time, massed practice is less successful (for long-term retention of the learned material) than spaced or distributed practice.

**Master teacher**   1. A talented, specially trained, and skillful teacher who is able to relate to other teachers and provide leadership, supervision, and consultation or mentoring. Master teachers must be able to help other teachers improve their abilities to better meet student needs. 2. In some school systems, master teachers must earn a masters degree in order to qualify for the title of "Master Teacher."

**Master's degree**   An advanced academic degree beyond a bachelor's degree usually accomplished in one to three years, but preceding a doctoral degree.

**Mastery learning**   An approach to learning that emphasizes performance-based outcomes. Such learning is often related to competencies that are taught and then evaluated for mastery.

**Mastery-oriented students**   Students who value high achievement and intend to improve their ability to learn and to know.

**Matching**   Equating groups on one or more variables (e.g., age, gender, SES [Socioeconomic Status], grade level, disability, etc.) so that direct comparisons can be made regarding the impact of some treatment/educational method, diagnostic assessment, etc.

**Materialism** 1. A philosophical belief characterized by the tenet that material things of life have greater value than the spiritual worth of life. 2. A theory that proposes that the basic reality of the world and universe is material in nature and/or derives ultimately from matter.

**Material previews** Previews of material to be read that can be compared to movie previews. Such previews can expose students to reading book titles, chapter titles, subheadings, pre- and post-questions, chapter introductions and conclusions, graphs, charts, pictures, etc. in order to make predictions about textual content that can be confirmed or disconfirmed after the reading.

**Maternal infection** A term used to describe an infection in a mother while pregnant. Possible damage to the unborn child with the potential for learning/physical disabilities and/or health impairments are of prime concern.

**Maternal rubella** German measles, a viral disease contracted by a pregnant woman. SEE: *congenital rubella*

**Maturation** The sum total of all relatively permanent changes of behavior that take place as the result of growth processes rather than learning experiences. Such developments are programmed by the individual's genetic endowment (i.e., they are attributable to heredity).

**Maturational lag** A theory which holds that the lack of readiness to learn results from a slower-than-average physiological/neurological development.

**MBD (Minimal Brain Dysfunction)** An outdated term that was synonymous with learning disabilities meaning minimal brain dysfunction. SEE: *Minimal Brain Dysfunction*

**MD** SEE: *Muscular Dystrophy*

**Mean** The arithmetic average of a distribution of scores.

**Mean test score** The score obtained by adding all of the scores to determine a total and then dividing that total by the number of scores. SEE: *mean*

**Meaningful instruction** A type of instruction that ties real life skills to teaching pedagogy.

**Meaningful verbal learning** Learning of verbal materials that have meaningful associations among themselves.

**Means-end analysis** A heuristic technique for solving problems. The various steps toward the final goal are treated as subordinate goals.

**Measles** SEE: *congenital rubella*

**Measurement** The evaluation of performance by means of assigning numerical scores to it.

**Measurement bias** Measurement results or data that are in fact inaccurate as a result of influences of one's cultural background, race, gender, ethnicity, etc. SEE: *test bias*

**Measures of central tendency** Scores that represent the typical or average performance of a group. SEE: *mean, median, mode*

**Measures of variability** Scores that represent how variable (i.e., what the spread is) a group is. SEE: *range, standard deviation, quartile deviation, variance*

**Median** The middlemost point in an ordered distribution above and below which are 50 percent of the scores.

**Mediation** The subconscious use of language wherein a verbal label is attached to some thing or activity in order to facilitate recall.

**Mediational strategies** Approaches used to convey and communicate information between parties in conflict. Mediation can be used in schools to bring about reconciliation between disagreeing students. For example, Student A and Student B bring their dispute before a student council of mediation, agreeing to accept the findings of the council after presentation of their sides of the issue.

**M**

**Medicaid**   A federally sponsored health care program for low-income person(s) with disabilities and others who may qualify. Medicaid pays for many medical services including early childhood screenings, immunizations, diagnosis, and medical treatment. Medicaid was established as a federal-state partnership program in 1965 and pays for persons receiving SSI (Supplemental Security Income) benefits. It also pays for families receiving welfare payments.

**Medical model**   A system which is based upon the assumption that a disorder has a medical cause and an effective treatment or cure for it. A disorder initially requires a diagnosis to determine the disease condition that caused it. Normal means that a person develops without biological disorders or problems; pathological means that biological disorders or problems emerge sometime during the person's development.

**Medically fragile**   Individuals with health problems who are medically at risk. Frequently, such persons are in need of technical/medical support or support systems such as in the case of kidney dialysis. Certain elderly individuals and children (e.g., those who take the drug Ritalin for hyperactivity) may require nutritional supplements as another example.

**Medicare**   A Title XVIII, Social Security Act program for persons over the age of 65 and retired persons over the age of 62 as well as eligible persons with disabilities. It is a national insurance program that pays for supplementary medical insurance and hospital insurance. Part A, which is required for inpatient hospital care is provided without cost to the Medicare recipient. Part B, pays for a wide range of medical services and supplies as well as doctor's bills. The recipient pays a fee if Part B is selected.

**Meditation**   A form of relaxation that differs from sleep. The person adopts the posture of contemplation. Thought is narrowly focused on a single object. Rhythmic and slow breathing is used. The striped muscles are relaxed; if necessary, one part of the body is made calm (usually this first part of the body would be the soles of the feet), then another part, and so on up the body until the whole musculature is at ease. The meditator may recite to oneself, in rhythm, a simple syllable such as "om" or the word "one." The meditator must have a passive, "let-it-be" attitude, without any effort to relax, which would be self-defeating anyway. This practice may prevent psychosomatic or stress-related disease.

**Medulla (oblongata)**   The oblong-shaped, hindmost part of the hindbrain. This is the part of the brain that meets the spinal cord. The medulla oblongata contains the "vital centers." These areas of the medulla are necessary for breathing, heart rate, and blood pressure.

**Megabyte (MB)**   One thousand Ks or about one million bytes. SEE: *bit, byte, kilobytes, Appendix 4: Computer Terms*

**Megavitamins**   The treatment of emotional disorders or learning disabilities by the intake of very high doses of vitamins, well above the RDAs (Recommended Daily Allowances). This approach to remediation or psychotherapy is known as orthomolecular medicine and is now considered controversial.

**Melting pot**   The nineteenth century and early twentieth century metaphor for the assimilation of various groups of immigrants into American society and is now considered controversial. The larger society may accept small individual contributions from each ethnic group, but the ethnic groups are expected to lose their distinctiveness and blend into a monolithic American society and culture. This view has been replaced with a more sensitive respect for the cultural diversity and uniqueness of the several ethnic groups now residing in the United States.

**Memory**   1. The storage and use of the information that one acquires by learning. 2. The total information remembered. 3. The ability to store learned information and to retrieve it at a later time. Depending on the context, therefore, memory can be considered a process (meaning 1), a thing (i.e., content), as in meaning (2), or a function (meaning 3). The three stages of memory are (1) sensory memory, (2) Short-Term Memory (STM), and (3) Long-Term Memory (LTM).

**Memory strength**   The ability of an individual memory to remain intact. The better learned the information was originally, the stronger the memory of it will be.

**Menarche**   The age of a young woman at her first menstruation (around the age of 12). SEE: *menstrual cycle*

**Meninges**   The three membranes that surround the spinal cord and the brain. They are, from the outermost inward, the dura mater, the arachnoid, and the pia mater. SEE: *meningitis*

**Meningitis**   An inflammation of the membranes encasing the spinal cord and the brain; it is bacterial or viral in nature. Symptoms include impairment of the senses, confusion, irritability, and drowsiness.

**Meningocele**   This is a type of spina bifida. It is an outward thrusting sac on the lower part of the spinal cord that contains cerebrospinal fluid and that has no nerve tissue; it protrudes through an opening in the spinal column. SEE: *spina bifida*

**Meningomyelocele**   Another term for myelomeningocele. SEE: *myelomeningocele*

**Menopause**   The point in time when a woman stops menstruating. The cessation of menstruation generally occurs when a woman reaches middle age or between the ages of 35 to 58. SEE: *estrus cycle*

**Menstrual cycle**   The monthly periodic cycle in which a woman's follicle and corpus luteum grow and recede, with correlated increases respectively in estradiol and progesterone. This occurs along with the maturation of the ovum, with menstruation marking the releasing of an unfertilized mature ovum.

**Mental Age (MA)**   The typical intelligence of all individuals in a given age group (usually indicated by the average test score of the age group). In early intelligence tests such as the Stanford-Binet, performance on the test was scored as a Mental Age (MA). This could then be divided by the person's true or Chronological Age (CA). The ratio would come out less than 1 if the individual performs less well than the average member of his/her age group; would equal 1 if performance is average; and would be greater than 1 if the individual performs above the average. The MA/CA ratio is then multiplied by 100 to yield the intelligence quotient (IQ). SEE: *basal age, ceiling age, intelligence, Chronological Age (CA)*

**Mental disorder**   Disorders marked by social deviance, personality disturbances, and emotional turmoil. According to DSM-IV, mental disorders are associated with present distress (a painful symptom), a disability (impairment in an important area of functioning), or with an increased significant risk of pain or disability. Mental disorders are considered to be a type of behavioral or psychological dysfunctioning with deviant and unacceptable behaviors present.

**Mental giftedness**   Giftedness is, in general, an extremely great talent that is genetically based. The example of a 10-year-old boy who graduated from college in May of 1994 is not only a record-breaker, he is a prototype (i.e., a fitting model) of the concept of giftedness.

**Mental retardation**   Intellectual functioning significantly below average for one's own age group, which is accompanied by inadequate adaptive functioning or adjustments to the physical and social environment. Three essential features for this diagnosis are 1. significantly lower-than-average general intelligence (generally below an IQ of 70), 2. significant inadequacy in social adjustment, and 3. these deficits appear before the age of 18. The American Association of Mental Deficiency (AAMD) defines mental retardation as "subaverage general intellectual functioning which originated during the developmental period and is associated with impairment in adaptive behavior." Impairments in adaptive behavior refer to general adaptations to the environment and performing such everyday skills as grooming/dressing oneself, preparing a meal, following directions, following through with a task, etc. Caution must be exercised when classifying an individual as mentally retarded. An IQ score should not be used alone to determine whether or not someone is mentally retarded. The following IQ subcategories are sometimes used along with measures of adaptive behavior functioning: 55–69, mildly mentally retarded; 40–54, moderately mentally retarded; 25–39, severely mentally retarded; less than 25, profoundly mentally retarded. Many practitioners now use the term "developmentally delayed" as opposed to "mentally retarded." There are about 200 known or suspected causes of mental retardation. Approximately 15–20 percent of those identified as mentally retarded were born prematurely or at least three weeks before the due date or weighed less than 5 pounds, 8 ounces. Genetic causes include chromosomal abnormalities as in the case of Down syndrome where the fetus develops 47 chromosomes instead of the usual 23 pairs (46). In most cases, it is difficult to determine the obvious cause of the mental retardation although it is thought one-fourth to one-half of the cases known relate to biological causes. In some cases, mental retardation can be prevented as in the instance of PKU. SEE: *mild mental retardation, moderate mental retardation, PKU, severe mental retardation, profound mental retardation*

**Mental set**    A readiness to think and act in a particular way. This readiness is established (i.e., "set") either by verbal instructions or by past experience. The "set" concept is a kind of bridge between "attention" (i.e., selection of the kind of stimulus to perceive and react to) and "attitude", a fixed disposition to behave in a particular way.

**Mental telepathy**    A form of Extrasensory Perception (ESP), an awareness of events without the need for using sense organs. Mental telepathy is the ability to read another person's thoughts when those thoughts are not expressed in speaking, writing, or gesturing. Telepathy, like all of ESP, is not accepted as real by most psychologists.

**Mentalism**    SEE: *idealism*

**Mentally handicapped student**    A term used to describe a student whose mental abilities are so delayed, immature, and/or deficient that the student is unable to progress and achieve in a normal fashion. The terms "cognitively disabled" or "mentally disabled" are more accepted.

**Mentor**    A term often used in education to designate a teacher who serves as a model and/or advisor for a less experienced professional. For example, in the state of Massachusetts, master's level teachers seeking standard (full) certification must be supervised by a "mentor" teacher.

**Mentorship**    1. An educational program wherein a student is paired with a teacher in order to learn in a practical sense from the teacher as the teacher models various techniques and behaviors. The student can be paired with an adult, not necessarily a teacher as such, to accomplish the purpose. Such approaches are also frequently part of programs for the gifted and talented. 2. A specially trained teacher who serves as a special supervisor to a provisional or otherwise not fully certified teacher. The mentor supervises the teacher's clinical internship, which is usually for a minimum of 400 class hours of teaching and includes an educational research project. Requirements vary in different states but at the conclusion of the clinical internship the mentor verifies that the provisional teacher has now achieved status as a fully certified and/or professionally certified (the title varies from state to state) teacher.

**Meta-analysis** (meta = Greek for beyond)    A type of statistical procedure that is used after or beyond initial analyses. Meta-analysis is a procedure that synthesizes completed research studies in a particular field or topic by generating effect sizes. The resulting statistic allows general conclusions to be drawn on a body of research after internal and external validity issues have been resolved. For example, the large overall numbers used in a meta-analysis help to reduce the likelihood of Type II errors (finding there are no real differences when there are actually differences) and the ability to generalize results because of increased numbers; a wider range of subjects; differing experimental conditions; etc. For educators, effect sizes can be reviewed to try to determine if, when effect sizes are combined, the magnitude of the overall average allows one to make cause-and-effect inferences when program planning or making recommendations.

**Metabolic disorders**   Disorders that affect metabolism or the breakdown of food into energy and materials needed for bodily maintenance and activity. It can be a result of genetics, disease, or bodily malfunction as in the case of diabetes and hyper- or hypothyroidism.

**Metabolism**   The breakdown and conversion of food into the energy and materials needed for body maintenance and action (functioning).

**Metacognition**   1. Awareness and understanding of one's own reasoning processes, learning style, and problem-solving behavior; 2. knowledge of one's own cognitive processes, or thinking about thinking. SEE: *metacognitive skills*

**Metacognitive abilities**   Specific metacognitive skills such as setting a learning goal and the strategies required to achieve the goal, analyzing errors or error patterns, self-assessing the degree of success in meeting a learning challenge, etc. SEE: *metacognition, metacognitive awareness*

**Metacognitive awareness**   Self-awareness or knowledge of one's own cognitive processes (e.g., ability to self-monitor, self-evaluate or reflect, and self-question).

**Metacognitive skills**   The skills necessary to understand one's own awareness and one's own reasoning processes.

Such skills assist one in understanding or comprehending learning activities. Metacognitive skills include self-evaluation, self-pacing, self-monitoring, self-questioning, and self-reflection. SEE: *metacognition*

**Metacognitive strategy instruction**   A method of using alternative thinking methods to enhance and/or improve learning and metacognitive skills. SEE: *metacognitive skills*

**Metacomprehension**   A term used in education and in general that refers to how one learns and comprehends from a reading/learning situation or task through the use of effective and appropriate teaching/learning strategies. How one plans, regulates, monitors, and self-evaluates one's comprehension are processes involved in metacomprehension. Metacomprehension relates to "metacognition" or "thinking about thinking."

**Metaethics**   A special area of analytic philosophy that concerns itself with the meaning of ethical terms and concepts such as obligations, responsibilities, the good life, right conduct, etc. It is also concerned with the validity of moral judgments. SEE: *analytic philosophy, ethics*

**Metalanguage**   Refers to an awareness of language use in reading/writing/oral language activities.

**Metalinguistic awareness**   One's understanding of his/her own use of syntax, vocabulary, word meanings, and other aspects of language ability.

**Metalinguistics**   A language used to talk about another language. Educationally speaking, metalinguistics refers to the individual's ability to focus on and think about the language, what the components are, and how the different language structures relate to one another. It involves the ability to make judgments and decisions about how to use the language (e.g., whether sentences are grammatically correct or are properly written, whether words have the same meaning, etc.).

**Metaphors**   A figure of speech wherein words, figures, examples, etc., are used to illustrate and explain an idea when in fact the name or quality is not literally connected. Examples: "nerves of steel," "heart of gold," "sharp as a tack," etc.

**Metaphysics**   A branch of philosophy that deals with the basic principles of things; the study of the nature of reality.

**Methadone**   A synthetic narcotic used as a substitute for such drugs as heroin. Its medical value lies in the fact that it rids the addict of the desire or craving for a drug without giving the addict that high feeling or euphoria. Its use has had limited success.

**Method of loci**   A disciplined routine for the enhancement of short-term memory (STM). A fictitious scene is created in one's mind where one can place information to be memorized in an organized type of mnemonic. For example, one could use a set of stores in a shopping mall (or a set of houses on a village square) as a framework. The first item (on the list to be memorized) is thought of as involved in the first house, the second item does something in the second house, etc. The word "loci" means "place," hence the name. SEE: *mnemonic device, Short-Term Memory (STM)*

**Method of savings**   The method of measuring memory quantitatively that was invented by pioneer psychologist Ebbinghaus in 1879. The materials are separate items on a list and going through the list one time = one trial. Trials continue until a criterion of learning (e.g., reciting the list correctly twice in a row) is met. Time is allowed to pass and forgetting sets in. The same list is then rememorized. The difference between the number of trials needed for original learning and the smaller number of trials needed for relearning is the amount of *savings*. This amount is only relative, so it is divided by the number of trials needed for original learning. The resulting fraction is multiplied by 100 percent to yield percent savings, which is the memory measure.

**Methodology**   A type of teaching procedure or focus used to teach in a particular subject area. For example, one

teaching methodology included in the presentation of a seminar class in education might be to have students use this dictionary to define introductory terms for special units.

**Microcephalus**   A condition characterized by an abnormally small skull with resulting brain damage and mental retardation.

**Microcephaly**   A craniofacial anomaly characterized by a head that is excessively small in proportion to the remainder of the body. The capacity of the skull must be less than 1350 cubic centimeters for this diagnosis to be made. This congenital disorder is associated with mental retardation and defective development of the brain.

**Microcomputers**   General-purpose computers that are small enough to fit onto a desktop in a classroom and can be used for classroom reinforcement of lesson presentations, word processing, spell checks, testing, data compilation, data analysis, and recording.

**Microdialysis**   A method for the delivery of a tiny amount of a chemical to a particular brain area or the extraction of a similar amount of chemical material from a brain area.

**Microglossia**   A condition in which the tongue is too small for the mouth as opposed to the condition of macroglossia. SEE: *macroglossia*

**Micrognathia**   A craniofacial anomaly characterized by a small chin or lower jaw and underdevelopment of the mandible or chin.

**Microphthalmus**   A condition characterized by very small eyeballs.

**Micropolitics**   Politics occurring within an organizational context (i.e., within a town or college). SEE: *macropolitics*

**Microsoft Disk Operating System (MS-DOS)**   A system used by IBM or IBM-compatible computers. This program activates the operating system so that the computer is able to read the information from a disk. This procedure is also called "booting" the system. SEE: *MS-DOS*

**Microteaching**   A type of instructional approach for teacher trainees in which the student/practitioner teaches a small group of college students or school-age children for an abbreviated amount of time. Typically a narrow topic is chosen at the level and within the area of certification desired and the college instructor and college peers provide constructive feedback and suggestions for improvement. Sometimes microteaching exercises involve videotaping and playbacks for feedback and reflection.

**Microtia**   A craniofacial anomaly characterized by a small outer ear.

**Midbrain**   One of the three main divisions of the brain, it is the smallest in size of the three. The other two are the hindbrain and the forebrain.

**Middle school**   A two- to four-year school that contains combinations of any or all grade levels 5–8. Middle schools are considered a bridge developmentally between elementary- and secondary-level programs.

**Migrant Student Record Transfer Service (MSRTS)**   A computerized network for migrant students. It handles migrant students' transcripts and health records nationwide. The service is based in Little Rock, Arkansas.

**Migration**   1. The movement of neurons in the developing brain toward the positions where they will ultimately settle in and go into action. 2. The movement of students into or out of state to attend other schools or colleges. Net migration in a state education system equals the number of students who come into a state minus the number of students who leave the home state to attend school.

**Mild mental retardation**   A condition characterized by somewhat poor adaptive behavior along with an IQ ranging between 50–55 to 69. A mildly retarded person can communicate reasonably well, usually has no major physical problems, has reasonable social adjustments, is able to achieve at the basic academic elementary upper elementary level, and has good potential for employment and independent living.

Mild retardation affects about 10 of every 1000 persons. These students need adaptations in their educational programs and are usually on an Individualized Education Plan (IEP). SEE: *moderate mental retardation, severe mental retardation, profound mental retardation, and educable mentally retarded*

**Mildly handicapped**   Refers to any individual who experiences a handicapping condition that is not considered severe. Any restriction caused by the handicap is slightly limiting to normal or expected behavior and/or performance (and not of a serious nature, educationally speaking). SEE: *handicap*

**Milieu therapy**   Treatment or therapy in which great pains are taken to control all aspects of the environment for consistency and enhanced therapeutic benefit.

**Mind-brain identity**   An answer to the mind-body problem, which holds that there is only one kind of reality that is both mental and physical. It can be thought of as neutral monism, neutral because it is neither idealistic nor materialistic. A variant of this viewpoint is panprotopsychic identism. SEE: *idealism, materialism, mind-brain problem, monism, panprotopsychic identism*

**Mind-brain problem**   The question of how it is possible that nonphysical things such as intentions and desires can actually cause such physical things as arms and legs to do things; and, equally puzzling, how physical and chemical events at our sense receptors can create nonphysical conscious experiences such as perceptions and memory images. SEE: *double-aspect theory, dualism, emergence theory, epiphenomenalism, epistemology, idealism, interactionism, metaphysics, mind-brain identity, monism, panprotopsychic identism, parallelism, materialism*

**Minicourse**   An abbreviated course offering in either a shortened semester (e.g., intersession course) or reduced course content (e.g., in a workshop for professionals).

**Minimal Brain Dysfunction (MBD)**   An obsolescent term used for the same children who are today listed as learning disabled. The idea is that the learning-disabled child has a subtle malfunctioning of some part of the brain that is not discoverable by the usual diagnostic tests for brain damage. The MBD concept has been abandoned because it has not been helpful in either theoretical research or therapeutic practice.

**Minimum competency testing** Exit-level tests designed to assess whether or not students have achieved basic levels of performance in areas like reading, writing, and math. Generally competency testing is given nationwide in grades 4, 8, and 12. Minimum standards in many school systems have been set before students can graduate from high schools now in an attempt to prevent students who cannot read or write from graduating with a diploma.

**Minority** 1. A way to categorize a group of people within a larger society. Minorities share distinctive identities based upon racial, religious, ethnic, political, and cultural characteristics or differences. At times individuals classified as minorities experience a subordination status sometimes involving occupations with lesser prestige, fewer educational/occupational opportunities, etc. On occasion, minorities may actually be in the majority, as is the case with women in today's United States. 2. Also, any group distinguished by its number (less than half of the total) or a group that is lesser in number and distinguished from the larger group by some characteristic(s) (e.g., individuals with orthopedic disabilities comprise a minority population of the disabled). Blacks, Hispanics, and Asians are also examples of minorities in the United States.

**Mirror writing** A condition whereby a student or person writes from right to left, backwards. This writing when viewed in a mirror appears normally written; that is, from left to right.

**Misapplied constancy** SEE: *theory of misapplied constancy*

**Miscue** In reading, a deviation in pronunciation from the printed page. Miscues are not considered to be reading

errors, but rather alterations to what is presented. Oral reading miscues provide valuable insights into the word analysis strategies of a reader. Miscues can significantly interfere with comprehension/reading fluency if they significantly alter or interfere with sentence/paragraph meaning. Nonsignificant miscues would not alter meaning especially if they are self-corrected (e.g., a dialect variation). Examples of miscues include but are not limited to: 1. letter(s)/word/sentence *omissions*—reading "It bright, sunny day" for "It is a bright sunny day" or "appy" for "happy"; 2. letter(s)/word/sentence *insertions*—reading "I really love my family" for "I really really love my family" or "running" for "run"; 3. letter(s)/word/sentence *substitutions*—reading "glad" for "happy." It is a significant miscue if meaning is altered— reading "sad" for "happy;" 4. letter(s)/ word/phrase *repetitions*—reading "I am going home going home" for "I am going home" or "Yes, yes" for "Yes"; 5. *self-corrections*—reading "Please pass the deesert/dessert" (self-corrected); 6. slow and laborious *word-by-word* reading—reading, "I (long pause) want to (long pause) see (long pause) the puppy." Teachers can diagnosis reader's miscues by using a formal system (e.g., informal reading inventory) or an informal checklist.

**Mission statement** The main goal or goals written by a school system, school, government agency, group, association, and the like. The main purpose of the written statement is to describe how a group perceives its obligations, goals, services, and challenges and so forth.

**MIT braille embosser** A system used for reading and writing by the visually impaired or blind. Developed at the Massachusetts Institute of Technology (MIT), it translates ink print into Grade 2 braille. It is used with a telewriter. Materials can be requested by phone from a computer center and they are returned via the telewriter in braille. Today braille translations are made by microcomputer.

**Mixed cerebral palsy** A cerebral palsy type in which several specific types of cerebral palsy are involved. For example, athetosis and spasticity occur concurrently. SEE: *athetosis, spasticity*

**Mixed dominance**   Sometimes referred to as mixed laterality, it is a term used to describe a mix of a student's or person's choice of preferred sides of the body. The student might be left-handed for writing but right-handed for batting a ball. The left-right side preference is not consistent for all activities.

**Mixed hearing loss**   A type of hearing loss involving both *conductive* and *sensorineural* impairments, which are two other types of hearing loss. Individuals with the mixed type can't hear decibels below a certain level and experience problems in sound and word distortions. Only the conductive type of hearing loss is treatable by normal means so that only the conductive elements involved in this type of loss are medically treatable. SEE: *conductive hearing loss, sensorineural hearing loss*

**Mnemonics** or **mnemonic device**   Any of several procedures used to enhance short-term memory beyond its limit of seven items plus or minus two. One example is the "method of loci." Another is the acrostic method (first letters of items on a list are used to form a word); for example, the word "HOMES" is the acrostic for the Great Lakes: Huron, Ontario, Michigan, Erie, and Superior. Some other common mnemonics include: "Thirty days hath September, April, June, and November except for February which has 28. All the rest have 31." "Roy G. Biv" represents the colors of the visible spectrum—red, orange, yellow, green, blue, indigo, and violet. "I before E, except after C or when sounded like A in neighbor." SEE: *method of loci, Short-Term Memory (STM)*

**Mnemonist**   An individual with greatly developed memory skills.

**Mobility**   The movement of individuals from one position to another within a particular stratification system. A teacher may obtain a higher level degree, for example, and then apply to become a principal.

**Mobility instruction**   SEE: *mobility training*

**Mobility training**   This is training that assists visually impaired or blind students or persons with the wherewithal to get about at large and to move from one place to another in spite of obstacles that may exist.

**Modality**   A method or sensory channel through which an individual learns better than through another. For example, a child may learn to read better with the phonic method rather than through a sight method (hearing vs. vision). SEE: *modality preference*

**Modality preference**   The belief that learners have preferred sensory channels for learning that include visual, auditory, and tactile-kinesthetic. Some authorities, for example, believe that some individuals with learning disabilities will learn better through the auditory sense.

**Mode**   The most frequently occurring score in a distribution.

**Model program**   A program that implements and evaluates new procedures or techniques in order to serve as a basis for development of other similar programs.

**Modeling**   Teaching by providing a guided example of desired behaviors or learning outcomes. The student in effect imitates the teacher. SEE: *imitation*

**Modem** (from "modulate-demodulate") A part of a computer system called a peripheral (not necessary for the operation of the computer as such) that is used to send information over a telephone line from one computer to another. SEE: *Appendix 4: Computer Terms*

**Moderate mental retardation**   A condition characterized by poor adaptive behavior along with an IQ ranging between 35–40 to 50–55. A moderately retarded person has difficulty communicating but can carry on simple conversations, usually has some health and motor difficulties, has some awkward social adjustment, can learn functional survival skills, can live in a supported environment, and can be gainfully employed in a supportive setting. Moderate retardation affects about three persons out of 1000. These students definitely need Individualized Education Programs (IEPs). Programs should emphasize basic self-care, social, elementary academic, and vocational skills. SEE: *mild mental retardation, severe mental retardation, profound mental retardation, educable mentally retarded, trainable mentally retarded*

**Modular scheduling**   The time arrangement of class periods in units of 15, 20, 30, 40 minutes, etc. in order to permit greater flexibility in scheduling. At the elementary level, 30-minute time frames are usually reserved for classes while 45–60 minutes are usual at the secondary level.

**Modules for learning**   The arrangement of learning and teaching time within a school schedule for a school day. It is the time arrangement of class periods. SEE: *modular scheduling*

**Mongolism**   A term used in the past to describe a person with Down syndrome. Currently, it is considered an undesirable term.

**Monism**   The belief that the whole universe is, at the least, of a single nature, be it material, mental/spiritual, or a combination of the two. Idealism or spiritualism, materialism, and mind-brain identism are three versions of monism. Most monists, Russell being one example, were materialists. Plato, Kant, and Berkeley, however, championed idealism. SEE: *idealism, metaphysics, mind-brain identity, mind-brain problem, panprotopsychic identism*

**Monitorial schools**   Schools developed by Joseph Lancaster and Andrew Bell in the early 1800s in which one teacher worked with a number of bright students as monitors teaching other groups of children. This type of school was closed in the 1840s because not enough children were benefiting from an adequate educational experience.

**Monocular cues**   Environmental stimuli that an observer can use to judge visual depth (i.e., front-back distance). These cues do not require the use of both eyes

to be effective, hence the name "monocular." Examples are: linear perspective, aerial perspective, relative size of known objects, light and shade, texture, and interposition.

**Monolinguals**   Persons who can speak only one language.

**Mononucleosis**   The so-called "kissing disease," which is a result of a virus. It is infectious and affects primarily tissues of the lymphatic system. It is characterized by abnormal liver functioning, enlarged and sometimes painful lymph nodes, and an enlarged spleen. SEE: *Epstein-Barr virus*

**Monoplegia**   The paralysis of one limb.

**Monotheism**   The belief that there is one personal God, from whom the universe is derived, including truth, beauty, and goodness. The major religions of the western world—Judaism, Christianity, Islam, and Buddhism—all adhere to this basic belief.

**Monozygotic**   A term that refers to the twins who are products of the same fertilized egg and thus are genetically identical. SEE: *zygote*

**Monroe approach**   A synthetic phonics approach developed by Monroe in 1932. This approach can be used with readers with severe oral reading difficulties as stress is placed on eliminating incorrect pronunciations of vowels and consonants and reading miscues such as omissions, substitutions, reversals, and repetitions. The synthetic phonics teaching is used in conjunction with correct motoric response training.

**Mood disorder**   A psychotic condition in which the main symptom is an uncontrollable emotional state (mood). These disorders include mania (extreme euphoria, feeling high, hyperactivity, and grandiosity), major depression (extreme sadness, despair, suicidal thinking, and possibly attempts at suicide), and bipolar manic-depression (alternating between the two extremes of mania and depression).

**Moon illusion**   The visual perception of the moon's size varies, depending on its position in the sky. The moon seems to

**M**

be larger when it is on the horizon than when it is at the zenith (at its height). Various explanations of the illusion have been offered. One is that the size of the horizon moon can be compared with the sizes of trees and houses; its relative size is obviously large. No such comparison is available for the moon at the zenith.

**Moonlighting**   A term in general use today that means holding down a second job in addition to what one does primarily to earn a living. The term implies working after a full day's work at night or "under the light of the moon," so to speak.

**Moral dilemmas**   Various social situations in which there is no clear-cut, right way to behave. As the saying in the legal profession goes, "hard cases make bad law."

**Moral reasoning**   Logical processes used to help decide whether a line of conduct is ethically right or wrong.

**Morality**   A collection of learned attitudes, beliefs, and opinions about social practices and behaviors or one's social conscience.

**Mores**   Societal rules governing acceptable behaviors and moral standards. Mores specify unacceptable behaviors (e.g., stealing and lying) even if legally acceptable.

**Moro's reflex** (Ernest Moro, German pediatrician, 1874–1951)   A defensive reflex wherein an infant will draw its arms across its chest in an embrace as it responds to the striking of the surface on which the child rests.

**Morpheme**   The smallest unit of language that involves meaning. Prefixes, suffixes, and root words are examples of morphemes.

**Morphine**   A narcotic drug that is addictive in nature. It is derived from and is the principal alkaloid of opium. Its primary medical use is for the relief of pain and/or for sedative purposes. SEE: *heroin, opium*

**Morphology**   In linguistics, the science that deals with the use of morphemes. SEE: *morphemes*

**Mosaicism**   Abnormal junction of chromosomal pairs after fertilization and after the fetus has developed normally for awhile. The infant has mixed chromosomal abnormalities with some tissue that is abnormal and some normal. Infants with "mosaicism" are normally less retarded than those with "trisomy-21" or "translocation." SEE: *trisomy-21, translocation*

**Motivation**   The entire set of factors (i.e., motives) that compel an individual to respond. Examples of motives include hunger, aggression, and the need for achievement. Hunger is a drive based on a physiological need (food deprivation). Aggression is an attempt to injure another organism or person, a motivational capacity produced by emotional reactions to the environment and a physiological release of brain circuits that control destructive activity. Achievement is a learned ("psychogenic") need, arising from being reared in a given society and culture. SEE: *need*

**Motive**   An internal process that directs one's behavior toward a goal.

**Motokinesthetic**   A speech training method for students or persons with hearing impairments. This approach emphasizes the touching of a person's face for cues as well as the reproduction and imitation of voice patterns and breathing.

**Motor cortex**   Areas of the cerebral cortex that, when active, direct motor acts such as movements of the limbs.

**Motor development**   Motor development refers to changes in motor activity in an ever-increasingly proficient manner such as in the case of a child who progresses to walking from crawling. It involves higher-level perception skills and analysis of visual and auditory input as well as one's ability to organize. SEE: *fine motor skills, gross motor skills*

**Motor habits**   Motor activities that are usually nonfunctional and repetitive such as tapping one's foot, thumb sucking, hair twisting, etc. Such behavior appears to be a response to anxiety or stress.

**Motor skills**   These are skills involving small and large muscle activities as well as fine and gross motor skills. SEE: *directionality, laterality, fine motor skills, gross motor skills*

**Movement management**   The ability of a teacher to keep the classroom lessons, homework assignments, and student activities moving in a smooth, orderly way.

**Mowat sensor**   A travel aid for blind students or persons, it is a hand-held ultrasonic travel aid about the size of a flashlight. It warns the user of objects in his/her path by vibrating at different rates, and is an alternative to the Hoover cane. SEE: *Hoover cane*

**MRI**   SEE: *Magnetic Resonance Imaging*

**MS-DOS**   SEE: *Microsoft Disk Operating System, Appendix 4: Computer Terms*

**MSRTS**   SEE: *Migrant Student Record Transfer Service*

**Mullerian ducts**   The forerunners in the early human fetus of a mature female reproductive apparatus. The Mullerian ducts will develop into the oviducts, uterus, and upper vagina.

**Multicultural**   A term used to show a condition that reflects more than a single culture (i.e., a state of cultural diversity). SEE: *multicultural education, multiculturalism*

**Multicultural education**   An educational process approach in which there is an emphasis on interactive communication, self-respect, confidence, and appreciation for one's own culture and the culture of others. A vital component to multicultural studies is the presentation of children's and adult's literature that is authentic as cultural awareness and understanding can be abstracted. Multicultural education also involves providing strategies to students in which their cultural backgrounds are viewed in positive ways and integral to the developing curriculum. Curriculum and instructional methods for all children involve cooperative learning, constructivism, critical thinking, problem solving, and investigative inquiry. Some major goals of multicultural education include social justice and an awareness, acceptance, tolerance, and appreciation for others with respect, dignity, and equitable treatment. Students are empowered to learn about their own culture and the culture of others while developing values and belief systems about society(ies) in general. Multicultural education is pervasive in that it is integrated throughout the school day and is not relegated to one lesson/activity in particular. Multicultural education is broad in scope and includes the study of culturally diverse learners, linguistically diverse learners, and individuals from varying religions, socioeconomic classes, abilities, family lifestyles, etc.

**Multicultural literacy**   Strategies for teaching ethnic and multicultural content in an effort to provide opportunities for students to interact in a wide range of meaningful and functional learning experiences.

**Multicultural literature**   1. Literature that focuses on people who are considered to be outside of the social/political mainstream. 2. Popularly, literature offerings (e.g., folktales, books) that highlight people of color such as Hispanic Americans, African Americans, Asian Americans, and Native Americans. There is some controversy regarding whether or not Euro-American ethnic groups should be included. The term "multicultural" is used so as to avoid use of the term "minority," which has a negative connotation (i.e., low status, inferior qualities). Multicultural literature books are important in providing a more equitable presentation of society and to sensitize students to the unique and significant contributions of all peoples.

**Multiculturalism**   A philosophy wherein people of many cultures work together with mutual respect in a spirit of cooperation. SEE: *multicultural education*

**Multidisciplinary team**   A team from two or more disciplines or academic areas that comes together for planning purposes but goes separate ways for delivery of services. There tends to be

M

less involvement (cooperation and communication) amongst members of this team collectively speaking than of any other types of educational teams. The planning and implementation of services for special-needs students usually are based on the pull-out model for each service to be delivered. SEE: *interdisciplinary team, pull-out model, transdisciplinary team*

**Multifactored assessment** Assessment and evaluation of a child with a disability with a variety of test instruments and observation procedures. This is required by P.L. 94-142 when assessment is for educational placement of a child who is to receive special education services. This type of assessment prevents the misdiagnosing and misplacing of a student as a result of considering only one test score.

**Multilevel instruction** An approach to teaching whereby different types of instruction and teaching methods are used in order to meet the individual needs of each student. The ability or functional level of each student is a factor, however. Outcomes are still based on the same curriculum for all.

**Multiple disabilities** A term used to designate a condition characterized by more than one handicap. SEE: *multiply handicapped*

**Multiple-factor theories of intelligence** SEE: *multiple intelligences*

**Multiple intelligences** In Howard Gardner's theory of intelligences there are eight varieties: interpersonal, intrapersonal, bodily-kinesthetic, musical, spatial, logical-mathematical, verbal and naturalistic. SEE: *theory of multiple intelligence*

**Multiple personality** A neurotic condition that is considered a dissociative disorder. An individual shifts from one personality to another. The rival personalities may vary in the amount that each is aware of the others. This condition is, erroneously, called "schizophrenia" by movie and television scriptwriters.

**Multiple sclerosis** A neurological disorder progressive in nature in that the myelin sheath which covers the nerves hardens. It is a chronic, slow, and progressive disease of the central nervous system (CNS). As a result of nerve damage weakness, spasticity, tremors, and muscular problems take place. Depending on the severity of the condition and on which nerves are affected, a person may have difficulty with the use of his/her limbs and may have difficulty walking. Dizziness, visual problems, and slurred speech may also be present. Remission or exacerbation also come into play.

**Multiply handicapped** A student or person with more than one special need or handicap. For example, a person who is deaf and also has a physical handicap, a mentally retarded person with a speech and language disability, or a person who is blind and deaf.

**Multipurpose high school** A comprehensive high school with diversified curriculum offerings such as college courses, business courses, technology courses, etc. Such a high school is designed to meet the needs of all students regardless of their backgrounds, interests, aptitudes, and abilities.

**Multisensory procedure** A teaching approach of particular value for those students with learning disabilities (as well as any student). This method uses two or more of the senses such as vision, hearing, kinesthetics, touch, etc. Some well-known systems are the Gillingham-Stillman, Slingerland, Traub, and the Fernald-Keller amongst others. SEE: *Fernald-Keller approach, Gillingham-Stillman approach, Vak approach, Vak method, Vakt approach, Vakt method*

**Munchausen syndrome** The syndrome named after Baron Karl von Munchausen who was famous for telling tall tales, it is a type of malingering in which a person feigns sickness. If the malingerer is discovered then he/she will go to another doctor or hospital for treatment. Patients with this syndrome are in need of psychiatric diagnosis as well as therapy.

**Muscle tone**   The underlying tension of muscles.

**Muscular Dystrophy (MD)**   A group of diseases characterized by progressive atrophy or the wasting away of the skeletal muscles without damage to the nerves. It occurs more frequently in males and generally appears at an early age. It is thought to be caused by a genetic defect in muscle metabolism.

**Mutation**   An abnormal change in one or more of the genes or chromosomes. The arrangement or number may be affected. SEE: *genes, Down syndrome*

**Myasthenia gravis**   An autoimmune disorder in which the body builds antibodies against the acetylcholine receptor sites at neuromuscular junctions. Symptoms include serious muscular weakness and fatigue.

**Myelodysplasia**   A generic term indicating defective formation of the spinal cord. Myelodysplasia is also a general term used to indicate spina bifida. SEE: *spina bifida*

**Myelomeningocele**   A protrusion on the back of a child with spina bifida, consisting of a sac of nerve tissue bulging through a cleft in the spine. The spinal nerves are usually damaged and paralysis is often present in the area of the body that functions below the myelomeningocele.

**Myopathy**   A disease of the striated muscles as well as any abnormal condition of the muscular tissue, it is characterized by the atrophy (wasting away) of muscles, progressive muscular weakness, and hyperthyroidism. SEE: *hyperthyroidism*

**Myopia**   (nearsightedness) The inability to see objects at a distance SEE: *hyperopia (farsightedness), presbyopia*

**Myositis**   A condition characterized by inflammation of the muscle tissue and in particular the voluntary muscles.

**Myringoplasty**   A surgical procedure used to reconstruct a perforated (pierced) eardrum.

**Myxedema**   A medical condition that results from an underactive functioning of the thyroid gland. SEE: *hypothyroidism*

**NAEP**   SEE: *National Assessment of Progress*

**NAEYC**   SEE: *National Association for the Education of Young Children*

**Naive realism**   The belief that the world is constituted exactly as it appears to human perception. The existence of optical illusions, the fact that the world is round, and the fact that the earth goes around the sun are disproofs of naive realism. SEE: *realism, representative realism*

**NARC**   SEE: *National Association for Retarded Citizens*

**Narcolepsy**   A sleep disorder. The individual has repeated attacks of drowsiness and sleep during the day (or normally awake time). This involves a sharp reduction in muscle tone and there is a risk of serious injury to the patient. In most people, REM sleep (the sleep stage in which the major skeletal muscles lose tone) occurs only at the end of a 90-minute sleep cycle. Fortunately, there is a medical treatment for narcolepsy.

**Narcotics**   A number of drugs that induce stupor, sleep, relaxation, relief from anxiety and pain, and reverie or dream-like contemplation. For example, opium, heroin, morphine, cocaine, etc.

**Narrative text**   A type of writing style or form of writing wherein the author/ writer tells a fictional or nonfictional story in the form of prose (the language of ordinary speech) or verse (poetry), and usually in a sequential manner. SEE: *text structure*

**Nasal retina**   The half of the retina nearest to the nose. Optic nerve neurons from the nasal half-retina run to the visual brain of the opposite side (i.e., the contralateral visual brain). Three of the six layers in the lateral geniculate nucleus in the brain's thalamus are reserved for contralateral (and necessarily nasal retina) inputs.

**Nasal sound**   The sound produced by the passing/flow of air through the nasal cavity when the oral cavity is blocked. Sometimes this is called talking through one's nose.

**Nasality**   The distinctive sound produced by a lack of a speaker's ability to control the flow of air into one's mouth and nasal cavity. The air escaping through the nasal cavity gives the speech sounds produced a peculiar nasal quality as is the case when one has a head cold and feels "stuffed up."

**Nasogastric feeding**   The administration of liquid foods through a tube that has been inserted through the nose, down the throat, and into the stomach. The tube may also be used to empty the stomach of liquids or gas.

**Nasopharynx**   The upper portion of the pharynx that is connected to (continual with) the nasal passages.

**Natal**   A word used to describe a relationship to birth or the birth process.

*Nation at Risk, A*   The 1983 National Commission on Excellence in Education Report on the state of educational affairs in the country at that time. It was the first national education report that warned educators of risking the decline of our educational excellence to mediocrity. Reforms were recommended to overhaul curriculum, goals, and teaching styles.

**National Academy of Early Childhood Programs**   A division of the National Association for the Education of Young Children (NAEYC). The National Academy is charged with the accreditation of early childhood centers and schools. SEE: *National Association for the Education of Young Children (NAEYC)*

**National accreditation**   SEE: *National Council for the Accreditation of Teacher Education*

**National assessment**   A nationwide testing program that aids in determining just how effective American schools are. The major question addressed is, "Have the schools effectively taught students and have the students learned?"

**National Assessment of Educational Progress (NAEP)**   A national assessment tool/report used to evaluate a sampling of American students in the areas of reading and writing. Begun in 1970, the NAEP samples a select group of students at ages 9, 13, and 17 every five years or so. The NAEP is often referred to as "our nation's report card." This rating of our schools is mandated by Congress and conducted by the National Center for Education Statistics which falls under the U.S. Department of Education. The NAEP began a state-by-state analysis after 1990 and overviewed and rated such domains as school climate, teaching quality, standards and assessments, resources, and student achievement.

**National Association for Retarded Citizens (NARC)**   An organization of parents and professionals who are dedicated to advancing the rights, learning and working conditions, and overall status of individuals with mental retardation.

**National Board for Professional Teaching Standards**  A private organization established in 1987 to create rigorous standards and assessments designed to recognize outstanding practitioners in the teaching field. Teachers who are considered complete year-long portfolios, videotape their classrooms, compile lesson plan presentations, take subject-matter examinations, etc. Several hundred teachers have been certified by this board.

**National Council for the Accreditation of Teacher Education (NCATE)**  A nationwide organization whose primary purpose is to evaluate teacher education programs in colleges and universities. NCATE revised accreditation standards in 1993 with the major goal of requiring teacher preparation programs to implement specific national standards. NCATE does not require all teacher preparation programs (especially college programs) to have the same teacher preparation programs or require a specific number of liberal arts/professional courses. There is a trend, however, for teacher preparation institutions to provide more of a liberal arts focus/background to education students. NCATE will accredit an institution if they meet 19 standards under the general areas of 1. the curriculum of professional education, 2. the assessment process, 3. faculty qualifications/responsibility, and 4. the unit (school, department, college, university) in terms of governance, accountability, resources, etc. NCATE has recommended that teacher preparation programs key in on individual teaching candidates, interdisciplinary connections, preservice/professional training opportunities, multicultural experiences, increased opportunities for mentored practice, using technology in the classroom, and forming vital teacher-parent-community-professional partnerships. Teacher preparation institutions voluntarily apply for NCATE certification although

many states require this process. All states require state accreditation of teacher education programs, thus placing more control over the requirements of teacher preparation with the individual states.

**National Association for the Education of Young Children (NAEYC)**  The largest professional organization devoted to the promotion of children's growth, development, and education.

**National Council of Teachers of Mathematics (NCTM)**  A nonprofit professional organization founded in 1920 whose mission is to improve the mathematics education for school-age children in Canada and the United States. The NCTM publishes *Teaching Children Mathematics*. The NCTM World Wide Web site is http://www.nctm.org.

**National economy**  The total wealth and debt of a society.

**National Education Association (NEA)**  The largest organization of education professionals in the United States whose primary focus is the quality of education delivered to the students and the working conditions of educators.

**National education goals**  SEE: *Goals 2000*

**National norms**  Quantitative test data that are obtained from a standardization group selected from all parts of the country. As a result, a student's score on a test that is provided with national norms can be interpreted in relation to the performance of all other students across the entire nation.

**National Research and Educational Network (NREN)**  A nationally planned network that will connect colleges, universities, research centers, and libraries to schools throughout the United States. SEE: *Appendix 4: Computer Terms*

**Native Americans**  Peoples native to North America

**Nativism**  The doctrine that behavior is the product of hereditary factors and that individual differences can be explained genetically. A specific teaching of nativism is that the mapping of the visual field on the visual brain is preestablished at birth, not shaped by experience.

**Natural concept**   A category that applies to the world of our experience, a familiar group of objects belonging to one category (e.g., "animals"). SEE: *concept*

**Natural setting**   The typical environment in which students and persons of similar age attend school, work, play, and live.

**Natural support**   Supportive service for students or persons with disabilities from nonorganizational or government agencies such as members of one's family, colleagues, peers, and friends.

**Naturalism**   The pure philosophical position which adheres to the belief that there is no reality beyond what humans can perceive; in other words, only the physical world as we know it is real. This is the oldest pure philosophical position, with Hobbes (1588–1679) and Spencer (1820–1903) strong proponents of the naturalist position. Rousseau (1712–1778), the most well-known naturalist, believed that a teacher should nurture students as a gardener would his plants by providing the optimal environment and nourishment. Rousseau also believed that all humans were innately good but were corrupted to some extent by society.

**Naturalistic observation**   A research method in the sciences. The phenomena of interest are observed as they occur in the natural course of events. Almost all of astronomy is based on data collected by this method. In the social sciences, participant observation is a major variety of naturalistic observation. The participant becomes a member of a group and observes it while participating in its activities.

**Nature**   1. One's genetically inherited characteristics such as skin, eye color, physical characteristics, temperament, and other inborn qualities. 2. The forces and laws that govern the physical universe and change therein.

**Nature vs. nurture**   A controversial theory involving the importance of and contribution to a persons intelligence that is derived from genetics/heredity (nature) and that which is derived from sociocultural/educational/environmental (nurture) influences. Most specialists in the fields of psychology and education feel that both are important factors.

**NCATE**   SEE: *National Council for Accreditation of Teacher Education*

**NCTM**   SEE: *National Council of Teachers of Mathematics*

**NEA**   SEE: *National Education Association*

**Near-death experiences**   A set of conscious experiences shared by people who have momentarily "died" and have been restored to life at the last moment. Correlating experiences of this phenomena are the view of one's own body from above and seeing a lighted tunnel entrance.

**Nearsightedness**   SEE: *myopia*

**Need**   A physiological innate condition (e.g., hunger, thirst) that causes arousal and the occurrence of responses (e.g., eating, drinking) that will satisfy the need. SEE: *motivation, motive*

**Negative correlation**   An orderly relationship between people's scores on one continuous variable and their scores on another variable is a correlation. In a negative correlation, the higher the score on one of the variables, the lower the score on the second variable. For example, more winning games for a pitcher in baseball results in a lower earned-run average. In education, greater absenteeism generally results in lower grades. SEE: *correlation, positive correlation*

**Negative reinforcement**   The conditioning of an operant ("voluntary") response by removal of an unwanted state of affairs right after the response occurs. This results in an increased probability that the response will be made the next time that unwanted circumstance happens.

**Negative skew**   Also known as skew to the left. A negative skew is actually a shape of a frequency distribution curve that is different from the normal curve in that it is asymmetrical (the normal curve is symmetrical): more scores occur at one end of the curve than the other. This is the type of skewed curve that shows most of the scores are high ones, piling up at the right part of the curve. The thin tail of the curve points to the left; this means the curve is skewed to the left, or negatively skewed. In skewed curves, the mean, median, and mode become separated, with the mean being pulled too far to the tail to be an acceptable measure of central tendency. For skewed distributions, the best policy is to report the median as the central score for the group. SEE: *positive skew*

**Negativism**   1. A lack of a positive attitude that can adversely impact relationships and overall functioning. 2. A condition whereby demands are made upon a student or person that are beyond one's abilities. This can lead to withdrawal, nonparticipation, refusal to speak, and even doing the opposite of what is suggested.

**Neglect syndrome**   A bizarre symptom of brain damage in which the person acts as if a part of his/her body does not exist. A man may fail to shave one side of his face, for example. This is most often a result of damage to the parietal lobe of the right cerebral hemisphere.

**Negligence**   The lack of use of common sense, or failure to use reasonable judgment and care to a point where one's actions result in injury to other(s).

**Neodissociation theory**   Ernest Hilgard's theory of hypnotism. The hypnotised person has had his/her consciousness divided into channels that operate independently. This allows the possibility of a "hidden observer" who sees what is "really going on" while the hypnotized subject is involved in the hypnotic trance.

**Neologisms**   A speech pattern typical in schizophrenics wherein unnatural or meaningless words are coined or used by the schizophrenic.

**Neonatal**   Refers to the time period between the onset of labor and the first six weeks of birth.

**Neonatal hypothyroidism**   A medical condition caused by an underactive, impaired, or even absent thyroid gland. Development can be impaired and mental retardation can take place. SEE: *cretinism, hypothyroidism*

**Neonatal Intensive Care (NIC)**   A separate special hospital section or unit designed to care for infants who are seriously ill and in need of constant medical care and monitoring.

**Nephritis**   A condition involving inflammation of the kidneys. This condition is characterized by symptoms that include digestive disturbances, eye disturbances, puffiness about the eyes and other parts of the body, fever, headache, weakness, nausea, vasomotor disturbances, high blood pressure, and anemia.

**Nephrosis**   A kidney disorder caused by infections, burns, poisoning, or other diseases. In general, this condition involves kidney degeneration to a point where poor filtering or elimination occurs and can cause puffiness, loss of appetite, malaise, etc.

**Nerve**   A bundle of axons in the peripheral nervous system.

**Nerve deafness**   That form of deafness that is a result of damage to the cochlea or the auditory nerve pathway. Nerve deafness cannot be relieved by a hearing aid.

**Nerve growth factor**   A protein that stimulates the survival and growth of neurons in the peripheral nervous system and also in the brain.

**Nervous system**   The entire set of the body's nerve cells, their interconnections, and their supporting cells. The two chief components of the nervous system are the central nervous system and the peripheral nervous system. The brain and spinal cord belong to the CNS. SEE: *peripheral nervous system (PNS)*

**Network**   A system in which two or more computers or other communication devices are connected for educational and/or informational purposes. SEE: *Appendix 4: Computer Terms*

**Neural graft**   An implantation of healthy nerve cells in an area of the central nervous system that has been damaged. Ordinarily, such a graft would not be expected to work because damage to neurons of the central nervous system (CNS) is permanent. Recent research utilizing chemical assistance from the nerve growth factor, however, seems to be promising. SEE: *central nervous system (CNS)*

**Neurasthenic neurosis**   Sometimes called neurasthenia, it is a condition with symptoms of chronic weakness and exhaustion. A neurasthenic person is often undernourished-looking in appearance, has small muscles, a long narrow thorax, and appears weak and easily fatigued.

**Neuroanatomy**   The anatomy of the nervous system.

**Neurofibromatosis**   An hereditary condition characterized usually by tumors of the skin. This genetic disorder affects growth of neural tissues and can be found in intercranial and interspinal locations as well as the skin.

**Neuroleptic**   The kind of antipsychotic drug that is prescribed for schizophrenia patients. Examples of neuroleptics are chlorpromazine, haloperidol, and clozapine.

**Neurologic impairment**   Any physical disability caused by damage to the nervous system (brain, spinal cord, ganglia, and nerves).

**Neurological**   Pertaining to the study of the nervous system or nervous diseases.

**Neurological dysfunctioning**   Refers to aberrations or abnormalities in some CNS (central nervous system) structure or system. Generally, abnormal behavioral manifestations lead practitioners to infer there are such neurological problems because new research developments (e.g., PET scans) are now validating earlier conjectures, especially in the area of learning disabilities. For example, it has been found with dyslexics that some have abnormal EEGs or visual thresholds.

**Neurological examination**   A medical examination usually conducted by a neurologist (a physician) of the sensory or motor responses. Reflexes are particularly noted as indicators of possible disorders of the nervous system. SEE: *neurological dysfunctioning, neurologic impairment, neurologists*

**Neurologists**   Physicians who study the brain and related disorders and diseases, as well as the science of the nervous system as it relates to other parts of the body.

**Neuromuscular disease**   A disease that affects both a person's nerves and muscles. Examples of such problems include muscular dystrophy, multiple sclerosis, myasthenia gravis, Huntington's chorea, and Parkinson's disease. SEE: *Muscular Dystrophy (MD)*

**Neuromuscular junction**   The functional link between a motor nerve ending and the membrane around a muscle bundle. In many ways, the neuromuscular junction works like a synapse between a sending and a receiving neuron. The nerve ending releases a chemical neurotransmitter that settles into a properly-shaped receptor site on the membrane.

**Neuron**   A cell that is specialized for the transmission of information from one part of the body to another. Collectively, neurons comprise the information-handling part of the nervous system. There are billions of neurons of various shapes and sizes. The other cells of the nervous system are the supporting cells known as neuroglia.

**Neurophonia**   A condition characterized by a spasm or tic of the muscles involved in speech. This results in an uncontrollable (involuntary) cry or sound.

**Neurophrenia**   A term used to describe conditions of mental disorder resulting from damage or disorder of the central nervous system (CNS). SEE: *neurological* *dysfunctioning, neurological impairment, neurosis*

**Neuropsychological examination**   Systematic testing of people with learning disabilities with a battery of test procedures. There are test batteries available that purport to screen patients for organic brain disorders and to indicate a probable diagnosis, such as the Halstead-Reitan battery and the Luria-Nebraska neuropsychological battery. Often, a neuropsychological assessment will include one of the Wechsler intelligence scales. Memory, somatosensory ability, picture-copying accuracy, and other skills may be tested in a neuropsychological examination. Clear indications of damage to a part of the brain are shown by "hard signs" while behavioral disturbances that are possible indications of brain damage are called "soft signs."

**Neurosis**   A diagnosis of mental/emotional disorder that is not serious enough to require hospitalization. A neurosis can be treated in visits to the office of a psychologist/psychiatrist/psychoanalyst. Examples of neuroses (plural) are anxiety disorders, panic attack syndrome, multiple personality, and obsessive-compulsive disorder.

**Neurotic disturbances**   SEE: *neurological dysfunctioning, neurologic impairment, neurosis*

**Neurotransmitters**   Chemicals released at the axon terminals of sending neurons that create electrical voltage changes on the membranes of postsynaptic (receiving) neurons, or, if the sending neuron is a motor neuron, the voltage change on the membrane of a muscle bundle. Neurotransmitters may either add a negative charge to the outside of the receiving neuron's membrane (which has an excitatory effect, helping to start a nerve impulse) or a positive charge, which tends to inhibit the receiving cell (i.e., hinder the formation of a nerve impulse). The amount of a particular neurotransmitter in the body at a particular time can have a significant impact on behavior (see nicotine) or the acquisition of certain disorders (e.g.,

schizophrenia—a disorder possibly caused by an excess of a neurotransmitter called dopamine). The best known neurotransmitter is acetylcholine.

**New England primer**   An introductory reader used in New England schools during the 1800s. This type of eclectic reader included poetry, prose, and Biblical references. This schoolbook was originally published in 1690 and emphasized the memorization of biblical text.

**Newbery Medal**   A special award given to the most outstanding children's book. The Newbery Medal is named after John Newbery, a famous American children's book publisher and writer. The award has been given annually since 1922. It is one of two major outstanding book awards in the United States. The other is the Caldecott Medal for the most distinguished children's book illustrator. SEE: *Caldecott Medal*

**NIC**   SEE: *Neonatal Intensive Care*

**Nicotine**   A chemical that produces acetylcholine-activation at some places in the nervous system. The acetylcholine-accepting receptor sites that can be activated by nicotine are called nicotinic receptors. These receptors are found on the membranes of the striped muscles. An overdose of nicotine could lead to an excessive rise in the muscle tone of the striped muscles, causing a rigid and tense form of paralysis called spasticity. Nicotine is extremely toxic and addictive. Cigarettes/tobacco contain nicotine.

**Niemann-Pick disease**   A severe metabolic disorder characterized by an enlarged liver and spleen. This disorder usually results in a variety of handicaps (multiple handicaps), including mental retardation and others. SEE: *Pick's disease*

**Night terror**   A frightening experience accompanied by a fast heartbeat and other "emergency reactions" that affect the sleeper in stage 4 sleep, not stage REM (dreaming) sleep. Most of the victims of night terrors are children who have difficulty coping with such an unusual experience. In this form of nightmare the individual awakens screaming in terror. This terror or fear continues for a period of time after the individual is awakened and conscious. SEE: *nightmare*

**Nightmare**   A dream with threatening, anxiety-arousing content. A nightmare is less serious than a night terror. SEE: *night terror*

**NMR**   SEE: *Nuclear Magnetic Resonance*

**Noise**   A term used to indicate a poor acoustical environment. Such an environment can make it difficult or even impossible to hear properly. The condition can be a result of poor acoustics in the room or even poor syntax of the speaker.

**Nominal aphasia**   An impairment of language that is characterized by an inability to recall and recognize names and objects. SEE: *anomia*

**Nominal data or scales**   Data or scales that classify information into discrete or separate categories. One person, place, or thing can be assigned to one (and only one) category and members of a category have attributes or characteristics in common. This can be considered "head counting" and nominal data is frequently used in polling and demographics work.

**Noncategorical**   The practice of grouping individuals with disabilities without labeling the disabling condition. In Massachusetts, for example, students are grouped by prototype status (meaning how much time is spent out of the mainstream classes) and are not labeled by their disabling condition.

**Noncertified teacher**   An individual who may have completed a teacher preparatory program but did not fully meet standards for state certification.

**Nondiscriminatory and multidisciplinary assessment**   A type of assessment required under the provisions of the Individuals with Disabilities Education Act (P.L. 101-476). Assessment procedures and tests must be administered in the primary language of the student. Such a procedure is designed to prevent racial and cultural discrimination. A multidisciplanary team should use varying types of assessments appropriate to the student's background in order to accurately determine a student's needs. SEE: *P.L. 94-192, P.L. 101-476, multidisciplinary team*

**Nondiscriminatory testing**   Testing or assessments that consider a student's background to include one's culture and language. SEE: *nondiscriminatory and multidisciplinary assessment*

**Non-English speakers**   SEE: *bilingual learners*

**Nonfamily householder**   A person who lives and maintains a household alone, or if she/he lives with others they are not related. SEE: *householder*

**Nongraded school**   A type of school wherein grade levels are eliminated sequentially for two or more years.

**Noninstitutional population**   Those individuals who do not reside in such institutions as residential homes, schools, hospitals, or residential settings for persons with physical or mental disabilities; hospitals or residential settings for mental, tubercular, or chronic-disease patients; homes for unmarried mothers; nursing, convalescent, rest homes, or assisted living quarters for the aged and dependent; orphanages; and prisons or other correctional institutions.

**Nonpaid supports**   Work of a voluntary nature involving ordinary assistance given to a person with a disability usually by family members, friends, or neighbors. The aid is at no cost to the individual with the disability.

**Non-parametric statistics**   Inferential statistics (e.g., chi-square) that are built on the assumption that the scores/ observations used were not obtained from a normal or bell-shaped distribution.

**Nonsheltered work environments**   Work sites for persons with disabilities that involve working alongside non-handicapped persons as equal co-workers. The work is legitimately competitive and no special accommodations other than those required by law are available to persons with disabilities.

**Nonsuppurative otitis**   A non-pus producing inflammation of the middle ear without an infection, it often precedes the infectious form of ear problem, otitis media with effusion. SEE: *otitis media*

**Nonverbal communication**   A condition in which a person is able to communicate ideas without the use of speech, such as in the use of hand and arm signals and sign language. This may include gestures and vocalization but no recognizable words.

**Norm**   That which is considered to be average or normal.

**Norm-based averages**   SEE: *Norm-Referenced Assessments*

**Norm group**   The group of students used to provide the data from which test norms are calculated. SEE: *norms*

**Norm-referenced**   The assessment of the quality of a student's performance by comparing that performance with that of other students (i.e., the norm group).

**Norm-Referenced Assessments** Assessments based upon averages normed at the local or national level. SEE: *norm, norms*

**Norm-referenced data**   Data which are based on local, state, regional, or national norms. SEE: *norms*

**Norm-referenced grading**   Marking "on a curve." A student's grade is based on how his/her performance compares with that of the other students in the group.

**Norm-referenced test**   A standardized test that compares a student's or other individual's performance with that of a group of persons on which the test has been standardized or normed.

**Normal curve**   A distribution of scores that forms what has come to be known as the "bell-shaped" or "normal" curve. Educators are familiar with grading practices based on the normal curve where a certain percentage of students receives grades of A, B, C, D, and F. Most students fall in the middle grade categories because the assumption is made that student abilities (via IQ) form

a normal curve. In order for a distribution to form a normal curve, there must be a "normal distribution." SEE: *normal distribution*

**Normal distribution**   A distribution that forms a normal curve where 50 percent of the scores fall above the mean and 50 percent of the score fall below the mean. The mode, median, and mean fall precisely at the same point in a normal distribution. Approximately 68 percent of the scores fall between plus or minus 1.0 Standard Deviations (SD) from the mean; 95 percent between plus or minus 2.0 SD, 99 percent between plus or minus 3.0 SD. There are a number of variables that form a normal distribution, including intelligence, aptitude, height, weight, etc. SEE: *normal curve*

**Normal school**   A college-level two-year training school for teachers. No longer in use, it was the first American institution solely dedicated to teacher training.

**Normalization**   The principle of allowing each person's life to be as normal as possible in all aspects, including residence, schooling, work, recreational activities, and overall independence. Similarities between people with and without disabilities of the same age are emphasized.

**Normative ethics**   A part of prescriptive philosophy. Normative ethics are concerned with answering questions of what people ought to do, what constitutes the right way to behave, what it means to be a good person, etc. SEE: *ethics, prescriptive philosophy*

**Norming sample**   A large group of persons who have been given the same standardized test. Their average scores (and the variability of scores around the average) are used as norms to decide how the scores of others who take the test should be interpreted.

**Norms**   Standardized test scores that describe performance on a given test for particular groups of individual (e.g., age and grade) in terms of the average scores for that particular group. Such average scores are termed norms. Norms can be local or national. SEE: *local norms, national norms*

**Novice teachers**   Teachers who are just beginning their work. Although they have done well in their training, they do not yet have a developed set of solutions for a number of typical classroom problems. Furthermore, there are many aspects of teaching that they will learn from experience.

**NREM sleep**   Sleep without rapid eye movements (NREM stands for non-REM). The NREM sleep stages include descending stage 1, stage 2, stage 3, and stage 4 sleep. After the first 90-minute cycle, stage 1 is of the ascending type. Another name for ascending stage 1 sleep is stage REM sleep.

**NREN**   SEE: *National Research and Educational Network*

**Nuclear Magnetic Resonance (NMR)**   SEE: *Magnetic Resonance Imaging (MRI)*

**Nucleus**   1. The central part of an animal's body cell, that contains the chromosomes that control hereditary characteristics. 2. A collection of nerve-cell bodies in the brain or spinal cord, making up part of the gray matter of the central nervous system (CNS). 3. The

central part of an educational program, system, or curriculum.

**Null hypothesis**   The hypothesis given that states there is no relationship or difference between variables under study and that any relationships that emerge are a result of chance and chance alone (i.e., sampling error). Rejecting the null hypothesis in a research study means that the results obtained were statistically significant and probably not a result of chance.

**Nursery school**   A school that provides education to students at the pre-kindergarten level. Nursery schools normally service children from ages 2–4.

**Nurturing attitude**   In education, that disposition expressed by a teacher or educational professional that displays encouragement, caring and concern for a student's needs, academically, behaviorally, socially, psychologically and the like. Such persons provide a supportive and favorable atmosphere for growth within the context of the classroom and/or school environment.

**Nystagmus**   A rapid, involuntary, rhythmic and cyclical movement of the eyes that may cause difficulty in reading or fixating on an object.

**OBE**   SEE: *Outcomes-Based Education*

**Obedience**   The readiness to change one's behavior in conformity with commands from an authority figure.

**Obesity**   An extremely overweight condition. The person has so much excess fat that the abdomen and other body

parts have a round and protruding shape. Generally, an obese person is 20 to 30 percent overweight or more based on recommended averages in height and weight tables.

**Object permanence**   A relatively mature stage of perceptual development.

Before this stage is reached an infant immediately forgets about an object when the object is hidden from the infant's view. An older child starts to search for the missing object (i.e., this child makes the assumption that the object is nearby and can be located).

**Objective**  In education, a specific purpose or goal to be reached/learned by the student.

**Objective idealism**  The view that reality is of a single nature and that it is mental. In this view, reality transcends the differences among individual human minds. When an individual gains knowledge, he/she is moving closer to oneness with the absolute. The author of this view is Hegel. SEE: *determinism, dialectic, idealism, metaphysics, monism, subjective idealism*

**Objective scoring**  The agreement by different judges, raters, or observers on the ratings, grades, or scores to be assigned for a given performance. Objective scoring occurs when the assessment procedure is a reliable one.

**Objective test**  A test that yields mathematically derived results that can be evaluated or scored by different people who will calculate identical outcomes. Multiple choice and true-false tests can be considered objective tests as they are scored in such a way that a chosen answer is either right or wrong and is scored accordingly.

**Observation learning**  A method of learning in which the student learns by observing what others do. It is usually the prelude to actually doing what one has observed or at least part of what has been observed.

**Observation techniques**  An organized system of observing various aspects of a school or classroom. Such procedures are systematic approaches to gathering statistical data. SEE: *observation learning*

**Observer prejudgment**  The premature labeling of a pupil on the part of a teacher on the basis of prior information. SEE: *self-fulfilling prophecy*

**Obsession**  A condition wherein an idea or thought persists to a degree that a person fixates or dwells upon it even when the person considers the idea or thought irrational.

**Obsessive-compulsive disorder**  A type of neurosis (i.e., a relatively mild behavior disorder) in which the individual keeps repeating the same activity (i.e., compulsive behavior) and rethinking the same thoughts, as when an old song lyric keeps "running through one's head" (which is obsessive thinking).

**Obstacle sense**  A term used to describe the skills possessed by the blind or severely visually impaired when they can accurately detect obstacles in the environment. It is a result of the ability to detect minute changes in the pitch of echoes of high frequency.

**Obstetrician**  A physician who is a specialist in the field of obstetrics. One who deals with a woman before, during, and after the birth of a child. SEE: *obstetrics, pediatrics*

**Obstetrics**  The branch of medicine that deals with the medical management of women and the puerperium period (the 42-day period after birth). SEE: *obstetrician, pediatrician*

**Obturator**  1. A device used to close a cleft palate (the roof of the mouth). 2. Any device that closes an opening. The device is artificial in nature.

**Occipital lobes**  The lobes of the brain that contain visual processing areas related to perception of visual stimuli in the environment. Damage to this area could result in blindness or visual deficits particularly related to object recognition, scanning, color discrimination, and visual recall.

**Occlusion**  A term used to describe how teeth close and fit together. Poor occlusion may cause speech problems.

**Occupational therapist**  A specialist who develops and maintains for a person with disabilities the functions and skills necessary for daily living such as dressing, mealtime activities, etc.

**Occupational therapy**  Service relating to expected or actual work activities. A professionally trained therapist designs and delivers such instruction or services. SEE: *occupational therapist*

**Ocular** A term used to describe things that involve or pertain to the eye.

**Ocular motility** The eyes' ability to move.

**Oculomotor** Motor activities that relate to the movement of the eye.

**Oedipus complex** The concept in Freudian psychology of the arousal of a boy's sexual interest in his mother. This is seen by the Freudians as the main event in the third stage of psychosexual development, the phallic (the first two being the oral and the anal). For normal development of the male, this complex must be resolved. The cause of the resolution is said to be fear of being castrated by the father.

**Official assessments** Pupil assessments that teachers are required to complete in the form of reports to their superintendents or other superiors. These reports may involve the placement, grouping, promotion, or graduation of pupils.

**Old Deluder Satan Act** Passed by the Massachusetts legislature in 1647, it is an old colonial education law. It required all towns with at least 50 households to provide schools (elementary education) for their children. The idea was for all students to learn to read the Bible, in particular, and thus the children would be able to gain the knowledge necessary to delude Satan (therefore, the name for the act).

**Old field schools** Unsuitable housing in old and worn tobacco fields in the South where poor white children received a rudimentary or basic education during the 1800s and early 1900s.

**Olfaction** The sense of smell.

**Oligodontia** A condition in which a person develops less than the normal number of teeth. An adult human normally has 32 teeth (second set). The normal two-year-old has 20 milk (deciduous) or baby teeth.

**OMEP** Organisation Mondiale Pour L'Education Prescolaire (World Organization for the Education of Preschoolers). An organization concerned with children's growth, education, and development. SEE: *NAEYC*

**Omission** The deletion of a phoneme such as saying "ca-" for "can" or "ha-" for "hat". SEE: *phoneme*

**On-the-job-training** A program of education wherein the skills necessary for a particular vocation or profession are taught primarily on the job site rather than in the classroom.

**Oncologist** A medical doctor who specializes in the treatment of tumors, especially malignant tumors (cancers).

**Oncology** The science of the study of tumors frequently associated with cancer (malignant tumor).

**One-room school** The so-called "one-room schoolhouse" was popular years ago in small communities, especially in rural areas. One teacher taught all students of all grade levels in a single room, thus the name.

**Onset** The consonant sounds that precede a vowel in a syllable. The onset is followed by the rime. For example, in the word pen, "p" is the onset and "en" is the rime. SEE: *rime, syllable*

**Ontology** The study of being and existence.

**Open-caption TV** Television captions (worded lines of explanation) that appear at the bottom of a TV screen. Since the 1970s, certain selected programs are captioned as an aid to the hearing impaired. Open-captioned programs can be seen on all television sets whereas closed-caption programs can only be seen on certain sets that subscribe to this special programming.

**Open classroom** Educationally speaking, a more modern innovation wherein self-contained or closed-off classrooms were replaced by an open space and open curriculum program. Individualized instruction for students is the key and students have the freedom to move about in the open area. SEE: *open education*

*O*

**Open education**   A philosophy of education wherein students are encouraged to explore courses and curriculum appropriate to their interests and abilities without losing the foundations of a good education. This approach allows individual differences to be met at the personal level and thus provide the student with a great deal of satisfaction during the schooling process.

**Open enrollment**   Also called school choice, this is the practice of allowing students to attend the school of their choice within a particular school system or district.

**Open institution**   An educational organization that is subject to conditions and pressures outside of itself (e.g., a school system is subject to the wishes and dictates of school boards or committees usually elected by the community at large—all citizens of the appropriate ages are eligible for admittance). Access is available from without.

**Open-space school**   The open-classroom concept or a school building without interior walls enclosing teaching areas.

**Operant conditioning**   One of the methods of behavior modification wherein the student learns that rewards are given or withheld based on whether or not the student's response is appropriate. For example, the reward for good behavior might be a treat or small gift whereas poor behavior would elicit no reward at all or even punishment.

**Operant conditioning audiometry**   A method of measuring hearing by conditioning the subject to make an observable response to sound. For example, a child may be taught to drop a block into a box each time a light and a loud tone are presented. Once this response is conditioned, the light is no longer presented and the volume and pitch of the tone are gradually decreased. When the child no longer drops the block into the box, the audiologist knows the child cannot hear the tone. This procedure is used to test the hearing of nonverbal children and adults.

**Operants**   Responses emitted by an organism that do not appear to be initiated by an environmental stimulus (e.g., a bird flying, babies babbling, dogs running on four legs, etc.).

**Operational definition**   The scientific way of defining a concept; that is, by reference to observable and measurable events. For example, one ice fisherman carved a giant-sized circular hole in the ice when ice-fishing with his child. Another ice fisherman cut smaller, more normal-sized holes. The first fisherman's child asks, "Daddy, what is an optimist?" The concept of "optimist" is thereby defined operationally.

**Operationalize**   To make an abstract concept measurable by redefining it in terms of observable procedures.

**Operations**   In the sense of "mental operations," these are actions that a person imagines herself/himself performing.

**Ophthalmia neonatorum**   An inflammation of purulent conjunctivitis in the front of the eyeball. Usually occurring during an infant's first week.

**Ophthalmologist**   A physician trained in the diagnosis and treatment of the diseases of the eye. An ophthalmologist can prescribe drugs for eye disorders, measure refractions, prescribe lenses, and/or perform eye surgery.

**Ophthalmology**   The study of or the science of diseases of the eyes. SEE: *ophthalmologist*

**Opiates**   A set of chemicals having drug effects similar to those of opium (namely, pleasant mood, relaxation, and sedation) and that become addictive. Opium derivatives such as morphine, heroin, codeine, and demeral are opiates. The body's own natural opiates are endorphines, enkephalins, and dynorphin.

**Opium**   A narcotic drug that is very addictive in nature, it is derived from the opium poppy flower (i.e., the unripe buds or capsules). The dried latex extracted from the poppy serves as the basis for the manufacture of morphine from which, in turn, heroin is derived. SEE: *heroin, morphine*

**Opponent-process theory** A nineteenth-century theory of color vision offered by Ewald Hering. The original theory was based on the two types of metabolism; namely, the anabolic buildup of body chemicals and the catabolic breakdown of body chemicals. Color receptors in the eye were hypothesized to have dual properties: a receptor gave the experience of red when its chemicals were broken down but the experience of green when the chemical parts were reassembled. The twentieth-century version of the theory was stated by R. DeValois. The two opposed processes were changed to neural excitation and inhibition. The neurons involved are no longer said to be the receptors; they are, instead, the retinal ganglion cells and some of the cells in the lateral geniculate nucleus. If a color sensitive neuron is excited by red (a result of red light affecting the cones leading up to it), then it is inhibited by green.

**Opportunistic infection** Infection that can penetrate the immune system. Such germs usually do not infect a normally healthy person but in this case a weakened or defective immune system allows the opportunity for infection to take place.

**Optacon** A special device that changes visual information to an exact tactile duplicate; of special use for the blind. It was developed at Stanford University and is comprised of 144 tactile pins that are activated by print and produce a vibratory image of the letter(s) on the finger(s).

**Optic atrophy** A term used to describe a degenerative disease of the nerve fibers leading from the retina to the brain.

**Optic chiasm** X-shaped structure at the base of the hypothalamus, marking the point where the two optic nerves arrive at the brain. The x-shape stands out because the white, myelin-sheathed axons contrast with the gray matter of the ventral hypothalamus. The optic nerve axons, once they travel in the brain, comprise the left and right optic tracts.

**Optic nerve** The nerve that carries impulses from the eye to the brain.

**Optician** A vision specialist who is trained to fit and grind lenses for eyeglass prescriptions and can fit and order contact lenses if trained to do so. SEE: *optometrist, ophthalmologist*

**Optimal level** An aspect of cognitive development according to Fischer's theory of academic skills. The "optimal level" is the highest level one can attain, with the benefit of the greatest possible amount of supportive assistance.

**Optimal pitch** That pitch produced by the speech or laryngeal mechanism (the voice box) effectively and with the least amount of effort on the part of the speaker.

**Options** The various choices offered a test-taker answering a multiple-choice question. The choices for one item include the correct answer and two or more distractors.

**Optometrist** A vision specialist who can prescribe and fit corrective eyeglass lenses and contacts. An optometrist is not a physician but like an ophthalmologist may prescribe drugs for eye disorders whereas an optician cannot. SEE: *optician, ophthalmologist*

**Oral** An approach to education of deaf children that stresses learning to speak as an essential element of integration into the hearing world.

**Oral-aural method** A method of teaching deaf students who have some residual hearing; amplification is used as well as speech reading (lip reading). Speech production and manual communications are emphasized. Reading and writing take place usually after oral communications or the oral-aural method is reasonably mastered.

**Oral method** A method of teaching deaf students how to communicate through the use of speech. First students are taught to pronounce syllables, which are then combined to form words and on to sentences. The acquisition of correct accents is stressed. SEE: *oral*

**Oral miscue analysis**   SEE: *miscue*

**Oral stage**   The first of Sigmund Freud's five stages of psychosexual development. In this stage, the infant seeks gratification and pleasure from oral stimulation.

**Ordinal data or scales**   Data that are rank ordered (e.g., first, second, third). Interval data can be converted to ordinal data. If two interval numbers have the same value, then each is assigned the same average rank (e.g., if assigned an average rank of 1 and 2, the assigned rank for each is 1.5).

**Organ of Corti**   The organ of Corti is housed in the snail-shaped cochlea that is filled with fluid. It converts sound waves into nerve impulses that are transmitted along the auditory nerve to the brain. SEE: *cochlea, sound waves, auditory nerve, brain*

**Organic**   Inborn or inherent causes. These are known abnormalities of a neurological or structural nature.

**Organic disability**   A disability that is caused by inborn or inherent causes. An individual born with cerebral palsy would be considered to have an organic disability as opposed to brain damage caused by a car accident.

**Organization**   The continuous process of rearranging experiences and observations into mental schemes. The orderly form of a network of interrelated items.

**Orientation**   The ability to establish one's position in relation to the environment.

**Orthomolecular medicine**   An unproven approach to remediation of learning disabilities and to psychotherapy of emotional disorders through the use of very high doses of vitamins (megadoses). SEE: *megavitamins*

**Orthopedic devices**   Such objects as braces, crutches, and wheelchairs that are used to aid persons with physical disabilities.

**Orthopedic disability**   SEE: *orthopedically handicapped*

**Orthopedic impairment**   Any disability caused by disorders to the musculoskeletal system.

**Orthopedically handicapped**   SEE: *orthopedic impairment, physically handicapped*

**Orthopedics**   A specialty area that deals with the science of prevention and correction of disorders of the body's skeleton, joints, and muscles; that is, the locomotor structures. It is sometimes used synonymously with the term orthotics. SEE: *orthotics*

**Orthoptist**   A vision specialist who uses eye exercises when prescribed by an ophthalmologist.

**Orthosis**   An aid or device like a crutch or brace that helps restore a lost bodily function. The assistance provided may result in partial or complete restoration of functioning.

**Orthotics**   The science of artificial devices for orthopedics. Examples include knee braces, arch supports, etc. SEE: *prosthetic devices, orthopedics*

**Oscillator**   A repetitive back-and-forth motion such as the flapping of wings by a flying animal or the scratching motions of a dog or cat performing a scratching reflex.

**Osmosis**   The passage of liquid, usually water, through a membrane that is semipermeable.

**Ossicles**   Three small bones (hammer, anvil, and stirrup) that transmit sound energy through the middle ear to the inner ear. SEE: *ossicular chain*

**Ossicular chain**   The three bones in the middle ear commonly called the hammer, anvil, and stirrup because of their shape. They are alternatively called the malleus, incus, and stapes, respectively.

**Osteoarthritis**   A type of arthritis that is prevalent among children with physical disabilities. Damage to muscle cartilage surrounding bone joints makes movement painful and difficult.

**Osteogenesis imperfecta**   Better known as "brittle bone disease," this is a rare hereditary disorder that adversely affects bone growth and causes bones to easily break. Other characteristics of this disorder can include early deafness, capillary bleeding, opalescent teeth, and translucent skin as well as joint instability. In most cases, it is an inherited autosomal dominant trait. Bones broken heal normally and as a person ages, fracturing decreases and sometimes disappears. At present, there is no known cure for osteogenesis imperfecta. SEE: *autosomes*

**Osteomyelitis**   Inflammation of the bone and especially the bone marrow. Chronic pain and pain following pressure of the affected area as well as swelling and inflammation are its chief characteristics.

**Other health impaired**   A general category of health impairments as described under the Individuals with Disabilities Education Act (IDEA), or P.L. 101-476.

**Otitis media**   An infection of the middle ear that can be treated with antibiotics.

**Otolaryngologist**   A physician whose specialty is diseases of the ear and throat.

**Otolith organs**   Also known as vestibular sacs, these are two sense organs of the inner ear, one of which, the utricle, detects horizontal acceleration of the head. The other otolith organ, the saccule, senses vertical head accelerations. The "oto" part refers to the ear, while the "lith" refers to stone. The mechanism of these organs depends on stones that rest against the hairs, or cilia, of the receptor cells (the hair cells).

**Otologist**   A physician whose specialty is diseases of the ear.

**Otology**   An area of medical specialty dealing with the ear and diseases of the ear.

**Otosclerosis**   An inherited disease involving chronic progressive deafness. This disease of the bone of the middle ear is caused by the formation of spongy bone around the stapes. SEE: *stapes, stapedectomy*

**Otoscope**   An instrument used by ear specialists to examine the auditory canal and eardrum.

**Otoxic drugs**   Drugs that have an adverse effect upon the organs of balance and hearing or the eighth cranial nerve (the acoustic nerve).

**Outcomes**   A term used to indicate the results or the expected results of an educational plan or program (e.g., achieving one year's growth in an academic area; completing a book report; preparing an oral presentation; etc.). Outcomes can also be the consequences of decisions made.

**Outcomes-Based Education (OBE)**   The demonstrations or activities generated from high quality, meaningful activities that are considered culminating activities and indicators of learning achieved. Outcomes-based assessments usually occur during such culminating periods of one's academic career as fourth or fifth, eighth, and twelfth grades. William Spady describes the "Demonstration Mountain" in OBE with 1. a *traditional zone* that involves discrete concrete learning tasks, 2. the *transitional zone* that moves to more complex unstructured learning tasks and higher-order competencies, and the 3. *transformational zone* that culminates in life-role applications and functioning and complex performances.

**Outer-directedness**   A personality trait wherein one is dependent upon others for direction in solving problems. It is a term indicating an external locus of control. SEE: *external locus of control*

**Outreach programs**   Special programs for students with special learning challenges/needs that are provided on site in the school system by private day or residential schools or by other centralized agencies such as a state regional education center. Conversely, town or city schools can have programs that reach out to other school systems for delivery of services that the assisted community might lack.

**Oval window**   The section of the ear that connects the middle with the inner. It is an oval-shaped aperature in which fits the base of the stapes. SEE: *stapes*

**Ovary** The female gonad that releases (at different stages of the menstrual cycle) the hormones estradiol and progesterone. The ovary also forms the ovum, which is the female reproductive cell or gamete.

**Overachievement** The performance of an individual above the level normally expected on the basis of innate ability or of ability measures.

**Overcorrection** A behavior modification procedure in which the learner must make restitution for or repair the effects of his/her undesirable behavior and then put the environment in even better shape than it was prior to the misbehavior. Used to decrease the rate of undesirable behaviors.

**Overextension** The use of a single word to cover a wide set of items that, more correctly, should be placed in separate categories.

**Overgeneralization** The inclusion of inappropriate items in a particular category. SEE: *overextension*

**Overlapping** Taking on the responsibility of supervising more than one academic activity at the same time.

**Overlearning** Repeated practice, drill, and review of material to be learned. Overlearning material can result in better memory recall. SEE: *memory*

**Overregularization** The application of a rule of syntax or spelling to words that are exceptional and do not follow the typical rules. An example would be using "throwed" as the past tense of "throw."

**Overregularize** To apply a learned rule to many instances, some of which are not really appropriate.

**Overt behavior** Behavior of a student that is obvious. There is no attempt to hide one's behavior and the behavior is easily observed.

**Ovum** The unfertilized mature egg released by a female at the beginning of the menstrual cycle.

**Oxycephaly** A genetic condition wherein the head is small and pointed, the hands and feet are webbed, and the student or person has severe mental retardation.

**p** Represents the probability or level of significance.

**Paired reading** Forming student pairs for the purpose of reading side-by-side. This technique can be used to help a student with reading difficulties by pairing him/her with a proficient reader. Students support each other in the reading process as they take turns reading aloud (usually a page apiece).

**Palate** The hard plate (palate) in the front of the mouth and the soft plate (palate) in the back (roof) portion of the mouth. The resulting structure is called the "palate."

**Palsy** Technically a synonym for paralysis but more commonly understood to mean a temporary or permanent loss of sensation or movement, frequently characterized by shaking or tremors.

**Pancreas**   A large organ situated near the stomach, it secretes digestive enzymes that are carried by duct to the duodenum. Specialized islet cells located on the pancreas have endocrine functions. Some of them, the alpha cells, release the hormone glucagon into the bloodstream. This hormone acts to increase the level of glucose in the blood. Other islet cells, the beta cells, release the hormone insulin. Insulin lowers blood sugar levels and helps convert glucose to glycogen, an animal starch that is stored in the liver. Diminished secretion of insulin by the pancreas results in diabetes. SEE: *diabetes mellitus, juvenile diabetes*

**Panic disorder**   An anxiety disorder involving the sudden onset of emergency reactions (panic attacks) such as rapid shallow breathing, rapid heartbeat, perspiration at the forehead and the palms of the hands, dizziness, nausea, loss of a sense of reality, depersonalization, fear of dying, fear of the loss of one's sanity, numbness, etc. There is no particular stimulus for evoking this reaction, so it is different from a phobia. H. Levinson attributes this condition to a disorder of the cerebellum and the vestibular senses. Some panic disorders are accompanied by agoraphobia, the fear of crowds. Situations such as riding in a bus, train, or automobile, standing in line, or being part of a group may bring on the panic reaction.

**Panprotopsychic identism**   The belief that the fundamental makeup of the universe is a mixture of the mental and the material. This view states that there is at least a minimal amount of consciousness (i.e., mentality) in all physical things. Panprotopsychic identism is a special type of mind-brain identity position; it is a type of neutral monism, being neither an idealism nor a materialism. SEE: *metaphysics, mind-brain identity, mind-brain problem, monism*

**Pantheism**   The belief that God is intertwined with the universe. God is a first cause and a prime mover, but God, according to this view, is not a person. Baruch (Benedict) Spinoza and Albert Einstein held pantheistic views.

**Papilloma**   Warty tumors, wartlike growths; epithelium tumors that are usually benign and thought to be virally related.

**Parallel processing**   The "division of labor" concept in the case of computing. A large computer functionally subdivides into a number of separate smaller computers, each performing a different part of a complicated task. The brain's visual perceptual processing is an example of parallel processing. Separate neural circuits deal with form, color, light-dark contrast, depth, motion, location in three-dimensional space, identification, etc.

**Parallel talk**   Talking about what the child hears, sees, experiences, feels, etc. For example, in relationship to what a child is doing, an adult might say, "You are building a big sand castle," or "That water feels cold."

**Parallelism**   The view that assumes the correctness of dualism (i.e., the mind and the body are two separate realities) and specifies that events in each reality occur separately but parallel to one another. Every mental event is therefore correlated with every physical event. It is just that one has no causal influence over the other. This view was spelled out by Leibnitz, but it is also contained in Spinoza's double-aspect theory. SEE: *double-aspect theory, dualism, epistemology, idealism, metaphysics, mind-brain problem, monism*

**Paralysis**   The loss of ability to move a striate muscle or group of striate muscles.

**Parametric statistics**   Statistical tests such as the *t* test that are built on the assumption of scores/observations derived from normal or bell-shaped distributions.

**Paranoia**   A tendency to be irrationally suspicious; a mental state or psychosis characterized by feelings of persecution or grandeur.

**P**

**Paranoiac**   A person suffering from paranoia; a condition characterized by feelings of grandeur or persecution.

**Paranoid schizophrenia**   A type of schizophrenia in which the patient exhibits delusions of being persecuted by all-powerful enemies. Hallucinations about threatening voices may occur. The condition requires institutionalization as the patient may constitute a threat to society.

**Paraphilia**   A condition of having an unusual choice of sexual object. Paraphilias include fetishism, necrophilia, narcissism, sadism, masochism, zoophilia, pedophilia, exhibitionism, transvestism, voyeurism, bestiality, coprophilia, etc.

**Paraplegia** (also known as diplegia) This is a condition that involves paralysis or functional loss (could be actual physical loss) of the lower limbs.

**Paraprofessionals** (in education) Trained classroom aides who assist teachers; may include parents.

**Parapsychology**   The study of the supernatural causes of mental events. The special areas of parapsychology include: mental telepathy, clairvoyance (telling what is occurring at a faraway place without the benefit of sensations), precognition (knowledge of future events), and psychokinesis (using thoughts to affect physical changes in material objects).

**Parasympathetic nervous system** That division of the autonomic nervous system that is responsible for the preservation of the individual and the species; it is involved in such processes as digestion, regular respiration, elimination, and reproduction. SEE: *autonomic nervous system (ANS), peripheral nervous system (PNS), sympathetic nervous system (SNS)*

**Parent Effectiveness Training (PET)** A plan for teaching effective parenting skills especially in the areas of drug abuse, child care and abuse, and schoolwork.

**Parent empowerment**   The policy of allowing parents to help make important decisions about their child's education, the school environment, and school-municipality relationships.

**Parent journal**   A communications technique in education wherein a journal is exchanged between the parent and the school for written exchange of information involving some problem or project pertaining to a student(s). Usually the student carries the journal between home and school.

**Parent surrogate**   A person who serves as an advocate for a student or individual in the absence of a parent or guardian. A parent surrogate/advocate represents the parents in situations requiring their presence, such as the case of team evaluation meetings for developing an Individualized Education Plan (IEP), other school business, court appearances, etc. The parent surrogate must have the written permission of the parent(s) or be legally appointed, as in the case of appointment by court order. SEE: *IEP*

**Parent training**   Training programs for parents that promote the needs of both the parents and students in adapting to special needs/circumstances that impact learning in school.

**Parental participation**   A policy of encouraging the student's parents to take part in developing an Individualized Education Program (IEP) for their child and letting them examine the school's records of their child's school progress. This can include parental input/active participation regarding the total educational scheme of running a school or school system.

**Parietal lobes**   The lobes of the brain's cerebral cortex that involve the sensation of touch and our sense of body position in space. Damage to this lobe may result in distorted self-images, a loss of the touch sensation, and disorientation and disorganization responses. Near the junction of the parietal lobe with the temporal and occipital lobes, the parietal lobe's angular gyrus (area 39) in the left cerebral hemisphere is involved in the ability to read and write. It lies in close proximity to the primary visual and auditory areas.

**Parkinson's disease**   A neuromuscular disorder resulting from a malfunction of the brain's basal ganglia. The basic problem is the lack of the neurotransmitter dopamine, which is normally sent from the substantia nigra of the midbrain to the caudate nucleus and putamen (parts of the forebrain's basal ganglia). There is an inability to complete an intended act because the limb goes into uncontrollable vibration (intention tremor) in the attempt. Other symptoms are slowness of movement and depressed mood. The condition is treated with the drug *l*-DOPA, which is a chemical precursor of dopamine.

**Parochial school**   An educational school or institution that is operated and administered by a religious organization.

**Part learning**   Memorizing a list of items by breaking it up into parts and learning each part separately.

**Partial inclusion**   Refers to the partial participation of students with disabilities and special needs within the regular classroom setting. These students attend other special education classes with students with similar needs. While in the regular classroom setting, the classroom teacher adapts and modifies curriculum materials to meet the needs of the student with a disability or special needs.

**Partial participation**   SEE: *partial inclusion*

**Partial reinforcement**   On-again, off-again reinforcement or reinforcement that places a student on an irregular schedule. This type of reinforcement is neither complete nor continuous and has different effects from those of continuous reinforcement for learning.

**Partial reinforcement schedule**   Partial reinforcement means the reinforcement of some, but not all, of the correct operant responses of a given type (e.g., disk-pecking by a pigeon in a Skinner box). A partial reinforcement schedule is an arrangement whereby those reinforcements are provided. Examples of such a

schedule are the fixed interval (FI), the fixed ratio (FR), the variable interval (VI), and the variable ratio (VR). SEE: *fixed-interval schedule, fixed-ratio schedule, variable-interval schedule, variable-ratio schedule*

**Partial seizure**   A seizure that takes place in and involves only a small area of the brain, very localized in nature. SEE: *focal seizure*

**Partial sightedness** or **partially sighted**   Refers to individuals with visual impairments who have limited sight and some residual vision. Visual acuity falls in the range of 20/70 to 20/200 for the better eye with the best corrective measure (i.e., contact lenses or glasses). Moderate loss ranges from 20/20 to 20/70, severe loss from 20/70 to 20/200, and profound loss 20/200 or over (the classification for being legally blind). One may be considered partially sighted for income tax purposes if the visual acuity is 20/200 in one eye and the other is no better than 20/70 (with correction). SEE: *legally blind*

**Participant modeling**   A method of psychotherapy based on observational learning or modeling. The model demonstrates the correct behavior and the client is asked to imitate that behavior one step at a time. The therapist actively encourages this imitation. The therapist and the model are often the same person.

**Participant observation**   A form of the naturalistic observation research method. The observer joins the group being studied and observes the behavior of the group members from the members' point of view. SEE: *naturalistic observation*

**Participant structures**   The complete set of rules for taking part in a given organized activity.

**Pasteur, Louis F.** (French chemist and bacteriologist, 1822–1895)   He was the "father" of microbiology who developed immunizations and vaccines, especially injections for the treatment and prevention of rabies. He is perhaps most famous for his pasteurization (named for him) process wherein milk was heated at 62° F for 30 minutes (can now be flash heated to higher temperatures for under a minute), thus destroying the pathogenic and undesirable bacteria.

**Path finder** SEE: *sonic guide*

**Pathology** A term used to describe causes of conditions caused by disease. It is the study of the causes and nature of diseases.

**Pathsounder** Similar to a sonic pathfinder or sonic guide, it is a sonic device worn by a blind person usually around the neck. This device emits a noise for the wearer as he/she approaches obstacles or objects. SEE: *sonic guide*

**Patterning** A method to assist students with learning disabilities/problems. It requires a planned sequence of specific movement exercises.

**Pauper school** An outdated term used to refer to free education facilities and opportunities for poor children.

**Pearson r** A measure of correlation that uses interval or ratio scales or data. Many education variables can be represented on interval scales so that the Pearson r is appropriate for determining relationships and the strength or degree of the relationship.

**Pedagogy** The science or the study of the profession of teaching. The pedagogy particular to a certification area would reflect that level and/or subject area.

**Pediatric AIDS** Acquired immunodeficiency syndrome in children or infants that is contracted from the blood of the mother through the placenta in utero or through blood transfusions. This incurable virus is most often fatal and causes a host of learning and physical problems. SEE: *Acquired Immune Deficiency Syndrome (AIDS)*

**Pediatric neuropsychology** The practice of neuropsychology with children who display pediatric neurological diseases or syndromes. The treatment of such problems involves a thorough diagnostic assessment and treatment

prescriptions that address the medical and behavioral symptoms.

**Pediatrician** A physician who is a specialist in the field of pediatrics, or one who deals with the medical care of children, especially children's diseases. SEE: *obstetrics, pediatrics*

**Pediatrics** The branch of medicine that deals with the medical management of the health and illnesses of children. SEE: *obstetrician, pediatrician*

**Pedophile** One who has an unnatural and abnormal sexual desire to relate to children.

**Peer acceptance** Acceptance by others of equal status (e.g., same age and grade).

**Peer coaching** 1. Student-to-student support where more able students frequently volunteer or are assigned to assist students who require extra support or academic assistance. 2. Teacher-to-teacher mentoring support programs that promote communities of professional practitioners who collaborate to create optimal school learning environments. Frequently, first-year or novice teachers participate in formal mentoring programs where a more veteran teacher is assigned as the "coach." When thoughtfully implemented, peer coaching has been found to improve morale and student/teacher effectiveness/learning.

**Peer counseling** 1. Student-to-student counseling programs usually mentored and monitored by a school-adjustment counselor or other adult in authority where students discuss problems, issues, alternative solutions, resources, etc. in such areas as substance abuse, conflict resolution, career planning, academic/home problems, etc. Cross-age counseling combined with peer counseling is especially effective when dealing with such problems as dropping out of school, delinquency, pregnancy, etc. Participation of older students in role-playing episodes or dramatic reenactments helps younger students acquire strategies to prevent or handle difficult situations. 2. Teacher-to-teacher programs where trained or experienced teachers provide advice/dialogue/strategies when problems/difficult situations arise.

**Peer influences**   Influences or pressures that are brought to bear on one by a member or members of a group to which one belongs or with which one identifies. For example, pressure from a classmate, team member, neighborhood friend, etc.

**Peer mediation**   A type of peer tutoring that involves the use of peers to facilitate appropriate social skills acquisition and to mediate disputes, disagreements, or problems.

**Peer ratings**   Ratings of performance by students that are made by their fellow students.

**Peer tutoring**   A type of cooperative learning activity involving students of varying or similar ability levels working together. Sometimes students with learning challenges are paired with more able students who have mastered the material/skills/strategies required by the teacher. In this instance, the peer mentor/teacher interacts with the other student in a tutorial format. Peer tutoring can also involve students of similar ability levels working collaboratively to scaffold the learning process. In this situation, interactive dialogue/questioning allows students to increase/expand their knowledge base.

**Peg-type mnemonics**   A memory-assisting method that uses cue words that are each associated with an item to be remembered.

**Pegword method**   One of the mnemonic devices that may be used to help complex learning material move from Short-Term Memory (STM) to Long-Term Memory (LTM). Cue words are associated with the information to be remembered.

**Pellagra**   A disease characterized by symptoms such as anxiety, depression, delirium, hallucinations, nausea, vomiting, and diarrhea. It is caused by a serious deficiency of niacin, the B vitamin. Anemia is also common. Treatments

involve an adequate diet of vitamins, minerals, and amino acids. Also, supplements of niacinamide are administered. Pellagra is found in certain parts of the world, particularly where people are more or less restricted to a corn diet.

**Penalty**   A punishment given for an infraction or offense (e.g., a demerit for being tardy).

**Peptide hormone**   Most hormones (which are secretions of the endocrine glands) take the form of a polypeptide, which is a chain of from 10 to 100 amino acids. A peptide is a chain of two or more amino acids. Over 100 amino acids comprise a protein.

**Per-capita income**   Refers to the average income per person in a specified population group (e.g., a state, a particular racial group, a particular age range, etc.).

**Per-pupil expenditure**   A state's annual spending on children in the public schools, grades K–12. This sum is divided by the total number of students and adjusted by taking into consideration how much it costs other districts to employ teachers with similar qualifications so that comparisons can be made.

**Percent (%) of attendance**   The aggregate present in attendance of a school during a reporting period (quarterly, half-year, or more typically a full school year) divided by the total sum of students present and absent for all of the days in the selected period equals the percent of attendance. SEE: *aggregate present, aggregate membership*

**Percentage grading**   Recomputing class performances as percentages and using cut-off points to determine letter grades.

**Percentile**   A number from 1 to 99 designating the relative ranking of a score on a test or other behavior measure. If a score is at the 25th percentile, 25 percent of the scores in the group are below that score and 75 percent of the scores are higher. If a score is at the 50th percentile, that score is the median. SEE: *median*

**Percentile band**   A range of percentile ranks where a student's test score would be expected to fall if tested repeatedly.

Percentile bands are given as one way to reduce the chance of error in one particular test score.

**Percentile rank**  A standardized test score that indicates the exact rank or score at which a student's test score falls. The rank indicates the percentage of scores that the student exceeded. For example, a good reader who falls at the 95th percentile rank in reading exceeds 95 percent of the other students in that category in terms of performance.

**Percentiles**  A percentile is the percentage of scores falling below a given score. For example, a dyslexic who scores at the 35th percentile in reading falls below 65 percent of the individuals taking this exam and exceeds only 35 percent.

**Perception**  Making use of the sensory messages we receive from our receptors and sensory nerve cells to recognize objects and relationships between them in the world around us. For example, one may sense low-frequency, high wavelength visible light, but one perceives a red stoplight.

**Perception without awareness**  The demonstration of perceptual knowledge by an individual who feels that he/she is only using blind guesswork. A dramatic example is "blindsight," whereby a person with injuries to the visual cortex is able to point out the location of an object that he/she "cannot see."

**Perceptual constancy**  The ability to understand the real and various characteristics of objects; that is, placement/ position, shape, size, etc. when the objects themselves present various impressions that may be misleading to the observer.

**Perceptual defense**  The failure to perceive clear stimuli that are well over the absolute threshold because the stimuli are frightening, threatening, or are unwelcome demonstrations of one's own weaknesses or shortcomings ( i.e., things that would cause one to be ashamed of oneself). This concept is an extension of Freud's concept of repression, which applies to failures of memory. The concept is considered dubious, however, because apparent instances of perceptual defense are much more readily explained by response suppression, the unwillingness to say something that might put the speaker in a bad light. SEE: *absolute threshold, subliminal perception, repression*

**Perceptual disorder**  A difficulty or an inability to organize and interpret information through any one sense or any combination of the senses. SEE: *perception*

**Perceptual expectancy**  The readiness to perceive a stimulus in a certain way because of previous experience(s). For example, a teacher squeaking chalk on a chalkboard would create a "cringing" response among students when the teacher is returning to the chalkboard.

**Perceptual handicap**  A term formerly used to describe some conditions now included under learning disability; usually referred to problems with no known physical cause.

**Perceptual illusions**  Illusions that surprise or startle the normal observer as a result of the action of misleading stimulus cues that create inaccurate perceptions. An example would be the illusion of induced movement, which involves the sensation of moving when sitting in a stationary vehicle. One seems to be moving backward because there is no point of reference to indicate that one is staying put. Looking at the ground may help to establish a frame of reference and correct the mistaken perception. This sort of illusion contrasts with physical illusions, which are quite common and do not elicit reactions of surprise. SEE: *physical illusion*

**Perceptual-motor approaches/ methods**  Methods that are concerned with the interaction of perception and motor activities. For example, Visual-Auditory-Kinesthetic-Tactile (VAKT) approaches to learning are perceptual-motor approaches. SEE: *perceptual-motor disabilities, visual-auditory-kinesthetic method, visual-auditory-kinesthetic-tactile method*

**Perceptual-motor disabilities**  Any sensory and/or muscular impairment that prevents the learner from responding correctly to such educational materials as pictures, models, words, letters, or numbers.

**Perceptual-motor functioning**  The combination of sensory information with controlled action. A perceptual-motor task might, for example, require hand-eye coordination, as in moving one's finger to follow a moving object that is being tracked by the eyes.

**Perceptual-motor match**  A concept based on the idea that motor development comes before sensory development, especially in the visual system. This theory by Newell and Kephart has not been substantiated by most researchers in child development.

**Perceptual skills**  Our abilities to use our senses (primarily hearing and vision) in order to selectively organize and interpret the environment around us.

**Perennialism**  A philosophical position based on the humanities and the great books (e.g., Shakespeare). This school of thought relies on absolute truths (e.g., honesty and truth) more than the physical world. The bases for the perennialist views stem from Thomas Aquinas (1222–1274), who emphasized the rational abilities of humans along with faith as the tools to obtain knowledge. Teachers adhering to this view stress the active learner as a rational and spiritual person. A structured disciplined approach is taken with the study of mathematics, the great books, languages, religious doctrines, etc. as important in disciplining the mind. The three R's (reading, writing, and arithmetic) are considered paramount to the young child. Emphases are placed on reasoning about moral principles and learning exercises.

**Performance assessment**  The judgment of a student's ability on the basis of observing the student's actual behavior (e.g., building a box or making a speech). SEE: *performance criteria, performance standards*

**Performance-based education**  A teaching and learning approach that is designed to produce achievement and accomplishment as compared to just knowledge. Accomplishment of predetermined goals takes precedence over mere knowledge.

**Performance contract**  An agreement between schools or other agencies and educators that guarantees a specified party will produce specific educational results.

**Performance criteria**  Those aspects of a student's performance that can be described and are therefore observable and gradable during a performance assessment. Those performance criteria that reflect the quality of the performance can be used as performance standards. SEE: *performance assessment, performance standards*

**Performance feedback**  Generally, information given to students by a teacher or other person (e.g., a counselor) in regard to a student's academic achievement, whether solicited by the student or not.

**Performance goal**  The intention of an individual to achieve a specified level of performance.

**Performance IQ**  A component of the Intelligence Quotient (IQ) on the Wechsler series of intelligence tests. It consists of the following subtests: object assembly, picture arrangement, picture completion, block design, digit symbol (coding), and, optionally, mazes.

**Performance standards**  Required ability levels that a student is expected to meet to achieve good grades while being observed during a performance assessment. SEE: *performance assessment*

**Perimeter**  In psychology, education, and medicine, it is a device that maps out a 360 degree field of view. Central vision is the middle of the visual field (indicated on a perimeter as the range from 0 to 30 degrees around the center), while peripheral vision is what is seen to the sides of central vision or the outer surfaces.

**Perinatal**   Refers to an event or condition that occurs during birth (e.g., lack of oxygen).

**Peripatologist**   A specially trained person who works with visually impaired students or persons. A peripatologist is concerned with mobility training to assist the visually impaired to travel independently.

**Peripheral**   Toward the outside. The antonym of "peripheral" is "central." The peripheral nervous system (PNS) is outside the bony coverings of the central nervous system's components, the brain and spinal cord; namely, the skull and backbone. What the peripheral nervous system (PNS) has that the central nervous system (CNS) lacks is the neurolemma (a thin membrane sheath). Within the peripheral nervous system are various nerves and ganglia.

**Peripheral nervous system (PNS)**   The peripheral nervous system (PNS) and the central nervous system (CNS) are the two major divisions of the nervous system. The peripheral nervous system (PNS) consists largely of afferent neurons that send messages to the central nervous system (i.e., the brain and spinal cord) and efferent neurons that send messages from the brain or spinal cord to the muscles or glands. The muscles and glands in general are called the effectors. As a mnemonic device to help one keep "afferent" and "efferent" straight, the efferent neurons communicate with the effectors. The PNS is made up of two main divisions; namely, the autonomic nervous system (ANS) and the somatic (or skeletal) nervous system. In its turn, the ANS is composed of two main parts, the sympathetic nervous system (SNS) and parasympathetic nervous system. SEE: *central nervous system (CNS), somatic nervous system, autonomic nervous system (ANS), sympathetic nervous system (SNS), parasympathetic nervous system*

**Peripheral vision**   The type of vision provided by the peripheral areas of the retina. Compared to central or foveal vision, peripheral vision is insensitive to color differences, poor in the resolution of details, and superior in sensitivity to faint light. In many dyslexics, however, peripheral vision permits some resolution of visual detail and the correct recognition of the color of a visual stimulus. SEE: *perimeter*

**Perkins brailler**   A six-keyed device used to print in braille; each key represents one of the six dots of the cell. SEE: *braille*

**Permanent certification** (also known as professional certification)   Teacher reform efforts in the 1990s have resulted in levels of certification (usually two). The initial or provisional teaching certificate can be followed by permanent or professional certification typically after the provisional teacher has completed additional appropriate coursework/training and sometimes a clinical teaching experience or internship. Many states/local communities require ongoing professional development in terms of workshops, courses, etc. in order for teachers to maintain their permanent teaching certificates.

**Perpetuating**   A term used in language arts and education in general to describe the concept of using language for the creation of records, histories, and oral histories.

**Perseveration**   1. Repetition of a meaningless answer, word, or phrase, which is not related to questions asked. 2. An inability to change from one point or focus to another. 3. A continued response that is no longer proper or appropriate.

**Person-centered therapy**   An approach to psychotherapy that stresses the person's ability to gain insight into his/her own problems and correct them. An example is the "client-centered" approach used by Carl Rogers.

**Personal care attendant**   An individual employed to assist a student or person with disabilities with such tasks as personal hygiene, bathing, grooming, cooking, eating, dressing, etc.

**Personal companion**   A technology apparatus/device that reacts to vocal instruction. When commanded by voice, this device is able to dial telephone numbers, read the newspaper by telephone, maintain a daily schedule of appointments, turn appliances off/on, etc.

**Personal construct** A statement of a goal that the individual uses to guide his/her own behavior (i.e., a standard for judging one's own success or failure).

**Personal development** The series of age-related changes of personality that occur as an individual grows older.

**Personal education** Education that is designed around the needs of the individual student.

**Personal unconscious** The portion of the unconscious mind that, according to Jung, applies to the individual and is most similar to the "unconscious" described by Sigmund Freud's psychoanalytic theory. Jung also postulates a "collective unconscious" that is shared by all persons.

**Personal wellness, the promoting of** Those strategies/activities/qualities/characteristics one needs to reduce the risk of being sick and to be optimally ready to approach learning/life situations. These include but are not limited to not using drugs, tobacco, or alcohol (if using alcohol, in moderation); engaging in safe sex practices; eating nutritious and well-balanced meals (maintaining a proper weight); exercising on a regular basis (daily if possible but at least 3 times weekly) and with the advise of a medical professional; using seat belts and bicycle helmets and protective gear; obtaining regular medical and dental checkups and following medical regimens; avoiding situations and friends who engage in destructive behaviors; cultivating long-lasting friendships that are positive and constructive; getting an adequate amount of sleep (usually 7–8 hours and longer for children/adolescents); and obtaining help when needed.

**Personality** The sum of all our behavioral/cognitive/emotional characteristics that can account for consistent patterns of behavior and thinking.

**Personality disorders** A long-lasting pattern of thinking, feeling, or behaving that interferes with everyday social and personal functioning and many times will diminish in intensity after age 40. Examples of personality disorders are paranoid schizophrenia, affective disorders, schizophrenia, explosive personality disorder, and antisocial personality disorder. SEE: *each disorder as listed*

**Personality psychology** The area of psychology dealing with the individual's characteristic patterns of acting, thinking, and feeling. Some theorists consider that there are types of personality, while others believe that a personality can be described by a list of behavioral traits. Tests have been developed to measure personality types or personality traits.

**Persuasion** A change of attitude resulting from the effort of another person to cause the change (i.e., socially caused attitude change).

**Perthes' disease** (George C. Perthes, German surgeon, 1869–1927) A disease that is characterized by a tuberculous hip joint. The disease causes deformity in the hip as a result of changes in the head of the femur, the thigh bone that extends from the hip to the knees.

**Pervasive developmental disorder** A severe social disorder that is characterized by impaired social functioning/interactions, abnormal mannerisms, delayed language/speech development, and unacceptable social behaviors.

**Pervasive language deficit** The presence in one individual of several language-related problems, such as the combination of poor spelling, poor reading, articulation difficulty, a lack of word fluency, etc. Whether some people can have extremely severe dyslexia (which would entail such widespread language deficits) and still not be classifiable as "garden-variety poor readers" (simply poor learners in anything) is controversial.

P

**P**

**Pestalozzi, Johann Heinrich (1746–1827)**   A Swiss educator known for his reforms and influence in the development of primary education.

**PET**   SEE: *Parent Effectiveness Training*

**Petit mal seizure** or **absence seizure**   A brief epileptic seizure usually accompanied by dizziness or fainting. It is a mild epileptic attack and the person may show signs of rapid neural firing in brain activity and eyeblinking, or conversely, a fixed stare. It is unlike grand mal in that there is an absence of convulsions. The seizure is sometimes so brief that it is frequently missed by teachers or the observer. SEE: *grand mal*

**Phallic stage**   One of Sigmund Freud's stages of psychosexual development. This stage is the third (following the oral and anal stages) and typically occurs in children aged 2 ½–5 years of age. SEE: *Oedipus Complex*

**Pharynx**   A musculomembranous tube extending from the skull base to the esophagus which serves as an airway from the nasal cavity to the larynx and from the mouth to the esophagus.

**Phenotype**   The actual physical or behavioral trait shown by a person. The trait may be a result of genetic or environmental factors or a combination of causes. For example, having brown eyes is one example of a phenotype. It may be a result of either of two genotypes: 1. a brown-eye allele from one parent and a recessive blue-eye allele from the other parent, or 2. two brown-eye alleles.

**Phenylalanine**   An amino acid formed from protein and found in such foods as milk or even NutraSweet, the artificial sweetner Aspartame.

**Phenylketonuria (PKU)**   A hereditary chemical disorder resulting from a missing enzyme. The body cannot metabolize the amino acid phenylalanine, which is a common component of the proteins in our diet. The urine will contain larger-than-usual amounts of unmetabolized phenylalanine along with an abnormal metabolic product of phenylaline, a phenyl ketone; namely, phenylpyruvic acid. In normal individu-als, the phenylalanine is simply converted to another dietary amino acid, tyrosine. The ketone is toxic to brain cells and if untreated PKU will lead to retardation. Chemical tests can detect the condition in the neonate and PKU can be avoided by putting the individual on a phenylalanine-free diet. This diet is low in proteins and includes high amounts of fruits and vegetables. This avoids the development of any retardation. The individual must stick to that diet for life. If this regimen is not followed, the individual will develop seizures and tremors and suffer mental retardation. All 50 states now require screening of infants for PKU at the time of birth. SEE: *phenylalanine*

**Pheromones**   Chemicals that provide a means of chemical communication and may be thought of as "social hormones." Some pheromones are airborne, olfactory stimuli. They are released by some organisms and affect other organisms of the same species. Variations of sexual development in female mice depend on the presence of male mice from the same colony or from afar, in large numbers or small, etc.

**Phi phenomenon**   A visual illusion of movement based on the spacing and timing of stationary lights in a dark surround. One light coming on and then turning off, with another light coming on after a short time, creates the impression of a single light traveling from the location of the first light to the position of the second light.

**Philosophy**   "The love of wisdom" in the literal sense. The study of knowledge and wisdom through observations, one's value system, previous knowledge, nature, etc. There are major branches (metaphysics, epistemology, and axiology) of philosophy and major schools of philosophy (realism, idealism, neo-Thomism, perennialism, existentialism, idealism, and experimentalism). SEE: *each branch or school as listed*

**Philosophy of education**   Basic principles of education that serve as guidelines for professional educators in their process of planning curriculum and general decision making. An example of a philosophy of education for a teacher would be the following: "To meet the social, academic, emotional, and psychological needs of all students in a multiculturally sensitive environment where parent-teacher-student-community partnerships are nourished and fostered."

**Philosophy of science**   A term used interchangeably with "logical positivism." The extreme version of this school of thought holds that only analytic philosophy is worth pursuing. In this view, its task is simply to clarify the meanings of scientific propositions.

**Phlegmatic**   A condition in which an individual displays a dull, apathetic, sluggish temperament or personality; motivation and interest in anything are markedly absent.

**Phobia**   A condition characterized by an unreasonable fear of some thing, person, place, situation, etc. This abnormal fear is not grounded in any real threat actually presented to the person. Behaviorists attribute phobias to the classical conditioning of reflexive actions to paired stimuli. Cognitive-behavior theory regards phobias as examples of biological preparedness.

**Phocomelia**   A congenital deformity. The limbs are very short and sometimes missing altogether. When the limbs are present, they are attached like flippers to the torso directly or by means of bones that are poorly formed. This condition was sometimes caused by a sleeping pill taken by pregnant mothers called thalidomide, which is presently not approved by the FDA. SEE: *thalidomide*

**Phonation**   The production of sound/voice by the vibration of the vocal cords in the larynx.

**Phonatory disorders**   Voice disorders that stem from problems with the mechanism of the larynx such as inflammation of the vocal folds (cords), growths on the vocal cords, etc.

**Phoneme**   The smallest unit of sound in speech such as "bl" in the word black. Combinations of phonemes form words. The word "smile" has three phonemes,

for example. A phoneme sometimes is an individual speech sound that can convey a meaning, such as a one-syllable word, a prefix, or a suffix.

**Phonic elements**   Various combinations of letter/sound correspondences.

**Phonics**   The application of speech sounds to reading. The student is given the sound(s) to associate with the letter, then syllables, and finally words. In the teaching of reading, the sound is given first and then related to the symbol; thus, the sound-to-symbol relationship or phonics.

**Phonics approach**   An approach to the teaching of reading that emphasizes the sound-symbol relationship and phoneme-to-grapheme match. Phonics knowledge is considered a prerequisite to fluent reading and spelling proficiency. SEE: *phonics*

**Phonogram**   A one-syllable word with at least one vowel followed by one consonant or the last two or more letters in a syllable. Another term for phonogram is rime.

**Phonological dyslexia**   This type of dyslexia is a developmental analog to Boder's dysphonetic dyslexic, Coltheart's acquired dyslexic, and Doering and Hoshko's phonological deficit type, which is marked by problems in interpretation or execution of the phoneme-grapheme correspondence match.

**Phonological process disorder**   A type of speech-processing disorder wherein the student's or individual's patterns of speech errors are identified and treated as deficits in the sound/speech system in reference to the rules for the production of speech sounds. This system approaches the deficit as a problem with the patterns of sound production rather than isolating single specific speech sounds for correction.

**Phonological processing**   This cognitive task is important to reading as Liberman and Shankweiler have demonstrated that dyslexics can 1. lack awareness of phonology rules and concepts, 2. lack proficiency in accessing phonological representations in memory,

**P**

and/or 3. lack a proficiency in accurate utilization of these rules and concepts. Mann has shown that good and poor readers differ in the rate at which they acquire phonological processing skills.

**Phonological rules**   Particular speech sounds as they should occur in language and the rules involving the formation of words through the combining of such speech sounds.

**Phonological skills**   The learned ability to understand and interpret grapheme-phoneme relationships or correspondences, the rules with which sounds are synthesized into words, and the ability to analyze a word into its sound components.

**Phonology**   The part of language that involves putting sounds together to make words. Phonology involves the study of speech sounds and the development of the ability to form sounds that convey meaning.

**Photophobia**   Extreme sensitivity of the eyes to light; occurs most notably in albino children. Also the fear of light.

**Photopigments**   Chemicals that undergo changes of structure when hit by light. Such chemicals (one of which is rhodosin) are contained in the eye's light receptor cells, the rods and the cones. When the light-induced chemical changes take place, neural messages are passed on from the rods and the cones to higher (more centrally located) neurons, beginning with the retina's bipolar cells.

**Photosynthesis**   The special process of photo (light) and synthesis (putting together) that allows plants to produce carbohydrates by combining water from the earth and carbon dioxide from the air (catalyzed by light energy and chlorophyll), which leads to the release of oxygen.

**Phrenology**   An old pseudoscience of personality based on the size and location of the irregular bumps on the skull. Each large bump is supposed to indicate a well-developed "mental faculty." The early nineteenth-century anatomist Franz Gall founded phrenology. It did

lead to the acceptance of the brain as the organ of the mind. Phrenology also led the way to localization theory, the idea that different small areas of the cerebral cortex perform different physiological functions.

**Physical development**   The series of age-related changes of body structure and body functioning that occur as an individual grows older.

**Physical disability**   A physical problem that interferes with one's ability to control and to use efficiently any part(s) of her/his body.

**Physical disorder**   A physical/body impairment wherein one's physical disability interrupts one's development as concerns learning, communication, motor coordination, mobility, etc.

**Physical prompting/fading**   A method of teaching or instructing a student or individual that requires physically/manually moving or manipulating a student to produce desired behavioral results. The physical assistance is reduced (faded) systematically as the student's behavior or actions become more appropriate until no prompting or assistance is required.

**Physical Therapist (PT)**   A person trained to prescribe and supervise physical activities such as range of motions, positioning, weight bearing, relaxation, stimulation, posture, gross motor, and other such therapeutic manipulations and exercises.

**Physical therapy**   A term used to describe the treatment of a student or person who is bodily/physically disabled. Such therapy involves special conditioning, exercises, and/or massage. SEE: *Physical Therapist (PT)*

**Physically handicapped**   Educationally speaking, this is a person of sound mental ability but some physical or health problem interrupts the normal learning process. The nonsensory problems are such that special education is frequently needed. For example, a quadriplegic or spina bifida student would require specialized seating, access to classrooms, etc.

**Piaget, Jean** (Swiss Psychologist, 1896–1980) Piaget was the most influential child psychologist of the 20th century. He developed a detailed and complete description of childrens' behavior and cognitive processes. He arranged the periods of cognitive development into four areas as follows: 1. the *sensorimotor period* which lasts for the first two years of life and is heavily influenced by external stimulation, 2. the *preoperational period* which lasts from about age two through seven. During this time the child's development is characterized by rapid language development and an ability to represent things symbolically, 3. the *period of concrete operations* which is from about age seven to twelve. This period is characterized by an ability to perform logical analysis and an ability to empathize with the feelings of others. It also marks the transition from childhood to adolescence, and 4. *the period of formal operations* which begins at twelve to adulthood. This period is characterized by the use of logic and symbolism of an adult nature. During this time the adolescent learns to reason deductively and indirectively as well as problem solve and reason formally.

**Pica** A perverse craving for substance(s) not fit for consumption. The affected person eats inappropriate things such as ashes, plaster, dirt, paper, etc.

**Pick's disease** 1. (Arnold Pick, Czechoslovakian physician, 1851–1924) A brain disorder involving presenile dementia and atrophy of the cerebral cortex. 2. (Friedel Pick, Czechoslovakian physician, 1867–1926) Nonrheumatic chronic pericarditis, inflammation of the pericardium (the membranous sac enveloping the heart). 3. (Ludwig Pick, German physician, 1868–1935) Niemann-Pick disease, which is a serious metabolic disorder of the spleen and liver. SEE: *Niemann-Pick disease*

**Pickwickian syndrome** From a character of Charles Dickens, this disease is characterized by obesity with decreased pulmonary functioning and polycythemia, which includes a flushing of the face as a result of an increased number and volume of red blood cells.

**Picture cues** Visual graphics (e.g., photographs) that provide a visual cue to read a word or complete a learning task (how to play a game). Picture cues are helpful for beginning readers and individuals with disabilities or learning problems.

**Pie graph** A method of comparing several things on one quantitative dimension. The area of a circle represents the total dimension. An object accounting for 25 percent of this dimension is depicted as a segment (pie slice shape; marked off by an arc and two radii), which contains 25 percent of the area of the circle. For example, 25 percent of all children with disabilities in the United States were educated in special classes in the academic year 1983–1984, 68 percent in the regular classes, 6 percent in separate schools, and 1 percent in still other settings.

*Pierce v. Society of Sisters* The 1925 Supreme Court ruling that overturned a law requiring all children to attend public schools. The Court ruled that parents had the constitutional right to control their children.

**Pineal gland** or **epiphysis** The endocrine gland attached to the top of the brain's diencephalon. Its hormone, melatonin, temporarily suppresses the gonads, maintaining childhood for years. Finally, its inhibiting role is removed and puberty occurs. It is believed that the release process is indirectly related to stimulation by sunlight; a neural pathway from the retina runs to the pineal gland.

**Pinkeye** Acute conjunctivitis caused by various organisms. This problem is highly contagious. The eye feels sore, gritty, and painful and is watery and red (bloodshot). SEE: *conjunctiva*

**Pinna** The outer, visible part of the external ear. SEE: *auricle*

**Pitch** The perceived frequency that is associated with voice quality. A high rate of vibration (frequency/cycles per second) equals a high-pitched voice and, conversely, a low pitched voice results from slower vibrations of the vocal folds (cords).

**Pitch disorder**  An impaired ability to control or regulate voice quality such as low and high pitches (i.e., the frequency of vibration of sound waves).

**Pitch perception**  The experience of the high or low frequency of a sound. This dimension of our hearing sense has a complex basis. Higher pitches are explained by the place-resonance mechanism. The basilar membrane of the inner ear has a tapering shape so its width changes continually. A given sound frequency (in the range from 4000 Hz to 20,000 Hz) corresponds to a certain width on the basilar membrane so that this local area vibrates much more than the rest of the membrane (resonant vibration). Thus, some of the hair cell sound receptors are strongly stimulated while other hair cells are quiet. The active hair cells create activity only in a small part of the auditory cortex. Lower tones (15 Hz to 1000 Hz) are explained by a telephone frequency mechanism. The frequency of the sound stimulus in Hertz is matched by the number of nerve impulses per second. Low tones cause indiscriminate resonating all over the basilar membrane so the resonance mechanism could not work for them. This leaves the middle tones (1000 Hz to 4000 Hz), because nerve fibers cannot fire impulses more rapidly than 1000 times a second. The volley theory comes into play here. The auditory nerve fibers are subdivided into four work units or squads that have different firing times. This allows the rate of firing in the whole auditory nerve to be four times the highest firing rate for a single auditory nerve fiber.

**Pituitary gland** or **hypophysis**  The endocrine gland that is attached to the hypothalamus (at the base of the brain) by a stalk called the infundibulum. There are actually two functional divisions of the pituitary gland. The first is the anterior pituitary (or adenohypophysis), which releases the growth hormone and the trophic hormones that

interact with other endocrine glands and the growth hormone. The second is the posterior pituitary (or neurohypophysis), which releases the antidiuretic hormone (vasopressin), oxytocin, and somatostatin (the growth-hormone suppressor).

**PK**  SEE: *Psychokinesis*

**PKU**  SEE: *Phenylketonuria*

**P.L. 45-186 (1879)**  This federal public law granted funds to the American Printing House for the Blind in order to manufacture braille materials.

**P.L. 65-178 (1918)**  This federal public law was in effect a World War I G.I. bill but was restricted to vocational rehabilitation services for World War I veterans.

**P.L. 66-236 (1920)**  This federal public law extended the vocational rehabilitation services authorized for World War I veterans (P.L. 65-178) to the civilian population.

**P.L. 74-732 (1936)**  This federal public law allowed and authorized the blind to operate vending stands in government (federal) buildings.

**P.L. 78-16 (1943)** (also known as the Vocational Rehabilitation Act)  This 1943 legislation provided education opportunities for disabled veterans.

**P.L. 78-113 (1943)**  This public federal law known as the Barden-LaFollette Vocational Rehabilitation Act authorized eligibility for vocational rehabilitation to the mentally ill and mentally retarded.

**P.L. 78-129 (1943)** (also known as the School Lunch Indemnity Plan)  In 1943, this legislation provided the precedent of funding all school lunch programs.

**P.L. 85-905 (1958)** (also known as the Captioned Films for Deaf Act)  The 1958 legislation that provided a library service of captioned films for the deaf.

**P.L. 85-926 (1958)**  A federal public law of limited measures that provided grant monies in the area of teaching of children with disabilities as it related particularly to special-needs children who were mentally retarded and/or deaf. These grants were directed toward research and the training of personnel dealing with the mentally retarded or deaf. They were direct grants to states and institutions of higher learning in order to train instructors who in turn would train teachers in the field.

**P.L. 87-715 (1962)** This federal public law made provisions for captioned films to be produced and distributed to the deaf.

**P.L. 88-164 Title III (1963)** This federal public law provided funds for research, demonstration projects, and teacher training as concerns the education of persons with disabilities. President John F. Kennedy is credited for much of the impetus in the renewal of interest in persons with disabilities, probably because of his sister's mental retardation. It was to her that the outstanding Kennedy Memorial Hospital for Children (in the Brighton section of Boston, MA) for special-needs children was dedicated.

**P.L. 88-352 (1964)** (also known as the Civil Rights Act of 1964) Support and monies were provided for schools to address problems associated with desegregation efforts.

**P.L. 88-452 (1964)** (also known as the Economic Opportunity Act of 1964) This legislation provided opportunities for work-study programs in colleges and support for Head Start programs, Job Corps, Upward Bound, and Volunteers in Service to America (VISTA).

**P.L. 89-10 (1965)** This federal public law is also known as the Elementary and Secondary Education ACT (ESEA) Title III. It deals with state-supported private and residential schools as well as state-operated schools. It was designed primarily to meet the educational needs of minority populations. It was one of the early federal laws to provide funding directly to local educational agencies.

**P.L. 89-36 (1965)** This federal public law's main feature resulted in the establishment of the National Technical Institute for the Deaf.

**P.L. 89-313 (1965)** This federal public law was an ESEA amendment to P.L. 89-10. It in effect provided the

means to award funds to the state departments of education in order to support state-operated programs for children with special needs.

**P.L. 89-522 (1966)** This federal public law expanded "talking book" services for the visually impaired to include persons with disabilities who were not able to use (hold or handle) printed materials.

**P.L. 89-750 Title VI (1966)** This federal public law was an ESEA amendment that provided funding to both state and local educational agencies for the education of special-needs children and youth.

**P.L. 90-170 (1967)** This federal public law added amendments to P.L. 88-164. It provided for monies to train personnel who cared for the mentally retarded. These amendments included individuals with neurological impairments related to mental retardation.

**P.L. 90-247 (1968)** This federal public law was an amendment to P.L. 89-10. It provided funds to create regional resource centers dealing with services for deaf-blind children and youth, and for evaluation of special-needs children and youth.

**P.L. 90-538 (1968)** This federal public law is also known as the Handicapped Children's Early Education Assistance Act. It provided funds in order to develop and implement experimental programs for special-needs children from birth to age six. These preschool programs were to serve as demonstration projects as well.

**P.L. 90-576 (1968)** This federal public law earmarked 10 percent of vocational education funds for persons with disabilities.

**P.L. 91-61 (1969)** This is the National Century on Educational Media and Materials for the Handicapped Act. This federal public law created a network nationwide in reference to materials and media for educating children and youth with disabilities.

**P.L. 91-205 (1970)** This federal public law required accessibility for the

P

physically handicapped to any building constructed with federal funds.

**P.L. 91-230 (1969)** This federal public law was an ESEA amendment to P.L. 89-10. It consolidated previous federal acts dealing with special-needs or children with disabilities into one act. Further, it included federal funding for the learning disabled and the gifted and talented.

**P.L. 91-516 (1970)** (also known as the Environmental Education Act) In 1970 this legislation established the Office of Environmental Education.

**P.L. 91-527 (1970)** (also known as the Drug Abuse Education Act of 1970) This established support for educational drug prevention/abuse programs.

**P.L. 92-424 (1972)** A federal public law involving Economic Opportunity Amendments designed to assist preschool children of low-income families. It requires that no less than 10 percent of the Head Start program enrollment be available to children with special needs.

**P.L. 92-255 (1972)** (also known as the Drug Abuse Office and Treatment Act of 1972) A Special Action Office for Drug Abuse Prevention provided coordinated efforts for policy planning/treatment programs.

**P.L. 93-112 (1973)** This is the Vocational Rehabilitation Act of 1973. It is a federal public law that is very similar in wording to the Civil Rights Act of 1964, which dealt with racial discrimination. Section 504 of this act deals with discrimination against persons with disabilities. The highlights of this section require the following: 1. employers are required to provide equal job recruitment, employment in assignments and compensation, and fringe benefits to persons with disabilities; 2. newly built public facilities must be handicapped accessible; 3. school children with disabilities are entitled to an appropriate public school education at no cost; 4. institutions of higher learning must have admission policies that do not

discriminate against persons with disabilities, and 5. health, welfare, and other social services and benefits will be available to persons with disabilities without discrimination. SEE: *section 504 of the Rehabilitation Act of 1973*

**P.L. 93-380 (1974)** (20 U.S.C. Sections 1701–1720, also known as the Equal Educational Opportunity Act of 1974) A law which states that schools with several children with little English-speaking ability are required to implement programs that overcome language barriers so that these students can participate on an equal basis in the educational opportunities available.

**P.L. 93-415 (1975)** (also known as the Juvenile Justice and Delinquency Prevention Act of 1974) A National Institute for Juvenile Justice and Delinquency Prevention was created.

**P.L. 94-142 (1975)** The Education for All Handicapped Act (now called Individuals with Disabilities Education Act) instituted in 1975 ensures that all students with disabilities by law receive the most appropriate education and in the least restrictive environment. It basically requires states to provide a free and appropriate education for all children with disabilities from 3–18 years of age.

**P.L. 95-49 (1977)** This federal public law amended P.L. 94-142, Education of the Handicapped Act (EHA), now known as the Individuals with Disabilities Education Act (IDEA). In particular, it included the definition of "learning disabilities" as per the federal interpretation.

**P.L. 95-178 (1978)** (Comprehensive Rehabilitation Services Amendment of 1978) An amendment that required delivery of comprehensive services to persons with disabilities even when they were not ready for vocational rehabilitation. Services were to be provided for all, not just the persons with the most severe disabilities.

**P.L. 95-561 Section 902 (1978)** The Gifted and Talented Children's Education Act. This federal public law expanded the definition of giftedness and included talented children based upon a definition that goes beyond mere intellectual ability.

**P.L. 95-602 (1978)** (The Developmental Disabilities Act) This federal public law required that a disability must occur before age 18 but there is no lower limit to age. Thus, students under three years old may be served by this act when they do not qualify for services in the public school. This act requires diagnostic evaluations and parental involvement.

**P.L. 98-199 (1984)** This federal public law was an amendment to P.L. 90-538. It provided funding for planning purposes relating to state-wide comprehensive services to special-needs children up to age 5.

**P.L. 98-525 (1984)** This federal public law amended the Developmental Disabilities Act to require states to adopt employment-related activities for persons with developmental disabilities. This included "supported employment" at or above the minimum hourly rate for persons with developmental disabilities who in fact would be unable to keep a job without support, supervision, transportation, and training.

**P.L. 99-457 (1986)** An amendment to the Education for All Handicapped Act (EHA) now renamed the Individuals with Disabilities Education Act (IDEA). It is a federal public law that requires services for children with special needs between the ages of three and five years in the form of the Preschool Grants Program, and provides incentives for early intervention programs for children with special needs from birth to age two in the form of the Handicapped Infants and Toddlers Program.

**P.L. 100-297 (1988)** The Javits Act (New York Senator Jacob Javits) This federal public law supported research and demonstration programs involving special needs of gifted students with physical disabilities from different cultures, and students who were economically disadvantaged.

**P.L. 100-407 (1988)** The Technology Related Assistance for Individuals with Disabilities Act. Also known as the "Tech Act," this federal public law provided funding to states concerned with providing assistive technology assistance to persons with disabilities of all ages. Funds may be used to survey, identify, assess, train, fabricate, and evaluate assistive technological devices. Many states are networking as concerns information about assistive technology.

**P.L. 101-336 (1991)** (also known as the Americans With Disabilities Act) It is a civil rights bill; its major premise is to eliminate discrimination against persons with disabilities. It guarantees equal opportunity in the areas of public accommodations, telecommunications, public services to include transportation, and employment.

**P.L. 101-476 (1990)** This federal public law changed the title of P.L. 94-142 from the "Education for All Handicapped Children Act (EHA)" to the "Individuals with Disabilities Education Act (IDEA)." Further, it required that transition services such as school to post-school programs be included in the educational plan (i.e., independent living, vocational training, sheltered workshop training, etc.). It also included the new categories; namely, autism and traumatic brain injury.

**P.L. 102-62 (1991)** (also known as the National Commission on Time and Learning Act) In 1991 this legislation enacted the National Education Commission of Time and Learning, which included legal education programs and an emphasis on research in teaching.

**P.L. 103-218 (1994)** This 1994 reauthorization of the 1988 Technology-Related Assistance for Individuals with Disabilities Act of 1988 provided support through 1998.

**P.L. 103-227 (1994)** (also known as Goals 2000: Educate America Act) This 1994 Act formalized national education goals and created a National Education Standards and Improvement Council (NESIC) and National Skill Standards Board. Part of this legislation in 1994 provided grant monies for education agencies to create violence-prevention activities/programs. SEE: *GOALS 2000*

**P.L. 103-239 (1994)**   This 1994 School-to-Work Opportunities Act provided monies for work-based learning programs and programs that lead to high school diplomas.

**P.L. 103-382 (1994)** (also known as the Improving America's School Act) This 1994 reauthorization of the Elementary and Secondary Education Act addressed Title I programs (the federal government's largest education program for disadvantaged children).

**Place theory**   Also known as resonance theory. The place on the basilar membrane of the inner ear that vibrates the most indicates the frequency of the sound stimulus. Helmholtz formulated this theory. It was found to be correct only for the higher-pitched sounds (above 4000 Hz). SEE: *pitch perception*

**Placebo**   An apparent treatment (e.g., pill, teaspoon of liquid, or injection) that has no physiological effect. The word means, "I shall please." In research, placebos are used on control subjects while the experimental subjects receive an active treatment (the real thing). This control assures that a subject cannot know whether he/she has gotten the experimental treatment or not. It is called a "single blind" control.

**Placement**   In education, the act of placing a student in a certain group, class, grade, program, or even school. This includes homogeneous placement (students of like ability) or heterogeneous placement (a mix of all abilities). SEE: *Individualized Education Program (IEP), mainstreaming, Least Restrictive Environment (LRE)*

**Plagiarism**   The use of the work authored by another individual(s) in the pretense it is one's own work. Not giving proper credit to other's written (e.g., thesis) or oral (e.g., a speech) work is unethical and in some cases illegal.

**Plane geometry**   The mathematical study of two-dimensional figures and their properties and relationships.

**Planned ignoring**   A type of behavior management technique whereby unwanted behaviors are ignored (e.g., gum chewing) with the hope that they stop after the student has had enough. Planned ignoring is also used in attention-getting situations (e.g., temper tantrums), again in the hope that the behavior will be extinguished because of a lack of reinforcement or attention. SEE: *reinforcement, extinction*

**Planned program budgeting**   A budgetary planning system used to analyze and allot resources to various areas of the school budget. The approach analyzes purposes and needs of each area (e.g., transportation, textbooks and supplies, etc.) through systematic planning, programming, actual budget building, and then evaluation and comparison for final decision-making.

**Plasma**   The liquid part of the blood. In the blood, platelets and corpuscles float in the plasma solution. Plasma is normally thin and colorless in appearance; it is a water-like fluid.

**Plasticity**   The property of being easy to change. This is a requirement for neural pathways for learned behaviors.

**Play audiometry**   A special method for children who are too young or unable to take regular audiometric tests. This hearing test is presented in a game format and the young children are taught to respond to audio signals.

**Pleasure principle**   The guiding rule for the activity of the libido (or of the Id) in Sigmund Freud's psychoanalytic theory. This primitive role of motivation involves the reduction of pain and the increase of pleasure; nothing else matters. More mature parts of the personality develop, however, such as the ego which is guided by the reality principle. This development is necessitated by the fact that an infant soon learns that pleasures are not always given simply because one screams for them.

**-Plegia**   A suffix that indicates and refers to an inability to move, as in the case of paraplegia, quadriplegia, or hemiplegia, for example.

**Plenary powers**   Full powers designated to a particular government unit. For example, local school boards/ principals have plenary powers to hire new staff members.

**Pluralism**   The doctrine that the United States has many components and that the members of no one limited subgroup (e.g., elderly male Christian caucasians) cannot speak for the entire country. William James held that reality itself has many components (e.g., processes, minds, laws, and things), not just one or two basic ones. In educational practice, the concept of pluralism leads to support for multicultural education. SEE: *multicultural education, pragmatism*

**Pluralistic perspective**   The basic view that various cultural groups have varying contributions that contribute to the richness of learning groups and experiences, which recognize the diversity of its learners. Jesse Jackson uses the term "salad-bowl theory" to refer to this pluralistic perspective; that is, each individual is like a rich, delicate, and unique vegetable which, when combined, produces a much different, cohesive, and even richer experience (i.e., salad).

**Pneumoencephalography**   A method of assessing brain structure. This method requires withdrawal of cerebrospinal fluid and the injection of gas or air in the lower spinal cord via a lumbar puncture. The procedure is tracked by x ray to determine abnormalities.

**Pneumonia**   An inflammation of the lungs normally caused by bacteria, viruses, and/or chemical irritants.

**PNS**   SEE: *peripheral nervous system*

**Podiatrist**   A synonym for a chiropodist, a professional who treats foot problems and diseases.

**Polio**   SEE: *poliomyelitis*

**Poliomyelitis** or **infantile paralysis**   Commonly called polio, it is a type of paralysis that is a result of a virus that attacks the motor neurons of the spinal cord. It frequently leads to paralysis of the muscles controlled by the nerves of

the spinal cord. Children seem especially susceptible to this serious infectious viral disease.

**Poliosis**   A premature graying of the hair. SEE: *poliosis circumscripta*

**Poliosis circumscripta**   Like poliosis, this is a condition characterized by premature graying of the hair but is limited to a particular area or shape.

**Political action committees in teacher education**   These can be any number of political action groups that support teacher education purposes and/or organizations such as the National Council for the Accreditation of Teacher Education (NCATE). Such groups can be at the local, state, or national levels.

**Polyarteritis**   A condition characterized by inflammation of several arteries simultaneously.

**Polychromatic**   Multicolored.

**Polydactylism**   A condition at birth whereby the infant has more than the normal number of fingers and/or toes.

**Polygenic**   A term that refers to several genes or a condition resulting from the interactions of several genes.

**Polygraph**   Also known as a lie detector. Physiological sensors are placed on the subject to be examined. These sensors are wired to amplifiers and then to electromagnetic controls of recording pens on a polygraph (a multipen recorder). The classical "lie detector" reads four functions: heart rate, blood pressure, breathing rate, and the galvanic skin response. When an emergency reaction occurs, the sympathetic nervous system activates a faster heartbeat, higher blood pressure (in blood vessels feeding the muscles and brain), more rapid breathing, and sweating of the palms of the hands (which lowers the skin's electrical resistance). The term "lie detector" is a misnomer. Synonym: *sphygmograph*

**Polyopia**   Also known as polyopsia, it is a condition of seeing multiple images; that is, two or more. SEE: *diplopia*

**Polyps**   Growths on or about the vocal cord that cause speech problems. There is a hoarseness or low pitch to the voice. Polyps are also tumorous membranes commonly found in vascular organs like the nose, throat, intestines, etc.

**Polyopsia**   SEE: *polyopia*

**Polytheism**   The belief that there is more than one god. An example would be Brahminism, the religion of many East Indians.

**Pons**   A part of the hindbrain. The name pons means "bridge." It is given the name because the nerve fibers that swing around the sides of the pons to the cerebellum above it resemble cables of a suspension bridge. These nerve fibers functionally connect the cerebellum to the rest of the brain. The pons contains areas involved in the control of REM sleep, non-REM sleep, and the waking cycle.

**Population**   The totality of all possible measurements of a specified kind. "Population" or "universe" is a technical term of statistical science. In research, one seldom is able to observe a whole population. Instead, we observe some cases (which make up a "sample") from the population.

**Pornography**   A legal term that refers to published (written, printed, drawn, or photographed) materials that are unacceptable morally as being too sexually explicit.

**Portable braille recorder**   This is an alternative (smaller) device to the Perkins brailler. It is a tape-cassette system used for the recording of braille.

**Portfolio** or **portfolio assessment**   A type of authentic assessment (assessments that relate testing to meaningful or significant life tasks) that reveals an individual's academic and personal accomplishments. Teachers provide guidance as to portfolio content. Portfolios are able to reveal progress in school as well as reflect student growth and development in a number of areas (e.g., participation in the school community, content-area progress, written language skills, speech-making proficiency [on audiotape], artistic and musical talent, etc.). Portfolio projects can encourage students to evaluate their own subject-area reading/language knowledge as well as listening and discussion abilities. Assessment portfolios are a type of evaluation portfolio used for any subject area (e.g., writing, music, art, math, etc.) that typically involves a year-long collection of learning outcomes generated from coursework/studies. Teachers and/or students create criteria/standards for acceptable work/outcomes. Teachers and students can assess growth and development over a period of a week/month/the school year with this authentic type of recordkeeping. In many instances, teachers periodically share such portfolios with parents during the course of the school year so as to justify grades/performance evaluations and to share/demonstrate growth and development.

**Portmanteaus**   Blends or combinations of words into new words (e.g., bit = binary + unit; smog = smoke + fog).

**Positive correlation**   An orderly relationship between people's scores on one continuous variable and their scores on another variable is a *correlation*. In a positive correlation, the higher the score on one of the variables the higher the score on the second variable. For example, more hits for a ballplayer in baseball results in a higher batting average. The upper limit of a positive correlation coefficient is +1.00. Values of positive correlation that are much lower (e.g., +0.06) indicate a very weak relationship, if any, exists. In education, more study time at home generally results in higher grades. SEE: *correlation, negative correlation*

**Positive practice**   Following-up an error by practicing the correct response immediately thereafter.

**Positive regard**   According to Carl Rogers, we all have a need for positive regard, which includes love, respect, sympathy, and acceptance.

**Positive reinforcement**   The conditioning of an operant ("voluntary") response by providing a needed or desired object or condition (in a particular environment) right after the response occurs. This results in an increased probability that the response will be made again the next time the need or desire arises when the individual is in that same environment.

**Positive skew**  A type of unbalanced frequency distribution in which most of the scores are low and high scores are very rare. The long tail (of the graph of such a distribution) points toward the right (to the high end of the score dimension, the x-axis). The mean of such a distribution will be too high to indicate the central tendency accurately. The median should be used instead.

**Positron-Emission Tomography (PET scans)**  A method for mapping active areas of the brain by detecting the radioactivity in the form of emitted positrons on a background of brain pictures. The radioactive material is added to glucose and ingested by the subject. Neurons have a prior call on available glucose over other body cells. Active neurons, in turn, are given priority over resting neurons. The background pictures are taken by the CAT-scan technique.

**Postconventional level**  The most advanced level of moral development in Lawrence Kohlberg's theory. People who have attained this level of moral development qualify as ethical leaders. Martin Luther King and Mohatma Gandhi are twentieth century examples. Thoreau and Tolstoi would be nineteenth century examples. The founders of the world's great religions, Buddha, Confucius, Laotze, Moses, Jesus, and Mohammed were also at the postconventional level. SEE: *conventional level, preconventional level*

**Post hoc tests**  Refers to statistics that are used to follow up after initial analyses are completed and there are more than two groups involved. Post hoc tests seek to find significant differences between individual pairs/sets of means so as to make individual comparisons. An example of a post hoc test would be Tukey's significant difference test.

**Posthypnotic suggestions**  Commands given to a hypnotized subject that are to be obeyed after he/she has been released from the hypnotic trance. When these commands are carried out and the subject is asked to explain the action, the subject can only offer some rationalization. This is because the subject is unaware of the real reason for the behavior.

**Postlingual**  Occurring after the development of language; usually used to classify hearing losses that begin after a person has learned to speak.

**Postlingual** or **postlinguistic deafness**  A hearing impairment that appears after speech and language development have been initiated. SEE: *postlingual, adventitiously deaf*

**Postlingual disorders**  Speech and hearing disorders that occur after one has developed the ability to speak. These disorders can occur at any age following speech development. SEE: *prelingual disorders*

**Postnatal**  Refers to conditions or events that occur after birth (e.g., jaundice).

**Postreading strategy**  In language arts, an activity that follows and relates to what has been read. The activity should prompt reflections on what has been read or serve as a base for launching further reading on related topics. An example of a postreading strategy would be to summarize orally what has just been read or retell what has just been read in one's own words.

**Postsecondary**  A term used to describe education that follows high school graduation. This includes but is not limited to education in a technical school, a junior or community college, a four-year college or university, and continuing-education programs.

**Postsecondary options**  Refers to programs that allow high school juniors and seniors to enroll at postsecondary (after high school) programs or institutions for free while receiving both high school and college credit for coursework taken.

**Posttraumatic Stress Disorder (PTSD)**  A severe stress reaction to a very

P

**P**

traumatic experience. Wartime battles, fires, floods, rapes, and other assaults are examples of events that can precipitate a PTSD. The symptoms include flashback memories, low startle thresholds, nightmares, and phobic reactions to objects that are connected (symbolically or otherwise) to the trauma.

**Postural drainage**   The draining of fluids from cavities in the body by changing the position of the body, such as in the case of drainage of the lungs by positioning the body upright, laying flat, head elevated, feet elevated, etc. Gravity allows the drainage to take place.

**Potain's disease**   Named after Pierre C. F. Potain (French physician, 1825–1901). This condition is a pulmonary edema or edema of the lungs (fluid in the air vesicles and tissues of the lung).

**Pott's disease**   Named after Percivall Pott (British surgeon, 1713–1788). This condition is primarily a disease of children and adults up to age 40. It involves destruction and compression of the vertebrae as a result of tuberculosis of the spine.

**Poverty index**   An estimate by the federal government of annual income necessary to meet the basic living costs in the United States. The Social Security Administration developed guidelines for this index in 1964 and revised them in 1969 and 1981. The index lists a series of incomes adjusted according to family size, number and age of children, gender of head of household, etc. The poverty level index changes each year according to the change (rise) in the consumer price index. SEE: *poverty level*

**Poverty level**   Annual income levels established by the U.S. Labor Department determined to be below the basic annual income requirements of a family based upon family size and other factors. SEE: *poverty index*

**Power**   SEE: *statistical power*

**PQ4R**   A method of systematic reading of text material for extracting and remembering meaningful content. It has the following six steps: preview, question, read, reflect, recite, and review.

**Practical intelligence**   The abilities required to carry out every-day life tasks or our adaptive functioning capability.

**Practicum**   A supervised practical experience. In particular, an on-the-job experience for students studying to become teachers and/or clinicians. It is the practical application of the theory studied in the classroom. Student teaching experiences are considered practicums. SEE: *internship*

**Pragmatics**   The understanding of the use of language and how it is used in communication (i.e., the social use of language). Speakers usually consider the "audience" when using language. Factors such as age, relationship to the audience, alertness, mental and health states, the presence of others, etc. all impact how one uses language in social situations. In other words, pragmatics involves the 1. study of the science of language usage for communication in a social sense and 2. the practical side of things and practical applications of principles.

**Pragmatism** (John Dewey's version is called experimentalism)   The philosophical position that is the only pure philosophical school to have originated in the United States. Pragmatism is based on the belief that truth can be obtained by what works in the present and that truth can change with the times and different circumstances. John Dewey (1859–1952) is probably the most famous pragmatist who emphasized the development of good citizens by teaching and modeling democratic principles. The major role of the teacher is believed by proponents of this school of thought to be a facilitator and resource person who works with students on becoming active problem solvers and independent learners.

**Preacademic instruction**   Instruction given in a preschool or kindergarten setting that prepares children for later instruction in reading, writing, and arithmetic.

**Preacademic skills**   The skills and behaviors that a child develops and needs before formally attending school. Preacademic skills include but are not limited to such things as play and peer cooperation; sharing; being able to identify shapes, numbers, letters, and colors; toilet training; self-help skills; etc.

**Precipitous birth**   Very rapid delivery of a child from the beginning of labor to the time of delivery. Generally, the period of labor is two hours or less.

**Precision teaching**   An instructional approach that involves pinpointing the behaviors to be changed; measuring the initial frequency of those behaviors; setting an aim, or goal, for the child's improvement; using direct, daily measurements to monitor progress made under an instructional program; graphing results of those measurements; and changing the program if progress is not adequate.

**Precocious**   1. A term used to describe a child who is prematurely developed physically or mentally and 2. a child who displays knowledge, skill, and/or ability at a younger-than-normal age.

**Precocity**   Early development that is unexpected or remarkable (e.g., a child who has an unusually well-developed vocabulary before the age of 4).

**Precognition**   One of the alleged variations of extrasensory perception. Precognition involves the accurate perception and knowledge of future events. SEE: *Extrasensory Perception (ESP)*

**Preconscious mind**   According to Sigmund Freud, the portion of the mind that is not in conscious awareness but can readily be presented to awareness. This is to be sharply distinguished from the unconscious mind, which the individual cannot bring to awareness. Unconscious memories have been repressed because they would otherwise produce intolerable guilt, anxiety, or shame.

**Preconventional level**   In Lawrence Kohlberg's theory, the immature stage of moral development in which the individual's choices are guided by fear of punishment and/or hope of reward (in other words, Freud's pleasure principle). SEE: *conventional level, pleasure principle, postconventional level*

**Prefix**   A letter or group of letters added to the beginning of a word, the "root" word, in order to change its meaning. For example, "un" before "natural" forms the word "unnatural," which differs in meaning from the word "natural." SEE: *affix root, suffix*

**Prefrontal cortex**   The front rim of the frontal lobe of the cerebral cortex. This was the part of the brain that was surgically separated from the rest in the once-popular operation called "frontal lobotomy." It is involved in our ability to perform the delayed reaction, holding a signal in memory for many minutes before acting on it. SEE: *prefrontal lobotomy*

**Prefrontal lobotomy**   The severance of the connection between the prefrontal cortex and the rest of the brain. The surgery was intended to relieve post-traumatic stress disorder, intractable pain, or otherwise untreatable psychosis. This type of surgery has been abandoned, partly because some undesirable side-effects accompanied it and partly because of the development of improved therapeutic techniques. SEE: *frontal lobe, prefrontal cortex*

**Prejudice**   Preconceived unfavorable/negative attitudes/ideas (that can lead to hostile feelings and unfair behavior) toward a group of people on the basis of an irrelevant criterion, such as race, ethnicity, sex, age, or membership in some organization. A prejudice is really a prejudgment that could be positive or negative. Most people experience both negative and positive prejudices in some form throughout their lives.

**Preliminary review**   Unlike a final review, it is the first look at data collected in reference to a student who is not progressing effectively in the regular school program. From such a review, a determination is made as to whether or not additional information and/or special education services are or might be needed.

**P**

**Prelingual**   Describes a hearing impairment that develops before a child has acquired speech and language.

**Prelingual** or **prelinguistic deafness**   A loss of hearing occurring before the development of speech and language. An individual with such a loss will ordinarily be both deaf and mute. SEE: *congenital deafness*

**Prelingual disorders**   Speech and hearing disorders that occur before one has developed the ability to speak. Disorders are classified as prelingual when they occur prior to age 2 or whatever age speech development really occurs. SEE: *postlingual disorders*

**Prelinguistic communication**   Communication by body language, oral gestures, or noises before words and sentences can be communicated.

**Premack principle**   A rule establishing the priority or the inferior status of two or more positive reinforcers. This rule derives from the research of David Premack. It says that the opportunity to perform a highly probable behavior will reinforce a less probable behavior. Thus, a thirsty rat will run in an activity wheel to earn sips of water, while a rat that has been confined in a small space will sip water in order to open the door leading to an activity wheel. As another example, a child may eat a vegetable she/he dislikes in order to have dessert. Premack's principle is also known as Grandma's law.

**Prematurity**   A term used to identify infants born in less than 37 weeks from the first day of last period of menses. SEE: *low birthweight*

**Premotor cortex**   A motor area of the frontal lobe (area 6) lying rostral to (in front of) the primary motor area (area 4). It is active during the planning of a movement, relating sensory data to the prospective action. The axons that leave area 6 are relatively short; many travel to the midbrain's basal ganglia, such as the substantia nigra and the red nucleus. These axons comprise (in part) the extrapyramidal motor pathways, so-called because they are outside of the main motor pathway, the pyramidal tract.

**Prenatal**   Occurring before birth.

**Prenatal asphyxia**   A lack of oxygen during the birth process usually caused by interruption of respiration; can cause unconsciousness and/or brain damage.

**Prenatal care**   The vigilant monitoring of a developing fetus by the mother and the attending physician.

**Preoperational stage**   The second stage of cognitive development in Jean Piaget's theory. The preoperational stage begins with the achievement of object permanence (objects remain real even when out of sight). Imaginative play occurs. The quality of thinking is marked by egocentricity; the 2–7-year-old child is unable to take another person's point of view. The child is easily fooled by rearrangement of objects into believing that the number or amount of the objects has been changed.

**Prepalate**   The section of the mouth that includes the ridge of the upper gum just above the upper front teeth (also called the alveolar ridge) and the upper lip.

**Prephonemic spelling**   In language arts, the earliest stage of spelling. It is characterized by 1. incorrectly formed or made-up numbers and letters, 2. basically unreadable forms and letters used in a random fashion, 3. unbroken lines of letters or wordlike spaced configurations, 4. an awareness/ability to carry out writing horizontally, 5. the knowledge that letters make up words, and 6. typically kindergarteners, first graders, and even older preschoolers display the above.

**Prepracticums**   Experiences in the classroom before student teaching. Prepracticum experiences allow the prospective teacher/practitioner to work with small groups of students and in tutorial situations in order to gain educational and social "hands-on" knowledge with students.

**Prereading activities**   Prereading activities (e.g., brainstorming, semantic mapping/webbing, surveying, graphic organizers, cognitive mediation, and vocabulary activities).

**Prereferral intervention**   When a student is not progressing effectively in the regular school program, prereferral intervention is considered before a referral is made for a special-needs evaluation. Children who are at risk for failure or who may need special services are examined in the light of what can be done to amend or adapt the regular curriculum to prevent school failure and/or referral for special education. Such action is referred to as prereferral intervention.

**Prereferral services**   Services directed to students identified as at risk for the development of a learning disability that are intended to help them adapt to the regular classroom. Later, some of these students may still be perceived as requiring special education services.

**Prereferral Team (PRT)**   A team consisting of professionals from regular and special education who work with regular classroom teachers to develop strategies, materials, and methods for children who are at risk for academic failure and special services. These actions are taken to minimize the number of children who are referred for special services who could otherwise be assisted within the regular classroom setting (with proper adaptations and modifications).

**Presbyopia**   Farsightedness, usually a part of the aging process and a result of the rigidity (loss of elasticity) of the lens, which makes accommodation of near objects extremely difficult. SEE: *accommodation, hyperopia, myopia*

**Prescriptive philosophy**   The attempt to establish well-reasoned standards for right behavior, beautiful art, and valid truth. Prescriptive philosophies are attempts to uncover the basis of good and evil, beauty and ugliness, and right and wrong, with the intention of stating rules that foster the good, the beautiful, and the right and reduce the amounts of evil, ugliness, and error in the world. SEE: *analytic philosophy, speculative philosophy*

**Presentation punishment**   The most familiar type of punishment: an aversive stimulus is presented to the individual immediately after an error in order to reduce the chances that the error will be repeated.

**Presentism**   Thinking only in terms of the present time and failing to consider the past or the future.

**Pressure**   The demands placed upon an individual by the external environment (both physical and social). A well-adjusted individual is one who has learned to cope with environmental pressures. SEE: *stress*

**Presymptomatic test**   An examination that can predict a long-delayed disease. Huntington's disease does not strike until middle age. An infant's chromosomes can be examined for the G8 marker, which occurs on chromosome number 4 in Huntington's disease cases.

**Pretest**   A test presented to learners before instruction or other treatment in order to measure their performance before they receive the specified treatment.

**Prevalence**   The number of people who have a certain condition at any given time.

**Prevention**   The act of avoiding or stopping the development of a disability.

**Primary cortical areas**   Most of the human neocortex consists neither of the terminals of sensory neural pathways nor the origins of motor pathways. Be that as it may, the cortical areas that do serve as terminals of sensory neural pathways are called the *primary sensory cortex,* while the area of the cortex from which the corticospinal and corticobulbar motor pathways originate is termed the primary motor cortex. Each primary cortical area has related areas around it called "secondary." For example, a number of secondary visual areas are located in the general neighborhood of the primary visual area. Also, the primary motor cortex has its neighbors called the premotor cortex and the supplementary motor cortex.

**P**

**Primary epilepsies** Seizure disorders that appear to be inherited. They are predictable disorders and normally appear at an early age. SEE: *secondary epilepsies, seizures*

**Primary reinforcer** A primary reinforcer is a type of stimulus that has an ability to influence behaviors that are not a result of learning. Examples of primary reinforcers are food, water, and sex. They are natural reinforcers as opposed to secondary reinforcers, which have to be learned. Primary reinforcers are also known as unconditioned reinforcers. SEE: *secondary reinforcer*

**Primary school** A school organization of the lower elementary grades. It includes grades one, two, and three and frequently kindergarten or their equivalents. In some school systems, preprimary grades are included (programs for 3- and 4-year olds).

**Principle** A relationship between observed variables. Often, a principle is a verified hypothesis.

**Private school** A school usually supported by nonpublic funds. Such schools are controlled and administered by persons not publically elected or appointed. There is no direct connection with public local educational agencies, state, or federal agencies; they are independently operated from these governmental agencies through the private sector.

**Private speech** Self-talking used to guide one's actions. This tactic is used more often by children than by adults.

**Proactive interference** The process in which previously learned material stored in memory interferes with new learning or information. For example, if a student learns French and then Spanish, the student could have difficulty with Spanish grammar because of the previously learned French grammar.

**Problem** A situation in which a goal is set and the way of attaining the goal has yet to be worked out.

**Problem finding** The ability of an educator or researcher to review a set of interrelated facts and observations and determine what aspect of that area requires further investigation and analysis.

**Procedural follow-up** In special education, a plan which requires the teacher to have on-going contact with a teacher support or evaluation team. The idea is to provide the teacher with an opportunity to stay abreast of the support being provided and/or available and to be able to tap into the expertise of the support team on an on-going basis in the best interest of the student(s).

**Problem solving** The activity of arriving at the solution of a problem through the systematic organization and the cognitive processing of the relevant data.

**Procedural knowledge** Know-how; the memories of skills needed to perform tasks successfully. Long-term memories of procedural knowledge are more resistant to traumatic effects than personal (names, dates) memories are. SEE: *procedural memory*

**Procedural memory** A part of long-term memory dealing with "know-how" as opposed to personal memories, names, and dates. Usually, traumatic conditions that interfere with the latter (called "semantic memory") have little or no effect on procedural memory. SEE: *semantic memory*

**Procedural safeguards** A system designed to protect the legal rights of an individual. For special education processing of students with disabilities, procedural safeguards include 1. zero reject, or all children with disabilities must be provided a free and appropriate education (hence, no one is rejected); 2. each special-needs student is entitled to a nondiscriminatory evaluation; 3. students in need of special education services must have a written "Individualized Education Plan" or IEP; 4. whenever possible, persons with disabilities must be educated in the least restrictive environment, as near normal as possible; 5. due process protection of one's rights; and 6. parents have the right to be included in the entire process.

**Procedures**   Systematic programs for the step-by-step performance of a given activity.

**Process/product debate**   The discussion of whether or not training a perceptual process (e.g., improving visual tracking skills) is more effective than direct instruction (e.g., teaching phonemic awareness to students with Learning Disabilities [LD]). This debate, which raged in the early 1970s, resulted in the finding that process (the perceptual approach) was infrequently effective in teaching academics.

**Process test**   A test or procedure, frequently of a perceptual or linguistic nature, that is used to help determine the effectiveness of psychological methods or processes.

**Process writing**   The teaching of the writing process after an initial brainstorming session(s) with reflection, three drafts, peer inquiry, and teacher feedback to follow. The teacher gives feedback, evaluates, and publishes the final product.

**Productions**   Rules that specify what steps to take if certain conditions are present.

**Professional autonomy**   The rights assumed or given to teachers and other professionals to collaborate, establish curriculum, implement classroom rules, etc.

**Professional-centered program**   Refers to an early intervention program that relies on the expertise of professionals to assist families in need of assistance.

**Professional library**   In education, a term used to describe a collection of professional and classroom materials for the use of the professional/instructional staff, primarily. Normally, such a library is maintained by the school district and can be housed within a school building and/or a central location.

**Profound mental retardation**   A condition characterized by extremely poor to nonexistent adaptable behavior along with an IQ of below 25 points. A profoundly retarded person has no effective speech, sometimes communicates through nonverbal gestures and sounds; communication skills are severely limited if they exist at all. Such persons have few motor skills and usually have serious physical problems. Social adaptation is frequently nonexistent as is independent functioning. It is unlikely that the profoundly retarded would benefit from training for employment. Their educational plans should concentrate on such skills as attending and positioning. Profound retardation affects less than one of every 10,000 persons. SEE: *mild mental retardation, moderate mental retardation, severe mental retardation*

**Profound multiple disorders**   SEE: *severe and profound multiple disorders*

**Profound visual disability**   A visual impairment severe enough to prevent the student from being able to learn from visually presented materials. This type of impairment fits the legal definition of blindness.

**Progeny**   Descendents or offspring.

**Progesterone**   The hormone released by the corpus luteum (which is a body produced in the ovary during the estrous cycle) that prepares the wall of the uterus for the implantation of the fertilized ovum (the zygote).

**Prognosis**   A prediction, or estimate of the course and eventual outcome of a disease or disorder.

**Program**   1. The courses and activities organized into an educational curriculum along with noncurriculum activities which have been designed to attain broad or specific educational objectives and goals as described by the school and institutions. 2. SEE: *Appendix 4: Computer Terms*

**Programmed instruction**   Teacher materials that are presented in a step-by-step format whereby a series of skills are presented with one skill building on the other. Programmed instructional materials are created so that the learner can progress at an individual pace with reinforcement provided as to correctness in responding. Only after a correct response is the next bit of instruction offered to the student. Such instruction has been found useful in areas such as math facts acquisition and spelling acquisition (rote types of subject presentations). Programmed instruction was a theory of education devised by B. F. Skinner, representing the use of Skinner's "teaching machine."

**Programmed learning**   Any learning material or device that when used by a student leads to a response to the student's activity with immediate feedback concerning the next step of operation. The student progresses from step to step to the completion of the program. SEE: *programmed instruction*

**Progressive education**   An educational philosophy emphasizing meaningful education to students, which is relevant to and in the spirit of a democratic society. Creativity and meeting the needs and interests of the individual student without losing sight of real world goals is paramount. The relationship between the school and the community is emphasized.

**Progressive relaxation**   A therapeutic technique worked out by an early behavior therapist, Edmund Jacobsen, who worked from 1908 to the 1930s. The patient lies in a supine position, concentrates on a given part of the body, and thinks of the body part as relaxed. When he/she feels no tension in that part of the body, the patient moves on to another part of the body. In this way, one can learn how to relax any given muscle group.

**Progressive tax**   A tax that is based on a scaled ability to pay. For example, federal income taxes are progressive.

**Progressivism**   A philosophy or theory of education that emphasizes the testing of ideas through experimentation. Learning by students is facilitated and rooted in the concept of answering questions as determined and developed by the students.

**Projection**   A characteristic of paranoia wherein an individual attributes to others, as a result of his/her own repressed and distorted perceptions, one's own traits and behaviors of an undesirable nature.

**Projective test**   A type of test instrument or assessment that involves asking a subject about a series of subjective and sometimes ambiguous stimuli. These tests are given in order to elicit thought patterns, which can give insights into the subject's personality and/or any thought disorders or problems. The Rorschach inkblot test and incomplete sentence tasks (e.g., "I will read this dictionary from cover to cover because . . .") are projective measures. Such tests are difficult to score and many times are not normed so that results have to be viewed with a cautious eye. SEE: *Rorschach inkblot test*

**Prolapse**   The act of collapse, slipping out of place, falling, or dropping down of an internal body part or organ.

**Prompt**   A reminder stimulus that is provided when an individual fails to supply the correct response to the programmed cue stimulus.

**Pronation**   1. A postural position in which a person is lying on one's stomach, stretched out, and face down. 2. The act of rotating the hand so that the palm is downward or backward.

**Property tax**   Any tax based on the value of property. This includes personal or real-estate property.

**Prophylaxis**   Preventative treatment and/or the prevention of a disease. Examples include innoculations (e.g., polio vaccine), teeth cleaning, braces, using condoms, etc.

**Proportionate tax**   A tax based on one's income or ability to pay.

**Propositional network**   A scheme of interrelated concepts and propositions that is held in long-term memory.

**Proprietary school**   A school, although private, that is subject to taxation on profits gained from revenues.

**Proprioception** or **proprioceptive system**   The proprioceptive receptors are housed in the joints, muscles, tendons, and nearby tissues. They react to the movement and/or positioning of the body and its members in space. Thus, there is an awareness of the position and movement of the body in space.

**Proprioceptor**    A receptor that is specialized in receiving information about the body's own movements, the contraction or elongation of the muscles, the level of muscle tone, etc. Proprioceptors are specifically found in the muscles, tendons, and joints.

**Proptosis**    A craniofacial anomaly characterized by bulging eyes.

**Prosocial behavior**    Activity that improves the welfare of persons other than the one doing the behaving.

**Prosocial education**    Education based on empathy and understanding of the unique abilities and needs of all learners.

**Prosody**    The flow or rhythm of our language, which involves intonation, word and sentence length, and stress patterns.

**Prosopagnosia**    A specific loss of the ability to recognize faces visually. SEE: *temporal lobes*

**Prosthesis**    1. Any device used to replace a missing or impaired body part. Examples would include a partial plate for dentures, a full set of false teeth, an artificial heart valve, etc., and 2. any device that augments impaired bodily function(s) such as a hearing aid.

**Prosthetic devices**    The actual artificial device that replaces a missing body part. It can be an artificial organ or part such as a heart valve or an artificial limb to replace a leg or arm. SEE: *prosthesis*

**Prosthetics**    A branch of surgery concerned with the replacement of body parts that are missing. SEE: *prosthesis, prosthetic devices*

**Prototype**    1. An object that has very typical characteristics of the category to which it belongs. For example, in regard to the concept "bird," a robin would be a prototype of "bird," but an ostrich or a penguin would not. 2. A classification system of students with special needs, based upon time spent out of regular class.

**Proxemics**    A term that describes the use of one's private space, personal territory, spatial arrangement, distance of comfort, or distance from other people and the use of this space in communications.

**Proximal**    Refers to being close to the body or trunk. It is the opposite of "distal." SEE: *distal*

**Proximity control**    A type of behavior management technique whereby students with unacceptable behaviors are moved to an area of close proximity to the teacher. This could be a front-row seat or an aisle seat.

**Proximodistal**    A term used to describe the muscular development of a child wherein the child first gains/develops control of those muscles closest to the trunk of the body (proximo-) or the center of the body and later develops those muscles located farther away from the body's trunk or center (-distal).

**PRT**    SEE: *Prereferral Team*

**Pseudohermaphrodite**    An individual who has not fully developed either as a male or a female but cannot be called a true hermaphrodite. A pseudohermaphrodite may be referred to as an intersex. SEE: *hermaphrodite, intersex*

**Psyche**    Sometimes referred to as the soul or the mind. The psyche is really everything that makes up the mind as well as how the mind processes information from the surrounding world.

**Psychiatrist**    A physician, a specialist in treating social, emotional, and mental disorders. A psychiatrist, unlike a psychologist, has a medical degree. SEE: *psychologist*

**Psychiatry**    That branch of medicine concerned with the diagnosis and treatment of emotional and behavioral disorders.

**Psychic determinism**    One of the assumptions of Sigmund Freud's psychoanalytic theory. According to this view, every psychic event is caused by some preceding event. SEE: *psychoanalysis*

**Psychoactive drugs**    Any drug is a chemical that affects the body's functions (i.e., the chemical has a physiological impact on the organism). A psychoactive drug has an impact on the behavior, the emotional adjustment, the sensory perceptions, or the personality

**P**

of an individual. There are five general categories of psychoactive drugs: 1. depressants, such as the barbiturates and ethyl alcohol; 2. stimulants, such as the amphetamines, cocaine, and caffeine; 3. opiates, such as opium, morphine, heroin, and methadone; 4. psychedelics (hallucinogens), such as LSD, mescaline, and marijuana; and 5. antipsychotics, such as the tricyclic antidepressants, the MAO inhibitors, and the neuroleptic drugs. As a mnemonic device to aid recall of these five categories, use the following acrostic: Does Santa open people's attics?

**Psychoanalysis**   A school of psychology founded by Sigmund Freud (1856–1939), an Austrian physician. Psychoanalysis is a method of tapping into and analyzing the psyche. It is based upon the premise of repressed past experiences that were painful or undesirable and that remain in the subconscious and thus cause abnormal phenomena. This psychotherapeutic system involves an ongoing dialogue between the analyst and the patient wherein the forgotten memories are brought into the conscious mind. · This resurrection of old memories enables the patient to view problems in the proper perspective, according to proponents of this school of thought. Solution(s) must involve confronting the repressed harmful experiences. In particular, psychoanalysis studies the "ego" in relation to reality as well as the "id" and "superego." SEE: *ego, id, psyche, repression, superego*

**Psychoanalytic perspective**   The interpretation of human behavior according to Sigmund Freud's psychoanalytic theory. Specifically, this could mean, in clinical practice, the attribution of an emotional/behavioral problem to a defense mechanism or to the interruption of psychosexual development. SEE: *psychoanalysis, psychoanalytics*

**Psychoanalytics**   A theory based on the principles of Sigmund Freud (1856–1939), an Austrian physician. This theory deals with the diagnosis and treatment of mental disorders such as schizophre-

nia through psychoanalysis. SEE: *mental disorders, psychoanalysis, schizophrenia*

**Psychobiology**   That school of thought that explains learning and behavior through biological mechanisms.

**Psychochemicals**   Chemicals or drugs that influence and change behavior. They normally produce short-lasting changes in the functioning of the activity of the brain.

**Psychodrama**   A diagnostic therapeutic technique invented by J. L. Moreno. The individual is first asked to play the role of herself/himself while other persons (colleagues of the therapist) play the roles of members of the person's family. After some time, the director announces role-switching. One of the cast members assumes the individual's role and the individual has to act like someone else. This provides the individual with perspective and helps her/him work out problems of interpersonal relationships.

**Psychodynamic**   An approach to the treatment of psychological disorders that is based on the precept that they are caused by unconscious conflicts and anxieties.

**Psychodynamic analysis**   A system (based on the psychoanalytic theory of Sigmund Freud) of investigating and analyzing one's subconscious feelings, emotions, and motivations.

**Psychodynamic modeling**   A term used to describe a concept wherein the behaviors of a student or individual are viewed as the expressions or symptoms of some underlying problem or disorder (e.g., acting out behaviors in school could result from prior angry encounters with family members/friends in situations unrelated to school). In other words, a disorder produces symptoms (e.g., conduct disorder), which are the observed behaviors (e.g., disobedience, fighting in school) of the underlying problem or disorder (e.g., anger emanating from outside conflicts with family members or friends). Therefore, in order to cure the disorder, one must first diagnose the underlying problem(s).

**Psychoeducational diagnostician** A trained specialist who tests, evaluates, and diagnoses a student's learning problems. SEE: *psychometrician*

**Psychogenic** A term used to describe psychological or functional disorders that are not related to an organic disease of the body.

**Psychogenic fugue** (also called dissociative fugue disorder) A dissociative disorder that combines amnesia with fugue, when the individual leaves his/her usual environment and wanders aimlessly. On rare occasions, the person may even adopt a new identity, settling down in an area distant from his/her home.

**Psychokinesis (PK)** (also known as Telekinesis) One of the varieties of extrasensory perception. PK is the alleged ability to move physical objects or to reshape them by the power of the unassisted mind. SEE: *Extrasensory Perception (ESP)*

**Psycholinguistic deficiencies** First studied in detail in 1961 when the ITPA (Illinois Test of Psycholinguistic Abilities) was developed. Refers to such weaknesses as the inability to use phonics to decode words from printed symbols and a failure to outgrow early language habits (in other words, the speaker-listener is unable to integrate the grammatical, and, in particular, the phonological knowledge he/she possesses).

**Psycholinguistics** A branch of linguistics, the scientific study of language, it merges psychological concepts with language science in order to explain the development of language and the universal features shared by all languages. Mostly developed by one innovative scientist, Noam Chomsky, psycholinguistics is concerned with the mental structures and operations that make language possible. The concepts of surface structure and deep structure are essential aspects of this point of view. This term covers all the processes involved in language acquisition and usage.

**Psychological hardiness** A trait possessed by some persons that involves resistance to the negative effects of psychological stress. These people are generally optimistic and have an internal locus of control. Stressful events are treated as occasions for learning and self-improvement. SEE: *stress*

**Psychological test** A psychological test is a sample of behavior that is measured objectively. These assessments may be used as the basis for inferences about some psychological concept such as special aptitude, general intelligence, personality type, adjustment or maladjustment, interests, values, attitudes, vocational interests, etc.

**Psychological trauma** A psychological injury or shock caused by an accident, violence, abuse, neglect, separation, or tension. SEE: *stress*

**Psychologist** A specialist trained in the theories, methods, and applications of psychology. A psychologist is not a medical doctor like a psychiatrist and, as such, cannot prescribe drug treatments. SEE: *psychiatrist, psychology*

**Psychology** The science of human and animal behavior and of human mental processes. The study of psychology is largely concerned with the genetic and environmental causes of our behavior. It focuses on how people interact with one another and respond to the physical and social environment. Psychology as a science is quite compatible with the physiological study of the functions of the body. One's own physical well-being is closely connected to one's cognitive and emotional processes. SEE: *psychologist*

**Psychometrician** A person trained in the measurement of mental data. Frequently psychometricians determine the educational, mental, and/or learning status of a student with a variety of social and education assessments. School psychologists frequently assume this role in school systems. SEE: *psychoeducational diagnostician*

**Psychometrics** The specialty within the field of psychology concerned with tests of intelligence, personality, aptitudes, achievement, attitude, interests, etc.

**Psychomotor** Motor activity that is directly related to or controlled by mental or psychological processes (e.g., playing basketball).

**Psychomotor domain** A set of physical skills that an individual is expected to acquire (e.g., walking, grasping, writing, etc.).

**Psychomotor epilepsy** A milder form of seizure wherein a person with epilepsy loses touch with reality but does not lose consciousness. The person appears more or less normal in functioning and is able to perform some motor activity. Normally the affected person has no memory of what has occurred during such an episode. SEE: *seizure*

**Psychomotor learning** The acquisition of fine and gross motor skills in conjunction with muscular development as they relate to the mental process. SEE: *psychomotor domain*

**Psychomotor seizure** A psychomotor episode that occurs concurrently with an epileptic seizure. SEE: *complex partial seizure, psychomotor epilepsy*

**Psychomotor tests** Motor skills tests that are concerned with physical activity and mental processes. Such tests would include sensory/perception-motor coordination tasks such as seeing a red light and hitting car brakes.

**Psychoneuroimmunology** The study of the linkages among psychological factors, immune responses, and the nervous system is named psychoneuroimmunology. For example, exposure to prolonged stress leads some neurons in the cerebral cortex to release endorphins, lowering the amount of responding to pain stimuli. Resulting high levels of endorphins may cause vulnerability to life-threatening diseases such as cancer.

**Psychoneurological disorder** (better known by the term learning *disabilities*) A condition wherein the learning problems or disabilities are symptomatic of central nervous system dysfunctioning. SEE: *Learning Disabilities (LD)*

**Psychoneurotic** A functional disorder of psychic or mental origin.

**Psychopath** An individual who lacks the ability to judge the difference between right and wrong and feels little guilt about destructive or unsatisfactory behavior. Psychopaths generally are in conflict with society and fail to learn from past experiences. For the most part, rewards and punishments do not impact how a psychopath will function. This term is sometimes used synonymously with the term "sociopath." SEE: *sociopath*

**Psychopathic personality disorder** SEE: *antisocial personality disorder*

**Psychopathology** The study of mental/emotional disorders.

**Psychophysics** An area of psychological research that involves the relationship of a physical variable (e.g., light intensity) to a subjective variable (e.g., experienced level of brightness of light). Particular approaches to measurement were developed originally in order to solve psychophysical problems (e.g., the method of limits, the method of constant stimuli, the method of average error, among others). Some of the psychophysical methods, with appropriate modification, have been used to measure attitudes. Traditional psychophysics has been challenged by a newer approach, signal detection theory, that considers the habitual and the motivational factors that enter into a perceptual judgment. While somewhat useful, the new approach has not replaced the older methods completely. SEE: *signal detection theory*

**Psychophysiological disorders** Also called psychosomatic disorders, they result from stressful emotions ("all in one's mind"). The organic physical symptoms are present even though the disease or illness is not. SEE: *psychosomatic disorders*

**Psychophysiology** The study of the relationships between mental life, motivation, and the emotions on the one hand and the physiological events such as the EEG, evoked responses, the galvanic skin response, respiratory rate, heartbeat, blood pressure, skin temperature, etc. on the other. Applications of psychophysiology include polygraphy, biofeedback, and the use of transcendental meditation (or the relaxation response) to relieve psychosomatic (stress-related) disorders.

**Psychosexual**   The workings of the mind as concerned with the emotional aspects of the sexual instinct.

**Psychosis**   Formerly a term used to describe any mental disorder, now psychosis is described as a mental/ emotional/behavioral disorder that is severe enough to require that the patient be institutionalized for the protection of the patient and of society in general. The psychotic loses contact with reality and many times suffers from delusions and hallucinations. Behaviors are abnormal, peculiar, antisocial, and maladaptive. Many times psychosis is used synonymously with schizophrenia. SEE: *schizophrenia*

**Psychosocial**   The term for the relationship between an individual's emotional condition and the interpersonal environment.

**Psychosocial ability/talent**   A unique ability of a person to lead others in the arenas of social, political, intellectual, and like pursuits.

**Psychosocial disadvantage**   Category of causation for mental retardation that requires evidence of less-than-average intellectual functioning in at least one parent and one or more siblings (when there are siblings). This condition is typically associated with inadequate medical care. The term is used, often synonymously, with cultural familial retardation when no organic cause can be identified.

**Psychosomatic disorders**   Illnesses involving physical damage to body tissues as the result of emotional reactions to stress. These include some cases of ulcers, asthma, colitis, high blood pressure, etc. The patient's life history and personality are important factors in the length and severity of the disorder. SEE: *stress*

**Psychosurgery**   A destruction of a part of the brain in order to repair or remove an emotional or adjustment problem affecting an individual. This is to be done only after the patient has failed to respond to psychotherapy, behavior therapy, or to psychoactive drug treatment, and where the condition presents a serious risk to the life of the patient and/or other persons. One example of such surgery is the Mark-Ervin procedure, which involves the specific destruction of a small portion of the amygdaloid nucleus. The area is burned out (by an applied direct current) in order to remedy outbursts of destructive aggression. An early and unfortunate example of psychosurgery was prefrontal lobotomy. SEE: *lobotomy, prefrontal lobotomy*

**Psychotherapeutic drugs**   1. Drugs normally used to relieve symptoms of individuals who are suffering from some sort of mental problem such as anxiety or depression, and 2. antianxiety drugs such as the tranquilizer Valium (diazepam), antidepressant drugs such as Tofranil (imipramine), or antipsychotic drugs such as Thorazine (chlorpromazine). SEE: *anxiety, depression, stress*

**Psychotherapy**   The practice of treating behavioral/emotional disorders by a "talking cure." The original form of psychotherapy was psychoanalysis (Freud's method). Other approaches to psychotherapy have emerged, each involving a basic disagreement with Freudian thought. Carl Rogers' system of client-centered therapy has the helpee participate actively in the therapeutic process; the helper is a counselor, whose task is to reflect feelings reported by the helpee. The reflection is done in a nonjudgmental manner, with the helper exhibiting unconditional positive regard (high esteem) for the helpee. SEE: *person-centered therapy, psychoanalysis*

**Psychotic**   One who is suffering from a severe personality disorder or affected by psychosis. SEE: *psychosis*

**Psychotic disorders**   SEE: *psychosis*

P

**Psychotropic drugs**   In effect, drugs that produce mood changes; that is, drugs that affect our behavior or psychic functioning.

**PT**   SEE: *Physical Therapist*

**PTA**   Ordinarily referred to as Parent Teacher Association, it is officially known as the National Congress of Parents and Teachers.

**PTSD**   SEE: *Posttraumatic Stress Disorder*

**Puberty**   The age at which reproductive behavior can begin. In today's society, it is 12 or 13 for girls and 13 or 14 for boys. The hypothalamus starts releasing the hormone LH releasing factor in hourly bursts. The pituitary releases both LH and FSH, stimulating the gonads into action. Estradiol from the ovaries leads to breast development, broadening of hips, and the start of menstrual cycles. Testosterone leads to beard growth, lowering of the voice, and the dropping of the testes into a scrotal sac. Precocious puberty strikes some children at such early ages as 8 or 9; it can be treated by drugs that inhibit the pituitary's release of FSH (follicle-stimulating hormone) and LH (luteinizing hormone).

**Public confidence**   Basically the real trust that the general public has in its institutions, to include its schools.

**Public law (federal)**   SEE: *public laws (P.L.)*

**Public school**   A school or institution operated and controlled by duly elected or appointed public officials. All school programs and activities are administered/controlled by these public officials and the schools are primarily supported by public funds.

**Pull-out model/program**   An educational model that involves "pulling" students out of their mainstream classes for remedial classes. Typically resource room programs and Title I programs utilize some pull-out models although many programs utilize "in-class" models. Speech therapists, occupational therapists, counselors, etc. may use pull-out programs for their students who need services in order to ensure privacy and

individualization of services. SEE: *Chapter I, resource room program, mainstreaming*

**Pulp**   1. The soft inner and vascular portion of a tooth. 2. The soft portion of an organ. SEE: *dentine, enamel*

**Punishment**   Providing a negative reinforcer (i.e., an aversive stimulus, which means an unwanted object or situation) to an organism after it makes an operant response, which results in a decrease in the chances that the response will be repeated in the same environment (in a few cases, punishment is accomplished by the removal of a positive reinforcer, although this variety is more rarely used). The concept of punishment is often confused with the idea of "negative reinforcement." What the two ideas have in common is aversive stimulation of the organism and some sort of tie-in to the consequences of responding. But punishment involves the presentation of the undesirable stimulus whereas negative reinforcement involves the removal of that stimulus (with a subsequent increase in response probability, which occurs in all instances of reinforcement). SEE: *operant conditioning, negative reinforcement*

**Pupil**   1. Analogous to the aperture of a camera, it admits light into the eye. The pupil is kept nearly closed in brightly lit settings and is widened where the light is dim. 2. A student in a school or some learning situation (e.g., pupil of piano).

**Pupil-teacher ratio**   In education, the number of students assigned to a single teacher at a given time. For multiple class periods, the pupil teacher ratio is the total number of pupils assigned for all periods divided by the number of class periods taught; this calculates the average pupil-teacher class size ratio.

**Pupillary reflex**   This is the constriction of the pupil of the eye in response to bright light (analogous to closing the aperture of a camera when taking a picture outdoors on a sunny day). The parasympathetic nervous system is acting to preserve the light-sensitive materials of the retina.

**Purdue Secondary Model for Gifted and Talented Youth** A high school program for gifted students that incorporates counseling and is intended to meet all the educational needs of such students. It includes "acceleration" and enrichment. SEE: *acceleration, enrichment*

**Pure philosophies** Refers to the four major "pure" philosophies of naturalism, idealism, realism, and pragmatism. Existentialism is also considered by some to be a pure philosophy. SEE: *naturalism, idealism, realism, pragmatism*

**Pure research** Research conducted solely for the purpose of gathering information/data to enhance understanding/creating a knowledge base.

**Pure sounds** A term used to describe sound waves of specific frequency used in pure tone audiometry to test an individual's range of hearing. SEE: *audiogram, frequency, hertz*

**Pure tone air conduction test** A test involving pure tones to determine hearing losses in the outer or middle ear. Various pure tone frequencies are listened to by the student or individual through a headset. The air conduction results are evaluated to determine what is referred to as a conductive hearing loss. Note: Bone conduction tests evaluate the inner ear by bypassing the outer and the middle ear. SEE: *air conduction (AC) test, bone conduction (BC) test, conductive hearing loss, pure tone bone conduction test, sensorineural hearing loss*

**Pure tone audiometric screening** A quick-screening test of hearing that uses pure tone signals. Various frequencies are listened to by a student or individual through a headset in order to determine possible hearing losses. This test is an initial test; if losses are determined, more intensive audiometric testing is indicated.

**Pure tone audiometry** The lowest intensity of sound (at various frequencies) that a person can hear within a normal range of –10 to +25 dB (decibels); especially useful at 500, 1000, and 2000

Hz (Hertz, or cycles per second), the normal speech range. Thus, the various frequencies and intensities that are measured can be used to determine a loss of hearing.

**Pure tone bone conduction test** A test involving pure tones to determine hearing losses in the inner ear. Various pure tone frequencies are transmitted through a vibrator applied to the bones of the skull. The outer ear and the middle ear are bypassed. If the bone conduction (BC) results show a loss, it may be concluded that the inner ear is not functioning properly. SEE: *air conduction (AC) test, bone conduction (BC) test, conductive hearing loss, pure tone air conduction test, sensorineural hearing loss*

**Pygmalion effect** The surprising academic improvement of a child after the teacher has been given a (false) record of previous academic successes. The name Pygmalion refers to a mythical sculptor whose statue of his ideal woman came to life.

**Pyramidal cerebral palsy** Refers to a type of cerebral palsy that is caused by damage to the pyramidal cells in the cerebral cortex. Individuals with this type of cerebral palsy cannot control voluntary movements and experience muscle spasms.

**Pyramidal tract** That set of nerve cell axons carrying nerve impulses from the primary motor area of the cerebral cortex of the brain. After they leave the brain, most of these axons comprise one of the three main descending tracts of the spinal cord. Damage to the pyramidal tract is usually involved in spastic cerebral palsy. The pyramidal tract is also known as the corticospinal tract, since it originates at the cerebral cortex (cortico-) and then travels down the spinal cord. The pyramidal tract is necessary for the smooth execution of our voluntary actions.

**Pyromania** A serious behavioral impulse control disorder that involves the lighting of fires for pleasure.

P

**Quadriplegia**   The paralysis or functional loss (could be actual) of all four limbs.

**Qualitative research**   Research efforts that are participant-oriented (e.g., collecting observations or interviews to create impressions/diagnostic hunches) and inductive in nature. Behavioral units are defined and many times quantified (e.g., observing a student with Attention-Deficit/Hyperactivity Disorder [ADHD] and the number of off-task behaviors during a specified time frame). Qualitative research usually focuses on a problem or issue at hand with little reference to previous research findings.

**Qualitative research data**   Data generated from qualitative research efforts that include observations, interviews, journal entries, and various assessment instruments (e.g., questionnaires, attitude and personality surveys).

**Qualitative sciences**   Sciences such as anthropology and ethnology that rely on qualitative research methods/data gathering.

**Quality disorders (of speech)**   Voice-quality problems characterized by hoarseness, nasality, nontypical tonality, etc.

**Quality of life**   A term used in education and special education in reference to the adjustment of students or persons who are cognitively/mentally disabled, learning/physically disabled, and/or health impaired. Quality of life examines how well one adjusts on a personal basis as well as adjustment to community life/living in general.

**Quality of teaching**   Observed characteristics that determine how effective teachers are in teaching/improving performances within the classroom. Several

key elements have been cited by the National Assessment of Educational Progress Board (NAEP) when assessing the quality of teaching within a particular school or state: 1. require high standards in such subject areas as math, science, English, and history; 2. match assessments to curriculum/standards; 3. hold teachers to high levels of competence and a commitment to teach to higher standards (look at % of teachers involved in professional development that includes new content standards); 4. organize/structure schools in ways to support teaching/learning; 5. hold all students to high expectations/standards (look at % of students taking AP (Advanced Placement) courses, remedial courses, and those dropping out of school); 6. challenge all students; 7. financial/ social support is needed from the community-at-large/parents (e.g., look at % of teachers who have access to advanced technology for teaching) along with a firm commitment to support public education.

**Quantitative research**   Research that involves the assigning of numerical values to observations (e.g., attitude survey toward math), behaviors (e.g., attention-behavior percentile standing as compared to peer group), learning outcomes (e.g., grades), test results (e.g., SAT scores), etc. as a way to screen large groups of students; make academic, behavioral, social comparisons; make predictions; determine academic strengths and weaknesses; etc. The information collected is expressed in the form of numbers/graphs and the like rather than through words/narrations as is the case in "Qualitative Research." SEE: *qualitative research*

**Quartile deviation**   A measure of variability that is one-half of the difference between the upper quartile (75th percentile) and the lower quartile (25th percentile) in a distribution.

**Quasi-experiment** (also called ex-post facto experiment)   Experiments or methods of research that do not have random group assignments, but researchers compensate for such statistical weaknesses by using various statistical procedures and methods (e.g., Bonferroni correction factor).

**Questioning**   A technique of instruction wherein the teacher guides the direction, understanding, and application of the information being taught through the use of questions. The teacher prompts students with questions and the students respond, hopefully, in an appropriate fashion. This approach can assist the students to think differently and develop new ideas and expand upon their knowledge base of the presented material.

**r**   Represents a correlation coefficient. "r" usually refers to the Pearson correlation coefficient.

**R**   Represents the multiple correlation coefficient.

**r²**   Represents the coefficient of determination.

**R²**   Represents the coefficient of determination when the coefficient is taken from a multiple correlation coefficient.

**Race**   A method of categorizing people who share geographical, national, and ethnic characteristics (usually sharing a number of physical features unique to their group—e.g., skin color) and are defined as a separate group by themselves and others. The race concept is controversial and a social one and is not used by anthropological scientists. Typically characteristics associated with race are biologically transmitted. Some racial characteristics have resulted from generations of families living in particular geographic regions. For example, in areas of intense heat, individuals developed darker skin (from melanin, a

natural skin pigment), and in areas with more moderate climates, individuals developed lighter skin colors. Many use the term race and ethnicity interchangeably. Race is considered to be more biologically distinctive and ethnicity more of a cultural description. SEE: *racial/ethnic group*

**Racial bias**   Prejudice against a race and the degree to which a person believes and behaves against members of a race in a prejudicial manner. SEE: *racism*

**Racial/ethnic group**   Category types that refer to one's ethnic or racial heritage. The Bureau of Census offers the following schemata for racial breakdowns:
White—persons or ancestors originating from Europe, North Africa, and the Middle East;
Black—persons or ancestors originating from any Black racial group in Africa;
Hispanic—persons or ancestors originating from Mexico, Puerto Rico, Cuba, Central America, South America, or any other Spanish culture regardless of race;
Asians or Pacific Islanders—persons or

ancestors originating from the Far East, Southeast Asia, Indian subcontinent, or the Pacific Islands. Included are Japan, Vietnam, India, Cambodia, China, Korea, the Philippines, and Samoa; Native Americans or Alaskans—persons or ancestors originating from any of the original people in North America with tribal or community recognition of cultural heritage

**Racism**   A type of destructive prejudice that involves the unequal treatment of a particular group of individuals because of social/physical/economic/linguistic or other characteristics that socially define a particular race. Racism involves a belief system whereby one racial (or several) category is considered to be superior or inferior to another. For example, the ancient Greeks viewed many peoples unlike themselves as inferior. For many centuries the enslavement of people of African descent occurred because of racism. Racism still exists in many countries in either open and direct forms (the refusal to hire an individual for a job because of race) or in less subtle ways (creating a social distance from another because of race). In more egalitarian cultures such as the United States, racism is less open but still practiced by some and is generally considered socially unacceptable. Such treatment of others usually results in hard feelings, poor social interactions, and discrimination.

**Radio-reading**   A type of script reading similar to a radio show or announcement that is delivered to an audience.

**Rainbow school**   A school that supports an atmosphere of tolerance, cooperation, and harmony amongst children of diverse cultures and races. Such a school promotes the fostering and protection of cultural similarities or differences.

**RAM**   SEE: *Appendix 4: Computer Terms*

**Random**   Occurring by chance, not according to an ordered plan. Selection of a sample of persons from a large population at random is done by giving each member of the population an equal chance to be chosen for the sample.

**Range**   A measure of variability that involves the difference between the high and low scores in a distribution.

**Raphe system**   A collection of nuclei along the midline (or "seam", which is what "raphe" means) of most of the brain stem (medulla, pons, and the posterior midbrain). The neurons in those nuclei release the neurotransmitter serotonin (5-HT) at their axon endings. The raphe cells are believed to cause the onset of non-REM sleep (slow-wave sleep) and to maintain a background of sleep when REM-sleep begins. SEE: *REM sleep*

**Rate (of behavior)**   A measure of how often a particular action is performed; usually reported as the number of responses per minute.

**Rating scale**   A written list of behavior descriptions that are each prototypes of a level of poor, mediocre, or good performance. The observer checks off the qualitative level of each type of performance covered by the scale. Before being put into widespread use, the rating scale should be checked for its inter-judge reliability. SEE: *checklist*

**Ratio scale**   A scale of measurement in which the consecutive numbers are spaced at equal intervals and the zero value indicates a total absence of the measured quantity or dimension. Scores obtained from measurements on a ratio scale may be added, subtracted, multiplied, divided, and raised to exponential powers. Other measurement scales do not permit the use of all these mathematical operations.

**Rationalism**   A philosophy or school of thought that postulates that certain rules of logic form the bases for all human thinking.

**Raw scores**   Raw scores are simply the number of correct responses on a particular measure of performance. For example, if a child correctly answers 40 out of 50 questions, he/she achieves a raw score of 40. In discussing raw scores with parents or other individuals unfamiliar with test jargon, it would be important to note that a raw score of

40 does not imply a score of 40 percent. Percentages are computed based on the number of correct responses out of the total number given. In the example we listed, the individual's percentage score would be 80 percent.

**Raynaud's disease**   (Maurice Raynaud, French physician, 1834–1881) A chronic blood vessel disease characterized by poor circulation to the hands and feet. This condition is a result of an abnormal spasm of the blood vessels in the extremities, especially as a response to cold or emotional stress. Heat provides relief. It seems to be alleviated by biofeedback. Also, this disease is rare in males.

**Reaction formation**   One of the defense mechanisms of the ego, according to Freud. In order to make denial of a shameful or frightening motive more effective, the individual adopts consciously the very opposite motive. SEE: *reversal (2)*

**Read Only Memory (ROM)**   A memory chip in a computer that stores information permanently. In this case, information containing instructions for the computer is not lost when the computer is turned off. SEE: *RAM*

**Readability**   A term used in language arts to rate or evaluate reading material as to its comprehensibility. An objective estimate in terms of reading level or grade level, the rating applies to certain quantified variables such as sentence length and difficulty of vocabulary.

**Readability formulas**   Formulas that have been developed to determine the difficulty of textual material by establishing grade levels. For example, the Fry Readability Graph involves randomly selecting passages from a story (usually three 100-hundred word passages at the beginning, middle, and end of the story), where the total number of syllables and sentences per 100 words are calculated and an average is taken of the three separate passages. The average number of syllables and average sentence length is plotted on a graph for the grade readability level of the story (e.g., sixth-grade level). Readability formulas

typically use vocabulary difficulty and sentence length as indirect measures of the semantic (meaning) and syntactic (grammar) difficulty of the reading material.

**Readability level**   The estimated grade level (e.g., first-grade level) of a book or selection based on reading formulas or experience. SEE: *readability formulas, reading grade level*

**Readable display**   In language arts, a term used to designate print that the reader finds easy to read.

**Reader-based problems**   Difficulties encountered during the reading task, which can be a result of lack of background knowledge/vocabulary/word recognition, lack of interest, intelligence/aptitude, a learning disability, or inadequate study skills. SEE: *Learning Disability (LD), dyslexia*

**Reader response theory**   The theory that purports that comprehension is derived from interactions between story content and the reader's prior schemata or knowledge. This theory also holds that there are developmental differences in reader responses and that comprehension of text varies with cultural diversity and the uniqueness of each individual.

**Reader's theatre**   A reading technique wherein two or more students read directly from a script. This technique reinforces skills in speaking, listening, viewing, and of course reading. Students begin by reading from prepared scripts but once they become familiar with the technique they can be allowed to prepare their own scripts. Generally, no props or costumes are used (sometimes a simple item may be employed such as a cap or bonnet to represent a character). It is a simpler form of a play.

**Readiness**   1. A term used to describe the preparedness of the learner in profiting from instruction/instructional materials/programs. 2. The basic and necessary skills accepted by educators (typically based on research and theoretical constructs) as required prerequisites to academic learning (e.g., the ability to pay attention; the ability to follow

R

233

directions; knowledge of letters and numbers, their names and meanings; etc.).

**Readiness testing**   Assessments that are given in order to determine whether a student is prepared to receive a more advanced course of education or training.

**Reading**   To understand language by 1. interpreting meaning from written symbol-sound correspondences and 2. constructing meaning from text. Reading involves the cognitive integration of bottom-up processing (sound, letter, word-level skills) and top-down processing skills (higher-order thinking skills) in order to construct meaning from the printed page. Bottom-up processing involves letter/sound recognition, phonological skills, word-level phonic skills, and sight-word recognition before top-down processing, which includes using schema-based comprehension for meaning, attention to text structure, metacognitive strategies, and sentence-level skills. Reading is viewed as an integrative processing between bottom-up and top-down cognitive processing skills. There are several components involved in the reading process: 1. Reading is interactive in the sense that the reader must interact with the printed page in order to derive meaning (e.g., use background knowledge concepts or schemata). 2. Reading is a social process and one of the most powerful tools of communication that we have, and as such, higher-order skills such as inferential thinking and drawing conclusions are required for text beyond the fourth-grade level. 3. Literacy or the ability to use reading and writing interconnectedly in everyday situations is vital for successful life adjustments/outcomes. SEE: *critical reading, creative reading, literal comprehension, inferential comprehension, reading ability*

**Reading ability**   The overall comprehension of the literal and interpretative aspects of reading text and interacting with and responding to the text in meaningful ways. Reading ability is impacted by an individual's overall

intelligence or IQ, conceptual and reasoning abilities, language competence, questioning abilities, state of health and emotional well-being, and social environment.

**Reading aloud**   A term used to describe a classroom process wherein students read aloud to the teacher or the teacher reads aloud to the students from the material, book, or text being studied for a prescribed period of time. The opposite from silent reading. SEE: *Drop Everything And Read (DEAR)*

**Reading attributes**   Characteristics observed in readers that impact reading success such as attitude, motivation, maturity level, prior knowledge base, experiences, and overall intellectual capacity.

**Reading autobiography**   A student's life history about his/her reading experiences. Students begin as far back as they can remember to their first reading experiences (e.g., what books they liked, who read to them, do they still like the same books, etc.). Questionnaires, checklists, narratives, or taped recordings can be used to record one's reading autobiography. Students who have reading problems can write or tell about their feelings surrounding their reading difficulties as well as analyze the source of their reading problems.

**Reading competency**   A term used to describe a measured ability or proficiency such as accurate identification of basic sight words. Typically school systems require overall minimum competency or proficiency levels in reading vocabulary and comprehension before a high school diploma will be awarded.

**Reading consultant**   An individual who is trained in the use of literacy materials/methods/remedial techniques for all learners whose main responsibility is to support the regular classroom teacher.

**Reading distance**   Refers to the normal reading distance of 12 to 18 inches using both eyes.

**Reading flexibility**   The adjustment of one's reading pace or rate to the purpose of the reading (e.g., skimming a newspaper for general information or enjoyment versus reading a science chapter relatively slowly for the purpose of preparing for a test). Reading flexibility also involves knowing what to do when experiencing reading problems (e.g., clarifying what is read after verbalizing a confusing point aloud).

**Reading formula**   SEE: *readability formulas*

**Reading grade level**   Also known as the readability of the printed page (i.e., grade-level functioning). Reading difficulty level or grade level functioning can be determined by the use of reading formulas, a teacher's best judgment, or the use of a cloze/informal reading test. SEE: *readability formula, cloze test*

**Reading instruction**   Teaching methods in reading instruction that are based upon a philosophy or orientation to reading. There are three major instructional methods/reading approaches used today: 1. the *basal-reader approach*, 2. the *literature-based approach*, and 3. the *whole-language approach*. The use of any reading instruction approach should take into account the individual learning styles/needs within the classroom, developmental appropriateness/interest, and curriculum requirements of the school/school system. Flexible programming efforts allow teachers to change instructional approaches when necessary. SEE: *bottom-up philosophy of reading, each approach as listed*

**Reading interests**   Reading material that is closely aligned with a person's present interests. One's reading interests vary over time depending on one's developmental level, environment, school situation, familial factors, etc. Teachers generally include reading materials that are of reading interest to all students in a particular program while at the same time trying to broaden interest areas.

**Reading laboratories**   A term used to describe some secondary reading classes that are equipped with a wide variety of reading materials for independent use

after the teacher has conducted some diagnostic prescriptive work.

**Reading maturity**   The ability to interact with written text with an emotional and intellectual detachment that allows for self-direction, self-reflection, and an objective evaluation of the reading situation. Mature readers can enjoy the reading task as a constructive and pleasurable activity which is both functional and critical to one's literacy development. SEE: *literacy*

**Reading programs**   The total combination of materials and methods used to teach readers in a particular class/program. Reading programs typically are based on a philosophy (e.g., whole language, basal readers, or a combination of both); which provides for individual levels of proficiency and achievement; follow a scope and sequence of reading skills work; supplements teacher-made materials/assists; incorporates audio-visual materials, computers, and other technology; and is based on some standard(s) of learning (e.g., a set curriculum).

**Reading rate**   The speed with which readers identify words while comprehending text. Reading rate is reported in the number of words per minute (wpm) accurately identified by the reader. Typically silent reading rates are faster than oral reading rates. Reading rates of 200 to 300 words per minute would be required for understanding of difficult material or when a high degree of comprehension of text is desired. An average reading rate would fall in the range of 250 to 450 wpm. Skimming of text for quick location of information can be accomplished with fast reading rates (over 450 wpm).

**Reading recovery**   An early intervention reading program developed by New Zealand teachers and described by Clay for children who are having a difficult time learning to read during their first year of reading. Generally, classroom teachers collaborate with a "Reading Recovery" specialist in order to establish a coherent reading program. The students in this program spend part

R

of their language arts instruction with a "Reading Recovery" teacher. Students receive instruction daily for about 30 minutes. The instruction is intense and individual and normally continues for 12 to 20 weeks.

**Reading-rehearsing strategy**   The rereading of text or repetition of information over and over again to enhance remembering and future application of the information. Students who are reading impaired or dyslexic especially benefit from reading-rehearsing strategies.

**Reading response groups**   Collaborative pairs or small groups of students who share responses to reading selections within the group and sometimes with the entire class. Purpose setting, learning-outcome expectations, and discussion prompts (i.e., questions posed by the teacher beforehand) can assist students in constructing meaning from the printed page. Students can share 1. what they know about a particular topic before a reading and then make predictions (confirming predictions afterward); 2. ideas they derive from a particular reading and their response to discussion prompts; and 3. meaning/ideas they can construct from the text that go beyond the scope of what is read (e.g., thinking about what one can do to improve the environment after reading an article on recycling). Reading response groups are used with literature-based and whole-language reading instructional programs. SEE: *literature-based approach, reading instruction, whole language*

**Reading response journals**   A type of learning log or journal primarily used in literature classes but also used in other content areas as well (e.g., science response journals). Typically, students read or listen to a portion of reading material and then write about it for less than five minutes afterward. Students alternate between writing and reading/listening after every chapter/poem/topical heading/appropriate break point. The teacher also writes while the students write and there is a sharing of responses between students and teacher

and/or students and students. SEE: *reading response groups, reader response theory*

**Reading-to-learn**   A reading situation where the individual reads for the purpose of remembering and applying the information read (e.g., how to fix a computer when one has to frequently use the computer).

**Readjustment**   Refers to an emphasis on learning situations that are socially useful and effective. Readjustment proponents support curricula that focus on social responsibility and civic training.

**Realism**   The philosophical position which adheres to the belief that the physical world is the real world as we know it. Inductive logic is used to look scientifically at cause-and-effect relationships. John Locke (1632–1704), John Comenius (1592–1670), and William James (1842–1910) are famous realists who believe that the role of teachers is to assist students in forming correct habits and to make connections between present knowledge and previous experiences. John Locke's famous "tabula rasa" phrase refers to the notion that students come into the world with a "blank slate" upon which experience in the real world writes.

**Real-time translation**   Almost simultaneous translation of speech into print through the use of a new system named c-print, which involves a type of computer shorthand. SEE: *c-print*

**Reason abstractly**   SEE: *abstract reasoning*

**Reasoning**   Generating new information by the cognitive processing of available data or knowledge.

**Reauditorization disorder**   An impairment in one's ability to recognize and understand words so that they can be recalled (remembered) for future use.

**Reception**   The receipt of information through hearing and/or vision. This occurs directly after the sensing of stimuli by the ears and/or eyes.

**Receptive aphasia**   SEE: *sensory aphasia*

**Receptive language**   The 1. oral (e.g., a personal interaction), 2. written (e.g., a

**R**

book), or 3. visual language (e.g., American Sign Language [ASL]) we receive from others to process. Receptive language involves decoding. SEE: *decoding*

**Receptive language disability**  Language problems that are the result of a student's lack of ability or inability to comprehend language. SEE: *receptive language, sensory aphasia, receptive aphasia*

**Receptors**  The cells or organs of the body that are specialized to be stimulated by environmental energies, such as lights, sounds, touches, temperature changes, odors, tastes, etc.

**Reciprocal determinism**  The theoretical position that assumes an interaction between the individual and the environment so that each can cause changes in the other.

**Reciprocal interaction**  A teaching technique and approach to learning wherein the teacher and student interact verbally and in writing. This exchange of information is designed to go beyond basic skills and is meant to elicit higher order thinking on the part of the student.

**Reciprocal movement**  Movement of both legs or arms and/or arms and legs simultaneously but in the opposite direction. An example of reciprocal movements would be walking.

**Reciprocal questioning**  An educational strategy using two- or three-person groups of students. Members of the group ask questions of the other members and answer the questions put to them by the other members, following (a) lesson(s).

**Reciprocal teaching**  A type of teaching whereby observational learning (modeling) is used as a method to teach reading comprehension in four domains: 1. self-questioning—students determine a reading purpose and main ideas/concepts/abstractions of what is read; 2. summarizing—students synthesize what is read in meaningful ways; 3. predicting—students hypothesis test during the reading situation whether reading predictions are confirmed or disconfirmed; 4. monitoring/evaluating—students self-monitoring

and self-evaluating during the reading process. The teacher tries to motivate and prepare the learner by first modeling learning activities. Corrective feedback is provided, which is supposed to facilitate the learning process so that the individual is able to develop independent reading skills, construct personal meaning from text, and apply what is learned. SEE: *constructivism*

**Recitation**  The combination of a teacher's questioning, the students' answers, and feedback from the teacher.

**Reconstruction**  A philosophical orientation that focuses on: 1. A curriculum that supports and encourages students to become part of the solution rather than part of the problem in society. It encourages students to become change agents in their society. 2. The use of memory, knowledge, logic, attitudes, etc. or other cognitive processes to reproduce a complex item of information.

**Reconstructionism**  An educational philosophy or theory that encourages schools to teach students to participate in the control of their institutions and organizations in accordance with basic democratic principles and ideals. SEE: *reconstruction, critical pedagogy*

**Rectangular distribution**  A particular shape of a frequency distribution of scores with many scores having equal frequencies. In a frequency distribution of scores, the scores are represented from lowest to highest along the x-axis (horizontal) and frequencies are shown increasing from the bottom to the top of the y-axis (vertical). With scores being tied in frequency, the top of the curve would be flat. As a result the entire figure (including the x-axis) resembles a rectangle. SEE: *shape, frequency distribution*

**Referral**  1. The act of processing a student for initial or further evaluation to an evaluation team in order to determine whether or not a special need exists. 2. The act of referral of a person to another (expert) in order to obtain initial, general, or more specific information. An example would be a referral made by a general practitioner of a

**R**

patient to a specialist. SEE: *evaluation team*

**Reflection**   The process of examining the merits and problems of one's actions, work, or learning; critical monitoring of one's progress, growth, and development; and receptivity to incorporating constructive suggestions within one's learning experiences as one develops as a learner and learner/practitioner.

**Reflective**   An adjective combining the ideas of being thoughtful and being creative. Reflective teachers think back on what they did in the past, how well it worked, and what changes might benefit students in the future.

**Reflective appraisal**   The utilization of the opinions of others in making self-judgments.

**Reflective cognitive style**   An approach to thinking and problem-solving that is deliberate, careful, and accurate.

**Reflective teaching**   A philosophical position taken by a teacher/practitioner that involves continual assessment, a looking inward, or reflection upon used teaching methods, materials, and subsequent outcomes. Reflection involves seeking constructive input from other professionals and students regarding pedagogy as well as participation in professional development activities.

**Reflex arc**   The simplest neural organization of a behavior. The reflex arc is the basic map of the nerve pathway for the performance of a reflex action, starting with the sense receptor that is stimulated to initiate the response, the afferent neuron connected to that receptor, the consecutive interneuron(s) that are affected, the efferent neuron carrying the motor command for the response, and the muscle bundle that executes the response. The reflex arc is an abstraction. It depicts only one cell at each level of activity. Moreover, any possible collateral neural activity is arbitrarily omitted from the layout of the arc.

**Reflex audiometry**   Observations of responses to sound as the initiator of a reflex action or an orienting response.

**Refraction**   Bending or deflecting light rays from a straight path as they pass from one medium (e.g., air) into another (e.g., the eye). This technique is used by eye specialists in assessing and correcting vision.

**Refraction error**   Errors or dysfunctioning of the eye's ability to bend light rays that strike the retina when forming an image.

**Refreshable braille**   Paperless braille. It is a system whereby a series of pins are raised or lowered electromechanically to present tactile impressions (messages) in braille; a temporary system of braille for the blind or braille reader.

**Regional Cerebral Blood Flow (rCBF)**   A method of visually revealing the more active regions of the brain through which the blood flows at a faster rate than through the quieter resting brain areas. A radioactive isotope of the gas xenon is inhaled and quickly enters the bloodstream. The radioactivity from a part of the brain will then be proportional to the rate of blood flowing through. The person can be required to go through a mental task or subjected to an emotion-arousing manipulation. The various psychological reactions can then be correlated with the brain activity data to develop a map of the functions of the various brain regions.

**Regression**   1. A natural occurrence as part of developmental learning and growth whereby the individual reverts to behaviors learned and used during earlier stages or periods of development (e.g., crying when a pet dies). 2. A defense mechanism which involves a person reverting back to an earlier stage of physical/psychological development in order to avoid a conflicting or painful situation that is generally not socially accepted (e.g., an 8-year-old sucking his/her thumb after experiencing a disappointment).

**Regression-based discrepancy formula**   A formula that involves the statistical correlation between Intelligent Quotient (IQ) scores and real academic achievement. In other words, this formula is designed to determine the difference between a student's achievement academically and his/her intellectual capacity.

**Regressions** Reversed saccades (rapid forward sweeps of the eye required for successful reading) observed in the attempts to read of some dyslexic individuals. Sweeping the eyes in a backward direction rather than forward. This is thought by some researchers to be an identifying symptom for a visual-perceptual subtype of dyslexia.

**Regressive tax** A tax that affects low- or lower-income groups in a disproportionate manner.

**Regular Education Initiative (REI)** A perspective that all students with mild disabilities, as well as some with moderate disabilities, can and should be educated in regular classrooms as part of general education program efforts.

**Rehabilitation** Sometimes referred to as rehab, it is a social service program designed to teach a newly disabled person basic skills needed for independence. The services can be therapeutic, psychological, social, occupational, etc. An example of rehabilitation would be to provide a physical therapist to an individual following an accident so that the individual can regain use of an injured limb. Another example would be the retraining of individuals who have lost their jobs for another profession.

**REI** SEE: *Regular Education Initiative*

**Reinforcement** The delivery of a pleasant condition to (or the removal of something unpleasant from) an individual following the performance of the correct response by that individual. Such an event raises the odds that the correct response will be made again. SEE: *positive reinforcement, negative reinforcement*

**Reinforcer** A stimulus following a response (within a reasonable time frame), which tends to increase or maintain the likelihood of that response occurring again (giving children food [reinforcer] for good behavior [response]). Sometimes a stimulus-response connection is made so that when the stimulus occurs, the response

will be naturally elicited (e.g. salivation response when food [reinforcer] is given to an animal). There are primary, secondary, and generalized reinforcers. SEE: *each reinforcer type as listed, negative reinforcement, positive reinforcement*

**Related services** Developmental, corrective, and other supportive services required for a child with disabilities to benefit from special education. Includes special transportation services, speech and language pathology, audiology, psychological services, physical and occupational therapy, school health services, counseling and medical services for diagnostic and evaluation purposes, rehabilitation counseling, social work services, and parent counseling and training.

**Relay service** The federal government (specifically, the Federal Communication Commission, the FCC) requires every state to operate a telephone system that can serve as a relay service for the deaf. A deaf person using a Teletypewriter (TTY) can place a call to others with the assistance of a nondeaf operator who can provide voiced messages via a relay service center. SEE: *telecommunication device for the deaf, TTY*

**Relearning** Returning to material that was learned in the past and learning it again (up to a certain standard or criterion of successful learning). Relearning was used by Ebbinghaus as a precise measure of memory during his original studies of the memory process.

**Reliability** The extent to which an assessment procedure yields consistent results. The same pupil should obtain the same score when retested. Different versions of the same test should yield the same score from the same pupil. Two different judges should observe that a pupil shows the same behaviors on a reliable checklist. Two different judges should rate the quality of various behaviors alike for the same pupil when using a reliable rating scale.

**Reliability engineering** The use of mechanical and engineering principles in creating devices to assist persons with disabilities as concerns their movement,

R

as in problems of sitting, bending, walking, and overall physical functioning.

**Religious-affiliated school** A private school that is normally controlled and operated by a religious denomination. Frequently, however, a parent-church group or council exercises some control over its operation and/or usually provides some type of funding.

**Reluctant readers** Readers who possess adequate reading skills but who do little voluntary reading. Usually reluctant readers dislike reading and choose to engage in other activities.

**REM sleep** The stage of sleep in which rapid eye movements (from side to side, usually) are exhibited. The REM stage is associated with dreaming to a much greater extent than any other stage of sleep. It is also associated with extreme relaxation of the larger, antigravity muscles. The EEG pattern is that of high-frequency, low-voltage activity, which is similar to the waking EEG pattern.

**Remedial courses** Courses that are designed to assist students who are not progressing effectively. They are designed to prevent further learning problems and to correct those problems that already exist. Examples of such courses are remedial math and remedial reading programs.

**Remedial readers** Students who are substantially behind their classmates in reading ability and who therefore are in need of special corrective reading instruction (remedial reading). Many reading specialists classify readers who are one-and-one-half to two grade levels behind in reading as children in need of remediation services.

**Remediation** An educational program designed to teach a person to overcome a disability through training and education.

**Removal punishment** A form of punishment in which a pleasant stimulus is taken away from an individual after an incorrect response is made. The effect is to lower the odds that the error will be repeated. SEE: *presentation punishment*

**Renaissance group** A consortium of eight teacher's colleges that produced a document in 1989 entitled *Teachers for a New World*. This group recommended that teacher training programs must ready teachers to instruct in a pluralistic society by establishing specific outcomes and expectations; creating rigorous learning expectations; and providing extensive training opportunities in schools/classrooms before graduation.

**Reorganization** The act of legally changing the geographical area of a school district and/or changing the designation or name of the school district. It can also include incorporating or regionalizing a part or all of a school district with another district. In this case, it usually is called regionalization.

**Replication** The redoing of an experiment or other research in order to learn whether the results of that study will be repeated.

**Representative realism** The type of realism that insists on a difference between the sensory experiences one has (sense data) and the reality represented by those experiences. Locke, for example, held that some of our experiences match real things closely; these are the primary qualities, such as the shapes and the hardnesses of things. Other sense experiences, such as colors, are not inherent in things but result from the interplay between our sense organs and brain on the one hand and real things on the other hand. These sense impressions Locke called the secondary qualities. SEE: *naive realism, realism*

**Representativeness heuristic** An assumption that may be made during the process of making a decision. The assumption is that a few cases (e.g., a sample) can be taken as typical of all cases (i.e., the entire population from which the sample was drawn).

**Repression** The removal of unpleasant thoughts or memories from consciousness. One may repress a particularly traumatic event such as an abusive situation because the memory is too painful. Psychotherapy and other types of counseling services assist individuals in recalling such traumas so that healing can take place.

**Reprimands**   Verbally administered punishment for improper behavior, by someone in authority. Scoldings, chastisings, rebukes, and harsh criticisms are all synonymous terms. Although usually verbal in the classroom, they may be presented in writing.

**Reproduction**   A curricular approach which stresses that school needs should mirror the values and needs of society within the classroom.

**Request**   A teaching approach which requires a paired question-answer technique. The teacher and the student spend time asking each other questions about the information taken/learned from the text or assignment. This can be done by pairs of students who design questions to ask each other in reference to the material being learned. Emphasis is placed upon training students to ask main idea and inferential questions rather than those which pertain solely to facts.

**Research**   The scientific and systematic study of a presented problem/ question/hypothesis.

**Research, educational**   The notion that education research that is rooted in the scientific method or other theoretical bases is useful to educators when seeking answers to challenges/problems. Learning outcomes can be identified and specific instructional methods/strategies can be employed/tested for effectiveness. Sometimes more accurate generalizations and conclusions can be drawn when instructional planning efforts are based on careful observations/ predictions/hypothesis testing. Data collection (e.g., test scores, writing quality, math proficiency) allows the reflective practitioner to self-assess efficacy in the classroom. The concept of "teachers being researchers" is widely accepted in the field as educational research is useful for curriculum planning, problem solving, identifying academic strengths and weaknesses, planning behavior management programs, etc. The Landmark Project keeps teachers up-to-date

with current research by publishing a monthly reference listing of literature offerings in the education field regarding over 200 topics. Access to this can be gained on the World Wide Web at http://www. landmark-project.com/ca/.

**Research design**   The proposal plan, procedural plan, or systematic outline to be used by a researcher for a specific research study.

**Research hypothesis**   The hypothesis under study that clearly or operationally defines expected relationships or differences between or among variables.

**Research logs**   A system of recordkeeping of research notes and information in the form of a log or journal. Students record books, experiments, environmental visits, computer programs, periodicals, articles, and other sources of information they have explored. Research logs also assist students in evaluating their progress and learning.

**Research plan**   A detailed action plan of a proposed study that typically involves a 1. statement of the problem, 2. review of the literature, 3. formulation of hypothesis(es), 4. description of subjects or the population studied and definition of terms, 5. description of the research design and procedures, and 6. discussion of results, conclusions, study limitations, and future research directions.

**Resegregation**   The occurrence of segregation in a school after desegregation and integration have taken place.

**Resident**   1. A physician who has completed an internship and furthers his/her clinical experience by continued training in a hospital/medical/clinical facility. 2. A person who resides in a facility (e.g., home, private school, special school, etc.) on a daily basis.

**Residential placement/school**   An institution providing both instruction and housing for individuals with disabilities. Residential schools house students on a 24-hour basis.

**Residual hearing**   The remaining hearing, however slight, of a hearing impaired person. Many hearing impaired persons have some semblance of hearing beyond the actual loss. This is also true to an extent for those who are deaf. Frequently amplification and other technological devices (i.e., hearing aids) are used to capitalize on any residual hearing.

**Residual vision**   The remaining amount and degree of visual acuity that a visually impaired person still has and which can be functionally used for learning and living.

**Resistance culture**   A set of attitudes, beliefs, and behavior tendencies on the part of the members of an oppressed group which involves the rejection of the cultural values of the larger society around them.

**Resonance**   The effect of sound passing through the vocal tract that gives the voice its particular characteristics.

**Resonance disorders**   Structural or functional problems in the vocal tract. Such problems as cleft palates, head colds, nasal obstructions, etc. could lead to hypo/hypernasality or deviations of resonance and voice tone.

**Resonating system**   The area in which speech sounds are formed; namely, the nasal and oral cavities. SEE: *resonance disorders, vocal tract*

**Resonation**   SEE: *resonance*

**Resource center for teachers**   Teaching resource centers that allow teachers to secure or prepare materials for instructional purposes. These centers many times contain photocopy equipment, typewriters, computers and software, literature books, reading kits, math manipulatives, laminating paper, construction paper, art supplies, tape recorders, overhead projectors, bulletin board materials, etc.

**Resource room**   A classroom in which special education students spend part of the school day and receive individualized special education services from identified special education staff (e.g., resource room teacher, aide, speech therapist, etc.) as noted on an IEP or Individualized Education Plan. Resource rooms are typically located within the same area as other classes not designated for special-needs purposes (e.g., the regular classroom) so as not to separate or stigmatize those students who require resource room instruction. SEE: *IEP, resource room program*

**Resource room program**   An instructional program, usually occurring within a classroom, where a student identified as "special needs" attends on a regular basis for IEP services. Students attending a resource room vary in the type of special need (e.g., learning disabled, emotionally disturbed, mentally retarded, physically impaired, visually handicapped, the gifted, hearing impaired, etc.) and in the length of service delivery time required in the resource room. Some resource rooms require that students be prototyped, meaning that students with the lowest prototype I (known as PP I) require monitoring only; prototype II students require up to one hour per day in the resource room, prototype III students require up to three hours per day, and PP IV students requiring services for most of the day. Time frames vary from state to state as do the prototyping designations. Typically numbers of students are limited to under 10 unless an aide is present. Most resource room programs require that students have an active Individualized Education Plan (IEP), progress reports, and ongoing assessments. SEE: *IEP, resource teacher*

**Resource services**   SEE: *resource room program*

**Resource teacher**   1. Sometimes referred to as a consulting teacher or a special education generic specialist, this is a special education teacher who consults with regular teachers who have students with special needs in their rooms. Advice is given to the regular teacher regarding methods and materials to use to better assist the special needs learner. 2. A special education teacher who works within a resource room to which special-needs students are sent for services. SEE: *resource room, resource room program*

**Respiration**   The act of inhaling and exhaling air from the lungs.

**Respiratory system**   In humans, the respiratory system involves those organs whose primary function is to breathe in oxygen and expel carbon dioxide, an exchange of gases. This system consists of the lungs, bronchi, trachea, larynx, pharynx, and nose.

**Respite care**   An opportunity provided by non-family members (e.g., paraprofessionals, professionals) made available to the parents and siblings of a child with a disability to spend time (a break from) away from the everyday problems of caring for their disabled family member. It is a time for recreation, relaxation, and/or vacation.

**Respondents**   B. F. Skinner's term for reflexive responses that are each elicited by a specific unconditioned stimulus. For example, you blink your eyes with puffs of air or wind. SEE: *unconditioned stimulus (US)*

**Response**   A measurable unit of behavior, it is the reaction to a stimulus or stimulation.

**Response set**   An attitude or mindset of a test taker that is frequently subconscious which results in improper or distorted answers. For example, the avoidance of extreme answers so that moderate or don't know choices are preferred; another example would be the tendency to answer "false" to almost every true-false question or vice versa.

**Restructuring**   1. Changing one's view of the elements of a problem so that a new and different approach to a solution can be attempted. 2. A general term that refers to various aspects and themes of an innovative nature as they relate to site-based decision making (teams). Decisions made are designed to improve school operations and thus improved educational performance by students.

**Resultant motivation**   The more influential of two needs; namely, the need to achieve or the need to avoid failure. If the former is stronger, one is inclined to take risks. If the latter prevails, one will tend to "play it safe."

**Resume**   A summary in written form of the experiences, preparations, and qualifications of an applicant for employment.

**Retarded depression**   A depressed state of psychosis of manic-depressive individuals. It is characterized by deliberate movement with little or no spontaneity. Gestures and verbalizations are limited.

**Retching**   A condition in which a person is attempting to vomit.

**Retention**   1. The holding back of a student in grade placement or the repeating of a grade. For example, a student who is retained in fourth grade actually participates in a fourth grade classroom two years in a row. 2. Retaining in one's body something that does not belong there or that which should be voided or excreted (such as urine and feces).

**Reticular formation**   A set of regions running through the brain stem (medulla, pons, and midbrain) that are neither white matter nor gray matter. It looks like a net, with criss-crossing white and gray strands; "reticular" means "netlike." The midbrain, anterior portion is the Ascending Reticular Arousal System (ARAS) and arouses the cerebral cortex. The reticular formation is responsible for waking from sleep, becoming aroused, and having heightened attention. SEE: *brainstem, medulla*

**Retina**   A sheet of nerve tissue at the back of the eye on which an image is focused. The retina contains the receptors or "cells of sight."

**Retinal defect**   An improper functioning or improper formation of the retina, the innermost part or back of the eye upon which light rays focus an image formed by the lens.

**Retina detachment**   A condition characterized by the separation of the inner sensory layer of retina from the outer epithelium. This condition leads to a loss of retinal function and vision problems.

**Retinitis Pigmentosa (RP)**   A progressive eye disease in which the retina gradually degenerates and atrophies, causing the field of vision to become progressively more narrow.

R

**Retinoblastoma**   An hereditary disease of the eye. It is a malignant tumor of the retina, usually unilateral, occurs in young children, and is associated with above-average intelligence.

**Retinopathy of Prematurity (ROP)**   A condition characterized by an abnormally dense growth of blood vessels and scar tissue in the eye. ROP often causes visual-field loss and retinal detachment. This disorder is usually caused by high levels of oxygen administered to premature infants in incubators also called Retrolental Fibroplasia (RLF).

**Retrieval**   1. The process of locating and then utilizing some information previously stored in long-term memory. 2. SEE: *Appendix 4: Computer Terms*

**Retroactive interference**   The process where new information interferes with previously learned information in memory. For example, learning and speaking a new language could interfere with remembering the previously learned and spoken language.

**Retrograde amnesia**   The loss of memory for events leading up to an injury to the brain or to a concussion.

**Retrolental Fibroplasia (RLF)**   SEE: *Retinopathy of Prematurity (ROP)*

**Revelation**   The view that miraculously revealed knowledge given to a great and saintly founder of religion is the most fundamental basis for truth. This is the view championed by the great monotheistic religions of the western world, including Judaism, Christianity, and Islam (in chronological order). SEE: *epistemology*

**Revenue sharing**   Distribution of federal government monies to state and local governments. The state and local governments can use this type of funding as they desire.

**Revenues**   External funds received along with net refunds and corrected transactions. This does not include non-cash transactions, commodities, "in-kind" receipts, liquidation, investment funds, issuance of department funds, and funds from nonroutine property sales.

**Reverberation**   The amount of time needed to decrease a sound to 60 decibels (dB) after the sound ceases. This is the amount of echo in an enclosed room. The reverberation in a room affects those with hearing impairments.

**Reversal**   1. Transposition of letters or symbols such as "6" for "9," "d" for "b," and "p" for "q." 2. In psychology, a change of an instinct to its opposite such as feeling hate for another and then love.

**Reverse discrimination**   A condition or situation wherein an individual or a group within the majority is denied certain rights because of preferential treatment given to a minority individual or group.

**Reversibility**   The ability to think one's way through a series of mental steps and then to retrace those steps mentally, returning to the starting point.

**Reversible thinking**   Thinking backward from the end of a chain of reasoning to the very beginning.

**Revise option**   The opportunity to revise work and improve its quality after having already submitted the work. The availability of a revise option is usually part of the contract between the work submitter (e.g., a student) and the evaluator (e.g., a teacher).

**Revisualization**   The ability of a person to write images of numbers, letters, words, etc. after they have been initially seen.

**Reye's syndrome**   A children's disease described by R. D. K. Reye (Australian pathologist) in 1963. Reye's syndrome usually occurs as a result of chicken pox or influenza. Symptoms include headaches, fever, vomiting, and disorders of the central nervous system. This disorder can be mild or progress to coma and sometimes death. Note that it is thought by many in the medical field that aspirin products can trigger Reye's syndrome. That is why in many cases young children are given alternate drugs to aspirin products.

**RF**   SEE: *community residential facility*

**Rh incompatability**   A reaction that destroys red blood cells in the fetus. It results from opposite Rh factors; that is, Rh-positive blood type in the infant and Rh-negative blood type in the mother. If not treated with Rh immune globulin within 72 hours after delivery, this condition often results in brain damage and other severe disabilities in the infant.

**Rheumatic fever**   A condition that may result in damage to the heart or kidney; symptoms include painful inflammation of the joints, swelling, and fever.

**Rheumatism**   A general term used to describe soreness and stiffness of muscles and pain in the joints. It includes arthritis, degenerative joints, myositis, fibromyositis, bursitis, etc. SEE: *myositis, bursitis*

**Rheumatoid arthritis**   This condition is a form of chronic arthritis that affects muscles and joints. It is characterized by symptoms including pain, deformity, and limited motion. The juvenile (onset before age 16) type of rheumatoid arthritis is also known as Still's disease (Sir George F. Still, British physician, 1868–1941).

**Rhinitis**   Inflammation of the mucous membrane of the nose.

**Rho-GAM**   Rh immune globulin. It is an anti-Rh factor gamma globulin used to counteract the adverse effects upon a child as a result of an incompatible blood type between a mother (Rh-negative) and a fetus (Rh-positive). Rho-GAM is normally administered within 72 hours of birth. SEE: *Rh incompatability*

**Rhythm**   A term used to describe gross motor movement in the sense of an ability to move smoothly and in syncopation; that is, a regularly or rhythmically timed fashion, an orderly flow of movement.

**Rickets**   A nutritional condition characterized by a lack of proper bone development. This condition involves a deficiency of vitamin D.

**Right-left disorientation**   A condition characterized by an inability to determine direction, especially an inability to determine right from left.

**Rigidity**   A condition in which muscle tone is seriously rigid or hypertonic to a point where it interferes with movement by a person or even by a therapist.

**Rigidity cerebral palsy**   A type of cerebral palsy characterized by low levels of rigidity or muscle stiffness; the muscles never quite relax.

**Rime**   The ending of a syllable (following the onset), specifically the vowel and any consonant sounds to follow. For example, in the word pen, "p" is the onset and "en" is the rime. SEE: *onset, syllable*

**Ripple effect**   The spreading of a behavior among group members by imitation. The so-called "wave" type of cheer in grandstands at major league sports events would be an example.

**Ritalin**   A psychostimulant drug used in the treatment of students or persons with Attention Deficit Disorder (ADD) with or without hyperactivity (ADHD). It is sometimes called Ritalin hydrochloride and is chemically known as methylphenidate hydrochloride. Other stimulant drugs used in the treatment of ADD and ADHD are Dexedrine and Cylert. SEE: *Attention Deficit Disorder (ADD), Attention-Deficit Hyperactivity Disorder (ADHD)*

**Robotics**   In education and in general, the use of high-tech devices of a sophisticated nature to assist the individuals with physical disabilities. Robotics are usually applied to motor movement as in the case of a robotic arm that can manipulate objects for the user. Another example would be a simple page turner that turns the pages of a book or magazine for the reader.

**Rochester method**   A multimodal approach to communications for deaf persons. The oral-aural method is used in combination with finger spelling. In addition, amplification for residual hearing is used along with speech reading (lip reading) and facial gestures.

**Role playing**   A system wherein students or persons practice the behaviors to be learned. This rehearsing or playing of a part is designed to provide the

**R**

student with the role of another or familiarize the student with the desired behavior.

**ROM**   SEE: *Read Only Memory*

**Root**   The smallest unit of a word that can carry its basic meaning. It serves as a base to which a prefix or suffix can be added in order to create another word having a different meaning. For example, the root word "natural" can be altered to form the words *"unnatural"* (prefix = un) and *"naturalize"* (suffix = ize). SEE: *affix, prefix, suffix*

**Rooting reflex**   An automatic response in infants. When one touches the child's face the infant will turn toward the stimulus.

**ROP**   SEE: *Retinopathy of Prematurity*

**Rorschach inkblot test**   A widely used projective personality test which involves a series of ten ambiguous inkblot designs in which subjects look at and then tell the clinician what they see in the design. Scoring is quite involved and subjective. Clinicians look for specific thought patterns or disorders that

give insights into an individual's personality. SEE: *projective test*

**Rote memorization**   Learning information by repetition (sometimes called learning "by heart"). One can recite the learned item but there is no assurance that he or she understands what it means.

**RP**   SEE: *Retinitis Pigmentosa*

**Rubella (or German measles)**   A viral disease that, if it occurs during the first ninety days of pregnancy, may cause hearing and visual impairments as well as mental retardation, heart defects, and other fetal defects. It is sometimes referred to as maternal rubella and there is now an inoculation individuals can take to prevent contracting this disease. SEE: *congenital rubella*

**Rule**   A method of teaching (Eg) by going from generalizations to specific cases, as in deductive logic. SEE: *eg-rule method*

**Rules**   Statements that describe what is permitted to be done and what is forbidden. Rules can be called "do's" and "do not's."

**Sabbatical leave**   A leave of absence given to a teacher generally for the period of a semester or a year and with or without pay or reduced pay. Teachers use this time to pursue educational endeavors (e.g., write a book, conduct research, pursue a higher degree, etc.) and their position is held open until they return.

**Saccades**   Rapid forward sweeps of the eyes that are the characteristic eye

movements required for effective reading. Each sweep is followed by a brief eye fixation, after which another sweep begins. SEE: *fixation, regression*

**Saccadic movement**   The type of eye movement used in reading. After having rested at a point on the page (i.e., a fixation), the eyes dart several letters ahead. Then the process repeats. The sudden jump from one fixation to the place of the following fixation is the saccadic eye movement or saccade. SEE: *saccades*

**SADD** SEE: *Students Against Drunk Driving*

**Safety net** A term used to describe measures taken to provide safety nets for disadvantaged youth who are at risk for dropping out of school and relying on governmental programs for life support. These measures usually include vocational training and support and are also intended to help individuals (e.g., severely retarded) who cannot provide for themselves with life-support systems (e.g., housing, custodial care, etc.).

**Salad-bowl ideology** A philosophy of life which embodies the idea that all people in the world should be together in peace and harmony. A salad as described by Jesse Jackson is exquisite in that it is composed of very different, unique, and satisfying vegetables that together give an entirely new and more wonderful taste and experience. Likewise, a culturally diverse society can provide that same experience; thus, the salad-bowl theory.

**Salary** The total amount of money paid regularly to a person. This figure does not include deductions. Such monies are paid to employees of a business or organization for services rendered. SEE: *salary schedule*

**Salary schedule** Refers to a schedule of pay levels for which teachers are compensated based on years of schooling and service to that school. Typically teachers with graduate degrees receive a higher level of pay on the salary schedule.

**Sales tax** A fixed percentage of sales (e.g., 5 percent) tacked on to the price of goods to raise revenue. Many times sales taxes are placed on what are considered nonessential items such as restaurant foods as opposed to life-sustaining items (e.g., milk and bread from the supermarket).

**Sample** A subset of a population of measured observations that constitutes all the observations actually made by the researcher. The researcher will attempt to generalize the data from the sample to the entire population.

**SAT** SEE: *Scholastic Aptitude Test*

**Satiation** Requiring the student to repeat an action (presumably, an undesirable one) until it is no longer pleasant or rewarding to do it.

**Saturation** 1. The purity of wavelength of a light wave (i.e., the extent to which it is not mixed with light of other wavelengths). 2. A point at which a student can absorb no more educational or academic information.

**Savant syndrome** The combination of mental retardation or autism with an unusual talent in mathematical computation, in music, or in one of the graphic arts. The term "savant syndrome" is replacing the less flattering term "idiot savant."

**Savings score** The percentage of trials saved during relearning of material that was also learned at an earlier time. The relearning will require fewer trials to complete than the original learning. The difference between the amount needed originally and the amount needed for relearning = the amount saved (presumably stored in memory). The absolute amount saved is not a satisfactory measurement because this number has to be considered in relation to the difficulty level of the material (which is indicated by the number of trials required for the original learning). Accordingly, the amount saved is divided by the number of trials needed for original learning and this decimal result is multiplied by 100 percent to yield the percentage saved.

**Scaffolding** The outwardly visible support an adult or teacher provides the learner so that problem-solving abilities can be nurtured. Examples of scaffolding are: step-by-step algorithms, clues, hints, supportive encouragement, demonstrating the correct approach, etc.

**Scales of independent behavior** Essentially, a formal and standardized testing instrument for assessing the adaptive behavior of a student or person.

**SCAN**  SEE: *Schedules for Clinical Assessment in Neuropsychiatry*

**Scanning**  The rapid search of text for key words or phrases without the intent of complete text comprehension. The purpose of scanning is to locate partial or certain information (e.g., name, phone number, movie time, etc.). SEE: *skimming*

**Scantron tests**  Tests that have accompanying machine-scorable answer sheets (typically multiple-choice exams).

**Scapegoating**  Placing the blame for a misfortune on the shoulders of an innocent but relatively defenseless minority group (e.g., German militarists blaming the loss of World War I on the German Jewish population). The schools were also blamed for the failure of the United States to place the first man in space. This is the social analogue of the Freudian defense mechanism known as displacement.

**Schachter-Singer theory**  The cognitive/physiological arousal view of emotion. Arousal sets the stage for an emotion. What decides which emotion is felt is the individual's cognitive evaluation of the situation. A model for this theory has been proposed to be the selection and the playing of a song on a jukebox. Putting the coin in the slot is analogous to the general physiological arousal; pushing the alphanumeric buttons (e.g., "C-2") to select the song to be played is analogous to deciding, after cognitive processes have evaluated the situation, what emotion to feel.

**Schedules for Clinical Assessment in Neuropsychiatry (SCAN)**  Schedules for the assessment, measurement, and classification of psychopathological disorders. American Psychiatric Press.

**Schedules of reinforcement**  Arrangements for the administration of reinforcements (including the counting of the correct responses and/or measuring time elapsed since an earlier correct response) to be given after operant responses occur. The response-reinforcement relationships that are programmed by the schedule are known as "contingencies."

**Schema (plural: schemata)**  A generalized idea that includes the essentials but not all the details of what is learned. A schema is a generalized idea about some object(s), person(s), or event(s).

**Schema-driven problem solving**  The solution of a problem by recognition of the fact that it is simply a revised version of a problem that one has solved at an earlier point in time.

**Schemes**  Organized sets of memories or perceptual categories; some schemes are equivalent to concepts.

**Schizophrenia**  A class of psychoses involving some or all of the following: hallucinations, delusions, inappropriate emotional reactions to the environment, disturbed or even bizarre thought processes, abnormal movements of the trunk and limbs, extreme introversion, and incoherent speech.

**Scholarships**  Scholarships may include direct grants of monies, stipends, awards, prizes, tuition, and fee waivers. Scholarships are frequently granted to undergraduate college students and are less likely to be awarded to graduate students.

**Scholastic Aptitude Test (SAT)**  A test published by the Educational Testing Service in Princeton, New Jersey, the purpose of which is to assess the readiness of high school students to complete college-level work.

**Scholasticism**  A philosophical inquiry and study of the logic and beliefs of the church (as per Christianity).

**School-based clinics**  A term usually used in conjunction with medical and other clinics held on-site in a school to assist students on a personal basis with any problems they might have involving sexuality or medical problems.

**School-based management**  A reform movement that encourages schools on an individual basis to be self-governing. Teachers are especially encouraged to participate along with administrators, parents, and others and become part of the decision-making process.

**School bond** A type of financing used for school buildings and repair expenses. Bonds are long-term financial obligations incurred by school districts.

**School choice** A type of student placement system that allows parents and/or students to actually choose the school he/she will attend. This permits schools to focus on particular disciplines or subject areas (e.g., schools that have a science focus, a gifted and talented school, etc.).

**School climate** How schools are organized and maintained on a daily basis to promote optimal learning and social interactions. School climate is frequently assessed by class sizes and the ratios of pupils-to-teachers; perceptions of safety by students and teachers; how schools are managed (e.g., site-based management); the amount of autonomy schools have; whether or not schools have clearly defined mission statements or goals; attendance; truancy; parent support; measures of learning; discipline; amount of conflict observed within the school; and so on.

**School context** The school environment.

**School district** Also known as the Local Educational Agency (LEA), it is the agency or organization that operates public schools or contracts for public school services. It is sometimes called the Local Basic Administrative Institution. (e.g., a school board or school committee).

**School diversity** The differences amongst the various schools throughout the nation. This includes the student population as such; local, state, and regional traditions and practices; and cultural, ethnic, and racial diversity.

**School finance plan** The financial plan of a school district based on local, state, and federal monies in regard to the disbursement of funds.

**School finance reforms** A movement initiated during the 1970s that focused on equalizing educational opportunities for all school-age students through the proper reimbursement and/or expenditure of local, state, and federal monies.

**School-finance system** Refers to the state formulas used to disburse funds targeted for education programs and the taxes used to raise revenue for the public schools.

**School houses** Separate and autonomous groupings of teachers (sometimes administrators) and students within a particular school. School houses have been used in some larger schools as a way to personalize and create a sense of community among the teachers and students.

**School phobia** A fear of school manifested by a reluctance on the student's part to go to school at all. Factors involved include fear of separation from the parents and/or the rest of the family, fear of failure, and/or some event occurring at school that triggers a reaction against attendance. Such events might cause the school to be perceived as a threatening, uncomfortable, or even dangerous situation. The symptoms may include stomachaches, headaches, profuse sweating, and/or other complaints.

**School social climate** The social atmosphere in a school, which is a composite of many factors to include student/teacher/administration attitudes and interactions; parent involvement and response(s) to educational programs; availability of resources and class sizes; student mobility; school dress/ behavior/attendance policies; grade policies; reward incentives; etc.

**School superintendent** The Chief Executive Officer (CEO) or chief administrator of a school system.

**School-to-work programs** Created by Congress in 1994 under the School-to-Work Opportunities Act, these programs prepare high school students for the workplace and college. Frequently, high school students are placed as interns in businesses and institutions where they can be compensated and receive school credit for their work.

S

**School-Wide Assistance Team (SWAT)**
A team of students, parents, teachers, administrators, and other professionals who work in unison toward the common goals of instructional support, curriculum improvement, identification processes for students at risk, overall school improvement, and improvement of the education process in general. SWAT teams are usually found at the local level.

**Schools without walls**   As the name connotes, a school that reaches out into the total community. It is a type of alternative education and stresses using the community as a resource for learning.

**Schwa**   A neutral vowel sound in an unaccented syllable of a word. It is symbolized as a lower case "e" upside down (ə). For example, when -"le" is the final syllable, the vowel has the schwa sound.

**SCID-D**   SEE: *Structured Clinical Interview for DSM-IV Dissociative Disorders*

**Scientific method**   The systematic and controlled basis for making generalized statements in scientific explanations. The processes of inductive and deductive reasoning are both involved. First, a number of facts about a natural phenomenon are observed. Then, by an inductive reasoning, a tentative explanation of the facts is expressed (i.e., inductive reasoning). This tentative explanation is called a hypothesis. The hypothesis is used as the basis of the prediction of the outcome of an appropriate experiment or observation. Deductive logic is used to make such a prediction. The study/experiment is done (or an observation is recorded/made) in order to see if the predicted results indeed occur. That would add credence to the hypothesis. If the prediction is not confirmed, the hypothesis is rejected. B. F. Skinner offered a variation of his own. If, in the midst of research, one encounters some unexpected novel data, drop the former plans and study the new phenomenon. In summary, the scientific method involves 1. identifying a problem(s), 2. observation, 3. formulating a hypothesis(es), 4. observation,

5. verifying, modifying, or rejecting the hypothesis(es), and 6. repeating steps 3 and 4 until a solution to the problem is presented.

**Sclera**   The outer white layer of the eyeball that protects the delicate eye and holds the eye in place.

**Scoliosis**   Sometimes called curvature of the spine, this is a congenital abnormality in which the spine (the vertebral column) is misaligned and curved laterally that is side to side. SEE: *kyphosis, lordosis*

**Scope of bargaining issues**   Refers to the type of issues that are subject to legal negotiations such as salaries, working conditions, and benefits.

**Scoring rubric**   A rating scale that employs descriptions of low, medium, and high levels of achievement in the process of assessing a given type of performance.

**Scratch reflex**   An example of an oscillator. This reflex can be seen when an irritation of the skin might cause a dog, for example, to lift its paw to the irritated area and make rhythmic scratching motions. This rhythm is paced by the nerve cells within the spinal cord's gray matter, not to the irritating stimulation.

**Screening**   Any system or instrument for quick testing for a general impression of the existence of a need for further, more precise assessment. For example, students in the schools are routinely screened for visual, auditory, and postural defects in order to determine whether a further workup is necessary.

**Script**   A sequence of stepwise procedures for performing a task, such as buying a home or assembling a bicycle.

**Scurvy**   A deficiency disease characterized by anemia, general weakness, limb and joint pain, spongy and bleeding gums, bad breath, etc. It is caused by a deficiency of vitamin C usually as a result of a lack of fresh fruits and vegetables in the diet. Infantile scurvy sometimes follows the protracted use of sterilized milk, condensed milk, or the like. Vitamin C is also known as "ascorbic acid." SEE: *Barlow's disease*

**Seasonal affective disorder**   A mood disorder that is restricted to one season of the year. Usually the problem is depression during the winter. The precipitating cause is the reduction of the hours of daylight. Symptoms include a craving for high-calorie foods, increased hours of sleep, and weight gain.

**Seatwork**   Work done in the classroom by the student as an individual.

**Second language acquisition**   Learning a new language; this process has similarities to the learning of one's own first language.

**Second stage facilitator** or **consigliere**   A leadership role for a teacher in a school wherein the teacher acts as a facilitator and offers assistance to other teachers as part of a school-based change process.

**Secondary appraisal**   The second stage in the cognitive evaluation of a stressful event, including the assessment of one's resources for coping with that event.

**Secondary emotions**   The primary emotions are those emotions that are common to all humans and are found in all types of cultures. These primary emotions, in turn, can be combined in various ways. These combinations, which are often unique to particular cultures, are called secondary emotions.

**Secondary epilepsies**   Seizure disorders that can occur at any age and are directly related to trauma, accidents, child abuse, brain lesions, other brain injury, meningitis, drug withdrawal, metabolic disturbances, etc. SEE: *primary epilepsies, seizures*

**Secondary reinforcers**   Reinforcers or stimuli that acquire reinforcing qualities by their association with primary reinforcers (e.g., food, water, and sex). For example, if a teacher rewards a class with a Bingo game on Fridays for good work (periodic praise during the week = secondary reinforcement, while play (Bingo) = the primary reinforcer), the Bingo game becomes associated with good work habits. Secondary reinforcers are also known as conditioned reinforcers. SEE: *primary reinforcer*

**Secondary school**   A school that may encompass grade levels beginning at the end of elementary or middle school education, such as grades 7–12 following an elementary setting of K–6 or grades 9–12 following a middle school arrangement of grades 5–8. In some systems, it includes junior high school, 7–9, and senior high school, 10–12.

**Secondary sex characteristics**   Physical changes that take place in the body following the arrival of puberty. In both sexes, pubic, and underarm hair growth occurs. Females manifest breast enlargement while males exhibit a deepening of the voice and facial hair.

**Secondary trait**   In Gordon Allport's trait theory of personality, a secondary trait is a tendency to behave consistently under most conditions, although the individual will abandon consistency in order to adjust to the requirements of a specific circumstance. As a result, a person's secondary traits require more observations to be identified than the person's cardinal or central traits.

**Secret ballot**   A type of voting procedure that involves a paper ballot and not a voice vote so that participants cannot be identified in any way.

**Section 504 of the Vocational Rehabilitation Act of 1973**   This act was the basis of the requirement that all public buildings built after its passage be accessible to all people. Older buildings require minimal or extensive renovations. Guidelines for this act include the following: 1. walkways at least 36 inches wide, no interruptions by steps or abrupt changes more than 1/2 inch; 2. ramps at least 36 inches wide, indoor with slopes no more than 1 foot every 12 feet and outdoor 1 foot every 20 feet; 3. entrances and doorways at least 32 inches wide with leveled thresholds of no more than 3/4 inch height; 4. accessible restrooms to easily accommodate a wheelchair, stalls being 60 inches wide and deep, door swinging outward. Grab bars must be mounted on each side of the stall while toilet seats should be 17 to 19 inches high. Sinks should be no more than 34 inches high with at least a 29-inch clearance underneath to accommodate a wheelchair. Mirror shelves and towel dispenser are to be within easy reach and no more than 40 inches high. SEE: *P.L. 93-112, Vocational Rehabilitation Act of 1973; Appendix 3: MARCS and MAPP*

**Secular education**   A type of education that emphasizes life experiences on earth (our physical reality) as opposed to an emphasis or inclusion of religious beliefs in the curriculum.

**Secure attachment**   Attachment is the bond acquired by an infant to his/her mother in response to being cared for and fed by the mother. This process has been used as the basis of the attachment theory of social relations. This view holds that there are three kinds of attachments: secure, avoidant, and ambivalent. The secure attachment is a comfortable one, without anxiety or worry being involved.

**Sedentary lifestyle**   An inactive pattern of living without doing regular exercising for time periods of at least 20 minutes three or more times a week.

**SEE I**   SEE: *Seeing Essential English (SEE I)*

**SEE II**   SEE: *Signing Exact English (SEE II)*

**Seeing Essential English (SEE I)**   A system of manual signing used by the deaf or the seriously hearing impaired. In syntax, the signs provide parallel meanings to those of English language symbols. Seeing Essential English is used primarily as a tool for learning English in contrast to American Sign Language (ASL), which is the language of the deaf community. SEE: *Signing Exact English (SEE II), American Sign Language (ASL)*

**Seeing-eye dogs**   SEE: *guide dogs*

**Segregated education facilities**   Separate schools or educational facilities that are separate from the mainstream of regular education classes. Individuals with disabilities are separated from those without disabilities. SEE: *self-contained programs, special class*

**Segregation**   Refers to the social or educational separation of one group of individuals from another (e.g., separating students with special learning challenges from students without special learning challenges) or separating legally or illegally different ethnic groups or races in regard to educational opportunities, housing, jobs, transportation, etc.

**Seizure**   Sometimes referred to as a fit or a convulsion. The condition is characterized by a loss of consciousness that is sometimes accompanied by a convulsion. A convulsion involves alternating involuntary spasms, which are contractions and relaxations of the striped muscles. This condition is usually brought about by abnormal electrical discharges in the brain. SEE: *epilepsy*

**Seizure disorders**   A variety of brain disorders (e.g., epilepsy) that partially or fully affect a person's consciousness. Usually such seizure disorders are accompanied by spasms and uncontrolled motor activity. SEE: *epilepsy, seizure*

**Selection bias**   Assigning of subjects to different groups by an experimenter in a way that permits the groups to differ on any measure correlated with the dependent variable. Such a selection process confounds the research so that a difference between the experimental and the control group could not be clearly attributed to the independent variable.

**Selection item**   An item on an examination in which the student has to select an answer from a set of presented choices. A selection item may be a true-false question, a multiple-choice question, or an item in a matching question.

**Selective attention**   1. The selection of a few stimuli for further neural processing. The sense organs (and particularly the eyes) are bombarded with many stimuli at once. From the sensory store, which is the initial stage of memory, a few of these stimuli (a manageable 7 plus or minus 2 bits of information) are processed for perception and recognition while the remainder are forgotten. This selection process is named attention or selective attention. The selected stimuli are promoted to a second memory stage, the short-term memory. There are stimulus factors as well as personal factors that participate in the selection process. Loudness of sounds and brightness of lights are examples of the stimulus factors. Personal needs are examples of personal factors. 2. A condition in which students often elect to focus on what interests them rather than attend to the central theme, task, or information being presented.

**Selective listening**   The ability of a student or person to focus or rule out all other auditory input except that which the listener is concentrating on. For example, paying attention to a lecturer (hearing just that person's voice) while blotting out all other sensory stimuli. SEE: *marginal listening*

**Self-actualization**   According to Maslow, the realization of one's potential. Also, the dedication of one's talents and abilities for the betterment or welfare of others.

**Self-advocacy**   1. A social and political movement in support of mentally retarded persons which espouses the philosophy that mentally retarded persons are able to speak for themselves. It was organized in Oregon in 1974 by persons who themselves were disabled or handicapped. The idea behind self-advocacy is to help persons with mental disabilities take charge of their own lives whenever they can and to make their own decisions. 2. Advocating and representing for oneself.

**Self-care skills**   Skills that are generally related to a student's or person's ability to care for oneself, especially in the areas of health, hygiene, dressing, and feeding.

**Self-concept**   The cognitive image one has of oneself. SEE: *self-esteem*

**Self-contained classroom**   1. In regular education the least restrictive educational setting within the public school. The self-contained classroom is the mainstreamed class. Typically found at the elementary level, one teacher teaches

all or most of the subjects to the entire class. Students with learning disabilities, emotional problems, sensory impairments, etc. are sometimes removed from mainstream classes for their special-needs services. Regular classroom activities can fall within this setting when children are placed in a substantially separate class for regular classroom activities (i.e., music, art, and physical education). 2. In special education, the self-contained classroom is the most restrictive for students with disabilities. The classroom is substantially separate from regular education activities or mainstreaming. SEE: *mainstreaming, self-contained programs*

**Self-contained programs**   In the sense of special education, an instructional setting where a special-needs child who is usually moderately or severely handicapped spends a great deal or all of his/her time out of the regular classroom; little or no time is spent with the regular students in the mainstream (also known as a substantially separate classroom).

**Self-determination**   A person's ability to decide for herself/himself, especially when making decisions involving one's education, vocation, avocation, and lifestyle in general. SEE: *internal locus of control*

**Self-efficacy**   These are our feelings or thoughts about how competent we are in various areas. Internal (e.g., self-perceptions of one's intellectual capacity) and environmental factors (e.g., social interactions whether they be positive or negative) affect our self-efficacy.

**Self-esteem**   One's own evaluation of oneself with regard to personal worth, life and school successes, perceived social status, etc.

**Self-evaluation**   How one views himself/herself in terms of negative and positive characteristics.

**Self-fulfilling prophecy**   The process by which teachers who have been provided with information about the characteristics of their pupils treat these pupils as if the information is absolutely correct, leading to a shift of the pupils'

**253**

responses to match the teacher's treatment of them. In this way, the teacher's expectation is made into a reality.

**Self-image**   The subjective perceptions one has of oneself in terms of abilities, physical appearance, strengths, weaknesses, personality, etc.

**Self-instruction**   Talking or thinking one's way through the performance of a complex task.

**Self-instruction training**   A cognitive behavior modification technique wherein the student asks himself/herself questions and gives answers to himself/ herself aloud. The student then asks questions (and responds internally) to himself/herself silently as a method of problem solving.

**Self-instructional device**   Any device or material used by a student as an aid to teaching oneself.

**Self-management control**   Control of one's own behavior by manipulating reinforcement schedules of oneself.

**Self-management technique**   A system or set of procedures wherein a student or person becomes responsible for self-instruction, self-monitoring, and/or self-reinforcement in order to change or to take control of one's own behavior, learning, and living. SEE: *cognitive behavior modification*

**Self-monitoring**   A type of assessment procedure which involves a person consistently and systematically recording one's own behavior(s) frequency and duration in order to modify or regulate such actions.

**Self-questioning**   A cognitive strategy whereby the individual formulates questions about text or material to be learned in order to enhance memory recall. For example, a student might ask himself/ herself what the main idea was of a story read along with typical who, what, why, where, and when questions.

**Self-reference effect**   A factor hindering communication and commerce attempts between members of different cultural groups. An individual judges relationships with members of another

culture and makes plans to deal with them on the basis of his/her own culture and/or experiences. This usually leads to costly mistakes.

**Self-regulated learners**   Students who have both the self-discipline and the academic ability to make learning easy.

**Self-regulation**   A person's ability to control his/her own behavior. SEE: *self-determination*

**Self-reinforcement**   Providing reinforcements for one's own correct responses or rewarding oneself for a job well done.

**Self-report**   A technique for obtaining biographical information on a subject. The subject provides data about himself or herself to the researcher.

**Self-report tests**   Questionnaires or item inventories that require a person to check off every item that describes himself/herself accurately.

**Self-serving bias**   The tendency to credit all our successes to good heredity or to some personal strength or talent and to attribute all our failure to environmental circumstances.

**Self-talk**   The act of verbalizing what one hears, sees, does, and/or feels. It is modeling speaking for a child who is reluctant to speak and interact. The adult might say, "I am washing my face," as one's face is being washed. There is no demand made on the child.

**Semantic memory**   The aspect of Long-Term Memory (LTM) that stores points of general knowledge, such as mathematical rules, geographic and historical data, spelling, grammatical rules, etc.

**Semantics**   The meaning of language that involves several aspects of language. Multiple word meanings, alliterations, figurative language, and slang all refer to the semantic or meaning aspects of language.

**Semicircular canal**   One of three balance receptor organs in the inner ear. Each receptor organ is orientated at a right angle to the other two. One semicircular canal responds to accelerations of the head in the vertical plane, a second to front-to-back or back-to-front accelerations of the head, and the third to left-to-right or right-to-left head accelerations. The semicircular canals are part of the structure called the vestibular apparatus of the inner ear. The nonauditory, inner-ear sense is known as the sense of balance.

**Semi-independent apartment** or **home** (also known as "Supported Living Arrangement" or SLA)    Describes a living condition wherein a person with a disability needs some level of support and/or supervision but not total care.

**Semilingual**    Lacking fluency in language.

**Semiotic function**    The capacity to use symbols to represent objects or actions. Such symbols could be pictures, gestures, words, etc.

**Senile dementia**    The general term for certain brain disorders, usually appearing in late middle age or afterward, that involve memory losses of personal acquaintances and of past events, the decline of reasoning ability, changing behaviors, etc. SEE: *Alzheimer's disease, Pick's disease*

**Senility**    SEE: *senile dementia*

**Senior high school**    A secondary school usually following junior high that incorporates grades 10–12, the final years of high school or secondary education.

**Sensation**    The reception of stimulus energy from the environment by sense organs and the initiation of nerve impulses in sensory neurons. SEE: *perception*

**Sensitive period**    A more judicious and careful term for critical period. SEE: *critical period*

**Sensitivity training**    Refers to teaching methods that emphasize teaching tolerance of others. Empathy, respect, and tolerance are keys to becoming sensitized to the uniqueness found in others.

**Sensorimotor**    A combination word referring to both the input to the central nervous system (CNS) from the sense organs and the motor activity output from the CNS. The term is used to cover cases of direct relationships between sensations and muscular movements when input from the senses of sight, sound, smell, touch, and/or taste is reflected in the appropriate motor activity. An example would be a baseball player sighting the location of a pitched ball and accurately striking the ball with his bat.

**Sensorimotor stage**    The first stage of cognitive growth, according to Jean Piaget. It lasts from birth to age two. The infant develops his/her senses and motor skills during this stage. The end of this stage is marked by the acquisition of object permanence (knowledge that objects continue to exist even when they are no longer seen), which entails the ability to hold in mind a "representation" (presumably a memory image of some sort) of the absent object.

**Sensorineural hearing loss**    A type of hearing loss that involves damage to the inner ear and auditory nerve. Such a loss prevents the delicate hair cells of the cochlea from properly transforming sound waves to electrical impulses that go to the brain through the auditory nerve. Damage can be caused by disease, high fevers, medicine, and congenital defects. Loud music can also cause this type of hearing loss. Unfortunately, this type of hearing loss is permanent and not treatable like a conductive hearing loss, which is the type of hearing loss resulting from outer or middle ear problems. A third type of hearing loss is called a mixed hearing loss. SEE: *auditory nerve, cochlea, conductive hearing loss, mixed hearing loss*

**Sensory**    Dealing with the senses, it is a term used to indicate knowledge or information received through the sense of touch, taste, smell, sight, or hearing.

**Sensory adaptation**    The tendency for a sense receptor, over time, to become less and less responsive to a continuously present stimulus.

**Sensory aphasia**    Sometimes called receptive aphasia or Wernicke's aphasia, this is a communication disorder in which the individual, as a result of a sensory deficit, has difficulty with language comprehension.

**Sensory deprivation**   The reduction of sensory inputs to a bare minimum. The individual may be blindfolded, be wearing earplugs, have on soft gloves, etc. People who experience sensory deprivation for several hours begin to manifest abnormal symptoms such as a change of their body image, hallucinations, extreme restlessness and irritability, declining ability to reason, etc.

**Sensory disorder**   A disorder of the senses, particularly those of vision and hearing, that interferes with academic (or nonacademic) performance.

**Sensory memory**   The first stage of memory according to the current three-stage view of memory storage. Sensory memory holds all the details of the stimulation presented to the senses but it is very unstable, lasting only a fraction of a second in most adults. This type of memory has also been called the sensory store or sensory register.

**Sensory-motor**   SEE: *sensorimotor*

**Sensory neuron**   A neuron that sends impulses from the sense receptors toward the central nervous system. Such neurons are also called afferent neurons.

**Sensory receptors**   Those cells (found in every sense organ) that are specialized in the transduction of the stimulus energy (e.g., light or sound) into electrical and chemical forms of energy used by neurons. SEE: *transduction*

**Sensory register**   The first stage of memory; the very brief retention of sensory information. SEE: *sensory memory*

**Sensory seizure**   A seizure that primarily involves the senses; this includes such areas as hearing, vision, smell, touch, and taste. SEE: *seizure*

**Separate but equal**   An educational doctrine that promotes separation of the races for schooling purposes. The idea is that those separated will receive equal services and treatment. This doctrine was rejected by the U.S. Supreme Court in its decision on the *Brown v. Board of Education* case in 1954.

**Separation anxiety**   The anxiety experienced by infants when they are left alone by their parents or guardians. This type of anxiety is strongest in the age range of 12 to 18 months.

**Sequential development**   A step-by-step procedure in which one level is built upon another in turn until the ultimate goal is reached.

**Serial position effect**   A phenomenon observed when people are required to memorize a series of items. The items at the beginning and the end of the list are much easier to remember than items in the middle of the list.

**Seriation**   The arrangement of items in an ordered series; for example, according to size.

**Serious emotional disturbance**   A term used in P.L. 101-476, the Individuals with Disabilities Education Act (IDEA) to define those students with severe emotional disturbances and behavioral disabilities (disorders) that significantly interfere with day-to-day functioning and success in the school environment. Students with severe conduct disorders or severe antisocial problems can be classified as serious emotionally disturbed.

**Serous otitis media**   An inflammation of the middle ear characterized by a secretion of a serous fluid buildup in the middle ear. This condition may or may not be infectious.

**Service coordination**   A term used to describe the cooperative effort of professional persons in working together with persons with disabilities and their families. This united approach is concerned with the ongoing program of supports and services for persons with disabilities; particularly assessments, planning, implementation, and follow-up of such services.

**Service delivery team**   The professionals or persons that perform the services required by an Individualized Education Plan (IEP) or an IFSP (Individualized Family Service Plan).

**Service manager**   A term used in special education to identify that person charged with supervising the implementation and evaluation of some special service (e.g., implementing an Individualized Family Service Plan [IFSP] as required under P.L. 99-457).

**SES**   SEE: *Socioeconomic Status*

**Set point**   The weight that body processes maintain and defend. If weight falls too far below the set point, the hunger drive sets in and eating is begun. This process persists until the set value of weight is restored. If too much weight is gained, hunger is suppressed and metabolic rate is increased until the set weight value is restored.

**Seven liberal arts**   A curriculum that consisted of seven parts. The trivium encompassed grammar, rhetoric, and logic while the "quadrivium" included arithmetic, geometry, music, and astronomy.

**Severe and profound multiple disorders**   These are combinations of disorders (such as mentally retarded and physically handicapped) wherein the student or person is classified at or near the very lowest end of the scale as it relates to the disorder. Usually the deficits are at least three standard deviations below the mean or average. For example, a profoundly retarded student with an IQ of 25 or below along with very poor adaptive behavior could also be so physically handicapped that he/she would be wheelchair bound.

**Severe discrepancy**   A difference between a student's ability and achievement that is large enough to indicate the existence of a learning disability.

**Severe mental retardation**   A condition characterized by very poor adaptive behavior along with an IQ that is lower than 35 points. A severely retarded person has very limited communication skills but is able to use simple verbal and nonverbal communication. Frequently, these persons have serious health and motor problems, poor social adjustment, and need assistance with activities of daily living. Employment possibilities are limited to supported or sheltered settings. These students need

an Individualized Education Plan (IEP) that concentrates on the necessary self-help skills and functional needs. Severe retardation affects less than one out of every 10,000 persons. SEE: *mild mental retardation, moderate mental retardation*

**Severe/multiple disabilities**   SEE: *severe and profound multiple disorders*

**Severely and profoundly handicapped**   SEE: *severely multiple handicapped, severe and profound multiple disorders*

**Severely handicapped**   Students or persons placed at or near the bottom category of the exceptionality or disability. An example would be a profoundly retarded child or a quadriplegic. Normally, the severely and profoundly handicapped are at least three standard deviations below the mean (average) in the category given. SEE: *profound mental retardation, quadriplegia*

**Severely multiple handicapped**   SEE: *severely handicapped, severe and profound multiple disorders*

**Seville statement**   A report by social scientists from a conference held in Seville, Spain. They concluded that destructive warfare is not inevitable and that it is theoretically possible for people to arrange conditions for lasting peace.

**Sex chromosomes**   One of the pairs (23rd) of chromosomes in the human organism. There are 22 other pairs of chromosomes, the autosomes. The sex chromosomes are paired in females, but the members of the pair are different in males. The kind of chromosome of which females possess two and males only one is the X chromosome. The other chromosome that males possess is the Y chromosome; that is, X X in the female and X Y in the male. The traits controlled by the genes on the X chromosome are called sex-linked traits.

**Sexism (sex bias)**   Unequal or prejudicial treatment of persons due to their gender.

**Sex-limited gene**   A gene that acts only in one sex because it depends on activation by a high level of one of the sex hormones. Both sexes may have the

S

gene, but it is made active only in one sex.

**Sex-linked inheritance** The inheritance of some trait, the gene for which is carried on the X chromosome. Some recessive, sex-linked traits are much more likely to occur in men than in women because the dominant form of the gene cannot be given to a male who carries the recessive gene on his only X chromosome. A female with a gene for a recessive, sex-linked trait might escape the trait because her second X chromosome could carry the dominant form of the gene. Examples of sex-linked traits are hereditary baldness, color blindness, and hemophilia.

**Sex role** The set of activities considered to be characteristic of one gender by the prevailing culture of the social group in which the person grows up. SEE: *gender identity*

**Sex role stereotype** The mental expectations (e.g., men will excel more in the math area) and images (it is the woman's job to care for the children) one has of the roles of men and women that can be based on inaccurate perceptions or interpretations.

**Sex typing** The process of acquiring the behaviors, biases, values, etc. that are considered typical of one's own sex in a given culture.

**Sexual abuse** A situation characterized normally by an adult who sexually mistreats a child or younger person (could be an adult as well). Sexual abuse includes incest, rape, assault, and/or exploitation of a sexual nature. It may also include fondling and inappropriate sexual touching. The abuse can be both physical and/or psychological.

**Sexual coercion** The culturally transmitted behavior pattern for males that dictates that the man should make the first move toward the sexual act and behave in a dominant and coercive matter.

**Sexual harassment** Unwelcome pressure (solicitations of sexual congress, request for dates, or simply making loud remarks or exhibiting sex-related materials) directed at a person in the workplace by a coworker or a superior.

**Sexually Transmitted Diseases (STD)** SEE: *STD*

**Shape (of a frequency distribution)** A distribution of scores after data compilation that can be represented on the x-axis (horizontal part) of a graph from lowest to highest and the frequency with which each score occurs shown on the y-axis (vertical part). The resulting shape or figure (a curve) will take one of several possible shapes, examples of which are the normal or bell-shaped (Gaussian), the skewed (which may be skewed to the right or to the left), the rectangular, and the bimodal. SEE: *frequency distribution, skewness*

**Shape constancy** An aspect of perceptual constancy. Changing the angle from which an object is viewed changes the shape of the object's image on the retina. Nevertheless, one still sees that the object has its normal shape, despite the change of viewpoint.

**Shaping** Also called successive approximations, this is a training procedure in which small achievements are reinforced, allowing a complex skill to be taught to a naive individual. Shaping begins with the reinforcement of only one small aspect of the skill, such as orienting the body correctly. After that first step is mastered, reinforcement is withheld. The individual must take another small step in the direction of the skilled activity before reinforcement is provided again. Again, reinforcement is delivered regularly until the second step has been mastered. The process continues in a developmental fashion until the final goal or behavioral objective is attained. SEE: *sequential development*

**Shared literature units** Literature packets that the teacher provides (activity units, guides, and books) to assist in the presentation of thematic units to students. Every few weeks or so the teacher presents a new topic or unit by reading a picture book to young children (elementary) or just a content chapter to older students (middle/secondary). The teacher then queries the students and writes their responses on a chart. This creative exercise includes and enhances higher order thinking about the reading and serves a basis for follow-up activities for language skills development.

**Shared responsibility** 1. The partnership that regular education and special education staff must have in order to best meet the educational needs/interests of all learners. 2. The sharing of responsibility by two or more persons toward a common cause.

**Sheltered English** Adaptive English-language presentations for bilingual learners. For example, modifying rate of speech or tonality; using supplementary visual aids or context cues; incorporating vocabulary related to a student's culture or background in lesson presentations, etc. SEE: *bilingual learners*

**Sheltered workshop** An area of employment, usually a factory, in which all employees have the same disability. For example, a sheltered workshop may employ blind workers or another sheltered workshop may have employees who are mentally retarded. The products of the workshop are sheltered from commercially competitive pressures in that the market for the workshop's products is established when the workshop is founded. This does not necessarily mean that the goods produced are second rate; they may be as good as commercially produced articles and often are less expensive.

**Shift schedule** Arrangements of work shifts and of changes from one shift to another. If these are unplanned they may upset workers' biological clocks. Industrial/organizational psychologists can provide a company with a suitable plan for designing shift schedules in such a way that workers are not stressed.

**Short attention span** The inability to keep attending to a source of stimulation for more than a very brief time (usually three to five minutes). A student with a short attention span is easily distracted. This can be a handicap in the student's efforts to learn from such traditional instructional methods as lectures and textbook reading assignments.

**Short-Term Memory (STM)** The second of three stages of memory, the one in which only a few items of information (seven plus or minus two bits) can be stored. These five to nine bits can be maintained without rehearsal for about a minute or so. After this, the information is either lost or is saved by being entered into the third type of memory, the Long-Term Memory (LTM). The first stage of memory is known as sensory memory.

**Short-term objectives** A list of described behaviors indicating what a student (especially students with special needs or learning challenges) is expected to be able to carry out after a given course of instruction. Such a list can be related to a statement of annual goals for the student and it can also be part of the student's Individualized Education Plan (IEP).

**Shunt** A tube used to drain excess fluid from some part of the body. Shunts are commonly used with individuals who have hydrocephalus to remove an excess of cerebrospinal fluid from the head area. The fluid is then redirected to the heart or intestines.

**Sibilant** Sibilants are the uttered "hissing" sounds such as the s, sh, and ch sounds.

**Sibling rivalry** The competitive nature of brother/sister relationships who mutually compete for parental attention, family status, etc. A competition among siblings for the attention of the parents, which may entail rivalry in the spheres of academics, sports, career, or social success.

**Sickle-cell anemia** A blood disorder (anemia) found almost exclusively among people of African ancestry. It is a result of the inheritance of the abnormal recessive sickle-cell gene from both parents. This gene produces an abnormal form of hemoglobin. The name "sickle-cell anemia" stems from the fact that the red corpuscles each have an abnormal, sickle-like shape. SEE: *anemia, hemoglobin*

S

**Sickle-cell trait** A term used to describe a person who carries the sickle-cell gene but actually does not suffer from the disease of sickle-cell anemia. SEE: *sickle-cell anemia*

**Side effects** Unexpected or unwanted effects of a drug, medical treatment, or educational technique that are unrelated to the purpose for the administration of the drug or treatment.

**Sight conservation** A philosophy that recommends limiting the use of sight in order to save what vision is remaining with individuals who have severe vision problems.

**Sight words** SEE: *basic sight words*

**Sighted guide person** A person with sight who has had special training and assists a visually impaired or blind person in moving about in the environment.

**Sign language** A system of communication involving hand gestures to represent actions, feelings, and objects. SEE: *American Sign Language (ASL), Seeing Essential English (SEE I), Signing Exact English (SEE II)*

**Sign systems** The use of systems in addition to sign language that use visual clues and manual signs to simulate an oral language equivalent. SEE: *sign language*

**Signal detection theory** A modern approach to psychophysics, the measurement of sensory perceptions as a function of stimulation, that does away with the concept of threshold. The subject is treated as a responsive system. The responses made by the subject are considered to be not merely correlates of sensory stimuli but dependent on the subject's value and expectancies as well.

**Signal-to-noise ratio** The ratio of the decibel (dB) level of the speaker (divided) by the decibel (dB) level of the noise in the rest of an enclosed room. This ratio impacts the receptive communication ability of hearing impaired individuals.

**Significance** SEE: *level of significance*

**Signing Exact English (SEE II)** A manual method of communication used by the hearing impaired or deaf, it is similar to American Sign Language (ASL) in that they share some signs—there is a different word order for both. In print it is displaced by a series of drawings. This system emphasizes standard word order in English; it also marks the tense of verbs and shows irregular verb forms as well. It is a manual code based on standard English and is used primarily in educating students for English. SEE: *American Sign Language (ASL), Seeing Essential English (SEE I)*

**Silent consonant** In the English language, the first or second of two adjacent consonants may be omitted in speech. For example, the k in "know," the p in "pneumonia," and the h in "chorus" are not sounded.

**Simile** A figure of speech in which two different things are indicated as being like one another, using the word "as" or "like." For example, his/her smile is like a ray of sunshine.

**Simulation** Sometimes referred to as gaming, it is a method of instruction that attempts to relate what is being studied to real-life experiences.

**Single-cell recording technique** The use of a microelectrode to record voltage changes taking place in a single nerve cell of an experimental subject. This is the very opposite approach to recording from taking an electroencephalogram, which uses large electrodes that each respond to thousands of neurons.

**Single subject curriculum** A curriculum that presents various subjects as single areas of study in isolation. The academic disciplines are not taught in relation to each other or interdisciplinarily but as areas to be studied as a separate entity.

**Single-word communication** This refers to children or persons who primarily use one-word utterances and appear to be unable to speak in word combinations.

**Site based** A term which indicates that the activity, event, instruction, and the like is taking place on the school campus, that is within the environs of the school building or grounds.

**Site-based management**   The sharing of school governance by administrators, teachers, parents, community members, students, and other professionals. Teachers and parents are given opportunities to make recommendations regarding curriculum, staffing, budgets, and the use of instructional/technology materials. The type of management system and level of school autonomy vary widely.

**Site license**   Refers to sites granted license or legal access to computer or other programs and disk or other materials within a particular school district typically for a period of a year. During this time, all schools within the district have access to these programs and materials and may copy them for their use.

**Situation attribution**   The tendency to attribute our own misfortune, errors, and mishaps to situational factors such as poor weather conditions, careless behaviors of other people, unfairness of societal rules, etc.

**Six-hour retardate**   An outdated term used to describe the unusual occurrence when a student appears/acts retarded during the regular school day (usually a six-hour day) and not outside of the school facility.

**Size constancy**   The ability to maintain a perception of the variations in the object's distance. The optical image of a far-away object is much smaller than the image of the same object close to us. Size constancy is the ability to disregard such changes in image size.

**Skepticism**   In its undiluted version, skepticism is a disbelief that science and/or philosophy can ever produce reliable knowledge. A less extreme form of skepticism holds that innovative scientific or philosophical ideas should be subjected to rigorous experimental and/or logical tests before they can be accepted. The ancient Greek philosopher Pyrrho founded the extreme form of skepticism. The French philosopher Descartes used moderate skepticism as a starting point for the development of his own system of thought.

**Skewed distribution**   A distribution of scores that is not normal or normally distributed. Such a distribution is not symmetrical and the values representing the mean, median, and mode are different. There are more extreme scores at one end of the distribution. In a negatively skewed distribution, the mean is lower than the median and both the mean and median are typically lower than the mode. In a positively skewed distribution, the mean is higher than the median and the mean and median are higher than the mode.

**Skewness**   A property of a frequency distribution having to do with a set of scores that fail to cluster around the central tendency (central value) of the frequency curve. If mostly low scores are obtained, the majority of scores occur on the left, with a thin tail-like part of the curve extending to the right. This kind of curve is said to be skewed to the right or positively skewed. If, however, most scores are high numbers, the majority of scores pile up toward the right end of the curve, and the thin tail points toward the left. This curve is described as skewed to the left or negatively skewed. SEE: *frequency distribution, shape*

**Skill-based**   Instruction which is directed toward a particular lack of or inability in a specific area of study such as reading, sight vocabulary, spelling, etc. Teaching is designed to develop those required skills necessary for the student to progress effectively in the appropriate skills area.

**Skill deficits**   In education, a term used to describe a lack of ability or even little or no ability in a particular area of study. For example, a student may have a "skill deficit" because the student has no command or mastery of phonics, or perhaps has a poor sight vocabulary and/or difficulty with spelling and the like.

**Skillful micropolitical action**   Developing relationships for political reasons within an organizational context (e.g., developing good relationships within a college setting). SEE: *micropolitics*

**Skill groups**   A term used to describe students who are grouped or clustered by need. That is, students who need serious remediation and support in some particular area of study such as in the case of poor readers. SEE: *skill deficits*

**Skillwork** In education, verbal or paper and pencil tasks given to students particularly from workbooks and practice books (e.g., from basal readers) or materials used to assist students in acquiring specific mastery of a skills area (e.g., using flashcards to master multiplication facts).

**Skimming** The rapid reading of text in order to obtain a general overview or impression of the text. SEE: *scanning*

**Slander** The leveling of charges or misrepresentations of facts, which can damage the reputation of another and are not based on facts; usually a false, oral, and insulting statement (as opposed to libel, a written or published statement). In the nonlegal sense, both can be written or stated.

**Slate and stylus** A system of writing in braille in reverse order, unlike the Perkins brailler. The paper is fastened in a slate and the stylus is pressed through openings to form a type of reverse braille. SEE: *Perkins brailler*

**Sleep** A complex phase of our daily lives that alternates with waking. In newborn infants, sleep accounts for most of the 24-hour day. Eventually, the need for sleep is lowered until it consumes only one third of the 24-hour day. Some say that dreaming is a third phase of living, but most regard dreaming sleep as simply one of the sleep stages.

**SLI** SEE: *Specifically Language Impaired*

**Slip of the tongue** An error of speech, such as saying aloud what one is thinking, making the sound of a forthcoming word too early, or omitting an important sound of a word. Freud found that many of these slips could be symbolically connected to the personal problems of the speaker.

**Small class size** A term, depending on what is being taught and at what grade level, which indicates a class of a certain number of students wherein a teacher is able to give attention on an individual

basis to every member. Classes of 15 students or less are usually considered small whereas classes of 20–30 are usually considered of normal size.

**Snellen chart/Snellen eye chart** (Herman Snellen, German ophthalmologist, 1834–1908) A special chart used for testing vision. The chart is designed so that the top letter at 200 feet would appear the same size as the standard letters when viewed from 20 feet. The test distance of 20 feet is the standard because light rays from an object at that distance are parallel and the eye muscles are at rest for the normal eye. This distance gives a truer picture of visual acuity than other distances in the normal eye. "20/20" means one can see clearly at 20 feet what the normal eye can see at 20 feet. "20/20" is considered normal vision.

**SNS** SEE: *sympathetic nervous system*

**Social cognition** An individual's understanding, ideas, belief systems, etc. of the actions and intentions of others. Social cognitions form the basis for our interpersonal interactions in the environment.

**Social cognitive approach** The tendency for some personality theories to account for the development of people's personalities by observational (i.e., social) learning and cognitive factors. For example, a personality trait of neatness could result from observing the behavior of one's neat and tidy parent.

**Social cognitive learning** The view that observations of people and environmental events influence the way we act and process information.

**Social-comparison theory** A theory of happiness which states that one's level of happiness is based on one's estimate of how his/her own life circumstances compare to those of others.

**Social facilitation** When there is another person present, one performs better on simple tasks but performs worse on difficult tasks. The influence of having someone else near is to bring out the dominant response, which is likely to be correct for a simple task but is probably incorrect for a difficult task.

**Social identity theory**   A social psychology theory about the stereotyping of groups of people. According to social identity theory, we think highly of our own group because this increases our own self-esteem. Putting down other groups contributes to this effect.

**Social intelligence**   The overall ability of an individual to understand social conventions and how to effectively interact within one's social environment.

**Social interference**   A dropoff in performance or impaired performance resulting from the actions/presence of others.

**Social isolation**   A disciplinary procedure; a disruptive student is set aside from the class for several minutes.

**Social learning**   SEE: *imitation*

**Social learning theory**   An explanation of gender-role development. For example, boys and girls obtain rewards for acting like other boys and like other girls, respectively. Secondly, they watch the behavior of other children and imitate the activities they observe.

**Social loafing**   A dropoff in effort on the part of the members of a work group resulting from the formation of a group norm.

**Social maladjustment**   SEE: *socially maladjusted*

**Social mobility**   The ability and freedom to move from one social level to another, up and down the scale as one chooses. Social levels are defined by the societal system in which one lives and functions.

**Social platform**   Major issues (e.g., wage practices and advancement of women and minorities in the work place) that can become politicized and used in general discussion and/or campaign purposes as in an election (e.g., the position of a candidate) or a policy decision (e.g., formulating a system-wide school policy).

**Social promotion**   The promotion of a student to the next grade based on the chronological age of the student instead of the student's achievement.

**Social psychology**   That subfield of psychological science dealing with the influence that group membership, including participation in social interactions, has upon the behavior of individuals.

**Social role theory**   Theodore Barber's theory of hypnotism. The hypnotized subjects act out the role of a hypnotized person. There are culturally prescribed expectations about the actions of someone in a hypnotic trance. The hypnotized person feels that the situation demands compliance with the hypnotist's commands.

**Social schema**   A model of the structure of a social group's internal relationships, the pattern of obligations and rights attached to a social role, the significant social relationships involved in some historic event, or the various roles, statuses, and environmental influences involving a particular person.

**Social-skills training**   A type of behavioral group therapy aimed at improving the patient's interpersonal skills.

**Social stratification**   In effect, the different class levels as identified by the society at large. Sometimes this term is called social class.

**Social system**   A system that groups people in a social, ethnic, cultural, racial, occupational, and/or socioeconomic fashion. The social groups share common interests, purposes, goals, expectations, etc.

**Socialization**   The process by which one acquires the customs, values, knowledge, and behavioral skills that enable her/him to be a functional member of her/his own society.

**Socialization mismatch hypothesis**   This is an explanation of the reasons why certain language-minority groups succeed or fail in school. This hypothesis states that the greater the match between the English language/ communication patterns reinforced at home and those reinforced in school, the greater is the likelihood that the child will succeed in school.

**Socialized aggression**   That type of behavior usually exhibited by an adolescent (but sometimes adults) that is contrary to and aggressive toward accepted social norms. A good example of aggressive and antisocial behavior would be gang membership.

**Socially maladjusted**   A person that has no sense of morality that separates right from wrong. Students who are socially maladjusted usually display a serious lack of ability to conform to even the basic social norms; they have as such no real social responsibility. SEE: *sociopath*

**Society**   A population sharing a given geographic area. People who live together and share a common culture. SEE: *social system*

**Sociobiology**   A school of thought that accounts for various types of group behavior by appealing to genetic and evolutionary causal factors. For example, an act of altruistic self-sacrifice on the part of an individual in order to save the lives of others is accounted for by appealing to the preservation of most of the sacrificed person's genes in the cells of the people whose lives were saved.

**Sociodrama**   A technique for diagnosing an individual's social adjustment difficulties. In sociodrama, the individual plays a role (or a series of roles) so that his/her perceptions of himself/herself and of others are brought out in a social context. The technique may have psychotherapeutic value by providing the individual with insight into one's own social adjustment problems.

**Socioeconomic Status (SES)**   One's social standing based on society's view of one's income, occupation, social contacts, value system, influence, etc.

**Sociolinguistic**   In language arts, the cognitive connection between reading and writing as a similar process in the sense of an interdisciplinary link between sociology and linguistics, such as the study of language in various social settings. This includes but is not limited to areas of social class, ethnicity, and regional dialects.

**Sociolinguistics**   The study of all the rules, both formal and informal, pertaining to holding conversations that apply to a given cultural and language group.

**Sociology**   The scientific study of the behavior of social groups and institutions and how such groups are organized.

**Sociology of race**   The scientific study of the causes and consequences of varying socially constructed racial groups.

**Sociopath**   1. A person who is not adjusted socially is, in a sense, amoral and does not feel guilt or remorse for misdeeds or misbehavior. 2. An antisocial disorder of personality. SEE: *socially maladjusted*

**Socratic discussion groups**   Refers to the use of discussion groups as in the time of Socrates whereby probing questions and abstract complex issues are presented (e.g., topic = what is a good teacher?).

**Socratic method**   The use of dialectical questioning while reasoning or discussing as in the time of Socrates. The student is expected to be able to generate the answer based on the student's own thought processes. SEE: *Socratic discussion groups*

**Soft neurological signs**   The absence of obvious neurological symptoms. These are behavioral symptoms that suggest minimal brain dysfunction or injury.

**Soft signs**   SEE: *soft neurological signs*

**Software programs**   Refers to computer programs that are stored on floppy disks and/or hard disks.

**Solid geometry**   The mathematical study of three-dimensional figures and their properties and relationships.

**Solipsism**   The most extreme form of idealism which holds that basic reality is mental or spiritual. The solipsist contends that the entire universe is a figment of his/her own imagination. While the solipsist may bother to defend his/her views, he/she is under no obligation to do so because other persons have no existence outside the mental life of the solipsist. While no eminent philosopher actually arrived at unqualified solipsism, George Berkeley came very close to it. He did concede, however, that the mind of God contains all reality. SEE: *idealism, metaphysics, mind-body problem, monism, subjective idealism*

**Somatic nervous system**   That part of the peripheral nervous system that receives its input from the exteroceptors (receptors covering the external environment) and sends motor commands to the striped (voluntary) muscles. SEE: *peripheral nervous system (PNS)*

**Somatoform disorder**   A psychological problem (of less severity than a psychosis) in which the patient complains of physical symptoms despite the absence of a relevant disease or injury.

**Somatosensory cortex**   That part of the parietal lobe receiving inputs from the general body senses (light touch, deep pressure, pain, warmth, cold, and kinesthesis). The sense receptors from which these messages are sent are distributed throughout the body.

**Somatosensory system**   A sensory input system that responds to touch, pain, and temperature stimulation through receptors on the surface of the skin.

**Somnambulism**   1. Also known as "sleep walking" wherein a person does things that are normally done during a state of waking; the actions are of an unconscious nature. 2. A type of hysteria wherein a person does not recall his/her actions or behaviors.

**SOMPA**   SEE: *System of Multicultural Pluralistic Assessment*

**Sonic glasses**   Developed in 1973 by L. Kay, these emit high frequency sounds and help to locate objects by echoes. SEE: *sonic guide*

**Sonic guide**   Used by the seriously visually impaired, it looks similar to a pair of glasses. The sonic guide emits high frequency sounds beyond the range of hearing, which reflect back to the device that produces audible noise, thus giving the wearer distance, direction, and some sense of the surface characteristics of objects in the path of travel of the user. Used for mobility and travel, it detects objects in about an eight-foot range. Sometimes referred to as a sonic pathfinder.

**Sonic pathfinder**   SEE: *sonic guide*

**Sonography**   A type of x ray that converts sound waves into a visual picture. Because there is no radiation used, this technique is considered to be safe when viewing the physical development or detecting major physical problems in an unborn fetus.

**Sound**   1. The mechanical energy wave stimulating the sense of hearing. The intensity of sound energy, or sound amplitude, is registered subjectively as loudness. Variations in the frequency of sound waves are experienced as changes of pitch. 2. The subjective experience resulting from stimulation of the inner ear and the auditory nervous system.

**Sound localization**   An aspect of auditory perception in which the hearer judges the location from which the sound stimulus is coming from.

**Sound-symbol association**   Simply, the ability of a student to identify and match the sound of a letter with the correct letter. Poor sound-symbol association is a signal of perceptual difficulty in a student. Students with this difficulty depend upon visual memorization. They have difficulty learning phonics and rely on repetition and practice as a means of learning sound-symbol association. Such students tend to have a slow reading rate as they struggle to associate sounds with symbols.

**Sound waves**   Mechanical energy passing through air (or another medium). The molecules of the sound medium are alternately compressed and spread out (rarefied). The rate at which compressions and rarefactions alternate is the frequency of sound. The amplitude of the wave corresponds to the sound's intensity. Most sounds are composed of a mixture of frequencies. These are measured separately for amplitude by a method called Fourier analysis (a mathematical/harmonic analysis method named after Baron Jean Baptiste Joseph Fourier, 1760–1830).

**Spasms** A condition characterized by a contraction (involuntary) of a muscle. They are "clonic" (alternating between contraction and relaxation) or "tonic" (sustained). They may affect skeletal muscles, which are striated, or visceral muscles, which are smooth. Strong and painful contractions or spasms are called "cramps."

**Spastic cerebral palsy** SEE: *spasticity*

**Spastic paralysis** A type of paralysis of the striped muscles which have high levels of muscle tone although they cannot carry out motor commands from the higher parts of the brain. This kind of paralysis is associated with damage to the primary motor cortex or, perhaps, to the dorsal roots of the spinal nerves. It could definitely not be a result of damage to spinal cord motor neurons or to the ventral roots, as such damage would cause flaccid paralysis, paralysis accompanied by very low muscle tone.

**Spasticity** (also called hypertonus) This is a type of cerebral palsy that is characterized by increased muscle tone or tension and stiffness in the muscles to a point of spasms.

**Spatial frequency filter theory** The view that visual perception involves the analysis of patterns of light and dark into their basic sine-wave components (with the high-frequency stimuli having narrow light and dark stripes and the low-frequency stimuli having wide light and dark bands).

**Speaking valve** Air exhaled through the stoma, which is below the vocal folds (cords), causes no vibration of the folds, thus no speech. The air can be pushed through the vocal folds by blocking off the tracheostomy tube at the stoma. While this can be done by touching the opening with one's thumb, the "speaking valve" eliminates this necessity. The valve stays open for inflation and open for "easy" exhalation but will close upon forceful exhalation, thus passing air through the trachea past the

vocal folds and vocal tract to produce vibration and the articulation of speech. SEE: *tracheostomy, stoma*

**Spearman rho** A measure of correlation that is used with ordinal scales or data and when the median and quartile deviations are used.

**Special children** or **special-needs children** Refers to children who are considered different from the so-called average or "norm." These children usually are thought to require special education services of some type, appropriate resources, and adaptations (i.e., curriculum). The basic criterion for this classification is that the child is not progressing effectively in a regular school program.

**Special class** An instructional classroom for special-needs children who are considered to be in need of a substantially separate program. They are mostly self-contained and are taught by a special education teacher. Children in these classrooms are mainstreamed infrequently, if at all. SEE: *mainstreaming*

**Special day schools** 1. Schools that educate special-needs students during the regular school day and usually during the regular school year. They are normally substantially separate programs. They can also provide services for up to a full 12-month year. 2. Day schools (i.e., students are not residents) that specialize in particular disorders/problems/handicaps/diseases (e.g., school for students with emotional handicaps, school for students with learning disabilities, etc.). These schools are separate from regular public/parochial schools. Frequently, special day schools are out-of-district placements wherein school systems must pay tuition/transportation expenses. Typically school systems do not have enough special students in a particular district to warrant such a school within that locale. School systems then must collaborate to form regional schools or collaborative programs or provide the funds for what becomes a private school situation.

**Special education** The supportive services or special-needs programs designed for children who are considered to differ from the norm and do not progress effectively in regular school programs.

**Special education classroom**   A classroom staffed and supervised by a certified special education professional(s) in which a special-needs student or student with special learning challenges receives a program of services as called for by his/her Individualized Education Plan (IEP).

**Special education technology**   Any kind of technology that would aid a disabled or special-needs person but particularly technology designed with that purpose in mind. SEE: *assistive technology*

**Special educator**   Refers to a professional or paraprofessional who is trained/mentored/educated to meet the unique learning challenges/needs of students with disabilities.

**Special-needs child**   SEE: *special children*

**Special schools**   This classification includes any out-of-district day school (educational services only) or residential program (student receives both educational and living/residential services). SEE: *special day school*

**Special self-contained class**   SEE: *special class*

**Special services committee**   A multidisciplinary team of professionals that comprises the evaluation team charged with determining whether or not a student has special needs and, if so, with the writing of the Individualized Education Plan (IEP). SEE: *evaluation team, Individualized Education Plan (IEP), Individualized Family Service Plan (IFSP)*

**Specialist consultation**   The use of highly specialized professionals such as speech, physical, and occupational therapists or vision/hearing specialists to provide teaching ideas, behavior management plans, and social adaptations for students with special needs in order to maximize regular classroom adjustment/success.

**Specialized supports**   Part of a system of supports provided for a person with disabilities/special learning challenges (e.g., speech therapists, counselors, and learning disabilities specialists). Other types of supports include generic services and nonpaid supports. SEE: *generic supports, nonpaid supports*

**Specific language disability**   In common use, a term used as a synonym for a learning disability. SEE: *learning disability, specifically language impaired*

**Specific learning disability**   SEE: *specific language disability, learning disability, specifically language impaired*

**Specifically Language Impaired (SLI)**   These are children who appear to have normal development in the other domains such as intelligence, motor ability, social skills, etc. but not in the area of communications.

**Speculative philosophy**   Systematic thinking about all that exists in the universe. Speculative philosophy attempts to reveal the order and meaning that are assumed to be inherent in the world around us. SEE: *analytic philosophy, metaphysics, prescriptive philosophy*

**Speech**   This involves the production of sound patterns in a systematic fashion, which results in communication.

**Speech and language disorder**   A condition in which the individual has difficulties effectively communicating by oral speech/language. SEE: *language disorder, speech disorder*

**Speech and language specialist**   An especially trained professional who is able to test, assess, diagnose and provide services and support for students or individuals with speech, language and/or communication disorders. SEE: *speech correctionists*

**Speech audiometry**   A process of testing the hearing of a person in order to determine levels at which speech-sound is heard. That is, to determine the Speech Reception Threshold (SRT), the decibel (dB) level at which a person can just barely hear speech and other sounds. SEE: *Speech Reception Threshold (SRT)*

**S**

**Speech correctionist**   Also known as a speech-language pathologist, this is a professional person trained to deliver services to persons with speech and language problems. Sometimes called a speech therapist or speech clinician. SEE: *speech, speech-language pathologist*

**Speech disorder**   Speech that is generally quite different from the speech of other people (so-called normal speech) to a degree where it is obviously unintelligible and/or extremely unpleasant.

**Speech flow**   The rhythmic sequence of speech sounds during conversation.

**Speech handicapped**   A person that has delayed development and/or speech impairments to a degree that interferes with normal communications. This handicap may also cause anxiety as a result of the attention the problem calls upon itself. SEE: *speech-language pathologist*

**Speech impairment**   An inability to make speech sounds clearly.

**Speech-language pathologist**   A specially trained professional who tests, diagnoses, and administers services to individuals with speech, language, or communication disorders.

**Speech mechanisms**   The various parts of the body that are necessary for oral speech. They include the mandible, palate, tongue, lips, teeth, etc. SEE: *resonating system, vibrating system, vocal tract*

**Speech pathology**   The science or the study of the diagnosis and/or treatment of delayed speech development or impairments of speech.

**Speech plus talking calculator**   A synthetic speech hand-held calculator with a vocabulary of about 24 words; inexpensive but not very extensive. This device repeats out loud the number(s) or answer(s) pressed.

**Speech reading**   Sometimes referred to as lip reading, this is more than lip reading. It is the visual interpretation of other communication clues in addition to lip reading such as gestures and facial expressions.

**Speech Reception Threshold (SRT)**   The decibel level at which an individual can interpret speech. That is, the level of loudness or intensity of sound measured in decibels (dBs) at which a person can understand speech, not just hear it.

**Speech therapist**   SEE: *speech-language pathologist*

**Spelling instruction**   Approaches to the teaching of spelling that generally move from basic letter-sound correspondences to consonant blends in various word positions to long vowel spellings, inflections, structural word parts, and so on. The major goal of spelling instruction is to provide children with the conventions and regularities of an alphabetic system. Spelling instruction assists children in finding word patterns and conventions for assembling word parts and whole words. Current research shows that children will become better spellers if they are directly taught how to analyze and synthesize sound-symbol correspondences.

**Sphygmograph**   SEE: *polygraph*

**Spina bifida**   A congenital malformation of the vertebra involving the failure of the bony spinal column to close during fetal development. It can occur at any point in the spinal column and is characterized by a vertebra that has failed to close at the midline. This condition can cause mental retardation and severe fine and gross motor problems, where individuals are at times confined to wheelchairs. SEE: *spina bifida cystica, spina bifida occulta, spina bifida meningocele*

**Spina bifida cystica**   A defect and malformation of the spine characterized by a tumorlike sac filled with spinal fluid. The sac has no nerve tissue. SEE: *spina bifida*

**Spina bifida meningocele**   A cystlike or tumorlike sac on the spine that causes malformation of the spinal column. As in the case of spina bifida cystica, the sac is filled with spinal fluid; but unlike spina bifida cystica, this condition does have nerve tissue. SEE: *spina bifida, spina bifida cystica, spina bifida occulta*

**Spina bifida occulta**   Spina bifida in which the spinal cord is not damaged even though the vertebra does not close. The protrusion commonly seen is absent and in the area concerned the only noticeable indication may be a hairy growth. SEE: *spina bifida*

**Spinal cord**   The part of the central nervous system (CNS) encased by the spine or backbone. Through it run the spinal reflex arcs. It also carries afferent (sensory) messages toward the brain and efferent (motor) messages descending from the brain.

**Spinal cord injury**   An injury involving spinal cord trauma, a cut across the long axis of the spinal cord or other damage as such caused by an accident.

**Spinal meningitis**   A condition characterized by inflammation of the outer layers of the spinal cord (the meninges). SEE: *meningitis*

**Spinal nerve**   A nerve connected to the spinal cord. There are normally 31 pairs of spinal nerves. The spinal nerves and the cranial nerves form the interface between the central nervous system (CNS) and the peripheral nervous system (PNS).

**Spiritualism**   SEE: *idealism*

**Splinter skills**   A term used to describe a condition wherein a student knows certain skills about an operation or task but does not have all the skills necessary to effectively complete the operation or task. What is known is well known but what is not known is completely lacking.

**Split-brain research**   Research on the separately specialized functions of the left and right cerebral hemispheres. Subjects for this type of research are epileptic patients who have had surgery done to sever the corpus callosum, which connects each hemisphere with the other.

**Spondylitis of adolescence**   A form of rheumatoid arthritis that affects the body in general and not just particular joints or areas. SEE: *rheumatoid arthritis*

**Spontaneous recovery**   The return of a conditioned response to its original strength (or, at least, an increase in strength) after extinction training has taken place and this training has been interrupted. When the experimenter returns after the interruption, the animal's response is at a higher level than it had been just before the interruption. This phenomenon may be observed in both classical (Pavlovian) and operant (Skinnerian) conditioning.

**Spontaneous remission**   The disappearance of an illness as the result of the passage of time rather than any medical treatment. This can occur with some emotional problems as well as with some physical ailments.

**Sport psychology**   A field of applied psychology in which psychological principles are used to help athletes perform better.

**Sputnik**   The name given to the original Russian space satellite launched in 1957. Its successful orbiting was considered a threat to the security of the United States and a blow to the pride of our nation. Sputnik's launching provided the impetus for a renewed national interest in education (especially math and science) as the space race began in earnest. Congress passed the National Defense Education Act (1958) as part of the response to the launching of Sputnik. Federal funding became available to promote programs for high academic achievement, particularly in mathematics and physical science.

**SQ3R**   A study method which is described as intentional reading. First, one reads only major headings. Then, one reads to get the information about the headings. Then, there is self-testing to check retention. Finally, the material is reviewed. The symbols stand for "Survey-Question-Read-Recite-Review."

**SQUIRT**   1. An acronym for sustained quiet uninterrupted individualized reading time. 2. SEE: *Detective Q. Squirt.*

**SRT**   SEE: *Speech Reception Threshold*

**SSR**   An abbreviation used to describe sustained silent reading. SEE: *Sustained Silent Reading (SSR), Uninterrupted*

*Sustained Silent Reading (USSR), Drop Everything and Read (DEAR)*

**STAD** SEE: *Student Team Achievement Divisions*

**Staff** In organizational groups, an arrangement of personnel wherein a person is not under the direct control of most others. The staff member in fact may serve many persons in authority but is not a direct subordinate of these persons, e.g., a secretary.

**Staff development** Ongoing education for the faculty and staff of a school. Usually the service is provided by consulting personnel on site at the school. SEE: *in-service education*

**Stage 1 sleep** The sleep pattern typical of falling asleep right after a state of waking with drowsiness. The EEG is rapid and of low voltage. Descending stage 1 specifies this dropping-off phase, but during a night's sleep Stage 1 is revisited two or three times in the form of ascending Stage 1 sleep, which is also called stage REM sleep.

**Stage 2 sleep** The sleep pattern that follows Stage 1 sleep. The EEG shows a background record of fast, low voltage activity (the Stage 1 picture) interrupted by slow-wave stretches (the sleep spindles) or by high-voltage negative spikes (the k-complexes).

**Stage 3 sleep** One of the two stages of slow-wave sleep. The Stage 2 sleep pattern alternates with delta-wave activity that takes up less than one half of the record. Delta waves are the slowest of all brain waves, ranging from one half per cycle to four cycles per second.

**Stage 4 sleep** The sleep stage in which delta waves (high voltage, low-frequency waves) take up half or more of the total EEG record. It is during this stage that sleepwalking may occur.

**Stage REM sleep** Also known as ascending Stage 1 sleep. This stage of sleep first appears following the second episode of Stage 2 sleep on the way "up the ladder" from Stage 4. The EEG record is low voltage and high frequency. It is during this stage that most dreaming occurs. The larger striped muscles (anti-gravity muscles) are fully relaxed. The eye muscles move rapidly back-and-forth (the rapid eye movements that give us the name REM).

**Stand-alone thinking skills programs** Programs that are purported to teach thinking ability directly, without requiring work with an academic subject.

**Standard deviation** A measure of variability that looks at how much each individual score in a distribution deviates from the mean. The standard deviation or SD is equal to the square root of the sum of squared differences between each score and the mean, known as the sum of squares (SS) for a sample distribution of scores divided by N–1 (number of scores–1). The standard deviation calculated on a population is the same except one needs to divide by N instead of N–1.

**Standard error of measurement** The statistical estimate of the amount of variation that a group of scores would exhibit if the subjects took the same test over again. There are approximately two chances in three that a test score obtained by an individual is within one standard error either above or below a person's obtained score.

**Standard scores** Standard scores are raw scores that have been changed statistically so that means and standard deviations can be compared. They tell how far an individual's score deviates from the mean in units of standard deviation. Two types of standard scores that are popularly used are called "z" scores and "T" scores. The "z" type standard scores range from +3.00 to –3.00 with a standard deviation of 1.00.

**Standardization** The establishment of precise test procedures for an objective test. The data from a test development group are statistically analyzed to produce norms such as the mean, the standard deviation, and percentiles. Such tests are called standardized tests. Manuals for them usually include data on test reliability and validity.

**Standardized** Refers to a type of assessment procedure that is required to be administered, scored, and interpreted in the same manner regardless of the time and place of the testing.

**Standardized scores**  Standard scores which are valid and reliable and which can be normed and made available to the educator or user. SEE: *standard scores*

**Standardized tests**  Commercially prepared tests containing a fixed set of questions that are administered to all students under the same time constraints and test directions. Standardized tests are normed, meaning they are given to a large national sample so that student performance can be compared on a national level. The two most common types of standardized tests are achievement tests and aptitude tests. SEE: *achievement test, aptitude tests, norms*

**Standards**  Specific definitions of what students should know or demonstrate. Performance standards enumerate how well students (and in what ways) demonstrate knowledge mastery while content standards specify what is to be known in the various academic subject areas by grade level.

**Stanford-Binet intelligence scale**  Originally known as the Binet-Simon scales, the scale is a standardized individual Intelligence Quotient test (IQ). This test was revised and standardized at Stanford University by Lewis Terman (1877–1956) who felt that IQ tests could be used to help identify gifted children, who throughout their lives tend to maintain intellectual superiority. Terman revised the Binet-Simon in 1916.

**Stanines**  A stanine (which is a contraction of a standard score 1 through 9) is a transformed raw score into a score that is based on the normal curve. These scores are represented in whole numbers from 1 through 9. This single-digit scoring system provides a mean of 5 and a standard deviation of 2. The percentage of scores falling within each stanine interval (again, based on the normal curve) are 4, 7, 12, 17, 20, 17, 12, 7, and 4 respectively.

**Stapedectomy**  A surgical process that involves replacement of the stapes (or

stirrups), a small bone in the middle ear, if it is defective. The stapes are replaced with prosthetic devices. SEE: *stapes*

**Stapes (or stirrup)**  A small bone in the middle ear that is stirrup-shaped. It is the third of the three auditory ossicles. SEE: *incus, malleus*

**State-adoption textbooks**  Those textbooks selected by a state governmental agency such as a State Department of Education which requires all school systems state-wide to adopt and use.

**State aid**  Tax revenue raised by the state is in turn appropriated to local school systems in support of local educational programs. It is frequently used as a means to finance and provide equal educational opportunity amongst various communities.

**State-dependent memory**  The superiority of recall when the memory test is given with the subject being in the same condition as he/she was during the original learning.

**State Educational Agency Operations Organization**  State educational activities designed to implement state laws and regulations as they pertain to education. Also, to assist the cities and towns in fulfilling state and local educational responsibilities. This organization is frequently referred to as the State Board of Education or the State Department of Education.

**Statistical power**  The robustness of a test to reveal/detect real differences, if they exist. When the significance level is established at a low value or the number of individuals/scores studied is lowered, the power of the statistical test is reduced. There are two types of statistical errors researchers can make when using statistical procedures, type I and type II errors. When statistical power is increased, the chance of type II errors are reduced. SEE: *type I research error, type II research error*

**Statistical relativity**  A method of comparison of the frequency of behavior or characteristic to an average frequency and the deviation from that average.

**Statistical significance**   The likelihood that the observed outcomes of a statistical procedure/test occurred by chance. Statistical significance is not the same as something that is socially or educationally important. Statistical significance is a mathematical way to state the probability that observed outcomes of statistical procedures are a result of chance variations (e.g., perhaps because of small sample size, unequal group sizes, unreliable test instruments) in scores. Typically three levels of significance are commonly used: .05, .01, and .001. SEE: *levels of significance*

**Status epilepticus**   A condition that involves experiencing frequent epileptic seizures and accompanying symptoms. SEE: *epilepsy*

**STDs**   Sexually Transmitted Diseases affecting more than 40 million Americans that are usually contracted after sexual contact. Many of these diseases are fairly common with unpleasant side effects and dangerous consequences occurring especially if the STD is left untreated. For example, *chlamydia* is a bacterial infection that affects more than 4 million individuals per year with gonorrhea, syphilis, and genital herpes also common STDs. AIDS is an STD with no known absolute cure. Program efforts that provide information and ways to change behaviors have been found to be effective, especially with "high risk" populations (e.g., IV-drug users). Particularly helpful are programs that involve small-group support sessions over a long-term basis with social support systems given for changing behaviors that lead to acquiring STDs. SEE: *Acquired Immune Deficiency Syndrome (AIDS)*

**Stem**   The part of a multiple-choice test item that precedes the three or more possible choices.

**Stereochemical theory**   The theory of olfaction that the quality of a smell is based on the shape of the chemical stimulus molecule and the shape of a matching receptor site for that chemical in the olfactory mucous membrane. Recently this theory has been extended to the sense of taste, resulting from dissatisfaction with conventional explanations of how the taste sense works.

**Stereotaxic atlas**   A pictorial map of the brain showing frontal, horizontal, and vertical spatial coordinates, it is used along with the stereotaxic instrument as a guide for brain surgery to help ensure that an electrode (whether for destruction, stimulation, or recording) is placed in the small location in the brain that the experimenter intends to investigate.

**Stereotaxic instrument**   A restraining device equipped with elaborately ruled controls that permits the placement of an electrode at a precise location in the brain of a person or an experimental animal. It has been likened to a drill press in a machine shop. Distances front and back, right and left, and up and down can be adjusted with precision. These distances can be related to positions in the brain with the assistance of a stereotaxic atlas.

**Stereotype**   (stereo = Greek for "hard" or solid") A type of prejudice that involves a generalized but oversimplified view of a group of people, such as "all people from the midwest are isolationists." Stereotypical behaviors often involve racial and ethnic minorities. For example, the Serbs and Croats have experienced great strife and conflict because of deep-seated stereotypes. In the United States, the wealthy sometimes stereotype the work habits of the poor and vice versa. SEE: *stereotypic behavior*

**Stereotype effect**   A type of bias in which someone judges or attributes certain characteristics or qualities to all people who fall into a certain category (e.g., children cannot speak in sentence form before the age of 2).

**Stereotyped movement disorder**   SEE: *stereotypic behavior*

**Stereotypic behavior**   A movement disorder characterized by repetitive and usually gross motor motions such as eye rubbing, head nodding, head banging, foot tapping, various tics, etc. The movement is considered to be abnormal. SEE: *tic*

**Sterilization** 1. The act of making an individual sterile and unable to reproduce. 2. The destruction of microorganisms by exposure to physically or chemically harmful agents, radiation, filtering, heating, freezing, sound, etc. 3. The act of making an object, a food, or person germ-free.

**Steroid hormone** The kind of hormone released by the gonads and the adrenal cortex. Most other hormones are polypeptides. Steroids are distinguishable by their molecular shape; they contain four interlocked rings of carbon atoms.

**Stigma** Refers to labeling a person in some socially disgraceful or unflattering manner (e.g., the label of emotional disturbance can be considered a stigma in the case where others shun or avoid individuals with this problem). A stigma can be felt by the individual himself/ herself and/or by others. A stigma can also be attached to labels not in and of themselves disgraceful or unflattering (e.g., deaf, gay).

**Still's disease** A chronic condition of children with polyarthritis, it is characterized by intermittent fevers and enlargement of the lymph nodes and spleen. The disease is named for Sir George F. Still (1868–1941), a British physician. SEE: *rheumatoid arthritis*

**Stimulants** A category of drugs that produce excitement as well as increased heart rate and blood pressure. Examples of stimulants are the amphetamines, cocaine, and caffeine.

**Stimulus** An individual change in the physical energy that affects a sense receptor; examples would be lights or sounds for the eye and the ear, respectively. A stimulus is a unit of the environment.

**Stimulus discrimination** A special type of training in classical conditioning in which the conditioned stimulus (CS) continues to be presented before the unconditioned stimulus. Another stimulus, however, one similar in some physical manner to the CS, is also presented and is never backed up by the unconditioned stimulus. The trained person/ organism will selectively react to the correct stimulus and withhold a reaction when the negative stimulus is presented. Ordinarily, without having had discrimination training, the person/organism would be exhibiting some generalized responses to the incorrect but similar stimulus. This sort of training can also apply to operant behaviors. For example, we act differently in the presence of a red traffic light from the way we behave with a green light.

**Stimulus generalization** In conditioning, the tendency to react to a neutral stimulus that has some resemblance to a conditioned stimulus (CS). The person/ organism acts as if the true CS had been presented. This can occur in operant conditioning although no CS exists. A discriminative stimulus can be the basis for the response in operant conditioning.

**Stimulus reduction** A teaching method wherein external stimuli, extraneous activities, and distracting events are reduced or eliminated, thus making the learning environment less distracting. This method works well for children who are easily distracted or hyperactive.

**Stirrup** A bone of the three-bone chain in the middle ear, it is also called the stapes. SEE: *stapes, ossicles*

**STM** SEE: *Short-Term Memory*

**Stoma** A hole in the neck that opens into the trachea just under the larynx, used as a breathing hole as part of a tracheostomy. SEE: *tracheostomy, speaking valve*

**Storage, memory** The second step in memory following the acquisition of learned information but coming before the retrieval of that information. There are physiological theories concerning the location in the brain of stored information. Certain short-term memories seem to arrive at the hippocampus where they are consolidated (i.e., converted) to long-term memories.

**Story grammar** The basic parts of a story. Although there are many variations of the specifics of story grammar, most would agree that narratives contain a setting, plot (one or more episodes), and major theme(s). A story's grammar is the structure or rules typically used for a certain type of story. The grammar of a story involves such elements as the characters and their motivations, setting, a story problem(s) with a resolution to solve the problem(s), a chain-of-events that leads to the story resolution, and a story conclusion or ending.

**Story graph**   In language arts, a type of graphic display (chart, list, diagram, etc.) that organizes a specific story or reading topic, theme, idea, or element from the start to the end of the story or reading. This is a type of graphic organizer. SEE: *network, graphic organizers*

**Story ladder**   A term used in language arts for a sequential and structured approach for interpreting a story for primary grade students. The teacher summarizes the story for the students then deletes the last half of each sentence in the summary. Thus students are presented with a series of open-ended statements. The student then attempts to finish each incomplete sentence rung in the ladder appropriately. One should not expect students to complete the sentences as originally summarized and arranged by the teacher (exactly).

**Story line**   In language arts a persuasive technique wherein a mini-story is presented to children emphasizing the main theme and concluding with a satisfactory ending. Also used in advertising to convey the main idea in a satisfactory fashion.

**Story map**   A planning tool that helps students and teachers to organize the structure and meaning of a story. It is a type of sequential listing or map of the important highlights or elements of a narrative that includes story grammar. As an example, a story map might highlight the initiating event(s) of a story, the protagonist's internal responses to the initiating event(s), an attempt by the protagonist to solve a problem(s), a positive or negative outcome and then resolution of the protagonist's attempts to solve the problem or achieve a goal, and

a reaction showing the feelings of the protagonist in the success or failure of story resolution. SEE: *story grammar*

**Story star**   In language arts, an interpretation of the main points of a story in the form of a five-pointed star. It can be used to compare stories, organize the basic themes of a story, stimulate individual or group thinking and participation, or it may be used as a method of organizing and creating a story.

**Strabismus**   A condition characterized by the inability of both eyes to focus on an object at the same time. The eye muscles pull unequally, laterally speaking. Internal strabismus results in the eyeballs being pulled in toward the nose while external strabismus results in the eyes being pulled outward toward the ears. In alternating strabismus, eyeballs can be pulled and shifted between internal and external positions.

**Strauss syndrome**   A series of symptoms in the brain-injured child that include, for example, hyperactivity, impulsivity, and distractability.

**Strephosymbolia**   An inability to distinguish letter direction of similar forms such as "p" and "q" and "b" and "d." It includes reversed perception of direction as well, such as "left" to "right."

**Stress**   1. Any condition that requires drastic adjustive behavior so that it can be removed. Causes of psychological stress include pressure, frustration, conflict, major life changes, minor but oft-repeated hassles, and self-imposed factors such as false self-evaluations. 2. Physiological stress refers to any threat to life or health, including extreme heat, extreme cold, burns, frostbites, infections, and injuries.

**Stress inoculation training**   A form of cognitive psychotherapy devised by Meichenbaum. Individuals are placed in high-stress situations and are then persuaded to shift from negative thoughts to positive ones.

**Stressor**   A factor that causes stress. For a list of psychological and physiological stressors, see the definition of *stress.*

**Stretch reflex**   A reflex running directly through the spinal cord that requires only two neurons because the level at which the stimulus message arrives is the same as the level from which the outgoing motor message leaves. No interneuron is required. The knee-jerk and similar reflexes of other joints are phasic types of stretch reflex in which an actual motion occurs. Other stretch reflexes are tonic; the motor outflow increases the tone of a muscle but does not make it contract.

**Striated muscle**   Also called striped or voluntary muscle. The muscles have horizontal dark and light bands. They are grouped into muscle bundles that have a common membrane.

**Stridor**   Noisy or harsh breathing usually resulting from obstructions in the air passages. SEE: *dyspnea*

**Stroke**   A vascular failure that leads to the death of brain cells. If the blood cannot supply oxygen to nerve cells on a regular basis, those neurons will die. The symptoms of a stroke victim depend on what part of the brain suffered damage. For example, a stroke in the anterior part of the left cerebral cortex may lead to a loss of the ability to speak.

**Structural analysis**   The assessment of a student's word recognition skills by having the student do syllabication, employ base words, identify contractions, notice plurals, detect possessive pronouns and possessive adjectives, etc.

**Structuralism**   1. The theory of Wundt, Titchener, and the other early experimental psychologists that focused on the mind as consisting of such elements as sensations, images, and feelings. The task of psychology, to these theorists, was to discover how these elements came to be assembled. 2. The theory of linguists that every society's language has a unique structure and that the task of linguists is to uncover the structure of every human language.

**Structure** or **structured program**   A program that is highly organized and teacher-directed with limited or no flexibility. Educational activities are formally arranged in a step-by-step fashion. This teaching approach is sometimes effective for hyperactive or easily distracted students.

**Structured Clinical Interview for DSM-IV Dissociative Disorders (SCID-D)**   A semistructured interview format assessing five disorders based on criteria in DSM-IV: Anxiety disorders, psychotic disorders, eating disorders, personality disorders, and substance abuse disorders. (American Psychiatric Press, Publisher DSM-IV.)

**Structured observations**   These are observations based on a predetermined process. Using this predetermined method, judgments and impressions can be validly made.

**Structured overview**   In language arts, a system of organizing vocabulary words in a hierarchial fashion. The teacher lists vocabulary words with the most important ones arranged at the top of the diagram. This assists students in reading and understanding the vocabulary words to be learned within a reading.

**Student**   The individual for whom every school, school system, or educational institution has been established. The student, the learner, or the pupil may receive educational programs at any level that are provided by any educational organization as stated above.

**Student-centered curriculum**   A curriculum designed so as to consider the needs and interests of the pupils in class; learning activities are geared toward student needs and requirements.

**Student empowerment**   The ability to participate and achieve as a learner by successfully determining academic and career goals and to participate in the total community by being an active and productive citizen/learner.

**Student motivation to learn**   A student's intention to work on academic tasks, which derives from placing a high value on the learning.

**Student service expenditure**   Funds expended outside of the regular curriculum on behalf of students in such areas as admissions and registration costs. Also, monies spent on the emotional and physical well-being of the students as well as funds expended for their intellectual, social, and cultural development beyond the curriculum.

**Student teaching**   A clinical teaching experience of approximately 150–450 hours depending on the state and level and area of certification. Prospective teachers actually work in classroom situations under the direction of a mentor or certified teacher. Student teachers must be enrolled in state approved college education programs (four to six years). Student teachers are required to observe; keep records; create lesson plans and units; conduct mini-research projects; self-evaluate and reflect on progress; work with individuals, small groups, and entire classes; and adapt curriculum to the individual needs and learning styles of all learners.

**Students Against Drunk Driving (SADD)**   An organization dedicated to the prevention of young people or anyone driving under the influence of alcohol and/or other drugs.

**Student Team Achievement Divisions (STAD)**   A form of cooperative learning where separate groups of students compete with each other to earn rewards for academic achievement. SEE: *cooperative learning*

**Students at risk**   This is an education term used to describe students who might be in a high-risk category for any school/social/occupational failure. This broad category includes but is not limited to potential schools dropouts, school dropouts, substance abusers, the homeless, the abused, the neglected, the poor, the educationally delayed or deprived, limited English-speaking students, the conduct disordered, and sometimes the disabled and learning disabled, etc.

**Stuttering**   A fluency disorder in which the speaker repeats and/or prolongs sounds, syllables, and words. The flow and timing of speech is inappropriate and is frequently accompanied by tension and extraneous movement. At one time it was thought to be a neurotic disorder based on rejection and critical reaction by listeners. Today, it is believed to involve heredity, environment, learning, and emotion. There appears to be a genetic disposition to stuttering and problems with the speech-motor processes.

**Subarachnoid space**   A space below the arachnoid membrane (the middle of three membranes around the central nervous system) that contains spent Cerebrospinal Fluid (CSF). From that space, the CSF is extruded by the arachnoid villi into the subdural space, which is filled with venous (i.e., spent) blood.

**Subculture**   A group in a society whose habits and values differ greatly from the dominant and/or majority culture.

**Subfamily** or **related subfamily**   1. A couple with or without children sharing the home of one spouse's parents. 2. One parent with one or more single (never-married) children under 18 years of age living in a home and related to the person or couple who maintain the household.

**Subject-centered curriculum**   A curriculum so organized as to center itself along with its learning activities and content around a subject field such as history or science.

**Subject structure**   The basic framework of an academic concept in the educational theory of Jerome Bruner (also called "structure of the discipline").

**Subjective idealism**   The view championed by Bishop George Berkeley that physical things owe their apparent existence to the ideas in the minds of those who observe them. Berkeley's motto was "To be is to be perceived." The view came very close to solipsism, which is the contention that only "I" exist and all else is a mere figment of "my" thoughts. Berkeley granted that God holds all reality in mind, so that even when Berkeley is not looking at something it continues to exist thanks to the divine mind. SEE: *idealism, metaphysics, mind-brain problem, monism, objective idealism, solipsism*

**Subjective scoring** The tendency for different judges (raters, observers) to disagree in their scoring of a behavior. The assessments of pupil performance are not consistent. The assessment procedure is, therefore, not reliable.

**Subjective well-being** The individual's self-rating of his/her own level of happiness and/or satisfaction.

**Subjects** The people or organisms studied in psychological research.

**Sublimation** A mechanism of ego-defense according to Sigmund Freud. The person harnesses libidinal energy (sexual desire, usually) into channels that produce socially valuable works of music, art, or literature. This defense mechanism may not exist, according to critics who point to great artists who had no problems fully expressing such desires.

**Subliminal perception** The perception (by the subconscious mind) of stimuli that are too faint or too well-hidden to be perceived by ordinary sensory perception. The existence of this phenomenon is a matter of controversy.

**Subliminal psychodynamic activation** The attempt to stimulate fantasy in the processes of the unconscious mind by providing related subliminal stimulus information.

**Submersion** A term used to define an educational placement for a bilingual student in a totally English-speaking classroom with native English-speaking students. No special language assistance is made available to the non-English-speaking student. It is a "sink-or-swim" approach. This approach has been judged to be illegal as a result of the *Lau v. Nichols* Supreme Court decision. SEE: *total immersion*

**Substance abuse** Refers to the improper and unhealthy use of drugs and alcohol. The use is of such proportion that its effects become detrimental to the emotional and/or physical well-being of the individual. Both legal and illegal drugs can be abused.

**Substance p** A neurotransmitter associated with pain sensations.

**Substantia nigra** One of the midbrain's basal ganglia. The cell bodies are naturally stained with melanin, the substance that tans the skin in the heat of summer. The axons from these cells run to the caudate nucleus and putamen (two of the forebrain basal ganglia), releasing the neurotransmitter dopamine. A failure of this system leads to the development of Parkinson's disease.

**Substantially separate classroom/ program** SEE: *self-contained programs, special class*

**Substitution** A condition that occurs when one sound is substituted for the correct sound or word such as "wip" for "rip" and "tan" for "can."

**Subtest** A set of items on a test that are scored as a group, although they are only a part of a larger instrument. For example, Arithmetic, Picture Arrangement, and Comprehension are three subtests of the Wechsler scales of intelligence.

**Successful schools** Research has shown that there are variables that can be identified in effective or successful schools. These include but are not limited to a community spirit where classrooms can be considered communities of learners; an emphasis on basic skills in reading, writing, and mathematics; strong leadership that is shared with administrators, teachers, parents, students, and other staff; high expectations for all students and teachers; an emphasis on professional development and teacher-learners who are reflective; ongoing assessment/evaluation schoolwide; a sense of purpose/formulation and constant evaluation of school goals/objectives; collegiality among and between professionals/parents/teachers/students; an orderly and safe school environment; and one in which resources are available to provide an optimal learning experience.

**Suffix** A letter or group of letters added to the end of a word, the "root" word, in order to change its meaning. For example, "ize" after the word "natural" produces a new word, "naturalize," which differs in meaning from "natural." SEE: *affix, prefix, root*

**Suicide**   The deliberate act of taking one's life. Suicide is considered the leading cause of death among youth ages 15 to 24 years of age. There are several precipitating events that can cause young people to take their lives: depression, serious conflict in the home, the divorce of parents, the death of a loved one, abuse, rejection by peers, poor performance in school, the breakup of a relationship, drugs, or any combination of the above. School/outside counseling has been found to be effective in working with suicidal students.

**Sum of squares**   In an equation, the sum of each score squared. In statistical work, the sum of the squared mean-deviation (i.e., score minus the mean) scores in a distribution. SEE: *standard deviation*

**Summative assessment**   Assessment performed at the end of a term of instruction to evaluate a pupil's total learning of a subject matter and arrive at a grade. This is the opposite of a formative assessment. SEE: *assessment, formative assessment, instructional assessment*

**Superego**   One of three classes of psychic functions, according to psychoanalytic theory. It is the part of the psyche that deals with the individual's social adjustment. The superego includes the conscience, which is the set of learned inhibitions concerning behaviors prohibited by the individual's society, and the ego ideal, which is the set of behaviors the individual is encouraged to practice, usually because they are actions of admired role models. The superego, according to Freud, is the source of one's ethics and morals, one's capacity for self-criticism, and conformity to community standards. When actions conform to the ego-ideal, the superego provides the rewards of satisfaction and contentment. When one behaves in ways that are prohibited by the conscience, the superego is the source of guilt, shame, and anxiety. SEE: *ego, id*

**Superior colliculus**   A structure located in the tectum, the roof of the midbrain. The superior colliculus is involved in some eye muscle reflexes and blindsight. Blindsight is the ability to tell where a particular visual object is while consciously unaware that one is seeing anything.

**Superphone**   An electronic device designed for use by deaf persons to communicate with hearing persons who have a push-button phone. The deaf person types messages on a keyboard and this is translated to a voice message for the push-button phone user. The hearing person then answers by typing on the phone keys, which appears as a message on the deaf person's special typewriter.

**Superstitious behavior**   Behavior that occurs because an accidental relationship was established between a response and either a reinforcement or a punishment. For example, if something unpleasant happens to someone right after he or she has seen a black cat, that person will proclaim to everyone else that having a black cat cross your path means bad luck.

**Supination B**   A term used in physical therapy to explain the movement of the hand in which the palm is turned upward or the movement of the arch of the foot into a raised (upward) position.

**Supported competitive employment**   A place of employment where individuals with disabilities or mental retardation can earn at least minimum wages with the support of others (e.g., job coach) who help the individual to satisfactorily function in the job.

**Supported employment**   Ways to integrate individuals with special needs into a competitive job environment by using support systems (e.g., job coach) to help the individual function on the job.

**Supported Living Arrangement (SLA)**   SEE: *semi-independent apartment or home*

**Supportive personnel**   Especially trained persons or teacher who provide support and assistance to regular classroom teachers by direct support in class from special educators and/or specialists. Such personnel usually have additional expertise in the areas of teaching methods, approaches, and systems as well as expertise in how to adopt curriculum for more effective teaching of students in need.

**Supportive services**   Those special services provided to a student in need of assistance correction and/or remediation. Such services may be delivered to both regular day and/or special needs students. They include but are not limited to such areas as learning disability instruction, occupational therapy, physical therapy, speech and language therapy, adaptive physical education, and the like.

**Surface aspects of language**   Basic language skills such as word pronunciation, grammar usage, and vocabulary acquisition.

**Surface structure**   The arrangement of verbal information according to grammatical rules. SEE: *deep structure*

**Surrogate parent**   A legally responsible person or guardian who acts on behalf of a child as a parent. Usually assigned by state or federal law (P.L. 94-142) to represent a parent when the natural or legal parent is unknown, unavailable, or incapable of performing parental duties. SEE: *P.L. 94-142*

**Survey method**   A research method in the social sciences. A large group of people are asked the same questions and the answers are described statistically. Practical means for gathering data surveys, including personal interviews, telephone surveys, and mail surveys, each of which has its own set of advantages and disadvantages.

**Survival skills**   Basic skills that are required to live in one's society today. Sometimes these skills are referred to as "life skills."

**Suspension**   The temporary exclusion of a student from the school setting usually from 1–10 days because of a school infraction(s).

**Sustained attention**   The maintenance of attention on a given source of stimulation for a time long enough to provide for the perceptual processing and retention of the stimuli.

**Sustained Quiet Uninterrupted Individualized Reading Time (SQUIRT)**   In language arts, a method that allows students to read independently and silently over a period of time as determined by the teacher. SEE: *Uninterrupted Sustained Silent Reading (USSR), Drop Everything and Read (DEAR), Detective Q. Squirt*

**Sustained Silent Reading (SSR)**   In language arts, a method that allows students to read silently for long periods of time, thus freeing up the teacher to assist others on an individual or group basis. Students are taught and realize they are expected to be able to read silently and value silent reading for extended periods of time. SEE: *Uninterrupted Sustained Silent Reading (USSR), Drop Everything and Read (DEAR)*

**Sustaining expectation effect**   The stabilizing of student performance at a given level as the result of the teacher's failure to observe any evidence of improvement.

**SWAT**   SEE: *School-Wide Assistance Team*

**Sweep test**   An audiometric screening test that detects loss of hearing. SEE: *audiometer*

**Syllable**   Syllables are the smallest units of speech that can be spoken in isolation. Every syllable contains a vowel sound. Syllables are composed of two distinct parts—the "onset" and the "rime." SEE: *onset, rime*

**Syllogism**   A type of deductive reasoning that has major and minor premises and a conclusion. Aristotle introduced this type of logic and rules, which lead the individual to a logical conclusion. Example: major premise—all people can share good will; minor premise—my sister and brother are people; conclusion—therefore my sister and brother can share good will.

**Symbolic interaction theory**   A social theory based on interaction between persons. This interaction gives meaning to situations and things. For example, a person has intelligence because others believe that she/he is intelligent. Thus, constructs are socially created.

**S**

279

**Symbolic racism**  The tending of the media in the 1980s and 1990s to report extensively on certain social problems of some African Americans such as crime, drugs, and long-term dependence on the social-welfare system. The media do provide a balanced view of the large numbers of African Americans who do not have such problems.

**Sympathetic nervous system (SNS)**  That division of the autonomic nervous system that is responsible for our "fight-or-flight" emergency reactions, as well as those associated with emotional expressions such as fear and anger responses.

**Symptom severity**  A standard of classification that alludes to the degree from the norm (average) the symptom deviates.

**Symptomatic epilepsy**  Also known as acquired epilepsy, this is a condition characterized by convulsions as a result of brain damage caused by such things as drug or alcohol intoxication, encephalitis, trauma, tumors, or other pathologies.

**Synapse**  The point of junction between two neurons through which transmission of nerve impulses takes place. In this neural pathway, the axon terminal of one neuron is in close proximity to the dendrites of another. The impulses travel in one direction from the first neuron to the second, and so on.

**Synaptic cleft**  The narrow space between the axon terminal of a sending neuron and the membrane of a receiving neuron. Often, the axon terminal is a swelling, shaped like a knob or bulb. In that case, the receiving membrane seems to form a pocket around the knob, as if a cleft had been chipped out of the membrane. These sending and receiving membranes are between 200 and 300 Angstrom units apart.

**Syndrome**  Symptoms characterized by certain patterns, collections, or groupings that are usually found in specific diseases or disabilities.

**Syndrome description**  A standard of classification that often describes special needs or special education disorders in technical language or medical terms.

**Synophrys**  Eyebrows that tend to grow together or meet.

**Syntax**  The grammar of our language that involves combining words to form sentences and paragraphs. In effect, syntax contributes to how we determine the meaning of our words and sentences.

**Synthetic speech**  The combination of sounds into phonemes and words to produce speech by means of a computer; usually resulting in (an) artificially produced speech sound(s); sometimes the sound produced is stunted and tinny in nature.

**Synthetic touch**  Pertains to the touching or feeling of an object; that is, synthetic touch involves the tactile handling and experience or the information one receives as a result. The object may be held in one or both hands and is usually of a size to be so handled (i.e., hand-held).

**Synthisophy**  The integration of socially pertinent information derived from the study of history into present culture.

**Syphilis**  A venereal disease caused by direct contact between persons usually as a result of sexual intercourse. The spirochete treponema pallidum enters through broken skin or mucous membrane. In the primary stage (two to four weeks), a lesion (papule to small ulcer to chancre) appears on the prepuce or vulva. In the secondary stage (six weeks after the primary lesion appears), an eruption of the skin involving a rash (reddish brown spots) appears; this stage may also include headache, malaise, and fever. In the tertiary stage, the heart, blood vessels, and the central nervous system are affected. Laboratory tests are available to diagnose this condition. The antibiotic treatment of choice is penicillin. SEE: *venereal disease (VD)*

**System of Multicultural Pluralistic Assessment (SOMPA)**  A special assessment developed in 1977 by J. Mercer and J. F. Lewis to help identify gifted minority children. It uses traditional measures of intelligence but weighs the results according to social and family characteristics. One of the purposes of such a test is to prevent the frequent test bias of using "white-middle-class standards" to norm the test.

**Systematic desensitization**   A technique devised by Joseph Wolpe that uses classical conditioning to free individuals from their phobias. The phobia-causing stimulus is introduced at a safe distance, posing no threat. When the individual is relaxed, the stimulus is presented at a shorter distance, which now seems safe to the patient. The condition of least threat is called the "bottom of the fear hierarchy." Gradually, the individual is worked up the hierarchy. Ultimately, the individual can even come into contact with the once-feared object.

**Systemic**   Relating to and affecting the entire body; a body-wide system.

**Systemic sign language**   An English system of manual signing for the deaf. SEE: *American Sign Language (ASL)*

**Systems analysis**   A systematic approach to analyzing educational objectives, making decisions about how to efficiently reach those objectives, and what resources and methods will work best in that pursuit. Steps are carefully measured, tested, and controlled to ensure the step-to-step process. The idea is to proceed efficiently from objective to objective in a scientific manner.

**T score**   A standard score obtained from a z score by multiplying the z score times 10 and adding 50. The mean $T = 50$ and the standard deviation of the T scores = 10.

**t test**   A statistical test that provides an estimation of the probability that the differences between the means of two groups (remember $\underline{t}$ test use by the mnemonic "tea for two") are likely to be the result of chance. The use of $\underline{t}$ tests is important when comparing: 1. mean values between an experimental and control group in a study (e.g., an experimental group is given instruction in the writing process and a control group of students is given no instruction); 2. pre- and post-test comparisons of mean scores for one group of individuals or subjects (e.g., math achievement scores of first graders are compared at the beginning of the school year and then at the end of the school year); and 3. the comparison of mean values/scores between two groups of subjects's (e.g., comparing males to females; individuals with disabilities to those without disabilities, third graders to fourth graders; etc.

**Tabula rasa**   The conceptualization of John Locke that our minds are "blank slates" upon which experience writes. This philosophical position posits that our experiences are the primary source of knowledge.

**Tachistoscope**   A reading machine that displays for a fraction of a second or a short period of time a certain amount of visual material. The idea being that with training one will be able to visualize or read what is displayed more rapidly and with accuracy.

**Tachylalia**   A condition characterized by extremely rapid speech. Speech is delivered in an extremely rapid fashion.

**Tactile**   1. Pertaining to or referring to the sense of touch. 2. Part of a multisensory method used to teach students to speak/read. Students are taught to associate cues of a tactile-visual-auditory nature in building a foundation of sound/speech/reading.

**Tactile perception**   Interpreting and critically evaluating sensory stimuli through the sense of touch.

**Tactual vocoder**   A machine or device that changes sound into vibrations.

**TAI**   SEE: *Team-Assisted Individualization*

**Talent**   Special abilities or aptitudes in specialized areas such as art, music, sports, crafts, etc. It is thought that all of us have some special talent(s) or skill(s) that can be developed. A special ability or aptitude is sometimes used synonymously with gift. SEE: *gifted, talented*

**Talented**   A term used to describe a student with some special ability, highly developed skill, or aptitude. The individual may not necessarily possess a superior intellect (high IQ) as in the case of a gifted person. Examples of talented persons could be a professional baseball player with average intelligence, a woodcarver with an average IQ, and a juggler with normal intellectual abilities. SEE: *gifted, Intelligence Quotient (IQ)*

**Talipes** (talus = ankle, pes = foot, [ankle foot])   More commonly called clubfoot. SEE: *clubfoot*

**Talking books**   Books that have been recorded in an auditory format. Such audio aids permit the visually impaired and the blind to listen to written materials. Talking books have been available through the Library of Congress since the mid-1930s, but one can find such material available in local libraries and bookstores. The audio format includes vinyl disc records, cassette tapes, and compact discs (CDs).

**Talking programs**   Programs that are designed to use digitized speech from a disk by means of the software on the computer.

**Tardive dyskinesia**   A motor disorder resulting from neuromuscular malfunctioning, it is the outcome of many years of using an antipsychotic drug. Tardive dyskinesia strongly resembles the natural neuromuscular disorder Parkinson's disease.

**Target behaviors**   A term used in behavior modification which identifies that behavior we wish to change, add, or eliminate; in effect, target for action (thus the term).

**Target effects**   The intended effects of a therapy, such as a drug. They are to be contrasted with side effects. SEE: *side effects*

**Task analysis**   The breakdown of a particular learning skill or lesson into smaller units of ability or content.

**Task-involved learners**   Students whose motivation is concentrated on the solution of a problem or the mastery of a task.

**Taste**   One of the chemical senses. The receptors for taste are found on the tongue as well as on the linings of the oral cavity. In humans, there are four elementary tastes; namely, sweet, salty, sour, and bitter. Taste buds, the receptors for this sense, are found on the papillae, the small vertical structures on the tongue. Flavor results from a combination of smell and taste sensations.

**Taste aversion**   A learned tendency to avoid foods with a particular flavor. This may be a result of an association between experiencing the flavor and having an internal illness (e.g., an upset stomach) after that experience; the unconditioned stimulus (US) (the illness) may occur hours after the conditioned stimulus (CS) (the flavor experience). This illustrates the principle of biological preparedness for particular kinds of CS-US pairings.

**Taste-aversion learning**   This is a type of one-trial learning first described by Garcia in which an organism will avoid a food associated previously with becoming ill, even if several hours intervene between the eating and the illness.

**TAT**   SEE: *Thematic Appreciation Test*

**Taxonomies**   A classification of thinking or learning levels. Benjamin Bloom organized levels of thinking in hierarchial fashion. Generally, those in the education field incorporate 1. cognitive objectives (develop critical thinking/intellectual capabilities); 2. affective objectives (address alues/interests/attitudes/opinions); and 3. psychomotor objectives (fine and gross motor skills) when developing educational taxonomies. SEE: *taxonomy*

**Taxonomy**   A system for the classification of varieties of a phenomenon. For example, biologists use a taxonomy of animal species. In the study of learning disabilities, researchers are endeavoring to achieve an agreed-on taxonomy of types of learning disabilities.

**Tay-Sachs disease**   (named for Warren Tay, English physician, 1843–1927, and Bernard Sachs, American neurologist, 1858–1944). A disease characterized by symptoms that include muscular deterioration, spasticity, and convulsions as well as mental and physical retardation and hand enlargement. It is an inherited disease involving a specific enzyme defect; namely, the absence of "hexosaminidase A," which is important in metabolizing certain lipids (fats). In Tay-Sachs disease, lipids accumulate especially within nerves and the brain, thus causing neurological deterioration. Death usually occurs within the first 18 months. This disease is especially prevalent amongst Jewish children (especially Ashkenazi Jews) at the rate of 100 times that of others. SEE: *lipid*

***Taylor v. Board of Education***   (New Rochelle, New York)   The 1961 federal district court ruling that outlawed attendance lines set by school districts if these lines result in de facto segregation. SEE: *de facto segregation*

**TDD**   SEE: *Telecommunication Device for the Deaf, TTY*

**Teachable moment**   That particular moment or point in class time when all conditions are just right to explain a concept, thought, or idea. A there-and-then opportunity to teach students and/or to make a point.

**Teacher Assistance Teams (TATs)**   SEE: *School-Wide Assistance Team (SWAT)*

**Teacher center**   In effect, a resource area for teachers rich in educational materials and supplies. It is a combination workshop, laboratory, and library.

**Teacher centered**   In language arts and education in general, instruction to students that is planned, prepared, and presented by the teacher with little or no student input.

**Teacher certification**   A certificate indicating endorsement of a state board of education as to the worthiness of a teacher candidate. This endorsement is based upon successful participation in four-year college teacher preparatory programs that have been properly accredited by the same state board of education. Individuals are granted certificates based on different levels (i.e., early childhood (pre k–3), elementary (1–6 or 1–8), middle (5–8), secondary (9–12), etc.) and areas of interest (i.e., early childhood [major focus on early childhood regular and special needs], elementary [minor in mathematics], moderate special needs, severe special needs, secondary English, middle school [minor in Social Studies], etc.). Most states have reciprocal certification programs for approved college sites. This means one can travel to another state and apply to that state for certification with very few and sometimes no additional requirements needed to be certified. Some of these additional requirements (which vary from state to state) include competency testing, National Teacher Exams (NTEs), a course in the state's history, U.S. history, etc. A prospective teacher is advised to seek an application from the state's department of education for certification purposes (usually housed somewhere in the state's capital). Most states require that teachers be competent in the following areas before certificates are issued: subject-area knowledge, communica-

T

tions, equity, assessment, instructional methods, and problem solving. Most states also require prepracticum field work and a practicum (also called student teaching) in a school site that could also be an internship or clinical experience. Many states now require a two-step process before final and full certification is issued. First, a provisional certificate is issued with a permanent certificate most often given after completion of a master's program, an additional practicum, and on-site supervised teaching experience. SEE: *prepracticums, internship, clinical experience, practicums, student teaching*

**Teacher contracts**   An agreement or a document that spells out the terms of employment and compensation for teachers. School committees or boards of education have the legal authority to enter into such agreements with teachers or their unions or associations.

**Teacher effectiveness**   Those conditions and activities that have a high rate of success in the teaching and learning process. For example, effective teachers have been found to be caring, empathic, and concerned with the learner as a person and attentive to the social/emotional/academic/physical well being of all students; sensitive to individual needs, learning styles, attitudes, aptitudes, and motivations of students both collectively and individually; competent in their field of knowledge; facilitating the development of strong oral and written communication skills; fair and equitable with all learners with high expectations and standards apparent for all; flexible, energetic, and enthusiastic about teaching with a passion for their chosen profession; possessing a good sense of humor; using a variety of materials, methods, and strategies in the various subject areas; using multiple measures of assessment of student learning; creating and nurturing strong parent-community-professional partnerships/resources; committed to reflective teaching practices and the notion that teachers are life-long learners; student-oriented with attention focused on scaffolding the learning process and encouraging students to become independent learners who are able to construct meaning from learning situations.

**Teacher empowerment**   A movement to provide teachers with the opportunity to actively participate in decision-making activities in order to help determine the nature of the educational system in which they are employed (e.g., participate in decisions regarding textbook adoptions, the hiring of new teachers, discipline procedures/codes, etc.).

**Teacher induction**   A process of orienting new teachers to a system, a new program, or field of study. This can include "hotlines" for teachers with colleges and universities and ongoing visitations to other school systems that are running programs in the new fields in which the teacher is about to embark.

**Teacher journal**   1. In education, an interactive journal or log kept by a teacher and shared with the students. Students are allowed to read the teacher's journal and respond and react to its content. In turn, students keep their own journal to which the teacher may react. 2. A type of recordkeeping that is not shared with students, wherein the teacher logs important observations and the like for academic, social, legal, and/or school or district purposes.

**Teacher power**   The embodiment of single teacher power in the form of organized teacher groups. These groups or organizations push (lobby) for improvements in education both for the teachers and the students.

**Teacher preparation programs**   Colleges with two- to four-year programs that are involved in preparing individuals for a four-year teacher certificate program. A student from a two-year program usually transfers into a four-year college that will subsequently confer the degree and stamp the college's transcripts to indicate fulfillment of state teaching certification standards. Many states now require a four-year baccalaureate program for initial or provisional certification, with a fifth year master's degree for full or permanent certification.

**Teacher ratings** Evaluations by teachers of student ability or achievement on each of several variables.

**Teacher resource model** A system which requires a skilled and trained consultant who prepares and trains certain chosen regular day and special educators to serve as a teacher resource team. This involves regular class teachers who have special education and/or at risk students in class.

**Teacher role** Generally, the duties and behaviors that are expected of a teacher.

**Teacher self-concept** In effect, how teachers see themselves and the roles they have as part of the profession of education.

**Teacher stress** Sometimes referred to as teacher "burnout," it is an all-too-common condition of stress as a result of the many pressures teachers experience on a day-to-day basis in their teaching positions. Stress if handled improperly may lead to teacher ineffectiveness, incompetence, and failure (burnout).

**Teacher supply and demand** The need for teachers based on a comparison of projected teachers available vs. the projected number of students. Fields of study by teachers vs. students projected for that field of study are also factors to be considered.

**Teacher's aide** A paraprofessional teacher's assistant who is not required to be certified. An aide generally assumes such duties as tutorial instruction, library work, noninstructional supervision, correcting of papers, and other nonprofessional duties (e.g., bus monitoring). The aide usually receives instructional directions and materials from the teacher. Teachers are most often required to be readily accessible for questions and directions.

**Teaching assistants** Trained personnel who assist teachers with their instructional duties. Teaching assistants are usually paraprofessional persons but sometimes are professional. Such persons support the teacher in the educational setting.

**Teaching efficacy** The teacher's confidence in her/his own ability to reach and to educate even the most difficult students.

**Teaching for exposure** A term used to describe the teaching of a subject, concept, idea and the like in a very general or broad sense. Topics are not covered in depth but are merely presented in a surface content manner.

**Teaching styles** Various teaching methods or approaches regarding teaching and learning as well as management of the classroom. Different teaching styles are usually based on different psychologies and philosophies of teaching held by the teacher himself/herself. Examples: Some teachers prefer to lecture to students while others use a coaching approach to learning, or peer tutoring/cooperative learning, combinations of the aforementioned, and so on. Team teaching or cooperative teaching is another example of teaching style. SEE: *quality of teaching, effective teachers, effective schools*

**Team-Assisted Individualization (TAI)** A cooperative teaching/learning instructional technique based on individual diagnosis of learning strengths and weaknesses. SEE: *collaborative teaching, team teaching*

**Team leader** The professional who runs and coordinates the meeting of an educational team of teachers or who heads up the group of professionals and/or paraprofessionals. The team leader is the person in charge of the project, meeting, group, assembly, council, curriculum team, etc.

**Team rewards** A term which indicates the granting of recognition in the form of reinforcers, prizes, or other awards which are based on the combined output of individual members of a group or team. In this case, awards are not based on team competition with other groups or teams but are contingent on the combined effort within the team.

**Team teaching** A type of teaching that involves teachers working in teams. Generally a team leader is chosen who networks and assists the team in determining which classes are individually taught and which are shared. Teachers also agree to a division of duties and classes. SEE: *collaborative instruction, collaborative teaching, Team-Assisted Individualization (TAI), team leader*

**Teams-Games Tournaments (TGT)** A cooperative learning method in which teams of students are established. After learning cooperatively within his/her team, a student must meet someone from another team in a tournament game format, trying to win points for his/her own team. SEE: *cooperative learning*

**Techniques of daily living** SEE: *daily living skills*

**Technologically dependent** A term synonymous with "medically fragile." SEE: *medically fragile*

**Technologically dependent children** Children who depend on high technology devices to maintain health and life. Such medically fragile children may use insulin pumps as in the case of students with diabetes, ventilators with children who experience breathing difficulties, etc. SEE: *medically fragile, ventilator.*

**Technology literacy** SEE: *Appendix 4: Computer terms*

**Technophobia** A phobia or fear of technology. These individuals fear using computers or word processors and other technological devices.

**Tectum** The roof of the midbrain, containing the inferior and the superior colliculi. SEE: *superior colliculus*

**Tegmentum** The middle level of the midbrain containing the nuclei of the third and fourth cranial nerves, the ventral tegmental area, the red nucleus, the substantia nigra, the periaqueductal gray matter, and the ascending reticular arousal system.

**Telecommunication Device for the Deaf (TDD)** Sometimes referred to as TTY (Teletypewriter). A special device that permits deaf persons to communicate on the telephone by typing messages. Typed messages are transformed into electrical signals which are then retranslated into print on a monitor screen at the other end of the line.

**Telecommunications network** A computer-based system that allows students, teachers, and research scientists to communicate with one another using a variety of electronic devices. The system is referred to as CISCONET. Individuals can access and send information over the network.

**Telegraphic speech** Young children, when learning to speak, may use the nouns and verbs but omit prepositions, conjunctions, and articles.

**Teleology** The theoretical position that purports that our behaviors are guided by a spiritual mind that acts on a concrete, materialistic brain.

**Teletext** An electronic system that presents information on a television screen. The user can access this at any time but it requires a decoder and keypad for information retrieval.

**Teletypewriter (TTY)** A communication device that is connected to a telephone with an adapter. This device allows individuals with hearing impairments to communicate with those who are not hearing impaired. SEE: *Telecommunication Device for the Deaf (TDD)*

**Temperament** The combined tendency or characteristics of a person in relation to one's emotions, intelligence, mood, disposition, ethics, and physical and mental reaction to one's environment.

**Temporal lobes** The lobes of the brain that contain auditory reception and some visual processing areas. Damage to these lobes can affect auditory or visual memory storage, sound discrimination, and voice recognition. In the posterior part of the uppermost (superior) temporal gyrus is located Wernicke's area for the recognition of speech sounds. Wernicke's area is included within the primary auditory projection area, areas 41 and 42. The middle temporal gyrus is involved in the perception of visually seen motion. The lowermost (inferior) temporal gyrus is involved in facial recognition; damage to it causes prosopagnosia. SEE: *prosopagnosia*

**Tenure**   An educational employment system that involves having educators serve three to five probationary years (usually) before granted lifetime job security. After an educator achieves tenure status, he/she cannot be fired unless legally removed for serious infractions related to job performance or moral turpitude.

**Teratogens**   Factors that interfere with normal fetal development by causing birth defects or deformities (e.g., cocaine has been known to cause cognitive and motor abnormalities that are permanent).

**Terminal buttons**   Also called end bulbs or synaptic knobs. The tips of the end-brush at the end of the axon are swelled up, giving the appearance of knobs or buttons. These contain vesicles in which are stored the chemical neurotransmitters of the axon. These chemicals are released after a nerve impulse has traveled down the axon. SEE: *synapse*

**Territoriality**   A drive that involves defending one's property or space. SEE: *drive*

**Test**   1. A method for collecting data. 2. In the broadest use, any assessment measure, method, or instrument. 3. In the more traditional sense, a particular set of printed questions (or set of detailed procedures) for sampling a student's performance. The test results form the basis for generalized descriptions of how the student is expected to perform in other situations involving similar behaviors to that sampled on the test. Tests can assess performance in a number of areas, to include intelligence, aptitude, behavioral functioning, social skills, feelings, personality types, etc.

**Test anxiety**   A condition displayed by a student or individual characterized by an uneasiness of mind, an apprehension, and/or a fear of an impending or anticipated test to be taken.

**Test battery**   A group of tests, each dealing with a different content area. All the tests comprising the battery have been standardized on the same sample of subjects (i.e., the standardization group). All the tests of the battery are to be administered to the same subjects.

**Test bias**   Tests or testing results/data that are in fact inaccurate or unfair to certain groups or individuals not because of a lack of ability but because of circumstances related to one's cultural background, race, gender, ethnicity, etc.

**Test form**   A version of a test. The test may be prepared at different difficulty levels so that different grades may each be given an appropriate version of the test. A test form is not identical with a test level; one form of a test should be the equivalent of another form. This permits the calculation of parallel forms of reliability, which is the correlation between the students' scores on one form of the test with their scores on another form of the test.

**Test manual**   That manual or set of directions provided for the test administrator in order to properly give a test, score a test, and evaluate a test, so as to provide proper validity and reliability of test results.

**Test norms**   SEE: *norms*

**Test-retest reliability**   The measure of reliability between the scores of the same individual in the same test given at two different intervals. Typically, 6- to 12-month intervals are recommended between test administrations. SEE: *reliability, correlation*

**Testis**   The male gonad. It releases the androgens such as testosterone in response to the pituitary hormone LH. The testis forms the sperm cells, the male reproductive cells or gametes, in response to the pituitary hormone FSH.

**Testosterone**   The main male hormone. It is a steroid and is produced by the testes when they are affected by the pituitary Luteinizing Hormone (LH).

**Text difficulty assessment**   Evaluating a student's understanding of textbook materials. Teacher-made inventories, standardized tests, etc. can be administered in group or individual formats.

**T**

Text-difficulty assessment involves evaluating both the literal and inferential comprehension of students and can involve measuring word reading/comprehension rates.

**Text frames**   The key questions and categories of information that correspond to some type of text pattern and subject area (e.g., chronology of U.S. history from 1812 to the present).

**Text pattern guides**   A written representation (often graphic) of the text organization/content of a book where a predominant pattern is evident (e.g., cause-and-effect text pattern guide, sequential text pattern guide, contrast/comparison text pattern guide, etc.). Text pattern guides allow students to readily make relationships among ideas/constructs and are useful study guides. SEE: *text patterns*

**Text patterns**   A type of organization used to summarize, outline, or describe a text. There are numerous text patterns created to organize the ideas in a particular book: series-of-events, problem-solution, comparison-contrast, cause-and-effect, etc. Text patterns are frequently illustrated in the form of an outline, network tree, concept web, matrix, Venn-Diagram, etc. SEE: *text pattern guides*

**Text structure**   1. The organization of a book. 2. In language arts, a term used to describe how books, texts, and other reading materials are organized in order to deliver different and/or certain messages to the reader. There are two common types of text structure: (a) narrative text, which is usually written in a sequential time-ordered manner, and (b) expository text, which shows cause-and-effect relationships such as problems/solutions and comparison/contrasts.

**Textbooks**   SEE: *texts*

**Texts**   Books typically used in content area subjects such as social studies, science, etc. One of the primary roles of the content area teacher is to assist students in effectively interacting with text materials. Text organizers, pattern guides,

and other strategies (e.g., using marginal glosses) assist students in handling the subject matter of the text.

**TGT**   SEE: *Teams-Games Tournaments*

**Thalamus**   The main part of the diencephalon or "between-brain." In the thalamus are found many of the sensory relay nuclei; examples of these are the nuclei related to hearing, vision, and the general body senses. It is shaped like a pillow or a football.

**Thalassemia**   In effect, an inherited anemia characterized by red blood cells that are abnormally thin. The earlier the disease appears in children, the more unfavorable the outcome. It is sometimes referred to as Cooley's anemia. In thalassemia major (characterized by severe anemia, enlarged heart, jaundice, etc.), death usually occurs in the teens or early 20s from anemia or heart failure. In thalassemia minor the prognosis is excellent. The prevalence of this disease is related to ethnic origin; it is found to occur more often among Southeast Asians and people bordering the Mediterranean such as Italians, for example.

**Thalidomide**   A drug used as a sleeping pill in Europe during the 1960s. It was banned by the U.S. watchdog agency, the FDA. Women who took the drug in early pregnancy were discovered to give birth to children with such congenital deformities as phocomelia. SEE: *phocomelia*

**Thanatos**   According to Freud, the death instinct that pushes people toward destructive and aggressive behaviors. Also, this is another term for death.

**Theism**   SEE: *monotheism*

**Thematic Apperception Test (TAT)**   A projective test that involves a series of black and white pictures containing one or more persons in ambiguous situations. Subjects are asked what led up to the situation, what will happen in the future, and what are the people depicted thinking about. Conflict resolution is also probed. This test, like all projectives, is subjectively scored and results must be viewed with caution. However, thought patterns and emotional states can be assessed giving insights into personality profiles and problems. SEE: *projective test*

**Thematic units** Sets of lesson presentations that organize classroom instruction around certain texts, activities, and learning episodes related to a topic(s). A thematic unit might integrate several content areas (e.g., teaching a unit on the solar system across the curriculum; math = calculating distances of the planets from the sun; science = analyzing the composition of the surface of various planets; art = making models of the planets; social studies = studying how countries cooperatively establish space stations; literature = reading and discussing a science fiction book related to the topics at hand; music = learning how to do the "moon walk" to music; etc.).

**Theoretical construct** A model or concept based on theory (i.e., an organized body of knowledge) rather than on practical or experiential knowledge.

**Theory** A logically coherent set of principles offered to explain observed data and to predict the outcome of further observations.

**Theory of cognitive dissonance** Leon Festinger's theory of attitude change. The incentive to change attitude is based on a discrepancy between what one believes to be true and one's own behavior, an incompatibility between two of one's beliefs, or the failure of a prediction based on a belief to come true. The state of dissonance is a tension that is similar to a motive such as hunger. The dissonance can be relieved either by changing what one believes or by changing one's behavior.

**Theory of learned helplessness** Martin Seligman's theory of ineffectual behavior. An organism may have had the experience that no attempt to escape from an aversive stimulus will succeed. After having reconfirmed this point enough times, the individual stops trying, even when a way out is available and is easy to find. Seligman has suggested that depression may be the result of this type of learning.

**Theory of misapplied constancy** A theory offered to explain some geometric visual illusions. Converging or diverging lines are cues used in judging depth by linear perspective. Even when the lines are in an abstract drawing this depth judgment may be made, although not appropriately. This may lead to errors in the judgments of the sizes of objects in such pictures or to a failure to find the correct continuation of an interrupted line.

**Theory of multiple intelligence** Howard Gardner's theory that intelligence is not a single, general talent but that there are eight varieties of intelligence: 1. language ability, 2. logical/mathematical reasoning, 3. spatial judgment, 4. kinesthetic judgment, 5. musical thinking, 6. intra-individual reasoning, 7. interpersonal thinking, and 8. naturalistic awareness.

**Therapeutic abortion** A term that refers to a medical action or procedure taken after the discovery of a defect in the unborn fetus after prenatal testing and evaluation.

**Therapist** A professional person with special training and licensing who delivers services or treatment to an individual with a temporary or permanent disability or disease (e.g., physical therapist, inhalation therapist, therapeutic counselor, etc.).

**Think-alouds** A reading strategy that involves thinking aloud and verbalizing one's thought processes during reading. This helps readers to self-monitor and self-regulate comprehension of text. Think-alouds should involve having the reader develop hypotheses or predictions that are then either confirmed or disconfirmed after further reading/rereading. Think-alouds that allow the reader to think about or visualize what is being read. Teachers need to model think-aloud strategies (e.g., how to question oneself so that one is linking new information with prior knowledge).

**Thinking** The mental manipulation of images of physical objects or of abstract symbols in order to arrive at a conclusive decision. Problem-solving,

**T**

concept-formation, and decision-making are all examples of thinking.

**Thyroid**   An endocrine gland located in the area of the pharynx (base of the neck) that secretes thyroxine, a hormone. This hormone regulates metabolism and influences the growth and development of a child.

**Thyroid hormones** (including thyroxine)   These hormones from the thyroid gland increase the metabolic rate, generating increased body heat. The synthesis of thyroid hormones requires iodine.

**Tic**   An involuntary and spasmodic muscular contraction. Frequently tics involve the head, face, neck, and shoulder muscles. A transient tic usually occurs as a result of undue stress and usually disappears when the stress is removed or reduced. Chronic tics differ from transient tics; they usually involve other factors and may continue for long periods of time.

**Tic disorders**   A term used to describe involuntary, rapid, and recurring vocalizations and movements that are stereotypical in nature (i.e., repetitive). SEE: *tic, Tourette's syndrome*

**Timbre**   The pattern of overtones of a voice or sound that are whole numbers of octaves above a basic, or fundamental, frequency. Pure tones from tuning forks or oscillators lack overtones. Every musical instrument, however, has its own characteristic overtone pattern (i.e., timbre), which allows the listener to recognize which instrument is being played.

**Time on task**   The amount of time actively spent working on a given task.

**Time out**   The removal of a student or person from a reinforcing situation for a very short period of time, usually a few minutes or so. For example, removal of a student from the classroom who is about to start fighting or is getting too physical with another student, removal of a child who is throwing a temper tantrum, etc.

**Tinnitus**   A consistent and distracting ringing in the ears.

**Tip-of-the-nose phenomenon**   A partial recognition of a familiar odor. One can tell that the scent is a familiar one, but the exact name of it cannot be retrieved.

**Tip-of-the-tongue experience**   The feeling that one can almost put (a) remembered idea(s) into words, yet, unfortunately, one is unable to retrieve these "remembered" items completely.

**Title 1**   SEE: *Chapter 1 and 2*

**Title 2**   SEE: *Chapter 1 and 2*

**T-lymphocytes**   White blood cells that excite or inhibit immunological responses to invading organisms.

**TMR**   SEE: *Trainable Mentally Retarded*

**Tocology**   The study of the science of giving birth to the young (parturition) and obstetrics. SEE: *obstetrics*

**Token economy**   The use of tokens as secondary reinforcers for students in school or other persons such as inmates of a hospital or penal institution. Good behavior, or the avoidance of forbidden actions, can earn tokens. These tokens may be exchanged for goods, rewards, or for rest periods. This economic system is a useful means of behavior modification. This system when used in classroom situations (e.g., providing homework passes for good behavior or good grades) is very effective.

**Token reinforcement system**   SEE: *token economy*

**Tolerance**   1. One of the criteria for drug addiction. The user requires greater and greater dosages to get the same effects as earlier because the body has begun to neutralize the drug's action. 2. The attitude that people of other societies and cultures are as legitimate as the people of one's own group and are fully deserving of respect and consideration.

**Tonaphasia**   A condition characterized by a serious difficulty or inability to recall or remember a tune as a result of a cerebral lesion.

**Tongue thrust**   A speech difficulty caused by a swallowing pattern whereby the tongue is thrust forward

T

pressing against the teeth or even protruding through the teeth. This condition usually, but not always, creates problems with "s" and "z" sounds.

**Tonic** 1. A condition characterized especially by muscular tension. The term pertains to tension or contraction. 2. A medicine that heals and restores strength. SEE: *tonic phase*

**Tonic/clonic seizures** Also called grand mal seizure. The brief loss of consciousness (up to five minutes) followed by both tonic and clonic muscle contractions of the head, trunk, and limbs. SEE: *tonic, clonic*

**Tonic phase** The second stage of a grand mal seizure, which is a severe form of an epileptic seizure (vs. petit mal). During this stage a person's body becomes very rigid and is subject to strong muscular contractions.

**Top-down** A term which implies that the direction and operation of a program curriculum, school, etc. is controlled by the subordinates (bosses, principals, superintendents, etc.) who send directives down to the faculty for initiation with little and usually no input from the workers on the line, teachers and/or subordinates and the like. It is the opposite of "bottom-up" administration.

**Top-down processing** The idea that perception involves higher mental functions, such as knowledge and interpretation. The context in which an object is seen decides whether recognition will be easy or difficult. If easy, it is because the observer has had prior experience with the object in the present context.

**Top-down philosophy of reading** SEE: *bottom-up philosophy of reading, top-down processing*

**Topical net** In education, a type of graphic organizer wherein the main topic, theme, or idea becomes the basis or the center (hub) for any number of related topics or ideas.

**TORCHS** An acronym used to describe a number of infections and diseases, namely: Toxoplasmosis, Rubella, Cytomegalic-inclusion, Herpes simplex virus, and Syphilis. SEE: *each infection as listed*

**Tort** A legal term for a wrongful action subject to civil suit taken by a person(s) against another person who causes injury or damage to that person or the person's property. It does not include a breach of contract.

**Torticollis** A condition that can be congenital or acquired. The neck muscles affected are those connected to the spinal accessory nerve. The spasmodic contractions of these neck muscles cause a "stiff" neck condition, drawing the head to one side with the chin pointing in the opposite direction. This can cause misalignment of the vertebral joints.

**Tortipelvis** Distortion of the spine and the hip resulting from muscular spasms.

**Total communication** A method used in educating the deaf whereby all methods of communication as concerns language development are used. This would include a mix of methods such as signing, amplification, finger spelling, speech reading, gesturing, reading, writing, and any oral, visual, manual, or other method deemed appropriate.

**Total expenditures per pupil in average daily attendance** This includes the entire school budget and/or all expenditures that are allocable to per pupil costs divided by the average daily attendance figure. Allocable costs include curriculum expenditures, expenditures for noncurriculum programs, interest on school debt, indirect costs, and capital outlay.

**Total immersion** A term used to define an educational placement for a bilingual student who is placed in a class taught entirely in English. In this type of class, there is no specific instruction in the home language as such. This type of program can be contrasted to bilingual immersion. SEE: *bilingual immersion*

**Total inclusion** That educational philosophy that would keep all students with disabilities in the regular classroom, regardless of the severity of their disability.

**Total staff approach** An approach to teaching wherein the entire faculty concentrates on a single theme or topic. This thematic approach requires all teachers to interweave the theme into their class instruction or activity. The total staff approach is for a brief or predetermined period of time but done at an intense level school-wide.

**Total time hypothesis** The view that the amount one learns depends on the total amount of time that one practices with the materials being learned.

**Touch-response screen** A computer screen that allows the user to touch the screen when interacting with various software programs as opposed to using a keyboard. This type of device is particularly helpful for deaf learners. SEE: *Appendix 4: Computer Terms*

**Tourette's syndrome** A neurological condition in which the onset is usually between the ages of 2 and 16. This disease is characterized by involuntary muscular "tics," inappropriate sounds and/or grunting, and the use of improper words (i.e., cursing). The symptoms exhibited are involuntary on the part of the person afflicted with this disease. SEE: *tic*

**Toxemia** An infection throughout the body caused by poisonous bacteria distributed from an infected local site. Such infections complicate childbirth and may cause handicapping conditions or other complications during the birth of a child (e.g., poisonous substances in the blood stream).

**Toxicomania** A condition characterized by an abnormal craving for intoxicants, narcotics, or even poisons.

**Toxin** A poison; its origin could be from an animal, plant, germ, etc. A toxin is usually produced by certain bacteria.

**Toxoplasmosis** An infectious disease caused by the protozoa toxoplasma gondii. This intestinal parasite can cause severe difficulties in the newborn child if it is contracted congenitally (e.g., damage to the central nervous system, anemia, jaundice, etc.).

**Tracheostomy** A medical procedure required as a result of disease, trauma, and/or various medical reasons. An opening (stoma) is made in the throat just under the larynx. A tube is inserted to maintain an opening for respiration. Sometimes a speaking valve is connected to the tracheostomy tube at the stoma. SEE: *stoma, speaking valve*

**Trachitis** A condition in which the trachea is inflamed; inflammation of the trachea.

**Trachoma** A contagious form of conjunctivitis characterized by inflammation of the inner surface of the eyelid. SEE: *conjunctivitis*

**Tracking** The grouping of students according to ability level in homogeneous classes (e.g., high- and low-ability math groups), with all students in a particular track given the same curriculum (e.g., college preparatory work vs. business education).

**Trade books** Non-textbook types of books of a fictional or nonfictional nature that are used to supplement the reading program. Also, any books published for general use rather than instructional use.

**Trainable Mentally Retarded (TMR)** A term not in popular use but sometimes used by educators to identify moderately retarded persons who have poor adaptive behavior as concerns personal independence and social behavior; coupled with an Intelligence Quotient (IQ) between 35–40 to 50–55. These persons are capable of being trained in the very basic academic and vocational skills (such as those required in sheltered workshops), self-care, and social skills areas. SEE: *educable mentally retarded*

**Trait** A tendency to behave in a particular way that is characteristic of an individual. Such a tendency is typical enough to be a recognizable property of that individual's personality. Like traits of physical appearance, some personality traits seem to be inherited.

**Trait approach** The preference of some personality theorists for studying individual differences in traits as the basis of doing psychological research on personality. Rival personality theorists prefer to classify personality types. Still other psychologists are situationists; they deny the validity of both types and traits.

**Transaction model**   A system of viewing instruction which focuses on the relationship between the reader and the text or written material. Students learn by their interaction between the known and the unknown in the reading(s).

**Transdisciplinary approach**   SEE: *transdisciplinary team*

**Transdisciplinary team**   A team of professionals across disciplines that is charged with the responsibility of placing students in special services programs. Professional personnel as well as family members and other professionals (e.g., family doctor, counselor, etc.) are usually involved. This model crosses lines of discipline; more team cooperation, planning, and delivery of services can exist if the model is properly utilized. It is normally the most cooperative and communicative form of teaming. SEE: *multidisciplinary team, interdisciplinary team*

**Transduction**   The transformation of one form of energy to another (e.g., in an automatic toaster, electrical energy is changed to heat). In our sense receptors, a given kind of energy (e.g., light) is changed to the electrical/chemical energy used in the nervous system. A transduction device is also used to alter sound into neural stimulating signals in the case of cochlear implants.

**Transfer**   The carry-over of learning in a given environment to a different situation. For example, the student wires a circuit board in a school laboratory and later uses the knowledge to rewire an appliance at home.

**Transference**   The formation of inappropriate emotional attachments to the psychotherapist by a patient in psychoanalysis. This is taken as a critical opportunity, being a chance to show the patient that he/she is acting irrationally in order to help the patient achieve insight into the nature of the emotional problem.

**Transformational grammar**   Chomsky's theory that all human languages involve the transformation of actual (spoken or written) phrases and sentences (the surface structure) into a deeper meaning-structure; every human has the innate ability to make such transformations.

**Transforming**   A term used to describe changing the function or layout of a school in a major way. This can include restructuring programs, redesigning curriculum, and/or major physical plant modifications such as internal restructuring or a major building addition.

**Transition**   A term used to describe the process of a student when moving from adolescence to adulthood. Such a process considers the cultural, socioeconomic, and legal factors involved in the transition from adolescence to young adulthood.

**Transition from school to adult life**   Refers to the period of time when a student graduates from school to the time one enters adult life. SEE: *transition plan, transition services*

**Transition plan**   As required by P.L. 101-476, the Individuals with Disabilities Education Act (IDEA), each student with special learning needs or challenges is required to have, as part of one's Individualized Education Plan (IEP), a statement in reference to services needed to effectively make the transition from being a student to entering adult life. SEE: *P.L. 101-476, transition services*

**Transition programming**   The gradual shaping of exceptional students to move from high school into advanced education, vocational training, employment, or community service.

**Transition services**   In special education, programs or services that assist the special-needs student to move from school to post-school, independent living, vocational training, sheltered workshop training, and the world of work and daily living in general. Now

T

required as part of an Individualized Education Plan (IEP) as per P.L. 101-476 (1990). SEE: *P.L. 101-476*

**Transition teams**   Committees that represent a wide spectrum of members of the local or state communities/areas/regions whose task is to facilitate individuals with disabilities transitioning or making successful adaptations to the community/workplace following secondary school graduation. Membership typically consists of individuals who represent the diversity in culture/ethnicity, socioeconomic levels, occupations, gender, age, etc. from the community at-large. There are several types of transition teams: 1. *Individual transition planning teams/committees* that design, provide ways to implement, and evaluate students' transition plans. These teams usually include the student, school nurses or physicians, parents or guardians, regular education and special education staff, school psychologists, counselors, occupational and physical therapists, school administrators, and transition coordinators. 2. *School-based transition teams/committees* initiate and evaluate school-wide transition practices (e.g., curriculum practices, assessment procedures, service delivery practices/options, etc.). Membership includes the same individuals as cited for individual transition teams and also the possibility of school-committee members, former students, social workers, and professionals/personnel involved in specialized service or program delivery. 3. *Community-based transition teams/committees* provide links from the school to the community that involve adult service programs/living arrangements/job training programs and the like (additional team members from #1 and #2: possibly representatives from Native-American tribes, vocational rehabilitation counselors, representatives from the Social Security Administration, representatives from local Chamber of Commerce groups, trade group representatives, etc.). Community transition teams also can involve the training of appropriate staff and provisions for sharing technical assistance and resources.

4. *Regional transition teams/committees* involve several communities/teams networking to provide services to a wider range of individuals with disabilities. Some communities share Department of Labor staff and other professional advisors. 5. *State-level transition teams* focus on state-level services needed to improve and develop services for individuals with disabilities. Additional staff available might include state department of education professionals, department of mental health staff, etc. SEE: *individualized transition plan*

**Transitional language programs**   Education programs designed to assist students in making a transition from bilingual education classes or English as a Second Language (ESL) programs to the English-speaking classroom. SEE: *bilingual learners*

**Transitional spelling**   In language arts, spelling that is more complete in form and generally readable and understood by others. This type of spelling is generally used by young students who have progressed beyond the beginning reading stage.

**Translocation**   A condition in which part of a chromosome is attached to another part of the same chromosome or more likely to another chromosome altogether. It is a type of Down syndrome. SEE: *Down syndrome*

**Transmission model**   A system of reading instruction which focuses on teaching isolated skills. The teacher presents/transmits skills and knowledge to the student in a discrete fashion.

**Transsexual**   1. An individual who has had a surgical external sex change. 2. A person who has an abnormal desire to be of the opposite sex.

**Trauma**   1. A physical injury or wound as a result of a violent external force such as an auto accident. 2. A psychological condition caused by the shock of physical and/or mental violence such as a soldier who suffers the trauma of being "shell-shocked" as a result of combat experience.

**Traumatic brain injury**   An accident or injury to the brain that results in impaired educational and/or social functioning. Such cognitive processes as memory, language, reasoning, judgment, and problem-solving abilities are adversely affected. Traumatic brain injury cases do not include conditions present at birth or degenerative diseases/conditions.

**Traveling notebook**   A type of journal or log that allows parents and professionals to communicate with students in a written format. The student keeps this traveling notebook in his/her possession in order to refer to and respond to communications given by those individuals involved in this type of dialogue format.

**Treacher-Collins syndrome**   Sensory defects characterized by many types of hearing problems both conductive and sensorineural. This syndrome usually is accompanied by abnormal jaw, face, and ear development.

**Treatment**   In statistics, the cause, event, or activity that is used to implement change or produce a desired result or outcome.

**Tremor**   A continuous convulsive and usually involuntary quivering of large muscles or parts of the body such as the lips, hands, arms, legs, etc.

**Tremor cerebral palsy**   Cerebral palsy that is characterized by involuntary muscular movement; certain muscles will move in a rhythmic fashion. It is a rare form of cerebral palsy. SEE: *cerebral palsy*

**Trial-and-error**   1. The basic method of learning, according to the learning theorist/educational psychologist Edward Lee Thorndike. All learning, to Thorndike, involved attaching a response to a situation by a positive (rewarding) effect of the response. A response is not learned if it fails to provide a rewarding consequence, which defines such a response as an error. 2. Refers to the type of learning where an individual tries a response (trial) and then will take errors as opportunities for learning, growth, and development.

**Triangular theory of love**   Robert Sternberg's three types of love—romantic love, compassionate love, and consummate love. Romantic love has been described as a combination of liking and passion. Compassionate love is the combination of commitment with liking. The combination of all three ingredients—liking, passion, and commitment—is consummate love.

**Triarchic theory of intelligence**   Sternberg's view of intelligence as coming in three forms. Componential intelligence is the kind measured on IQ tests, involving reasoning ability and academic aptitude. Experiential intelligence is the ability to solve problems creatively and do original work. Contextual intelligence involves "street smarts" (i.e., practical intelligence).

**Trichinosis**   A disease caused by the ingestion of the parasite trichinella spiralis commonly found in uncooked or improperly cooked meat, especially pork.

**Trichomonas vaginalis**   A condition in women caused by a genus of flagellate parasitic prologa found especially during pregnancy or after vaginal surgery. When found in the male it settles in the urethra and is transmitted through intercourse. It is considered one of the venereal diseases but is not always contracted as a result of sexual intercourse. SEE: *Venereal Disease (VD)*

**Trichromatic theory**   The Young-Helmholtz theory of color vision. This theory holds that there are three types of light receptors in the retina—one type is most sensitive to red light, another is most responsive to green, and a third to blue. An even mix of stimulation to all three results in white. The remaining colors are produced by various mixtures of high and low amounts of stimulation to the three groups of light receptors. At the receptor level this theory has been supported by data; there are three photopigments each used by one of three groups of cones, or color receptors.

**Trigger**   The stimulus, event, or impulse that initiates some particular behavior, response, or happening.

**Trigonometry** That area of mathematics involving the study of relationships and measurements of the sides and angles of triangles.

**Triplegia** A condition that is characterized by the loss of use ( may be actual) or paralysis of three limbs of the body. SEE: *paraplegic, quadriplegic*

**Trisomy-21** SEE: *Down syndrome*

**Trophic factor** A chemical that promotes activity and growth for survival. One example of a trophic factor is the nerve growth factor. SEE: *nerve growth factor*

**Trophology** The study or the science of nutrition.

**True experiment** A procedure or experiment undertaken where an experimental group and a control group are considered equal in all variables with random assignment of individuals or subjects to each group (distinguishable from quasi-experiments). It is difficult if not impossible in the social science and education fields to conduct 100 percent pure "true" experiments.

**True score** The expected average of an individual's scores on a test if that individual should take the test repeatedly.

**TTY or TYY** Teletypewriter and printer. SEE: *Telecommunication Device for the Deaf (TDD)*

**Tuberculosis** A disease caused by the tubercle bacillus, it commonly affects the respiratory system and, while it causes tissue destruction in many parts of the body, it particularly affects the lungs. However, the larynx, bones, skin, gastrointestinal tract, heart, and genitourinary tract can also be infected. It is usually contracted from an infected person or by drinking contaminated cow's milk.

**Tuberous sclerosis** A biochemical disorder and a rare brain disease, it is caused by an abnormal dominant gene and can result in mental retardation. The retardation can range from mild to severe if present.

**Tukey's Honestly Significant Difference Test (HSD)** A type of post hoc test used to ferret out significant individual differences/comparisons when using ANOVA procedures.

**Tunnel vision** A condition characterized by a loss of peripheral vision to a point whereby the field of vision is the same regardless of distance. The effect of looking through a tube or tunnel is present. This condition is frequently a result of advanced glaucoma.

**Turner's syndrome** (H. H. Turner, American physician, 1892–1970) Condition of females characterized by defective or abnormal development of the ovaries particularly during the embryonic stage. Usually only one X chromosome is included in the chromosomes. The female is usually short in stature and may be retarded.

**Twice exceptional student** A term used to refer to a student who in fact has two exceptionalities. For example, a student who is gifted but also learning disabled.

**Twin, fraternal** Sometimes referred to as biovular or dizygotic, fraternal twins are developed within the uterus at the same time from two separate ova fertilized during the same impregnation. Fraternal twins resemble each other closely but are not identical; in fact, they can be of the same or different sex. SEE: *twin, identical*

**Twin, identical** Identical twins (also called monovular or monozygotic) are developed in the uterus at the same time from a single ovum, fertilized during the same impregnation. Identical twins have a striking physical and physiological resemblance in addition to mental characteristics. They are of the same sex. SEE: *twin, fraternal*

**Twin studies** Research on the development of intelligence has often used data from identical twins reared separately. These persons have the same heredity but different environments. The differences in IQ between the two members of an identical twin pair must be a result of the environment. The method may overstate the role of heredity because the separate environments may be too similar to one another.

**Two-way bilingual education**  A sharing of two languages in an integrated fashion. Students who speak two languages are placed together in a bilingual classroom or program of studies. The concept is based on the premise that students will learn each other's primary language and thus become able to work academically in either language.

**Tympanic membrane**  This thin membrane, also known as the eardrum, separates the middle ear from the outer ear.

**Type**  Patterns of personality characteristics that define a particular syndrome. SEE: *type A individuals, type B individuals*

**Type A individuals**  This is a personality type that is characterized by impatient, sometimes hostile, and highly competitive individuals who tend to rush through life.

**Type B individuals**  This is a personality type that is characterized by calm, patient, and even-tempered individuals.

**Type I research error**  An error in statistical analyses that happens when a researcher finds statistical differences or real differences which in truth could be a result of chance. When significance levels are established above .05, for example, there is an increased likelihood for Type I errors (that is, finding significance when there is none).

**Type II research error**  An error in statistical analyses that happens when a researcher fails to find statistical significance or relationships that could exist. If significance levels established are set too low (e.g., .01 instead of .05), there is an increased chance of committing type II research errors (that is, not finding significance when there is a relationship/difference).

**Typhlolexia**  In effect, the condition of being word blind; it is a condition wherein the student or person has an inability to recognize words whether spoken or written.

**Typhlology**  The study of the science of blindness to include especially its etiologies (causes) and effects.

**Tyrosine**  An amino acid found in some dietary protein, it is the basic catecholamine compound that serves as a precursor to a group of neurotransmitters, neuromodulators, and hormones such as dopamine, norepinephrine, and epinephrine. Tyrosine is also formed by the metabolism of another amino acid, namely, phenylalanine. In Phenylketonuria (PKU), if left untreated in an infant, mental retardation can result. The body is unable to oxidize phenylalanine, an amino acid, to tyrosine. SEE: *PKU*

**UADD**  SEE: *Undifferentiated Attention-Deficit Disorder*

**UFONIC speech system**  A speech synthesizer to be added to a computer. Produced by Jostens Learning Corporation.

**Ulalgia**  Receding or shrinking of the gums.

**Ulcer**  A lesion or open sore on the skin or mucous membrane of the body. It may be caused by caustics, intense heat or cold, and trauma.

**Ulcer, gastric**   Also referred to as a peptic ulcer, it is an ulcer of the mucosa of the duodenum resulting from the caustic effects of gastric juices. SEE: *ulcer*

**Ultrasound**   Sound in the frequency range of 20,000 to 10 billion cycles per second. Sound of such high frequency is inaudible to humans. Ultrasound differs in velocity in different tissue according to tissue density and elasticity. Thus, it can be used to outline the shape of various bodily tissues and organs. It is now used medically for diagnostic and therapeutic purposes.

**Umbilicus**   A recessed (sometimes popped out) spot marked by a depression in the middle of the abdomen; also referred to as the navel. It is in effect the scar marking the spot of the former attachment of the umbilical cord from the fetus to the placenta of the mother. SEE: *umbilical cord*

**Umbilical cord**   The cord or tube that nourishes the unborn child and joins the fetus to the placenta of the mother. SEE: *umbilicus*

**Unconditioned positive regard**   The attitude of complete acceptance and respect that a clinician of the client-centered therapy school practices. Carl Rogers, creator of this form of psychotherapy, insists that there should be complete respect with no reservations. He also says that good parents ought to practice it.

**Unconditioned response**   A natural reaction or unlearned response to a specific condition or stimulus. For example, smiling when pleased or crying when hurt, or in the case of an infant, when hungry. SEE: *conditioned response (CR)*

**Unconditioned stimulus (US)**   The kind of stimulus that leads to a reflective action without the need for training. This is because the nervous system's inborn structure sets up the link between the unconditioned stimulus and the unconditioned response. The unconditioned stimulus, in classical conditioning, is given after the presentation of a neutral stimulus until the latter can substitute for the unconditioned stimulus and elicit the reflexive response. The once neutral stimulus then has been made a conditioned stimulus (CS).

**Unconscious**   A part of the mind, according to the theories of Freud, Jung, and some neo-Freudian theories. Freud's concept holds that primitive drives, and repressed memories that would lead to too much anxiety or shame if made conscious, constitute the unconscious portion of mind. Jung added to the Freudian idea of a personal unconscious an extended concept; namely, the racial or collective unconscious which is shared by all human beings, despite the cultural differences between them.

**Underachiever**   Refers to an individual whose academic proficiency, grades, or achievement fall below expectations (what would be expected considering one's overall intellectual capacity or abilities).

**Underextension**   An error of word usage. The verbal concept is used in a very narrow sense so that its meaning is applied only to some but not to all of the appropriate examples.

**Undergeneralization**   Leaving out some of the examples that belong to a category. SEE: *underextension*

**Undifferentiated Attention-Deficit Disorder (UADD)**   A disorder in a student or person who has difficulty concentrating, paying attention, and staying on task. Impulsive actions are present but hyperactivity is not. SEE: *Attention Deficit Disorder (ADD), Attention-Deficit/Hyperactivity Disorder (ADHD)*

**Unemployed**   Refers to civilians who during a survey time period had no employment while seeking work and 1. actively sought work in the past four weeks, 2. were waiting for a call-back if laid off, or 3. were waiting to begin a new waged or salaried job within 30 days.

**Unemployment rate**   This is the number of individuals who are unemployed but who are seeking employment. This rate is shown in both state and national percentages of the civilian labor force. Rates vary between states and an overall national average is used as a gauge from which states can assess their own rates.

**Ungraded school** A nongraded school where students progress through curricular materials at their own pace. Students are not classified according to the traditional first, second, third, . . . eleventh, twelfth grade levels.

**Unified phonics method** A method (1962) of teaching children to read through the use of "phonics" as per R. B. Spalding and W. T. Spalding. The idea is to have the child, using the rules of English spelling, write down the sounds heard in spoken English. Then, conversely, the child is able to pronounce any written word.

**Uninterrupted Sustained Silent Reading (USSR)** In language arts, a method that teaches students the value of being able to read for protracted periods of time, silently, and individually, without interruption. SEE: *Sustained Silent Reading (SSR), Drop Everything and Read (DEAR)*

**Unionism** Major national teacher organizations in the United States such as the National Education Association (NEA) and the American Federation of Teachers (AFT). The National Education Association (NEA) stipulated in 1960 that teacher organizations that were unionized must stress professional standards as well as job issues related to employment.

**Unit of learning** An organized series of learning activities and materials that key in on a specific topic related to the curriculum as a whole. For example, a unit on the solar system within the science curriculum could include textbook content, a visit to the planetarium, a movie on the planets, creation of the planets from paper mache balls, etc. The use of many and varied activities is believed to provide a more in-depth look at the subject area and an enhancement of learning through high-interest activities.

**Unlearned reflexes** Responses that are basic in nature such as coughing, ducking, blinking one's eyes, etc. These reactions are elicited automatically when specific conditions or stimuli are present or presented.

**Unit study** An approach to teaching wherein students are presented a broad topic from which subtopics or units are assigned or selected for exploration. Thus this approach allows for a more global or complete understanding of the topic, theme, or unit.

**Unrelated subfamily** A family unit consisting of two or more individuals who are related by birth, marriage, or adoption but who are not related to the householder. This type of subfamily may involve boarders, houseparents in a private school, resident employees and their families living in a private home or school, etc.

**Urea** The diamide of carbonic acid $CO(NH_2)_2$ found in blood lymph and urine. It is the final product of protein metabolism and the major nitrogenous part of urine. Excess urea is one of the causes of uremia. SEE: *uremia*

**Uremia** A toxic condition associated with renal (kidney) dysfunction. The blood retains excessive amounts of urea and nitrogen wastes to a point of toxicity.

**Urethra** The tube that connects the bladder to the exterior of the body. It passes through the penis in the male and in the female it discharges in the area between the vagina and the clitoris.

**U.S. Department of Education** Also known as the Department of Education, this cabinet-level department was formed in 1979 by President Carter and assumed the responsibilities of the U.S. Office of Education that was created in 1953. The U.S. Department of Education supports and distributes educational research, administers federal grants, and assists in establishing educational policies/practices/agendas. World Wide Web site: http://www.ed.gov

**Use** A term used in reference to the proper application of language and its appropriate usage. SEE: *pragmatics*

**User fee**   A fee paid by a parent(s) for nonrequired courses (e.g., summer school), sports activities (e.g., after school baseball), and other such activities (e.g., clubs) in order to help financially support the extracurricular activities.

**User friendly**   This concept usually refers to technical materials (such as this dictionary) and equipment such as computer equipment and software that are readily usable by the consumer. SEE: *Appendix 4: Computer Terms*

**Usher's syndrome**   A condition of multiple handicaps involving vision and hearing impairments that is inherited.

**USSR**   An abbreviation used in language arts that stands for uninterrupted sustained silent reading. SEE: *Sustained Silent Reading (SSR), Drop Everything and Read (DEAR)*

**Uterus**   The female organ, it is a pear-shaped, muscular, and hollow structure situated in the mid-pelvis area. Its specific function is to contain and nourish the embryo and fetus from the time of fertilization to birth.

**Utility value**   The value an activity has for an individual based on its possibilities of achieving that individual's goals.

**Uvula**   The rear part of the soft palate in the mouth. The uvula can be seen hanging down in the back of the throat.

**Vaccination**   Inoculation with a vaccine in order to become resistant to a specific infectious disease; sometimes called immunization.

**VAK approach**   SEE: *Visual-Auditory-Kinesthetic method*

**VAK method**   SEE: *Visual-Auditory-Kinesthetic method*

**VAKT approach**   Acronym for visual-auditory-kinesthetic-tactile approach. Same as visual-auditory-kinesthetic method except for the addition of tactile. SEE: *Visual-Auditory-Kinesthetic-Tactile method*

**VAKT method**   SEE: *Visual-Auditory-Kinesthetic-Tactile method*

**Validity**   The extent to which a measuring device is accurately measuring the phenomenon it is purported to measure.

A valid test makes accurate predictions about future performance.

**Values**   One's conscience or personal principles that guide social interactions and decision making.

**Values clarification**   A type of model that involves active discussions leading to clarification of one's values involving a wide range of topics.

**Variability**   The extent to which scores have a tendency to differ among themselves. In some frequency distributions, all scores are close to the central tendency (mean, median, or mode), there is little or no variability. In other frequency distributions, many scores lie in the lower and higher tails; these have great variability. SEE: *range, standard, deviation, variance*

**Variable**   Any measurable characteristic that can change values. The opposite of a variable is a constant.

**Variable-Interval schedule (VI)**   A plan for the presentation of reinforcements following some, but not all, of the correct responses. In this schedule, after a reinforced response, an interval begins following which the next response made will get reinforced. That interval varies from one time to the next, however. Usually the average time between reinforcements is specified and used to define the schedule (e.g., VI2' means that, on the average, a reinforcement is set up every two minutes). This schedule produces a steady rate of work.

**Variable-Ratio schedule (VR)**   An arrangement for delivering reinforcements following some, but not all, correct responses. After a reinforced response, a certain number of responses must be made for the next reinforcement to occur. In a VR schedule, this required number varies from one occasion to another. The average number of responses required per payoff is specified and used to designate the schedule. VR 10 means that, on the average, every tenth response gets reinforced, although there may be a requirement of 20 responses one time and a requirement of only two for another.

**Variance**   A score representing the square of a standard deviation. The amount of variance observed describes how individual scores/observations differ in a particular distribution/population. Researchers work hard to identify those factors or influences that account for variance(s) observed.

**Vascular**   The circulatory system (i.e., pertaining to blood vessels, the heart, and lymphatics).

**Vascular accident**   SEE: *cerebrovascular accident*

**Vasomotor**   Pertaining to the nerves that control the circularly arranged smooth muscles of the veins and arteries, thus controlling the blood vessel walls.

**VD**   SEE: *Venereal Disease*

**Velopharyngeal incompetence**   The escaping of air from the nasal cavity while speaking.

**Velum**   The soft palate at the upper rear of the mouth.

**Venereal Disease (VD)**   A disease that pertains to or results ordinarily from sexual intercourse or direct contact with an infected partner. The diseases include chancroid, gonorrhea, and syphilis. Trichomonas is also included but is not always contracted through intercourse. SEE: *syphilis, gonorrhea, chancroid, trichomonas vaginalis*

**Venn diagram**   A visual depiction of two circles that are horizontally aligned and intersect in the middle. The portion of the diagram that shows overlap between the two circles is generally where one writes similarities/comparisons between two ideas/concepts. The outermost independent portions of the circles can represent different or related ideas. For example, one can compare how two sports are alike and how they are different (comparison/contrast). How the sports compare can be summarized where the circles intersect. The uniqueness attributed to each sport could be listed in the nonintersecting space of each circle. Literature teachers have used Venn diagrams to graphically display key story elements/ structure, character development, etc.

**Venous**   Pertaining to the blood vessels (the veins) that carry the blood back to the heart after it has circulated throughout the body; or to the blood in those veins.

**Ventilator**   A machine that artificially ventilates the lungs and controls the flow of air. It is used to assist a person who has difficulty breathing.

**Ventricle**   Either of two lower chambers of the heart: the right forces blood into the pulmonary artery into the lungs while the left ventricle forces blood through the aorta to the remaining arteries.

**Ventromedial Hypothalamus (VMH)**   An area of the brain important for motivation and emotion. Injury to the VMH leads to overeating because normal satisfaction mechanisms are damaged. Another symptom of VMH damage is aggressive rage.

**Verbal expression**   The ability to communicate one's ideas through speaking.

**Verbal unreality**   Inappropriate verbal responses by a non-sighted person that are not based on observed experiences such as an inability to understand how color relates to feelings and situations (e.g., blue Monday, green with envy, pure as the driven snow [white = purity], etc.).

**Verbalism**   1. An expression that is wordy and has little meaning and appears to be more important than the reality it represents. 2. A word or words that usually are not backed by real experiences.

**Verbalization**   Expressing one's plans and reasoning processes in words.

**Verbomania**   1. The use of more words than is necessary, a state of verbosity; or 2. the flow of words in a verbose fashion indicating certain types of psychoses.

**Vermis**   Part of the brain, the median-connecting lobe of the cerebellum. In children with autism the vermis is characteristically undeveloped. SEE: *autism*

**Vernacular**   A term in language that refers to an informal way of speaking. The common language or dialect of a region or ethnic group.

**Vernal**   Pertaining to spring or occurring during the season of spring, springtime.

**Versabraille system**   A system that stores braille on a cassette tape. Information from the tape is sent to the user by microcomputer in braille or in print on a screen.

**Vertebra** (plural, vertebrae)   The bony segment of the spine. The spinal column has 26 bony sections. These sections or segments are separated by disks made of fibrous cartilage. Thus, the vertebrae are able to articulate with each other and the spine has movement.

**Vertigo**   Also known as dizziness, vertigo is the feeling that one is moving

around in space or that objects are moving or spinning around one's self.

**Vestibular mechanism**   Three semicircular canals and two otolith organs in the inner ear. This mechanism is located in the upper part of the inner ear and is filled with fluid. The vestibular mechanism is involved in the control of our equilibrium senses and movements of the head.

**Vestibular system**   The vestibular set of receptors housed in the inner ear; it detects head position or movement and is primarily concerned with the orientation of the head in space.

**VI**   SEE: *Variable-Interval schedule*

**Vibrating system**   A term used to describe the orderly function of the larynx and vocal cords; their ability to vibrate and produce pitch and sound. The larynx is also referred to as the voice box. SEE: *larynx, resonating system, speech mechanisms, vocal cords*

**Vibrotactile aid**   A special device used by persons with disabilities that transforms sound to tactile vibrations.

**Vibrotactile pulser**   A device that pulsates in the palm of the hand. It has been used to regulate the speed of reading and in behavior modification as a signal or stimulus.

**Vicarious punishment**   A part of the mechanism for observation learning, according to Bandura. The observer watches another student or person perform an incorrect response and receive punishment afterward. The observer then refrains from making that response, even though the observer never got punished for doing it.

**Vicarious reinforcement**   A part of the mechanism for observation learning, according to Albert Bandura. The observer learns what to do by watching another organism perform the correct response and receive the reinforcement. The observer will then perform the same action although never having obtained a reinforcement for that response.

**Video digitizer**   A device used in computers that changes video images to still graphics. SEE: *Appendix 4: Computer Terms*

**Video disk**   A system that stores graphics, text, video, and sound; frequently used for high quality stills and movies. Playback is accomplished by means of a video disk player.

**Video materials**   Materials that involve picture/sound recordings that can be played on a television monitor/video player system.

**Videodisc instruction**   A method of teaching that uses videodiscs containing narrations of visual images on the disc. This approach is effective with students with learning disabilities but may be used with all students. It is an alternative to Computer-Assisted Instruction (CAI). SEE: *Computer-Assisted Instruction (CAI)*

**Videoscript**   A translation of the visual software program into a text format. Videoscripts can be prepared in ASL (American Sign Language) or in other languages to assist the hard-of-hearing, ESL (English as a Second Language) students, etc. SEE: *Appendix 4: Computer Terms*

**Viewscan**   A print enlarger for persons with serious visual impairments. It uses a small camera that tracks print on a page and displays it in enlarged form on a screen to be read by the user.

**Viremia**   A condition in which viruses are present in the blood. It is also referred to as virusemia. SEE: *virusemia*

**Virtual reality**   SEE: *Appendix 4: Computer Terms*

**Virus**   1. Once thought to be any organism that could cause an infection (now an obsolete definition), it is a minute submicroscopic organism and parasite depending on its metabolic and reproductive needs. It is able to pass through bacterial filters and shares some features with bacteria. Viruses cannot be seen by ordinary microscopy but can be seen through the use of the electron microscope. Their composition and method of replication make viruses a much simpler organism than bacteria. They are comprised of a strand of Ribonucleic Acid

(RNA) or Deoxyribonucleic Acid (DNA) but not both RNA and protein (CAPSID). Viruses cause many infections, including the common cold and most childhood diseases. 2. SEE: *Appendix 4: Computer Terms*

**Virusemia**   Also known as viremia, a condition in which viruses are present in the blood. SEE: *viremia*

**Visible speech**   A method of instruction that explains how the vocal folds (cords) operate in the production of speech. The deaf are able to model what they are seeing.

**Vision**   A measure of acuity, a term used to describe how well an individual can see the visual stimuli received. SEE: *visual acuity*

**Visual acuity**   The sharpness or keenness of the sense of vision; a term used to describe how well a person sees or one's sensitivity to visual stimuli.

**Visual aphasia**   A condition characterized by a person's inability to comprehend what is written. SEE: *alexia*

**Visual association**   The ability of a person to relate what is seen to concepts, ideas, comparisons, and understandings.

**Visual-Auditory-Kinesthetic method (VAK)**   A remediation system for reading disabilities. The method uses a combined (eclectic) approach with sight (e.g., seeing the word "dog"), sound (e.g., hearing the word "dog" and a dog bark), kinesthetic (tracing the word "dog" in the air with one's finger), and other sensory experiences tactile (such as touch). SEE: *Visual-Auditory-Kinesthetic-Tactile method (VAKT)*

**Visual-Auditory-Kinesthetic-Tactile method (VAKT)**   Same as Visual-Auditory-Kinesthetic method except tactile/touching is added (e.g., feeling a letter made of wood or plastic in order to determine its shape and identification). SEE: *Visual-Auditory-Kinesthetic method*

**Visual closure**   The skill or ability of a person to identify a visual presentation when only able to see a partial visual presentation of a person, place, or thing.

**V**

**Visual cortex** The part of the cerebral cortex contributing to vision. The entire occipital lobe as well as parts of the temporal and parietal lobe play some role in visual perception. The central portion of the occipital lobe is the primary visual cortex or striate area.

**Visual discrimination** The ability to identify and distinguish in a visual fashion (through sight) objects or stimuli and their similarities, exactness, and/or differences.

**Visual efficiency** How well and to what degree a person is able to utilize one's eyesight or vision to include visual acuity, closure, discrimination, memory, etc.

**Visual efficiency scale** A system of testing visual functioning but not visual acuity. For example, visual discrimination ability might be assessed in terms of spatial perspective/position and dark-light intensity thresholds. SEE: *visual efficiency*

**Visual field** SEE: *field of vision*

**Visual fusion** Also referred to as binocular focusing, it is the coming together of the separate images from each eye into one image.

**Visual impairment** A common term used to describe all types of visual problems such as colorblindness, hyperopia, astigmatism, blindness, etc.

**Visual memory** The ability to remember the visual stimuli to which one has been exposed. In effect, remembering what one sees and one's ability to recall it. SEE: *visual sequential memory*

**Visual motor** A term used to describe the relationship between a visual stimulus and a motor response. SEE: *visual-motor coordination*

**Visual-motor coordination** A term used in special education and in general to describe one's ability to coordinate what one sees with bodily movement. For example, hitting a baseball, threading a needle, driving a car, etc. require good visual-motor coordination abilities.

**Visual perception** The ability of a person or student to critically evaluate and come to conclusions in order to selectively organize and interpret what he/she sees. SEE: *perceptual skills*

**Visual reception** The perception/receiving of (a) visual stimulus (i) and the ability to draw conclusions and meanings from what one sees. SEE: *perceptual skills*

**Visual Reinforcement Audiometry (VRA)** A test that commonly presents an auditory signal followed by a head-turn response that is reinforced with an attractive visual stimulus such as a toy or food treat.

**Visual sequential memory** Like visual memory, the ability to remember what one sees and to recall it; visual sequential memory deals with remembering and recalling visual stimuli in sequence (i.e., the order in which each stimulus was seen). SEE: *visual memory*

**Visual-spatial perception** One's ability to accurately perceive the arrangement of objects and symbols in space or locale such as in the case of properly perceiving drawings, numbers, letters, etc.

**Visualization** The ability to create a mental image or to picture in one's mind what one has seen or heard in the past. In some cases, the ability to project a mental image based on what one expects to see or hear.

**Visually handicapped/impaired** A generic term which includes persons with a large range of visual problems or impairments that require special adaptation in order to properly learn and/or see such as lighting, glasses, large print books, talking books, etc. The term includes persons with hyperopia, myopia, the legally blind, blind, etc. SEE: *each term as listed*

**Visuoauditory** In effect, the relation between sight and sound or vision and hearing.

**Vitalism** The belief that the origin of life does not lie in chemical, physical, or mechanical forces; life had its origin through some other means.

**Vitamin** Vitamins are complex chemical substances. Organic in nature, they are absolutely essential for the body and its proper development, normal metabolism, and growth. They do not include proteins, fats, organic salts, carbohydrates, and minerals.

**Vitiligo**   Also known as piebald skin, it is a cutaneous condition characterized by milky white patches. These white or bleached patches are surrounded by normally pigmented skin. The condition has an unknown etiology and is more common in tropical climates and amongst the black race.

**Vitreous humor**   A transparent jelly-like substance that fills the space between the retina and the lens of the eye. SEE: *retina, lens*

**VMH**   SEE: *Ventromedial Hypothalamus*

**VOCA**   SEE: *Voice Output Communication Aid, synthetic speech*

**Vocables**   The use of consistent sound patterns (usually by very young children) that refer to objects or people in the environment. For example, a child might hear a parent say "powder" and then say "pow-pow" when powder is wanted.

**Vocabulary**   The words or terms an individual acquires that can be recalled or recognized during oral and/or written communications. There is a reciprocal relationship between vocabulary knowledge and reading comprehension. Typically students with large vocabularies read a great deal and reading increases vocabulary knowledge (thus becoming better readers). Students with poor vocabularies typically find reading tedious and cumbersome whereby reading is limited in breadth and scope (thus acquiring more reading problems in terms of fluency and/or comprehension). There are approximately 100,000 word meanings associated with English vocabulary.

**Vocabulary, depth of**   The number of meanings attributed to a word.

**Vocabulary development**   The acquisition of words and word meanings or the expansion of our vocabulary. Great vocabulary growth is seen between the ages of 1 and 2 when young children can

go from 6-word vocabularies to 250-word vocabularies. By age 6, it is estimated that many children have between 2500 and 10,000 word vocabularies. One's intellectual capacity or abilities, experience, and motivation impact vocabulary development.

**Vocabulary instruction**   Approaches to teaching vocabulary knowledge that include both spoken and written vocabulary. Organized approaches to vocabulary instruction have been found to be most effective when teaching is explicit in terms of structural word parts; vocabulary usage in a variety of contexts; and learning strategies to determine the meaning(s) of new vocabulary encountered in reading.

**Vocabulary journals**   Also called vocabulary log, this is a structured way for students to record, review, and think about new vocabulary words/meanings. Students can organize such a journal alphabetically, by subject matter, chronologically, by interest area, or a combination of the above. Vocabulary words can be chosen by the student or teams of students.

**Vocabulary log**   A type of journal, diary, or recording method that is used with VSS and other such methods. Students record vocabulary terms, definitions, how to use terms in context, etc. These can be organized alphabetically, chronologically, by subject matter, or a combination of the above. SEE: *Vocabulary Self-Collection Strategy (VSS)*

**Vocabulary meaning, flexibility in**   The ability to select the meaning of a word most appropriate to the context.

**Vocabulary rating**   A teaching strategy used as a prereading activity wherein the teacher provides the student a list of words to be classified into one of three areas: 1. Can define, 2. Seen or heard before, and 3. Not sure or do not know. While this vocabulary teaching strategy does not teach vocabulary directly, it does give a student an opportunity to build on known words, become familiar with unknown words, and fosters an interest in reading and vocabulary development.

**Vocabulary Self-collection Strategy (VSS)** A vocabulary instruction strategy after reading in context. VSS keys in on words children want to learn. Words are chosen for class lists after word nominations are discussed. Final lists are recorded in vocabulary journals or maps (Haggard, 1982; Ruddell, 1993). SEE: *vocabulary log*

**Vocabulary types** There are four general types of vocabulary one acquires and uses for oral and written communications: 1. *Listening vocabulary* or terms an individual understands through hearing. The acquisition of listening vocabulary begins during the first year of life and serves as the foundation for other types of vocabulary. 2. *Reading vocabulary* or all printed words a reader recognizes and understands. 3. *Speaking vocabulary* or all words an individual can use in oral speech. 4. *Writing vocabulary* or all words an individual can use in written expression. Listening and reading vocabulary are termed "receptive" in nature and speaking and written vocabulary are "expressive" forms of language. Most individuals learn new vocabulary words through reading and listening in context.

**Vocal nodules** Nodes on the edge(s) of one or both vocal folds (cords). These calloused growths can cause the voice to have a breathy quality and a corresponding reduction in loudness.

**Vocal symbols** Speech sounds are in fact vocal symbols. They are an oral means of communication.

**Vocal system** Those parts of the respiratory system involved in producing speech; namely, the diaphragm, chest, and muscles of the throat.

**Vocal tract** The area from the larynx to the edge of the lips or nostrils.

**Vocational aptitude tests** Tests that measure particular abilities that are required in certain occupations.

**Vocational counselor** A counseling psychologist who focuses on providing individuals with job guidance by assessing aptitudes, intelligence, interests, and financial resources.

**Vocational education** Job training within an educational institution that is intended to prepare an individual for a particular job (e.g., mechanic or dress designer), as opposed to college preparatory training. Students are given education and job training skills needed to be successful at a particular job and in the community in general. Vocational education is sometimes referred to as occupational education.

**Vocational interest tests** Tests measuring likes and dislikes. Various like-dislike patterns have been found to be typical of workers in certain occupations. The test-taker's like-dislike pattern is taken as an indication of his/her interest in a certain type of occupation; namely, the one that has a similar like-dislike profile to that of the test-taker.

**Vocational rehabilitation** A type of training program for individuals with learning challenges that keys into skills required in the job market.

**Vocational training** SEE: *vocational education*

**Vocomotor skills** Skills involving the control of the tongue, lips, and jaw as they relate to the production of speech.

**Voice disorder** A spoken language problem characterized by any number of disorders or impairments to include hypernasality, stuttering, irritating pitch or dialect, monotone speech, etc.

**Voice Output Communication Aid (VOCA)** A communication device that produces speech electronically. SEE: *synthetic speech*

**Voiced sounds** Refers to all sounds that use vocal fold vibration(s) (e.g., "d" sound). You can feel your throat vibrations when you vocalize the "d" sound as in "dictionary."

**Voiceless sounds** Those sounds produced by air turbulence in the vocal tract when the larynx is open such as "s" and "h."

**Voicing problems** SEE: *voice disorders*

**Volition** One's self-control, use of willpower, or willingness.

**Voluntary reading**   Reading done by the individual on her/his own and not assigned by the teacher. The student reads on his/her own initiative independently.

**Von Recklinghausen's disease**   Also known as neurofibromatosis, it is an inherited disease characterized by tumors of nerves, organs, and skin. Mental retardation may be present with this disease.

**VOTRAX personal speech system**   A speech synthesizer added to a computer. Produced by Votrax, Inc.

**Voucher plan**   Milton Friedman's notion that the government should guarantee every child an equal but minimum level of education, which can be achieved by school choice. The government in essence would give parents vouchers or certificates that would be redeemable as cash stipends and then used to pay tuition(s) at approved school sites.

**VR**   SEE: *Variable-Ratio schedule*

**VRA**   SEE: *Visual Reinforcement Audiometry*

**VSS**   SEE: *Vocabulary Self-collection Strategy*

**Vygotskian principles of learning** (Lev Semenovich Vygotsky, 1896–1934)   The belief that children learn best when an adult or more learned peer is present, two-way communication ensues, and that the responsible teacher provides a learning experience within the learner's zone of proximal development or area of potential.

**Waardenburg's syndrome** (Petrus Johannes Waardenburg, Dutch ophthalmologist, 1886–1979)   An inherited disease that may include symptoms of congenital sensorineural hearing loss, growing together of the two sets of the eyebrows, a white forelock, bicolored eyes, and a broad abnormally large nose. A cleft palate may be associated with this disease as well as mental retardation.

**WAIS-R**   SEE: *Wechsler Adult Intelligence Scale, Revised*

**Wallace v. Jaffree**   The 1985 Supreme Court ruling that overturned laws authorizing prayers in the public schools. The Court held that the practice of having a moment of silence for prayers or meditation in the public schools was unconstitutional.

**Wallenberg's syndrome**   (Adolph Wallenberg, German physician, 1862–1949) A group of symptoms as a result of the occlusion of the posteroinferior cerebral artery supplying the lower portion of the brain stem characterized by muscular weakness, impairment of the senses of temperature and pain, as well as other cerebellar dysfunctions.

**Wavelength**   A feature of an energy wave such as a light wave or sound wave. The wavelength is inversely related to frequency (i.e., high frequencies mean short wavelengths and low frequencies indicate long wavelengths). For light, the longer wavelengths are at

**W**

the red end of the spectrum while blue and violet have the shortest wavelengths.

**WCI**    SEE: *Whole Child Initiative*

**Weave**    A term used in education to indicate the use of a graphic organizer (chart, topical list, diagram, etc.). The display shows how the various components of an idea, theme, or topic connect to form a whole.

**Webbing**    Refers to a form of graphic organizer where ideas or topics are related to one common theme. Typically a visual map lists the key theme at the top of a diagram with branches pointing to one-word/brief phrase descriptions of related ideas/topics. Webbing is considered an effective study technique when outlining texts/studying for exams. SEE: *graphic organizer*

**Weber's law**    A rule for the amount of stimulus change that will be just barely enough to make a detectable difference. This just noticeable difference (jnd) or difference threshold (s) depends on the amount of stimulation already present. For a faint, small stimulus, a very small change is all that is needed, whereas a strong stimulus requires a relatively large amount of change before the change can be noticed. The expression for Weber's law is: $\Delta s/S = K$ where $s$ is the difference threshold, $S$ is the size of the stimulus before the change, and $K$ = a constant. For judging weights that are lifted in the palms of the hands, $K$ is equal to .10.

**Wechsler Adult Intelligence Scale, Revised (WAIS-R)**    The 1981 version is the latest edition of an intelligence instrument introduced in 1939. The WAIS-R, a well-standardized and reliable IQ measure, contains 11 subtests that are grouped into verbal and performance areas and IQs. The six verbal subtests are: Information, Digit Span, Vocabulary, Arithmetic, Comprehension, and Similarities. The five performance subtests are: Picture Completion, Picture Arrangement, Block Design, Object Assembly, and Digit Symbol. The WAIS-R can be administered to those individuals between the ages of 16 years, 0

months to 74 years, 11 months. It does overlap with the WISC-R from ages 16 years, 0 months to 16 years, 11 months. The WAIS-R is useful in clinical and psychoeducational settings when trying to determine innate abilities or strengths/weaknesses.

**Wechsler Intelligence Scale for Children, Revised (WISC-R)**    Now updated to the WISC-III but still in use, it is an intelligence test. This intelligence test was originally published in 1949 (WISC), revised in 1974 (WISC-R) and 1991 (WISC-III). SEE: *Wechsler Intelligence Scale for Children III (WISC-III)*

**Wechsler Intelligence Scale for Children III (WISC-III)**    The 1991 version is the latest edition of an intelligence instrument introduced in 1949. The WISC-III contains 11 subtests that are grouped into verbal and performance areas and IQs. The six verbal subtests are: Information, Digit Span, Vocabulary, Arithmetic, Comprehension, and Similarities. The five performance subtests are: Picture Completion, Picture Arrangement, Block Design, Object Assembly, and Digit Symbol. The WISC-III can be administered to those individuals between the ages of 6 years, 0 months to 16 years, 11 months. It does overlap with the WAIS-R from ages 16 years, 0 months to 16 years, 11 months.

**Wechsler Preschool and Primary Scale of Intelligence, Revised (WPPSI-R)**    The 1976 version is the latest edition of an intelligence instrument introduced in 1963. The WPPSI-R contains 11 subtests that are grouped into verbal and performance areas and IQs. The six verbal subtests are: Information, Vocabulary, Arithmetic, Comprehension, Sentences, and Similarities. The five performance subtests are: Animal House, Picture Completion, Block Design, Mazes, and Geometric Design. The WPPSI-R can be administered to those individuals between the ages of 4 years, 0 months to 6 years, 6 months.

**Weighting**    The readjustment of the size of a school class achieved by counting each exceptional student as more than a single full-time enrolled student. This allows such classes to be "filled" with a smaller number of students than classes that include no exceptional student. A regular full-time equivalent student is classified as a 1.0 (FTE) pupil. Special education students may be classified as 1.5, 2.0, etc. depending on the amount and type of service needed.

**Well-controlled study**   A research study conducted so that the observed changes or differences can be attributed only to the independent variable and not to a confounding variable. Furthermore, the study should be performed in a standardized way and on many subjects so that the observed changes are not attributed to chance.

**Wernicke-Korsakoff syndrome**   This is a disorder that can be characterized as two separate syndromes: Wernicke's disease or syndrome and Korsakoff's syndrome. Wernicke's disease is caused by a lack of vitamin B1 (thiamine) and can affect a person's physical state and mental abilities (i.e., unsteadiness, profound fatigue, double vision, and the absence of emotion). When the symptoms of Wernicke's become severe, and if the individual survives to a point of losing much long-term memory, the Korsakoff's psychosis takes over as well. It is characterized by changes in behavior, memory loss, and problems in learning, thus the name Wernicke-Korsakoff syndrome.

**Wernicke's aphasia**   An impaired ability or actual loss of ability to comprehend the spoken word (speech). It is a combination of word deafness and visual aphasia as such. SEE: *visual aphasia (alexia)*

**White matter**   The material within the central nervous system (CNS) that is glistening white in color and stands out from the gray matter. The white matter gets its color from myelin, a lipid substance that forms the sheaths that surround many of the CNS axons. White matter consists of groups of axons.

**Whole Child Initiative (WCI)**   The conceptualization that parents, teachers, professionals, and community members will work together to seek academic excellence and a positive and enjoyable learning experience for all students/learners.

**Whole language**   A view of literacy and learning that focuses on 1. presenting material in the child's natural language, 2. relevant language usage, 3. functional reading materials, 4. a meaning-based approach, 5. the use of literature offerings, 6. making the reading-writing connection, and 7. avoiding skills/phonics work in isolation. Key features to the whole language approach include: providing the learner with background experiences/knowledge, learning in cooperative environments so as to increase positive social interactions, and nurturing reader-writer interactions with the printed page. The whole language approach is most like the literature-based approach in that complete literature-selections are used with an emphasis on the child's response to the printed page. The whole language approach differs from the literature-based approach in that there is more emphasis placed on creating/maintaining reading-writing connections. This is considered a top-down instructional approach to reading. SEE: *bottom-up philosophy of reading, reading instruction, whole language teaching*

**Whole language teaching**   The teaching of reading by using words in context (e.g., with literature books) so that the contextual meaning clues the children into the word name. Phonics is introduced as needed.

**Whorfian hypothesis**   A relativistic linguistic theory that states that the vocabulary of a cultural group shapes the ways of thinking and reasoning used by members of that group. This view is not compatible with Chomsky's idea that the deep structures of all languages are alike.

**Win-lose approach**   This applies to an area of social psychology called conflict analysis. In this approach, one party's win is balanced by the opposing party's loss (as in a sports event).

**Win-win approach** This applies to an area of social psychology, namely conflict analysis. In the win-win approach, both parties cooperate with one another and both gain.

**WISC-R** SEE: *Weschler Intelligence Scale for Children, Revised*

**WISC-III** SEE: *Wechsler Intelligence Scale for Children III*

**Wisconsin v. Yoder** The 1972 Supreme Court decision that held that compulsory education for Amish children (requirement was to age 16) violated the Amish's free exercise of religion.

**Withdrawal symptoms** Physical and psychological reactions of a transient nature; usually the body's reaction to the absence of a drug.

**Withdrawal** or **withdrawal reaction** A drawing away from reality wherein a person exhibits signs of anxiousness, shyness, and withdrawing into one's self; living in a world of fantasy rather than reality.

**Within-class ability grouping** An educational plan in which members of a class are assigned to separate groups on the basis of their ability.

**Withitness** Kounin's concept: the extent to which one is aware of all the events taking place in the classroom. Kounin posits that good teachers know what's going on in their classrooms.

**Wolffian duct** Precursors in the early human fetus of the male reproductive organs. SEE: *mullerian ducts*

**Word analysis** Using phonic, sight-word, configuration, structural, and other strategies to identify words/word meanings.

**Word classes** The major parts of speech identified in linguistics: namely, nouns, verbs, adjectives, adverbs, etc.

**Word processing** The typing of data on a computer keyboard which is recorded, stored, and easily retrieved via computer disks or hard drive (within the computer itself). Word processing saves much labor by providing automatic commands (e.g., alphabetizing, justifying a paper, easy erasure of text, the abil-

ity to cut-and-paste in seconds, etc.). SEE: *Appendix 4: Computer Terms*

**Word recognition** The identification of printed symbols by some word strategy so that the word can be pronounced and understood in terms of meaning(s). Word recognition ability is fundamental to reading ability. SEE: *word recognition strategies*

**Word recognition strategies** The use of cognitive abilities to identify and understand word units. Readers have a number of strategies available to them to help pronounce/understand words: 1. Apply *phonetic analysis* and *synthesis* skills or make proper phoneme (sound)-grapheme (letter) correspondences. Analysis = breaking words into their component parts; Synthesis = building a whole word from its component parts. 2. Rely on *context cues* or clues by using the words or sentences surrounding the word to be identified. 3. Use the "whole word" or "look-and-say" method, which is identifying the word by sight as a whole (also known as the sight-word method). 4. Apply structural analysis and synthesis abilities in breaking down words (analysis) and building up (synthesis) word parts to form whole units by using prefixes, suffixes, and roots (bases). 5. Ask someone else to pronounce the word or give the word meaning. 6. Use the dictionary for assistance.

**Word salad** A pattern of speech in which phrases and words are stated in disorganized fashion. The combining of the words and phrases seems to lack meaning, has no rhyme or reason, and is illogical; this speech pattern can be indicative of schizophrenia.

**Word superiority effect** When letters are flashed rapidly on the screen of a tachistoscope (high-speed slide projector), the subject finds it easier to recall a letter included within a word than to recall a single letter flashed alone.

**Work experience** Educationally speaking, this involves simulated, partial, or real work situations experienced by students in order to give them a feel for the real life experiences and responsibilities involving the skills and knowledge required in the world of work. It includes "career education" as well as "prevocational" and "vocational training." SEE: *vocational education, work-study program*

**Work-study program**   A type of program that involves part-time/full-time schooling and gainful employment in the community, school, or industry. The purpose of such a program is to provide on-the-job training or an opportunity to earn expense money while attending school.

**Worker's compensation**   Payment given by insurance companies to injured workers as a result of job-related injuries (e.g., hurting oneself on school property).

**Working backward strategy**   A heuristic approach. The problem-solver starts with the solution and tries to work back, step by step, to the starting point.

**Working memory**   According to the traditional three-stage model of memory, the Atkinson-Shiffrin model, Short-Term Memory (STM) is used in the retrieval of information from storage in Long-Term Memory (LTM). Some researchers insist, however, that there are differences between the STM and working memory.

**Working self-concept**   1. In Roger's client-centered therapy, the acceptance of the client with complete empathy and unconditional positive regard on the part of the therapist will lead the client to make positive changes in the client's own self-concept. These changes involve more understanding of oneself, greater self-confidence, and greater independence. 2. Child psychologist John Bowlby's view that an individual goes about with a working model of the world, a working model of oneself, and a working model of one's caregiver. The formation of two working models of the caregiver by an insecure child leads to the formation of different conscious and unconscious working models of the self. 3. The view of Hazel Markus that the self-concept regulates behavior. The concept, at a given time, includes all available information about oneself. The

working self-concept may turn worse if you see yourself in the mirror and something is wrong with your clothes. On the whole, though, the working self-concept tends to be stable.

**Working through**   The final stage of psychoanalytic therapy in which the patient gives up neurotic behaviors and adopts mature and well-adjusted patterns of behavior.

**Workshop approach**   In education a type of instruction which emphasizes learning by doing. For example, students learn to write by writing and learn to read by reading. The teacher supervises the process and both the teacher and student peers provide the learner with feedback.

**World Confederation of Organizations of the Teaching Profession**   An organization of approximately 100 nations, the purpose of which is to foster international understanding and appreciation for such universal principles as peace, freedom, and human dignity within educational systems. Included within this organization are the AFT (American Federation of Teachers) and NEA (National Education Association).

**WPPSI-R**   SEE: *Wechsler Preschool and Primary Scale of Intelligence, Revised*

**Writing process**   An approach to writing that focuses on developing literate/sophisticated writers who can think about, plan/prepare, and follow through with a writing task. Good writers are able to self-evaluate and monitor writing growth/progress. Eight general steps are key to this approach to writing: 1. prewriting stage (i.e., brainstorming ideas/finding story starters/creating story maps); 2. drafting stage (i.e., jotting notes/scribbling key ideas); 3. revising stage (sharing work/receiving input/using a dictionary or computer); 4. editing stage (rewriting based on input from stage 3); 5. sharing stage (teacher/peer/class conferences, bring work home to a family member); 6. revisit stages 3,4,5 until satisfied with the final product (especially books!); 7. self-evaluation stage—this stage should be ongoing throughout the entire writing process but especially before a final publishing; and 8. publishing stage (pop-up books, construction-paper books, completed poem, a computer-generated book with visuals, etc.). The mechanics of writing (i.e., spelling/grammar) are handled within the context of the writing assignment and usually not until the editing stage. SEE: *writing records, writing workshop*

**Writing records** Maintaining formal or informal documentation of a student's writing progress. An informal procedure could consist of a *writing log* of conferences held with the student. Notes could include student accomplishments, skills learned/used, skills requiring additional support (e.g., spelling of sight-words), etc. Portfolio assessments can also provide an informal assessment of a student's writing strengths and weaknesses. Formal measures (e.g., Test of

Written Language [TOWL]) can provide information regarding grade-level functioning, thematic maturity, etc. SEE: *portfolio assessment*

**Writing workshop** Classtime that is set aside each day for a writing activity. Emphasis is placed on improving writing fluency and sophistication. Writing workshops usually involve conference times with the teacher, cooperative sharing of work, think-time, rewritings of drafts, writing responses from the teacher or classmates, etc. The teacher models good writing habits and emphasizes writing mechanics (e.g., spelling) in the context of writing assignments/pieces. SEE: *writing records*

**Written expression** The expression of ideas through writing in the broadest sense, to include spelling and even handwriting.

**X** 1. Represents an individual score/observation. 2. Represents the mean of a distribution.

**X chromosome** The female chromosome. A normal female has two X chromosomes (XX). The male has one X and one Y chromosome (XY). SEE: *chromosome*

**XXY chromosome condition** SEE: *Klinefelter's syndrome*

**XYY chromosome condition** A chromosomal abnormality with the male having one extra Y chromosome. An XYY tends to be taller than average and less sexually active than average. They have an higher-than-average imprisonment rate which may be a result of lower-than-average intelligence rather than of an aggressive personality. Their crimes tend to be "white collar" in nature rather than violent.

**Y chromosome**   The determining male chromosome. A male has one X and one Y chromosome (XY). SEE: *chromosome*

**Z score**   A standard score that represents how far an individual score deviates from the mean of a distribution in terms of standard deviation units. A Z score can be calculated by subtracting the mean of a distribution from an individual score and dividing by the standard deviation of the distribution.

**Zeigarnik effect**   An effect characterized by the remembering of incomplete or interrupted events better than those that have been completed or concluded. For example, a teacher might remember better that he/she has not completed report card grades for reading but has placed out of immediate memory the fact that grading was done for the other subjects.

**Zeitgeber**   The environmental stimuli used to reset our biological clocks. Daylight is the principal zeitgeber. Others include tidal effects, temperature, and of course sundials, watches, and clocks.

**Zeitgeist**   The prevailing theoretical leanings of a particular time. For example, the Zeitgeist of reading theory in the 1990s appears to center on whole language/writing process activities.

**Zero correlation**   The score on one variable cannot help to predict the score on a second variable. For example, a high score on variable 1 is accompanied by a low score on variable 2 in some cases, by a medium sized score in other cases, and by a high score in still other cases. This situation is described as a lack of correlation, or, the correlation coefficient is equal to zero.

**Zero reject**   Used in the context of P.L. 101-476, the Individuals with Disabilities Education Act (IDEA) (formally known as the Education for All Handicapped Children Act or P.L. 94-142), it provides for a free and appropriate education for children with special needs. The principle is that no child with special needs

**Y**

**Z**

will be denied a free and appropriate education; thus, no student with disabilities is to be rejected.

**Zone of proximal development**   One of Vygotsky's cognitive development concepts. A stage of learning at which the unaided child will fail, but the child can pass with the appropriate assistance of other persons.

***Zorach v. Clauson***   The 1952 Supreme Court ruling that endorsed the practice of releasing students during the school day in order to attend religious classes or centers to receive religious instruction. The Court ruled that a New York state law upholding release time for religious centers was constitutional.

**Zygote**   A cell produced by two gametes (i.e., the union of the female egg and the male sperm to form the fertilized ovum).

# Appendix 1
# Abbreviations in Education

**4R-F** Four Relationship Factor Questionnaire

**16PF** Sixteen Personality Factor Questionnaire, fifth edition

**AA** Achievement Age

**AABP** Aptitude Assessment Battery: Programming

**AAC** Achievement/Ability Comparison

**AACD** Augmentative and Alternative Communication

**AAHPERD Health Related Physical Fitness Test** American Alliance for Health, Physical Education, Recreation and Dance

**AALI** Ann Arbor Learning Inventory

**AAMD** American Association on Mental Deficiency

**AAMR** American Association on Mental Retardation (formerly known as the American Association of Mental Deficiency)

**AAPEP** Adolescent and Adult Psychoeducational Profile

**AAPS** Arizona Articulation Proficiency Scale

**AATF** American Alliance of Teachers of French

**AATG** American Association of Teachers of German

**AATSP** American Association of Teachers of Spanish and Portuguese

**AB** Adaptive Behavior

**ABA** Applied Behavior Analysis

**ABA** Apraxia Battery for Adults

**ABC** Assessment Battery for Children; Assessment of Basic Competencies

**ABCD** Arizona Battery for Communication Disorders of Dementia

**ABE** Adult Basic Education

**ABES** Adaptive Behavior Evaluation Scale

**ABI** Adaptive Behavior Inventory

**ABIC** Adaptive Behavior Inventory for Children

**ABLE** Adult Basic Learning Examination

**ABR** Auditory Brainstem Response

**ABS** Affects Balance Scale; Adaptive Behavior Scales; Assessment of Basic Skills

**AC** Air Conduction or Alternating Current or Adrenal Cortex

**ACALD** Association for Children and Adults with Learning Disabilities

**ACDM** Assessment of Career Decision Making

**ACEI** Association for Childhood Education International

**ACER Advanced Test** Australian Council for Educational Research

**ACh** Acetylcholine

**ACL** The Adjective Checklist: American Classical Language

**ACLC** Assessment of Children's Language Comprehension

**ACLD** Association for Children with Learning Disabilities; American Committee on Learning Disabilities, now known as Learning Disabilities Association (LDA)

**ACPT** Auditory Continuous Performance Test

**ACRMD**   Association for Children with Retarded Mental Development

**ACS**   American Chemical Society; Assessment of Coping Styles

**ACS-NSTA**   American Chemical Society—National Science Teachers Association

**ACT Assessment Program**   American College Testing Program

**ACTeRS**   ADD-H Comprehensive Teacher's Rating Scale

**ADA**   Americans with Disabilities Act (P.L. 101-336) of 1991; average daily attendance

**ADAEP**   Alcohol and Drug Abuse Education Program

**ADD**   Attention-Deficit Disorder; Affective Domain Descriptor Program

**ADD-H**   Attention Deficit Disorder with Hyperactivity

**ADHD**   Attention-Deficit/Hyperactivity Disorder

**ADHDT**   Attention Deficit/Hyperactivity Disorder Test

**ADIS**   Anxiety Disorders Interview Schedule

**Adj**   Adjective

**ADL**   Activities of Daily Living

**ADM**   Average Daily Membership

**ADP**   Aphasia Diagnostic Profiles

**ADT**   Auditory Discrimination Test; Wepman's Auditory Discrimination Test

**Adv**   Adverb

**AE**   Age-Equivalent

**AERA**   American Educational Research Association

**AFDC**   Aid to Families with Dependent Children

**AFEES**   Armed Forces Examining and Entrance Stations

**AFSC**   Assessment of Fluency in School-age Children

**AFI**   Adaptive Functioning Index

**AFT**   American Federation of Teachers

**AG**   Annual Goal

**AGCT**   Army General Classification Test

**AGE**   Adult Growth Examination

**Ags**   Affiliated Groups

**AGS**   American Guidance Service

**AHSME**   American High School Mathematics Examination

**AHVS**   AH Vocabulary Scale

**AI Survey**   Alienation Index Survey

**AIB**   Australian Item Bank

**AIDS**   Ahr's Individual Development Survey; Assessment of Intelligibility of Dysarthric Speech; Acquired Immune Deficiency Syndrome

**AIME**   American Invitational Mathematics Examination

**AIM-TO**   Achievement Identification Measure—Teacher Observation

**AIR**   Assessment of Interpersonal Relations

**AJHSME**   American Junior High School Mathematics Examination

**AKT**   Applied Knowledge Test

**ALB**   Assessing Linguistic Behaviors

**ALD**   Automated Learning Device

**ALDA**   Analytic Learning Disability Assessment

**ALEM**   Adapted Learning Environments Model

**ALS**   Amyotrophic Lateral Sclerosis (Lou Gehrig's disease)

**ALST**   Adolescent Language Screening Test

**ALT**   Academic Learning Time

**AMA**   American Medical Association

**AMAP**   Alternative Model Assessment Package

**AmE**   American English

**AmInd**   American Indian

**AmSp**   American Spanish

**ANE**   Assessment in Nursery Education

**ANS**   Autonomic Nervous System

**ANSER**   Aggregate Neurobehavioral Student Health and Educational Review

**Ant**   Antonym

**AOB**   Automated Office Battery

**AP**   Advanced Placement

**APA** American Psychological Association; American Psychiatrical Association

**APART** Adelphi Parent Administered Readiness Test

**APF** Additional Personality Factor Index

**API** The Adult Personality Inventory; Affective Perception Inventory; Application Program Interface (computers)

**APP-R** Assessment of Phonological Processes, Revised

**APS** American Psychological Society

**AQSDOR** Assessment of Qualitative and Structural Dimensions of Object Representations

**ARAS** Ascending Reticular Arousing System

**ARC** Aids Related Complex

**ARI** Advanced Reading Inventory; Abuse-Risk Inventory for Women

**ASC** Assessment of Skills in Computation

**ASCD** Association for Supervision and Curriculum Development

**ASCII** American Standard Code for Information Interchange (computers)

**ASES** The Adult Self-Expression Scale

**ASHA** American Speech-Language-Hearing Association

**ASI** Reiss-Epstein-Gursky Anxiety Sensitivity Index

**ASIEP** Autism Screening Instrument for Educational Planning

**ASIEP-2** Autism Screening Instrument for Educational Planning, second edition

**ASK** Analysis of Skills Criterion referenced tests

**ASL** American Sign Language

**ASLPR** Australian Second Language Proficiency Ratings

**ASNLAS** Assessment of School Needs for Low-Achieving Students

**ASQ** The IPAT Anxiety Scale Questionnaire; Conners' Abbreviated Symptom Questionnaire

**ASS** Affective Sensitivity Scale

**ASSET** Assessing Semantic Skills through Everyday Themes

**ASVAB** Armed Services Vocational Aptitude Battery

**ATA** American Teachers Association

**ATAMS** Australian Test for Advanced Music Studies

**ATB** Advanced Test Battery

**ATFR** Arlin Test of Formal Reasoning

**ATMS** Attitudes Toward Mainstreaming Scale

**ATNR** Asymmetrical Tonic Neck Reflex

**AUD.DIS** Auditory Discrimination

**AVA** American Vocational Association

**AWM** Attitudes Toward Working Mothers Scale

**B-HPRS** Brief Hopkins Psychiatric Rating Scale

**BAB** Ball Aptitude Battery

**BALI** Behavior Analysis Language Instrument

**BAS** The British Ability Scales

**BASA** Boston Assessment of Severe Aphasia

**BASC** Behavior Assessment Scale for Children

**BASE** Behavioral Academic Self-Esteem; College Basic Academic Subjects Examination

**BASIC** Beginner's All-Purpose Symbolic Instruction Code

**BASIS** Basic Achievement Skills Individual Screener

**BAT** Bristol Achievement Test

**BBRS** Burks' Behavior Rating Scales

**BBTOP** Bankson-Bernthal Test of Phonology

**BC** Bone Conduction

**BCAS** The Barclay Classroom Assessment System

**BCCI** The Barclay Classroom Climate Inventory

**BCD** The Maryland/Baltimore County Design for Adult Basic Education

**BCI** Basic Concepts Inventory; Behavior Change Inventory

**BCP** Behavioral Characteristics Progression

**BCS** Battered Child Syndrome

**BCT** Basic Competency Test; The Booklet Category Test

**BD** Behavior Disorder

**BDAE** Boston Diagnostic Aphasia Examination

**BDCIBS** Brigance Diagnostic Comprehensive Inventory of Basic Skills

**BDI** Battelle Developmental Inventory; Beck Depression Inventory

**BDP** Behavioral Deviancy Profile

**BDRS** Behavior Dimensions Rating Scale

**BEA** Bilingual Education Act

**BEH** Bureau of Education for the Handicapped

**BEOG** Basic Educational Opportunity Grant

**BES-2** Behavior Evaluation Scale, second edition

**BEST** Basic Educational Skills Test; Basic English Skills Test; Bedside Evaluation and Screening Test of Aphasia

**BET** Basic Economics Test

**BETA-II** Revised Beta Examination, second edition

**BGMA** Hughes Basic Gross Motor Assessment

**BGT** Bender-Gestalt Test

**BHI** Bilingual Home Inventory

**BHS** Beck Hopelessness Scale

**BIAB** Brief Index of Adaptive Behavior

**BICS** Basic Interpersonal Communication Skills

**BINET** Stanford-Binet Intelligence Test

**BINL** Basic Inventory of Natural Language

**BINS** Bayley Infant Neurodevelopmental Screener

**BIP** Canter Background Interference Procedure for the Bender-Gestalt

**BK** Back

**BLAT** Blind Learning Aptitude Test

**BLCT** Basic Language Concepts Test

**BLNAI** Barclay Learning Needs Assessment Inventory

**BLSI** Barsch Learning Style Inventory

**BLST** Bankson Language Screening Test

**BLT** Bloomer Learning Test

**BLT-2** Bankson Language Test-2

**BMAT** Basic Motor Ability Test

**BMCT** Bennett Mechanical Comprehension Test

**BNAS** Brazelton Neonatal Assessment Scale

**BOA** Behavioral Observation Audiometry

**BOAE** Bureau of Occupational and Adult Education

**BOCES** Board of Cooperative Educational Services

**BOLT** Bilingual Oral Language Test; USES Basic Occupational Literacy Test

**BPI** Biographical and Personality Inventory

**BPS** Brigance Preschool Screen; Brickling Perceptual Scales; Bits per Second (computers)

**BPSM** Behaviour Problems: A System of Management

**BPVS** British Picture Vocabulary Scales

**BRI** Basic Reading Inventory, second edition

**BRIAAC** Behavior Rating Instrument for Autistic and other Atypical Children

**Brit** British

**BRP** Behavior Rating Profile

**BRP-2** Behavior Rating Profile Test, second edition

**BRS** Behavior Rating Scale; Behaviordyne Retirement Service

**BSA** Basic Skills Assessment

**BSCS** The Bloom Sentence Completion Survey

**BSI** Basic Skills Inventory; The Brief Symptom Inventory

**BSID-2** Bayley Scales of Infant Development, second edition

**BSL** The IOX Basic Skills Word List

**BSM II** Bilingual Syntax Measure II

**BSRI**   Bem Sex-Role Inventory

**BSS**   Beck Scale for Suicide Ideation

**BSSI**   Basic School Skills Inventory

**BSSI-D**   Basic School Skills Inventory—Diagnostic

**BSSI-S**   Basic School Skills Inventory—Screen

**BST**   Bessemer Screening Test; Basic Skills Tests; Behavior Study Technique

**BTBC-PV**   Boehm Test of Basic Concepts—Preschool Version

**BTBC-R**   Boehm Tests of Basic Concepts, Revised

**BTHI**   Brief Test of Head Injury

**BTORP**   Biemiller Test of Reading Processes

**BTRSP**   The Boder Test of Reading-Spelling Patterns

**BVMAT**   Basic Visual-Motor Association Test

**BVMGT**   Bender Visual Motor Gestalt Test

**BVRT-R**   Benton Visual Retention Test, Revised

**BWAP**   Becker Work Adjustment Profile

**C-L**   Cain-Levine Social Competency Scale

**C-PAC**   Clinical Probes of Articulation Consistency

**CA**   Chronological age

**CAAP**   Child and Adolescent Adjustment Profile

**CAAS**   Children's Attention and Adjustment Survey

**CAB**   Career Adaptive Behavior Inventory; Comprehensive Ability Battery; Clerical Abilities Battery

**CABR**   Children's Adaptive Behavior Report

**CABS**   Children's Adaptive Behavior Scale

**CAD**   Computer-Aided Design

**CAD/CAM**   Computer-Aided Design/Computer-Aided Manufacturing

**CADET**   Communication Abilities Diagnostic Test

**CADL**   Communication Abilities in Daily Living

**CAGS**   Certificate of Advanced Graduate Study Degree

**CAHPER**   Canadian Association for Health, Physical Education and Recreation

**CAI**   Computer Assisted Instruction; Career Assessment Inventories for the Learning Disabled; Career Assessment Inventory; Computer-Aided Instruction

**CALD**   Cognitive/Academic Language Deficiency

**CALIP**   Computer Aptitude, Literacy, and Interest Profile

**CALS**   Checklist of Adaptive Living Skills

**CALP**   Cognitive-Academic Language Proficiency

**CAM**   Computer-Aided Manufacturing

**CAP**   Callahan Anxiety Pictures; Comprehensive Assessment Program; Creativity Assessment Packet

**CAPE**   Clifton Assessment Procedures for the Elderly

**CAPPS**   Current and Past Psychopathology Scales

**CAPT**   Computer Aptitude Profile Test

**CAQ**   The Class Activities Questionnaire; Clinical Analysis Questionnaire

**CARS**   The Childhood Autism Rating Scale

**CAS**   Character Assessment Scale; Child Anxiety Scale; Cognitive Abilities Scale

**CASE**   Council of Administrators of Special Education of CEC; Comprehensive Assessment of School Environments

**CASI**   Career Attitudes and Strategies Inventory

**CAST**   Children of Alcoholics Screening Test

**CAT**   California Achievement Test; Children's Apperception Test; Cognitive Abilities Test; Canadian Achievement Tests

**CAT-SCAN**   Computerized Axial Tomography Scan

**CATIM** Class Achievement Test in Mathematics

**CAVAT** Carrow Auditory-Visual Abilities Test

**CBC** Camelot Behavior Checklist

**CBCL** Child Behavior Checklist

**CBE** Competency-Based Education

**CBED** Children with Behavioral and Emotional Difficulties

**CBI** Competency-Based Instruction; Creative Behavior Inventory

**CBRS** Cognitive Behavior Rating Scales

**CBRSC** Comprehensive Behavior Rating Scale for Children

**CBRT-R** The Clymer-Barrett Readiness Test, Revised

**CBRU** Computer Based Resource Units

**CBS** Criterion Test of Basic Skills

**CBTE** Competency Based Teacher Education

**CCB** Cognitive Control Battery

**CCBD** Council for Children with Behavioral Disorders of CEC

**CCC** Certificate of Clinical Competence

**CCEI** Crown-Crisp Experiential Index

**CCGI** Community-College Goals Inventory

**CCh** Creativity Checklist

**CCP** High School Career-Course Planner

**CCQ** The California Child Q-Set

**CCSI** Classroom-Communication Skills Inventory

**CCSPEA** Classroom Communication Screening Procedure for Early Adolescents

**CCT** Children's Category Test

**CCTT** Cornell Critical Thinking Tests

**CCTV** Closed-Circuit Television

**CDA** Child Development Associate

**CDB** Cognitive Diagnostic Battery

**CDC** Center for Disease Control

**CDCQ** Child Development Center Q-Sort

**CDI** Career Development Inventory; Children's Depression Inventory; Child Development Inventory; MacArthur-Communicative Development Inventories

**CDM** The Harrington-O'Shea Career Decision-Making System

**CDM-R** The Harrington-O'Shea Career Decision-Making System, Revised

**CDMT** California Diagnostic Mathematics Tests

**CDRT** California Diagnostic Reading Tests

**CDS** Communications Disorders Specialist; Career Decision Scale; Children's Depression Scale

**CDT** Chromatic Differential Test

**CEAI** Continuing Education Assessment Inventory

**CEC** Council of Exceptional Children

**CEC-DR** Division for Research of CEC

**CEC-MR** Division on Mental Retardation of CEC

**CEC-PIO** Pioneers Division of CEC

**CED** Committee for Economic Development

**CEDS** Council for Educational Diagnostic Services of CEC

**CEEB** College Entrance Examination Board

**CEFT** Children's Embedded Figures Test

**CEH** Classes for Emotionally Handicapped

**CELF-3** Clinical Evaluation of Language Functions—Diagnostic Battery, third edition

**CELF-R** Clinical Evaluation of Language Fundamentals, Revised

**CELI** Carrow Elicited Language Inventory

**CERI** Counselor Effectiveness Rating Instrument

**CES** Career Exploration Series

**CETA** Comprehensive and Employment Training Act

**CF** Cystic Fibrosis

**CFI**   Course-Faculty Instrument

**CFIT**   Culture Fair Intelligence Test

**CGI**   Career Guidance Inventory

**CGP**   Comparative Guidance and Placement Program

**CHAP**   Child Health Assessment Program

**ChilDSTest**   Visco Child Development Screening Test

**CHP**   Comprehensive Health Planning; Community Health Planning

**CI**   Content Inventories English, Social Studies, Science

**CIA**   Central Intelligence Agency

**CIBS**   Brigance Diagnostic Comprehensive Inventory of Basic Skills

**CIC**   Composite Indicators of Changes in average salaries and wages paid by public school systems

**CII**   Career Interest Inventory; Chart of Initiative and Independence

**CILD**   Career Inventories for the Learning Disabled

**CIRP**   The Cooperative Institutional Research Program

**CIT**   Career Interests Test

**CKST**   Cambridge Kindergarten Screening Test

**CLA**   Community Living Arrangement

**CLD**   Concept Learning and Development

**CLEP**   College-Level Examination Program

**CLIP**   Clinical Language Intervention Program

**CLOS**   Community Living Observational System

**CLP**   Comprehensive Language Program

**CLS**   Classroom Learning Screening

**CLSST**   Community Living Skills Screening Test, second edition

**CMAD**   Computer-Managed Articulation Diagnosis

**CMH**   Classes for Multiply Handicapped

**CMHC**   Community Mental Health Center

**CMI**   Computer-Managed Instruction; Career Maturity Inventory; Cornell Medical Index-Health Questionnaire

**CMMS**   Columbia Mental Maturity Scale

**CMS**   Children's Memory Scale

**CNS**   Central Nervous System

**COACH**   Cayuga-Onaondaga Assessment for Children with Handicaps

**CogAT**   Cognitive Abilities Tests

**COH**   Committee on the Handicapped

**COII**   Canadian Occupational Interest Inventory

**COL**   Comprehension of Oral Language

**COMPAS**   Oetting's Computer Anxiety Scale

**COMPS**   Clinical Observations of Motor and Postural Skills

**COMS**   Clyde Mood Scale

**Conj**   Conjunction

**COS**   Classroom Observation System

**COTNAB**   Chessington O.T. Neurological Assessment Battery

**CP**   Cerebral Palsy

**CPA**   Conditioned Play Audiometry

**CPAB**   Computer Programmer Aptitude Battery

**CPAS**   Computer Performance Appraisal Scale

**CPCI**   Couple's Pre-Counseling Inventory

**CPCL**   Career Problem Checklist

**CPI**   California Psychological Inventory; Consumer Price Index; Characters Per Inch (computer)

**CPI-R**   California Psychological Inventory, Revised

**CPQ**   Children's Personality Questionnaire

**CPR**   Cardio Pulmonary Resuscitation

**CPS**   Carlson Psychological Survey; Comrey Personality Scales; Characters per second (computers)

**CPT**  Conners' Continuous Performance Test Computer Program

**CPU**  Central Processing Unit

**CPVT**  Carolina Picture Vocabulary Test

**CQ**  Cree Questionnaire; The Custody Quotient

**CR**  Conditioned Response

**CRAC-Kit**  Crogt Readiness Assessment in Comprehension Kit

**CRC**  Civil Rights Commission

**CRI**  Classroom Reading Inventory, fourth edition

**CRS**  Communication Response Style; Customer Reaction Survey

**CRT**  Criterion-Referenced Testing; Cloze Reading Tests; Creative Reasoning Test

**CRTB**  Critical Reasoning Battery

**CRTM**  Curriculum-Referenced Tests of Mastery

**CS**  Clear-Screen Computers; Conditioned Stimulus

**CSAB**  Cognitive Skills Assessment Battery; Counseling Services Assessment Blank

**CSAE**  Cosmetology Student Admissions Examination

**CSAP**  Career Skills Assessment Program

**CSBS**  Communication and Symbolic Behavior Scales

**CSC**  Cognitive Symptom Checklists

**CSCS**  Piers-Harris Children's Self-Concept Scale (The Way I Feel about Myself)

**CSE**  Committee on Special Education

**CSF**  Cerebrospinal Fluid

**CSI**  Communication Sensitivity Inventory; Culture Shock Inventory

**CSSA**  Comprehensive Scales of Student Abilities

**CT-SCAN**  SEE: *CAT-SCAN*

**CTA**  Watson-Glaser Critical Thinking Appraisal; Context-Text-Application Approach

**CTAB**  Comprehensive Test of Adaptive Behavior

**CTBS**  Canadian Test of Basic Skills; Comprehensive Tests of Basic Skills

**CTBS/4**  Comprehensive Tests of Basic Skills, fourth edition

**CTI**  Clerical Task Inventory

**CTLESS**  Caso Test for Limited English-Speaking Students

**CTONI-2**  Comprehensive Test of Nonverbal Intelligence, second edition

**CTP**  California Test of Personality

**CTRS**  Conners' Rating Scales

**CTS**  Carey Temperament Scales

**CVLT**  California Verbal Learning Test

**CVLT-C**  California Verbal Learning Test for Children

**CYO**  Catholic Youth Organization

**DA**  Developmental Age

**DAB**  Devereux Adolescent Behavior Rating Scale

**DAB-2**  Diagnostic Achievement Battery-2

**DACL**  Depression Adjective Check Lists

**DALE**  The D.A.L.E. System: Developmental Assessment of Life Experiences

**DAM**  Diagnosing Abilities in Math

**DANTES**  DANTES Subject Standardized Tests

**DAP**  Draw-a-Person Test

**DAPQSS**  Draw-A-Person: A Quantitative Scoring System

**DAP:SPED**  Draw A Person: Screening Procedure for Emotional Disturbance

**DARD**  Durrell Analysis of Reading Difficulty

**DARE**  Diagnostic Analysis of Reading Errors; Drug Awareness Resistance Education

**DART**  Diagnostic Analysis of Reading Tasks

**DARTTS**  Diagnostic Assessment of Reading with Trial Teaching Strategies

**DAS**  Differential Ability Scales; Draw-a-Story; Dyadic Adjustment Scale

**DASH**  Developmental Assessment for the Severely Handicapped

**DASI** Developmental Activities Screening Inventory

**DASI-II** Developmental Activities Screening Inventory II

**DAST** Denver Audiometric Screening Test

**DAT** Differential Aptitude Tests

**DATA-2** Diagnostic Achievement Test for Adolescents, second edition

**DATP** Dental Admission Testing Program

**DAVLS** Dos Amigos Verbal Language Scales

**dB** Decibel (1/10th of a Bel)

**DC** Direct current

**DCAT** Developing Cognitive Abilities Test

**DCCD** Division for Children with Communication Disorders of CEC

**DCD** Division on Career Development of CEC

**DCDT** Division on Career Development and Transition of the CEC

**DCI** Developmental Communication Inventory

**DCMHQ-R** Denver Community Mental Health Questionnaire, Revised

**DD** Developmental Disabilities

**DDST** Denver Developmental Screening Test

**DDT** Dyslexial Determination Test

**DEC** Division for Early Childhood of CEC

**DECAD** Departmental Evaluation of Chairpersons Activities for Development

**DEJ** Double Entry Journal

**DEQ** Depressive Experience Questionnaire

**DESB II** Devereux Elementary School Behavior Rating Scale II

**DEST** Denver Eye Screening Test

**DHA** Denver Handwriting Analysis

**DHEW** Department of Health, Education and Welfare

**DI** Decoding Inventory

**DIAL-R** Developmental Indicators for the Assessment of Learning, Revised

**DIAM** Diagnosis: An Instructional Aid: Mathematics, Levels A and B

**DIQ** Deviation Intelligence Quotient

**DISC** Diagnostic Inventory for Screening Children

**DISES** Division of International Special Education and Services of the CEC

**DIT** Defining Issues Test

**DL-TA** Direct Listening-Thinking Activity

**DLD** Division for Learning Disabilities of CEC

**DLO** Desired Learning Outcomes

**DM** Diabetes Mellitus

**DMI** Diagnostic Mathematics Inventory; Decision-Making Inventory; Defense Mechanism Index

**DMI/MSIOI** DMI Mathematics Systems Instructional Objectives Inventory

**DMO** Decision-Making Organizer

**DMT** Distar Mastery Test

**DNA** Deoxyribonucleic Acid

**DOBS** Description of Body Scale

**DOCS** Developmental Observation Checklist System

**DOES** Dimensions of Excellence Scales

**DOF** Direct Observation Form

**DOSC** Dimensions of Self-Concept

**DP** Data Processing

**DPCL** Dating Problems Checklist

**DPH** Division for the Physically Handicapped of CEC

**DPHD** Division for Physical and Health Disabilities of CEC

**DPICS** Dyadic Parent-Child Interaction Coding System: A Manual

**DPII** Developmental Profile II

**DPST** Dallas Pre-School Screening Test

**DQ** Developmental Quotient

**DRA** Directed Reading Activity; Diagnostic Reading Activity

**DRI** Diagnostic Reading Inventory

**DRP** Degrees of Reading Power

**DRS**   Dementia Rating Scale

**DRS-81**   Diagnostic Reading Scales

**DRT**   Deductive Reasoning Test

**DRTA**   Directed-Reading-Thinking Approach

**DSA**   Developmental Sentence Analysis

**DSB**   Diagnostic Skills Battery

**DSFI**   Derogatis Sexual Functioning Inventory

**DSI**   Daily Stress Inventory

**DSM-III-R**   Diagnostic and Statistical Manual of Mental Disorders, Revised (third edition)

**DSM-IV-R**   Diagnostic and Statistical Manual of Mental Disorders, Revised (fourth edition)

**DSMD**   Devereux Scales of Mental Disorders

**DSP**   Digital Signal Processing (computers)

**DSPT**   Diagnostic Spelling Potential Test

**DST**   Decoding Skills Test; Diagnostic Screening Test; Diagnostic Spelling Test

**DTAS**   Diagnostic Test of Arithmetic Strategies

**DTKR**   Developmental Tasks for Kindergarten Readiness

**DTLA-3**   Detroit Tests of Learning Aptitude, third edition

**DTLA-A**   Detroit Tests of Learning Aptitude—Adult

**DTLA-P:2**   Detroit Tests of Learning Aptitude—Primary: Second Edition

**DTLS**   Diagnostic Test of Library Skills; Descriptive Tests of Language Skills

**DTMS**   Descriptive Tests of Mathematics Skills

**DTP**   Desktop Publishing (computers)

**DTVP-2**   Developmental Test of Visual Perception, second edition

**DVH**   Division for the Visually Handicapped of CEC

**DVI**   Digital Video Interactive

**DVR**   Division of Vocational Rehabilitation

**DVRT**   Drumcondra Verbal Reasoning Test 1

**DVSCB**   Dole Vocational Sentence Completion Blank

**DWPT**   Diagnostic Word Processing Test

**E**   English; Eastern; East

**EA**   Educational Age

**EAGT**   Emporia American Government Test

**EAI**   London House Employee Attitude Inventory

**EARLY**   Chicago Early Assessment and Remediation Laboratory

**EAS**   Educational Abilities Scales

**EASE**   Elicited Articulatory System Evaluation

**EBC**   Emotional Behavioral Checklist

**EBIS**   The Employment Barrier Identification Scale

**ECBI**   Eyberg Child Behavior Inventory

**ECDI**   Early Child Development Inventory

**ECEH**   Early Childhood Education for the Handicapped

**ECERS**   Early Childhood Environment Rating Scale

**ECI**   Early Coping Inventory

**ECIA**   Education Consolidation and Improvement Act of 1981

**ECPE**   Examination for the Certificate of Proficiency in English

**ECT**   Elementary cognitive task; End-of-Course Tests

**ED**   Emotionally disturbed

**ED or ed**   Education, Edited, Editor, Edition

**EDA**   Electrodermal Audiometry

**EDI**   Eating Disorder Inventory

**EDIBA**   Enright Diagnostic Inventory of Basic Arithmetic Skills

**EDS**   Educational Development Series

**EEG**   Electroencephalogram

**EEOC**   Equal Employment Opportunity Commission

**EEOG**   Equal Education Opportunity Grant

**EETS**  The Emotional Empathic Tendency Scale

**EFA-3**  Examining for Aphasia, third edition

**EFT**  Embedded Figures Test

**EGA**  Enhanced Graphics Adapter

**EH**  Emotionally Handicapped

**EHA**  Education of All Handicapped Act PL 94-142

**EI**  Emotionally Impaired; Educationally Impaired

**EII**  Educational Interest Inventory, revised edition

**EIP**  Elementary Intern Program

**EIRS**  Endeavor Instructional Rating System

**EIS**  Employee Involvement Survey

**EISP**  Early Identification Screening Profile

**EKG**  Electrocardiogram

**ELAD**  Early Learning: Assessment and Development

**ELC**  External Locus of Control

**ELD**  Electroluminescent Display

**ELI**  Environmental Language Inventory

**ELM-2**  Early Language Milestone Scale, second edition

**ELP**  Estimated Learning Potential; English-Language Proficient

**ELPI**  Educational Leadership Practices Inventory

**ELS**  ESL/Literacy Scale

**ELSA**  English Language Skills Assessment in a Reading Context

**EMDK**  Early Mathematics Diagnostic Kit

**EMH**  Educable Mentally Handicapped

**EMI**  Employability Maturity Interview

**EML**  Early Mathematical Language

**EMR**  Educable Mentally Retarded; Emotionally Mentally Retarded

**EMS**  Effectiveness Motivation Scale

**ENH**  Educable Neurologically Handicapped

**EOG**  Educational Opportunity Grant

**EOM**  End of Month

**EOWPVT-R**  Expressive One-Word Picture Vocabulary Test, revised

**EOWPVT-UE**  Expressive One-Word Picture Vocabulary Test-Upper Extension

**EPB**  Environmental Prelanguage Battery

**EPI**  Eysenck Personality Inventory

**EPPS**  Edwards Personal Preference Schedule

**EPQ**  Eysenck Personality Questionnaire; Educational Process Questionnaire

**EPS**  Executive Profile Survey; Encapsulated Postscript

**EPT**  Entry-Level Professional Test

**EQ**  Educational Quotient; Emo Questionnaire

**ER**  Erase screen (computers)

**ERB/CTP II**  ERB Comprehensive Testing Program II

**ERG**  Electroretinogram

**ERIC**  Educational Resources Information Center

**ERS**  Educational Research Services

**ESA**  English Skills Assessment

**ESC**  Escape Key (computer)

**ESEA**  Elementary and Secondary Education Act (PL 89-10, 1965)

**ESI**  Early Screening Inventory; Employability Skills Inventory

**ESL**  English as a Second Language

**ESLOA**  English as a Second Language Oral Assessment

**Esp**  Especially

**ESP**  Early Screening Profiles

**ESS**  E. S. Survey; Emotional Status

**EST**  Employment Screening Test and Standardization Manual

**ETR**  Experience-Text-Relationship Method

**ETS**  Educational Testing Service

**ETSA**  Educators'/Employers' Tests and Services Associates

**EWAT-X**  Ennis-Weir Argumentation Test, Level X: An Essay Test of Rational Thinking Ability

**F**  French

**FAA**  Federal Aviation Administration

**FACES III**  FACES III

**FAPE**  Free Appropriate Public Education

**FAS**  Fetal Alcohol Syndrome

**FAST**  Firestone Assessment of Self-Destructive Thoughts; Frenchay Aphasia Screening Test

**FBI**  Federal Bureau of Investigation

**FBLA**  Future Business Leaders of America

**FCC**  Federal Communications Commission

**FD**  Forward

**FDA**  Food and Drug Administration

**FDCRS**  Family Day Care Rating Scale

**FDIC**  Federal Deposit Insurance Corporation

**FDT**  Fine Dexterity Test

**FEC**  Foundation for Exceptional Children

**FEP**  Fluent English Proficient; Front-End Processor (computers)

**FES**  Family Environment Scale

**FF**  Form Feed (computers)

**FFA**  Future Farmers of America

**FGST**  First Grade Screening Test

**FHA**  Federal Housing Administration

**FIDPVCP**  Florida International Diagnostic-Prescriptive Vocational Competency Profile

**FIP**  Family Involvement Process

**FIPI**  The Facial Interpersonal Perception Inventory

**FIRO**  The Fundamental Interpersonal Relations Orientation

**FirstSTEP**  Screening Test for Evaluating Preschoolers

**FISS**  The Flint Infant Security Scale

**FKSB**  Florida Kindergarten Screening Battery

**FLT**  Functional Literacy Test

**FmHA**  Farmers Home Administration

**Fn**  Function Key (computers)

**FOME**  Fuld Object-Memory Evaluation

**FPT**  Four Picture Test, third revised edition

**fq**  Frequency range (involved in hearing)

**FRI**  Formal Reading Inventory

**FRT**  Family Relations Test

**FSH**  Follicle-Stimulating Hormone

**FSS**  Fear Survey Schedule

**FST**  Firefighter Selection Test

**FTA**  Future Teachers of America

**FTC**  Federal Trade Commission

**FY**  Fiscal Year

**G**  German

**GA**  Grade Age

**GAEL-P**  Grammatical Analysis of Elicited Language—Pre-Sentence Level

**GAIM**  Group Achievement Identification Measure

**GALT**  Gates Associative Learning Tests

**GARS**  Gilliam Autism Rating Scale

**GATB**  General Aptitude Testing Battery

**GATSB**  Guide to the Assessment of Test Session Behavior for WISC-III and WIAT

**GC CATS**  Guidance Centre Classroom Achievement Tests

**GDS**  Gesall Developmental Schedules

**GE**  Grade Equivalent

**GED**  General Education Development; General Equivalency Diploma; Tests of General Educational Development

**GEFT**  Group Embedded Figures Test

**GES**  Group Environment Scale

**GFTA**  Goldman-Fristoe Test of Articulation

**GFW**  Goldman-Fristoe-Woodcock Test of Auditory Discrimination

**GGF**  The Gross Geometric Forms Creativity Test for Children

**GHDT**  Goodenough-Harris Drawing Test

**GHQ**  General Health Questionnaire

**GIFFI**  Group Inventory for Finding Interests

**GIFT**   Group Inventory for Finding Creative Talent

**GIS-II**   Guidance Information System

**GIST**   Gochnour Idiom Screening Test

**Gk**   Greek (Homer circa 700 B.C.–300 A.D.)

**GLA**   Group Literacy Assessment

**GLD**   General Learning Disability

**GLI**   Grade Level Indicator

**GMA**   Group Mapping Activity

**GMAT**   Graduate Management Admission Test

**Gmc**   Germanic (the parent language of English, Dutch, German, Gothic, and Scandinavian languages)

**GMRT**   Gates-MacGinitie Reading Tests

**GMT**   Group Mathematics Test, second edition

**GNP**   Gross National Product

**GNT**   Graded Naming Test

**GOCL**   Gordon Occupational Check List II

**GOIT**   Goyer Organization of Ideas Test

**GORT-3**   Gray Oral Reading Tests

**GORT-D**   Gray Oral Reading Test—Diagnostic

**GPA**   Grade Point Average

**GPP-I**   Gordon Personal Profile—Inventory

**GREGT**   Graduate Record Examination—General Test

**GRT**   Group Reading Test, second edition

**GSCF**   Geriatric Sentence Completion Form

**GSIT**   Group Shorr Imagery Test

**GSR**   Galvanic Skin Response

**GTSF**   Gifted and Talented Screening Form

**GZTS**   The Guilford-Zimmerman Temperament Survey

**HABGT**   Hutt Adaptation of the Bender-Gestalt Test

**H-T-P**   House-Tree-Person Technique

**HAP**   Hilson Adolescent Profile; Human Activity Profile

**HAT**   Health Attribution Test

**HBDI**   Herrmann Brain Dominance Instrument

**HCEEP**   Handicapped Children's Early Education Plan

**HEEA**   Home Economics Education Association

**HELP**   Henderson-Moriarity ESL/Literacy Placement; Hawaii Early Learning Profile

**HESB**   Hahnemann Elementary School Behavior Rating Scale

**HESI**   Hudson Education Skills Inventory

**HEW**   Department of Health, Education and Welfare

**HGSHS**   Harvard Group Scale of Hypnotic Susceptibility

**HHSB**   Hahnemann High School Behavior Rating Scale

**HI**   Hearing impaired

**HILS**   High Intensity Learning System

**HIMR**   Hearing Impaired Mentally Retarded

**Hindu**   A native of India; Hindustani (a common language from India)

**HIP**   Hospital Improvement Project; Human Information Processing Survey

**HIT**   The Holtzman Inkblot Technique

**HIV**   Human Immune Deficiency Virus

**HM**   Happiness Measures

**HMACL**   Howarth Mood Adjective Checklist

**HMO**   Health Maintenance Organization

**HMS**   The Hearing Measurement Scale

**HNCAF**   Humanics National Child Assessment Form

**HOME**   Home Observation for Measurement of the Environment

**HOS**   Krantz Health Opinion Survey

**HPB**   High Probability Behavior

**HPP/SQ**   Hilson Personnel Profile/Success Quotient

**HPQ** Howarth Personality Questionnaire

**HPSS** Hogan Personnel Selection Series

**HRDR** Human Resource Development Report

**HRNB** Halstead-Reitan Neuropsychological Test Battery

**HRRA** Heart Rate Response Audiometry

**HSFCT** Harding Stress-Fair Compatibility Test

**HSMT** Henshaw Secondary Mathematics Test

**HSPAC** Help for Special Preschoolers Assessment Checklist

**HSPQ** High School Personality Questionnaire

**HSQ** Home Screening Questionnaire

**HS-WBLT** Watson-Barker Listening Test—High School Version

**HT** Hand Test; Hall-Tonna Inventory of Values

**HTL** Hearing Threshold Level

**HTLD** Houston Test for Language Development

**HTLV III** Human T-Lymphotrophic Virus Type III

**HTTP** Hypertext Transfer Protocol (computers)

**Hz** Hertz (cycles per second)

**I & R** Information & Referral

**IAAT** Iowa Algebra Aptitude Test

**IAHD** Institute for Applied Human Dynamics

**IAS** Integrated Assessment System

**IBAS** Instructional-Based Appraisal System

**IBQ** Illness Behaviour Questionnaire

**IBS** Interpersonal Behavior Survey

**IBT** Irrational Beliefs Test

**ICAP** Inventory for Client and Agency Planning

**ICD** International Classification of Diseases; Inventory for Counseling and Development

**ICEQ** Individualized Classroom Environment Questionnaire

**ICES** The Instructor and Course Evaluation System

**ICF** Intermediate Care Facility

**ICFMR** Intermediate Care Facility for the Mentally Retarded

**ICLAT** Illinois Children's Language Assessment Test

**ICP** Initial Communication Processes

**ICRH** Information Center-Recreation for the Handicapped

**ICRT** Individual Criterion-Referenced Test

**ICS** Interpersonal Conflict Scale

**IDA** Infant-Toddler Developmental Assessment

**IDEA** Individuals with Disabilities Education Act (1990); Instructional Development Effectiveness Assessment (PL 101-476)

**IDEAS** Interest Determination, Exploration and Assessment System

**IDS** Instrument for Disability Screening

**IDT** Interdisciplinary Team

**IED** Brigance Diagnostic Inventory of Early Development

**i.e.** (id est) That is

**IEP** Individualized Educational Plan (for special-needs students)

**IES** Brigance Diagnostic Inventory of Essential Skills

**IEU** Intermediate Education Unit

**IFSP** Individualized Family Service Plan

**IGE** Individually Guided Education

**IHE** Institute of Higher Education

**IHO** Impartial Hearing Officer

**II** Individualized Instruction

**IIP** Individual Implementation Plan

**IIPGC** Inventory of Individually Perceived Group Cohesiveness

**ILBC** Independent Living Behavior Checklist

**ILC** Internal Locus of Control

**ILDCSI**   Individual Learning Disabilities Classroom Screening Instruments

**ILS**   Independent Living Skills; Integrated Learning System

**ILSA**   Interpersonal Language Skills Assessment

**IMAGE-CA**   Imagery of Cancer

**IMBS**   Individual Motor Behavior Survey

**IMC**   Instructional Materials Center

**IMI**   Impact Message Inventory; Incentives Management Index

**IMMA**   Intermediate Measures of Music Audiation

**IMTS**   Independent Mastery Testing System for Writing Skills

**Infant MSEL**   Infant Mullen Scales of Early Learning

**INQUEST**   Investigating Questioning Procedure

**INT**   Integer

**Interj**   Interjection

**IOI**   Ilyin Oral Interview

**IOX**   IOX Basic Skill System

**IPBA**   Iowa Parent Behavior Inventory

**IPC**   Index of Personality Characteristics

**IPI**   Individually Prescribed Instruction; Initial Placement Inventory; Inwald Personality Inventory; IPI Job-Tests Program

**IPMA**   International Personnel Management Association

**IPP**   Individual Program Plan

**IPS**   Inventory of Perceptual Skills

**IQ**   Intelligence Quotient

**IRA**   International Reading Association

**IRF**   Intermittent Reinforcement

**IRI**   Informal Reading Inventory(ies)

**IRS**   Infant Rating Scale; Internal Revenue Service

**IRT**   Industrial Reading Test; Infant Reading Tests

**ISCS**   Iowa Social Competence Scales

**ISEE**   Independent Schools Entrance Examination

**ISI**   Informal Spelling Inventory; Interpersonal Style Inventory; Canfield Instructional Styles Inventory

**ISM**   Integrated Skills Method

**ISO**   International Standard Organization

**ISRT**   Iowa Silent Reading Test

**ISS**   Information System Skills

**IST**   Incomplete Sentences Task

**ISTEP**   Indiana State Practice Tests

**Ital**   Italian

**ITBS**   Iowa Tests of Basic Skills

**ITED**   Iowa Tests of Educational Development

**ITPA**   Illinois Test of Psycholinguistic Ability

**ITV**   Instructional Television

**IWI**   Informal Writing Inventory

**IWRP**   Individualized Written Rehabilitation Program

**IWRT**   Instant Word Recognition Test

**J3MSLS**   Joliet 3-Minute Speech and Language Screen

**JAI**   Job Awareness Inventory

**JAPQ**   Job Activity Preference Questionnaire

**JAS**   Jenkins Activity Survey; Job Attitude Scale

**JCE**   A Job Choice Decision-Making Exercise

**JDI**   The Job Descriptive Index

**JDQ**   Job Disposition Questionnaire

**JEPI**   Junior Eysenck Personality Inventory

**JIIG-CAL**   Job Ideas and Information Generator—Computer-Assisted Learning

**JLRRT**   Jordan Left-Right Reversal Test

**JOB-O**   Judgment of Occupational Behavior—Orientation

**JPI**   Jackson Personality Inventory

**JRA**   Juvenile Rheumatoid Arthritis Inventory

**JTPA**   Job Training Partnership Act

**JVIS**   Jackson Vocational Interest Survey

**K-A**  Kuhlman-Anderson Intelligence Test

**K-ABC**  Kaufman Assessment Battery for Children

**K-BIT**  Kaufman Brief Intelligence Test

**K-SEALS**  Kaufman Survey of Early Academic and Language Skills

**K-SNAP**  Kaufman Short Neuropsychological Assessment Procedure

**K-TEA**  Kaufman Test of Educational Achievement

**KAI**  Kirton Adaptation-Innovation Inventory

**KAIT**  Kaufman Adolescent and Adult Intelligence Test

**KCT**  Knox's Cube Test

**KDS**  Kinetic Drawing System for Family and School

**K-FAST**  Kaufman Functional Academic Skills Test

**KID**  Kent Infant Development Scale

**KIDS**  Missouri Kindergarten Inventory of Developmental Skills

**KIEI**  Kundu Introversion Extraversion Inventory

**KIPS**  Kaufman Infant and Preschool Scale

**KLMT**  Kerby Learning Modality Test, revised

**KLPA**  Khan-Lewis Phonological Analysis

**KNPI**  Kundu Neurotic Personality Inventory

**KOIS**  Kuder Occupational Interest Survey

**KPAG**  Keele Pre-School Assessment Guide

**KPC**  Kohn Problem Checklist

**KPMI**  Kraner Preschool Math Inventory

**KPR**  Kuder Preference Record

**KQM**  Kolson Quick Modality Test

**KSCS**  Kohn Social Competence Scale

**KST**  Keyboard Skills Test

**KTI**  Keegan Type Indicator

**KTPI**  Khatena-Torrance Creative Perception Inventory

**KVST**  Keystone Visual Survey Test

**KWL**  A reading approach based on 1. what you Know about a topic, 2. what you Want to learn or know, and 3. what you Learned after reading.

**L**  Latin (classical language from 200 B.C.–300 A.D.); Late Latin today

**LA**  Learning aptitude

**LAAP**  Language Arts Assessment Portfolio

**LAB**  Language Assessment Battery

**LAC**  Lindamood Auditory Conceptualization

**LACT**  Lindamood Auditory Conceptualization Test

**LAD**  Language Acquisition Device; Test of Lateral Awareness and Directionality

**LAI**  Love Attitudes Inventory

**LAP**  Learning Ability Profile

**LARR**  Linguistic Awareness in Reading Readiness

**LARS**  Language-Structured Auditory Retention Span Test

**LAS**  Language Assessment Scales

**LASSI**  Learning and Study Strategies Inventory

**LAV**  Lymphadenopathy-Associated Virus

**LBC**  Louisville Behavior Checklist

**LBDQ**  Leader Behavior Description Questionnaire

**LBP**  Learned Behaviors Profile

**LBS**  Learning Behaviors Scale

**LCGT**  Listening Comprehension Group Tests

**LCPC**  Learning Channel Preference Checklist

**ld or LD**  Learning Disabled

**LDA**  Learning Disabilities Association (formerly known as American Committee on Learning Disabilities)

**LDES**  Learning Disability Evaluation Scale

**LDRP**  Learning Disability Rating Procedure

**LDTC**   Learning Disabilities Teacher Consultant

**LEA**   Local Education Agency; Language Experience Approach

**LEADR**   Law Enforcement Assessment and Development Report

**LEAP**   Louisiana State Practice Tests

**LEI**   Learning Environment Inventory

**LEL**   Learning Expectancy Level

**LEP**   Limited English Proficient

**LES-C and LES-A**   Life Event Scales for Children and Adolescents

**LET-II**   Learning Efficiency Test II, revised

**LFMT**   Listening for Meaning Test

**LFT**   Language Facility Test

**LH**   Learning Handicapped; Luteinizing Hormone

**LI**   Language Impaired

**LIFE II**   Longitudinal Interval Follow-Up Evaluation, second edition

**LIPS**   Leiter International Performance Scale

**LIT**   Language Imitation Test; Language Inventory for Teachers

**LL**   Late Latin (300 A.D.–700 A.D.)

**LLQ**   Leatherman Leadership Questionnaire

**LMT**   Learning Methods Test

**LNNB**   Luria-Nebraska Neuropsychological Battery

**LOI**   Life Orientation Inventory

**LOTCA**   Loewenstein Occupational Therapy Cognitive Assessment

**LOVE**   Linguistics of Visual English

**LPB**   Low Probability Behavior

**LPI**   Learning Preference Inventory

**LPQ**   Learning Process Questionnaire

**LPR**   Local Percentile Rank

**LPS**   Laterality Preference Schedule

**LPT**   Language Proficiency Test

**LQ**   Learning Quotient

**LRE**   Least Restrictive Environment

**LRS**   Least Restrictive Setting; Light's Retention Scale

**LRT**   London Reading Test

**LS**   Learning Screening

**LSA**   Language Sampling and Analysis

**LSAT**   Law School Admission Test

**LSES**   Salamon-Conte Life Satisfaction in the Elderly Scale

**LSI**   Leadership Skills Inventory; Learning Styles Inventory; Lessons for Self-Instruction in basic skills

**LSIS**   Learning Style Identification Scale

**LSQ**   Life Style Questionnaire

**LST**   Library Skills Test

**LT**   Computer Command of Left

**LTI-C**   Let's Talk Inventory for Children

**LTIT**   Lorge-Thorndike Intelligence Tests

**LTM**   Long-Term Memory

**LTP**   Language Proficiency Test

**M-C**   Milani-Comparetti Motor Development Screening Test

**M-G-L**   Move-Grow-Learn Program

**M-M-F**   Major-Minor-Finder

**MA**   Mental Age

**MAACL**   Multiple Affect Adjective Check List

**MAB**   Multidimensional Aptitude Battery

**MAC-K**   Maculaitas Assessment Program, commercial edition

**MACPH**   Mossford Assessment Chart for the Physically Handicapped

**MACR-R**   Southern California Motor Accuracy Test, Revised

**MADD**   Mothers Against Drunk Driving

**MAE**   Multilingual Aphasia Examination

**MAE-S-MAE**   (Spanish): Examende Afasie Multilingue

**MAI**   Mathematics Attitude Inventory; Motivation and Achievement Inventory

**MAP**   Miller Assessment for Preschoolers; Multidimensional Assessment and Planning Form; Managerial Assessment of Proficiency

**MAPI**   Millon Adolescent Personality Inventory

**MARS** Mathematics Anxiety Rating Scale

**MAS** Manifest Anxiety Scale; Management Appraisal Survey; Memory Assessment Scales

**MASI** Multilevel Academic Skills Inventory

**MAST** Multilevel Academic Survey Tests

**MAT** Miller Analogies Test; Motivation Analysis Test

**MAT7** Metropolitan Achievements Test

**MBA** Mini-Battery of Achievement

**MBD** Minimal Brain Dysfunction; Minimal Brain Damage

**MBDCT** The McGuire-Bumpus Diagnostic Comprehension Test

**MBHI** Millon Behavioral Health Inventory

**MBI** Maslach Burnout Inventory

**MBO** Management by Objectives

**MBSP** Monitoring Basic Skills Progress

**MBTI** Myers-Briggs Type Indicator

**MCAT** Medical College Admission Test

**MCD** Minimal Cerebral Dysfunction

**MCDI** Minnesota Child Development Inventory

**MCH** Management Change Inventory

**MCI** Marital Communication Inventory; My Class Inventory; Managerial Competence Index

**MCMI-III** Millon Clinical Multiaxial Inventory-III

**MCR** Management Coaching Relations; Managerial Competence Review

**MCT** Minimum Competency Test; Minnesota Clerical Test

**MD** Muscular Dystrophy

**MDE** Marketing and Distributive Education

**MDI** Mental Development Index; Multiscore Depression Inventory

**MDQ** Menstrual Distress Questionnaire

**MDRP** The Macmillan Diagnostic Reading Pack

**MDS** McCarron-Dial System

**MDT** Manual Dexterity Test

**ME** Manson Evaluation; Middle English (1100 A.D.–1500 A.D.)

**MEAP** Multiphasic Environmental Assessment Procedure

**Med** Medieval

**MEI** Marriage Expectation Inventories; Medical Ethics Inventory; Military Environment Inventory

**MEM** Bessell Measurement of Emotional Maturity

**MEPS** Management Effectiveness Profile System

**MET** Minimum Essentials Test

**MFAQ** OARS Multidimensional Functional Assessment Questionnaire

**MFAS** Marriage and Family Attitude Survey

**MFD** Memory for Designs Test

**MFFT** Matching Familiar Figures Test

**MFVPT** Motor-Free Visual Perception Test

**MGIB** Management and Graduate Item Bank

**MGLD** Mild General Learning Disability

**MH** Multiply Handicapped

**MHVS** Mill Hill Vocabulary Scale

**MHz** Megahertz

**MICR** Magnetic-Ink Character Recognition (computers)

**MicroCog** Assessment of Cognitive Functioning

**MIDRI** McCarthy Individualized Diagnostic Reading Inventory

**MIFV** Maferr Inventory of Feminine Values

**MILI** Multilevel Informal Language Inventory

**MILM** Management Inventory on Leadership and Motivation

**MIMC** Management Inventory on Managing Change

**MIMV** Maferr Inventory of Masculine Values

**MIPAC**  Management Inventory on Performance Appraisal and Coaching

**MIPS**  Millon Index of Personality Styles

**MIQ**  Minnesota Importance Questionnaire

**MIRBI**  Mini-Inventory of Right Brain Injury

**MITM**  Management Inventory on Time Management

**MKAS**  Meyer-Kendall Assessment Survey

**M-KIDS**  Metropolitan Early Childhood Assessment Program

**MLD**  Measurement of Language Development

**MLST**  Merrill Language Screening Test

**MLU**  Mean Length of Utterance

**MMAT**  Missouri State Practice Tests

**MMI**  Meta-Motivation Inventory

**MMMT**  Meanings and Measures of Mental Tests

**MMPI**  Minnesota Multiphasic Personality Inventory

**MMPI-2**  Minnesota Multiphasic Personality Inventory-2

**MMPI-A**  Minnesota Multiphasic Personality Inventory—Adolescent

**MMY**  Mental Measurements Yearbooks

**Mo**  Mode

**MO**  Mathematical Olympiads

**MOANS**  Mayo's Older Americans Normative Studies

**MP-JFI**  Managerial and Professional Job Functions Inventory

**MPAPS**  Motivation and Potential for Adoptive Parenthood Scale

**MPD**  Measures of Psychosocial Development

**MPDT**  Minnesota Percepto-Diagnostic Test

**MPFB**  Revised Minnesota Paper Form Board Test

**MPI**  Maudsley Personality Inventory; Minnesota Preschool Inventory

**MPR**  Manager Profile Record

**MPRE**  Multistate Professional Responsibility Examination

**MPSI**  Minneapolis Preschool Screening Instrument

**MPT-R**  The Michigan Picture Test, Revised

**MPU**  Management Practices Update

**MR**  Mental Retardation

**MREI**  A Marriage Role Expectation Inventory

**MRFI**  Mutually Responsible Facilitation Inventory

**MRI**  Magnetic Resonance Imaging

**MRS**  Management Relations Survey

**MRT**  Metropolitan Readiness Test

**MS**  Multiple Sclerosis; millisecond

**MS-DOS**  Microsoft Disk Operating System (trademark system)

**MSAS**  Minnesota School Attitude Survey

**MSAT**  Minnesota Scholastic Aptitude Test

**MSCA**  McCarthy Scales of Children's Abilities

**MSCC**  Mental Status Checklist for Children

**MSCS**  Miner Sentence Completion Scale; Multidimensional Self-Concepts Scale; Multisensory Disorder

**MSEI**  The Multidimensional Self-Esteem Inventory

**MSGO**  Miskimins Self-Goal-Other Discrepancy Scale

**MSI**  Marital Satisfaction Inventory; Motor Skills Inventory

**MSKP**  Medical Sciences Knowledge Profile

**MSQ**  Minnesota Satisfaction Questionnaire

**MSRT**  Minnesota Spatial Relations Test

**MST**  McCarthy Screening Test

**MVPT**  Motor-Free Visual Perception Test

**MVS**  My Vocational Situation

**MWM**  Minskoff, Wiseman, Minskoff (program for language development)

**MZSCS** Martinek-Zaichkowsky Self-Concept Scale for Children

**N** Number of participants in a sample or study; Nano; North; Noun

**NABC** Normative Adaptive Behavior Checklist

**NABE** National Association for Bilingual Education (bilingualism)

**NABT** National Association of Biology Teachers

**NACH** National Advisory Committee on the Handicapped

**NADI** North American Depression Inventories for Children and Adults

**NAEP** National Assessment of Education Progress

**NAESP** National Association of Elementary School Principals

**NAEYC** National Association for the Education of Young Children

**NAGC** National Association for Gifted Children

**NART** National Adult Reading Test

**NASA** National Aeronautics and Space Administration

**NASBE** National Association of State Boards of Education

**NASDC** New American Schools Development Corporation

**NASDE** National Association of State Directors of Special Education

**NASP** National Association of School Psychologists

**NASSP** National Association of Secondary School Principals

**NASTEC** National Association of State Directors of Teacher Education and Certification

**NAT** National Achievement Test

**NATB** Nonreading Aptitude Test Battery

**NATIE** National Association for Trade and Industrial Education

**NATO** North Atlantic Treaty Organization

**NBPTS** National Board for Professional Teaching Standards

**NCATE** National Council for Accreditation of Teacher Education

**NCME** National Council on Measurement in Education

**NCSS** Navran Component Scoring System; National Council for the Social Studies

**NCTE** National Council of Teachers of English

**NCTM** National Council of Teachers of Mathematics

**NDEA** National Defense Education Act

**NDOC** Neurological Dysfunctions of Children

**NDRT** Nelson-Denny Reading Test

**NEA** National Education Association

**NEAT** Norris Educational Achievement Test

**NEDT** National Educational Development Tests

**NEGP** National Education Goals Panel

**NELT** Nelson English Language Tests

**NEO-PI** The NEO Personality Inventory

**NEP** Non-English Proficient

**NEPSY** Comprehensive Neuropsychological Assessment

**NFIE** National Foundation for the Improvement of Education

**NFSHSA** National Federation of States High School Association

**NH** Neonatal Hypothyroidism

**NI** Neurologically Impaired

**NIMH** National Institute of Mental Health

**NITDHS** Non-Verbal Intelligence Tests for Deaf and Hearing Subjects

**NJCLD** National Joint Committee on Learning Disabilities

**NJTRS** New Jersey Test of Reasoning Skills

**NL** New Latin (after 1500 A.D.)

**NLQ** Near-Letter Quality (computers)

**NMR** Nuclear Magnetic Resonance

**NMSA** National Middle Schools Association

**NNAT**   Naglieri Nonverbal Ability Test

**NOCTI**   National Occupational Competency Testing Institute

**NOW**   National Organization for Women

**NPSS**   National Proficiency Survey Series

**NQP**   Nisonger Questionnaire for Parents

**NREM**   Non-REM Sleep

**NREN**   National Research and Educational Network

**NRIT**   Non-Readers Intelligence Test

**NRM**   Norm-Referenced Measurement

**NRT**   Norm-Referenced Testing

**NS**   Nanosecond

**NSE**   National Spanish Examinations; Neuropsychological Status Examination

**NSF**   National Science Foundation

**NSST**   Northwestern Syntax Screening Test

**NSTA**   National Science Teachers Association

**NTCS**   Nonverbal Test of Cognitive Skills

**NTE**   National Teachers Exam

**NTLA**   Nebraska Test of Learning Aptitudes

**NVIT**   Non-Verbal Intelligence Test

**NVSH**   Non-Vocal Severely Handicapped

**NYC**   Neighborhood Youth Corps

**O**   Old

**O-A**   Objective-Analysis Test Battery

**OA**   Osteogenesis Imperfecta (brittle-bone disease)

**OAAAT**   Ohio Apparel and Accessories Achievement Test

**OABMAT**   Ohio Auto Body Mechanic Achievement Test

**OAMAT**   Ohio Automotive Mechanics Achievement Test

**OACCAT**   Ohio Accounting/Computing Clerk Achievement Test

**OAGBAT**   Ohio Agricultural Business Achievement Test

**OAGMAT**   Ohio Agricultural Mechanics Achievement Test

**OASIS-2**   Occupational Aptitude Survey and Interest Schedule, second edition

**OASIS-AS**   Occupational Aptitude Survey

**OASIS-IS**   Occupational Interest Schedule

**OAT**   The CHILD Center Operational Assessment Tool

**OBE**   Outcomes-Based Education

**OCAAT**   Ohio Commercial Art Achievement Test

**OCAT**   Ohio Carpentry Achievement Test

**OCEAT**   Ohio Construction Electricity Achievement Test

**OCHSAT**   Ohio Community and Home Services Achievement Test

**OCI**   Organizational Competence Index

**OCIW**   Our Class and Its Work

**OCOAT**   Ohio Cosmetology Achievement Test

**OCPEAT**   Ohio Communications Products Electronics Achievement Test

**OCSAT**   Ohio Clerk-Stenographer Achievement Test

**OCTAT**   Ohio Clerk Typist Achievement Test

**ODAAT**   Ohio Dental-Assisting Achievement Test

**ODAT**   Ohio Drafting Achievement Test

**ODEFSPAT**   Ohio D.E. Food Services Personnel Achievement Test

**ODHOAT**   Ohio Diversified Health Occupations Achievement Test

**ODMAT**   Ohio Diesel Mechanic Achievement Test

**ODPAT**   Ohio Data Processing Achievement Test

**ODS**   Orton Dyslexia Society

**ODSS**   Organic Dysfunction Survey Schedules

**OE**   Old English (before 1100 A.D.)

**OECHC**   Office for Education of Children with Handicapping Conditions

**OEI-R** Observational Emotional Inventory, Revised

**OEO** Office of Economic Opportunity

**OEP** Office of Emergency Preparedness

**OE/SPPT** Oral English/Spanish Proficiency Placement Test

**OFMAT** Ohio Farm Managerial Achievement Test

**OFMKEAT** Ohio Food Marketing Key Employee Achievement Test

**OFSAT** Ohio Fabric Services Achievement Test

**OGMAT** Ohio General Merchandising Achievement Test

**OGOCAT** Ohio General Office Clerk Achievement Test

**OHARAT** Ohio Heating, Air Conditioning, and Refrigeration Achievement Test

**OHAT** Ohio Horticulture Achievement Test

**OHEFSAT** Ohio H. EC. Food Services Achievement Test

**OHI** Other Health Impaired

**OHS** Organization Health Survey

**OIEAT** Ohio Industrial Electronics Achievement Test

**OIRS** Occupational Interest Rating Scale

**OJT** On-the-Job Training

**OLDM** Oral Language Dominance Measure

**OLE** Optimal Learning Environment

**OLPAT** Ohio Lithographic Printing Achievement Test

**OLPM** Oral Language Proficiency Measure

**OLSAT** Otis-Lennon School Ability Test

**OLSIDI-F** Oral Language Sentence Imitation Diagnostic Inventory—F

**OLSIST** Oral Language Sentence Imitation Screening Test

**OMAAT** Ohio Medical Assisting Achievement Test

**OMAT** Ohio Masonry Achievement Test

**OMEP** Organisation Mondiale Pour L'Education Prescolaire

**OMI** Orientation and Motivation Inventory

**OMTAT** Ohio Machine Trades Achievement Test

**OODQ** Oliver Organization Description Questionnaire

**OP** Outpatient

**OPAAT** Ohio Production Agriculture Achievement Test

**OPI** Omnibus Personality Inventory

**OPQ** Occupational Personality Questionnaire

**ORV** Off-Road Vehicle

**OSERAT** Ohio Small Engine Repair Achievement Test

**OSHA** Occupational Safety and Health Administration

**OSI** Occupational Stress Indicator; Occupational Stress Inventory

**OSIQ** The Offer Self-Image Questionnaire for Adolescents

**OSLMT** Ohio School Library/Media Test

**OSMSE** The Oral Speech Mechanism Screening Examination

**OT** Occupational Therapist

**OTC** Occupational Training Center

**OVIS-II** Ohio Vocational Interest Survey, second edition

**OVR** Office for Vocational Rehabilitation

**OWAT** Ohio Welding Achievement Test

**OWLS** Oral and Written Language Scales

**OWPAT** Ohio Word Processing Achievement Test

**P** Probability; Percentile

**P-F Study** The Rosenzweig Picture-Frustration Study

**P-MAC** Perceptual-Motor Assessment for Children

**P & MTT** Production and Maintenance Technician Test

**P-TPT**  Portable Tactual Performance Test

**PA**  Physical Age

**PAAM**  Projective Assessment of Aging Method

**PAAT**  Parent as a Teacher Inventory; Programmer Analyst Aptitude Test

**PAC**  Parent Advisory Council; Progress Assessment Checklist; Progress Assessment Chart of Social Development; Placement and Counseling Program; Political Action Committee

**PACI**  A Parent-Adolescent Communication Inventory

**PAI**  Personality Assessment Inventory

**PAIP**  Preverbal Assessment-Intervention Profile

**PAIR**  Performance Assessment in Reading; Personal Assessment of Intimacy in Relationships

**PAIS**  Psychosocial Adjustment to Illness Scale

**PAK**  Practical Articulation Kit

**PAL-C**  Profile of Adaptation to Life—Clinical Scale

**PAL-H**  Profile of Adaptation to Life—Holistic Scale

**PALD-ESA**  Prescriptive Analysis of Language Disorders—Expressive Syntax Assessment

**PALS**  Program for the Acquisition of Language with the Severely Impaired

**PARS**  Personal Adjustment and Role Skills Scale

**PAS**  Programmer Aptitude Series

**PaSaT**  Paced Auditory Serial Attention Test

**PASES**  Performance Assessment of Syntax

**PASS**  Program Analysis of Service Systems; Personnel Assessment Selection System; Phoenix Ability Survey System; Perception of Ability Scale for Students

**PAT**  Persian Achievement Tests; Photo Articulation Test; Predictive Ability Test; Progressive Achievement Tests in Reading

**PAT/Study Skills**  Progressive Assessment Tests/Study Skills

**PATHS**  Peer Attitudes Toward the Handicapped Scale

**PATMATHS**  Progressive Achievement Tests in Mathematics

**PAYES**  Program for Assessing Youth Employment Skills

**PB**  Peg Board

**PBCL**  Pre-School Behaviour Checklist

**PBI**  Personal Background Inventory; Pollack-Branden Inventory

**PBQ**  Preschool Behavior Questionnaire

**PBR**  Portable Braille Recorder; Parent Behavior Form

**PBRF**  Phoneme Baseline Recording Forms

**PBRS**  Pupil Behavior Rating Scale

**PBTE**  Performance-Based Teacher Education

**PC**  Personal Computer

**PC-DOS**  A DOS-Operating System that is trademarked

**PCB**  Printed Circuit Board (computers)

**PCDP**  Personal Career Development Profile

**PCI**  Premarital Communications Inventory

**PCK**  Premarital Counseling Kit

**PCL**  Printer Control Language (computers)

**PCL-R**  Hare Psychopathy Check List, Revised

**PCT**  Preliminary Competency Test

**PD**  Pen Down (computers); page down

**PDI-R**  Psychiatric Diagnostic Interview, Revised

**PDIS**  Personal Distress Inventory and Scales

**PDMS**  Peabody Developmental Motor Scales and Activity Cards

**PDQ**  Denver Prescreening Developmental Questionnaire; Preliminary Diagnostic Questionnaire

**PE**  Physical Education; Pen Erase (computers)

**PEB**   Psycho-Educational Battery

**PECC**   The Prior Early Childhood Curriculum

**PEER**   Pediatric Examination of Educational Readiness

**PEET**   Pediatric Extended Examination at Three

**PEEX**   Pediatric Early Elementary Examination

**PEI**   Personal Experience Inventory

**PEIPD**   The Prior Evaluative Instrument for Perceptual Development

**PEP**   Pupil Evaluation Program; Psychoeducational Profile; Primary Education Program; Psycho-Epistemological Profile

**PEPS**   Productivity Environmental Preference Survey

**PES**   Progress Evaluation Scales

**PEST**   Patterned Elicitation Syntax Test

**PET**   Pupil Evaluation Team; Parent Effectiveness Training

**PET Scan**   Positron Emission Tomography Scan

**PF**   Sixteen Personality Factor Questionnaire

**PFPS**   Potential for Foster Parenthood Scale

**Pg**   Portuguese

**PH**   Physically Handicapped

**PHC**   Pupils with Handicapping (ed) Conditions

**PHCA**   Personal History Checklist for Adults

**PHI**   The Psychap Inventory

**PHS**   Public Health Service

**PHT**   Paired Hands Test

**PI**   Personal Inventory; Proactive Inhibition

**PIAT-R**   Peabody Individual Achievement Test, Revised

**PIC**   Personality Inventory for Children

**PICA**   Programming Interpersonal Curricula for Adolescents; Porch Index of Communicative Ability

**PICAC**   Porch Index of Communicative Ability in Children

**PIL**   Purpose in Life Test

**PIM**   Personal Information Manager (computers)

**PIN**   Personal Identification Number

**PINS**   Persons (usually juveniles) In Need of Supervision

**PIP**   Parent Involvement Project; PIP Development Charts

**PIPS**   Peabody Intellectual Performance Scale

**PIQ**   Purdue Interest Questionnaire

**PKU**   Phenylketonuria

**PL**   Public law (federal); Plural

**PLA**   Psycholinguistic Age

**PLAI**   Preschool Language Assessment Instrument

**PLDK**   Peabody Language Development Kits

**PLS**   Parsons Language Sample

**PLS-3**   Preschool Language Scale-3

**PLSPS**   Performance Levels of a School Program Survey

**PMA**   Primary Mental Abilities Test

**PMCI**   Premarital Communications Inventory

**PMHP**   Program for Multi-Handicapped Pupils

**PMI**   Prescriptive Math Inventory; Power Management Inventory

**PMMA**   Primary Measures of Music Audiation

**PMP**   Power Management Profile

**PMPQ**   Professional and Managerial Position Questionnaire

**PMR**   Profoundly Mentally Retarded

**PMRT**   Peabody Mathematics Readiness Test

**PMS**   Participative Management Survey

**PMT**   The Porteus Maze Test; The Perceptual Memory Task

**PNS**   Peripheral Nervous System

**POHI**   Physically or Otherwise Health Impaired

**POI**   Personal Orientation Inventory

**POM**   Personal Opinion Matrix

**POMS**   Profile of Mathematics Skills; Profile of Mood States

**PONS**   Profile of Nonverbal Sensitivity

**POS**   Profile of a School

**PP**   Pre-Placement

**PPAIP**   Phonological Processes Assessment and Intervention

**PPBC-R**   Portland Problem Behavior Checklist, Revised

**PPM**   Pages per Minute

**PPMS**   Purdue Perceptual Motor Survey

**PPP**   Prescriptive Parent Programming

**PPPI**   Personnel Performance Problems Inventory

**PPRS**   Perceptions of Parental Role Scales

**PPS**   (Post Postscriptum) An additional postscript

**PPS**   Productive Practices Survey

**PPST**   Pre-Professional Skills Tests

**PPVT-R**   Peabody Picture Vocabulary Test, Revised

**PQ**   Personal Questionnaire; Perceptual Quotient

**PQRST**   Personal Questionnaire Rapid Scaling Technique

**PR**   Percentile Rank

**PRCS**   Psychological Response Classification System

**PRE-LAS**   PRE-LAS English

**Pre-TOEFL**   Preliminary Test of English as a Foreign Language

**Prep**   Preposition

**PRETOS**   Proof-Reading Tests of Spelling

**PRF**   Personality Research Form

**PRI**   Personal Reaction Index; Personal Relations Inventory; Prescriptive Reading Inventory

**PRI/RS**   Prescriptive Reading Inventory/Reading Systems

**PRIDE**   Preschool and Kindergarten Interest Descriptor

**Pro**   Pronoun

**PRPT**   Prescriptive Reading Performance Test

**PRQ**   Personal Resource Questionnaire

**PRS**   Parent Rating Scales; Psycholinguistic Rating Scale

**PRSP**   Pre-Reading Screening Procedures

**PS**   Post script; Partially Sighted

**PSA**   Public Service Announcement

**PSAT**   Preliminary Scholastic Aptitude Test

**PSB-HOAE**   PSB-Health Occupations Aptitude Examination

**PSE**   Present State Examination

**PSEN**   Pupils with Special Educational Needs

**PSI**   Personalized system of instruction; London House Personnel Selection Inventory; Parenting Stress Index; Psychological Screening Inventory; Problem-Solving Inventory

**PSLT**   Picture Story Language Test

**PSM**   Personal Sphere Model

**PSP**   Revised Pre-Reading Screening Procedures

**PSPCSA**   Pictorial Scale of Perceived Competence and Social Acceptance

**PSPI**   Psychosocial Pain Inventory; Prout-Strohmer Personality Inventory

**PSR**   Psychological Stimulus Response Test

**PSRS**   Process Skills Rating Scales

**PSS**   Parenting Satisfaction Scale; Preschool Screening System

**PSSI**   Preschool Screening Instrument

**PSTT**   Picture Spondee Threshold Test

**PT**   Physical Therapist; Physical Therapy

**PTA**   Parent Teachers Association; Pure Tone Average (hearing)

**PTB**   Personnel Test Battery

**PTI**   Pictorial Test of Intelligence

**PTM**   Progress Tests in Maths

**PTO**   Parent Teacher Organization

**PTR**   Personality Test and Reviews

**PTS** Prescriptive Teaching Series

**PU** Pen Up (computers); Page Up

**PVCS** Pre-Verbal Communication Schedule

**PVS** Picture Vocabulary Screen

**PVT** Picture Vocabulary Test

**q, qu,** or **ques** Question

**QAR** Question-Answer Relationships

**QCI** Quick Cognitive Inventory

**QLAI** Quick Language Assessment Inventory

**QLQ** Quality of Life Questionnaire

**QNST** Quick Neurological Screening Test

**QOLI** Quality of Life Inventory

**QRS** Questionnaire on Resources and Stress

**QS** Quickscreen

**QSAT** Quick-Score Achievement Test

**QSI** Quick Spelling Inventory

**QSL** The Quality of School Life Scale

**QSP** Quick Screen of Phonology

**QT** Quick Test

**QUALT** Queensland University Aphasia and Language Test

**R** Response

**R-CRAS** Rogers Criminal Responsibility Assessment Scales

**R-FVII** Reading-Free Vocational Interest Inventory

**R-PAS** Riverside Performance Assessment Series

**RADS** Reynolds Adolescent Depression Scale

**RAM** Random Access Memory (computers)

**RAS** Reading Ability Series

**RASI** Resident Assistant Stress Inventory

**RATC** Roberts Apperception Test for Children

**RBPC** Revised Behavior Problem Checklist

**RCBA** Reading Comprehension Battery for Aphasia

**rCBF** Regional Cerebral Blood Flow

**RCDS** Reynolds Child Depression Scale

**RCI** Reading Comprehension Inventory

**RCT** Regents Competency Test

**RDA** Recommended Daily Allowance

**RDLS** Reynell Developmental Language Scales

**READ** Reading Evaluation Adult Diagnosis

**REAL** Reading/Everyday Activities in Life

**REEL-2** Receptive-Expressive Emergent Language Test, second edition

**REFER** Rapid Exam for Early Referral

**REI** Regular Education Initiative

**REM** Rapid-Eye-Movement sleep, the stage of sleep in which most dreaming occurs.

**req** Required; Request

**REQUEST** Reciprocal Questioning (a reading strategy)

**RFP** Requests for Proposal

**RFS** Red Fox Supplement

**RFT** The Reversals Frequency Test

**RGEPS** Rucker-Gable Educational Programming Scale

**RI** Retroactive Inhibition

**RIAP-3** Plus-Rorschach Interpretation Assistance Program Version 3.1

**RIBLS** Riley Inventory of Basic Learning Skills

**RICO** Racketeer Influenced and Corrupt Organizations (Act)

**RIDES** Rockford Infant Developmental Evaluation Scales

**RIF** Reduction in Force; Reading is Fundamental

**RIPA-2e** Ross Information Processing Assessment, second edition

**RIPELB** Rhode Island Profile of Early Learning Behavior

**RIPIS** Rhode Island Pupil Identification Scale

**RISA** Responsibility and Independence Scale for Adolescents

**RISB** Rotter Incomplete Sentences Blank

**RISC** Rust Inventory of Schizotypal Cognitions

**RITLS** Rhode Island Test of Language Structure

**RLF** Retrolental fibroplasia

**RMC** Regional Media Center

**RMPFBT** Revised Minnesota Paper Form Board Test

**RMPI** Riley Motor Problems Inventory

**RNA** Ribonucleic Acid

**ROBS** Rating of Behavior Scale

**ROCI** Rahim Organizational Conflict Inventory

**ROLI** Receptive Oral Language Inventory

**ROM** Range of Motion; Read Only Memory (computers)

**ROTC** Reserve Officers' Training Corps

**ROWPVT** Receptive One-Word Picture Vocabulary Test

**ROWPVT-UE** Receptive One-Word Picture Vocabulary Test, Upper Extension

**RPAB** Rivermead Perceptual Assessment Battery

**RPAI** Rogers Personal Adjustment Inventory

**RPM** Response to Power Measure Series

**RR/RS** Reid Report/Reid Survey

**RRC** Regional Resource Center

**RRI** Reading Readiness Inventory

**RSA** Rehabilitation Services Administration

**RSDT-III** Reading Skills Diagnostic Test III

**RSI** Reading Style Inventory

**RSK** Communication Knowledge Inventory

**RST** Nelson Reading Skills Test

**RSVP** (respondez s'il vous plait) Please Reply

**RT** Recreational Therapist; Recreational Therapy; Recreation Time; computer command of Right; Reciprocal Teaching

**RTBS** Richmond Tests of Basic Skills

**R*TECS** Regional Technology in Education Consortia

**RTT** Revised Token Test

**RY** Reading Yardsticks

**s** Standard Deviation

**S** Stimulus; South

**S-B** Stanford-Binet Intelligence Scale

**S-CPT** Swanson Cognitive Processing Test

**S-FRIT** Slosson Full-Range Intelligence Test

**S-MCP** Self-Motivated Career Planning

**S-R** Stimulus-Response

**SA** Social Age

**SACL** Sales Attitudes Check List

**SACQ** Student Adaptation to College Questionnaire

**SADD** Students Against Drunk Driving

**SAGES** Screening Assessment for Gifted Elementary Students

**SAGES-P** Screening Assessment for Gifted Elementary Students—Primary

**SAI** Self-Actualization Inventory; Skills and Attributes Inventory; School Abilities Index

**SAM** School Attitude Measure; Skills Assessment Module

**SAMI** Sequential Assessment of Mathematics Inventories

**SAP** Self-Awareness Profile

**SAPQ** South African Personality Questionnaire

**SARPI** New Sucher-Allred Reading Placement Inventory

**SAS** Clarke Reading Self-Assessment Survey; Sex Attitudes Survey and Profile; Statements about Schools; Scholastic Aptitude Scales

**SASB** Structural Analysis of Social Behavior

**SASI** Sexual Abuse Screening Inventory

**SAT** Senior Apperception Technique; Scholastic Aptitude Test; Scholastic Assessment Test

**SAT-8**  Stanford Achievement Test, eighth edition

**SATA**  Scholastic Abilities Test for Adults

**SBA**  Social Behavior Assessment

**SBC**  School Behavior Checklist

**SBCT**  Standardized Bible Content Tests

**SBMCT**  Silver Burdett Music Competency Tests

**SBMI**  Swassing-Barbe Modality Index

**SBS-HP**  Staff Burnout Scale—Health Professionals

**SCA**  Sickle-Cell Anemia

**SCALE**  Scaled Curriculum Achievement Levels Test

**SCAN**  A Screening Test for Auditory Processing Disorders

**Scand**  Scandinavian

**SCAT**  School and College Ability Tests

**SCATBI**  Scales of Cognitive Ability for Traumatic Brain Injury

**SCC**  Selection Consulting Center

**SCCT**  Sexual Concerns Checklist

**SCGI**  Small College Goals Inventory

**SCI**  Spinal Cord Injury

**SCII**  Strong Campbell Interest Inventory

**SCLB**  Study of Children's Learning Behaviors

**SCOM**  Supervisory Communication Relations

**SCORE**  Supervisory Coaching Relations

**SCOSD**  Southern California Ordinal Scales of Development

**SCPNT**  Southern California Postrotary Nystagmus Test

**SCREEN**  Senf-Comrey Ratings of Extra Educational Need; Screening Children for Related Early Educational Needs

**SCRP**  Supplemental Conventional Reading Program

**SCS**  Smoker Complaint Scale

**SCSIT**  Southern California Sensory Integration Tests

**SCT**  Sentence Comprehension Test; Short Category Test

**SD**  Standard Deviation

**SDI**  Self-Description Inventory

**SDI-II**  Jacobsen-Kellog Self Description Inventory II

**SDLRS**  Self-Directed Learning Readiness Scale

**SDMT**  Stanford Diagnostic Mathematics Test

**SDPMP**  The Steenburgen Diagnostic-Prescriptive Math Program

**SDRT**  Spadafore Diagnostic Reading Test

**SDRT-4**  Stanford Diagnostic Reading Test, fourth edition

**SDS**  Self-Directed Search

**SDSS**  Single and Double Simultaneous Stimulation Test

**SDT**  Stromberg Dexterity Test; Silver Drawing Test

**SDTI**  Student Developmental Task Inventory

**SDTLI**  Student Developmental Task and Lifestyle Inventory

**SE**  Standard Error

**SEA**  State Education Agency; Special Education Administrator

**SEAI**  Meadow-Kendall Social-Emotional Assessment Inventory for Deaf and Hearing Impaired Students

**SEARCH**  Scanning Instrument for the Identification of Potential Learning Disability, second edition, expanded

**SEE I**  Seeing Essential English

**SEE II**  Signing Exact English

**SEED**  Sewall Early Education Development Profile

**SED**  State Education Department; Seriously Emotionally Disturbed; School of Education; Special Education Department; standard error of difference between means

**SEDS**  Social-Emotional Dimension Scale

**SEI**  Coopersmith Self-Esteem Inventories; Culture-Free Self-Esteem

Inventories for Children and Adults; Self-Esteem Index

**SEIMC** Special Education Instruction Materials Center

**SELF** Self-Concept Evaluation of Location Form

**SEQ** School Effectiveness Questionnaire

**SERVS** Spanish/English Reading and Vocabulary Screening

**SES** Socioeconomic Status

**SESAT** Stanford Early School Achievement Test

**SESBI** Sutter-Eyberg Student Behavior Inventory

**SET** Short Employment Tests; Sports Emotion Test; Student Evaluation of Teacher Instrument

**SETRC** Special Education Training Resource Center

**SEWEP** Sheltered Employment Work Experience Program

**SFAB** Survey of Functional Adaptive Behaviors

**SFVCS** San Francisco Vocational Competency Scale

**SH** Severely Handicapped

**SHARP** Senior High Assessment of Reading Performance

**SHEIK** Study Habits Evaluation Instruction Kit

**SHORS** School/Home Observation and Referral System

**SHR** Supervisory Human Relations

**SHSS** Stanford Hypnotic Susceptibility Scale

**SI** Speech Impairment; Stanton Inventory; Salience Inventory

**SIB** Scales of Independent Behavior; Self-Injurious Behavior

**SIB-R** Scales of Independent Behavior, revised

**SIC** Supervisory Inventory on Communication

**SICCS** Social Interaction and Creativity in Communication System

**SICD** Sequenced Inventory of Communication Development

**SIFT** Skills Inventory for Teachers

**SIG** Special Interest Group

**SIHR** Supervisory Inventory on Human Relations

**SIL** Skills for Independent Living

**SILS** Somatic Inkblot Series; Shipley-Institute of Living Scales for Measuring; Intellectual Impairment

**Sing** Singular

**SIP** Skills Inventory for Parents

**SIPI** Short Imaginal Process Inventory

**SIPT** Sensory Integration and Praxis Tests

**SIQ** Suicidal Ideation Questionnaire

**SIRI** Suicide Intervention Response Inventory

**SIS** Scale for the Identification of School Phobia; Supervisory Inventory on Safety

**SIST** Sentence Imitation Screening Tests

**SIT** Shorr Imagery Test; Slosson Intelligence Test; Sensory Integration Training; Small Identification Test; Social Intelligence Test

**SJD** Supervisory Job Discipline

**SJI** Supervisory Job Instruction

**SJS** Supervisory Job Safety

**SKI** Sex Knowledge Inventory

**SKOLD** Screening Kit of Language Development

**Skt** Sanskrit

**SLA** Supported Living Arrangement

**SLD** Specific Learning Disability

**SLEP** Secondary Level English Proficiency Test

**SLI** Specific Language Impaired

**SLIP** Singer-Loomis Inventory of Personality

**SLOTE** Second Language Oral Test of English

**SM** Socially Maladjusted

**SMAT** Stanford Mental Arithmetic Test

**SMI** Sales Motivation Inventory

**SMMLS** Simons Measurements of Music Listening Skills

**SMP** Survey of Management Practice

**SMR** Severely Mentally Retarded

**SNS** Somatic Nervous System; Sympathetic Nervous System

**SNST** Stroop Neuropsychological Screening Test

**SO** Syntax One

**SOBAR** System for Objective-Based Assessment-Reading

**SOC** Survey of Organizational Culture

**SOI** Structure of Intellect Learning Abilities Test

**SOLAT** Style of Learning and Thinking

**SOLST** Stephens Oral Language Screening Test

**SOMPA** System of Multicultural Pluralistic Assessment

**SOMT** Spatial Orientation Memory Test

**SON** Snijders-Oomen Non-Verbal Intelligence Scale

**SONG** Seeking of Noetic Goals Test

**SOON** Sequential Organization of Needs Test

**SORT-R** Slossan Oral Reading Test, Revised

**SOS** Simultaneous Oral Spelling; Self-Observation Scales; Survey of Organizational Stress

**Sp** Spanish

**SPAS** Student's Perception of Ability Scale

**SPCI** Couple's Pre-Counseling Inventory

**SPED** Special Education

**SPELT** Structured Photographic Expressive Language Test

**SPES** Surveys of Problem-Solving and Educational Skills

**SPH** Severely or Profoundly Handicapped

**SPI** Self-Perception Inventory; Stuttering Prediction Instrument for Young Children; Supervisory Practices Inventory

**SPIB** Social and Prevocational Information Battery

**SPINE** Speech Intelligibility Evaluation

**SPLIT** Shutt Primary Language Indicator Test

**SPQ** Study Process Questionnaire

**SPQS** Self Profile Q-Sort

**SPR** Supervisory Profile Record

**SPS** Suicide Probability Scale

**SPSI** School Problem Screening Inventory

**SPT** Supervisory Potential Test

**SQ** Social Quotient

**SRA** Science Research Associates

**SRBCSS** Scales for Rating the Behavioral Characteristics of Superior Students

**SRI** Standardized Reading Inventory

**SRPI** Self-Report and Projective Inventory

**SRS** Social Rehabilitation Service; Student Rights Scales; Social Reticence Scale; Stress Response Scale

**SRT** Speech Reception Threshold; School Readiness Test

**SSA** Social Security Administration

**SSAT** Secondary School Admission Test

**SSCS** Student Self-Concept Scale

**SSD** Scale of Social Development

**SSHA** Survey of Study Habits and Attitudes

**SSI** Supplementary Security Income or Social Security; Supervisory Skills Inventory; Social Skills Inventory

**SSKAT** Socio-Sexual Knowledge and Attitudes Test

**SSQ** Student Styles Questionnaire

**SSR** Sustained Silent Reading

**SSRS** Social Skills Rating System

**SSSQ** Street Survival Skills Questionnaire

**SST** Slingerland Screening Tests

**ST-LNNB** Screening Test for the Luria-Nebraska Neuropsychological Battery

**STAD** Student-Assisted Divisions

**STAI** State-Trait Anxiety Inventory

**STAL** Screening Test of Adolescent Language

**STAP** Screening Test for Auditory Perception

**STAXI** State-Trait Anger Expression Inventory

**STC** Staffordshire Test of Computation

**STEP** Sequential Tests of Educational Progress

**STEPS** Screening Test for Educational Prerequisite Skills

**STI** Styles of Teamwork Inventory

**STM** Short-Term Memory

**STO** Short-Term Objective

**STT** Students Typewriting Tests

**SUR** Supervisory Union Relations

**SV** Study of Values

**SVH** Severely Handicapped

**SVT** Stycar Vision Tests

**SW** Southwestern

**SWAT** School-Wide Assistance Teams; Special Weapons and Tactics

**Syn** Synonym

**T-JTA** Taylor-Johnson Temperament Analysis

**T-MAC** Test of Minimal Articulation Competence

**TA** Task Analysis; Transactional Analysis

**TAAS** Test of Auditory Analysis Skills

**TAAS-RAS** Test of Academic Achievement Skills—Reading, Arithmetic, and Spelling

**TABC** Temperament Assessment Battery for Children

**TABE** Tests of Adult Basic Education

**TAC** Test of Auditory Comprehension

**TACL-R** Test for Auditory Comprehension of Language, Revised

**TAD** Toward Affective Development

**TAG** The Association for the Gifted of CEC

**TAGS** Teacher Assessment of Grammatical Structure

**TAI** Team Assisted Individualization; Test Attitude Inventory; Therapy Attitude Inventory

**TALPS** Transactional Analysis Life Position Survey

**TALS** Test of Awareness of Language Segments

**TAM** Technology and Media Division of CEC

**TAP** Tests of Achievement and Proficiency; Test Anxiety Profile; Test of Articulation Performance

**TAPS** Test of Auditory-Perceptual Skills

**TAPT** Task Assessment for Prescriptive Teaching

**TARC** TARC Assessment System

**TARPS** Test of Auditory Reasoning and Processing Skills

**TAS** Trustworthy Analysis Survey; Test of Ability to Subordinate; Teamwork Appraisal Survey; Test of Attitude Toward School

**TASK** Stanford Test of Academic Skills

**TAT** Thematic Apperception Test

**TAWF** Test of Adolescent/Adult Word Finding

**TB** Tuberculosis

**TC** Temperament Comparator

**TCAM** Thinking Creatively in Action and Movement

**TCAP** Tennessee State Practice Tests

**TCB** Themes Concerning Blacks

**TCLA** Test of Children's Learning Ability

**TCS** Communication Screen; Test of Cognitive Skills

**TCSM** Test of Cognitive Style in Mathematics

**TCSW** Thinking Creatively with Sounds and Words

**TDD** Telecommunications Device for the Deaf

**TDI** Team Development Inventory

**TEA** Test of Economic Achievement

**TeachERS** Teacher Evaluation Rating Scales

**TEAF** Team Effectiveness Analysis Form

**TED**   Teacher Education Division of CEC

**TEEM**   Test for Examining Expressive Morphology

**TEK**   Test of Economic Knowledge

**TEL**   Test of Economic Literacy; Tests for Everyday Living

**TELD**   Test of Early Language Development

**TELS**   Test of Early Learning Skills

**TEMA-2**   Test of Early Mathematics Ability-2

**TEMAS**   Tell-Me-a-Story

**TEPL**   Test of English Proficiency Level

**TERA-2**   Test of Early Reading Ability-2

**TERA-D/HH**   Test of Early Reading Ability—Deaf or Hard of Hearing

**TERC**   Technical Educational Research Center

**TESOL**   Teachers of English to Speakers of Other Languages

**TETC**   Transitional Educational Training Center

**TEWL-2**   Test of Early Written Language-2

**TGMD**   Test of Gross Motor Development

**THINK**   Test of the Hierarchy of Inductive Knowledge

**TI**   Temperament Inventory

**TIES**   The Instructional Environment Scale

**T.I.M.E.**   Toddler and Infant Motor Evaluation

**TIMSS**   Third International Mathematics and Science Study

**TINR**   Test of Individual Needs in Reading

**TIP**   Teachers Instructional Plan

**TKFGRS**   Test of Kindergarten/First Grade Readiness Skills

**TLC**   Scale of the Assessment of Thought, Language, and Communication

**TLC-E**   Test of Language Competence, expanded edition

**TM**   Transcendental Meditation

**TMH**   Trainable Mentally Handicapped

**TMI-R**   Test of Motor Impairment Henderson, Revision

**TMJ**   Temporomandibular Joint

**TMR**   Trainable Mentally Retarded

**TNR**   Tonic Neck Reflexes

**TO**   Time Out

**TOAL-3**   Test of Adolescent and Adult Language, third edition

**TOBE**   Tests of Basic Experiences

**TOEFL**   Test of English as a Foreign Language

**TOEIC**   Test of English for International Communication

**TOES**   Test of Enquiry Skills

**TOESD**   Test of Early Socioemotional Development

**TOI**   Teacher Opinion Inventory

**TOIL**   Test of Initial Literacy

**TOLA**   Test of Oral and Limb Apraxia

**TOLD-2**   Test of Language Development-2

**TOLH**   Test of Legible Handwriting

**TOMA-2**   Test of Mathematical Ability, second edition

**TOMAL**   Test of Memory and Learning

**TONI-2**   Test of Nonverbal Intelligence, second edition

**TOPA**   Test of Phonological Awareness

**TOPICS**   Test of Performance in Computational Skills

**TOPL**   Test of Pragmatic Language

**TOPS**   Test of Problem Solving

**TORC-3**   Test of Reading Comprehension, third edition

**TOSCA**   Test of Scholastic Abilities

**TOSI**   Transit Operator Selection Inventory

**TOSRA**   Test of Science-Related Attitudes

**TOVA**   Test of Variables of Attention

**TOWK**   Test of Word Knowledge

**TOWL-3**   Test of Written Language-3

**TPBA**  Transdisciplinary Play-Based Assessment

**TPI**  Time Perception Inventory

**TPK**  Test of Practical Knowledge

**TPRI**  The Canfield Time Problems Inventory

**TQ**  Time Questionnaire

**TRC**  Test of Relational Concepts

**TRF**  Teacher Report Form

**TRS**  Teacher Rating Scale

**TSA**  Test of Syntactic Abilities

**TSCS**  Tennessee Self-Concept Scale

**TSE**  Test of Spoken English

**TSFI**  Test of Sensory Functions in Infants

**TSH**  Thyroid Stimulating Hormone

**TSI**  DeGangi-Berk Test of Sensory Integration

**TSI**  Teacher Stress Inventory

**TSPT**  Texas State Practice Tests

**TSWE**  Test of Standard Written English

**TTB**  Technical Test Battery

**TTC**  Token Test for Children

**TTCT**  Torrance Tests of Creative Thinking

**TTY**  Teletypewriter device for the deaf

**TUCE**  Revised Test of Understanding in College Economics

**TVA**  Tennessee Valley Authority

**TVAS**  Test of Visual Analysis Skills

**TVI**  Teacher Values Inventory; Temperament and Values Inventory

**TVIP**  Test de Vocabulario en Imágenes Peabody

**TVPS**  Test of Visual-Perceptual Skills

**TWE**  Test of Written English

**TWF**  Test of Word Finding

**TWFD**  Test of Word Finding in Discourse

**TWI**  Transition-to-Work Inventory

**TWS-3**  Test of Written Spelling, third edition

**UAF**  University-Affiliated Facility

**UAP**  University-Affiliated Program

**UCR**  Unconditioned Reflex; Unconditioned Response

**UCS**  Unconditioned Stimulus

**UFT**  United Federation of Teachers

**UPAS**  Uniform Performance Assessment System

**US**  Unconditioned Stimulus; United States

**USES**  U.S. Employment Service

**USOE**  U.S. Office of Education

**USSR**  Uninterrupted Sustained Silent Reading

**UTLD**  Utah Test of Language Development

**UTLD-3**  Utah Test of Language Development-3

**V**  Verb

**VA**  Veterans Administration

**VABS**  Vineland Adaptive Behavior Scales

**VADS**  Visual Aural Digit Span Test

**VAK**  Visual-Auditory-Kinesthetic

**VAKT**  Vision, Auditory, Kinesthetic, Tactual

**VAP**  Voice Assessment Protocol

**VARS**  Vocational Adaptation Rating Scales

**VBC**  Vocational Behavior Checklist

**VCCG**  VITAL Checklist and Curriculum Guide

**VCM**  Vocational Competency Measures

**VCM:ACAT**  VCM: Agricultural Chemicals Applications Technician

**VCM:AS**  VCM: Apparel Sales

**VCM:C**  VCM: Carpenter

**VCM:CO**  VCM: Computer Operator

**VCM:CS**  VCM: Custom Sewing

**VCM:DA**  VCM: Dental Assistant

**VCM:DM**  VCM: Diesel Mechanic

**VCM:ET**  VCM: Electronics Technician

**VCM:FEM**  VCM: Farm Equipment Mechanic

**VCM:FS**  VCM: Fabric Sales

**VCM:GC**  VCM: Grocery Clerk

**VCM:HMFO**   VCM: Hotel (Motel) Front Office

**VCM:PTA**   VCM: Physical Therapist Assistant

**VCM:RS**   VCM: Restaurant Service

**VCM:WPS**   VCM: Word Processing Specialist

**VCM:WTT**   VCM: Water Treatment Technician

**VCM:WWTT**   VCM: Wastewater Treatment Technician

**VCS**   Verbal Communication Scales

**VD**   Venereal Disease

**VEDS**   Vocational Educational Data System

**VEIK**   Vocational Exploration and Insight Kit

**VES**   Visual Efficiency Scale

**VFAT**   Visual Functioning Assessment Tool

**vg**   Very Good

**VI**   Visual Impairment; Visually Impaired; Variable interval; Values Inventory

**VICA**   Vocational Industrial Clubs of America

**VICTA**   Valett Inventory of Critical Thinking Abilities

**VIESA**   Vocational Interests, Experience, and Skill Assessment

**VII-R**   Vocational Interest Inventory, Revised

**VISTA**   Volunteers in Service to America

**VL**   Vulgar Latin

**VMD**   Vincent Mechanical Diagrams Test

**VMI**   Visual Motor Integration Test; Developmental Test of Visual-Motor Integration

**VOCA**   Voice Output Communication Aid

**VOI**   Vocational Opinion Index

**VPI**   Vocational Preference Index; Vocational Preference Inventory

**VPR**   Visual Pattern Recognition Test and Diagnostic Schedule; Vocational Personality Report

**VPSI**   Visual Perceptual Skills Inventory

**VR**   Variable Ratio; Vocational Rehabilitation

**VRA**   Visual Reinforcement Audiometry; Vocational Rehabilitation Act

**VRAM**   Video Random Access Memory (computers)

**VRII**   Vocational Research Interest Inventory

**VRS**   Visual Response System

**VSA**   Visual Skills Appraisal

**VSAT**   Visual Search and Attention Test

**VSMS**   Vineland Social Maturity Scale

**VSS**   Vocabulary Self-Collection Strategy

**VTST**   Vocational Training Screening Test

**VVT**   Visual-Verbal Test

**W**   West

**W-GES**   Work-Group Effectiveness Scale

**WAB**   Western Aphasia Battery

**WAC**   Women's Army Corps

**WACS**   Wachs Analysis of Cognitive Structures

**WAI**   Work Adjustment Inventory

**WAIS**   Wechsler Adult Intelligence Scale; Wide Area Information Servers

**WAIS-R**   Wechsler Adult Intelligence Scale, Revised

**WAN**   Wide Area Network (computers)

**WAPS**   Work Aspect Preference Scale

**WAQ**   Work Attitudes Questionnaire

**WASC**   Williams Awareness Sentence Completion

**WAVES**   Women Accepted for Volunteer Emergency Service

**WBI**   Work Behavior Inventory

**WBRS**   Wisconsin Behavior Rating Scale

**WBSS**   Watkins Bender-Gestalt Scoring System

**WCAT**   Weiss Comprehensive Articulation Test

**WCI**   Whole Child Initiative

**WCOAT**   Wolfe Computer-Operator Aptitude Test

**WCQ**   Ways of Coping Questionnaire

**WCST** Wisconsin Card Sorting Test

**WEI** Work Elements Inventory

**WES** Work Environment Scale

**WFRC** Word Finding Referral Checklist

**WFPT** Welsh Figure Preference Test

**WIAT** Wechsler Individual Achievement Test

**WII** Work Interest Index

**WIS** Word Identification Scale

**WISC** Wechsler Intelligence Scale for Children

**WISC-R** Wechsler Intelligence Scale for Children, Revised

**WISC-III** Wechsler Intelligence Scale for Children, third edition

**WIST** Whitaker Index of Schizophrenic Thinking

**WJ-R** Woodcock-Johnson Psycho-Educational Battery, Revised

**WKT** Word Knowledge Test

**WLA** Written Language Assessment

**WLPB-R** Woodcock Language Proficiency Battery, Revised

**WLST** Written Language Syntax Test

**WLW** William, Lynde, and Williams

**WMS** Walker-McConnell Scale of Social Competence and School Adjustment

**WMS-III** Wechsler Memory Scale, third edition

**WNAI** Word and Number Assessment Inventory

**WOCT** Word Order Comprehension Test

**WP** Without Prejudice; Work Preference Questionnaire; Word Processing; Word Processor

**WPAB** Eosys Word Processing Aptitude Battery

**WPAI** Wilson-Patterson Attitude Inventory

**WPAT** Wolfe Programming Aptitude Test

**WPBIC** Walker Problem Behavior Identification Checklist

**WPI** Western Personality Inventory

**WPOAB** Word Processing Operator Assessment Battery

**WPP** Writing Proficiency Program; Work Personality Profile

**WPPSI** Wechsler Preschool and Primary Scale of Intelligence

**WPPSI-R** Wechsler Preschool and Primary Scale of Intelligence, Revised

**WPT** Western Personnel Tests

**WPT** Wonderlic Personnel Test

**WRAML** Wide Range Assessment of Memory and Learning

**WRAT** Wide Range Achievement Test

**WRAT-3** Wide Range Achievement Test-3

**WRAVMA** Wide Range Assessment of Visual-Motor Abilities

**WREST** Wide Range Employability Sample Test

**WRIOT** Wide Range Interest-Opinion Test

**WRMT-R** Woodcock Reading Mastery Tests, Revised

**WSSAB** Weller-Strawser Scales of Adaptive Behavior

**WTRSD-C** Wisconsin Tests of Reading Skill Development: Comprehension

**WVAST** Washer Visual Acuity Screening Technique

**WWSAD** Wolfe-Winrow Structured Analysis and Design Concepts Proficiency Test

**WWW** World Wide Web

**YOC** Youth Opportunity Center

**YOF** Youth Self-Report

**YRS** Youth Research Survey

**z** Standard Score

# Appendix 2
# Legal Terms and Issues Related to Education

The following appendix contains court citations that will allow further reading of the subject-matter presented. Sometimes this is a confusing process. The reader will first be instructed as to how to read a court citation in layperson's terminology. Hopefully this will facilitate the interpretation of what sometimes appears as mathematical formulas embedded within case-history terms and names. Most of the cases cited in a dictionary of this nature would be those decided by the Supreme Court as this body supersedes, in law, decisions made by lower courts.

Reading a Court Citation

Example: (an original citation)

Citation: *Board of Curators of University of Missouri v. Horowitz,* 435 U.S. 78, 89-90 (1978).

1

Citation: \Board of Curators of University of Missouri v. Horowitz\,
 2 3 4 4 5
\435\ \U.S.\ \78\,\89–90\ \(1978).\

1 = The name of the case.
2 = The volume of the "reporter" or official document where the case can be found.
3 = The name of the reporter; in this case, *United States Reports. United States Reports* records decisions of the U.S. Supreme Court. The court making the decision in the case cited is assumed to be the Supreme Court unless otherwise noted.
4 = Pages in the reporter where the court decision can be found (in this case, pages 78, 89-90).
5 = Year decided.

## Legal Terms/Rights/Situations Important to Educators

**Ability tracking**   The grouping of students according to aptitude, interests, or ability levels. Ability tracking has been ruled as acceptable by the courts as long as such grouping does not result in the segregation of minorities. Otherwise, the courts are compelled to evaluate ability-tracking policies. Such grouping of students must be based on multiple criteria to include test results, teacher referrals, and adaptive behavior assessments.

**Absences**   Excessive and unexcused absences are a growing concern to educators. The courts have generally ruled that academic sanctions (and not corporal punishment) can be given to students who are excessively absent (without just cause). Such sanctions include the loss of course credit and grade reductions.

**ADA**   SEE: *American With Disabilities Act*

**Age discrimination**   Age discrimination (refusal to hire professionals because the individual is considered too old or too young) in employment is prohibited if the individual is willing and able to satisfactorily fulfill job responsibilities. Citation: Age Discrimination in Employment Amendment of 1986, P.L. 99-592, 29 U.S.C.| 621 (1991).

**Americans with Disabilities Act (ADA)**   The 1990 federal law that protects individuals with physical or cognitive disabilities (or both) from discrimination in employment, public transportation and housing, and telecommunications. Citation: 42 U.S.C.A. | 12101 et seq. (1991).

**Antidiscrimination**   The law is clear when discrimination issues are brought forward. Discrimination of individuals based on age, race, religion, political affiliation, gender, etc. is clearly prohibited. Specifically, 1. Title IX of the Education Amendments of 1972 (Citation: Title IX 20 U.S.C. |1681 (a) (1988)) states that federally funded programs can be terminated if *gender discrimination* exists. 2. Title VII of the Civil Rights Act of 1964 prohibits *discrimination* of employees based on race, color, religion, sex, or national origin. 3. The Age Discrimination Act of 1975 prohibits *discrimination* in hiring/ firing *based on age*. 4. The 1990 Americans with Disabilities Act of 1990 (ADA) protects individuals from *discrimination based on physical and/or cognitive disabilities* in employment, public transportation and housing, and telecommunications (Citation: 42 U.S.C.A. | 12101 et seq. (1991)). There is one exception where discrimination can be overt and permissible: Title VII [Citation: 42 U.S.C. | 2000 e (j)(1988)] exempts religious institutions from banning religious discrimination (e.g., a private religious school may require attendance at a religious service and not offer alternative religious services because students voluntarily attend said school). The courts take discrimination practices so seriously that they are empowered to order hiring and promotional preference based on race or gender if prior discrimination can be proved.

**Appeal**   The instance where a higher court (e.g., Supreme Court) is asked to review the decision of a lower court (e.g., state Supreme Court).

**Appellant**   A party who has lost a court case and is now asking to have the decision reviewed by a higher court. SEE: *appellee*

**Appellee**   A party who has won a court case and argues against an appeal to a higher court that would reverse this decision. SEE: *appellant*

**Arraignment**   A court hearing where a defendant appears before a judge and is identified and given his/her legal rights. Specific charges are read and recorded and the defendant enters a plea to the guilt or innocence of the charges read.

**Arson**   The intentional and malicious burning or torching of the property of another with the intention to defraud.

**Assault**   A threat to commit battery. Aggravated assault involves the threat with the use of a deadly weapon. SEE: *battery*

**Assessments**   Standardized testing is typically used to assess the effectiveness of curriculum and teaching. States have been given a clear mandate in establishing standards for student performance [Citation: Board of Curators of Univ. of Missouri v. Horowitz, 435 U.S. 78, 89-90 (1978)]. Under IDEA, the use of tests is legitimate only if there is a purpose for use and the tests accurately reflect aptitude and achievement. Educators should take precautions to ensure that 1. students are prepared for testing/assessments, 2. tests are nondiscriminatory and culture-fair to the maximum extent possible, 3. students who fail given tests are given remedial opportunities and other occasions for test "retakes," and 4. test modifications or accommodations are made for students with special needs.

**Athletics, access to**   Interscholastic athletic programs should be made available to male and female students on an equal basis. Such programs can include mixed gender groupings or comparable segregated teams. Title IX of the Education Amendments [Citation: 34.C.F.R.|106.41 (b) (1990)] clearly states that schools should provide coeducational sports activities in noncontact sports if gender segregated teams are not available. Gender bias in sports activities can result in the termination of federal funds for other educational purposes.

**Battery**   The illegal physical abuse of another through beating or offensive "roughing," which is often accompanied by an assault or the threat of force. SEE: *assault*

**Beyond a reasonable doubt**   In order for a crime conviction to occur, the prosecution must prove "beyond a reasonable doubt" or with certainty that the facts presented implicate the defendant in crimes for which he/she is charged. SEE: *charge, crime, defendant, prosecution*

**Bond**   A written agreement between a defendant and the courts secured by monies (posted by the defendant or other interested parties) assuring the attendance of the defendant at a required court proceeding or arraignment. Lack of compliance results in the loss of the security or bond to the courts

and the possibility of additional penalties.

**Burglary**   The illegal or forcible entry into a dwelling with the purpose of committing a crime (usually theft).

**Capital punishment**   A sentence of death given by the courts in some states for some capital crimes (typically first-degree murder).

**Censorship**   The removal of curriculum materials by school boards/committees who have been given broad and discretionary authority to make, "legitimate and substantial decisions for the community interest in promoting respect for authority, and traditional values, be they social, moral, or political" [Citation: Board of Educ. Island Trees Union Free School Dist. No. 26 v. Pico, 457 U.S. 853, 864 (1982)]. Curriculum and censorship issues are generally state issues.

**Certification**   1. The process educators follow to become approved teacher/practitioners within a particular state. Typically, stringent guidelines, curriculum, and practicum experiences are required before certification will be granted. 2. The process or transfer within the juvenile court system of juveniles who are removed from juvenile court jurisdiction to that of the adult criminal court system. SEE: *juvenile court system*

**Charge**   In a legal sense, the formal allegation that an individual is guilty of a particular crime or offense.

**Civil action**   A judicial action taken to provide redress to an individual whose civil rights have been violated as opposed to criminal actions.

**Civil law**   Law that pertains to the private or civil rights of citizens. Civil laws generally pertain to family and property matters such as divorce actions, the neglect of children, and property inheritance disputes. Civil law can overlap with criminal law with "Tort Cases." Generally, court cases involving civil law issues do not involve as serious social and penal repercussions as criminal law cases. SEE: *civil right, criminal law, torts*

**Civil right**   A right of citizenship that is bestowed to an individual as a result of legal residency. U.S. citizens are given the civil right of voting privileges for local, state, and national elections, for example. Other civil rights include the right to free speech and the right to practice religious beliefs.

**Community service**   The alternate to incarceration whereby an individual convicted of a crime is assigned community activities (i.e., cleaning streets, painting homes for the poor, working in soup kitchens, etc.). Community service can be combined with parole or be assigned following a reduced prison term.

**Contempt of court**   An act initiated by an individual/group/institution intended to undermine or embarrass the power of the court. The judge makes a determination as to whether or not the contempt is civil or criminal and can impose a fine or prison sentence or both. SEE: *civil law, criminal law*

**Continuance**   The adjournment of a court proceeding to another day and time.

**Contraband**   Materials such as weapons, drugs, alcohol, and fireworks for which possession is illegal and punishable under the law.

**Contract**   A written or oral (or both) agreement between two or more parties who can be judged as competent in the decision-making process in which legal relationships are created, altered, or dissolved.

**Copyright infringement**   Educators need to carefully monitor the use of the photocopier and other technology (i.e., videotaping) that relies on the use of others' work. The owner of copyrighted (and noncopyrighted material that has been made public) material has exclusive control over original work. The "fair use" doctrine has been used to define instances when one can reasonably copy and use the work of others [Citation: 17 U.S.C. | 101 et seq. (1988)]. Specific guidelines regarding the fair use of copyrighted material by teachers can be found in "The Educators Rights to Fair Use of Copyrighted Works," *Education Law Reporter,* vol. 51 (1989), pp. 711–724. When making more than a few copies, teachers must consider the issues of 1. *brevity* or not copying more than 10 percent of a work (longer works—not to exceed 1000 words; poems—not to exceed 250 words), 2. *spontaneity* or copying materials (directed by a teacher and not an administrator) within a time frame that precludes seeking permission, and 3. *cumulative effect* or limiting multiple copying of the same source to no more than nine instances. Consumables such as workbooks may not be reproduced. Videotaping restrictions are clear with Congress issuing guidelines for educators in 1981 (Citation: *Guidelines for Off-the-Air Recording of Broadcast Programming for Educational Purposes,* Cong. Rec. | E4751, October 14, 1981). Videotaping is restricted to: 1. use within the first 10 days of taping, 2. reinforcement or evaluation purposes after the 10-day limit, and 3. the tape must be erased after 45 calendar days if permission is not obtained from the appropriate party. Certain publishers of videotapes will charge a fee at this point in time. Frequently tapes from popular news/educational programs are available for sale through the corresponding television station at reasonable rates. Other options include rentals at video stores or library loans.

**Corporal punishment**   1. The physical punishment of a student (e.g., spanking, hitting, etc.) for reasons of misconduct. The 1977 Supreme Court case of *Ingraham v. Wright* [Citation: *Ingraham v. Wright* 430 U.S. 651 (1977)] established the legality of corporal punishment and ruled that such punishment does not violate a student's due process guarantees under the Constitution. However, the Supreme Court has made this issue a state issue and most states have policies or laws governing the use of corporal punishment in the schools. The Supreme Court has also supported the right of students to file assault and battery charges if corporal punishment was excessive or arbitrarily given.

Safeguards should always be in place when corporal punishment is administered to include: notifying the student in advance of the punishment with time given for the student to discuss the punishment; ensuring that the punishment is not malicious, cruel, or excessive; providing a witness to the punishment; notifying the principal of the intended punishment with careful consideration given to community and state standards; notifying the parents of the intended punishment; and the logging of the events that lead to the punishment as well as the who, what, why, where, when the day the punishment is given. 2. A legal punishment for criminal activities in some countries. In the United States, corporal publishment is not an option. The last state to end such practice was Delaware in 1973 when the state's whipping statute was repealed.

**Crime**   An act of commission or omission that is against the law(s) of a particular group/society that is punishable under the law. Unfortunately, most crimes are not made known to the police in the United States because of the reluctance of many of the victims to report a crime. It is estimated that less than 50 percent of the violent crimes of assault, robbery, and rape are reported; 40 percent or less of larceny, burglary, and car thefts; and less than 30 percent of personal larceny cases without contact.

**Criminal action**   A judicial action sought by the state against a person/party charged with a public offense/crime.

**Criminal law**   Law that defines acts which threaten the well-being of citizens and are so offensive that the government seeks punishment or compensation for the alleged victim(s) if the crime has been adjudicated as having been committed. Sometimes criminal law overlaps with civil law. There are more serious legal and social repercussions encountered in criminal law cases vs. civil cases. Court cases involving criminal law can involve extended prison sentences, the loss of a job, etc. SEE: *civil law, crime*

**Curriculum standards**   States typically mandate minimum curriculum standards with standardized tests used to assess effectiveness in implementation. Individual states can mandate what textbooks will be used in the classroom and who will purchase and distribute said materials. Some states offer the privilege of choosing textbooks to their respective school boards/committees. Typically the courts have left teaching curriculum issues to the individual states and local education agencies. The courts will only intervene if a constitutional right is clearly violated. Most states require instruction on the U.S. Constitution, U.S. history, and frequently English, math, science, drug education, health, and physical education. In particular, English-deficient children are entitled to compensatory instruction to overcome language barriers. Some states will target specific grades at which specific subject-matter will be taught. Many states require special education programs, bilingual education, and vocational education.

**Damages**   Award(s) (usually monetary) given to an individuals whom the court(s) feels has(have) been wronged to compensate for the damages incurred.

**Date rape**   SEE: *rape*

**De facto segregation**   The separation of ethnic groups based on extenuating facts/circumstances as opposed to actions taken by the state/community. For example, the "white flight" from some cities has resulted in some city schools having more than 50 percent of its student population represented by a particular minority group(s). This is "de facto" segregation because it was not caused by an action of the state or its agents (i.e., courts).

**De jure segregation**   The separation of ethnic groups by laws and/or state/community actions.

**De minimis**   A term used to signify that something is not worthy of judicial review.

**Defamation**   A false or misleading oral or written communication that leads to the disgrace or ridicule of another person's reputation. Spoken defamation is called slander and written defamation is called libel.

**Defendant** The individual/party who initiates a judicial action.

**Defense attorney** The attorney for an individual in a court proceeding who is accused of criminal activity. The defense attorney's main responsibility is to protect the legal rights of the accused. If an individual is indigent or cannot afford an attorney, a public defender is appointed by the government to represent the accused.

**Deposition** Testimony secured from a witness for one of the opposing parties in a court case. This testimony is taken out of court, but under oath, in the presence of the attorneys for the defense and prosecution. This testimony is formally recorded and can be used if the witness cannot attend the court proceeding.

**Detention center** A temporary facility for juveniles who are in the court system waiting for the disposition of a court proceeding/case.

**Discipline** The manner in which behavior standards are created, implemented, and modified needs careful attention to the law. The Supreme Court relies on the 1871 Civil Rights Act [Citation: Section 1983 of the Civil Rights Act of 1871, 42 U.S.C. | 1983 (1988)] in allowing the award of damages to students who have been unfairly subject to extreme disciplinary measures. If misconduct is related to a disability that falls under IDEA (1990), a student cannot be expelled from school. Rather, the school system must provide internal alternative disciplinary measures. The courts have uniformly upheld the rights of school systems to enforce behavior standards through such measures as expulsions and suspensions as long as students are given due process under the law. SEE: *expulsions, freedom of speech, suspensions*

**Discretionary power** Authority that is given to a party/individual which necessitates decision-making based on opinion, a subjective process. Principals are frequently given discretionary power to hire new teachers for their schools.

**Discrimination** SEE: *antidiscrimination*

**Due process** The legalities involved in ensuring that all students (especially those with disabilities) have equal educational opportunities.

**Expulsions** The removal of students from school for long periods of time, usually in excess of 10 days, for disciplinary reasons. Grounds for expulsion can include school infractions during school hours and before or after school (on school property) or any time a school activity occurs. Expulsions can also be based on occurrences en route to or from school or on field trips or other school functions held off-premises. Courts have generally ruled in favor of school-initiated expulsions based on the following reasons: possession of a weapon or intoxicant of any kind; the use or encouragement of the use of violence, force, noise, or comparable conduct that interferes with the daily routine of the school; vandalism/stealing of valuable personal/school property or repeated vandalism/stealing of personal/school property with relatively small values; refusal to obey reasonable school rules; assault and/or battery; and engaging in criminal activities (i.e., gambling). Student safeguards include the following: the right to a third party or legal counsel; written notice of the reasons for intended expulsion with adequate time given for repudiation of or defense against said charges; the right to present witnesses or to cross-examine accusatory witnesses; and the right to a full and impartial hearing before an impartial third party/adjudicator. The Supreme Court established in the *Goss v. Lopez* case of 1975 strict adherence to due process guarantees under the law for expelled students [Citation: *Goss v. Lopez* 419 U.S. 565 (1975)].

**Extradition** Legal proceedings initiated when one state requests the transfer of a convicted offender from another state to the requesting state in order to participate in any part of the judicial process.

**Fact finding**   A process which involves a third party who mediates when an impasse in negotiations is reached between two opposing parties (e.g., school committee vs. teachers' union). The fact-finder collects the facts pertaining to the case, identifies relevant issues, and recommends a settlement that is nonbinding to both parties. In most instances, the opposing parties will accept the fact-finder's recommendations.

**FERPA**   The Family Educational Rights and Privacy Act of 1974. This act ties federal funding to certain privacy issues related to students and their families. School systems can lose federal funding if they 1. fail to provide parents access to a child's educational records or 2. distribute information (some exceptions—i.e., the use of said information for data compilation by the federal government during program assessments/review) to third parties without parental permission or, at age 18, without the student's permission. Student names, addresses, dates of birth and birthplaces, major fields of study, and degrees and awards given can be released without parents' permission. The school system must give adequate notice, however, to the public and provide opportunities for discussion if there are reasons parents feel would preclude the publishing of such information. School records can be released to a transferring school where a student will be enrolled.

**Fourteenth Amendment (of the U.S. Constitution)**   The courts have ruled that a student is guaranteed a state-created property right to an education under this amendment. The Fourteenth Amendment was added to the Constitution in 1868 and reads as follows: "Section 1. All persons born or naturalized in the United States, and subject to the jurisdiction thereof, are citizens of the United States and of the State wherein they reside. No State shall make or enforce any law which shall abridge the privileges or immunities of citizens of the United States; nor shall any State deprive any person of life, liberty, or property, without due process of law; nor deny to any person within its jurisdiction the equal protection of the laws."

**Freedom of speech**   Students may express opinions or thoughts on controversial issues in the classroom, hallways, cafeteria, playground area, gym, etc. as long as such speech does not substantially interfere with the requirements of appropriate discipline in the operation of the classroom or school or disrupt the rights of others. School personnel must have substantial reasons to curtail student expression, which must be more than a desire to repress unpleasant or uncomfortable viewpoints [Citation: *Tinker v. Des Moines Independent School District* (1969) 393 U.S. 503, 508 (1969)].

**IDEA**   SEE: *Individuals with Disabilities Education Act (P.L. 101-476; 1990)*

**Impasse**   A deadlock in negotiations between opposing parties/individuals that typically results in the recruitment of a third party (i.e., fact-finder) to "break the impasse."

**In loco parentis**   Literally means, "in place of the parent." According to the law, caretakers are charged with the same responsibilities of a parent when infants or juveniles are entrusted in their charge. For example, teachers fall in the category of "in loco parentis" because they are entrusted with the social/emotional/academic well-being of students who are away from the care of their parents.

**Individuals with Disabilities Education Act (P.L. 101-476; 1990)**   The 1990 Individuals with Disabilities Education Act, IDEA was formally known as the Education for All Handicapped Children's Act (EHA). This federal legislation provides federal monies for state and local education programs that offer appropriate education programs for students with disabilities. States are required under IDEA to provide a free and appropriate public education (FAPE) for all children with disabilities [Citation: 34 C.F.R. ||(104.35 (b)] 3. and 300.532 (c) 1990).

**Juvenile**   A young person under an age established by the community/courts (varies from 16 to 21 years of age depending on the state) who is denied certain privileges because of the young age (e.g., the right to vote, smoke, and drink alcoholic beverages). Typically punishments imposed by the courts are diminished for individuals who are considered juveniles at the time of the commission of a crime.

**Juvenile delinquent**   An individual under a certain age limit (18 years in most states) who has been judged by the courts to be in violation of a criminal law or statute. Contrary to what many believe, juveniles under the age of 18 do not commit the majority of the violent crimes. However, close to 50 percent of the violent crimes (e.g., robbery, murder, forcible rape, aggravated assault) are committed by those under the age of 25. Most crimes committed by juvenile delinquents are running away from home, curfew violations, car theft, arson, vandalism, burglary, and larceny.

**Larceny** or **theft**   The illegal removal of another's property without permission with the intent of keeping it permanently.

**Liability of school administrators**   School officials cannot be held liable for the actions of their subordinates under Section 1983 of the Civil Rights Act of 1871. Liability would occur only if the administrator (i.e., principal) participated in or had knowledge of wrongdoing and did not act in a responsible manner.

**Liability of teachers**   According to Section 1983 of the Civil Rights Acts of 1871, teachers or other public school employees are liable for infringing upon or abridging the constitutional rights of a student or other teacher/professional [Citation: Section 1983 of the Civil Rights Act of 1871, 42 U.S.C. | 1983 (1988)].

**Libel**   SEE: *defamation*

**Locker search**   Locker searches are generally allowed by the courts on the premise that lockers are school property and the schools and students hold joint control to said property. A search of a locker should only be undertaken if there is reasonable doubt or suspicion of illegal activities (e.g., possession of drugs and weapons) [Citation: People v. Overton, 229 N.E. 2d 596, 598 (N.Y. 1967)].

**Mediation**   The process deadlocked parties or individuals use when at an impasse in order to settle an issue(s)/dispute (e.g., salary). Mediation involves the recruitment of a third, neutral party to serve as an intermediary or consultant in determining ways to settle the problem(s) presented. Mediation can simply involve having teenagers serve as intermediaries when other classmates are involved in disputes.

**Miranda warning**   Legal precedent established in the Miranda v. Arizona case, which protects the rights of individuals in custody for offenses that might involve incarceration at some point in time. It is the responsibility of the law-enforcement official to warn the suspect of his/her legal rights before questioning occurs that may be incriminating. Included would be the right to remain silent without an attorney present and the right to an attorney who could be appointed if one cannot be afforded. If the Miranda warning is not given to a suspect, information or evidence obtained may become inadmissible in a future trial [Citation: *Miranda v. Arizona*, 384 U.S. 436, 444, 445 (1966)].

**Negligence**   The failure of an individual to exercise reasonable care. This neglect results in harm to another (i.e., a student getting hurt on the playground while unsupervised) which, under the law, is considered preventable with due care and responsibility.

**Parens patriae**   A term derived from old English common law meaning, "parent of the country." Parens patriae refers to the responsibility of the juvenile court system in the United States to protect the rights of children.

**Per curiam**   How a court disposes of a case in regard to a decision. However, an opinion of the court is not rendered, just the decision.

**Plaintiff**   An individual/party who initiates a judicial action.

**Plea bargaining**   Negotiations held between a defense attorney(s) and prosecuting attorney(s) before the commencement of a trial on behalf of the accused. Essentially, attorneys on both sides are "bargaining" to avoid a trial situation by reducing or dropping some of the charges in exchange for an admission of guilt on another lesser charge(s).

**Plenary power**   Refers to absolute or complete power. Some town meeting bodies/mayors/town managers, for example, are given full plenary power in regard to the approval of a school budget.

**Precedent**   The case when a judicial decision serves as an authority or model for subsequent cases that present similar questions under the law.

**Pregnant students**   Title IX of the Education Amendments specifies that schools/institutions receiving federal funding cannot make parental status an admission standard. Schools cannot exclude pregnant students from school other than for health reasons.

**Prejudicial error**   Errors committed during court proceedings that affect the legal rights of an involved party and that could result in the reversal of a court decision.

**Presumption of innocence**   An important concept to the judicial system in the United States; that is, an individual is presumed to be innocent until the prosecution in a court case proves beyond a reasonable doubt that the individual is guilty of a crime.

**Prima facie**   Literally meaning "on its face." Something is presumed to be true (on the face value) unless contrary evidence is provided.

**Probable cause**   1. Situations involving the use of search warrants whereby facts and circumstances presented dictate that a "probable" cause or belief exists that items related to a crime and criminal activity could be present in a specific place. 2. Facts and circumstances presented which give "probable cause" or belief that a suspect has committed a crime.

**Probation**   The most frequently used consequence given to individuals convicted of criminal activities(y). This is an alternate to fines, community service, or imprisonment whereby a convicted offender is supervised by a probation officer within a particular locale. Sometimes the court gives a convicted individual a "split sentence" or a period of incarceration followed by some probation time. In other instances, courts will "modify" or reduce the sentence of a prisoner (i.e., for good behavior) and substitute the remaining prison time for probation. There is also the situation of "intermittent incarceration" or a combined prison/probation sentence wherein the individual might be incarcerated during the week and spend time on probation in the community on weekends.

**Probation officer**   An individual who works on behalf of the government in the capacity of a supervisor who monitors individuals on probation. Written reports must be filed for offenders of probation. SEE: *probation*

**Prosecution**   A prosecuting attorney representing the state or federal government who is charged with the responsibility of initiating and maintaining criminal proceedings against a person or party accused of having committed a crime(s). SEE: *defense*

**Pro se**   Acting as one's own attorney or "on behalf of self."

**Promotion**   The promotion of students to the next grade is clearly a state issue. States have the right to set standards for all students (including those with disabilities) in regard to grade promotion and receipt of diplomas. Students with special needs must be given opportunities to acquire the knowledge necessary to achieve these ends [Citation: *Board of Educ., Northport-East Northport Union Free School Dist. v. Ambach*, 457 N.E. 2d 775 (N.Y. 1983), cert. denied, 465 U.S. 1101 (1984)].

**Proprietary function**   An action/ activity performed by a state or municipality for monetary reasons that could otherwise be performed by a private corporation or institution. For example, some consider the overseeing of postsecondary (i.e., colleges) institutions a proprietary function. There are some state-sponsored colleges and many private institutions.

**Public defender**   SEE: *defense attorney*

**Rape**   Intercourse with a woman or man that is against the will of that person. *Forcible rape* is the term used when the rape is both against the will of the person and the use or threat of violence/ force is used. *Statutory rape* is the term used when the rape involves a minor or person under the age of consent. *Date rape* is the term used to describe sexual intercourse initiated and forced by a person known to the other on a social occasion where the victim might have agreed to some intimate interaction but not to intercourse. Most rape victims are females. A relatively small percentage of rapes are reported.

**REI**   SEE: *Regular Education Initiative*

**Recidivist**   One who continually commits crimes. Most violent crimes are committed by individuals who are recidivists.

**Regular Education Initiative (REI)**   The movement that advocates the restructuring of regular education and special education initiatives so that students with special needs are integrated within the regular classroom to the greatest extent possible.

**Released on Recognizance (ROR)**   The practice which allows the courts to release an offender before trial without a request of bail because the court believes that the accused will not flee prosecution.

**Right to counsel**   The right of a student, teacher, or any individual to be represented by an attorney during any critical stage of the criminal justice system (from an arrest to a trial).

**Robbery**   The use of violence, force, or threat(s) to take property belonging to someone else.

**ROR**   See: *Released on Recognizance*

**Searches**   The Supreme Court has ruled that school searches of student property can be held if "reasonable" grounds exist that lead a teacher or administrator to believe that the rules of the school or a law have been broken.

**Sentence**   The punishment or consequence for breaking a law that is given by a judge or jury in a court of law.

**Sexual abuse**   The psychological and/or physical mistreatment of any person with regard to their sex organs. This would include child pornography.

**Sexual harassment**   Providing a hostile or offensive working environment in which concrete incentives and promotions are tied to sexual favors is clearly prohibited [Citation: *Meritor Savings Bank v. Vinson,* 477 U.S. 57 (1986)].

**Slander**   SEE: *defamation*

**Status offenses**   Offenses committed by juveniles that would be perfectly legal for adults such as running away from home, being truant from school, breaking curfew, etc.

**Statute**   An act initiated by some legislative branch of government (e.g., state senate, district court) that expresses the will of the district concerned, and, in effect, becomes law within that district (e.g., statutes on curfews found in several towns and cities; a state statute on the requirement of wearing seat belts; etc.).

**Statutory rape**   SEE: *rape*

**Strikes**   Strikes are considered to involve a number of activities to include work stoppages and/or slowdowns, excessive absences in the name of sick days, and the refusal to perform duties expected as part of the job. Most states have statutes on the books or common law that dictate that teachers shall not strike. A few states allow the right to strike but under very restricted conditions. For example, negotiations have broken down to the point of one or more of the following: 1. mediation steps have been exhausted, 2. precautions have been taken to ensure public safety and health, 3. an adequate time frame has elapsed between the cessation of negotiations and the strike with public notice considered adequate, and 4. the contract has expired. If teachers threaten to strike, the employer can request an injunction from a court. Violation of the court injunction is considered contempt of court with fines and/or imprisonment possible. SEE: *contempt of court*

**Student privacy**   SEE: *FERPA, locker search*

**Subpoena**   A written order of the court demanding the appearance of an individual at a specified time, day, and place before a court of law in order to give testimony in a specific case. The subpoenaed individual may be ordered to bring documentation relating to the case.

**Summons**   Formal written notification by a court to an individual that his/her presence is needed and required at a specified time and day(s). Prospective jurors receive such documentation.

**Suspensions**   The removal of students from classroom activities because of infractions of school policy that are considered secondary in magnitude to those meriting a school expulsion (total removal from school). Suspensions can involve short-term (less than 10 days) removal from school or in-school suspension classrooms/places. The *Goss vs. Lopez* case [Citation: *Goss v. Lopez*, 419 U.S. 565 (1975)] established the standard of ensuring due process under the law to students even in cases where suspensions are for brief periods of time. The following standards have been recommended by the courts before suspensions are implemented: 1. notification of the reasons as to why the suspension is being given with an opportunity by the student to rebut and discuss the charge(s), 2. disclosure of evidence causing the suspension to be given, and 3. the opportunity to bring the case before a decision-maker (i.e., peer mediator, teacher, school administrator) who can offer a fair and impartial opinion of

the legitimacy of the suspension based on the facts presented. One- or two-day suspensions generally do not involve such formal procedures as obtaining legal counsel, calling witnesses, etc. Expulsion from school for longer periods of time would allow the student to invoke more formal procedures. SEE: *expulsion*

**Tenure**   A statutory right (SEE: *statute*) of an individual who works for a city, town, academic institution, etc., that grants permanent employment status to the individual after a probationary time period and attainment of certain job-related goals and requirements.

**Theft**   SEE: *larceny*

**Tort**   A civil action brought before a court by an individual/party who is seeking damages for some wrong-doing that is independent of contractual agreements. Torts can involve negligent acts involving death or injuries whereby the law permits the victim(s) or injured parties(y) to sue the person/institution responsible for the injury(ies). Most tort actions in court revolve around damages resulting from physical injuries and in some cases injuries to a person's reputation. SEE: *defamation*

**Trial**   In reference to criminal law, court actions or proceedings which involve a judge, or judge and jury, who listens to the charges and evidence presented by defense and prosecution teams so as to determine the guilt or innocence of a defendant beyond a reasonable doubt. SEE: *beyond a reasonable doubt, defendant, prosecution*

**UCR**   SEE: *Uniform Crime Reports*

**Uniform Crime Reports (UCR)**   Crime reports issued by the Federal Bureau of Investigation (FBI) containing crime data based on "crimes known to the police."

**Vacate**   A decision of the court to nullify or make void a judgment or verdict.

**Verdict**   A decision rendered by a court in regard to some question(s) presented to a jury.

**Victimology**   The study of the nature, causes, and treatments of crime victims so as to provide appropriate and effective treatment programs and to prevent victimization.

**Videotaping**   SEE: *copyright infringement*

**Voir dire**   Literally means "to speak the truth." Voir dire refers to the process of questioning the qualifications or abilities of prospective jurors sought to provide impartial and fair decisions in a court case.

**Waiver**   The relinquishing of one's legal rights (i.e., the right to an attorney or counsel) by a defendant knowingly and intelligently. Some rights may not be waived. One of the rights that may be waived is the right to have extradition proceedings. SEE: *extradition*

**Warrant**   A writ issued by a court directing a court officer (e.g., police officer) to make an arrest or to search the premises of a locale for evidence in a case.

**White-collar crime**   The illegal actions of individuals or corporations during the course of legitimate business activities. Examples would include stealing school materials, embezzling funds, etc.

**Writ**   SEE: *writ of certiorari*

**Writ of Certiorari**   1. A writ is a court directive informing a party that an act is to be carried out (e.g., warrant). 2. A Writ of Certiorari (certiorari = to be informed of) is written notice of which cases a court has decided to hear. The Supreme Court will frequently use this process.

# Appendix 3
# MARCS and MAPP

≈≈≈≈≈≈≈≈≈≈≈≈≈≈≈≈≈≈≈≈≈≈≈≈≈≈≈≈≈≈≈≈≈≈≈≈≈≈≈≈≈≈≈≈≈≈

## Dr. Cheryl A. Stanley & Dr. Carol Spafford

There is much evidence to show that effective schools rely on research-oriented databases and information when making informed decisions. Although certain aspects of the school day do not require in-depth analyses, other educational processes require systematic and reflective thought so those in a position to do so initiate appropriate practices/strategies/plans. Action-based research plans allow educators and reflective practitioners to extend their knowledge base and provide optimal learning environments for the students they serve. A sample of activities is provided within a mathematics action-research classroom so that teachers can visualize various planning steps depending on the needs of the class. Part of the action-based classroom involves the creation of portfolios as alternative learning and assessment tools. MAPP provides some ideas for the classroom teacher as to mathematics portfolio inclusions with special consideration given to ethnic minority students.

## Professional Portfolio Inclusions for MARCS

### MATHEMATICS ACTION-BASED RESEARCH CLASSROOMS (MARCS)

I.  Identify Math Strengths/Problem Areas

    A.  Data Sources

| | |
|---|---|
| | Observations |
| Achievement/Aptitude Tests | Parent Surveys/Feedback |
| Attitude Scales | Portfolio Assessments |
| Authentic Assessments | Readiness Surveys |
| Behavioral Checklists | Running Records |
| Creativity Measures | School Records |
| Criterion-Referenced Tests | Self-Reports |
| Culture-Fair Tests | Social Assessments |
| Curriculum Guides | Student Surveys/Feedback |
| Interviews | Teacher-Constructed Tests |
| IQ Tests | Vocational Assessments |

B. Technical/Professional Research Support for Data Sources

Professional Recommendations
School System Research Department—Test Results
School System/School Curriculum Committees/Coordinators
Mental Measurements Yearbooks (MMYs)
Tests in Print
Journals (Example: *Journal of Educational Measurement*)
Test Publisher Manuals/Guides/Books
College Courses Pertaining to Assessment Practices
Internet Workshops
Consultants

C. Library Indexing of Educational Research (ERIC)

*Psychology (Psych) Abstracts*
*Educational (Ed) Index*
*British Education Index*
*Reader's Guide to Periodical Literature*
*Social Science Citation Index (SSCI)*
*New York Times Index*
*Dissertation Abstracts International*

D. Hypothesis Testing—Focus on:

Brevity
Ongoing Assessment
Reviewing/Revising/Reexamining
Reflective Practices
Testable Observations
Authentic Practices
Interdisciplinary Links
Performances in Group and Individual Situations
Culturally Relevant Screening/Considerations
Special Adaptations for Students with Learning Challenges

E. Authentic Purpose Setting

Establish Learning Outcomes
Establish Objectives/Goals
Establish Philosophies/Theoretical Bases
Incorporate Rsearch-Based Standards (e.g., NCTM or National
    Council of Mathematics Standards for the 1990s)
Review Usefulness of Information/Strategies/Material Presented
Continuously Reflect on the Impact of Culture, Special Learning
    Challenges/Needs, and Cognitive/Learning Styles

F. Cultural Factors

Communicataion Styles of Individuals/Groups Taught

Oral/Written Math Communication Styles/Skills
Native Language Proficiency
Testing/Learning Styles of Population Taught
Cultural/Familial Styles or Factors that Impact Learning
Student Choices/Preferences/Interests
Teacher Interest Areas
Contributions of Family Members/Community-at-Large

G. Method

Hypothesis Testing/Observation
Authentic Purpose Setting
Review Literature/Resources—What's Available?
Identify Class Data Required for Instructional Purposes/
  Diagnoses/Remediation
Operationally Define Problem Areas/Strengths/Learning
  Outcomes Expected/Instructional Courses of Action
Time Line
Continually Review/Assess/Refine/Redefine

H. Assessment

Pre/Post Reflections/Testing/Observations (Formal and Informal
  Measures)
Math Journals
Math Portfolios—Students and Teachers
  (See: MAPP—STANLEY & SPAFFORD)
Math Communication/Connections
Open-Ended Questions
Running Records
Future Directions

I. Appendices

Community Resources
Parents
Tutors
Technology Enhancement
Free Materials
List of Assessment Tools
NCTM Standards
Free Materials
Guest Speaker Lists
Literature Books with Math Connections
Science/Social Studies Materials with Math Connections
Creative Ideas/Lessons/Bulletin Boards
Running Records
Environmental Materials

J. The Ethics Involved

Personal: Privacy/Confidentiality Issues, Sharing Results, Labeling Issues, Informed Consent, Colleague/Peer Review, Research Review Committees

Ethical Standards:
American Psychological Association (APA)
Council for Exceptional Children (CEC)
Society for Research in Child Development (SRCD)

## Mathematics Assessment Portfolios-Personalized (MAPP)

Dr. Cheryl A. Stanley          Dr. Carol S. Spafford

**SPECIAL SENSITIVITY TO ETHNIC MINORITY STUDENTS
INTERPERSONAL FACTORS & SOURCE MANAGEMENT**

| Student Personalization | Teacher Sources |
|---|---|
| Who? Consider | Where? Consider |
| Math autobiographies/histories | Content area books/math links |
| Math likes/dislikes/feelings about math | National Education Goals |
| Math fears/difficulties/needs | Scope-and-Sequence Guides |
| Favorite math classroom/activities | Curriculum Frameworks |
| Math achievements | Task Analyses |
| Favorite math teacher | NCTM Standards |
| Math journals/responses from teachers/peers | Literature Books with math links |
| Math attitude/motivation/interest | Math learning styles assessments |
| Shared personal anecdotes | Patterns in Music/Arts |
| Successful math lessons/activities | Observations of Math use in daily activities |
| Family/personal experiences with math | Visits to other math classrooms/workshops |
| Cultural factors | Homework Hotlines |
| Math study groups | Math visuals (graphs/math art/tables) |
| Bilingual issues | Collections of artifacts that express cultural identities/family & community resources |
| Math aptitude/goals | |
| Math buddies/tutors | |
| Flexible non-threatening math environments | Videotaped math problems |
| | Math puzzles, trivia |
| | Computer Assisted Instruction (CAI) Materials |
| | Internet Access |
| | Calculator Checks |
| | Math manipulatives/games/electronics |

| Student Personalization | Teacher Sources |
|---|---|
| | MARC's Recommendations |
| | Number lines/charts |
| | Research/Journals/Books |
| | College courses |
| | Acted out math problems |
| | Constructivism/Scaffolding Techniques |
| | Math investigations & homework reinforcement |
| | Formal and authentic assessments |

## Mathematics Assessment Portfolios-Personalized (MAPP)

Dr. Cheryl A. Stanley    Dr. Carol S. Spafford

Special Sensitivity to Ethnic Minority Students
MAPP Process Components

Math Portfolios Will Nurture:

| Student Participation | Teacher Strategies |
|---|---|
| How? Why? | What? When? |
| NCTM applications practice | Cooperative activities and individualized instruction |
| Interactive dialoguing in math | |
| Peer coaching opportunities | Write out step-by-step how student/and/or teacher solves a problem |
| PALMS applications | |
| Math linkages to other subjects | |
| Daily math communications | Mutually discover math patterns |
| Math vocabulary knowledge development | Error-pattern analysis |
| | Hypothesis test |
| Reviewing the impact of technology on math learning | Math inventories/supplement basals & curriculum |
| International exchanges and Cross-cultural learning | Discovery/Inquiry Learning |
| | Videotape math problem-solving |
| Math connections are made | Consider cultural factors that impact math learning/embed in math |
| Vocational and life skills linkages | |
| Empowered math learners | |
| Math learning outcomes generated | Continually assess growth as a math learner |
| Specific Family Math Opportunities | |
| Self-assessment of math growth and development and independent, confident, reflective, competent math learners | Expand math vocabulary knowledge/integrate across the curriculum |

Student Participation              Teacher Strategies

Assess own math knowledge/
   successful lessons/attitudes
Math portfolios for teachers/
   students alike
Process assessment/Holistic
   scoring
Constructivist Approach
Math journals/Double entry
   journals (daily)
Checklists/Observations (weekly)
Running records (available to
   students)
Computer-Aided Instruction/
   Internet access
Student assessment of math
   proficiency (weekly)
Standardized tests—strengths/
   weaknesses: apply to
   curriculum
Task analysis of difficult math
   concepts
MARCS Activities

Basic Tenets

_____ All children will learn mathematics

_____ Provide equal math opportunities for all learners

_____ Hold high expectations for all math learners

_____ Teacher/student math learners will scaffold/interact as life-long
math learners

_____ Communities of math learners can reach math potentials

# Appendix 4
# Computer Terms

**AAC** SEE: *Augmentative and Alternative Communication*

**Access time** The required time to retrieve a word or file from memory storage.

**Acoustic coupler** A modem that works with an ordinary telephone handset (that piece with speaker and microphone ends) that can be inserted into matching cup-like sockets. Data can be sent over phone lines, as with any modem.

**Actuator** A component of a disk drive that contains the read/write heads for taking data onto the disk.

**Adaptive Firmware Card (AFC)** An input device (analogous to a keyboard) for persons who cannot use a standard keyboard. The device simulates the activity of a keyboard and a mouse. Some procedures it might support include scanning, Morse code, or an alternative keyboard.

**Add-on** A peripheral (additional mechanism) attached to a computer that allows for the transmission of data over the telephone. SEE: *modem*

**Address** A data storage location for information in RAM (Random Access Memory).

**ADP** Automatic Data Processing. Basically, this is what computing is.

**AFC** SEE: *Adaptive Firmware Card*

**AI** SEE: *Artificial Intelligence*

**Aided scanning** A helping procedure (for computer users with disabilities) in which an assistant points out menu choices to the person.

**Alerting device** A source of visual or tactile signals to gain the attention of a hearing-disabled computer user.

**Algorithm** The logically arranged steps for carrying out a plan, spelled out in ordinary English. Composing the algorithm is the first thing one must do in writing a software program.

**Alphanumeric** The various numbers, letters, and other symbols used by a computer when interacting with the user.

**Alta Vista** A World Wide Web (www) site that organizes and indexes large quantities of information on www (http://altavista.digital.com/). SEE: *World Wide Web*

**ALU** The arithmetic logic unit, which is part of the CPU (central processing unit). The ALU carries out four basic math functions (adding, subtracting, multiplying, dividing) and also performs comparison and sorting operations.

**Analog** A continuous form of information (as opposed to digital). The height of the mercury in a thermometer is an example of analog data; so is the position of the hands of the clock. Analog computers summate varying forms of continuous information as opposed to processing in discrete steps as is the case of digital systems. SEE: *digital*

**Anonymous ftp** A way to transfer computer files or other information/data from public FTP servers. In order to log-on to an anonymous ftp server, one keys in or types "anonymous" along with one's e-mail address as the password. SEE: *electronic mail or e-mail*

**ANSI**   American National Standards Institute. Standardized codes shared by all computers. These codes control such devices as keyboards and monitors. The ANSI command in MS-DOS allows the keys of the computer keyboard to be reassigned to different symbols.

**Apple DOS**   The disk operating system used by the Apple II group of computers.

**Apple Prodos**   An operating system for Apple II computers that is more advanced than Apple DOS. It is suitable for work with the hard drive.

**Apple Soft**   A version of the BASIC programming language that is built into ROM in Apple II computers.

**Apple II**   The first line of computers to emerge from the Apple computer company founded by Steve Jobs and Steve Wozniak.

**Applications software**   Those computer programs that are concerned with meeting users' needs, as opposed to the maintenance and operation of the computer. Such applications as word processing, databases, spreadsheets, graphics, and games are examples.

**Archie**   A database of "anonymous ftp" sites/information contents. Archie is available on the Internet and assists users in locating, organizing, and accessing files with an FTP server. Archie allows the user to type in a keyword and then search to find a given file. SEE: *anonymous ftp, FTP*

**ARPANET**   The original Internet program designed in 1969 by ARPA (Advanced Research Projects Agency) in the U.S. Department of Defense so as to allow communication between scientists in four sites.

**Arrays**   Related sets of fields and records arranged by rows and columns. Information in arrays is used by spreadsheet and database software programs.

**Artificial Intelligence (AI)**   The use of computer processing to simulate problem-solving by human experts.

**Askeric**   SEE: *Education Resources Information Center*

**ASCII (American Standard Code for Information Interchange)**   The standard system for relating particular machine functions to particular symbols such as numbers, letters, punctuation marks, and other symbols.

**Assembler**   A device for translating alphanumeric codes into machine language. This is necessary to allow the computer hardware to carry out the tasks required by computer programs.

**Assembly language**   A low-level computer language that is one step above machine language. It uses short code words rather than the human-like language forms of the higher level computer languages.

**Asynchronous**   The sending of data over a cable one character symbol at a time, with start and stop bits marking the boundaries of each character. This is called serial processing and is much slower than parallel processing.

**Asynchronous communicator**   A method for use in data processing in which clock timing (i.e., synchroneity) is replaced by a set of simple "stop" and "go" signals. Asynchronous communication can allow otherwise incompatible computer systems to exchange information.

**ATM**   Acronym for asynchronous transfer mode. This computer networking mode allows networks to transfer large amounts/types of data (e.g., live videos).

**Audio device**   Any part of, or attachment to, a computer that receives sound signals or produces them. A high-tech example would be a voice-recognition device that converts spoken commands to writing either on a monitor screen or on printed sheets of paper. The MIDI (Musical Instrument Digital Interface) device is another example.

**Audio digitizer**   A device for coding sound input into machine language for use by a computer. SEE: *audio device, MIDI*

**Audiodescription**   Spoken narration of visually presented scenes in television plays or films for the benefit of visually handicapped persons.

**Augmentative and Alternative Communication (AAC)**   Any procedures that can assist a person with disabilities to communicate with others or to work at a computer.

**Authoring language**   An easy-to-use computer language for teachers that enables them to construct "author" software programs for their classes. One example of an authoring language is PILOT.

**Authoring program**   A software program enabling an educator to create computer-presented lessons.

**AUTOEXEC.BAT**   A file consisting of a set of batch commands (i.e., each command triggers the next command automatically) in MS-DOS/PC-DOS. The commands start up the user's computer system. A command called PATH sets up the sequence of start-up actions.

**Auxiliary storage**   Any memory-storing device beyond the ROM and the hard and floppy disks available to a computer system. Such additional storage may be on tape cartridges or tape cassettes.

**Back up**   The making of duplicate files of data so that a failure of the computer system on the storage media (disks or tapes) does not result in the total loss of information.

**Band printer**   A printer having the characters on a horizontal, rotating band (analogous to a type ball on IBM selectric typewriters or to a daisy wheel on some computer printers). It operates more rapidly than a daisy wheel printer.

**Bandwidth**   The bit rate or velocity (i.e., speed of transmission) by which computer data is transferred. Data can flow more readily with wider bandwidths.

**Barcode**   A rectangular symbol consisting of black and white vertical lines of various widths. The black lines (bars) carry information. It can be used for inventory control and for pricing merchandise. Barcodes can be used as computer input devices.

**Barcode reader**   A computerized device that accepts data inputs in the form of barcode symbols.

**BASIC**   A programming language that is fairly easy for beginners. It stands for beginner's all-purpose symbolic instruction code.

**Batch processing**   A set of programs arranged in a series. The entire batch is processed as a matter of routine, without requiring a series of specific commands from the user.

**Baud**   The number of state shifts carrying information each second. It is not to be confused with the number of bits per second. The speed of a modem is measured in baud.

**BBS**   SEE: *Bulletin Board System*

**Binary digit**   A number on the binary number scale. This binary number scale employs only digits 0 and 1, omitting digits 2 through 9. "01" = 1, "10" = 2, "11" = 3, "100" = 4, etc. The words "binary digit" are collapsed to produce the word "bit."

**BIOS**   Basic Input-Output System. The part of ROM that enables a computer to receive data (input) and process the data (output).

**Bit**   A unit of information; a binary digit. Physically it takes the form of a single "on" or "off" switch operation. Kilobit = transmission of 1000 bits per second. Megabit = transmission of one million bits per second.

**Bitnet (because it's time network)**   Created by Fuchs and Freeman from CUNY and Yale, respectively, in 1981, this academic network (found on the Internet) provides mailing lists on a variety of topics/subjects. Access: listserv@bitnic.bitnet. SEE: *bitnic*

**Bitnic**   An organization in Washington, D.C., that maintains a listing of Bitnet discussion groups. SEE: *bitnet*

**BK**   A "primitive" command in the computer programming language, LOGO. "BK" means "back up."

**Block**   Refers to the ability of a user to "block" or make inaccessible certain computer sites/programs/information through the use of certain computer programs/assists. Blocking allows adults to help determine where children learn and explore in places like the Internet. Computer program features can include preapproved e-mail addresses and sites; creation of customized lists of appropriate on-line areas; and simplified instructions/navigation rules. SEE: *internet*

**Block move**   A feature of word-processing programs that involves moving a part of a document from one location in the document to another. In print editing, this is commonly known as "cut and paste."

**Board**   A large board (made of nonconductive materials) into which semiconductors such as computer chips are inserted. The mother board of a computer contains the CPU, memory chips, and control devices for disks, slots for the insertion of smaller boards (cards), etc.

**Boiler plate**   A standard set of words (of a paragraph to a page in length) that can be inserted into an appropriate document "as is." For example, part of a contract can be "boilerplate" insertions.

**Boolean**   Relating to Boole's system of symbolic logic, Boolean algebra. Boole showed that logical symbols can be manipulated in the same way as algebraic quantities are. Boolean algebra is useful in the design of computers.

**Booting**   Starting a computing session on a microcomputer by getting the disk operating system running. SEE: *Apple DOS, MS-DOS*

**BPI**   (Bits Per Inch) A measure of a disk's capacity for holding information. SEE: *double density, high-density floppy drive, single density*

**BPS**   Bits per second. For example, a 14.4 modem would allow for the transmission of data at 14,400 BPS. SEE: *baud*

**Branching**   A method of programming that allows the software to offer a variety of procedures to the user, according to the ways that the user responds.

**Broadband**   Generally, any video system (e.g., cable-television system) that delivers several channels to subscribers. It is also known as "wideband."

**Broadband communications**   A type of video communication system that is either a fast data-rate digital system or wide bandwidth analog system. SEE: *Cable-Television System (CATV)*

**Broadcast**   Refers to the sending of simultaneous messages to a number of receivers (e.g., electronic mail, networking).

**Browse**   A fast way to view information on computer programs without working with or manipulating the data. SEE: *browser*

**Browser or Web browser**   A type of software that allows computer users to make "point-and-click excursions" or to leap from computer to computer through the World Wide Web, a multimedia computer system that organizes information on the Internet. Examples of www browsers are Alta Vista (http:// altavista.digital.com/) and Yahoo (http:// www.yahoo.com/) SEE: *Internet, www*

**Bubble memory**   A form of information storage. The data are stored magnetically, in a way similar to the tracks on a cassette tape.

**Buffer**   A storage area for holding information temporarily during the processing of other data that have been inputted earlier in the sequence. Today's computer printers have buffer capabilities. This speeds up their performance.

**Bug**   An error in a computer design or a software program. The origin of the word comes from the fact that a real insect was found trapped in a relay during the pioneer days of the computer.

**Bulletin Board System (BBS)**   An organized service for subscribers whose computers are equipped with modems. Messages can be posted by any member of the BBS to be read and responded to by other members.

**Bus**   A strip of multiple connectors inside a computer for the inputting and outputting of data. Today, an advanced videocard will have its own bus—this enables the running of high-resolution, multiple-color video monitors.

**Byte** A unit of information equal to eight bits. A byte is the amount of information required to encode a character such as a digit or a letter of the alphabet. SEE: *bit*

**C** A programming language originally developed in support of Bell Lab's UNIX operating system. SEE: *unix*

**CA** SEE: *Computer-Aided*

**Cable-Television System (CATV)** A type of broadband communication system that delivers multiple program channels via satellite transmission and coaxial cable. There are various companies who offer CATV service and this service varies from community to community.

**Cache** A location in a computer's memory for holding data that have been processed earlier in the computing session. If the user requires some of these data again, the processing time will be greatly reduced, since these data are reaccessed speedily. A cache is similar to a buffer but holds a larger amount of memory.

**CAD** SEE: *Computer-Aided Design*

**CAD/CAM** The combination of computer-aided design and manufacturing operations in the same computer software program.

**CAI** SEE: *Computer-Assisted Instruction, Computer-Aided Industry*

**CAM (Computer-Aided Manufacturing)** A type of software program hat controls the operation of assembly lines in factories and performs similar industrial tasks.

**CAP** SEE: *Computer-Aided Planning*

**CAQ** SEE: *Computer-Aided Quality Assurance*

**CAR** SEE: *Computer-Aided Retrieval*

**Card** 1. A small board that can be inserted into an expansion slot of a board (e.g., the mother board). A card may control a peripheral device such as a modem. 2. An IBM card using

punched holes to carry information. Early macro computers used punch cards as their inputs. IBM cards were earlier known as Hollerith cards.

**Card reader** The device on an early macrocomputer that accepted punched IBM cards as input and translated the data into machine language for processing.

**CASE** SEE: *Computer-Aided Software Engineering*

**CATV** SEE: *Cable-Television System*

**Cause-effect software** Software that permits the user to operate a switch to make something happen on the screen of a computer monitor.

**CBI** Computer-Based Instruction.

**CBX** SEE: *Computerized Branch Exchange*

**CCD** SEE: *Charge-Coupled Device*

**CCIRN** Acronymn for The Coordinating Committee for Intercontinental Research Networks whose mission is to promote global research.

**CCSO** Acronym for Computing and Communications Service Office. This is a computer service that allows a user to search for students or faculty at a given school. SEE: *CSO*

**CCTV** SEE: *Closed-Circuit Television*

**CD-I** SEE: *Compact Disk Interactive*

**CD-ROM or Compact Disk-Read Only Memory** Read-only memory on a compact disk. Such storage has a very high capacity, approximately 600 times that of standard computer disks. The information in it can consist of text, sound, and graphics.

**CD-ROM drive** A drive for running a CD-ROM disk in a computer. Also known as a CD-ROM reader.

**CD-ROM reader** SEE: *CD-ROM drive*

**Cell** A component of a spreadsheet (which in turn is a product of a type of computer software program). The cell is located uniquely in a particular row and a particular column. SEE: *spreadsheet*

**Central Processing Unit (CPU)** The central intelligence component of a computer, it is physically in the form of a complex semiconductor chip. This is the unit through which all of the computing work passes. It is also known as a processor; in a personal computer it is called a microprocessor.

**CERN**   The particle physics laboratory locations in France and Switzerland which are the famed locations where Tim Berners-Lee established the World Wide Web in 1989.

**CGI**   Common Gateway Interface or a standard for running programs in the World Wide Web for a web server. SEE: *web server*

**Chain printer**   A type of printer used with large macrocomputers. The characters are placed on a rotating chain.

**CHAR**   Character.

**Character**   A letter, digit, punctuation mark, or symbol that can be expressed by one byte of information.

**Character**   1. One of a set of elementary symbols used to represent or to organize data. 2. A letter, digit, or symbol used in the representation or the organization of data. 3. In the programming language COBOL, a basic unit of that language.

**Character constant**   1. A string of any of the characters being represented, enclosed within apostrophes. 2. A character value (i.e., a symbol, a quantity, or a constant) that is part of the data rather than a reference to a field that includes the data. 3. In some programming languages, a character in apostrophes.

**Character graphic**   A visually represented character, usually picture elements with tone provide the image by contrast with untoned picture elements ("pels"). Occasionally, however, the image may consist of untoned pels surrounded by toned pels, as in a photographic negative. This is called reverse character.

**Character printer**   A printer that impresses a completely formed letter, digit, or symbol with one stroke. Many of these were known as "daisy wheel" printers because a metal disk had arms radiating from it like flower petals. Each arm ended in a print key for a symbol.

**Charge-Coupled Device (CCD)**   A memory storage device. It consists of a silicon chip. The data are stored as electrical charges distributed over the chip.

**Chip**   A rectangular piece of silicon (a semi-conducting element) having electrical circuits etched on it. The very heart of a computer, the CPU, is a complex example of a chip. Chips also are used for the computer's memory, both the ROM and the RAM.

**CHKDSK**   A command (in MS-DOS/PC-DOS) that is used to check the status of a disk (floppy or hard). Information revealed by this command includes the total disk space; the size and number of hidden files, user files, and directories; the number of bytes in bad sectors, and the number of bytes available.

**Chordic keyboard**   An alternative type of keyboard with relatively few keys. Two keys or more often need to be pressed simultaneously.

**CIM**   SEE: *Computer-Input Microfilm, Computer-Integrated Manufacturing*

**Circuit board**   A set of electrical circuits photographically etched on a plastic board. SEE: *board, motherboard*

**ClariNet**   A commercial computer network service of news and other information features for USENET groups. SEE: *usenet*

**Class A network**   An Internet computer network used by colleges/universities, businesses, and organizations with an Internet Protocol (IP) number of 1 to 127.

**Class B network**   An Internet computer network used by corporations, large businesses, and organizations with an Internet Protocol (IP) number of 128-191.

**Class C network**   An Internet computer network used by small businesses and organizations, schools, and service providers with an Internet Protocol (IP) number of 192-221.

**Classroom computer needs**   Today's classroom requires that teachers consider the following when creating computer-access centers in the classroom: 1. computer memory or RAM with 15–32 megabytes (MB) of memory fairly standard and a 3¼" disk drive; 2. adequate storage capacity either on hard-drive space (preferably 2 gigabytes (GB) or 3¼" disks; 3. a CD-ROM drive/ capabilities; 4. monitors, preferably color monitors (15-inch screens with over 200 colors); 5. sound options either built-in or sound cards; 6. modems that allow on-line access; 7. fax modems optional; 8. mouses, balls, or other pointing devices; 9. keyboards and storage capacities for keyboards and other equipment/software; 10. printers (preferably laser quality) with speeds that allow one ppm (page per minute) for color copies and three ppm for black-and-white copies; 11. access to hotlines for assistance; 12. access to the Internet and www; 13. support systems during all phases of computer use; 14. software access/evaluation mechanisms/record-keeping components/graphics programs; and 15. home-school connections/information sharing.

**Clearinghouse**   An information center that shares bodies of information. The federal government, for example, will provide up-to-date information about current trends in educational technology through the Department of Education (technical assistance provider network), which involves an on-line library, ERIC (Educational Resources Information Center) Clearinghouses, a Regional Technology in Education Consortia (R*TECS), a Technology-Related Assistance Program for Individuals with Disabilities, the Department of Energy's special technology centers, and the Eisenhower National Clearinghouse on Math and Science Education. Web access to ERIC is http://ericir.syr.edu.

**Click**   The operation of a button on a mouse to input a command to the computer. The mouse button is first pressed, then released. Some operations may require a double click. The mouse in most cases may have two or three buttons.

**Client**   A type of computer system configuration in a client/server network that allows one program on a personal computer or workstation ("a client") to request services from a larger (usually) computer ("the server"). SEE: *client-server network, server*

**Client-server network**   A common means of networking personal computers with a larger computer or "server" connected to and providing information/services to several smaller personal computers or workstations ("clients"). SEE: *client, server*

**Clip art**   Graphics (individualized pictures) that are stored as software and can be "clipped" (i.e., inserted) into documents, provided these are produced by word processing programs compatible with the clip art software.

**Clipboard**   In Macintosh computers, a location for RAM data that has been copied for transfer to another software application. SEE: *clip art*

**Clock**   A timing device in a microcomputer that puts out periodic signals, which synchronize the computer's operations.

**Clone**   A computer that works like another brand of computer, accepts the same accessories (i.e., is cable-compatible), and runs the same software. Most often the "other" make is a clone of the IBM-PC.

**Closed-caption decoder**   A device that causes a VCR or television to reveal closed captions, making television plays or films accessible to the hearing-impaired.

**Closed-Circuit Television (CCTV)**   A video enhancement in which enlarged images of text and other visual data are presented on a monitor, which benefits visually impaired viewers.

**CNC**   SEE: *Computer-Numerical Control*

**Coaxial cable** or **Coax**   This type of cable is used by cable television systems for broadband data.

**COBOL**   A computer language, COBOL commands resemble English, making it relatively easy to learn. Its use is mainly for business applications.

**Cochlear implant**   An alternate source of auditory input for an individual with a nerve-deafness disability. Electrodes are implanted in the auditory nerve near the cochlea, the organ of hearing in the inner ear; each electrode is connected to its own microphone and sound wave band-pass filter.

**Coding**   The entering of data (i.e., input) into a computer from a keyboard, mouse, or other device.

**COM**   SEE: *Computer-Output Microfilm*

**Command**   A specific order to the computer (provided by the input from the user) to perform an operation.

**Common carrier**   Refers to a telecommunications business or company that sells communications services to the community at large via shared circuits and published tariff rates. The Federal Communications Commission and state public utility commissions regulate the business practices (i.e., rates) of common carriers.

**Communication aid**   Any device that can help a person with disabilities communicate.

**Communication board**   A board marked with symbols that a person with a speech disability can point at, in order to indicate choices.

**Compact Disk Interactive**   A CD-ROM program that permits the user to provide inputs from a hand-held device so that there is an interplay between the CD-ROM data disk and the user's chosen actions.

**Compatibility**   The ability of one computing device to interact with another. There are two main types of compatibility: 1. cable compatibility, which allows printers, keyboards and monitors to be plugged into the computer's chassis and 2. software compatibility, which allows the RAM information on disk to be processed by the computer's central processing unit.

**Compile**   To translate a program written in a high-level computer language into a mid-level, assembly, or machine language.

**Compiler**   Software that converts high-level language programming into machine-language form, making it accessible to the computer. SEE: *compiling*

**Compiling**   Translating a higher-level computer language (e.g., C, or COBOL) into binary commands readable (in machine language) to the computer. SEE: *language*

**COMPUSEC**   SEE: *computer security*

**Computer**   An independent object capable of performing computations, to include logical arithmetic operations. The computer may be a stand-alone, or alternatively, one of several linked units.

**Computer abuse**   Any activity that interferes with the availability or use of computer resources. This category includes embezzlement, fraud, malicious mischief, unauthorized use, denial of service to those authorized to use the service, and theft.

**Computer-Aided (CA)**   Having to do with work done with the help of a computer. CA can also stand for "computer assisted," which is synonymous with "computer-aided."

**Computer-Aided Design (CAD)**   A type of software program used for designing the construction of houses, engines, and other complex items.

**Computer-Aided Industry**
1. Computer-Assisted Instruction. The computer performs some functions of a teacher by providing information, asking quiz questions, etc. 2. Computer-Aided Industry.

**Computer-Aided Planning (CAP)**   The use of computers to prepare operations on data pertaining to industrial processes.

**Computer-Aided Quality Assurance (CAQ)**   The use of computers throughout the life of a product, to include planning, monitoring, and controlling all processes and components. Quality control is affected on all levels from the production line to top management.

**Computer-Aided Retrieval (CAR)**
Software programs that combine the functions of a micrographics program with the indexing and retrieval functions of a database program.

**Computer-Aided Software Engineering (CASE)** Automated development and control of a product from its design through its production and testing. CASE may consist of programs and tools or of tools that work within other programs.

**Computer-assisted graphics** In multimedia applications, the activation of graphics from a computer rather than as part of the showing of a film or videotape.

**Computer-Assisted Instruction** The computer performs some functions of a teacher by providing information, asking quiz questions, etc.

**Computer conferencing** Communication among scattered computer users who share text and graphic data through interlinked terminals.

**Computer crime** A crime committed by the use of software or of computerized data.

**Computer cryptography** By the use of an algorithm, a computer can perform encryption and decoding functions. This may be done to prevent data from falling into the hands of unauthorized parties.

**Computer-dependent language** SEE: *computer-oriented language*

**Computer fraud** A computer crime involving the alteration of computer data for monetary or other gain, or the use of a computer for deception in order to obtain unlawful gain.

**Computer generation** A category of computers manufactured at the same stage of computer history, based on their technology. For instance, first-generation computers were based on relays, vacuum tubes, and IBM cards. Second-generation computers were based on semiconductors (e.g., transistors), and third-generation computers have been based on integrated circuits etched on chips.

**Computer graphics** 1. Any method of converting data either to or from graphic form by the use of a computer. 2. Computer graphics is the science and

technology for transforming digital data to graphics or vice versa by using computers.

**Computer language** SEE: *language, machine language*

**Computer-Input Microfilm (CIM)** The transformation of pictorial data to digitized information and the condensing of the data into OCR-A font-size or OCR-B font-size. The data can be inputted at a workstation for updating or to be included in a document. SEE: *OCR, OCR-B*

**Computer instruction set** The full set of instructions for a computer, to include definitions of various computer functions.

**Computer-Integrated Manufacturing (CIM)** Total automation of a manufacturing plant by the integration of computer operations, communications, and organizational processes.

**Computer micrographics** Methods for converting digital data to microform or vice versa that employ a computer.

**Computer name** In the programming language, COBOL, a system's name. It identifies the particular computer on which a program will be run or compiled. SEE: *compile*

**Computer network** An arrangement of two or more computers interconnected for the exchange of data. SEE: *network*

**Computer-Numerical Control (CNC)** Control exerted by a CAD/CAM software program of machine-tool processes using numerically coded instructions.

**Computer-oriented language** Either a low-level computer language (in the digital form easily handled by the hardware) or, in general, any programming language.

**Computer-Output Microfilm (COM)** Microfilm on which there are computer-generated digital data.

**Computer program** SEE: *program*

**Computer science** The pure and applied science of automated data processing.

**Computer security (COMPUSEC)** Techniques and procedures for the protection of computer hardware, software, and data against theft, destruction, or loss.

**Computer system**   A complete functional unit, including one or more CPUs, the necessary disk drives and memory, the necessary software (programs and data), etc.

**Computer time sharing**   An obsolete term for having a mainframe computer operate several terminals at different places; the operating costs can be shared among several users. The current term is "networking."

**Computer word**   A collection of bytes forming a word that can be processed by a computer.

**Computerization**   The use of computers to automate a process.

**Computerize**   To make a process automatic by having computer control over it.

**Computerized Branch Exchange (CBX)**   A central part of a communications network. A central node serves as a switch to form direct links between any pair of attached nodes.

**Concatenation**   Stringing together a series of characters or paragraphs.

**CONFIG.SYS**   A system file in MS-DOS/PC-DOS, it contains the particulars about the computer's setting. The file contains buffers, files, and device entries. Buffers are data stores that readily provide information as needed. Devices include disks, the keyboard, the mouse, the monitor, etc. The device entry in CONFIG.SYS provides software (called device drivers) for running each hardware device.

**Consortium for School Networking (CoSN)**   A nonprofit organization created by educators, computer dealers, and Internet providers to provide information about the information capabilities and availability within the Internet network.

**Copy**   The replication of part of a document that may be sent to a printer, to a disk, or to another location in the document.

**Copy program**   A kind of software program that facilitates the copying of information from one disk onto a different disk.

**CoSN**   SEE: *Consortium for School Networking*

**CP/M**   A once-popular disk-operating system for personal computers. CP/M was the original operating system for the IBM personal computer. IBM switched to Microsoft's MS-DOS, which is called PC-DOS by IBM, and the makers of IBM clones followed suit. CP/M stands for "Control Program/Microcomputers."

**CPU**   SEE: *Central Processing Unit*

**Crash**   Refers to the failure of a computer program or disk drive, which can result in the loss of data.

**CRT**   Cathode ray tube. The monitor screen of a personal computer. A television screen is another example of a cathode ray tube.

**Cursor**   A symbol (sometimes flashing) on the screen of a computer monitor showing where the next input will be inserted. A cursor is a kind of electronic bookmark.

**Cut and paste**   The removal of a part of a document and its placement into another location in the document. SEE: *block move*

**CWIS**   Acronym for Campus Wide Information Systems. These computer systems provide news/library/information/databases to colleges and universities.

**Cyber patrol**   Refers to Internet resources that allow parents or adults to block computer use certain times of the day. There are databases available that can provide information regarding computer sites [which is helpful in monitoring computer use with children (e.g., uses profanity)].

**Cyberspace**   Refers to the "total universe" of networked computers. If you use e-mail you are considered to be "flowing" through computer "cyberspace." SEE: *electronic mail*

**Daisy wheel**   SEE: *character printer*

**Data**   The information stored in, and processed by, a computer.

**Database**   A type of software program holding information so that it can be readily accessed, retrieved, and brought up to date. Databases can be organized into "fields." For example, a database of colleges might consist of one field for names of colleges, one field for addresses, one field for type of college, one field for cost, etc. Database Management Systems (DBMS) are computer programs that can manage or organize databases of information. DBMS programs can organize information on personal computers, networks, or large mainframes.

**Database Management System (DBMS)**   A type of software designed for the management of databases.

**Data disk**   A disk used to store work files (i.e., information generated by the user). This is to be differentiated from a program disk, which holds a software program.

**DBMS**   SEE: *Database Management System (DBMS)*

**DBS**   SEE: *Direct Broadcast Satellite*

**Decimal tab**   A tab key (or memory-held function) that allows a computer to align columns of numeric data within word processing programs.

**Dedicated**   A type of computer system or hardware that can perform only one particular task (e.g., a "word-processor" or a "chess computer").

**Default values**   The regular preset settings of various computer functions such as the length of a document page, the location of the preferred work drive, the protocol settings for modem use, etc. These values can be changed by specific commands from the user.

**Desktop accessories**   Software-provided tools such as a calendar, a calculator, and an appointment book.

**Desktop publishing program**   Software used to control the printing of text and graphics that is advertised as producing the kind of documents produced by a publishing company.

**Dictionary**   In word-processing programs, a file of words containing the correct spellings and hyphenation.

**Digital**   A type of information transmission used in computer systems that involves the use of discontinuous or discrete electromagnetic or electrical signals that vary in frequency, amplitude, or polarity. Digital systems are different from analog systems, which have continuous functions, although analog forms may be specially encoded for use on digital systems. Digital systems process numbers encoded in binary (on-off) forms.

**Digitized speech**   Speech translated into digital form to be used by electronic devices such as computers.

**Digitizer**   SEE: *audio digitizer, video digitizer*

**Direct Broadcast Satellite (DBS)**   A type of satellite system that is used relatively inexpensively by several earth stations at once.

**Directory**   A listing of files on a disk. Entering the command DIR leads to a display of the disk's directory.

**Discovery program**   A type of program in computer-aided instruction. The learner is enabled to experiment and to discover facts for herself/himself.

**Disc or disk**   A flat, round object placed in a plastic jacket. It is inserted into a disk drive that either "reads off" its information contents or "writes" new information onto it. Disks can be floppy (i.e., flexible) or hard. The hard disk is contained within a "hard drive" and seldom has to be removed or reinserted. Hard disks hold many megabytes or even a gigabyte of information whereas most floppy disks are limited to less than two megabytes.

**Disk notcher**   A punch tool used to make a square hole in a double-density floppy disk at a particular place on the disk. This enables the disk to store at least twice as much data as before; thus, 360 K disks can be made to carry 1.2 Mg or 720 K diskettes can be made to carry 1.44 Mg of information.

**Diskette**   A so-called floppy disk that holds from 360 kilobytes to 1.44 megabytes of information. Currently, diskettes are either 5¼" square and mounted in soft plastic or 3½" square and mounted either in metal or hard plastic. The smaller diskettes have the greater capacity for information storage. Double-density 5¼" diskettes hold 360 K; double-density 3½" diskettes hold 720 K; high-density 5¼" diskettes hold 1.2 megabytes (Mg); and high-density 3½" diskettes hold 1.44 megabytes.

**Display screen**   SEE: *CRT*

**Distributed network**   A network linking computer terminals at various locations within a school system or suite of offices. SEE: *computer time sharing, LAN*

**Documentation**   Written material explaining the use of computer programs, computer hardware, or peripheral devices.

**DOSKEY**   A command that is executed as part of MS-DOS/PC-DOS. A program by this name is installed in memory when DOSKEY is first executed. Thereafter, DOSKEY records your commands. Pressing the "up" arrow key orders your last command previous to the one displayed to appear on-screen. The "down" arrow orders the last command made after the command displayed to appear.

**Dot matrix**   A type of computer printer in which an array of dots is used to form characters. Each dot is formed by pressing an ink-filled pin onto the paper. Printheads usually have nine pins or 24 pins. Multiple passes of the printhead (going over the same line repeatedly) are required to produce letter-quality print. A single pass produces the grainy-looking "draft mode."

**Double density**   Floppy disks capable of storing 360 kilobytes of data. At one time, the development of these disks was an upgrade over the previously used single-density disks, which could carry only 180 Kb of information. Today, double-density disks are being replaced by high-density disks; 5¼" high-density floppies can hold 1.2 megabytes, or 1200 kilobytes, of information.

**Double-sided drives**   Most floppy disk drives are capable of writing to both sides of a diskette. Single-sided drives became obsolete in the early 1980s; they left the microcomputing scene early on.

**Download**   To receive data on a personal computer by modem from a larger central computer. This may occur on a BBS, a LAN, or an information service such as CompuServe.

**Dragging**   The act of moving a mouse across the desktop (so that the cursor covers the desired positions on the monitor display) while one of the mouse's buttons is held down or clicked repeatedly.

**Drill and practice program**   A software program in CAI that requires the learner to go through a set of guided practice procedures.

**Dump**   To place a segment of information from part of a computer's RAM or main memory on the computer screen (or to print said information).

**Dvorak**   A kind of typewriter or computer keyboard developed as a more efficient alternative to the conventional "QWERTY" keyboard.

**Dynamic display**   A display on the CRT that keeps getting erased and replaced by newer incoming data.

**Editor**   A text-modification subprogram found in MS-DOS. This type of software editor is suitable for the modification of computer-operating files such as the AUTOEXEC.BAT or COMMAND.COM files. It is not very useful for document editing.

**Education Resources Information Center (ERIC)**   A computerized clearinghouse of education resources that functions via Askeric, an Internet site. ERIC receives information and other support from the U.S. Department of Education. SEE: *Internet*

**Educational game**   A kind of learning software in which the learner plays a game, earning points by showing proof of learning.

**EFTS**   SEE: *Electronic Funds Transfer System*

**Electronic archive**   A set of files containing information to be used as reference materials or as back-up versions of documents and/or files stored on disks.

**Electronic bulletin board**   SEE: *Bulletin Board System (BBS)*

**Electronic education**   Refers to actual classes or learning that occurs via the computer (e.g., Internet and World Wide Web). SEE: *virtual classroom*

**Electronic Funds Transfer System (EFTS)**   A computer system used for the deposit and/or withdrawal of funds, the transfer of funds between accounts, and the reporting of financial data.

**Electronic mail (e-mail)**   Messages/correspondence sent via modem to people's computers, word processors, and facsimile devices.

**Electronic mailbox**   A file consisting of electronic mail data.

**Electronic messaging**   The encoding, sending, storing, and retrieving of data (in the form of text, graphics or voice information) electronically.

**Electronic worksheet**   The product of a spreadsheet program; the entire spreadsheet is encoded in RAM and may be scrolled for viewing on a computer monitor.

**E-mail**   SEE: *electronic mail*

**Emoticons**   Refers to symbols one can use to convey emotions when conversing on the Internet.

**Emulator**   A device that works the same way as another device. For example, a software program has been sold that purports to do the same work as a math co-processing chip (a semiconductor component of a computer that speeds up mathematical calculations). We could call this software a math co-processing emulator.

**Environmental control unit**   A device that allows the user to control various electrical appliances all over the house, such as lights, television sets, telephones, alarms, etc.

**ERIC**   SEE: *Education Resources Information Center*

**Error message**   A short statement on a computer screen telling the user that a procedure was incorrect. Examples are "incorrect command or file name" or "directory does not exist."

**ES**   SEE: *Expert System*

**Expanded memory**   MS-DOS/PC-DOS was formerly limited to a size of only 640 kilobytes (Kb) of memory. A combination of software and hardware was devised that raised the size of memory to 32 megabytes. The "near" memory above 640 Kb but below 1 megabyte is divided into 4 buffers, each 16 Kb in size. A program loaded into conventional memory (the lower 640 Kb) is divided into 16 KB-sized pages. The data contained in those pages are sent to the page buffers. Expanded memory became outdated with the development of Intel's 80286, '386, '486, etc., CPU's which allow for extended memory.

**Expansion slot**   A gap left inside the chassis of a personal computer near the motherboard. A plastic card (called an accessory board) can be placed there. Some accessory boards hold additional memory chips; they are used to boost the amount of RAM that the computer can handle. Some are interface boards, enabling the computer to work with a new peripheral component such as a modem.

**Expert System (ES)**   A computer program provided with sufficient data and appropriate algorithms to enable it to function in a way similar to a trained human professional. This is an application of AI (Artificial Intelligence). This is also called a knowledge-based system.

**Extended memory**   MS-DOS/PC-DOS normally has had a size limit of 640 kilobytes. With the development of the Intel CPU 80286 for IBM-AT computers and clones, more than 640 Kb of memory, called high memory or extended memory, was made available. Software programs must load their instructions in conventional memory (the "lower" 640 Kb) but the data manipulated by these programs can be stored in high memory.

**External memory** Computer memory (of work done by the user) that would be lost if it remained only in electronic memory and the computer was turned off. This information may be stored on hard drive, floppy disks, magnetic tapes, bubble memory, etc. External memory is also called "removable memory" and "mass memory."

**FAQ (Frequently Asked Questions)** Such lists of questions and answers assist computer users with information typically needed to be effective/efficient users of the Web. For example, the ERIC Clearinghouse on Disabilities and Gifted Education provides a FAQ guide for teachers at http://www.cec.sped.org.

**FAT (File Allocation Table)** A record of the location of each file on a disk. The FAT also keeps a log of the unused spaces on the disk.

**Fax** A facsimile. Black-and-white reproductions of documents, graphics, etc. are transmitted via a telephone or communications system. Schools can "fax" contracts, schedules, and other documents through fax systems.

**FCC** SEE: *Federal Communications Commission*

**Federal Communications Commission (FCC)** A board of commissioners appointed by the President who are entrusted to regulate interstate communications to include the computer industry.

**Fiber-optic cable** A cable that contains at least one optical fiber.

**Fiber optics** A relatively new technology that allows light beams to be projected and manipulated (e.g., reflected and bent) through very thin glass fibers (also called "optical fibers" and "glass optical wave guides").

**Field** A unit of information in a set of data. A field could consist of a name, an address, a telephone number, etc.

**File** Any document created by a software program, given a name, and stored on a computer disk. Word-processing files are the best-known examples.

**File Transfer Protocol (FTP)** A File Transfer Protocol is a communications protocol that allows for the transfer of files via telephone lines/networks on the Internet. FTP's specify how to convert/transfer data through the computer Internet system when different types of computers are used and how to detect errors. Some popular FTP's are Kermit, XModem, YModem, ZModem. SEE: *ftp, Internet*

**Firmware** Computer programs that are stored in ROM and that are used in operating the computer system.

**Fixed disk** SEE: *hard disk*

**Flexible disk** SEE: *diskette*

**Floppy disk** SEE: *diskette*

**Font** A typeface (a particular style and size of type). Fonts may be built into the hardware of character printers or provided for other printers in software accompanying the printer or provided with a word-processing or desktop publishing software program.

**Footer** A type of information placed at the bottom of all pages of a word-processed document. Such data could be the page number or the date, as examples.

**FORTRAN** A higher-level computer language. The name stands for "FORmula TRANslator." This language is intended mainly for mathematical applications, especially in the physical sciences.

**Freeware** Refers to computer software that is available to users of the Internet free-of-charge.

**ftp** A type of client used to download information on the Internet using FTP. SEE: *File Transfer Protocol (FTP)*

**FTP** File Transfer Protocol. An Internet tool that allows the transfer of computer files from one computer to another in the Internet system. SEE: *ftp, file transfer protocol, Internet*

**Galaxy** An encyclopedic listing of public and commercial Internet services. Access: http://www.einet.net/galaxy.html

**Gateway**   A device that interconnects two computer systems (or networks) with differences in network architecture.

**Geostationary satellite**   A type of stationary satellite viewed from earth that has a circular earth orbit 22,400 miles in space.

**Gigabyte**   A unit of computer memory equal to one billion bytes (i.e., 1000 megabytes). SEE: *byte, kilobyte, megabyte*

**Glass optical wave guides**   SEE: *fiber optics*

**Global Learning and Observations to Benefit the Environment (GLOBE)**   A program developed by NASA that links educators, scientists, students, and others around the world so as to make/record observations about the environment and to share this data via the Internet.

**GLOBE**   SEE: *Global Learning and Observations to Benefit the Environment*

**Gopher**   A type of computer software tool developed at the University of Minnesota that allows one to search for and access files on the Internet via a file menu of text/graphics. SEE: *Internet*

**Gopherspace**   Refers to the global universe of "gophers." SEE: *gopher*

**Gradebook**   A software program keeping a record of the names of the students in a class, the assignments given to the class, and the grades earned by each student. The program can also compute each student's grade for the semester.

**Grammar checker**   A type of software program that scans the text of a word-processed document and signals errors of grammar. Sometimes such programs also calculate a "readability index." These programs are also called "style checkers."

**Graphical User Interface (GUI) (pronounced "gooey")**   A feature of a disk-operating system which allows the user to select a visual symbol or icon that clearly indicates what function the computer will perform. This was always the standard procedure for Macintosh computers and the Microsoft Windows software now provides it for MS-DOS users.

**Graphics**   A type of software by which pictorial information is stored in digital form. Graphics may be integral to a desktop publishing program. They may also be stored as clip art and be imported into desktop publishing or word-processing programs.

**Grid**   A division of the CRT screen into evenly spaced horizontals and verticals. This allows for the precise location of visual images on the screen, using row and column coordinates.

**GUI**   SEE: *Graphical User Interface*

**Handshaking**   An exchange of signals at the beginning of a communication session between two computer systems. Handshaking is sometimes managed by hardware and sometimes through the use of software.

**Hard copy**   A word-processed document on paper. The document is in user-readable form instead of being in potentially printable form on a disk.

**Hard disk**   A high-capacity storage device capable of holding many megabytes of information. It is kept inside the hard drive almost all the time. The contents of the hard disk are often backed up (i.e., copied) onto other storage devices such as magnetic tapes or floppy disks.

**Hard drive**   The drive that contains, reads, and writes to a hard disk. SEE: *hard disk*

**Hardware**   Physical (mechanical and electrical) computer and telecommunications equipment. In regard to computers, hardware is the computer itself, the monitor, the disk drives, the modem, the keyboard, the mouse, etc. Computer software is the programs and files used in the hardware. SEE: *software*

**Headend**   A term used to refer to the control center for a cable-television system.

**High-density floppy drive**   A name for the type of floppy drive with memory capacity beyond the double-density level. A 5¼" high-density floppy disk holds 1.2 megabytes of information, while a 3½" high-density "floppy" disk (it is really quite rigidly encased in metal or hard plastic) holds 1.44 megabytes.

**Hit**  Refers to accessing or entering a particular file. Some organizations monitor the number of "hits," or people entering the file.

**Hits**  Refers to the number of data finds after a database search. Upon entering a keyword, if a user finds 23 entries, these are known as "hits."

**Home page**  The opening page at a World Wide Web site that typically gives an overview of the site such as location, contact persons, type of program, an introduction, etc.

**Horizontal scrolling**  A feature of some software programs. Text displays wider than the width of the standard display can be fully examined on the monitor screen because of this feature.

**Host**  A computer that is directly linked to the Internet.

**Host-name**  The computer name of a specific computer linked to the Internet.

**Hotlinks**  SEE: *hotlist*

**Hotlist**  Hypertext listing of hyperlinks that are valuable or hot sites in the World Wide Web in the opinion of some organization, group, or individual. SEE: *hyperlink*

**HTML**  SEE: *Hypertext Markup Language*

**HTTP**  SEE: *Hypertext Transfer Protocol*

**Hyper-ABLEDATA**  A CD-ROM version of ABLEDATA database software. This is a Macintosh-compatible database containing descriptions, pictures, and audio data of thousands of assistive technology devices. It is available to individuals with disabilities.

**Hypercard**  A monitor display that is part of an interactive computer technology developed for the Macintosh class of Apple computers. A "card" is a computer display used with other hypercards that are linked in a Hyper-media system, which consists of multi-media (text, sound, pictorial) programs. The hypercards are linked logically, not by alphabetical ordering or any other arbitrary system. The hypercards can be

grouped into larger units called "stacks." SEE: *hypermedia*

**Hyperlink**  A means (e.g., color change, bolding, underlining, and so on) to access related documents on hypertext files. Hyperlinks are the vehicle in which information is linked in the World Wide Web. One can click on a hyperlink in order to connect to other documents in the World Wide Web. Examples of hyperlinks might be *education*, which when clicked on might open access to *mathematics, science*, etc. When science is clicked, access might be given to the topics of *astronomy, space exploration*, etc. Under *space exploration*, one might encounter the *StarChild Project* by NASA, which will then reveal the URL or World Wide Web address for the StarChild Project which is: http:// heasarc.gsfc.nasa.gov/docs/StarChild/ StarChild.html. SEE: *hypertext, hyperlinking*

**Hyperlinking**  The ability of a network user (e.g., Internet user) to access information through a complex network of computers throughout the world. The computer user accesses information about various subjects that contain additional highlighted references that refer the user to other systems within the network.

**Hypermedia**  A system for linking computer programs that carry text, sound, and pictorial information. SEE: *hypertext, hypercard*

**Hypertext**  A setup for a group of computer software programs that are linked logically rather than by a simple linear sequence. These programs contain encoded textual, auditory, and graphical information. For example, you could read a text on plants and use a mouse to click onto words or phrases that could access more detailed information, pictures, and graphics. SEE: *hyperlink, hypermedia*

**Hypertext links**  SEE: *hyperlink*

**Hypertext Markup Language (HTML)**  Hypertext Markup Language which is the type of formatting code or language that create hypertext links (also called hyperlinks or links) in a World Wide

Web document and are many times underlined, highlighted, or in color. SEE: *hyperlinks*

**Hypertext Transfer Protocol (HTTP)** Hypertext Transfer Protocol. It is the manner in which HTML documents are exchanged between different computers using the World Wide Web. SEE: *hyperlink, url*

**IC** SEE: *Integrated Circuit*

**IAB** SEE: *Internet Architecture Board*

**ICMP** SEE: *Internet Control Message Protocol*

**Icon** A picture symbolizing a type of computer operation. A mouse may be used to select the icon for the desired operation. Such procedures are found in Apple computers and in Microsoft Windows shell software for the IBM personal computer and its clones.

**IDE** A type of interface (called a "driver") between a computer's CPU and its disk drives. IDE can control hard drives, floppy drives, and CD-ROM drives.

**IIPS** (Institutional Information Processing System) A hardware and software program/system for administering the geographically scattered community colleges of the state of North Carolina. This successful system is offered as a model for the administration of other statewide systems in the United States.

**ILS** SEE: *Integrated Learning System*

**Information service** A telecommunications system that computer users can join in order to receive data, do computer shopping, upload and download information, play games such as bridge or chess with faraway opponents, exchange electronic mail, etc. Some of these services are: The Source, CompuServe, Delphi, and Prodigy.

**Information superhighway** A label given to the Internet. SEE: *Internet*

**Information utility** The computer and information-related services offered to subscribers of a particular program/service/network. As examples, CompuServe and the Dow Jones News Retrieval services are considered "information utility" programs.

**Ink jet printer** A nonimpact printer (i.e., there is no element that presses onto the paper and the paper roller, as in the cases of daisy wheel or dot-matrix printers); the characters take shape from a pattern of ink droplets falling on the paper.

**Input** The information coming into the computer.

**Input device** Any physical tool for feeding information to a computer. Input devices include: keyboard, mouse, organ keyboard, tape drive, disk drive, microphone, light pen, optical scanner, digitizer, trackball, etc.

**Insert mode** In word processing, the data input from the user's strokes on the keyboard is inserted at the place marked by the cursor. In insert mode, all the previously entered material is left intact; the new data is simply inserted into the document at the place marked. This can be used when one has forgotten a letter in a word; one can go back to the point where the letter should be and type it in.

**Instructional software** Software that provides academic information or that facilitates learning in some way. SEE: *CAI*

**Integrated Circuit (IC)** A semiconductor chip on which a complete circuit is etched. IC chips can be used as microprocessors (the central processing unit), RAM chips, etc.

**Integrated Learning System (ILS)** A software curriculum placed on a network for simultaneous use by a number of computers. This system provides management aids for teachers as well as instructional software.

**Integrated Services Digital Network (ISDN)** A type of cable communication that allows for the transmission of video, data, and graphic images via digital connections on a public switched telephone network. SEE: *public switched telephone network*

**Integrated software** Software applications such as word processing, spreadsheet, database, and PIM provided by one company. The different programs are able to exchange data and to work on the same data. Major software companies that have issued their own versions of integrated software include Microsoft, Lotus, Borland, and Word Perfect.

**IntelliKeys**   A modified type of computer keyboard on which overlays may be placed to guide the user in various applications. The IntelliKeys board can be programmed.

**Interactive media**   A type of telecommunications system that permits individuals in one location to participate in two-way communications with individuals in other locales via computers/televisions. One can teach, take courses, send information, etc. through interactive media.

**Interactive Television (ITV)**   The use of the television medium for two-way communications. ITV is popular now on home-shopping networks and can be useful in the education field when processing information, teaching, etc.

**Interactive videodisk**   A videodisk controlled by a computer user employing such input devices as a joystick, a mouse, a trackball, a keyboard, etc. so that the user is able to interact with the information on the disk.

**Interlaced**   A manner of scanning the screen of a cathode ray tube (i.e., CRT, television, or computer monitor) that scans all even-numbered lines first, then does the odd-numbered lines, etc. This is considered to provide more annoying flicker than noninterlaced scanning would.

**Interleaving**   A method for the arrangement of data on a disk so that it conforms to the way that the disk controller reads the disk.

**internet**   A TCP/IP computer network that is a separate entity from the worldwide Internet. SEE: *TCP/IP*

**Internet (also known as the information superhighway)**   A large international computer network that provides users with e-mail, telephone interactions with other users, library search tools, and a bulletin board. This public computer system was developed by the U.S.

military and links several smaller-sized computer networks. Internet uses packet-switching networks that are interconnected by Internet Protocol gateways. Information services provide access to the Internet. For example, Delphi offers full access to Internet if you call 1-800-695-4005 or address e-mail to Delphi at INFO@delphi.com. Internet offers a glimpse of high-tech services to come in the future as seen in the first rock 'n' roll concert (Rolling Stones) played live worldwide over the Internet computer networks (both audio and video) on November 18, 1994. The history of the Internet can be accessed via http://world.std.com/~walthowe/history.htm) (author = W. Howe, May 9, 1996, When did the Internet Start? A Brief Capsule History). SEE: *archie, ARPANET, bitnet, bitnic, block, browse, browser, bulletin board system, class A network, class B network, class C network, cyberpatrol, electronic mail, ftp, File Transfer Protocol (FTP), galaxy, gopher, hyperlink, hyperlinking, information superhighway, Internet Architecture Board (IAB), Internet engineering task force, Internet Protocol (IP), Internet sites in education, Internet society, Internet tools summary, port, TCP/IP, telnet, usenet, VERONICA, web crawler, World Wide Web, Yahoo*

**Internet address**   A numeric coding system in TCP/IP Internet communications that specifies with which network the user will communicate. Internet addresses are expressed as dotted decimal numbers.

**Internet Architecture Board (IAB)**
Previously known as the Internet Activities Board, this board coordinates research and development for TCP/IP protocols and monitors standards for the Internet society. SEE: *Internet society*

**Internet Control Message Protocol (ICMP)**   A protocol that a gateway uses to send a message to a source (e.g., to report an error). ICMP is built into Internet Protocol (IP). SEE: *gateway*

**Internet engineering task force**   A task force of the Internet Architecture Board that develops and modifies standards for Internet protocols and architecture. SEE: *Internet Architecture Board (IAB)*

**Internet Protocol (IP)** A protocol for directing data traffic in an Internet setting. IP specifies the addressing mechanism to transfer data/information to a destination computer. SEE: *Internet, TCP/IP*

**Internet router** A device that lets an Internet host system serve as a gateway for the passage of data from one network to another; the two separate networks must use a particular kind of adapter. SEE: *gateway*

**Internet sites in education** *Gopher Sites: Askeric* (askeric@ericir.syr.edu); *Educational Journals* (gopher://info.asu. edu:70/11/asc-cwis/education/ journals); *K–12 Internet Resources* (informs.k12.mn.us); *Kidsphere Discussion* (kidsphere@vms.cis.pitt.edu); *National Aeronautics and Space Administration* (spacelink.msfc.nasa.gov); *National School Network Testbed* (copernicus.bbn.com); *WELL or Whole Earth 'Lectronic Link* (gopher.well.sf.ca.us); World Wide Web sites: *Book Nook* (database of book reviews compiled by children: http://www.schoolnet. ca/arts/ lit/booknook/index.html); *Cisco Ed Archive* (http://sunsite.unc.edu/ cisco/edu-arch.html); *Classroom Connect* (http://www.classroom.net); *Cyberkids* (http://www.mtlake.com/cyberkids); *EdWeb* (http://k12.cnidr.org:90); *Gifted and Talented Homepage* (http://www. eskimo.com/user/kids.htm/); *Guides/Tutorial/Lists* (http://library.tufts. edu/www/internet_guides.htm/); *Humanities/Literature/Genres/Childrens/ Authors* (http://www.yahoo.com/ Arts/Humanities/Literature/Genres/ Children_s/Authors/); *Institute for Learning Sciences* (http://www.ils. nwu. edu/ e_for_/index.htm/); *Internet in the Classroom* (http://www.schnet.edu.au); *Internet Public Library's Story Hour* (http://ipl. sils.umich.edu/youth/Story Hour/); *National Reading Conference* (http:// www.iusb.edu/webacts/ edud.EleEd/nrc/nrcindex.html/); *Publisher's Weekly Children's Bestseller Lists* (http://www. bookwire.com/pw/bsl/

childrens/current.childrens.html); *Roadmap for the Information Superhighway Interactive Internet Training Workshop* (http://www.ll. mit.edu/Roadmap/); *Scholastic* (http://scholastic.com.2005/ b); *Tales of Wonder* (folk and fairy tales from around the world) (http://www. ece.ucdavis. edu/~darsie/tales.html); *United States Department of Education Office of Educational Research and Improvement (OERI)* (http://www.ed.gov/); *Wishbone* (PBS series that fosters reading) (http:// www.pbs.org/wishbone/ index.html).

**Internet society** An organization that is dedicated to the growth and development of the Internet and Internet-related services. This organization provides assistance to groups involved with the Internet.

**Internet tools summary** An encyclopedia of Internet tools and their use. Access: http://www.rpi.edu/ Internet/ Guides/decemj/itools/top.html

**Internetwork** A wide area network that links two or more networks.

**Internetworking** Communications taking place among several networks.

**Interpreter** A kind of system software. It translates high-level languages into machine language form, step by step. Interpreters work more slowly than compilers.

**Inverse scanning** A scanning process in which the user holds the scanning switch (e.g., the down arrow key of a computer keyboard) and the cursor continues moving down the document. To select a position on the document, the user stops the cursor by releasing the switch.

**IP** SEE: *Internet Protocol*

**IRC (Internet Relay Chat)** These are sites or networks where individuals can conduct interactive conversations via the computer.

**ISDN** SEE: *Integrated Services Digital Network*

**ITV** SEE: *Interactive Television*

**JAVA** A type of programming language by Sun Microsystems that creates interactive formats, animation, and speed for World Wide Web documents.

**JPEG or Joint Photographic Experts Group**  A type of standard used on the Internet for compressing color or gray digital images of real-life depictions.

**Jughead**  A software tool that investigates gopher services for a local area of the Internet (such as a college). SEE: *archie, FTP, gopher, VERONICA*

**Justification**  Keeping the left (and right, in some cases) margins of a document straight. Word-processing programs allow the user to choose no justification, left-margin justification only, or both left and right justification.

**Ke:nx**  A device giving access to a Macintosh computer. The inputs may be provided by keyboard, switch, or Morse code.

**Keyboarding**  Entering data by typing on a computer keyboard.

**Keylock**  A mechanism for locking one computer key when another key is pressed.

**Keywording**  Refers to a word, code, or phrase that can access or identify a record or document. Keywords can be used in searching for or sorting information/data.

**KidNews**  This World Wide Web service allows children to access stories for free and to submit stories as well. Access: http://www.vsa.cape.com/~powens/Kidnews.html.

**Kilobyte**  A unit of computer memory equal to 1000 bytes. SEE: *byte*

**Knowledge-based system**  SEE: *Expert System (ES)*

**LAN**  SEE: *Local Area Network*

**Language**  A unified system of commands for a computer. Low-level languages are geared to the mechanical actions of switches in the computer. The lowest-level language is machine language. Higher-level languages tend to be more like English than do the lower-level languages.

**Laser printer**  A nonimpact printer (i.e., there is no element that presses onto the paper and the paper roller as in the cases of daisy wheel or dot-matrix printers); characters are formed by the action of a laser beam upon a photosensing material, followed by the application of a toner to make the characters visible. This is followed up by a process that transfers these developed images of characters onto paper.

**LATA**  SEE: *Local Access and Transport Area*

**LCD**  Liquid crystal display. The display mode most commonly used for the monitor screens of laptop computers. The characters are black against a gray background.

**LEC**  SEE: *Local Exchange Carrier*

**Letter quality printer**  A printer that produces output comparable to that of an office typewriter in quality. Daisy wheel printers, ink-jet printers, and laser printers usually create letter-quality products. Dot-matrix printers can do so also, especially if they have twenty-four pins on the printhead rather than nine and if they are used with a compatible word-processing software program. SEE: *character printer, ink-jet printer, laser printer*

**Light pen**  A data-inputting device. The tip of the pen emits a light. The user holds the tip against the monitor screen and draws or writes input messages.

**Linear Predictive Coding (LPC)**  A particular form of speech synthesis. The digitized speech is compressed so that it takes up less memory on a disc or other storage device.

**Link**  SEE: *hyperlink*

**Listserv**  A computer service that allows for the distribution of a message or letter to several e-mail users at the same time.

**ListServ mailing lists**  Mailing lists sent to a ListServ address which then distributes e-mail messages to list subscribers. Lists are generated from e-mail discussion or chat groups. SEE: *e-mail*

**Local Access and Transport Area (LATA)**  Refers to a telephone service region with local exchanges and is typically smaller than a state region.

**Local Area Network (LAN)**   A network linking computers within a fairly small area (e.g., in one school building or one classroom). SEE: *computer time sharing, distributed network*

**Local Exchange Carrier (LEC)**   Refers to a local telephone company or one that handles a particular exchange or locale (e.g., 413) with access to other carriers (long-distance).

**Log in**   SEE: *logon*

**Log out**   SEE: *logoff*

**LOGO**   A computer language that emphasizes graphics and is suitable for helping children acquire computer programming skills.

**Logoff**   A procedure by which one ends a computing session. In some programs, exiting by simply turning off the computer, without performing a logoff routine, would result in a loss of data.

**Logon**   A procedure for beginning a computing session. Logging on to a computer typically involves typing in or keywording your user name and a password. This protects the system or network from unauthorized use or abuse of computer time.

**LPC**   SEE: *Linear Predictive Coding*

**Machine language**   A computer language at the very lowest level. SEE: *language*

**Macintosh**   A line of computers from the Apple Corporation. These computers provide a graphical user interface. They have been found especially valuable for desktop publishing applications, easily managing the coordination of text and graphics.

**Macro**   A command that substitutes for a number of commands. Word processing programs allow the user to create customized macros. For example, a macro consisting of ".PI" may mean "Leave a line blank and indent the next line five spaces." Its use would be to start a new paragraph economically. Without this macro, the user would have to hit the Enter key twice and the space bar five times.

**Main memory**   The internal memory of a computer kept in its circuitry; the computer's ROM.

**Mainframe**   A large computer typically more powerful than a personal computer that can be connected to several smaller terminals as in a bank or insurance company.

**Manual scanning**   Aided scanning for a person with disabilities using a computer. An assistant points to options that the person selects.

**Megabyte**   A unit of computer memory equal to 1,000,000 bytes (i.e., 1000 kilobytes). SEE: *byte, kilobyte*

**Membrane keyboard**   A keyboard with a flat surface. The user's fingers can depress push-button switches underneath the membrane. The membrane is the stretched material that covers the keyboard.

**Memory**   The stored information within a computer, which may be measured in kilobytes, megabytes, or, soon, gigabytes. Some of it is hard-wired ROM ("Read-Only Memory") and some is RAM ("Random Access Memory").

**Menu**   A set of options offered to the user by a software program. The user must make a choice before anything more can be done. Not all programs are menu-driven, however.

**Message coding**   In Augmentative and Alternative Communication (AAC), a kind of speed-up device. Depressing one or two keys produces a complex message that would otherwise require pressing, in order, a large number of keys. SEE: *Augmentative and Alternative Communication (AAC), macro*

**Microcomputers**   A personal computer that can be placed on the user's desk. It is run by a microprocessor.

**Microprocessor**   A silicon chip containing the circuits of a microcomputer. Such a chip serves as the computer's Central Processing Unit or CPU.

**MIDI**   Musical Instrument Digital Interface. A system for connecting a computer to an electrical musical instrument in order to facilitate musical composition or to help a musician practice his/her art, for example.

**Minicomputer**  A computer that is too large to be classified as a microcomputer but smaller than a mainframe (wall-sized) computer.

**Mirror site**  When a server has duplicated or mirrored the files of another server or user of the Internet.

**Modem**  Modulator-demodulator. A device for sending computer information over telephone lines. Electrical pulses are converted to audible sounds. In addition, the device receives tones coming from telephone lines and converts them to the electrical pulses that are used by the computer.

**Monitor**  The viewing screen of a computer. SEE: *CRT*

**Mosaic**  A popular Web browser. SEE: *web browser*

**Motherboard**  A large card with slots into which other cards can be placed. The motherboard holds the CPU, the drivers for the hard and floppy disk drives, and RAM chips.

**Mouse**  An input device that cooperates with the information displayed on a computer screen. The user moves the mouse around on a flat surface until the cursor arrow on-screen is at the desired position. The user then clicks the appropriate mouse button. SEE: *click, input device*

**MPEG**  Moving pictures experts group. A standard for transmitting moving-picture images on the Internet.

**MS-DOS**  Microsoft disk-operating system. The disk-operating system used by all IBM clones. The IBM personal computers themselves use PC-DOS, which works like MS-DOS, but PC-DOS is slightly different (having a few less files).

**Multimedia**  The use of several types of information at one time in a computer application. For example, text, graphics, and sounds may be presented in an integrated manner, as in a CD-ROM encyclopedia.

**Muppet learning keys**  A computer keyboard for younger children with an inviting, colorful surface.

**National Information Infrastructure (NII)**  Broad-based proposals initiated by the federal government of guidelines and standards for digital-data information transmission.

**National Research and Education Network (NREN)**  An information network planned to link up various research centers, libraries, and colleges.

**National Telecommunications and Information Administration (NTIA)**  The office of the U.S. Commerce Department that supports the National Information Infrastructure through grants and other offerings in an attempt to broaden education programs/endeavors that further the field.

**Navigate**  Refers to the act of moving from one computer file or program to another. Also refers to moving from one computer server to another on the World Wide Web (www) using Web-browser computer software (e.g., Alta Vista, Netscape, and Yahoo). SEE: *World Wide Web*

**Navigator**  A software program for controlling the operation of a complex application such as running a videodisc. Navigators allow users to access current information on the Internet and access interactive text pages, audio presentations, animation, e-mail, newsgroups, etc. SEE: *navigate*

**Netiquette**  The commonly accepted "good manners" one should use when using the Internet. The Netiquette home page provides such information.

**Netscape**  An Internet navigator that provides 1. what's new on the Internet, 2. a search and directory for particular interest areas, and 3. an address file that allows one to return to particular Web sites (http://www.netscape.com).

**Network**  A coordinated group of computers that can communicate with one another (i.e., through telephone cables). SEE: *distributed network, Local Area Network (LAN)*

**Newsgroups**   Usenet discussion groups that can be accessed via the Internet (not the same as the Internet). SEE: *usenet*

**NII**   SEE: *National Information Infrastructure*

**NREN**   SEE: *National Research and Education Network*

**NTIA**   SEE: *National Telecommunications and Information Administration*

**Nybble**   A unit of information equal to four bits, or to half a byte.

**OCR**   SEE: *Optical Character Recognition*

**Off line**   Any information or equipment that is currently not available to the computer. A printer not properly connected or switched on so that it cannot accept data for printing from the CPU is said to be off line, for example.

**On line**   Any information or equipment that is currently connected with the computer and is ready to be run.

**On-line processing**   Continuous communication between a central computer and a remote terminal. When data have to be steadily inputted from the remote location, this type of processing is more efficient than batch processing.

**Open-network architecture**   The guidelines or standards set for telecommunications entrepreneurs when interconnecting with a computer network.

**Operating system**   A software system by which computer hardware (the CPU) can manage software programs and handle information. The best-known example is MS-DOS. Other examples include CP/M, AppleDOS, UNIX, TRSDOS, AmigaDOS, and XENIX.

**Optical Character Recognition (OCR)**   A photoelectromechanical device for transforming printed text and/or graphics into machine language (digital) form for use by a computer.

**Optical fibers**   SEE: *fiber optics*

**Orphan**   A term used in word processing that refers to the first line of a paragraph if it appears as the last line of a page. Most word processing packages allow one to repaginate or move the line to the next page of text. SEE: *widow, word processing*

**OS/2**   A new IBM operating system that is intended to replace, gradually, the still popular PC-DOS operating system.

**Output**   Information, processed by a computer, appearing in print or on the CRT.

**Output device**   Any device by which a computer displays information to the user, such as a printer or a monitor.

**Overlay**   A sheet of marked paper that can be laid atop a membrane keyboard. The markings on the paper indicate which keys will perform which tasks. Such keyboards can be customized to meet the needs of each individual student, after which the student can use the appropriate overlay. SEE: *membrane keyboard*

**Packet**   A set of binary digits, including both data and commands, that is transmitted as a unit. SEE: *Internet protocol*

**PASCAL**   A high-level programming language. More difficult to use than BASIC, but more flexible and powerful.

**Password**   Secret word(s) or sequence(s) of characters that are used to access computer files, programs, computers, or networks. Without this password(s), the user cannot gain access into the computer program or system. This is a security precaution to protect organizations from unauthorized use or abuse.

**PC-DOS**   The IBM version of the MS-DOS operating system, it has a few less files than MS-DOS does. The missing files are made up for by a hardware fix that is unique to IBM and not shared by the IBM clones that use the MS-DOS software program.

**Peripheral**   A part of the computer that is not essential for its basic functioning. Peripherals include printers and modems. They are usually connected to the computer by cables. Peripherals may be considered the interface between the computer and the human user.

**Personal listening device**   Any device that amplifies auditory outputs.

**PGP or pretty good privacy**   A type of encryptic computer application created by Phil R. Zimmerman that provides the

Internet user with the means to transmit information/messages in privacy.

**PIM** (Personal information manager) A software program that provides an agenda for the user as well as time-budgeting aids.

**Ping** A type of computer utility that allows a user to check to see whether or not a host is reachable. SEE: *host*

**Plotter** A device for drawing lines, in various colors, under computer instructions. These devices are no longer widely sold, inasmuch as color computers and color printers, run by today's software (which includes improved graphics programs) have rendered plotters obsolete.

**Pneumatic switch** A switch activated by a sudden change in air pressure. It may be mounted inside a tube that the user can sip from or puff into, depending on whether the air pressure has to be lowered or increased, respectively.

**Point-and-click excursion** To leap from computer to computer through the World Wide Web, a multimedia computer system that organizes information on the Internet. SEE: *Internet, World Wide Web*

**POP** or **postoffice protocol** A computer application that allows one to obtain e-mail on the Internet. See: *e-mail*

**Port** A specific location designation for a particular program on an Internet host computer. SEE: *Internet*

**PowerPak** An alternate keyboard having a flat but touch-sensitive surface. SEE: *membrane keyboard*

**Primitive** A simple command in the LOGO programming language that can serve as part of a more complex command. SEE: *LOGO*

**Problem-solving program** A type of software program that lets the user practice solving problems.

**Program** A set of instructions for performing a computer application. The instruction sequence carries out an algorithm. Programs need to be written in a programming language.

**Programming language** A set of coded rules used in the preparation of computer programs. Examples of programming languages include: *BASIC, C, COBOL, FORTRAN, and PASCAL*

**Protocol** A set of rules specifying how one's computer should be set up in order to establish a link, via modem, with another computer.

**Public domain program** Any software program that has not been copyrighted so that anyone may use it legally without having to pay a fee.

**Public switched telephone network** Another name for a commercial telephone company and its operating companies. SEE: *integrated services digital network*

**Public utility commission** Typically a state commission or other governing body that sets public utility rates (e.g., for telephone companies).

**Pull-down menu** A menu (a listing of choices) that is hidden offscreen from the computer user until the user "pulls" it "down" by giving a keyboard or mouse command.

**Quick time** A video-information compression device that is used to input graphic data into the memory of software programs running on a Macintosh computer.

**RAM** Random Access Memory. Computer memory that is available to carry out computer operations and for the storage of information. A RAM memory can be addressed at any desired location in the file, hence the name.

**Rapid captioning** The caption on a video monitor runs across the screen in the same time used for the audio information to be sent over the speaker (i.e., in real time).

**Receiver** The computer(s)/individual(s) on the receiving end of computer messages/services. SEE: *sender*

**Record** In database software programs, the set of fields pertaining to one item or individual.

**Refreshable braille** A braille display provided by having the pins rise and then fall back by electromechanical means. It is also called paperless braille.

**Regular scanning**   In the scanning of options on a monitor, the user is allowed to make a selection by pressing a switch. SEE: *aided scanning, inverse scanning, step scanning*

**Retrieval**   The reading of stored data for processing.

**RISC**   A type of memory chip.

**ROM**   Read Only Memory. This kind of memory is stored permanently in the computer's hardware. It controls the operations of the computer. ROM must always be retrieved from the very beginning so that it cannot be considered randomly accessible. ROM cannot be rewritten by the user.

**Rotary scanner**   An on-screen display of options in which the choices are presented in a circular array.

**Router**   A computer system used to direct computer traffic.

**Run**   To execute or carry out a program. SEE: *on line*

**Scanner**   A peripheral device that allows printed material (text and graphics) to be electronically entered into a computer. The computer's word processing and graphics software can later be used to edit the scanned materials.

**Scheduling program**   A software program that serves as the equivalent of an appointment book. SEE: *desktop accessories*

**Screen**   The CRT or computer monitor. SEE: *CRT*

**Screen dump**   A software program (usually provided in the ROM of a personal computer) causing the data shown on the monitor to be printed on paper.

**Screen magnification program**   A software program that causes the visual details (text and graphics) on the monitor to be increased in size.

**Screen reader software**   Software that sends the information on the monitor to a speech synthesizer to be read aloud.

**SCSI**   (pronounced "scuzzy") A type of interface between the CPU and the disk drives. SCSI can control hard drives, floppy drives, and CD-ROM drives.

**Search and replace**   A convenient feature of word processing software programs. A particular set of text symbols is searched for and replaced, whenever it is found in a file, by another specified set of symbols.

**Search engines**   Computer tools that allow Internet users to find information.

**Sender**   The source of a computer message/information. SEE: *receiver*

**Server**   Typically a larger computer in a client-server network that stores information/files/graphics and provides them upon request to "clients." SEE: *client, client-server network*

**Setup**   A set of programming commands used to arrange for the operation of an input device such as Ke:nx, an Adaptive Firmware Card, a Unicorn Expanded Keyboard, IntelliKeys, or Muppet Learning Keys.

**Shareware**   Any software program that is distributed for only the cost of a floppy disk but for which the user is asked to pay after using the program to the user's satisfaction. The user is also asked to register, thereby admitting an acknowledgement of and support for the program.

**Shell**   A type of software program that permits the user to change her/his work to a different program easily and quickly. Examples of shell programs include Microsoft Windows, DOSSHELL, and QuickMenu.

**Shockwave**   A type of computer application that allows World Wide Web users to transform Web pages into interactivemedia productions.

**Sign-off**   The orderly disconnecting of a computer by the user at the end of a work session.

**Sign-on**   The initiation of computer use by the operator.

**Signature**   Refers to the unique signature or message at the end of one's e-mail or correspondence that might contain your name, address, personal information, a favorite quote, etc.

**SIMM**  A type of memory chip.

**Single-density**  A kind of floppy disk, now obsolete, that provided only 180 kilobytes of memory storage.

**SLIP or PPP**  A type of dial-up connection to Internet Services. SEE: *Internet.*

**Smart drive**  A device driver, with the MS-DOS designation of SMARTDRV. SYS, that allows disk-caching, using extended or expanded memory. This drive is made part of CONFIG.SYS and is loaded from that file at the start of the computing session.

**Software**  Computer programs for running applications. These programs are written in program language and take up RAM. They are usually stored on a hard or floppy disk. Categories of software include word-processing programs, spreadsheets, databases, graphics programs, desktop publishing programs, desktop accessories, personal information managers, accounting software, statistics programs, instructional programs, and games. In contrast, computer hardware involves the actual physical equipment (e.g., the computer). SEE: *hardware*

**Sound card**  A peripheral that greatly enhances the quality and the volume of the sound provided with some software on floppy disks or CD-ROM disks.

**Source diskette**  When backing up data by copying from a diskette to a hard drive, another diskette, tape, or one of the other storage media, the diskette containing the data to be copied.

**Special education technology**  Any technology of assistance to students with disabilities. This includes assistive technology but can apply to any useful technical aids.

**SpecialNet**  An information system and computer network for persons involved in special education.

**Spreadsheet**  Software for a worksheet permitting planning and budgeting. "If-then" equations are tested by substituting different values for one variable in an equation. The spreadsheet then exhibits the consequences of each change of value. The first such program was named Visi-Calc and later spreadsheets were called "VisiClones."

**Stack**  1. A kind of program involved in HyperCard usage. Screen displays (individual "cards") are grouped into collections called "stacks." 2. When MS-DOS has had an interruption (resulting from a device completing an input/output task), DOS puts aside its own current task to deal with the device interrupt. In order for DOS to be able to resume the interrupted task later, this task is stored in a memory location. That location is called a stack.

**Step scanning**  A method of scanning options on a computer monitor. Pressing and releasing the switch moves a cursor from one option to the next. The user makes a selection by releasing the switch and pausing. SEE: *inverse scanning, regular scanning*

**Suite**  A set of protocols. SEE: *protocol*

**Surge suppressor**  A protective device consisting of a power strip provided with a circuit breaker. Current surges and sudden voltage increases ("spikes") trigger the circuit breaker, protecting all appliances plugged into the surge suppressor.

**Switched video**  A video service that allows businesses, schools, and private individuals to order video services on demand via the television, computers, and other telecommunications equipment (known as video dial tone).

**System**  Any integrated set of programs, set of computers, or combination of software and hardware dedicated to a specific project.

**System software**  Programs such as MS-DOS that are needed to operate the computer. This term is in contrast with applications software.

**T1**  An extremely fast and expensive way to transmit computer data at the rate of 1.544 megabits or million bits per second.

**Talking programs**  Programs using digitized speech information stored on disk to enable a speech synthesizer to deliver spoken output.

**Target diskette**   When data are to be backed up (from a source diskette or from the hard drive, for example) the target diskette is the diskette onto which the data are copied.

**Tariff**   The established charge for computer/telecommunications services, equipment, or facilities that is established by a communications common carrier.

**TCP**   Transmission Control Protocol, a part of the Internet transport layer. TCP controls data/information transport so that it arrives in its original form.

**TCP/IP**   Transmission Control Protocol/Internet Protocol. Refers to a set of protocols that define how computers on the Internet transport/exchange information/data/graphics. SEE: *Internet, IP, protocol, TCP*

**Teacher utilities**   Software designed to be used by teachers. SEE: *gradebook*

**Technology goals**   President Clinton signed the Telecommunications Act of 1996 so as to ensure that U.S. students will be technology literate as they enter the twenty-first century. Four major goals call for community-school-parent partnerships to ensure that: 1. all teachers will have the training and support they need to help students become computer literate and access the information superhighway (Internet); 2. all teachers and students will have access to multimedia centers/computers in their classrooms; 3. all classrooms will be connected to the information superhighway (Internet); and 4. effective computer software and on-line learning resources will be an integral part of every school's curriculum.

**Technology literacy**   Basic knowledge and understanding of how to use computers and other technology to effectively learn and apply knowledge in school and the workplace. Fundamentals include being able to use the Information Superhighway or Internet, integrating technology throughout all school disciplines or areas of work, using mul-timedia computer systems, being able to access resources on-line, critically examining software benefits/problems, and using technological advances to improve the quality of life/learning.

**Telecommunication phone networks**   Computer communications networks for which memberships are sold by private sector vendors. Information can be sent via modem to computers or even to television monitors. For example, writing programs are sold that allow writers to carry on interactive conferences and exchange materials at their computer terminals.

**Telecommuting**   1. Refers to computer/telecommunications initiatives via private homes. 2. The use of telecommunications to replace transportation.

**Teleconference**   Long-distance conferencing whereby the individuals who are participating in the communications can see and talk to each other.

**Telnet**   An Internet tool that allows users to manipulate and retrieve data from remote or distant computers. This service allows college students, for example, to search various college libraries by entering the word "telnet" on the keyboard followed by the address of the site.

**Terminal**   A cut-down version of a microcomputer that is connected to, but isolated from, a larger central computer.

**Test scoring program**   A software program that can calculate scores on objective tests.

**Tool**   A computer program that can create, modify, or analyze other computer programs (e.g., an editor). In graphic programs, tools can provide such dimensions as color, shape, and depth.

**Touchscreen**   An input device fitted over a computer monitor and activated by touching the device according to guidance from the data on the monitor.

**TouchWindow**   A kind of touchscreen. When removed from the monitor, it can act as a keyboard.

**Trackball**   A computer input device that has replaced the mouse, especially on notebook-sized computers. A ball (attached to the computer, usually on the keyboard) is rotated to simulate movements of the mouse.

**Turnkey system**   A complete ready-to-function minicomputer. The term refers to the idea that all the user needs to do is to "turn the key" to start the machine.

**Twisted pair**   Refers to the wires that connect local telephone circuitry to a centrally located facility.

**Two-way cable**   A type of telecommunications system that provides both "downstream" transmissions (from cable "headend" to private customer) and "upstream" transmissions (from the private customer to the cable "headend").

**Unicorn keyboard**   A programmable type of alternate keyboard. There is a larger model, the Expanded Unicorn Keyboard, as well as a smaller one, Unicorn Keyboard Model 510.

**Uniform Resource Locator (URL)**   An address for accessing a site on the World Wide Web (www).

**UNIX**   A higher-level operating system that is considered ideal for networks.

**Universal service**   Telecommunication services such as "voice mail" that are generally available to the public (in an affordable manner).

**Upload**   To send data from a personal computer by modem to a larger central computer. This can be done on a BBS or a LAN. Transmitted information from a personal/individual computer to a computer network (i.e., Internet) is made available for others to use.

**URL**   Universal Resource Locator or the address for a World Wide Web site. For example, students can visit the White House in the World Wide Web document "White House" via http://www.whitehouse.gov. The http represents "hypertext transfer protocol" and www. signifies "World Wide Web," with the remaining code specifying the location of the document and whether or not the sponsor is in the .gov (government), .edu (education), .com (commercial field), .org (nonprofit organization), etc.

**Usenet (or user network)**   A user's network created in 1979 by Ellis and Truscott from Duke University. Usenet is a public network available on the Internet and other networks that is accessible with special computer software. This world-wide service provides an enormous database of newsgroups by topic. One can read or access several items on a topic as well as respond to messages through newsgroups or one-on-one via e-mail. SEE: *e-mail, Internet*

**User-friendly**   Either hardware or software that is reasonably easy for an unsophisticated human operator to use, or learn to use. User-friendly software gives the user ample chance to avoid errors or to correct errors.

**Utility**   A software program that somehow enhances the usefulness of the computer and/or makes it easier for the user to operate the system. A screen saver and a menuing program would be two examples of utilities.

**Veronica**   Stands for Very Easy Rodent-Oriented Netwide Index to Computerized Archives. This is a computer utility that allows the user to type in keywords in order to search for gopher file names. VERONICA offers a service similar to Archie but regarding Gopher items. SEE: *gopher, Internet*

**Very Small Aperture Terminal (VSAT)**   A type of satellite dish used by individuals/schools/businesses that interact with various networks.

**Vibro-tactile aid**   A device that converts audio input into vibrations that are presented to the user's tactile sense.

**Video dial tone**   SEE: *switched video*

**Video digitizer**   A device that scans pictorial material and converts it into digital form to be inputted as data for a computer. SEE: *audio digitizer*

**Virtual classroom**   Refers to computerized long-distance classes that can be accessed via the Internet and www (World Wide Web). This distance learning allows classes to be taken at universities or colleges via the Internet and www. Students participate in these computerized classrooms using the interactive technology available on www. College lectures can be video-recorded and played live or in a delayed manner. The Open University (http://www.open.ac. uk/), for example, converts lectures to a virtual classroom format that can be used on the Internet via www. SEE: *Internet, World Wide Web*

**Virtual reality**   An advanced type of simulation. The user is enabled to experience, through a number of senses, the "presence" of a computer-generated "world."

**Virus**   A self-replicating program that interferes with computer operations. Some viruses attack the file allocation table; some attack the booting system commands; some contaminate data. Some viruses are timed to attack at some future date. For example, the "Michelangelo Virus" is arranged to take effect on Michelangelo's birthday, March 9th.

**VOCA**   SEE: *Voice Output Communication Aid*

**Voice Output Communication Aid (VOCA)**   A type of speech synthesizer.

**VRML** or **Virtual Reality Modeling Language**   Computer language simulations that create a 3D effect.

**VSAT**   SEE: *Very Small Aperture Terminal*

**WAIS**   Acronymn for Wide Area Information Servers. This program allows one to use keywords to search various databases.

**Web**   SEE: *World Wide Web*

**Web browser**   A type of computer software that allows users to "browse" through the World Wide Web (a multimedia hyperlinked system for organizing information on the Internet). SEE: *hyperlink, Internet, multimedia, World Wide Web*

**Web crawler**   A World Wide Web (www) site at the University of Washington that continually updates/adds to a database information on www. You merely enter a keyword you need searched and then query Web crawler. Access: http://webcrawler.cs.washington.edu/-WebCrawler/WebQuery.html

**Web page**   One of many pages that constitute a World Wide Web site that are connected by hyperlinks or links. Just about anyone can place a web page on the Internet, from schools to nonprofit organizations to businesses and so on.

**Web site**   Refers to a place on the World Wide Web, a part of the Internet, that allows individuals to travel for information, converse, interact, etc.

**WebTV**   Access to the Internet via a special terminal which plugs into one's television set through video and audio cable inputs or an RF adapter that is able to convert units' output to broadcast frequencies. A telephone cord is connected from the back of the WebTV terminal to a telephone jack. WebTV is available through WebTV Networks Inc., which was founded in 1994. WebTV subscribers are able to dial up access to the World Wide Web and can use optional infrared wireless keyboards.

**Wide-area network**   State-wide or regional computer network areas which are banded by a common use.

**Wide-band**   SEE: *broadband*

**Widow**   A term used in word processing that refers to the last line in a paragraph if it appears as the first line of a page. SEE: *orphan, word processing*

**Word prediction programs**   A type of software program that accelerates the inputting of text by "predicting" an entire word from just one or two keystrokes.

**Word processing**   Computer programs that allow one to create and edit text as well as to print and store information. Text can easily be "cut and pasted" or moved, modified, or deleted. Most programs have editing commands that allow one to modify or word process in seconds. Retyping text is no longer necessary. Additional features include but are not limited to finding synonyms, antonyms, dictionary definitions, and correct spellings for word entries; search and replace commands; copying portions or complete text/folder units; and word wrapping.

**Word processor** Either 1. a type of software, a word-processing program, or 2. a machine dedicated to word processing only and that is unable to perform other computer functions.

**Word wrap** The ability of a word processor to move an entire word to the following line. With word wrap available, it is not necessary to break up words at the ends of lines and hyphenate them.

**Workstation** A type of computer that is usually more powerful than a personal computer because of its ability to use graphics and complete several tasks at one time. Workstations are many times used in science-related environments and math fields and can be linked in a Local Area Network (LAN).

**World Wide Web** This widely used multimedia, hyperlinked Internet service allows users to secure hypertext and visual graphics from different sites. The World Wide Web was developed in Geneva, Switzerland, at the CERN or the European Laboratory for Particle Physics. Described by Barrie and Presti (October, 1996, *Science Magazine*, p. 371) as a "graphically attractive, user-friendly modality" that is composed of multiple servers allowing documents or pages to be sent to Internet users who are able to navigate from server to server via Web-browser software. Barrie and Presti list three educational uses in which www can be used: 1. to access information that is organized at various indexing sites (e.g., Vista and Yahoo); 2. as an integrative interface for distance learning also known as the "virtual classroom" (e.g., University On-Line found at http://www.online); 3. as a classroom supplement rather than a replacement. Multimodal capabilities include interactive text, pictures, sound, sound and pictures, movies, etc. Such browsers as Cello and Mosaic can access the World Wide Web (www). There are many "child friendly" www sites. As examples, "The Family Surfboard" (Access: http:// www.sjbennet.com/users/sjb/ surf.html) and KidNews (Access: http:// www. umassd.edu/specialprograms/ isn/kidnews3.html) are easily accessed by even young children. SEE: *browsers, hyperlinking, Internet, Yahoo, homepage, HTML, HTTP, hypertext links, URL*

**Worm** SEE: *worm disk*

**Worm disk** A kind of CD-ROM disk that allows the user one chance to enter information onto it. The acronym WORM stands for "write once, read many." This optical disk has an enormous storage capacity and is used to store data archives.

**WP** SEE: *word processing*

**Write-protect** A method of making it impossible to add to, or to modify, the data on a disk. A floppy disk can be write-protected by blocking an opening or a notch.

**Writing aids** Such software programs (or features of word-processing or desktop publishing programs) as spelling and grammar checkers and outlining programs.

**www** SEE: *World Wide Web*

**WYSIWYG (pronounced "wizzeewig")** "What you see is what you get." The ability of a desktop publishing program to show, on the monitor screen, the exact appearance of the document being processed. Ordinary word-processing software programs are unable to deliver WYSIWYG because they require too many coding symbols for punctuation, font changes, space changes, etc.

**Yahoo** A World Wide Web (www) site developed by Yang and Filo from Stanford University that is actually a collection/catalog of resources/information available in www. Access: http://www. yahoo.com/

# Appendix 5
# Important Federal Legislation, Milestones, and Reports which Relate to Education Affairs in the United States: Past and Present

1635 **First school** Boston Latin Grammar School.

1636 **First College** Harvard College.

1647 **Mandatory Schools Act in Massachusetts**

1687 **First primer was published** *New England Primer.*

1705 **Reverend Samuel Thomas** Goose Greek, South Carolina; enrolls 60 African Americans in school.

1740 **Education to African Americans was denied** South Carolina.

1751 **Philadelphia Academy was formed** Ben Franklin, founder.

1783 **American Speller published** Noah Webster's *American Spelling Book.*

1787 **Northwest Ordinance** Provided land grants for educational institutions.

1798 **Boston, Massachusetts** A separate home school for African Americans was established, Elisha Sylvester, headmaster.

1820 **First primary school for African-American children** Boston, Massachusetts.

1821 **First endowed secondary school for women** Troy, New York; Emma Willard, founder.

1821 **Establishment of first high school in the United States** English Classical High School, Boston, Massachusetts; George B. Emerson, headmaster.

1823 **First private normal school** Vermont.

1827 **First Legislation Mandating High Schools** In Massachusetts.

1837 **Massachusetts establishes a board of education** Horace Mann, secretary.

1839 **First public normal school** Lexington, Massachusetts.

1855 **First Kindergarten**

1862 **First Morrill Land Grant Act** Established agricultural and mechanical colleges.

1865 **Abolition of slavery signals new efforts to educate african americans**

1867 **Department of Education Act**

1872 **Legalization of tax collection for high schools** Kalamazoo Case.

1887 **Hatch Act**

1890 **Second Morrill Land Grant Act**

1892 **"Committee of Ten"** The National Education Association sets purposes for high school education.

1896 **Plessy vs. Ferguson Supreme Court decision** Support for racially separate-but-equal facilities.

1911 **The State Marine School Act**

1909 **First junior high school** Berkeley, California.

1914 **Smith-Lever Agriculture Extension Act**

1917 **Smith-Hughes Vocational Act**

| 1918 | Cardinal Principles of Secondary Education Report |
| 1918 | Vocational Rehabilitation Act   Provided grants for WWI veterans. |
| 1919 | Education Facilities Act |
| 1920 | Smith-Bankhead Act |
| 1932 | New Deal education programs |
| 1935 | Bankhead-Jones Act |
| 1935 | Agricultural Adjustment Act |
| 1936 | The Act to Further the Development and Maintenance of an Adequate and Well-Balanced American Merchant Marine Academy |
| 1937 | Public Health Fellowship Program   Established by the National Cancer Institute Act. |
| 1938 | Purposes of Education in American Democracy Report   By the Education Policies Commission of the National Education Association (NEA). |
| 1940 | Vocational Education for National Defense Act |
| 1941 | Amendment to the Lanham Act of 1940   Authorized aid for schools in federally impacted areas. |
| 1943 | Vocational Rehabilitation Act |
| 1944 | GI Bill of Rights |
| 1944 | Surplus Property Act   Allowed transfer to educational concerns. |
| 1944 | Education for All American Youth Report   By the National Education Association (NEA). |
| 1946 | National School Lunch Act |
| 1946 | George-Barden Act   Provided additional support for vocational education efforts. |
| 1948 | U.S. Information and Educational Exchange Act |
| 1949 | Federal Property and Administrative Services Act |
| 1950 | National Science Foundation established |
| 1950 | Housing Act   For college facilities. |
| 1952 | Imperative Needs of Youth Report   By the Educational Policies Commission. |
| 1954 | Brown vs. Board of Education of Topeka Supreme Court decision   Support for eliminating racial segregation in schools; overturned Plessy vs. Ferguson of 1896. |
| 1954 | Cooperative Research Act |
| 1954 | National Advisory Committee on Education Act |
| 1954 | School Milk Program Act |
| 1956 | Library Services Act |
| 1957 | Launching of Russian Sputnik (first space launch)   Leads to increased federation education funds |
| 1957 | Practical Nurse Training Act |
| 1958 | National Defense Education Act   Leads to funds for math, science, and foreign language programs. |
| 1958 | Education of Mentally Retarded Children Act |
| 1958 | Captioned Films for the Deaf Act |
| 1961 | Area Redevelopment Act   Retraining individuals in redevelopment areas. |
| 1961 | Peace Corps Establishment Act |
| 1962 | Communications Act of 1934 Amendment   Provided monies for education concerns. |
| 1962 | Manpower Development and Training Act |
| 1962 | Migration and Refugee Assistance Act |
| 1963 | Vocational Education Act |
| 1963 | Health Professions Educational Assistance Act |
| 1963 | Manpower Development and Training Act |
| 1963 | Higher Education Facilities Act |
| 1964 | Civil Rights Act   Protections against race discrimination. |
| 1964 | Economic Opportunity Act |
| 1964 | Head Start Program |
| 1964 | Job Corps Program |
| 1965 | Elementary and Secondary Education Act |
| 1965 | Higher Education Act |
| 1965 | Health Professions Educational Assistance Amendments |
| 1965 | National Foundation on the Arts and Humanities Act |
| 1965 | National Technical Institute for the Deaf Act |
| 1965 | National Vocational Student Loan Insurance Act |
| 1965 | Medical Library Assistance Act |

| 1965 | School Assistance in Disaster Areas Act |
|---|---|
| 1966 | National Sea Grant College and Program Act |
| 1966 | International Education Act |
| 1966 | Adult Education Act |
| 1966 | Model Secondary School for the Deaf Act |
| 1966 | Elementary and Secondary Education Amendments |
| 1966 | Coleman Report |
| 1967 | Public Broadcasting Act |
| 1967 | Education Professions Development Act |
| 1968 | Elementary and Secondary Education Amendments |
| 1968 | Handicapped Childrens' Early Education Assistance Act |
| 1968 | Vocational Education Amendments |
| 1968 | Higher Education Amendments |
| 1970 | Elementary and Secondary Assistance Programs |
| 1970 | National Commission on Libraries and Information Science Act |
| 1970 | Office of Education Appropriation Act |
| 1970 | Environmental Education Act |
| 1970 | Drug Abuse Education Act |
| 1971 | Comprehensive Health Manpower Training Act |
| 1972 | Title IX Education Amendment   Prohibits sex discrimination in the schools. |
| 1972 | Drug Abuse Office and Treatment Act |
| 1972 | Education Amendments |
| 1972 | Indian Education Act |
| 1973 | Rehabilitation Act   Provided vocational rehabilitation services for students with disabilities. |
| 1973 | Older Americans Comprehensive Services Amendment |
| 1973 | Comprehensive Employment and Training Act |
| 1974 | Women's Educational Equity Act   Expands opportunities for females in science, math, technology, and athletics. |
| 1974 | Educational Amendments |
| 1974 | White House Conference on Library and Information Services Act |

| 1974 | Juvenile Justice and Delinquency Prevention Act |
|---|---|
| 1974 | Women's Educational Equity Act   Expands opportunities for females in science, math, technology, and athletics. |
| 1975 | Education for All Children Handicapped Act (P.L. 94-142) |
| 1975 | Indian Self-Determination and Education Assistance Act |
| 1975 | Indochina Migration and Refugee Assistance Act |
| 1976 | Magnet schools begin to become popular. |
| 1976 | Education Amendments |
| 1977 | Voucher Schools become popular in some states. |
| 1977 | Youth Employment and Demonstration Projects Act |
| 1978 | Career Education Incentive Act |
| 1978 | Tribally Controlled Community College Assistance Act |
| 1978 | Education Amendments |
| 1978 | Middle Income Student Assistance Act |
| 1979 | Department of Education Organization Act   Federal department of education is now a reality. |
| 1979 | Cabinet-level Department of Education is established |
| 1980 | Asbestos School Hazard Protection and Control Act |
| 1980 | Amendments to the Higher Education Act of 1965 |
| 1981 | Education Consolidation and Improvement Act |
| 1983 | *A Nation at Risk: The Imperative for Educational Reform*   A book and report issued by the National Commission on Excellence in Education. |
| 1983 | High School: A Report on Secondary Education in America   Issued by the Carnegie Foundation. |
| 1984 | P.L. 98-377   Science and math programs added. |
| 1984 | Education for Economic Security Act |
| 1984 | Equal Access Act   Allows religion clubs to hold meetings on school properties. |
| 1984 | Perkins Vocational Education Act |
| 1984 | Talented Teachers Fellowship Act |

1984 **Equal Access Act** Allows religion clubs to hold meetings on school properties.

1985 **NCATE standards updated**

1986 **Holmes Report**

1986 **Carnegie report** Entitled *A Nation Prepared: Teachers for the 21st Century,* a report on teaching as a profession.

1986 *First Lessons: A Report on Elementary Education in America,* U.S. Secretary of Education Report.

1989 **Renaissance Group Report** Entitled *Teachers for a New World,* specified goals for teacher-trainees.

1989 **Presidential Education Summit** with state governors.

1989 **Carnegie Foundation Report,** *Turning Points: Preparing American Youth for the Twenty-First Century* Recommended the elimination of tracking and the creation of learning communities.

1989 **Children with Disabilities Temporary Care Reauthorization Act**

1989 **Drug-Free Schools and Communities Act**

1989 **Childhood Education and Development Act**

1990 **Excellence in Mathematics, Science and Engineering Act**

1990 **Children's Television Act**

1990 **Student Right-to-Know and Campus Security Act**

1990 **Americans with Disabilities Act**

1990 **National Assessment of Chapter I Act**

1990 **National and Community Service Act**

1990 **School Dropout Prevention and Basic Skills Improvement Act**

1990 **Tribally Controlled Community College Reauthorization Act**

1990 **National Environmental Education Act**

1990 **Public Service Assistance Education Act**

1990 **U.S. Supreme Court ruled that schools could have Bible clubs**

1991 *America 2000* An education strategy report.

1991 **Civil Rights Act** Expands protections to disability, sex, religion, and national origin.

1992 **Higher Education Amendments**

1992 **National Commission on Time and Learning** Reauthorized civic education programs.

1992 *Winners All* A document on inclusion produced by the National Association of State Boards of Education (NASBE).

1992 **Ready-to-Learn Act** Provided TV educational support programs/materials.

1992/ **Amendments to the Rehabilitation**
1993 **Act of 1973**

1993 **Higher Education Technical Amendments Act**

1993 **NAEP Assessment Authorization**

1993 *Leading and Managing for Performance* A document on inclusion produced by the National Association of State Directors of Special Education.

1993 **Student Loan Reform Act**

1993 **National Services Trust Act** Provided opportunities for national service for those in postsecondary programs over 17 years.

1994 **Federal government adopts National Education Goals 2000**

1994 **"School to Work"** Where children learn "on the job" becomes implemented in 50 states.

1994 **Safe Schools Act**

1994 **Educational Research, Development, Dissemination, and Improvement Act**

1994 **Technology-Related Assistance for Individuals with Disabilities Amendments of 1993**

1994 **Improving America's Schools Act**

1996 *Third International Mathematics and Science Study* Assessed mathematics and science education in several countries from 1991–1995; 1996, 1997, 1998 addendums.

1996 **Getting America's Students Ready for the 21st Century** Report on meeting the technology literacy challenge.

# Appendix 6
# Supreme Court Decisions
# Related to Education

| Case | Decision |
|------|----------|
| Pierce vs. Society of Sisters (1925) | The Court ruled that the law requiring public school attendence by all children was unconstitutional and infringed on the rights of parents to control their children. |
| Cochran vs. Louisiana Board of Education (1930) | The Court ruled that state monies for secular textbooks to nonpublic school children was acceptable. |
| Everson vs. Board of Education (1947) | The Court ruled that reimbursement funds for schools do not violate the first amendment. |
| People of the State of Illinois ex rel. McCollum vs. Board of Education of School District No. 71, Champaign, Illinois (1948) | The Court held that religious programs violated the principle of separation of church and state when held in public schools. |
| Zorach vs. Clauson (1952) | The Court upheld a New York law that allowed release time for children in religious centers for religious instruction. |
| Brown vs. Board of Education of Topeka (1954) | The Court ruled that separate but equal education opportunities violated the fourteenth amendment. |
| Engle vs. Vitale (1962) | The Court held that religious prayer violated the first amendment. |
| Schempp vs. School District of Abington Township (1963) and Murray vs. Curlett (1963) | The Court held that reading the Bible and reciting the Lord's Prayer in public schools violated the first and fourteenth amendments. |
| Green vs. County School Board (1964) | The Court ruled that freedom-of-choice school plans are acceptable only if they lead to desegragation of schools. |
| Board of Education of Central School District No. 1, Town of Greenbush vs. Allen (1968) | The Court ruled that the loaning of books to nonpublic schools alone did not show an unconstitutional degree of support for a religious institution. |
| Epperson vs. State of Arkansas (1968) | The Court held that teaching of evolution as a theory was allowed by the first amendment. |
| Swann vs. Charlotte-Mecklenburg Board of Education (1971) | The Court ruled that desegregation of schools does not mean that all schools |

Lemon vs. Kurtzman (1971)

Wisconsin vs. Yoder (1972)

Milliken vs. Bradley (1974)

Milliken vs. Bradley II (1977)

Wolman vs. Walter (1977)

Crawford vs. Board of Education City of Los Angeles (1982)

Grand Rapids School District vs. Ball (1985)

Wallace vs. Jaffree (1985)

Bethel School District vs. Fraser (1986)

Edwards vs. Aguilard (1987)

Hazelwood School District vs. Kuhlmeier (1988)

Franklin vs. Guinneth County Schools (1992)

must always reflect the racial composition of the school system as a whole.
The Court ruled that the legislation providing salaries and texts for nonpublic schools was unconstitutional.
The Court held that state laws requiring children to attend school until sixteen years of age violated the free exercise of religion (Case in point: Amish).
The Court overturned the lower-court rulings requiring cross-district busing unless "it is shown that there has been a constitutional violation within one school district that impacts significantly another school district resulting in segregation".
The Court ruled that a district court can order compensatory or remedial programs for school children who have been subjected to past acts of de jure segregation.
The Court ruled that providing remedial services to nonpublic school pupils was unconstitutional.
The Court upheld a ruling prohibiting state courts from ordering mandatory busing unless a federal court does so to remedy a federal constitutional violation.
The Court ruled that having public school teachers instruct nonpublic school students in supplemental subjects violated the establishment clause in that it promoted religion.
The Court held that one minute of silence for meditation or prayer led by teachers was unconstitutional.
The Court ruled that the determination of whether or not the manner (type) of speech in a school by students is appropriate or inappropriate rests with school boards.
The Court held that a state cannot require schools to teach the Biblical version of creation.
The Court ruled that school administrators may control student expression in official school publications, theater productions, etc. The Court stated that such publications were not public forums but rather supervised learning experiences.
The Court reaffirmed Title IX provisions regarding sexual discrimination against students by allowing money damages to be awarded when discrimination occurs.

# Appendix 7
# Sample Individualized Education Plan (IEP)

Individualized Education Plans (IEPs) are required under the IDEA or Individuals with Disabilities Education Act (20 U.S.C. 1400et seq.) of 1990. Specifically, under 1401 (a)(2) and 34CFR Parts 300.340-350, IEPs are designated as written statements of program planning efforts designed for children with disabilities. IEPs are developed in a meeting by a representative of the local education association or a qualified intermediate educational unit. The IEP is supposed to describe a specially designed individual program of instruction/remediation to meet the unique learning styles and challenges of the child with disabilities. The components of an IEP are listed in the model presented below by the State Department of Education for the State of Massachusetts. The format may differ from state to state, but the basic components are present in the various state forms. IEPs must contain statements of present levels of academic performance, annual goals, short-term instructional objectives, the specific educational services to be provided, the child's participation in regular program efforts, transition services if needed, projected date(s) of program commencement, duration of program services, and program evaluation criteria and schedules.

PPS-8

## COMMONWEALTH OF MASSACHUSETTS
## DEPARTMENT OF EDUCATION
INDIVIDUALIZED EDUCATIONAL PLAN (IEP)

School District: _____

**MEETING**
Date:
Type:
❑ Initial Evaluation
❑ Review # _____
❑ Reevaluation

### PART A: INFORMATION SECTION

**1. STUDENT INFORMATION**

Student name: _____ Identification number: _____
      last         first        middle

Birth date: ____/____/____ Age: _____ Grade: _____ Primary language: _____

Address: _____ Home telephone: ( ) _____

School name/address: _____

School telephone: ( ) _____

**2. PARENT INFORMATION**

Information below pertains to: ❑ Parent ❑ Foster parent ❑ Guardian ❑ Educational advocate ❑ Student
Name: _____ Name: _____

Address: _____ Address: _____

Home telephone: ( ) _____ Home telephone: ( ) _____

Other telephone: ( ) _____ Other telephone: ( ) _____

Primary language of the home: _____ Primary language of the home: _____

**3. INITIAL EVALUATION AND REEVALUATION INFORMATION**

Prereferral activities (for initial evaluation only)

Prereferral activities were implemented: ❑ Yes, documented in student record ❑ No

If no, explain: _____

**Eligibility Determination**

Existence of disability: ❑ Yes ❑ No

Student is making effective progress in regular education: ❑ Yes ❑ No

Eligible for special education services: ❑ Yes ❑ No

**If student is not eligible for special education, complete Parts C & D on last page of IEP form. If student is eligible for special education, complete the IEP form.**

**4. IEP INFORMATION**

Liaison name: _____ Position: _____ Telephone: ( ) _____

IEP period: _____ to _____ Next scheduled annual review date: _____

Scheduled three year evaluation date: _____

Cost share placement: ❑ Yes, cost share participants: _____ ❑ No _____
                                                              Page 1 of ____

Student Name: _____ Date of Birth: _____ IEP Period: _____

**PART B: STUDENT SECTION**

1. **STUDENT PERFORMANCE PROFILE**

    Describe: (a) student's areas of strength; (b) student's area(s) of need; and (c) the current level(s) of performance for each area of need that corresponds to attached goal(s) and objectives.

2. **STUDENT INSTRUCTIONAL PROFILE**

    Describe: (a) student's approach to learning; and (b) instructional approaches and/or modifications in the classroom and other settings that will facilitate successful accommodation and education for the student, including teaching approach, curriculum methods, equipment, assistive technology, staff, facilities, grading, testing, etc.

❑ Check box if information is continued on another page

Page _____ of _____

Student Name: _____ Date of Birth: _____ IEP Period: _____

### 3. GOALS AND OBJECTIVES

Annual Goal # _____:

| Objectives and Evaluation Procedure and Schedule |
|---|

1 Objective:

   Evaluation Procedure:

   Evaluation schedule:

2 Objective:

   Evaluation procedure:

   Evaluation schedule:

3 Objective:

   Evaluation procedure:

   Evaluation schedule:

4 Objective:

   Evaluation procedure:

   Evaluation schedule:

| Progress Report Information |
|---|

Progress reports shall be at least semi-annual. For students in collaborative and private school placements, progress reports shall be quarterly. The annual a review meets the requirement for the annual progress report.

Page _____of _____

Student Name: _____ Date of Birth: _____ IEP Period: _____

4. **SPECIAL EDUCATION SERVICE DELIVERY**

**School District Cycle:** ❑ 5 day cycle  ❑ 6 day cycle  ❑ 10 day cycle  ❑ Other _____

A. Consultation (Indirect Services to School Personnel and Parents)

| Type of Service | Focus on Goal # | Person(s) Responsible | Start Date | Freq/Duration per Day/Cycle | Total Time/ Cycle | Comments (if applicable) |
|---|---|---|---|---|---|---|
| | | | | | | |
| | | | | | | |
| | | | | | | |
| | | | | | | |

B. Special Education and Related Services in Regular Education Classroom (Direct Services)

| Type of Service | Focus on Goal # | Person(s) Responsible | Start Date | Freq/Duration per Day/cycle | Total Time/ Cycle | Nature of Service (if Applicable) |
|---|---|---|---|---|---|---|
| | | | | | | |
| | | | | | | |
| | | | | | | |
| | | | | | | |
| | | | | | | |
| | | | | | | |

C. Special Education and Related Services in Other Setting (Direct Services)

| Type of Service | focus on Goal # | Person(s) Responsible | Start Date | Freq/Duration per Day/Cycle | Total Time/ Cycle | Location |
|---|---|---|---|---|---|---|
| | | | | | | |
| | | | | | | |
| | | | | | | |
| | | | | | | |
| | | | | | | |
| | | | | | | |

**Service Delivery totals Per Cycle**

Total consultation time (A)    _____

Total service delivery time in regular education classroom (B)    _____

Total service delivery time in other setting (C)    _____

**Time and Prototype Determinations**

Total time in student's school cycle

Total time of special education/related services in regular education and other settings (B + C)    _____

Total time in regular education without special education/related services (school cycle – (B + C))    _____

Prototype: Total time outside regular education with special education/related services (C + school cycle)    _____

Page _____ of _____

Student Name: _____ Date of Birth: _____ IEP Period: _____

5. **SCHOOL DAY/SCHOOL YEAR**

The length of student's school day and/or school year is modified:

❑ Yes _____ Days per year _____ Hours per day ❑ No

If yes, basis for modified duration: _____

6. **TRANSPORTATION PLAN**

A special transportation plan is needed: ❑ Yes ❑ No

If yes, check one of the following and describe:

❑ Regular transportation with modifications

❑ Special transportation

❑ Parent-provided transportation with reimbursement at state rate

Describe: _____

7. **DISCIPLINE CODE**

The student's disability interferes with his/her capacity to meet the regular discipline code: ❑ Yes ❑ No

If yes, describe modifications: _____

_____

8. **PARTICIPATION IN REGULAR EDUCATION**

State the student's participation in regular education for the duration of this IEP (including academic; non-academic; physical education, adapted as necessary; and extracurricular activities): _____

_____

For students receiving special education and/or related services outside of the regular education classroom, provide a justification: _____

_____

For students who are not in a regular education classroom 100% of the time, identify steps to increase the student's participation in regular education: _____

_____

9. **GRADUATION/DIPLOMA**

For students 14 years or older, the TEAM has determined that the student is expected to graduate from high school: ❑ Yes ❑ No If yes, anticipated date of graduation: _____

Criteria for graduation includes modifications: ❑ Yes ❑ No If yes, describe: _____

_____

10. **ATTACHED INFORMATION**

| | |
|---|---|
| Statement of Needed Transition Services | ❑ Yes ❑ No |
| State Mandated Testing Attachment: | ❑ Yes ❑ No |
| Other: _____ | ❑ Yes ❑ No |

Page ____ of ____

# Appendix 8
# Sample Literacy Activities

Literacy activities need to occur at all levels. Emergent and proficient readers and writers acquire implicit and explicit knowledge of language systems and conventions by reading and writing endeavors that occur throughout the day from home and the community, to the school, and back to home and the community again. The use of technology at all levels provides motivation, background building, resources, and critical applications. Literacy activities naturally take into consideration cultural contexts and the backgrounds students bring to the learning situation. The following samples are meant to provide ideas for teachers and parents with concrete ways to engage learners into the reading-writing process.

## Early Childhood Samples (Nursery School through Grade 3)

Parents/teachers reading words, pages, and short stories and environmental terms (e.g., cereal box) to children and modeling good reading behaviors
Pointing to pictures
Matching pictures and words
Showing understanding of the parts of a book
Reciting the title, author, and illustrator of a book
Reading wordless books
Listening to language and language patterns
Listening to nursery rhymes and rhyming words
Listening to stories being read
Listening to tapes of stories
Reading or reciting stories for memorization
Reading signs and materials in the environment or classroom
Writing one's name
Spelling/vocabulary word banks
Creating semantic webs
Writing one's address and phone number
Writing simple questions
Pretending to read
Pretending to read to another

Reading alphabet letters and the entire alphabet
Writing letters of the alphabet
Writing the entire alphabet
Identifying beginning letters and sounds of words
Sounding out or decoding words
Copying letters and words
Inventive spelling
Reading and writing sight words
Reading and writing important environmental terminology (e.g., entrance, poison, flammable)
Copying letters
Copying words
Copying sentences
Reading simple books
Making predictions
Confirming/disconfirming predictions
Dictating stories
Reading dictated stories
Creating stories and storybooks
Writing a simple autobiography
Reading or repeating predictable stories and words
Journal and diary writing
Spelling accurately
Using literature books
Buddy reading
Using basals

Skills work
Writing drafts of work
Writing and sharing stories
Writing telegrams
Using resources such as the library
Beginning use of the Internet and computers
Beginning use of computer browsers
Reading and writing second/foreign language words and sentences
Identifying words and pictures from the newspaper
Writing poems
Writing simple math problems
Labeling words and pictures
Writing to prompts
Creating art activities to accompany print (e.g., mobiles, collages, story boxes, posters)
Creating word puzzles
Using music with print
Writing thank-you notes
Writing simple letters
Keeping simple portfolios
Parent-child trips to the library
Cooperative reading/writing activities (e.g., brainstorming a topic)

**Elementary Samples (Grades 1–6 or 1–8) (when appropriate, the same activities listed under early childhood)**

Peer coaching activities (e.g., how to help improve another's writing)
Parents/teachers reading to students
Teachers reading a chapter a day from a book
Maintaining portfolios in an organized manner with reflective
Writing pieces
Writing interrogative pieces
Writing about one's strengths and weaknesses in a particular area
Using stories/activites to create/write dialogue
Creating graphic outlines/complex webs
Writing responses to literature
Confirming/disconfirming predictions and providing details for either
Reading and writing different kinds of text
Response journals
Double-entry journals
Learning logs
Creating story maps

Content-area journals such as math and science
Spelling journals
Reading and writing second/foreign language stories and books
Reciting the publisher of a book and how to obtain a book
Reading and using various library systems
Browsing and reading information on the Internet/World Wide Web
Publishing books using word processors and computer technology
Reading original source documents
Reading the newspaper for enjoyment and information
Writing personal assessments of progress in an area of study
Writing essays and biographies
Writing a thumbnail sketch of a person, place, thing, or event
Maintaining written assignment records
Writing notes for test taking
Outlining text material
Keeping notes, observation logs, lab reports
Taking a position on an issue
Writing about a current event
Writing requests
Writing business letters
Writing persuasive letters
Writing story recollections
Writing about fantasy, adventure stories
Writing about fiction, nonfiction, and science fiction
Writing historical pieces
Writing dialogue
Writing summaries
Writing book reports
Writing about other cultures
Writing math problems and processes used to arrive at solutions
Creating and writing cartoons
Creating/narrating a video or slide presentation
Reading maps, graphs, charts, tables
Reading road maps
Reading household manuals
Reading instructions to a purchased item
Writing class newspapers/newsletters
Writing a proper letter
Writing buddies/penpals
Writing to politicans, environmental groups, etc.

Writing responses and rebuttals to prompts/popular press
Creating word search puzzles
Rewriting a television episode
Writing and submitting work for publication in newspapers, magazines
Writing songs
Writing book and movie reviews
Maintaining an organized study system
Writing about good citizenship

## Middle School/Secondary Samples (Grades 5/6/7-12) (when appropriate, the same activities listed under elementary)

Being reading/writing consultants to others
Parents/teachers reading to students
Using portfolios to document and reflect individual goals/objectives and to be organized, reflective, evaluative, with multiple measures of learning outcomes/assessment
Writing about one's metacognitive abilities
Writing about one's literacy development
Written debates
Writing the pros and cons to a current issue
Analyzing the quality of a writing piece using criteria/rubrics
Writing scripts (e.g., radio/play)
Writing conversations
Creating vocabulary circles/maps/classification systems
Creating text pattern guides
Writing commentaries
Writing and responding to multicultural presentations
Explaining or teaching the writing process to another
Creating a class/school booklet/newspaper
Writing a resume
Completing a job application
Completing a driver's license application
Writing an editorial
Writing a research proposal
Writing about what one wants to learn in a particular area
Writing about an interview
Writing a case study
Writing a character study

Writing an anecdote from experience or as told by another
Creating rubrics or evaluation criteria for writing endeavors
Creating subject dictionaries
Writing complex math solutions
Writing about science issues
Writing content area research reports
Creating Venn diagrams
Writing about environmental/national/state/local concerns/issues
Writing a how-to guide
Writing about career decisions/options
Writing about qualifications
Writing about training needs/options/choices
Writing about military service
Writing about public and community service
Writing about college choices/information
Writing songs and lyrics
Full responsibility for publishing schoolwide
Programs/guides/yearbooks/newspapers
Full responsibility for parent newsletters
Creating questions for interviews
Writing summaries of interviews
Writing about a computer search
Writing an explanation
Using literacy skills to help another
Improving the literacy skills of another
Writing or explaining good reading/writing strategies
Creating an organized study system
Microteaching
Mentoring others
Using literacy skills to further own/family/friends career goals

## Technology Literacy—All Levels

Connecting to the Internet
Connecting to on-learning resources
Using multimedia computers
Using multimedia centers
Accessing libraries, museums, and cultural resources
Critically evaluating software used
Expanding own's knowledge base
Reinforcing own's knowledge base
Using word-processing programs for written work
Using dictionaries/spell check/grammar programs to improve writing quality

On-line reading of books/materials/ people/news and other areas of interest during leisure reading

Using on-line resources to find needed information

Using interactive technology on the computer (e.g., encyclopedias)

Using technology to improve learning strategies/skills

Maintaining running records of progress/learning

Making vocational/job connections

Communicating via bulletin boards, e-mail

Accessing reading/writing materials

Visiting reading/writing centers/organizations via the Internet